MASTERS OF THE REFORMATION

Qui sunt isti, quaeso, moderni,
Si 'moderni' Latinum vocabulum est.

Laurentius Valla (1407–57)
Opera, Basel 1540, folio 434.

MASTERS OF THE REFORMATION

THE EMERGENCE OF A NEW INTELLECTUAL CLIMATE IN EUROPE

HEIKO AUGUSTINUS OBERMAN

Professor of Church History, University of Tübingen
Director of the Institüt für Spätmittelalter und Reformation, Tübingen

Translated by
DENNIS MARTIN

CAMBRIDGE UNIVERSITY PRESS

Cambridge
London New York New Rochelle
Melbourne Sydney

Published by the Press Syndicate of the University of Cambridge
The Pitt Building, Trumpington Street, Cambridge CB2 1RP
32 East 57th Street, New York, NY 10022, USA
296 Beaconsfield Parade, Middle Park, Melbourne 3206, Australia

First published 1981

This book is a revised and abridged version of
Werden und Wertung der Reformation,
first published by J. C. B. Mohr (Paul Siebeck) Tübingen, 1977

Printed in Great Britain
at The Pitman Press, Bath

British Library Cataloguing in Publication Data
Oberman, Heiko Augustinus
Masters of the Reformation.
1. Theology, Doctrinal—History—16th century
I. Title
230'.09'031 BT27 80–41508

ISBN 0 521 23098 5

Contents

Preface

O, stulti, O Sautheologen . . .!

Martin Luther, *Romans Commentary* (*WA* 56, p. 274, line 14), Wittenberg 1515

Vous ne ferez rien de durable pour le bonheur des hommes parce que vous n'avez aucune idée de leur malheur . . . l'essence de notre malheur est surnaturelle.

Georges Bernanos, *Les grands cimetières sous la lune*, Paris 1938

Though a conceptual unity in itself, this work is the companion volume to *The Harvest of Medieval Theology*, published in 1963 in that other, latter-day Cambridge graced by Harvard University. There, based in the late fifteenth century, I looked back over the medieval heritage invaded by changing perceptions, new scientific discoveries and political conflicts. Now I have turned around to reconnoitre a terrain crisscrossed by late medieval expectations, theological moral optimism and social critique, the sixteenth-century Reformation's lines of advance.

As the title suggests, the significance of academic tradition will be granted its full weight. Nevertheless, a religious movement originating in one of the youngest German universities, Wittenberg, would never have achieved the social relevance, the political power, the *permanence* it did in fact achieve had not many of its 'masters' been self-made men who proved themselves charismatic leaders in the marketplace and in the city council.

From the very outset this division between the rarefied and the practical lent to the Reformation movement a kind of antiphonal complexity far beyond that suggested by the colourful medieval clashes between 'town' and 'gown'. In the cities the Latin-schooled leaders of the first years found themselves accused of importing a new ideology, ill suited to the stabilization of peace and concord pursued by the *politiques* among the city fathers. The coincidence of 'intellectual' and 'urban' renewal was by no means complete, and remained in precarious balance throughout the first half of the century: the case of Zürich illustrates this for the period of the ascendency of the Reformation in the early 1520s as well as that of Strassburg does for the crises of the Interim period. Characteristic of the *whole* Reformation, however, is the conviction that a deeper grasp of the misery of man and the power of sin is the necessary precondition for a realistic reform of church and society. This point is crucial to any true understanding of the period. The present-day debate about the alleged 'failure of the Reformation' because of its 'starry-eyed confidence' in the betterment of man and his potential for education transforms the movement into a morality play more in keeping with the spirit of the later Middle Ages than with sixteenth-century thought itself.

An observation by George Bernard Shaw, formulated in another Preface (*Fanny's First Play*, 1911) applies exactly to our period:

> Mere morality, or the substitution of custom for conscience, was once accounted a shameful and cynical thing: people talked of right and wrong . . ., of sin and grace, of salvation and damnation, not of morality and immorality. The word morality, if we met it in the Bible, would surprise us as much as the word telephone or motor car.

Luther and Shaw: an unexpected and indeed improbable team. Yet the rare combination of irreverent irony and historical insight which characterizes both is likewise a fundamental quality of Reformation thought: a quality which continues to baffle and to fascinate.

The completion of these two first volumes paves the way, I trust, for a presentation, in a third volume, of Martin Luther: a Luther approached not as a desk-bound research scholar, but rather as a man besieged by and responsive to the conditions and convictions of his day and age.

Among all to whom I feel obliged for help rendered, I owe a special debt of gratitude to Professor G. R. Elton of Clare College, Cambridge, for his support, and to Professor R. W. Scribner of King's College, London, for his suggestions, extending even to the jacket illustration of this book.

HEIKO A. OBERMAN

Tübingen, November 1980

Abbreviations

ADB	*Allgemeine Deutsche Biographie*. 55 vols. and index. Leipzig, 1875–1912; reprinted Berlin, 1967–71.
AGBR	*Aktensammlung zur Geschichte der Basler Reformation in den Jahren 1519 bis Anfang 1534*, vol. 1: *1519 bis Juni 1525*. Edited by E. Dürr. Basel, 1921; vol. 3: *1528 bis Juni 1529*. Edited by P. Roth. Basel, 1937.
ARG	*Archiv für Reformationsgeschichte.*
Blarer-Gedenkschrift	*Der Konstanzer Reformator Ambrosius Blarer 1492–1564. Gedenkschrift zu seinem 400. Todestag*. Edited by B. Moeller. Constance, 1964.
Brev. OP	*Breviarium FF. Praedicatorum*. See the list of editions in Hanns Bohatta, *Bibliographie der Breviere 1501–1850*, 2nd edn, Stuttgart, 1963, pp. 144–53.
BWKG	*Blätter für württembergische Kirchengeschichte.*
CCath	*Corpus Catholicorum. Werke katholischer Schriftsteller im Zeitalter der Glaubensspaltung*, vol. 1ff. Münster i.W., 1919ff.
CChr	*Corpus Christianorum. Series latina*, vol. 1ff. Turnhout, 1954ff.
CIC	*Corpus Iuris Canonici*, vol. 1: *Decretum Magistri Gratiani*; vol. 2: *Decretalium collectiones*. Compiled by E. L. Richter, edited by E. Friedberg. Leipzig, 1879; reprinted Graz, 1959.
CICiv	*Corpus Iuris Civilis*, vol. 1: *Institutiones*. Edited by P. Krüger; *Digesta*. Edited by Th. Mommsen; vol. 2: *Codex Iustinianus*. Edited by P. Krüger; vol. 3; *Novellae*. Edited by R. Schoell, G. Kroll. Berlin, 1872–1908.
CR	*Corpus Reformatorum*, vol. 1ff. Halle a.d. Salle, 1834ff; reprinted Frankfurt a. M., 1963.
CSEL	*Corpus scriptorum ecclesiasticorum Latinorum*, vol. 1ff. Issued by the Wiener Akademie der Wissenschaften. Vienna, 1866ff.
Egli, *Acten*	Egli, Emil, ed., *Actensammlung zur Geschichte der Zürcher Reformation in den Jahren 1519–1533*. Zürich, 1879; reprinted Aalen, 1973.

Gregory, *Sent.* — Gregorius Ariminensis. *Super Primum et Secundum Sententiarum*. Venice, 1522. Cf. Cassiciacum (American Series). Studies on St Augustine and the Augustinian Order, 4. New York, Paderborn, 1955. Also found in Franciscan Institute Publications. Text Series, 7. St Bonaventure, N.Y., 1955.

Hain — Hain, Ludwig. *Repertorium bibliographicum*. 4 vols. Stuttgart, Paris, 1826–38; reprinted Frankfurt a.M., 1903; Milan, 1948.

Haller, 1 and 2 — Haller, Johannes. *Die Anfänge der Universität Tübingen 1477–1537*, vol. 1: *Darstellung*; vol. 2: *Nachweise und Erläuterungen*. Stuttgart, 1927–29; reprinted Aalen, 1970.

Itinerarium Italicum — *Itinerarium Italicum. The Profile of the Italian Renaissance in the Mirror of its European Transformations*. Festschrift Paul Oskar Kristeller. Edited by H. A. Oberman, Th. A. Brady, Jr. SMRT 14. Leiden, 1975.

Krebs, *Protokolle* — *Die Protokolle des Konstanzer Domkapitels*, 6. Lieferung: *Januar 1514 bis September 1526*. Nos. 4841–9024. Edited by M. Krebs. Beiheft zur Zeitschrift für die Geschichte des Oberrheins, 106 [N.S. 67] (1958).

LB — *Desiderii Erasmi Roterodami Opera omnia*. Edited by J. Clericus. Leiden (Lugduni Batavorum), 1703–6; reprinted London, 1962.

Opp. Zw. — *Opera D. Huldrychi Zwinglii cum Apologia Rodolphi Gvalteri*, vols. 1 (Zürich, 1545); 2 and 3 (Zürich, 1544); 4 (Zürich, n.d.).

PG — *Patrologiae cursus completus. Series Graeca*. 161 vols. Edited by J. P. Migne, Paris, 1857–96, Indices, 1912.

PL — *Patrologiae cursus completus. Series Latina*. 221 vols.; Indices 1–4. Edited by J. P. Migne. Paris, 1844–64; Suppl. 1–5. Paris, 1958–74.

QFRG — Quellen und Forschungen zur Reformationsgeschichte, vol. 1ff. Issued by the Verein für Reformationsgeschichte. Gütersloh, 1911ff.

RE — *Realencyklopädie für protestantische Theologie und Kirche*. 24 vols. Edited by A. Hauck. 3rd edn, Leipzig, 1896–1913.

Festgabe Reuchlin — *Johannes Reuchlin 1455–1522. Festgabe seiner Vaterstadt Pforzheim zur 500. Wiederkehr seines Geburtstages*. Edited by M. Krebs. Pforzheim. [1955].

RGG — *Die Religion in Geschichte und Gegenwart*. 6 vols. and index. Edited by K. Galling. 3rd edn, Tübingen, 1957–65.

RGST — Reformationsgeschichtliche Studien und Texte. Edited by J. Greving, W. Neuss.

Roth, *Urkunden*	Roth, Rudolph von, ed., *Urkunden zur Geschichte der Universität Tübingen aus den Jahren 1476 bis 1550*. Tübingen, 1877; reprinted Aalen, 1973.
Schiess, *Briefwechsel*	Schiess, Traugott, ed., *Briefwechsel der Brüder Ambrosius und Thomas Blaurer 1509–1548*, vol. 1: *1509 – Juni 1538*. Freiburg i.Br., 1908.
SHCT	Studies in the History of Christian Thought. Edited by H. A. Oberman.
SKRG	Schriften zur Kirchen- und Rechtsgeschichte. Darstellungen und Quellen. Edited by Ekkehart Fabian.
SMRT	Studies in Medieval and Reformation Thought. Edited by H. A. Oberman.
Staehelin, *Briefe*	Staehelin, Ernst, ed., *Briefe und Akten zum Leben Oekolampads. Zum 400 jährigen Jubiläum der Basler Reformation*. 2 vols. QFRG 10 and 19. Leipzig, 1927–34.
Thomas Aquinas, *STh*	Thomas Aquinas. *Summa Theologiae*. 3 vols. and index. Edited by P. Caramello. Turin: Marietti, 1952–62.
Vergenhans, *Chronicle*	Vergenhans, Johannes (Nauclerus). *Memorabilium omnis aetatis et omnium gentium chronici commentarii . . .* , vol. 2. Tübingen, 1516.
VIEG	Veröffentlichungen des Instituts für Europäische Geschichte Mainz. Abteilung für Abendländische Religionsgeschichte. Edited by Joseph Lortz.
WA	*Luthers Werke. Kritische Gesamtausgabe*, Abteilung Schriften, vol. 1ff. Weimar, 1883ff; reprinted Graz. 1964ff.
WABr	*Luthers Werke. Kritische Gesamtausgabe*, Abteilung Briefe, 15 vols. Weimar, 1930–78; reprinted Graz, 1969ff.
WATR	*Luthers Werke. Kritische Gesamtausgabe*, Abteilung Tischreden, 6 vols. Weimar, 1912–21.
ZKG	*Zeitschrift für Kirchengeschichte*.
ZSRG.K	*Zeitschrift der Savigny-Stiftung für Rechtsgeschichte*. Kan. Abt.
ZThK	*Zeitschrift für Theologie und Kirche*.
ZW	*Huldreich Zwinglis sämtliche Werke*, vol. 1ff. Edited by E. Egli, G. Finsler, *et al.* = *CR* 88ff. Berlin, 1905; Leipzig, 1908ff.; Zürich, 1957ff.

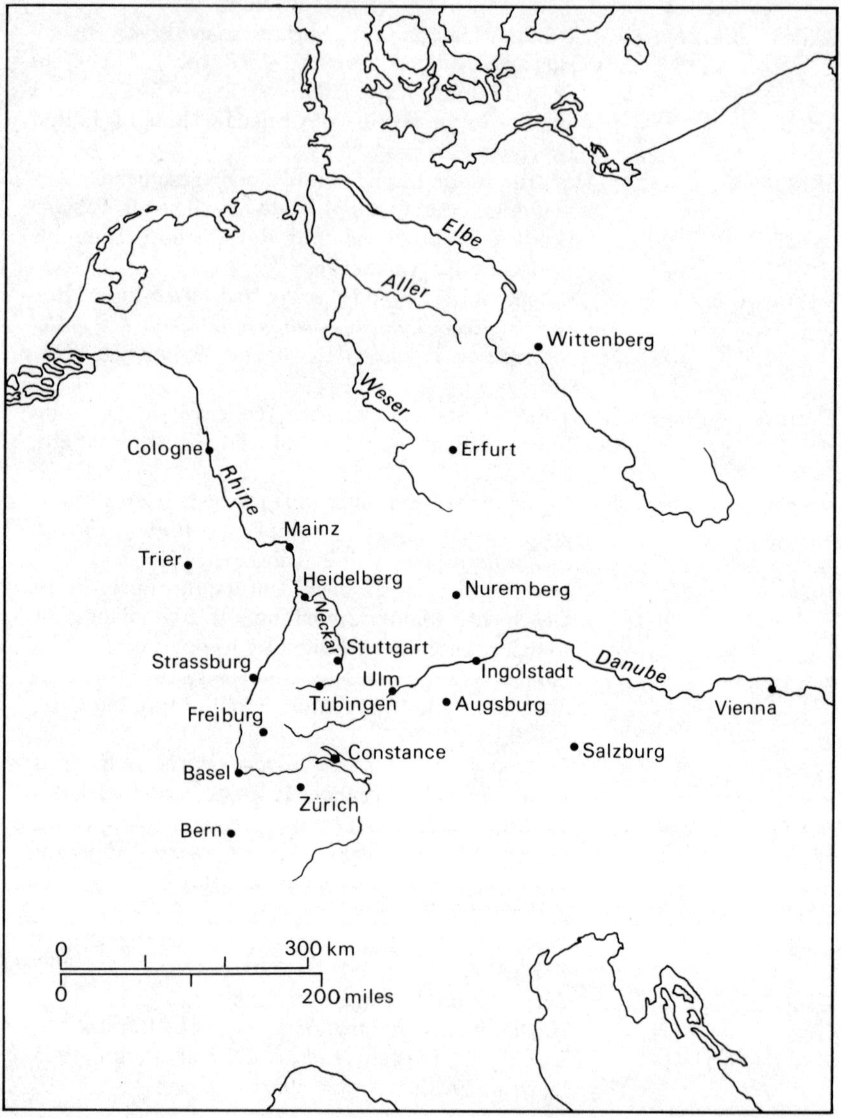

Elbe
Aller
Wittenberg
Weser
Cologne
Erfurt
Rhine
Mainz
Trier
Heidelberg
Nuremberg
Neckar
Stuttgart
Strassburg
Ulm
Ingolstadt
Danube
Tübingen
Augsburg
Vienna
Freiburg
Constance
Salzburg
Basel
Zürich
Bern
0
300 km
0
200 miles

Part I

INTELLECTUAL RENEWAL

1

The ivory tower: the university as observatory

GABRIEL BIEL died on 7 December 1495 as prior of an experimental house of the Brethren of the Common Life, St Peter's at the Hermitage, near Tübingen. Like the university which Biel served from 1485 to ca. 1490, St Peter's had been founded on the initiative and with the healthy support of Count Eberhard im Bart of Württemberg. In a previous study[1] we examined the late medieval system of theology and philosophy known as nominalism, especially as exemplified in the life and works of Biel, and concluded with some remarks on the catholicity of that much maligned theology. In the following pages we shall pursue the legacy of Gabriel Biel and the adherents of his *via moderna* as they walked and warred with the *via antiqua* amid the tempests that would eventually transform a catholic Europe into three separate 'confessions' plus an assortment of left-wing splinter groups.

The centrality of the university to any understanding of this period is as unquestionable as it is ill-defined. Early parochial chronicles portray the university itself as the mainstream, the source of a supposed 'golden era' in which the evils of a disintegrating society would be abolished. University erudition not only signified the growing pride of a German nation ready to compete as an equal on the playing fields of cultured Europe; it also meant escape from the dark ages, now sensed to be at their most threatening. These hopes become joint themes in numerous contemporary chronicles and account in part for their exuberant tone.

Today, intellectual history written from a university perspective may at first seem an anachronism: a throwback to these romantic excesses. The writing of university history has become a field of its own, demanding the scholar's complete energies and a lifetime of dedication. Standards have been set by the work of Astrik Gabriel on the Sorbonne and the University of Paris, Erich Kleineidam on Erfurt, Walter Friedensburg on Wittenberg, and Gerhard Ritter on Heidel-

[1] *The Harvest of Medieval Theology*.

berg: standards by which future work must be measured.[2] Moreover, fifty years ago Johannes Haller described the origins of the University of Tübingen in a study so carefully documented that Heinrich Hermelink's earlier history of the theological faculty lost much of its long-standing prestige.[3]

As the notes will eloquently testify, it is with far more than mere formal gratitude for these earlier efforts that I take them as my point of departure. Nor do I consider it my task to offer petty emendations. From the beginning I have been drawn and then driven by a different question, one which apparently did not similarly engross previous students of the history of the university: how can a grasp of the founding and reform stages of a single university such as Tübingen present more than the summary recapitulation of local events? How can such a history provide us meaningful access to the complex reality of the late Middle Ages and the Reformation?

These concerns, at first glance recalling the early understanding of the university's centrality, lead me in fact in quite a different direction. They have brought me outside the normal boundaries of the domain usually thought proper to university historians. One danger that I will hope to avoid is academic myopia: the ivory tower will not itself become the object of my study. I do not seek to view history *within* the university, but rather *from the viewpoint of the university*. The platform has been selected for its perspective, not for its loftiness. Other perspectives beckon to the observer wishing to do justice to the agitated period from the late Middle Ages to the Reformation. The panorama takes in everything from the papal curia and the headquarters of individual monastic orders to episcopal sees and the municipal preaching endowments: from the imperial court and the representatives to imperial diets to the city council chambers and guild halls. From the vantage-point of the ivory tower our glance will fall upon all these, permitting us to compile information regarding the times and society under study.

But this same ivory tower functioned also as a broadcasting tower. Tübingen's contribution to the intellectual life of Europe consisted not solely in the preservation and transmission of scholarly methods and conclusions limited to the academic community. Contemporary social, religious, economic and political questions intruded into lecture

[2] *Auctarium Chartularii Universitatis Parisiensis*, vol. 6; Kleineidam, *Universitas Studii Erffordensis;* Friedensburg, *Geschichte der Universität Wittenberg; idem, Urkundenbuch der Universität Wittenberg*, pt 1; Ritter, *Die Heidelberger Universität.*

[3] Haller, 1 and 2; Hermelink, *Die theologische Fakultät in Tübingen vor der Reformation 1477–1534.*

halls, disputations and literary controversies: questions which otherwise would tantalize today's historian even more. These were not always burning issues. They often involved the intellectual winnowing of inherited answers to unresolved questions from the high Middle Ages. Yet such answers were not simply irrelevant intellectual ballast overloading a ship. In Tübingen it was precisely fourteenth-century developments in epistemology and the emergence of a clearer distinction between the arts and natural sciences that played vital roles. In combination with a seemingly abstract and academic process of clarification, these fourteenth-century developments aided the diffusion of a heightened social and economic awareness. The late medieval university was capable of greater accomplishments and covered a broader and more vital spectrum than its former and present critics wish to admit. To establish the truth of this thesis is one aim of this book.

The view from the other European universities founded either before or after Tübingen would offer us different perspectives. Glancing briefly at these other institutions we find Heidelberg to have been a rallying-point for a 'pre-Erasmian humanism' for which the term 'scholasticism' had not yet become an insult. Cologne furnishes insights into that form of Thomism against which the aspiring German cultural and educational world would react allergically. Erfurt exhibits the philosophical creativity of the *via moderna* and Wittenberg brings us to the brink of the new Reformation theology. But Tübingen's significance lies in three areas at once: the *via moderna* was imported from England and Paris, the modern devotion brought in from the Netherlands, and the amazingly innovative coalition between the two *viae*.

The first area is concerned with the powerful legacy of the academic *via moderna*. We are in the process of discovering – or, in a better phrase, uncovering – the significance of late medieval nominalism.[4] My goal is to make visible the central thrust of the so-called *via moderna* and to free it from the overgrowth of distorting confessional interests. How much remains to be done can be seen in scholars'

[4] William J. Courtenay provided what I consider to be convincing arguments for restricting the label 'Occamism' to Occam and his disciples and not identifying it with 'nominalism' – at least in reference to the fourteenth century. Yet at the new German universities during the fifteenth century, the conflict between *via antiqua* and *via moderna* was equated with the controversy between realists and nominalists. Tübingen's Gabriel Biel was considered at the same time the leading mind among the nominalists and the most faithful disciple of Occam. See Courtenay, 'Nominalism and Late Medieval Thought. A Bibliographical Essay'; *idem*, 'Nominalism and Late Medieval Religion'.

stubborn use of the word 'disintegrating' to describe the effect of nominalist sacramental doctrine, and from accounts of Luther's victory over a supposedly nominalist concept of a 'capricious' God. Nevertheless, the work of recent years has been far from fruitless, and the discussion has become considerably more objective and source-related.

Acquitted of the charge of heresy, nominalism has gradually been acquiring a new image. Looking beyond epistemology and dogma, we discover that the study of physical phenomena, released from a metaphysical superstructure, found its own basis in *experimentum* and *experientia*, in observation and experience. Probably as a result of this empirical orientation, nominalism also pursued questions ranging in theme from economics to the care of souls, thereby extending itself far into the inchoate modern era which it to some extent made possible. These tendencies bear little resemblance to the image of hypercritical logical hairsplitting that has enjoyed such abiding popularity. One of the consequences of such distortion is that, much to our detriment, the nominalist heritage has yet to be completely incorporated into the modern arts disciplines. The defamation of the university as an ivory tower was not encouraged by the nominalist insistence on clearer definitions and reasoning. It was rather the *via antiqua*'s 'realist' faith in the eternal orientation of ideas glimpsed both professorially and prophetically, and the realist confidence in the priority of abstraction before and beyond experience, that helped to construct the ivory tower. Where experience is not ushered in it rushes in, causing uncontrolled shockwaves. To express our aim in terms suited to the object of our investigation: abandoning the often-encountered but groundless confinement of Gabriel Biel in a pigeon-hole labelled 'the last scholastic', we wish to free our view in order to observe the vitality of the first 'Tübingen school', previously camouflaged by a confessionally determined periodization.

Alongside the *via moderna*, the *devotio moderna*, although absent from the university statutes, constitutes a second factor deserving our attention. Unlike the *via moderna*, which reached Tübingen from the centres of medieval scholarship in Oxford and Paris, the *devotio moderna* pushed its way up the Rhine from the Overijssel valley and the Netherlands. Of still greater significance is its origin far from university lecture halls in the monasticized communities of the Brethren of the Common Life and the monasteries of the Windesheim canons. The Modern Devotion made its way into Württemberg and found a congenial complement in the experience-oriented Tübingen *via moderna*. And even after 1517, already institutionally expelled from Württemberg by Duke Ulrich and overwhelmed by the Reformation, the concerns of the *devotio moderna* remained vital and visible to the present day, especially in that complex phenomenon known as Swabian Pietism.

In 1490, nearly one hundred years after the movement's founding, and therefore at a point relevant to this study, the rector of the Hildesheim fraterhouse, Pieter Dieppurch (†1491), summarized in one sentence the goals of this historically elusive movement: 'Non sumus religiosi sed in seculo religiose vivere nitimur et volumus.'[5] No literal translation can do justice to the double meaning of the term *religiosus* which connotes both 'monk' and 'genuine Christian'. But freely rendered, Dieppurch's sense is clear: 'We are not cloistered monks but we endeavour to be Christians in the world.' Although it stops short of overt rejection, an attitude critical of the monastery[6] is clearly present in this self-portrayal; a critical spirit not shared to the same extent by all the brethren. Yet common to all was the goal of imitating Christ in a monastery as large as the world and under a rule older than all existing rules, i.e., the will of Christ as expressed in the Gospel. Thus formulated, Dieppurch's description could have been written by Gabriel Biel, the earliest and the foremost representative of the *devotio moderna* in Württemberg.[7]

During the fifty years after Biel left Urach for Tübingen in 1484, the brethren pursued and transmitted theology at the University of Tübingen within an unbroken tradition that sought to combine scholarship and devotion. Aspiring to more than the simple promotion of piety or internalized edification, they desired to prepare for the imitation of Christ in the profane world outside the monastery walls. Consequently we shall deliberately avoid using the term 'piety', so closely associated in the modern mind with 'inner

[5] *Annalen und Akten der Brüder des Gemeinsamen Lebens im Lüchtenhofe zu Hildesheim*, ed Doebner, p. 113. On Dieppurch see Post, *The Modern Devotion*, pp. 427ff. Cf. Naber, *Vrouwenleven in Prae-Reformatietijd bezegeld door den marteldood van Wendelmoet Claesdochter*, p. 68.

[6] This critical attitude toward monasticism found clear expression in the final comments which reduced the key concerns of the Lüchtenhof confraternity's statutes to basic essentials: 'Expedit enim pro nobis, ut non more religiosorum faciamus mencionem laborum, vigiliarum, disciplinarum, castigacionum, jejuniorum, abstinenciarum etc. in litteris confraternitatum nostrarum, de quibis nobis coram deo et hominibus non est gloriandum sicut ipsis gloriosis'. *Annalen*, ed. Doebner, p. 331.

[7] Dieppurch did indeed refer to Biel, who had convinced him that to use external force against backsliding brethren was to deny Christian liberty and was a practice best left to monastics: 'resipui [Dieppurch] audiens magistrum Gabrielem super hec respondisse, quod sufficerent religiosi'. *Ibid.*, p. 113.

emigration'; preferring the word 'devotion' for the reciprocity between surrender to God and mission to the world that was characteristic of the *devotio moderna* even in its later stages.

The pulpit offered to the Modern Devotion by the lecterns of the University of Tübingen had no equal in a Europe on the eve of Reformation and revolution,[8] when the movement reached both its geographical limits and the summit of its social and pedagogical achievements. But it was by means of a personal union with the *via moderna* that the burden of reform was shouldered by the brethren with such considerable success. For the bonds of coalition between the two 'modern' movements consisted neither in the destructive ecclesiology commonly postulated as characteristic of these movements and their times, nor in the total absence of an ecclesiology. On the contrary: they were linked by their mutual efforts on behalf of the unity of the church. Whatever the differences in their origins, a common concern is evident on various fronts in the course of the fifteenth century: a desire to mediate in the conflicts of the cloistered orders and arbitrate in the squabbles of the 'schools'.

Within the framework of the history of European universities the respectful cooperation between the major representatives of the two *viae*, Gabriel Biel (†1495) and Conrad Summenhart (†1502), illustrates a third aspect of Tübingen's significance. The two 'ways' intersected in a desire to clarify the socially and economically induced tensions of their times and to remedy abuses. The controversies arising in connection with investment interest illustrate how theologians began to reclaim an entire tangle of social and economic questions from the canon lawyers. This realization leads in turn to a phenomenon not entirely unknown, yet inadequately interpreted in this context.

Prohibited by the official church, charging interest was permissible for Jews alone, fanning the flames of 'Christian' anti-Jewish sentiment. But receiving interest had long been customary in Italian banking circles and, although not properly sanctioned by ecclesiastical lawyers, the practice had been interpreted in a manner suited to the economy's requirements. In contrast, bankers north of the Alps found themselves unable to shake off their conflicts of conscience when drawing up money-lending contracts. Jacob Fugger, probably the most powerful commercial magnate in Europe, assured himself and potential critics of the legitimacy of a five per cent rate of interest by commissioning a theological opinion in 1514. In observing how the University of Tübingen, responding to its alumnus Johannes Eck,

[8] Cf. Post, *The Modern Devotion*, pp. 444f.

faced the problem, we are confronted with the question: how could that which had long been standard procedure in Florence or Venice have led to an ethical dilemma in Augsburg? One could point to Johannes Janssen's explanation whereby the spiritual boom on the eve of the Reformation revealed 'the most profound essence of the German being and character' in piety, education and art, 'especially in the noble and stirring efforts stemming from a sense of Christian community'.[9] And thus it would seem that an excess and not a lack of piety plagued Germany: abuses tolerated elsewhere triggered the Reformation. Or one could apply the thesis of Janssen's Lutheran counterpart Johannes Haller, whereby the German spirit, which is 'Protestant by nature', had been fitted with a properly tuned conscience as standard equipment.[10] At the very least, a glance at the chequered confessional map of present-day Europe should suffice to render suspect such explanations based on national characteristics.

A widespread esteem for Jean Gerson (†1429) added impetus toward bridging the gap between the *via antiqua* and *via moderna*. Gerson and his admirers sought a new balance between canon law and theology which, devoid of Occam's vehement criticism, evolved into an intensive reappraisal of church law on the basis of scripture and tradition. This led to conclusions regarding the system of tithes that were restricted to the lecture hall to avoid triggering unrest. And the rising academic elite left those lecture halls supplied with ideas that filtered into wider reservoirs of public opinion in the following decades, conferring theoretical legitimacy on social ferment and criticism of the church long before the peasant tumults of the 1520s. This process illustrates how, rather than gazing inward as we recount the history of an ivory tower, we can use the university at Tübingen as a crow's-nest from which to catch sight of developments that might otherwise have eluded us. It is true that the current state of research does not permit us to posit the Tübingen perspective as generally valid for the intellectual history of the late Middle Ages and Reformation. Nevertheless, a segment of that history becomes visible from our vantage-point, an angle of vision encompassing reform attempts and alternatives which the subsequent upheavals of the Reformation should not obscure.

Despite his later sharp criticism of the university's defensive posture in the face of new classical educational ideals, Philip Melanchthon recognized the achievements of turn-of-the-century

[9] Janssen, *Geschichte des deutschen Volkes seit dem Ausgang des Mittelalters*, vol. 1, p. 567.
[10] Johannes Haller, *Die Epochen der deutschen Geschichte*, p. 175, trans., p. 126.

Tübingen. His reference to Wittenberg as a 'colony of Tübingen'[11] was certainly intended as more than mere formal praise. But we find this label disturbing since we are accustomed to retain the 'Reformation' niche of history for the church renewal that began with Martin Luther and to relegate all medieval attempts at renewal, however programmatic, to the company of the 'reform movements'. And in so doing we have not completely missed the mark. The Reformation did rearrange the subtle triangular balance between the individual spheres of influence of church, governmental authority and university. There can therefore be no talk of a 'colonia Tubingensis' since Wittenberg points to a new epoch.[12] On the other hand, focusing on the new era blurs other portions of the landscape. The secularization of the sciences and the recognition of the autonomy of the laws under which they operate had long been projects of the *via moderna*, although subject to the limits set by loyalty to the church. The sciences and especially the natural sciences, did not reach majority after bringing a successful court action against a guardian *Mater Theologia*; they eloped after a successful courtship by the *via moderna*. By leading theology back to its own sources, nominalism both delimited and inaugurated a newly understood range of validity for empirical scientific observation. In contrast, within the field of theology, the use of theological sources was so unmistakably regulated by the masters that a head-on collision became inevitable where the claims to theological majority were pressed in the face of the doctrinal and dogmatic prerogatives of the *Mater Ecclesia*.

We shall study the manner in which this confrontation took shape by considering the solid front presented by Tübingen in reaction to the budding Zürich Reformation. 'Modern' Tübingen became the academic centre of the south German Counter-Reformation and, under Austrian tutelage, a source of anti-Protestant propaganda. But the Counter-Reformation phase was then interrupted – until the Interim of 1548 and the accession of Duke Christopher on 7 Novem-

11 'Deinde nos in hac Academia non prorsus alienum esse ducamus, Cum enim sit οἰκιστής Academiae Tubingensis, unde quasi Colonia deducta est haec nostra Academia, decet nos ipsius quoque gratam memoriam retinere.' *CR* 11, col. 1023. Julius Köstlin's publication of the earliest matriculation register for the Wittenberg arts faculty confirms the image of a 'colony'. The first dean of the faculty, Sigmund Epp (1503) was one of two *Sententiarii* who accompanied Johann von Staupitz when he left Tübingen to enter the *Leucorea* and in 1505 two more Tübingen *Baccalaurei* were registered in Wittenberg as part of the steady influx of Swabian students. Köstlin, ed., *Die Baccalaurei und Magistri der Wittenberger Philosophischen Fakultät 1503–1517*, pp. 1, 6.

12 See my article, 'Reformation: Epoche oder Episode'.

ber 1550[13] – by Duke Ulrich's return and the accompanying political reversal of 1534. The reform decree, issued by Duke Ulrich and probably written by the Tübingen alumnus Ambrosius Blarer, was composed in the language of the south German Reformation, a language well understood in Zürich. Its declared purpose was to 'reform the university to suit the present circumstances and to bring into better order that which we have found disorderly'.[14] Reform of philosophy rather than of theology became the primary goal since the study of philosophy had become so inscrutable that the younger generation was losing interest and inclined to 'migrate to other universities and to forsake this our own place of higher learning'.[15] But the changes consisted of more than mere modernization for the sake of a better competitive position in relation to other universities. In addition to the innovations in curriculum, students of theology were freed from the obligation of ecclesiastical ordination. It was still possible to enter clerical orders, but the theology student was no longer to be 'forced or compelled thereto by the professors of theology'.[16]

A direct extension of the basic regulations of 1525 can be seen in the 1535 decree, with its emphasis on languages and insistence on clarity and practicality in the area of philosophy. In 1525 it had already been prescribed that in those cases where the scholastic questions from Peter Lombard's textbook were treated alongside the Bible, they were to be expounded concisely and clearly (*quanto brevius et lucidius*) since 'we become children of God by faith and not by vain and frivolous questioning'.[17] But contrasting the reforms of philosophy in 1525 and theology in 1535 would be too simple an approach. In both cases the university was to be reformed from the top and opened to the language-oriented educational ideals by means of the elimination of the two *viae* and their student hostels or *bursae*, so typical of Tübingen. Both attempts, the first under the pressure of the Habsburg Counter-Reformation and the second in the course of the equally politically motivated introduction of the Reformation under Duke Ulrich, met with resistance from a university determined to

[13] Heinrich Hermelink offers a useful but undocumented survey of events from the Battle of Lauffen on 13 May 1534 to the end of the Interim (Peace of Passau, 2 August 1552) in his *Geschichte der evangelischen Kirche in Württemberg von der Reformation bis zur Gegenwart. Das Reich Gottes in Wirttemberg*, pp. 60–84.

[14] Roth, *Urkunden*, pp. 176f. ('Ordnung' of 30 January 1535).

[15] *Ibid.*, p. 176.

[16] *Ibid.*, p. 177.

[17] '. . . per fidem efficimur Filii Dei et non per inanes et frivolas questiones . . .' *Ibid.*, p. 143.

defend its identity and academic privileges. Coalitions between the *devotio moderna* and *via moderna* and between the *via antiqua* and *via moderna* proved to have deep roots.

The statutes of 1525 never achieved their intended effect, and the reform of 1535 could only be completed after the territorial sovereign, as once previously in 1498, pledged himself to respect the privileges of the university insofar 'as they do not counter the divine order'.[18] Ecclesiastical authorization in the form of papal approval had clearly given way to 'divine order' and those successors of Biel and Summenhart who were ready to renounce Catholic observance only after defeat at disputation had to hold their tongues or relinquish their chairs. The confusion that accompanied the struggle for a correct understanding of this 'divine order' in the territory and the university forced the University of Tübingen back into its original bounds, pushing Ambrosius Blarer aside in the process. The university again became primarily what it had been at its foundation: a territorial, even provincial, university bypassed by the cultural thoroughfares of Europe. We could be satisfied with this conventional conclusion if the concluding chapter's comparison between 'urban' and 'princely' Reformations did not reveal that the very same university and ecclesiastical reorganization necessitated by princely *raison d'état* managed to maintain a role for research in areas of knowledge crucial to the development of the modern natural sciences.

But does not the term 'cultural' or 'educational thoroughfare' suggest a greater significance than is applicable to any late medieval university? Were not the professors, their schools and their influence transformed into pawns of territorial self-interest in the process of the provincialization of academic education in the late Middle Ages? Were they not in fact the prisoners of economic and political interest?

The pent-up resentment against the history of ideas evinced in the above objections and not at all uncommon in present-day historical scholarship leads us astray in our pursuit of the expectations of the period under study. It is true that the dogmatic prestige of the faculties suffered as the legal and theological opinions they wrote became pawns in a confessional struggle. The earlier collective statement of faculties or entire universities increasingly gave way during the Reformation to verdicts issued by leading individuals. But where the 'new doctrine' was able to accommodate the 'new learning', enormous authority and influence was ascribed to a university that was 'autonomous', at least within the context of its era. And

[18] *Ibid.*, p. 177.

through its strategic importance for the cause of Reformation in south Germany, Tübingen enjoyed a special degree of authority and influence.[19]

In 1536 the university floundered toward disaster as Blarer, a university reformer lacking a local power-base, ran aground on a combination of Lutheran suspicion of his Swiss connections, a defence of academic freedom, and a congealed scholastic traditionalism. The situation appeared so grim, and the university's potential for shaping culture was valued so highly, that two major leaders of the Reformation rushed from opposite directions toward Tübingen in order to salvage the operation: Melanchthon hurried from Wittenberg, Bucer from Strassburg. While Bucer attempted in vain to arrange a meeting with Blarer,[20] Melanchthon had already received news of Blarer's dismissal from Duke Ulrich. A university professor himself, Melanchthon was convinced that the reorganization could be assured of success only if put in motion from within the university. Acting in accord with ducal instructions, he urgently requested Johannes Brenz to take a leave of absence from his duties as pastor at Schwäbisch Hall to assume the care of the Tübingen Reformation. And a quotation from Melanchthon's letter forms a fitting conclusion to this introductory chapter, for Melanchthon expressed here, in contemporary language but certainly not for his contemporaries alone, what was at stake for the entire territory. His letter documents how inextricably the university and education, the educational crisis and vision for the future were bound up with faith and politics:

> I ask you therefore, for the sake of Christ and the good of the church, to come to Tübingen for a time. You owe this service in the first place to the glory of Christ, secondly for the sake of a church in distress and finally to the honour of your fatherland which is worthy of your special consideration.
>
> You know how important it is that the pursuit of knowledge and the finer arts be maintained. If you permit the pursuit of truth to perish there, what kind of barbarity will henceforth reign in most of Germany? Such barbarism would then be accompanied by confusion in Christian doctrine and practice, and the ignorant fanatics would carry the field.

[19] Luther considered the appointment of Blarer to be so telling that he feared for the success of the Wittenberg Reformation in all of south Germany: 'Et scribitur mihi, Ducem Wirtembergensem habere in deliciis Blaurerum. Quodsi verum est, quid speres de tota illa superiore Germania?' Letter to Justus Jonas, 17 December 1534; *WABr* 7, p. 130, lines 10–12.

[20] After two days of impatient waiting in Tübingen Bucer penned another moving letter from Herrenberg on 20(?) October 1536: 'Per Christum, qui nobis merito est omnia, te obtestor, ne sinas me expectare frustra.' Schiess, *Briefwechsel*, 1, p. 825.

If you do not come – of this I am convinced – many learned men who have thus far clung hopefully to Tübingen will depart.

As you well know, scholarship is neglected in all of south Germany. For that reason we must now concentrate all efforts on the restoration of the university at Tübingen. And I cherish the presumption, certainly not without reason, that the university in Tübingen, once it has been resuscitated, will prove to be of more lasting significance than all the others.[21]

[21] Wittenberg, 17 October 1536; *CR* 3, col. 170.

2

The impact of humanism: fact and fancy

'IN THAT same year of our Saviour 1477, thanks to the initiative of the renowned Count Eberhard of Württemberg and Montbéliard and his illustrious mother, Lady Mechthild, a university was established with papal approval in the city of Tübingen in the diocese of Constance, located in the ecclesiastical province of Mainz . . .' With this matter-of-fact notice Johannes Vergenhans (Nauclerus) recorded the founding of the University of Tübingen in his account of world history.[1] That the event found mention at all in a broadly conceived history of humanity may well be ascribed to local pride, while the modesty of the university's first rector may be responsible for the chronicler's silence regarding his own role in the school's planning and preparation. In contrast, Nicholas Baselius, a monk of Hirsau and the editor of Vergenhans' chronicle,[2] concluded his supplement for the years 1500–13 with a proclamation of the rebirth of Germany; a rebirth

[1] Vergenhans, *Chronicle*, fol. 295^{v}. Vergenhans repeated himself in almost identical words in his lively eulogy for Count Eberhard. *Ibid.*, fol. 301^{v}. In this case he fitted the founding of the university into the context of Eberhard's policy of reunification for Württemberg.

For the significance of this chronicle see Joachimsen, *Geschichtsauffassung und Geschichtsschreibung in Deutschland unter dem Einfluss des Humanismus*, vol. 1, pp. 91ff. Joachimsen termed it 'das erste kritische Geschichtswerk Deutschlands'. *Ibid.*, p. 92. The monk of Hirsau, Nicholas Baselius, brought the chronicle up to date in an appendix that commenced with the year 1501 and had the work published by Thomas Anshelm in Tübingen in 1516.

[2] Baselius thereby continued the monumental historical task of his renowned fellow monk Abbot Johannes Trithemius who had likewise used Vergenhans' work. Before his move to Würzburg in 1506 Trithemius had assembled a large library which was used by Gabriel Biel and, in 1515, by Conrad Pellikan.

Prior to 1520 Baselius procured for Willibald Pirckheimer a Sponheim codex containing works of Fulgentius and Maxentius. Lehmann, *Merkwürdigkeiten des Abtes Johannes Trithemius*, p. 53. See the list of visitors and a reconstruction of the catalogue, *ibid.*, pp. 21ff., 29ff. In 1535–6 Frecht, Capito and Bucer expressed great interest in a projected edition of the *Annales Hirsaugienses* and expected Blarer to have it published in Tübingen. The extant correspondence surrounding these plans 'is a significant testimony to the appraisal accorded Trithemius by the south German reformers'. Schreiner, 'Abt Johannes Trithemius (1462 bis 1516) als Geschichtsschreiber des Klosters Hirsau', p. 83. On Baselius see Irtenkauf, 'Bausteine zu einer Biographie des Nikolaus Basellius'.

furthered from the outset by Tübingen professors and students and transmitted in a golden chain fashioned link by link in the minds of men such as Johannes Reuchlin, Gabriel Biel, Wendelin Steinbach and Johannes Eck.[3]

To attribute this pompous assessment of Tübingen's significance for the history of ideas to mere provincial chauvinism would be too simple, since nearly the same judgment appears in a contemporary comparative account of European university history: 'Tübingen was one of the earliest universities to welcome first the new learning and then the Reformation. It numbers Reuchlin among its teachers and Melanchthon and Eck among its students.'[4] Thus Tübingen would seem to have been a southern metropolis of early German humanism. Baselius, at least, left no doubt concerning his own enthusiasm for humanism when, one month before the publication of 'his' history of the world (February 1516), he solicited a dedicatory epistle from Erasmus, begging in exuberant language for permission to call the Dutch humanist his friend and teacher. The Tübingen 'golden chain' of ordinary mortals would certainly have disintegrated under the weight of the superlatives that Baselius hung around the neck of the 'omnium doctissimorum doctissimum' (i.e. Germanorum omnium) Prince of the humanists: 'O Blessed Germany, that through you alone Erasmus dares to eliminate and erase the long and well-established barbaric debasement of the Latin language and to take up the sword against the arrogant Italians. . . .'[5]

Erasmus delivered – although with anything but dispatch – what was at the same time the desired dedicatory letter for Vergenhans' *Chronicon* and an unmistakable reply to Nicholas' panegyric. His letter of 1 April arrived so late that it could be included only by adding it to the reverse of the already printed title page.[6] He politely pointed out that Baselius' martial sentiments were foreign to the German–Italian competition for honour. His reference to Vergenhans' and Baselius' history was restrained in comparison to his usual dedicatory

In his *Collectio judiciorum de novis erroribus (1100–1652)*, Charles Du Plessis d'Argentré made use of Baselius' (Vergenhans') chronicle for the reproduction of the Ten Articles of the Bruchsal peasants' revolt of 1503. Vol. 1, pt. 2, p. 346b.

3 Vergenhans, *Chronicle*, fol. 316^{v}.

4 Rashdall, *The Universities of Europe in the Middle Ages*, vol. 2, p. 280.

5 'O felix iam nunc Germania! quae te uno atque solo Germano veterem Latinae linguae barbariem explodere, abstergere, abradere, ac cum Italis, hominibus alioqui gloriole cupidissimis, iam manus conserere ausit . . .' *Opus Epistolarum Des. Erasmi Roterodami*, ed. Allen, vol. 2, p. 203, lines 40–1; cf. p. 204, lines 72f.

6 *Opus Epistolarum*, ed. Allen, 2, p. 221; cf. especially Allen's introduction to this letter.

statements and contrasted sharply with his praise for the typographically outstanding editions with which the Tübingen printer Thomas Anshelm had served the international scholarly world in all three biblical–classical languages.[7]

Does this mean that Tübingen was indeed a centre of German humanism? Erasmus was aware from his own experience that the publisher's desk was far more important than the professor's lectern for promoting the *bonae litterae*. Yet, shortly after the publication of Vergenhans' *Chronicon*, Thomas Anshelm concluded five years of publishing activity in Tübingen, moving in July 1516, for unknown reasons, to Hagenau.[8] One could perhaps insist that the young Philip Melanchthon, who continued to work with Anshelm in Hagenau[9] from the time of his activity in Tübingen until his move to Wittenberg, formed a link between the university and the so-called 'Tübingen Academy' theretofore gathered around Thomas Anshelm; a company of scholars enjoying respect and adulation well into the climactic year 1516.[10]

It would be more accurate to speak of an 'Anshelmian Academy' and thus to avoid the impression that Tübingen managed to keep pace with humanist centres such as Strassburg, Erfurt or Nuremberg. A propensity in Tübingen for what Rashdall generously termed the 'new learning' is not at all conspicuous. Moreover, stressing the first half of the somewhat ambiguous label 'early humanism' makes clear just how late humanism took root there. The *via moderna* and *devotio moderna*, but certainly not the *eloquentia moderna*, characterized the early years of the university of Tübingen. But the constringency of this assertion depends on two preliminary verdicts: the evaluation of the circle around Heinrich Bebel (†1518), the first occupant of the chair for rhetoric, and the degree of Melanchthon's influence ten years later.

[7] '. . . tua officina laudatissimos autores suppeditat Latinis, Graecis, et Hebraeis formulis excusos, et his quidem longe elegantissimis.' *Opus Epistolarum*, ed. Allen, 2, p. 222, lines 3f. Cf. Melanchthon's gratitude for Anshelm's publication of his edition of Terence which likewise appeared in March 1516; *CR* 1, col. 9, no. 3.

[8] The vacuum created by Anshelm's departure was not filled until 1523 when Ulrich Morhart set up printing operations in Tübingen. See Steiff, *Der erste Buchdruck in Tübingen (1498 bis 1534)*, p. 26. Steiff was also unable to explain the move. *Ibid.*, p. 24. Cf. Widmann, *Tübingen als Verlagsstadt*, p. 42.

[9] Rau, 'Philipp Melanchthons Tübinger Jahre', pp. 20 and 25, n. 25. Cf. Wilhelm Maurer, *Der junge Melanchthon*, vol. 1, p. 217, n. 24.

[10] Maurer called the Anshelm press 'with its staff of scholars, an academy in miniature'. *Der junge Melanchthon*, vol. 1, p. 30. Johannes Haller also used the term 'small academy' but in reference to the circle surrounding Heinrich Bebel; a '*Genossenschaft* on the Neckar'. Haller, 1, p. 286.

The events of Whitsunday 1501 in Innsbruck, where Bebel was decorated as poet laureate by the emperor Maximilian, inflated both Bebel's self-esteem[11] and the reputation accorded him by succeeding generations. It would perhaps be more realistic to consider the imperial award an expression of relief that cultural life had finally begun to rouse itself in German-speaking Europe. We can agree that Bebel deserved 'a place of honour . . . in the chorus of the most adroit Latin-language German poets.'[12] But compared with the cultivated spirit of a Conrad Celtis or even with such a traditional author as Jacob Wimpfeling, Bebel merits the title of versifier rather than *poeta*.[13] Not only do his *Facetiae*, when heard with modern ears, parody the humour they were intended to convey, but they clearly lack the *esprit* of Bebel's contemporary, Poggio.[14] And if we take knowledge of Greek as an additional criterion, we note that Bebel had to turn to Johannes Reuchlin in 1501 with the most basic questions about elementary Greek. The Pforzheim humanist's attempt at politeness could not disguise his judgment that his questioner had not progressed much beyond the rudimentary stages.[15]

It is true that Johannes Reuchlin mentioned the 'robust defenders of refined letters in Tübingen' in a letter to Thomas Anshelm regarding his reluctant assent to the pleas of his compatriots that he return late in life to teach the biblical languages at Tübingen. But Reuchlin continued by remarking that, to be frank about the matter (*ut libere loquar*), it was a case of beginners who still needed to learn basic grammar.[16] Reuchlin's epitaph credits him with having snatched the ancient languages from the brink of destruction in Germany and restored the 'finer arts', but Tübingen was his last and least successful sphere of influence.[17]

11 Bebel, *Facetien. Drei Bücher*, ed. Bebermeyer.

12 *Ibid.*, p. xxi.

13 Avoiding a general judgment on Bebel by referring to Haller, 1, pp. 212ff., Otto Herding treated Bebel as a progressive pedagogue who took the poets 'seriously as being more than mere mediators of moral teachings . . .' Herding, ed., *Jakob Wimpfelings Adolescentia. Jacobi Wimpfelingi Opera selecta*, vol. 1, pp. 71–4; here p. 73. But it is precisely the gap between his technical skill and his less developed thematic profundity that justifies terming Bebel a versifier.

14 For Poggio's significance see Bebel, *Facetien*, ed. Bebermayer, pp. xxiiff.

15 'Redigere me vis ad incunabula et vagitus puerorum, ut Paulum Tarsensem cum suis Galatis jurgantem audiamus: quomodo convertimini iterum ad infirma et egena elementa, quibus denuo servire vultis' (Gal. 4.9). *Johann Reuchlins Briefwechsel*, ed. Geiger, p. 70. Here Reuchlin echoes the humanist longing for investigation instead of pontification, for the academy instead of the university. See below, nn. 19 and 26.

16 Letter of 13 January 1522; *ibid.*, pp. 334f.

17 'Musas elegantiores . . . restituit ac hebraicam simul et grecam linguam ab interitu reduxit . . .' *Ibid.*, p. 363. For Reuchlin's relationship to the medieval church see

Because the reputation of early humanism in Tübingen rests not merely on Heinrich Bebel's slender shoulders but has often been founded on the fame of the later *Praeceptor Germaniae,* Melanchthon's own evaluation of his time in Tübingen warrants our attention. Reflecting on his educational past on 31 October 1524, seven years after the posting of Luther's theses, Melanchthon remarked that Wittenberg had provided the first impetus to his intellectual development. Self-taught and mentorless, he had found himself, before going to Wittenberg, at a 'university where it was considered a capital crime to pursue the finer arts'.[18] But it was not merely the temporal distance and an understandable inclination to honour his new *Alma Mater* that elicited such harsh judgments from the Württemberger. Already on 12 July 1518 he had complained from Tübingen to his great-uncle and patron, Johannes Reuchlin, expressing his longing to be released from the Tübingen 'reform school' where he was not only making no progress, but found himself being forced back to the education level of schoolchildren.[19]

It would certainly be misleading to portray Melanchthon's entire Tübingen experience from September 1512 to the end of July 1518 with such sombre strokes. In all likelihood the departure of Thomas Anshelm in the summer of 1516 first darkened the skies of the Swabian university town for Melanchthon. Up to that point he had not only educated himself (*sine duce*) with the aid of books so generously furnished by Reuchlin, but had attracted his own circle of admirers among Anshelm's staff of *lectores*, a circle including Paul Altmann (Geraeander);[20] the later reformer of Reutlingen, Matthaeus Alber;[21] Bernard Maurus;[22] and Melanchthon's tutor in philosophy,

Decker-Hauff, 'Bausteine zur Reuchlin-Biographie', pp. 83–107. At one time a member of the Dominican confraternity, he had a family crypt constructed in the cloister of the Stuttgart Dominican monastery in 1501. Most likely as a result of the Pfefferkorn controversy, he entered the Augustinian confraternity. Decker-Hauff demonstrated that Reuchlin also entered the Stuttgart Salve-Confraternity, probably in the final days of his life. He must have died as an ordained priest since his name appeared in the Salve membership list under the rubric 'sacerdotes', leading Decker-Hauff to conclude: 'Reuchlin was ordained and became a priest prior to his death, probably in the last year of his life.' *Ibid.*, p. 102.

18 'Defuerant enim puero praeceptores, eramque in ea versatus schola, ubi capitale erat attingere meliores literas.' *CR* 1, col. 680.

19 'Salve, Suavissime, mi Capnio, mi Pater. Ut anxius sum, ne diutius in hoc me ergasterio agi, tundi, cruciari oporteat!' *CR* 1, col. 31. The improved reading, 'agi, tundi, cruciari' instead of 'agi, inde cruciari' is found in *Melanchthons Briefwechsel*, ed. Clemen, vol. 1, p. 36. Hans Volz follows Clemen in his edition, *Melanchthons Werke in Auswahl*, vol. 7, pt. 1, p. 32, line 6.

20 Maurer, *Der junge Melanchthon*, vol. 1, p. 77.

21 Haller, 1, p. 281.

22 Haller, 2, p. 110.

Franciscus Stadianus.[23] Above all Melanchthon found in Ambrosius Blarer a friend with whom he shared both his books and his knowledge of Greek. Even following Blarer's entry into the monastery of Alpirsbach in the Black Forest's Kinzig valley, an exchange of letters and occasional visits to Tübingen kept their intellectual intercourse alive.[24]

Blarer sought peace in the Benedictine monastery, 'in a place', so he wrote in an attempt to persuade his sister Margareta to follow, 'where unimpeded you will be able to accomplish the will of God'.[25] Melanchthon also dreamed in 1518 of a quiet refuge for learning, but envisioned a retreat as free of restrictive visible walls as it was devoid of people and the noise of the populace.[26] But this not infrequent humanist daydream stood small chance of realization in the Wittenberg career that lay before him. And in 1518, the humanist air of Tübingen had, in the absence of Anshelm and company, grown musty and oppressive for Melanchthon.[27] Despite all the vitality surrounding Thomas Anshelm, no circle comparable to that of Heidelberg in those same years – Brenz, Pellikan, Jacob Sturm and Bucer – was available to Melanchthon in Tübingen.[28]

Our reservations about exaggerated claims for Tübingen's role in the rise of humanism, claims increasingly incapable of meeting the

[23] Haller, 1, p. 280.

[24] After Melanchthon had left Tübingen, Stadianus gave testimony to his pupil's respect for Blarer: 'Magister Philippus Tubingam deseruit . . . Tu pro eius salute missam legas; est enim tui valde studiosus adeoque honeste de te et sensit et loquutus est semper ut nil supra.' Tübingen, 12 August 1518. Schiess, *Briefwechsel*, 1, p. 18.

[25] Alpirsbach, after New Year's 1510 (?); Schiess, *Briefwechsel*, 1, p. 3. Klaus Schreiner has demonstrated that a lengthy development reached its conclusion in the early sixteenth century as the social structure of the Alpirsbach monastery was transformed: the nobility was not 'completely excluded', but the leadership of the convent was now composed of 'sons of the Strassburg, Constance, Bregenz and St Gallen patricians . . .' *Sozial- und standesgeschichtliche Untersuchungen zu den Benediktinerkonventen im östlichen Schwarzwald*, p. 88. Blarer's flight should not be interpreted as the result of an external crisis: 'An religiöser Aufgeschlossenheit und geordneten Wirtschaftsverhältnissen scheint es also in Alpirsbach um die Jahrhundertwende nicht gefehlt zu haben.' *Ibid.* One and a half years before his exodus (July 1522) Blarer was still prior of his monastery, a post he must have assumed only shortly before, as indicated by the salutation of Melanchthon's letter from Wittenberg on 1 January 1521. Schiess, *Briefwechsel*, 1, p. 29 (no. 27); cf. p. 34 (no. 30).

[26] '. . . nihil gravius animo sedet quam in populo diutius versari, et auram vulgi longius obstrepere Musis meis, cupiebam Κἂν τρόπαν ἀπανθρωπότερον vitam in otio literario degere inter sacra silentia τῆς φιλοδοφίας . . .' *CR* 1, col. 32.

[27] Haller tried to maintain his thesis of the existence of a Tübingen (early) humanism by explaining Melanchthon's judgment as the result of 'personal experiences'. Haller, 1, p. 290.

[28] See Ritter, *Die Heidelberger Universität*, 1, p. 483.

demands of a more sober definition of humanism,[29] by no means constitute the final word on the young university's share in the 'new learning'. Tübingen's quest for a link between scholarship and wisdom could only win esteem in *later* humanism. In the course of this quest, the profusion of medieval eloquence was again displayed in all its splendour as in Summenhart's *Oratio funebris* or still more movingly in Wendelin Steinbach's portrayal of the Eucharistic mystery,[30] a work clearly indebted to Bernard of Clairvaux and yet testimony to an independent spirit. But to seek an omnipresent 'early humanism' in late medieval sources with the aid of the magnifying glass of a mature humanism leads to precisely the same illusion as does the attempt to survey the late Middle Ages through the lens of Luther and the Reformation and thereby to sprinkle one's field of vision with so-called prereformers. New beginnings that properly merit the label of 'new learning' were abundantly present in Tübingen, but they were nourished by traditions which managed to survive for a surprisingly long time without humanist scholarship and which then emptied themselves so gently into that new cultural stream that they scarcely accelerate the historian's category-generating mental turbines. To understand this era for its own sake demands, in fact, a rigorous renunciation of the standard categories and a rejection of every attempt and temptation to explain the period 'metaphysically' from the vantage point of its historical or metahistorical destination.

It was a late medieval territorial prince, Count Eberhard im Bart (†1496), and not a famous academic such as Marsilio Ficino in Florence or a far-sighted publisher such as Aldus Manutius in Venice or Johannes Froben in Basel, who stimulated and shaped the 'Tübingen Renaissance'. We have used 'renaissance' in a figurative sense and shall immediately retract it. At the outset and for a long time to follow we can detect no rebirth of the *humaniora*, the classical languages or the 'finer arts'. It is rather a coalition between late medieval devotion and scholastic investigation in the service of territorial unity that greets us as we survey the Tübingen university landscape. And Count Eberhard's active control over much of the life of the church in his territories prefigures in many ways one of the most important consequences of the coming Reformation.

[29] See my 'Quoscunque tulit foecunda vetustas. Ad Lectorem'. Cf. Joachimsen, 'Der Humanismus und die Entwicklung des deutschen Geistes'. See also Herding, 'Probleme des frühen Humanismus in Deutschland', pp. 344ff; and Wuttke, *Deutsche Germanistik und Renaissance-Forschung*, pp. 20ff.

[30] For earlier literature see Linsenmann, *Konrad Summenhart*, p. 77, n. 1.

We make no attempt to deny Count Eberhard's religious motivation and genuine interest in reform.[31] But we cannot help noticing that his consistent support for the monastic observance movement and church reform guided the ecclesiastical institutions in his territories in an independent path which simultaneously merited formal approval from ecclesiastical officialdom in Constance, Mainz and Rome and meshed with his territorial policy. The founding of his own territorial university had filled similar multiple functions. The Württemberg prince's policy prefigured the territorial ecclesiastical structure of the Reformation only in liberating and deploying existing forces for reform and channelling vital intellectual currents that collided, fused and surfaced within the university – a concentration of forces that sheds light on the otherwise obscure and elusive 'spirit of the age'.

Previous research on Tübingen between 1477 and 1516 has placed special emphasis on two questions: how does one evaluate the conflict between the *via moderna* and the *via antiqua* which, according to the university statutes, coexisted side by side in Tübingen; and, how open was the university scene, or which points of contact could the existing Tübingen tradition offer humanism as it arrived? Neither question can be filed away as long since answered, because the most recent quarter-century of research has shifted the range of interrogation, sharpened the focus and generally objectified the portrayal of both the *via moderna* and humanism. Above all, it has become clear that any appraisal of either intellectual current must take account of the numerous national and regional variables and novel tendencies as well as the historically constant factors. These same factors of time and space must be applied to a question which unfortunately has been all too hastily abandoned: the significance of the *devotio moderna* in Württemberg amid swirling contemporary intellectual currents.

[31] At the university's memorial service on 9 May 1496, Conrad Summenhart stressed in his eulogy Count Eberhard's religious motivation for founding the university: 'Annon iterum religione magnus convincitur, qui huius nostri ecclesiastici atque catholici gymnasii fundamenta primus iecit omnium atque patronus extitit?' Conrad Summenhart, *Oratio funebris*, fol. a6^{v}a–b. For Count Eberhard's less than pious adolescence, see Himmelein, *Eberhard, der mit dem Barte*, pp. 27f.

3

The scholastic rift: a parting of the ways

AT THE founding of the University of Tübingen the *via moderna* had already outgrown the stormy but inescapable phases of childhood and adolescence in which a movement discovers and develops its mature profile through contrast and definition. Karl Feckes even termed the modern way's 'Venerabilis Inceptor', William of Occam (†1349), a 'Stürmer und Dränger'.[1] But Occam's comprehensive programme found only limited realization in the first phase of the dissemination of nominalism.

Occam's thought had a twofold thrust and subsequent generations were unable to maintain the organic unity of this dual impulse. Existentially linked in Occam's person, his specific epistemological point of departure and his corporative ecclesiology each found a standard-bearer, the one in the lecture hall, the other in the convent. The radical Franciscans, or *Fraticelli,* could easily identify with his position regarding the church without paying much attention to what they considered to be his overly speculative epistemology. And Occam's earliest students in England could absorb completely his initiatives toward a new philosophical theology[2] while remaining untouched by his Franciscan spirit shaped in the quarrel over monastic poverty. Indeed, their indifference often gave way to an unmistakable aversion to Occam's ecclesiological writings.

It simply cannot be denied that Occam, as a disciple of St Francis and defender of the Franciscan ideal of poverty, favoured a basic renunciation of power on the part of the church and called for opposition to the exaggerated conception and the tyrannical application of spiritual power which he observed in the Avignon papacy.

1 Feckes, 'Gabriel Biel', p. 52.

2 Gordon Leff has announced a significant reversal of his earlier interpretation of Occam but at the same time traces his own error to Occam's disciples. 'In earlier books I have been guilty of just this misrepresentation through viewing Ockham from the same false perspective of Ockhamism.' *William of Ockham*, p. xiii. Cf. 'a new outlook . . . which within a decade had gone to extremes far beyond anything held by Ockham'. *Ibid.*, p. 476.

With pointed irony he referred to the 'ecclesia Avionica' and 'doctrina Avionica'[3] in portions of his writings which must have seemed politically anachronistic to readers in the period following the papal return to Rome. Even the French circles around Pierre d'Ailly (†1420) and Jean Gerson (†1429), although quick to quote Occam, made use only of the arguments that he had culled from the canons, decretists and decretalists of the twelfth and thirteenth centuries,[4] but were shy of adopting Occam's specific ecclesiological conclusions.

Without prejudicing certain interpretive nuances of recent research,[5] we may proceed from the assumption that Gerson appropriated the basic principles of Occam's philosophical theology.[6] Yet ecclesiologically Gerson rejected the Englishman's radical denial of the autonomy of church law.[7] Within the body of Christ, which includes the theologians and decretists,[8] he did recognize the historical necessity of ecclesiastical law.[9] But as a theologian Gerson insisted on a subordinate role for canonists, because the resolution of the Schism (1378–1415) depended on the capitulation of positive church law in the face of divine law, the *norma normans*.[10] And Luther's proud acknowledgment of his debt to Occam – 'sum enim occanicae factionis'[11] – refers not to specific ecclesiological theses[12] but rather to Occam's skill in dialectics.[13]

[3] Note the repeated use of these terms in the final chapter (XXVII) of the *Tractatus de imperatorum et pontificum potestate* edited by W. Mulder wherein Occam once more outlined his theological–political reform programme shortly before his death; *Archivum Franciscanum Historicum* 17 (1924), p. 72, lines 95f.

[4] See Tierney, 'Ockham, the Conciliar Theory, and the Canonists', p. 70.

[5] Martin Bauer places Gerson directly within the Occamistic wing of nominalism. *Die Erkenntnislehre und der Conceptus entis nach vier Spätschriften des Johannes Gerson*, p. 394.

[6] Gerson referred to Occam in his *Liber de vita spirituali animae* as the decisive authority on the question of universals. 'Si autem in oppositum allegetur Augustinus de ideis, quod alia ratione conditus est homo, alia equus, et quod illae rationes sunt incommutabiles et aeternae, remitto ad intellectum, quem dat Occam in hac materia super primo Sententiarum, in qua explicatione si rudis iudicetur, nescio quid appellabitur subtilitas.' *Gerson, Oeuvres*, ed. Glorieux, 3, pp. 125f.

[7] Cf. the 'Recommendatio licentiandorum in decretis' of April 1410. *Gerson, Oeuvres*, ed. Glorieux, 5, pp. 219f. The theme of the 'dimensions and limits of ecclesiastical law' was of such great significance that he had already twice addressed himself to it: 'Conversi estis nunc ad pastorem' (April 1406), *ibid.*, pp. 168–79; 'Pax vobis' (April 1408), *ibid.*, pp. 435–47.

[8] For the concept of the *corpus* see *Gerson, Oeuvres*, ed. Glorieux, 5, p. 178 (1406); 5, p. 443 (1408); 5, p. 218 (1410).

[9] *Gerson, Oeuvres*, ed. Glorieux, 5, p. 172 (1406).

[10] *Gerson, Oeuvres*, ed. Glorieux, 5, p. 443 (1408).

[11] *WA* 6, p. 600, line 11.

[12] See Johns, *Luthers Konzilsidee in ihrer historischen Bedingtheit und ihrem reformatorischen Neuansatz*, pp. 127ff.

[13] See *WATR* 5, no. 6419.

The writings of both Luther and the Paris conciliarists lack that Franciscan ferment and fervour which brought the dispute over poverty to a boil and permitted the most boring analyses and the endless accumulation of arguments in Occam's polemical writings to appear as stirring appeals to arms. It is true that the immediacy of the apocalyptic anticipation found among the *Fraticelli* and the prophetic vision of the speedy seizure of power by the elect that were characteristic of a Peter John Olivi (†1298) are absent in Occam. But whereas Olivi anticipated a renewal of the church as a result of direct divine action, Occam constructed a model for the restructuring of church and state through this world's forces, liberated by obedience to the dictates of scripture and human reason.

Although Occam's most recent interpreters[14] have likewise failed to establish tangible points of contact between Occam's personal involvement in the ecclesiastical conflict of his age and his philosophical theology, we cannot casually dismiss the ecclesiological question. In the first place, Occam's vision of the church as a corporation formed by all believing Christians, instead of an indivisible body or organism permeated with unidentifiable and numinous vital forces, corresponded to the spirit of his age.[15] And this understanding of the church as a corporation also complemented Occam's epistemological emphasis on the individual as a dependable basis for comprehending the whole. Thus Gabriel Biel spoke in the spirit of his mentor and model when he called the reversal and perversion of Occam's corporative ecclesiology the product of Platonic fantasies; a perversion that treated the church as if it were independent of time and place.[16]

But Occam's ecclesiology was aimed as much at Joachimite targets as at papal pretensions. Just as he rejected the identification of the pope with the Pauline *homo spiritualis* (1 Cor. 2.15) to whom all men

[14] Jürgen Miethke detects, in my opinion, quite correctly, the theoretical basis for Occam's political activity in his social philosophy. *Ockhams Weg zur Sozialphilosophie*, pp. 554f.

[15] But note Brian Tierney's critical evaluation of the too simple antithesis between 'Genossenschaft' and 'Anstalt' as constructed by O. von Gierke (*Das deutsche Genossenschaftsrecht*): Tierney, *Foundations of the Conciliar Theory*, pp. 98–103.

[16] Lectio 26 I: The value of the mass varies depending upon the occasion: 'ecclesia autem accepta est propter membrorum suorum et gratiarum in eis existentium merita, quoniam ecclesie meritum non est universale platonicum seu meritum abstractum extra homines particulares per se existens, sed est personarum et membrorum ecclesiam constituentium. Cum autem uno tempore sint plures homines boni et virtuosi quam alio, sequitur quod ecclesia uno tempore magis accepta est quam alio.' *Canonis misse expositio*, vol 1, p. 246.

owed obedience,[17] so he found the spiritual church of the *Fraticelli* incomprehensible. Occam reserved a certain degee of ecclesiastical elbow room for the Holy Spirit within established institutional channels.

These channels were in themselves neither the cause nor the guarantee, but rather the prerequisite for the working of the Holy Spirit. Like the sacraments they were *causa sine qua non*. Here we may have penetrated to that hidden point where Occam's fate and fortune in life merged with the foundations of his philosophical theology.

The critique of the ecclesiastical Establishment implicit in Joachimite anticipation of a divine reign of peace became, for Occam, a political programme: the faithful of church and state were summoned to resist a papal tyranny which threatened the Spirit's freedom of action. Yet to Occam's later readers this programme must have resembled temporary emergency legislation proposed for the Avignon crisis, since he drew his arguments and examples from the dispute over monastic poverty and the Avignon exile. The censorious blade of his ecclesiological programme gradually lost its keenness when wielded by his pupils in subsequent generations and was finally sheathed in the sixteenth century.

In what is assumed to have been his final treatise, 'Concerning the power of popes and emperors' (1347), Occam nevertheless censured the papacy in a voice that echoed and re-echoed in the Reformation epoch, leaving the limited horizons of dated polemics far behind. Indeed, Occam's claim that the tyranny of Avignon hindered scientific progress by forcing the learned and intelligent to bow in blind obedience and thereby to betray both reason and scripture[18] was elevated to a basic principle by humanist and enlightened minds of the Reformation. We search in vain within the intellectual atmosphere of the young Tübingen Academy for similar pointed criticism of the church or even for a slight suggestion that church dogma was capable of threatening secular scientific investigation. But it is precise-

[17] As in the bull, 'Unam Sanctam' of Pope Boniface VIII, 18 November 1302. Denzinger and Schönmetzer, eds., *Enchiridion Symbolorum Definitionum et Declarationum de Rebus Fidei et Morum*, no. 873 (469).

[18] It was typical of the Ecclesia Avionica that its leadership stifled all of Christendom: 'doctrinas catholicas et que fidei christiane non obviant, condempnando et profectum scientie multipliciter impediendo et cogendo litteratiores et intelligentiores eis, ut in eorum obsequium suum intellectum contra rationem et scripturas sacras captivent'. Scholz, *Unbekannte kirchenpolitische Streitschriften aus der Zeit Ludwigs des Bayern (1327–1354)*, vol. 2, p. 479. Occam considered the basic principle, 'lex evangelica est lex libertatis', to have been violated. See the convincing account by McGrade, *The Political Thought of William of Ockham. Personal and Institutional Principles*, pp. 140–9.

ly according to the same criteria of reason and scripture, and above all under the testimony of experience as expressed in the popular motto, *experientia teste*, that the ecclesiastical authorities were expounded there.

Although Tübingen's first great theologian can be called a 'loyal disciple of Occam', we must not overlook the fact that the political–prophetical aspects of the master's programme were sharply curtailed, internalized and personalized by the disciple. At peace with his prince and his pope, Biel was driven by the undisputed zeal for reform characteristic of the *devotio moderna*; a reform ideal that showed few signs of Occam's prophetic impatience.

But despite the shifting political and ecclesiastical presuppositions, there were lasting structures that shaped the *via moderna* in the course of its long trek from Occam (†1349) by way of Gregory of Rimini (†1358) to Pierre d'Ailly (†1420) and Jean Gerson (†1429); patterns of thought that informed the early Tübingen theology through Gabriel Biel (†1495) and his successor, Wendelin Steinbach (†1519). Unlike those historians who wish to treat the 'late Middle Ages' as a homogenous epoch and who thereby sacrifice the multidimensional vision,[19] we must not underestimate as factors in the *Wegestreit* the length and diversity of the path stretching from Occam to Steinbach. Three sets of circumstances that were of significance for the intellectual environment in Tübingen during the last half of the fifteenth century merit special attention.

1. Although the meaning of the qualification 'modern' in the term *via moderna* will later claim our consideration, we note that the nominalists by no means unanimously chose to identify themselves as 'Occamists'. At most, 'Occamism' serves as a label for one direction or school within the nominalist movement. In Paris the more inclusive term, *nominales*, was often linked with the names of Jean Buridan (†ca. 1359)[20] and Nicholas Oresme (†1382).[21] In Heidelberg *nominales* were associated with Marsilius of Inghen (†1396)[22] and in the statutes of the University of Wittenberg – probably under the influence of the Augustinian Eremites – with Gregory of Rimini.[23] We are of course dealing here with national or local factors of the interests of certain monastic orders, each intent on documenting the independent roots

19 See above, p. 10.

20 Paqué, *Das Pariser Nominalistenstatut. Zur Entstehung des Realitätsbegriffs der neuzeitlichen Naturwissenschaft*, esp. pp. 260–3.

21 See my study, 'Reformation and Revolution', pp. 407ff.

22 Ritter, *Studien zur Spätscholastik*, vol. 1, p. 46.

23 See the statutes of the arts faculty of 25 November 1508 edited by Friedensburg, *Urkundenbuch der Universität Wittenberg*, 1, pp. 53 and 56.

of its own scholarly pursuits. But this state of affairs still forces us to take seriously the characteristic features of the proposed central figure of each nominalist school.

2. The above observation would be self-evident had not students of the history of ideas unnecessarily exposed their views to reproach – only partly justified – from proponents of social and economic history. It is unwise for students of intellectual history to persist in manoeuvring behind the banner of *via antiqua* thought patterns, arraying 'universals' on a metahistorical horizon as if they constitute the 'real' *Stoff* of history while blissfully ignoring the unique and the momentary. To ensure a proper survey of the Tübingen landscape at the end of the fifteenth century, we must bear in mind the peculiarities of time and place even while drawing the equally indispensable comparisons with Heidelberg and Paris.

Serious consideration of the specific situation in Tübingen opens our eyes to conspicuous parallels between the most prominent and influential representatives of the two ways, Conrad Summenhart in the *via antiqua* and Gabriel Biel in the *via moderna*, while at the same time acknowledging their basic differences. The parallels lie in the area in which Tübingen's contribution was the most significant: in moral theology. It is here that Biel and Summenhart stand so close to each other, indeed, shoulder to shoulder, that they deserve to be called co-founders of the 'first Tübingen School', the intellectual pillars of a cooperative effort that had far-reaching consequences for an emerging social and economic ethic.[24]

Does this mean that the dispute between the two *viae* had become superfluous in late medieval Tübingen? Not at all. Although Summenhart considered himself a follower of the *via antiqua*, he would have refused the Thomist label mistakenly assigned to him in a modern study.[25] His prime authority was clearly John Duns Scotus (†1309), which placed him in the 'left lane' of the *via antiqua* where criticism was directed above all at Thomism.

On the other hand, Gabriel Biel followed wherever possible his *Inceptor Venerabilis*. Where Occam's trail left Biel stranded, especially in the region of ethics as treated in the fourth book of Lombard's Sentences, he was forced to cross over to Scotus.[26] Thus, starting

[24] See below, Chapters 7 and 8.

[25] Joseph Höffner in his otherwise valuable dissertation, *Wirtschaftsethik und Monopole im fünfzehnten und sechzehnten Jahrhundert*, pp. 85f.

[26] Luther commented in one of the *Tischreden*: 'In moralibus Scotus et Occam idem sunt. Scotus in quatuor sententiarum, Thomas in secunda secundae maxime laudantur.' *WATR* 1, no. 329.

from radically different presuppositions, Biel and Summenhart arrived at the field of practical theology engaged in lively and largely amiable discourse. The precise pattern of the intersection and the extent of the merger of these two routes remains to be considered; it suffices for the present to note that in Tübingen the *via antiqua* oriented itself toward Scotus and was capable of coalition with the *via moderna* without eliminating or suppressing epistemological differences.

3. Because we must attend not only to local variables but also to temporal alterations, we are especially grateful for evidence that sheds light on the last years of the period under study. We refer to the biography of Philip Melanchthon, Tübingen M.A. (1514) by Joachim Camerarius (†1574).[27] This is of exceptional historical value since Camerarius was able to draw from Melanchthon's own experiences and recollections, especially in describing his time in Tübingen. We are interested above all in the account of the conflict between the *viae*.[28]

Since we are dealing here with a story at third hand (Melanchthon recounted incidents from his student years to his friend and pupil, Camerarius, who passed them on in print), we must reckon with a degree of cosmetic surgery on the part of time and memory. But the emphasis on a Tübingen 'schism' between nominalists and realists fits well into the humanist landscape where younger humanists desired to overcome the old scholastic squabbles in their new republic of letters. And perhaps even a trace of Reformation image-making lies behind the desire to remind the reader that philosophical feuding and theological partisanship had not been invented in 1517.

Humanist historiography is certainly a more likely source for the portrayal of Plato and Aristotle as senior propagandists for the *via antiqua* and *via moderna* than is any late medieval testimony. But it also seems likely that Melanchthon experienced and evaluated the *Wegestreit* under the influence of this polarity. Luther also explained his own adherence to the *via moderna* in a manner similar enough to Melanchthon to suggest a certain consensus: the dialectical clarity of the nominalists and their effort to define individual concepts with precision made possible the standardization of terminology necessary for communication within the Wittenberg intellectual community.[29]

[27] Cf. the masterful sketch by Theodor Kolde in *RE* 3, pp. 687–9.

[28] *Joachimi Camerarii De vita Philippi Melanchthonis narratio* [1566], ed. Strobel, pp. 22f.: 'Philosophi scissi in duas factiones, Reales et Nominales; posteriori adhaerens Melanchthon amicitiam inter ambas partes conciliare studet.' Variant in *Melanchthons Briefwechsel*, ed. Clemen, 1, p. 19, n. 1.

[29] See *WATR* 5, no. 6419.

Unlike Luther, Melanchthon took up a mediating position between the two fronts. It may well be that the tutelage of the Heidelberg *via antiqua* thus left its mark on him.

This account of the controversy between the two ways is the product of a humanist orientation demonstrable for Tübingen even as early as Melanchthon's time (1512–18). Yet in Tübingen, 'humanism' also coincided with the *via moderna*. For along with his colleagues and friends, Franz Kircher, George Simler, Oecolampadius, Reuchlin and Pirckheimer, Melanchthon planned a new and 'refined' edition of Aristotle until his call to Wittenberg put an end to the undertaking.[30] And, despite being well-informed about the quarrel over universals, Melanchthon was actually attracted to the *nominales* by their studied and scientifically decanted language. Thus a newly acquired love of eloquence by no means displaced a respect for dialectics.

In an attempt to clarify three easily misunderstood but significant presuppositions, we have had to anticipate our analysis of the course of the Tübingen *Wegestreit*. As Camerarius reports, in Tübingen, the term *nominales* was synonymous with *moderni* in 1516. Often combined in the form 'doctor modernus' or with less precision as 'quidam modernus', the term 'modernus' was a temporally relative expression implying no value-judgment. It meant simply, 'modern', 'a contemporary', 'one of the recent ones'.[31] The label was employed in this sense throughout the middle ages by the representatives of all schools of thought, including the nominalists Gregory of Rimini (†1358), Gabriel Biel (†1495), and Johannes Eck (†1543); the Scotist John of Ripa (†second half of the fourteenth century); and the Thomist John Capreolus (†1444).

It is difficult to determine when the term *modernus* was first employed as a philosophical–theological *terminus technicus*.[32] A statement in a Tübingen document sheds some light on the question. The festive and 'forever valid' edict concerning the structure of the theological faculty, issued on 9 October 1496, prescribed that the faculty's four chairs be equally divided between the two ways. In practical terms this meant that two professors would be linked to each of the two *bursae*, to the two houses of living and learning which in

30 See Maurer, *Der junge Melanchthon*, 1, p. 76.

31 This comparative usage can result in a niche even for Boethius among the *moderni*. See Prantl, *Geschichte der Logik im Abendlande*, vol. 3, p. 255, n. 343.

32 Walter Freund considered it 'terminological rigidity', when, 'in der Mitte des 14. Jahrhunderts der Begriff der *via moderna* fest auf den ockhamistischen Nominalismus bezogen wird, was für die gegnerische Richtung der Skotisten und Thomisten die Bezeichnung der *via antiqua* hervorrief'. *Modernus und andere Zeitbegriffe des Mittelalters*, p. 113.

Tübingen, significantly enough, though divided by a wall, shared a common roof. The decree described the content of the *via antiqua* with the term 'via realium'; hence the use of 'modernorum' must also be viewed as a statement of the subject matter treated according to the 'modern way'. Two professors were expected to lecture in the old way and two according to the new: 'duo de via realium et duo de via modernorum'.[33] Four years later the revised statutes prohibited attempts to woo newly arrived students under the pretext of 'academic counselling' and forbade 'sheep-stealing' among those who had already opted for one of the two *bursae*.[34]

Generally speaking, only after the proclamation of the statutes of the arts faculty in 1488 had an attempt been made to achieve a rough balance between members of the two *viae* within the teaching staff.[35] But even the earliest minutes reveal that allegiance to one of the two ways was a consideration in naming examination committees as well as in the elections to the council of the university.[36] On the other hand, the unchallenged assumption by historians that both *viae* were granted equal rights in Tübingen from the outset[37] is inaccurate. In the university routine of both the theology and arts faculties, allowance was indeed made for potential rivalry. But a carefully planned parity in theological teaching appointments never came into question during the first twenty years, when the faculty had only three chairs at its disposal. As we have seen, this number was increased to four[38] only considerably later (1496).[39]

The early years in Tübingen must have resembled those at the University of Basel which in many ways acted as godparent to the new Swabian school. The Basel institution took four years from its foundation (4 April 1460) to agree to the official admission and parity of both ways.[40] But aside from this parallel, there was at least one

33 Roth, *Urkunden*, p. 264.

34 *Ibid.*, pp. 102f.

35 *Ibid.*, p. 378 ('De collegiatis').

36 *Ibid.*, p. 42. Cf. the excerpts from the minutes for 28 December 1477 (!) in Haller, 2, p. 25.

37 'Ingolstadt (1472), Tübingen (1477) und Mainz (1477) müssen schon von ihrer Gründung an beide Richtungen zulassen.' Hermelink, *Die Theologische Fakultät*, p. 135. Georg Kaufmann noted that in Ingolstadt the two ways alternated in supplying the deans of the arts faculty after 1477. *Zwei katholische und zwei protestantische Universitäten vom 16.–18. Jahrhundert*, p. 5. The *Wegestreit* did not fade away. On the contrary, two years later the *antiqui* attempted, *contra ordinem*, to regain the office of dean. *Ibid.*, p. 6.

38 Roth, *Urkunden*, pp. 70, 83ff. See also Haller, 1, pp. 28, 60 and 2, pp. 7, 19.

39 Fear of a disparity is still visible in documents from 1509. Roth, *Urkunden*, p. 113.

40 Vischer, *Geschichte der Universität Basel*, pp. 140ff.

significant difference between the two universities. Whereas in Basel the early years were dominated by the 'modern way',[41] events at Tübingen proceeded in reverse order. After the *via antiqua* had been admitted to Basel,[42] Heynlin of Stein (Ioannes de Lapide, †1496) left Paris to be accepted as a master by the Basel faculty of arts in August 1464. In 1467 he returned to Paris where in 1472 he was awarded the degree of doctor of theology. By 1478 he was referring to himself as a professor of theology and parish priest in Tübingen: 'sanctae Theologiae professor, plebanus huius loci Tuwingen'. Ten years after holding the office of rector at the Sorbonne,[43] he was elected in 1478 to the same position at Tübingen.

Hence from 1478 until the addition of Gabriel Biel in 1484, Tübingen hosted the *via antiqua* in the person of Heynlin of Stein. And Heynlin was no disinterested theologian who followed his own sublime path high above the terminological factiousness of the faculty of arts. He realized to a far greater degree than have many contemporary scholars[44] that the *Wegestreit* affected the foundations of theology. Heynlin had conferred his full authority as an ex-rector and former prior of the Sorbonne upon the Paris decree against the nominalists on 1 March 1474. And thus with the appointment of this Paris foe of nominalism at Tübingen, the *via antiqua* acquired a position of influence which, under Heynlin's successors, Conrad Summenhart (†1502) and Jacob Lemp (†1532), extended beyond the Tübingen 'higher school'.[45]

If the purpose of the Paris condemnation of 1474 was to check the influence of 'Guillelmus Okam et consimiles', Count Eberhard's attempt to protect his young university from a one-sided realist domination by appointing Gabriel Biel ten years later must be judged a positive development. Biel himself, his pupil Wendelin Steinbach, who received his doctor's cap on the same day as Summenhart, and

41 See Gabriel, '"Via antiqua" and "via moderna" and the Migration of Paris Students and Masters to the German Universities in the Fifteenth Century.' 'In the early years . . . only nominalism was taught.' *Ibid.*, p. 474.

42 Vischer detected the influence of Heynlin in this development and attributed 'this striking success in Basel' to his efforts. *Geschichte der Universität Basel*, p. 161.

43 See the data and references in the exemplary edition edited by Gabriel and Boyce, *Auctarium Chartularii Universitatis Parisiensis*, 6, pp. 249f. Cf. Monfrin, 'Les lectures de Guillaume Fichet et de Jean Heynlin'.

44 Gerhard Ritter thought 'that the historical significance of the fifteenth-century scholastic controversies between *via antiqua* and *via moderna* has been overestimated, at least as far as Germany is concerned'. *Studien zur Spätscholastik*, vol. 2, p. 144. I would accept his comments as valid for one phase around the turn of the century and to some degree as the result intended by the nominalists themselves.

45 See Karl Konrad Finke, *Die Tübinger Juristenfakultät 1477–1534*, pp. 239ff.

Peter Braun of Kirchheim on the Neckar (†1553), were Brethren of the Common Life. Since Steinbach taught until his death in 1519 and only the ducal decree of 30 January 1535 'persuaded' Braun to exchange his chair for early retirement,[46] these professors represented an unbroken tradition in the *via moderna* until the restructuring of the university in the course of the Reformation.

Given the preceding description of developments, how should one evaluate the relationship between the two ways in Tübingen? How is the intellectual atmosphere of the young university to be perceived? Overwhelming his reader with a stream of factual data and literary elan, Heinrich Hermelink conspicuously wove the scarlet thread of the *Wegestreit* into his historical account. According to Hermelink, after an initial period of paralysis during Biel's tenure,[47] the *via antiqua* rebounded to form the bridge to the future, 'leading the way to the new aspirations of the humanists'.[48] Johannes Haller, on the other hand, pursuing an objectivity that became noticeably burdensome whenever he discussed Hermelink's work, declared that it was 'probably the most unfortunate notion thinkable that Hermelink tried to construct the history of the theological faculty, and thereby of the university in general, primarily on a supposed abrupt antithesis between the old and new ways'.[49] Haller himself saw no noteworthy difference between the representatives of the two *viae*, Summenhart and Biel. Only the structure of the university forced them into 'confrontation' but 'that makes little difference'.[50] Haller's judgment seemed confirmed by the results of Gerhard Ritter's investigations. Extrapolating from Heidelberg to the rest of Germany at the close of his excellent account, Ritter could discover only a boyish and boisterous rivalry between the *viae*,[51] perhaps resembling a tug of war between two college fraternities.

The entire discussion is further complicated on the one hand by historians' insistence on reducing the dispute between the ways to a conflict entirely within the faculty of arts,[52] although clearly, as the later Tübingen statutes testify, it was a matter of concern to theologians as well. On another level, the precise understanding of the significance of nominalism and thereby of the *via moderna* is not

[46] Roth, *Urkunden*, p. 184.
[47] Hermelink, *Die Theologische Fakultät*, p. 80.
[48] *Ibid.*, p. 151.
[49] Haller, 2, p. 26.
[50] Haller, 1, p. 173.
[51] See above, n. 44.
[52] See Weiler, 'Antiqui/moderni (via antiqua/via moderna)'.

merely in flux in our era[53] but already in the fifteenth century revealed varied accents. It is of decisive importance whether we cull the characteristics of nominalism and the *via moderna* from the biting prohibition of the Paris nominalists in 1474, the balanced Basel resolution of reunion in 1492[54] or the satirically misleading *Letters of Obscure Men* of 1515,[55] to say nothing of older documents. But nothing has so blocked our access to the *Wegestreit* as the humanist assumption that the *via antiqua–via moderna* antithesis sustained by the scholastic *viri obscuri* would shrink to its *real* dimensions – i.e. trifling, ludicrous and scurrilous – when faced with the new antique–modern polarity born of the humanist recovery of classical antiquity and the liberation from barbarity. In that assumption and in the popularity of caricatures such as the *Letters of Obscure Men* lies an important explanation for the still-current disparaging references to the logical sophistry of that era.

We turn first to contemporary sources outside Tübingen, to return better informed to the early years of the Württemberg university. Our attention is drawn to two Heidelberg authors as appropriate informants: Stephan Hoest (†1472) the author of a carefully balanced treatment of the two ways;[56] and Wessel Gansfort (†1489), in contact with Gabriel Biel during the latter's Urach years[57] and a 'fellow traveller' with Heynlin of Stein on the Paris *via antiqua* before Gansfort, by his own account, managed to struggle free to nominalism.[58]

Although Stephan Hoest, in his function of vice-chancellor of the University of Heidelberg, delivered public addresses at the gradua-

53 A judicious treatment of this theme distinguishes between the state of the question (1) before 1930, (2) to 1965, and (3) during the appearance of 'new perspectives 1965–1972'. See Courtenay, 'Nominalism and Late Medieval Religion'.

54 See the 'Compactata unionis . . . tam moderne quam antique viarum' of the arts faculty. Vischer, *Geschichte der Universität Basel*, Beilage XIV, pp. 319–21.

55 See Gerschmann, '"Antiqui–Novi–Moderni" in den "Epistolae Obscurorum Virorum"'.

56 Stephan Hoest also served as Ritter's main example. See the excerpts from the two speeches delivered at the graduation ceremonies of the *via antiqua* (18 October 1468) and *via moderna* (12 March 1469) in Ritter, *Studien zur Spätscholastik*, vol. 2, Beilagen, pp. 147–53. We use the excellent unabridged edition with introduction and translation by F. Baron, *Hoest, Reden und Briefe*, pp. 146–79.

57 In the fragment, 'De Wesselo Groningensi', which was probably written by Wessel's *famulus* Goswinus van Halen and which has been dated ca. 1500 by Maarten van Rhijn, we are told: 'Aliquot annos cum Gabriele Byel ab Urach, viro doctissimo [egerat], ut eius monumenta testantur.' van Rhijn, *Wessel Gansfort*, Beilage A I b.

58 'ante annum inceptae viae Scoti cum omni diligentia, quantum potui, perspecte graviores in ea quam in via Realium errores deprehendens etiam corrigi paratus mutavi sententiam et Nominales adprehendi.' Wessel Gansfort, *Opera*, p. 877.

tion ceremonies of both *viae* in 1468 and 1469, he himself belonged to the modern way. Despite the heading added by its modern editor, the first speech, on the occasion of the graduation of the masters of the old way, was scarcely a 'defence' of the *via antiqua*.[59] The address would have been well suited to a university where the *Wegestreit* was unknown. Nonetheless a pair of timely barbs strike the reader just as they must have struck Hoest's listeners. With a mixture of commendation and caution[60] he pointed out that texts – in this case the works of Aristotle – must be understood within their own framework and context and not submerged under a flood of subtle glosses: 'Circa substantialia textuum permanendum esse, et non in curiosis supervacuisque ut nominant subtilitatibus immorandum.'[61] It appears to me that we have encountered here a fundamental intrascholastic criticism of the scholastic method which is valid for both schools, although addressing the *via antiqua* with greater force. Hoest added a second caution. Coupling the admonition with what was probably a pun on the *Wegestreit*, he urged his audience not to become mired in details *underway* but to proceed *via* the chosen path to one's destination: 'Circa singula morosi in via herent non per viam eo, quo tendendum est, gradiuntur.'[62]

In the concluding portion of his speech[63] where Hoest referred again to his introduction, he clarified the purpose of education in the arts faculty. This path's goal was none other than the proclamation of the gospel: 'per eam [scil. vestram institutionem] ad evangelii pergendum esse predicacionem'.[64] In short, it was his listeners' task 'to prepare a shelter for Christ in their listeners' hearts by teaching and preaching true doctrine'.[65] The function of the *Artes* in the actual *educatio* to Christ was propaedeutic and Hoest emphasized not the *via antiqua* as such but the *via* as a transit phase, literally as an access route. One should also note that the emphasis on the ancillary function of the *Artes* in relation to theology[66] was a characteristic and even a prerogative of the *via antiqua* for Hoest. He was by no means

59 *Hoest, Reden und Briefe*, ed. Baron, p. 147. To term the second speech a 'defence of the *via moderna*' is equally misleading. *Ibid.*, p. 165.

60 'Oraciuncula quedam habenda est, que laudibus permixtam habebit exhortacionem.' *Hoest, Reden und Briefe*, ed. Baron, p. 148, lines 28f; cf. pp. 35 and 39–41.

61 *Ibid.*, p. 154, lines 133–5.

62 *Ibid.*, p. 154, lines 144f. Baron relates *singula* to *via*.

63 'Precepta philosophie ad intelligenciam sacrarum litterarum . . .' *Ibid.*, lines 149f.

64 *Ibid.*, pp. 61; 150, lines 92f. Baron confuses the path and its destination in his translation.

65 'Per sanam igitur doctrinam in mentibus auditorum venturo Christo habitaculum preparate!' *Ibid.*, p. 158, lines 199–201.

66 Aquinas referred to their subordination or 'subalternatio'. See *STh* I, q.1 art. 5 ad 2.

alone in his judgment. An intentional subordination of philosophy to theology was more easily reconciled with the humanist ideal of *philosophia*, the devout wisdom, than with the nominalist attempt to establish the autonomy of philosophy and to free it from the bear-hug of theology. With that observation we have exhausted, so far as I can see, the basis for a thesis postulating an affinity between the *via antiqua* and 'humanism'. Yet this factor may well constitute the decisive perspective for understanding the Florentine Academy to which Kristeller has devoted special attention.

The second discourse, delivered six months later at the promotion ceremonies for the new masters of the *via moderna*, recounted the advantages of that way with far less timidity than had been evident in the treatment of the *via antiqua*. But it was really more of a eulogy than an apologetic. One notes the barely disguised innuendos directed at the old way whose graduation ceremonies were held 'fittingly' on the eve of winter, in a month in which nature begins to reveal the weakness of old age: '. . . omnia antiquitate et vetustate consenescunt'.[67] The *via moderna*, on the other hand, has associated itself with springtime in unfolding a new method and inaugurating a new access to philosophy (*aditum ad philosophiam fecit*). Yet there is no need to disparage one way in order to acknowledge the assets of the other. For 'moderna' means first of all 'increment' or 'expansion', the addition of the newly discovered to scholarship's existing stock. 'Moderna' further implies a new method clarifying the limits to the perception of truth when dealing with an artificially constructed set of problems.[68] To summarize Hoest's address: by means of a careful use of language (*dicendi proprietatem*), the modern way is able to overcome apparent contradictions (*apparenter adversa concordans*) and by demythologizing the universalia and redefining them as collective terms for individual observations, the new method can further the precise investigation of particulars. The conception of the nature of the universals, with all of its implications as set forth by Occam, Marsilio and Buridan,[69] constituted for Hoest the real distinction between *via*

[67] *Hoest, Reden und Briefe*, ed. Baron, p. 164, line 10.

[68] Hoest desires to have 'modernes' understood not as a temporal term but in terms of its ideational content. *Ibid.*, pp. 168, lines 95–170, line 101.

[69] Except for his evaluation of Henry of Ghent, Hoest's 'history of nominalism' remains valid even today. He traced its beginnings to Henry of Ghent and Duns Scotus and considered Occam the first representative of a purified strain: 'qui rubiginem omnis vetustatis detergens hanc viam primus dicitur purificasse . . .' *Hoest, Reden und Briefe*, ed. Baron, p. 176, lines 219–21. He used the temporal term, 'recenciores' instead of 'moderni' for Occam's disciples: 'recenciores commemorabo'. *Ibid.*

moderna and *antiqua*.[70] He concluded by warning once more against straying from the essence of the fundamental Aristotelian text.[71]

We have lingered over the two addresses by Hoest because no other contemporary source outlines the strife between the two ways so concisely and at the same time so comprehensively, while offering such valuable insight into the sources of the modernists' enthusiasm. Nothing in the two speeches indicates that late fifteenth-century Heidelberg merely gazed with amusement at a boisterous rivalry between two college fraternities. On the contrary: the *via moderna* has claimed credit for the discovery of a method whereby the rampaging flood-waters of a capriciously speculative thirteenth-century river of learning with its confluence of physics, metaphysics and theology could be mastered and confined to useful channels. Particulars have been programmatically advanced as an indispensable point of departure and dependable foundation for all perception. The *moderni* have insisted on a disciplined and puritanical use of language in which only a clearly established meaning verified by the respective context may be ascribed to a term (*proprietas dicendi*). Much scholarly strife has thereby been exposed as mere semantic skirmishing that could be laid to rest in a spirit of unruffled objectivity.

Hoest did not hide his sympathies. But he was no uncritical partisan of the modern way, for he feared that the 'modern' objective–scientific inclination might overwhelm all interest in the Aristotelian text itself. We might for the moment fancy that with this observation we have once more found a prop for the bold thesis that, at least in Germany, humanism sprang from the root of the *via antiqua*.[72] But the assertion is no more than a bold thesis and the newly discovered prop quickly begins to wobble. In the first place, in 1468 Hoest was by no means convinced of the *via antiqua*'s unswerving faithfulness to the Aristotelian text. Furthermore, Camerarius explicitly linked Aristotle to the Tübingen modernists in 1514. Generally speaking, we find many of Hoest's observations reappearing in

70 *Ibid.*, p. 176, lines 205–13.

71 As a successor to Peter Luder and an instructor in the *studia humanitatis*, Hoest was one of the earliest Heidelberg humanists who enthusiastically propagated rhetoric and literature. Yet he had no difficulty reconciling Aristotle's position as 'philosophorum princeps' with his own humanist inclinations. *Hoest, Reden und Briefe*, ed. Baron, p. 108, line 44. As late as 1513 Jacob Wimpfeling issued an edition of Hoest's *Modus praedicandi* (Strassburg, 1513). See Herding, *Wimpfelings Adolescentia*, p. 379, n. 160.

72 'Die Realisten sind es, denen wir die humanistischen Studien verdanken.' *Sebastian Brants Narrenschiff*, p. xx. See also Hermelink who likewise adopted this thesis: *Die Theologische Fakultät*, p. 151.

Melanchthon's recollections of his student days with the same conspicuous preference for the modern way which we noted in Hoest.

Finally, Hoest's espousal of the *via moderna* was not an isolated case. Within fifteen years of Hoest's oration Wimpfeling had assembled a chorus of young 'poets' in Heidelberg, lauding the *via moderna* and celebrating the 'divine Marsilio' of Inghen in classical metre.[73]

In all three cases we are dealing with a respect for the scientific openness and semantic discipline of the modernists on the part of those circles that were soon to develop into the nuclei of German humanism. Their members felt themselves allied in a common front against a scholasticism identified with the *via antiqua*, in their mutual effort at ecclesiastical and educational reform, and in their unanimous esteem for the unofficial fifth 'church father', Jean Gerson. But the consequences of the nominalist programme, a craving to experience and apprehend the world free from the tutelage of faith, proved irreconcilable with the platonically inspired humanist propensity for a *sancta philosophia*, a pursuit of the wisdom of piety and devotion. As a result, the ever-widening chasm between emerging humanism and the *via moderna* swallowed up the traces of former cooperation.

Before returning to Tübingen we turn to Wessel Gansfort who, unlike Hoest, was not active exclusively in Heidelberg but made an educational swing through the academic capitals of the Europe of his time (1420–89).[74] For all his humanist overtones and independently critical postulates, Gansfort never doubted the significance of scholastic theology or questioned the need for the scholastic method. Drilling in argument and counter-argument on the exercise field of the schools toughens and trains the mind for the battle for truth. Are not 'the trees strengthened by the winter storms?'[75] This conviction made it all the more important that Gansfort discover the particular school of scholasticism that would best enable him to comprehend the truth, to find the regiment in which nothing contrary to the faith was tolerated. As a Heidelberg realist he journeyed to Paris in order to convince two famous Scotists (famous at least to their fellow low-countryman Gansfort), Heinrich of Zomeren and Nicholas of Utrecht, of the error of their *via*. Before long he had hitched his own wagon to

[73] Ritter, *Die Heidelberger Universität*, 1, p. 483.

[74] See van Rhijn, *Wessel Gansfort*, pp. 47–110.

[75] 'Et hinc liquido elucessit, quantum conferat Scholastica Theologorum exercitatio, ubi dum argumenta contra veritatem facta solvuntur, adsertio veritatis sicut arbores vento et hyeme roboratur.' Wessel Gansfort, *Opera*, p. 432.

theirs but soon left the Scotist caravan for the *via moderna*.[76] That the *Wegestreit* had faded into insignificance in the Paris of those years is clearly untrue.

Wessel Gansfort recognized the possibilities and limitations of his school. When one of his opponents[77] entangled himself in contradictory assertions while seeking to defend papal plenary indulgences, Gansfort pointedly remarked that a nominalist was simply unable to put up with such bloated and ambiguous statements: 'Nosti, schola nostra Nominalis talem verborum dissidentiam et discohaerentiam non admittit.'[78] What concerned Wessel here was what Hoest captured with the term *proprietas dicendi*, a precision of language that left no doubt as to which term stood for what concept. As a general principle Wessel called for an end to the propaganda campaign against logic. Theologians need logic, and in large doses, as proved by the example of Gerson who prevailed thanks to training in logical argumentation by his mentor Pierre d'Ailly.[79] Or, for those who preferred a negative example, Wessel offered that of the condemned John of Wesel (†1481) who would have been better equipped to defend himself against his critics had he passed through the hands of the Paris drillmasters.[80]

But in preaching, Wessel realized, there is no guarantee that a clear and transparently logical assertion, however necessary, will reach the deepest level and innermost impulses of the human soul.[81] And logic has even less to do with meditation and mystical ecstasy, for in these it is the wedding-band of love[82] that signifies the final and decisive pledge and bond between God and man. *In summa*: just as logic leads to philosophy, so love is the sure path to the loftiest wisdom: 'Certa via in summam sapientiam gloriae nuptialis.'[83]

And thus the *via moderna* made its decisive contribution for both

[76] *Ibid.*, p. 877. Thus Wessel distinguished between three and not two schools: the 'Reales' (Albert and Thomas), the 'Formales' (Scotus) and the 'Nominales'.
[77] Wessel's correspondent and opponent, Jacob Hoeck (†1509), became rector of the University of Paris in 1473, shortly before the prohibition of the nominalists began (1473–81). In addition he was twice named *Prior Sorbonnae* (1474–6).
[78] Wessel Gansfort, *Opera*, p. 890.
[79] *Ibid.*, p. 895.
[80] *Ibid.*, p. 920.
[81] *Ibid.*, p. 270. No matter how gifted the preacher might be, he remains unable to reach the inner man, the heart or *mens* of his listeners. He can only make use of a conventional language that is accessible to the intellect and agreed upon by men; for 'voces nisi ex pacto non significant'. Language has no 'inherent' power of revelation or implicit 'allegorical' level of meaning.
[82] Wessel Gansfort, *Opera*, p. 603.
[83] *Ibid.*, p. 917.

Hoest and Gansfort in its stance on semantic clarity and methodical reasoning. But it was also as nominalists that they realized how the modern highway narrowed as it left the region of philosophy, entering the realm of theology as a single lane road, a useful route for apologetics and instruction.

The first occupant of a chair of theology at Tübingen, Johannes Heynlin of Stein, showed himself a less partisan patron of the *via antiqua* during his brief time in Tübingen than had been the case previously at Paris and Basel.[84] A longtime friend of Vergenhans,[85] he may well have been involved in the planning stages of the new university, since his sermon notes[86] confirm his presence in Urach, the residence of Count Eberhard, in February 1476 and May 1477.[87] Entered in the matriculation register for the summer term of 1478,[88] he filled the office of rector during the winter term of 1478–9 before leaving Tübingen permanently in the summer of 1479.[89]

In his last extant Tübingen sermon, preached in the Collegiate Church on 4 April 1478, Heynlin treated the role of logic in a discourse on St Ambrose which, aside from a thin veneer of humanist influence, was devoid of all charm and cerebral agility. In contrast to later humanist caricatures, Heynlin forewent the opportunity to blame logic as responsible for the 'dark ages'. On the contrary: the pursuit of this discipline placed one in the academic footsteps of St Ambrose both practically and speculatively. The sticky question – of crucial importance in the *Wegestreit*[90] – regarding the presuppositions

84 Haller questioned Heynlin's adherence to the *via antiqua*, even in his pre-Tübingen period. Haller, 2, p. 6.

85 Cf. Rau, 'Der Beitrag der Basler Hochschule zu den Anfängen der Universität Tübingen', pp. 15ff.

86 See Haller, 2, pp. 43 and 83.

87 See Stolz, 'Die Patrone', p. 9.

88 Heynlin was matriculated at Tübingen as no. 70 and Conrad Summenhart shortly thereafter as no. 76, both under the rectorate of Conrad Vessler. Hermelink, *Die Matrikeln der Universität Tübingen*, vol. 1, p. 21.

89 Stolz conjectured the existence of 'Zwistigkeiten, in die er mit seinen Vorgesetzten und Kollegen geraten wan'. 'Die Patrone', p. 10. The list of publications of Heynlin's Paris press in the 'House of the Golden Sun' (rue St Jacques), which employed three German typesetters, documents his broad educational experience. Nothing in Tübingen points to such wide-ranging learning and he could scarcely have aroused great interest there for such pursuits. That lack of interest may provide a partial explanation for his departure soon afterwards.

90 'Philosophia, ut Platoni placuit, in tres partes divisa est logicam sive rationalem, phisicam sive naturalem vel realem, ethicam sive moralem. Logicae finis est discernere verum a falso, bonum a malo. Phisice finis est cognoscere verum et illi assentire, Ethice finis est operari bonum. Quivis igitur scholasticus, Ambrosii dignus (volens), cupiens esse discipulus, bonum et malum temptabit in omnibus. In omnibus quidem speculabilibus temptabit, hoc est probabit, vera et falsa per logicam et reiecto falso adherebit vero per phisicam. Item in omnibus agibilibus probabit

according to which logic was to be applied, was absent, as might be expected in a festive sermon.[91] Had we not been forewarned by Stephan Hoest, the fact that Heynlin's insistence on a pursuit of logic 'in imitation of St Ambrose' was merely a typical desideratum of the *via antiqua* might well have escaped us. The Tübingen theologian's modernist listeners must certainly have accused him, and justifiably, of abusing the feast of the university's patron saint to lobby for his own partisan concerns. On the one hand, nominalists were sharply critical of logicians' unwillingness to limit logic to a mere classifying function. It was such insolence that gave birth to their presumptuous attempt to interfere formatively in the realm of theology. On the other hand, the *moderni* generously granted logic, within its own philosophical boundaries, a free hand to apprehend and investigate the world in conformity with reason and experience.

It seems clear to present-day understanding that the modern way was able to clear a path for the modern natural sciences precisely because the nominalists shifted the proverbial order of the horse and cart. The decision between truth and error was a cart following instead of preceding the horse of experience and observation.[92]

It was long assumed that Heynlin's sudden departure from Tübingen in the summer of 1479 could be traced to the *Wegestreit* and possibly to a direct confrontation with Gabriel Biel.[93] Opinions have since become more cautious, with E. Stolz alluding more generally to friction with the university administration and with colleagues.[94] Max Hossfeld is even more careful, pointing first to Heynlin's poor health[95] and then to 'the proverbial humanist *Wanderlust*' as well as to the dead-end streets of psycho-historical interpretations.[96] Tübingen's first theologian, and the best known outside Württemberg, Heynlin had endorsed the *via antiqua* in Paris and Basel with a special emphasis on loyalty to Aristotle.[97] During his Tübingen sojourn he could not have directly crossed swords with Gabriel Biel,

bona et mala per logicam et reiecto malo faciet bonum per ethicam.' Stolz, 'Die Patrone', p. 48.

91 'De speculabilibus non est hic disputandi locus, sed Aristotelice discipline preceptoribus committenda sunt.' *Ibid.*

92 See my 'Reformation and Revolution', pp. 410 and 412.

93 Summary of the literature in Max Hossfeld, 'Johannes Heynlin aus Stein', 2, p. 213, n. 1.

94 Stolz, 'Die Patrone', p. 10.

95 Hossfeld, 'Johannes Heynlin aus Stein', 2, p. 219, n. 5.

96 *Ibid.*, p. 219. As author of the Preface to Amerbach's Ambrosius edition (Basel, 1492) he must have felt a greater affinity to Basel than to Tübingen.

97 See Prantl, *Geschichte der Logik im Abendlande*, vol. 4, pp. 229f.

whom he may have met in the course of Urach planning sessions but who was never his teaching colleague.[98] Evidence of a direct confrontation with Biel would surely afford us a valuable breath of the intellectual atmosphere of those years. But unfortunately Heynlin was never more than a short-term guest in Tübingen.

Still, the fact that both Biel and Heynlin wrote treatises on the mass does make a limited comparison possible. Compared with Biel's rapidly and widely distributed comprehensive commentary, the *Canonis misse expositio*,[99] Heynlin's roughly contemporary effort to draw up a catalogue of questions dealing with the mass was a very modest work. But, probably just because of its limited size, the booklet enjoyed considerable popularity. Reprinted thirty-eight times before the Reformation,[100] its twenty-one pages contain more than previous discussion of it would indicate.[101] The treatise is so little known that an unauthentic commercial title, *Resolutorium*, has gone unchallenged.[102]

Like Biel when he produced his commentary on the Sentences,[103] Heynlin considered himself a compiler. For Heynlin that involved an unacknowledged pursuit of Aquinas and above all, of Scotus; whereas Biel explicitly set out to follow Occam and to answer in Occam's vein certain additional questions never expressly posed by the *Inceptor*. In general, though, Biel hoped to achieve through his two major works, the *Collectorium* and the commentary on the mass, precisely that harmony which Stephan Hoest had emphasized as a characteristic of the *via moderna*; a concord made possible by the Occamist unmasking of many apparently substantial problems as mere squabbles over words. Heynlin's motivation was different. He hoped to make clear that the Eucharist is not only the most sublime but also the most dangerous of the sacraments. For no human duty can compete in degree of difficulty with the task of properly celebrating the mass; with the responsibility for consecrating and consuming the sacrament of the body of Christ. To celebrate even a single mass is no small matter, and 'Happy is he who is equal to the task.'[104]

98 Adolph Franz placed Heynlin's first appearance in Tübingen in 1488. See *Die Messe im deutschen Mittelalter*, p. 558.

99 See the introduction to the critical edition, vol. 1, pp. xiiff.

100 Hossfeld, 'Johannes Heynlin aus Stein', 3, pp. 329f.

101 A. Franz dealt only with the external structure of the work and commented, 'It has a completely casuistic cast.' *Die Messe im deutschen Mittelalter*, p. 559.

102 'Tractatus dubiorum ac difficultatum circa officium misse . . .' (Basel, 1492).

103 See Biel's note, 'haec mea collecta' in Biel, *Collectorium, Prologus*, p. 7.

104 'In qua (scil. missarum celebratione) sacramentum corporis et sanguinis Jhesu Christi redemptoris nostri consecratur, immolatur et sumitur sacro canone attes-

Reverence for the sacrament of the altar was likewise a frequent theme and purpose of Biel's comments, and Wendelin Steinbach gave moving expression to that concern in rhetoric modelled on Bernard of Clairvaux in his dedicatory epistle for Biel's *Canonis misse expositio*. Biel chose his words with academic reserve; Heynlin apparently had the edification of the less educated local clergy in mind. His emphasis on the priest's responsibility to examine his conscience carefully in preparation for the mass indicates clearly how easily reverence in the presence of the *mysterium tremendum* could lead to a painful and fearful *scrupulositas*.[105] But it is difficult to demonstrate that this difference of emphasis concerning a question of spirituality stemmed from the *Wegestreit*. An important factor leading from confrontation to a partial convergence of the ways in Tübingen was precisely Biel's resolve to combine a respect for the older theology with an openness toward the special contribution of the new.[106]

Within the realm of physics, the specific achievement of the thirteenth- and fourteenth-century Paris and Oxford nominalists was the clearing away of the speculative underbrush then choking the tender saplings of the modern natural sciences. In the thicket of theology such a radical approach was hindered by the elevation of one particular philosophical explanation of the mystery of the doctrine of transubstantiation to ecclesiastically sanctioned dogma at the Fourth Lateran Council (1215). The nominalists first called attention to this philosophical presupposition of the Fourth Lateran, and subsequently relativized its validity by pointing to alternative explanations for the mystery of the altar.[107]

The full-scale nominalist attack on *curiositas*, i.e. on philosophy's attempt to infiltrate the secrets of divine revelation, meant a significant curtailment for theology. Theology and metaphysics were eventually found to have served not as essential supports for, but as impediments to, genuine exploration in the world accessible to the human senses and reason. Within theology, the *via moderna* pushed speculation into the corner and thereby made room for new efforts. Thus when Wendelin Steinbach set out to depict the presence of

tante. Non modica, inquit, res est unam missam facere. Et valde felix est, qui unam digne celebrare potest.' Heynlin, *Resolutorium*, fol. a5r.

105 For the theological and pastoral context of the concept *scrupulositas* see Werbeck, 'Voraussetzungen und Wesen der *scrupulositas* im Spätmittelalter'.

106 'ita inter novos et veteres theologos sese medium posuisse, quod nec illorum simplicem sprevit maiestatem nec horum magnificam horruerit subtilitatem'. Biel, *Collectorium, Prologus*, p. 5.

107 See Hilgenfeld, *Mittelalterlich-traditionelle Elemente in Luthers Abendmahlsschriften*, pp. 393ff.

Christ in the Eucharist, he called upon Eucharistic piety to fill the role formerly demanded of Eucharistic theology. In reverent awe he gathered the most diverse elements from the abundant medieval tradition, elements which were to be elevated to dogma by the various sixteenth-century parties (Luther, the Council of Trent, the sacramentarians) and linked these elements together in a chain of devout rhetoric.

Here we reach one boundary of the *via moderna*'s capacity to cooperate with the blossoming love for rhetoric. The modern way's strength lay from the beginning in the realm of dialectics and in the strict definition and use of words and concepts. Above all, it sought to prevent bloated semantic solutions from parading disguised as the genuine solutions to 'real' problems.

4

The devotio moderna*:*
movement and mystery

WHEREAS HEYNLIN aimed his treatise on the mass at the theologically uneducated clergy; at 'sacerdotes simplices, qui notitiam canonum non habent',[1] Gabriel Biel's commentary was clearly conceived for an academic audience.[2] But the two works differed not merely in regard to the educational level of their prospective readerships. As attested by Wendelin Steinbach[3] in his introduction to Biel's commentary, Biel hoped particularly to reveal Catholic truth in all its richness. He intended more than a mere quantitatively exhaustive treatment. His central aim was to overcome the conflict between the schools, in the service of catholic doctrine. This attempt to attain a unity in theology was basic to the 'modernist' programme and was by no means limited to contemporary theological controversies. The growing importance of an anti-Pelagian Augustinianism thoroughly tested the Tübingen tradition inspired by Biel and demanded the deployment of the most 'modern' interpretive tools in order to attain the desired doctrinal unity.[4]

But another factor was of particular importance for circumstances in Tübingen. The first three 'modernists' in Tübingen, Gabriel Biel, Wendelin Steinbach and Peter Braun,[5] were also Brethren of the Common Life and thereby at the same time members of both the *via moderna* and *devotio moderna*. Originally emanating from *petit bourgeois* and artisan circles, this *devotio* with its distinctive blend of devotion and zeal for reform, decisively influenced the theological atmosphere in pre-Reformation Tübingen in a manner unequalled at other univer-

1 Heynlin, *Resolutorium*, fol. a2r.

2 See the introduction to the critical edition of the commentary on the mass (*Canonis misse expositio*), 1, p. x, and my account in *The Harvest of Medieval Theology*.

3 We must be careful not to base our analyses on direct comparisons between differing types of treatises, e.g. Biel's dogmatics, his *Collectorium* and Steinbach's commentaries on scripture.

4 Feld went so far as to claim: 'Der Einfluss des Augustinus auf seine [Steinbachs] Theologie ist vermutlich grösser als der seines Schulhauptes Ockham.' *Wendelini Steinbach Opera*, ed. Feld, vol. 1, p. xx.

5 For Peter Br[a]un, who succeeded Steinbach, see Hermelink, *Die Theologische Fakultät*, p. 200.

sities. And so we devote a portion of the present study to the Modern Devotion.

This revival movement on the eve of the Reformation had more than the word 'modern' in common with the nominalists. Both *via moderna* and *devotio moderna* sought to transcend the scholastic and above all, the monastic, controversies, in pursuit of a synthesis of *scientia* and *sapientia* that would further a renewal of the Christian charity characteristic of the primitive church. It is the *devotio moderna*'s readiness to take its inspiration for reform and observance from the golden age of the church's history and the movement's pedagogical concerns that have so often attracted the attention of scholars prospecting for humanism in the Low Countries or even in all of northern Europe. As a result the *devotio moderna* has been transformed into 'Christian humanism'.[6]

Sifting through the mass of scholarly ore mined in the process one comes upon deceptive fool's gold: the supposed link between humanism and Christianity north of the Alps, juxtaposed with an Italian humanism indifferent or even inimical to liaison with devotion. That Italian humanism underwent significant modification in its journey from south to north is beyond dispute.[7] The northern recipients were concerned with the defence against immoral tendencies. And even if Heinrich Bebel evidenced no qualms about mining the entire lode of the Latin inheritance, a more cautious Wimpfeling carefully examined and refined his material to avoid damage to youthful minds and morals. At approximately the same time Erasmus took Poggio to task for his frivolous *Facetiae*. In 1508 he turned his attention to the church fathers, above all to Jerome,[8] the patron saint of the *devotio moderna*, in order to further the union between scholarship and Christian ethos in a new capacity as theologian and not as *poeta*. Yet despite these conspicuous tensions, which were definitely discernible to leading contemporary humanists, the historian's carefully constructed model of a north–south axis with an alpine continental divide between a profane and a Christian humanism has buckled beneath the weight of recent research on humanism.[9]

A second proviso is even more fundamental. Recent investigation

[6] See Post, *The Modern Devotion*, pp. 15f, 673, 675.

[7] Jozef IJsewijn has directed attention to the '*transitus humanismi ad christianismum*'. 'The Coming of Humanism', p. 223.

[8] See below, p. 73, nn. 48, 50.

[9] Kristeller, 'The European Diffusion of Italian Humanism', p. 87; Bouwsma, *Venice and the Defense of Republican Liberty*, pp. 27–33; Trinkaus, *In Our Image and Likeness*, vol. 1, p. xxiii.

has surrounded the significance of the *devotio moderna* for the spread of humanism in the Low Countries and the Rhine valley with a circle of question marks. A shadow of doubt has fallen over the supposed teaching activity of the Brethren of the Common Life or the canons of the Windesheim Congregation. Peering up from under the mass of R. R. Post's arguments and evidence, scholars will be obliged to make much more cautious judgments in this regard than in the decades following the work of Albert Hyma.[10] That the Brethren were not directly involved in instruction in the schools has been convincingly demonstrated.

But however healthy Post's debunking may be – not unlike the aftermath of Paul Oskar Kristeller's work in the area of Italian humanism – it is equally pressing to realize that from the outset the Brethren were unusually active in furthering education. Their concern ran more in the direction of *sapientia* than *scientia*, but by means of continually changing combinations they did pursue an ultimate synthesis of wisdom and knowledge. The movement's 'founder', Geert Groote (†1384), helped advance the chapter school at Deventer with its already established curriculum in all disciplines of the *quadrivium* to a reputation extending far beyond the IJssel valley. Less than fifty years after Groote's death the movement's reform ideal was explicitly formulated as a pedagogical task: 'The reformation of the church can be best achieved by those who in the prime of their youth have been trained in the exercise of virtue.'[11]

Thomas a Kempis reports that Groote's 'successor', Florens Radewijns (†1400), concerned himself with the welfare of the schoolboys in a special way, seeking board and lodging with Deventer families for those coming from outside the city. The description of Florens as having been characterized not by 'saecularis eloquentia' but by 'humilis informatio morum'[12] serves the historian as a fitting caption for this phase of the *devotio moderna*: the burning issue was not the pursuit of eloquence but an unpretentious formation and reformation of morals. Moulded by and adapted to the small-town environment of Gelderland and the IJssel valley, 'devotio' was unmistakably attired in anti-intellectual, perhaps also in anti-Italian, fashions. It was understood above all as a matter of the heart, a pursuit of that

[10] Hyma, *The Brethren of the Common Life*; cf. more recently the revised edition of *The 'Devotio Moderna' or Christian Renaissance (1380–1520)*, which appeared originally in 1924.

[11] G. Dumbar, *Analecta*, p. 184.

[12] *Thomae a Kempis Opera*, ed. Pohl, vol. 7, p. 176. In Van der Wansem, *Gemene Leven*, p. 130, n. 7.

wisdom whose summit Florens was acknowledged to have reached when he was described as 'expertissimus in spiritualibus'.[13] The *Frensweger Chronicle*, one of the oldest and richest sources for the history of the brotherhood to 1483, yields a further example of this anti-intellectual posture. The chronicle reports the radical change of heart on the part of Evert of Eza (†1404), a Jewish doctor and later rector of the sister-house in Almelo, as one of the most significant results of Groote's preaching. Evert, once 'puffed up with worldly learning' (*scientia*) and the captive of presumptuous 'curioesheit', finally cast aside all the arrogance of his previous learning under the influence of the preacher's words.[14] In socio-psychological terms, we detect here the devout self-consciousness of the (as yet) non-academically inclined urban *petite bourgeoisie*.

Adherents of the movement had serious reservations[15] about academic education, fearing that the mental training of the schools might lead to moral derailment.[16]

The early *devotio moderna* – and here we must acknowledge Post's contribution – was not concerned with founding new schools but rather with the reformation of monasteries and the para-academic care of the pupils in existing institutions. The Brotherhood was deeply concerned with the problems resulting from the rapid growth of the urban schools and devoted itself to procuring physical shelter and providing pastoral care, especially for the *extranei* forced to find lodging in strange cities throughout the week, or for the entire term.

But this state of affairs changed in the course of the fifteenth century and the Brethren became increasingly involved in the new

[13] *Thomae a Kempis Opera*, ed. Pohl, vol. 7, p. 182; Van der Wansem, *Gemene Leven*, p. 132.

[14] Alberts and Hulshoff, eds., *Het Frensweger handschrift betreffende de geschiedenis van de moderne devotie*, pp. 149f.

[15] 'Quomodo quis docere potest, quod nunquam didicit?' 'Consilium . . . ad iuvenem cui collata fuit ecclesia curata', in *Gerardi Magni Epistolae*, ed. Mulder, pp. 310–21; here p. 316.

[16] Hyma's claim that Celle 'inaugurated, upon Groote's advice, the reform which turned into the revival of learning in Northern Europe', is clearly exaggerated. *The 'Devotio Moderna'*, p. 127. Post points out that Groote's correspondence with Celle deals with many aspects – especially pastoral care – but that 'there is no word at all about education or teaching or the carrying out of innovations'. *The Modern Devotion*, p. 97. As we can only briefly indicate here, it would be most unfortunate for research on the *devotio moderna* should Hyma's exaggerated claims be permitted to obscure totally the elements of truth in his argumentation. His extreme position is considered with justification to be so completely superseded that his accounts have unjustifiably become unfamiliar territory to most scholars. Although frequently cited, he is seldom read.

pedagogical boom.[17] Alexander Hegius (†1498), closely associated with although not a member of the Brethren,[18] extended the former pastoral concern for moral development to his reform of school books while noting that 'the Italians love their children too much to stuff them with useless and thereby injurious material'.[19] Hegius himself began to write poetry and his school became a centre for the cultivation of young poets.[20] To use language more cautious than

[17] This combination of reform attempts, pastoral efforts and new enthusiasm for scholarship, centred to a large degree around monastic houses, can be termed 'monastic humanism' – the nearly unnoticeable transition from pious reading of the Fathers to a programmatic pursuit of pre-scholastic sources.

The *devotio moderna* documents a parallel development. The crucial stages marking the long road from Groote to Erasmus are: 'monastic reform', the 'pastorate to schoolboys', 'pedagogical activism', 'Latin school humanism' and scholarly '*sodalitates*'. Indeed, *de facto* there were three and not merely two branches of the *devotio moderna* which increasingly came to support the new interest in education: (1) the Brethren and Sisters of the Common Life – two lay communities which we here consider as one; (2) the Windesheim Congregation and (3) the rectors and teachers in the newly founded or newly resuscitated Latin schools that were linked to the Brethren of the Common Life by means of student hostels. Whether Geert Groote's original ideal was preserved in this threefold division can be answered affirmatively for the Windesheimer and demonstrated institutionally for the succession of rectors.

For the relationship between Erasmus and the Deventer educators, Alexander Hegius and Jan Synthen, see the balanced account in Tracy, *Erasmus, The Growth of a Mind*, pp. 21–9. The 'devout' concept of a monasticism 'as broad as the world',can be found in Erasmus' statement to the provost of his convent, Steyn, Servatius Roger. Here he very skilfully played off a characteristic ideal of the *devotio moderna* against the Windesheim Congregation's adaptation to monasticism: 'Quanto magis est e Christi sententia totum orbem Christianum unam domum et velut unum habere monasterium, omnes concanonicos et confratres putare; baptismi sacramentum summam religionem ducere, neque spectare ubi vivas sed quam bene vivas.' *Opus Epistolarum*, ed. Allen, 1, pp. 296, 568, lines 84–8. A variant of this same thought – 'quid aliud est civitas quam magnum monasterium?' – can be found in his letter to Paul Volz which found wide dissemination as a foreword to the 1518 edition of the *Enchiridion militis Christiani*. *Opus Epistolarum*, 3, p. 376, line 561.

[18] In his later retrospective account, the *Compendium vitae Erasmi* of 1524, Erasmus described how he had been sent to Deventer at the age of nine: 'Ea schola tunc adhuc erat barbara . . .; nisi quod Alexander Hegius et Zinthius coeperant aliquid melioris litteraturae invehere.' *Opus Epistolarum*, ed. Allen, 1, p. 48, lines 34–40. Together with Jan Synthen († before 1493), Hegius published a new and, before long, popular Latin grammar. See Post, *The Modern Devotion*, p. 576.

[19] 'Eos cariores habent quam ut eis tam inutilia tamque noxia inculcent.' In IJsewijn, 'The Coming of Humanism', p. 245.

[20] 'Hegius' school at Deventer became a kind of seminar for young student poets.' *Ibid.*, p. 253. The document in which Hartman Moller, a canon of the chapter of St Bartholomew at Frankfurt, endowed the newly founded house of the Brethren (St Mark's) in Butzbach – where Biel became provost – with the task of caring for needy pupils, indicates the degree to which Deventer and Zwolle served as examples: 'zeu der ere gotts in nutze armer und ander schuler dy darin uffgnomen werdent sollent nach wyse der schulen zu Devender und Schwolle'. Diehl ed., *Die Schulordnungen des Grossherzogtums Hessen*, vol. 1, p. 475; cited by Franz Joseph Burkard, *Philosophische Lehrgehalte in Gabriel Biels Sentenzenkommentar unter besonderer Berücksichtigung seiner Erkenntnislehre*, p. 41, n. 142.

Hyma's, the *devotio moderna* at this stage proved capable of *coalition* with the new pedagogical forces. And the movement's influence extended far beyond territorial frontiers, even penetrating Paris[21] although admittedly in Jean Standonck's more restorative than reformative application of Groote's ideals at the Collège de Montaigu. [22]

It was no accident that Count Eberhard im Bart permitted and promoted the expansion of the *devotio moderna*'s monastic branch, the Windesheim Congregation, into Württemberg during the years of the university's founding. With the consent of Sixtus IV (1476), Eberhard converted the assets of the wealthiest Württemberg religious establishment, Sindelfingen's collegiate chapter, into the basic endowment for his new university. Even when freed of all compulsory services, rents and taxes on 1 August 1477, the formerly affluent chapter could support[23] no more than the simple life style of the Brethren to which the newly regulated house now belonged.[24]

Conrad Summenhart probably intended no allusion to this skilful fusion of provision for the university with the promotion of the interests of the Windesheim canons in his university eulogy of Count Eberhard on 9 March 1496. Summenhart asked rhetorically whether the count had not testified to his deeply religious nature (*religione magnus*) in having furthered monastic reform[25] and at the same time

21 The following entry of 1495 in the *Acta capituli generalis* of the Windesheim Congregation, apparently unknown to Renaudet (see the following note), must refer to this fact: 'Commissum est prioribus de Monte et de Fonte cum alio priore e Brabantia assumendo, pergere ad domum iuxta Parisios . . .' *Acta capituli Windeshemensis*, ed. van der Woude, p. 94.

22 See Renaudet, *Préréforme et humanisme à Paris pendant les premières guerres d'Italie (1494–1517)*, pp. 172–81, 213, 246. Standonck attempted to transplant the *devotio moderna* to the kingdom of France and to assist it in taking root under the protection of Charles VIII. It was the Windesheim Congregation, the third branch of the movement characterized by strict monastic observance, that appealed to Standonck.

23 Meyer, *Die Brüder des gemeinsamen Lebens in Württemberg*, p. 11; also in *BWKG*, 17 (1913) (=1), pp. 107f. Regarding the partial transfer of the Sindelfingen endowment and the founding of a monastery, see the documents that are printed as an appendix to Waldemar Teufel's *Universitas Studii Tuwingensis*.

24 How far in advance plans must have been laid can be seen from a decision by the central chapter shortly after Easter of 1477: 'Concessum est visitatoribus in Wormacia et Heghe incorporare capitulo domum in Zinderinghe [Sindelfingen] et ibi ponere fratres qui priorem eligant.' *Acta capituli Windeshemensis*, ed. van der Woude, p. 74.

25 Summenhart was probably referring to the reform of the Augustinian monastery in Tübingen but his statement was certainly not limited to that reform: 'An non et iterum religione magnus fuit, qui collapsarum religionum tot vel instauravit vel in melius reformavit monasteria, ita ut non solum his, qui de sua provincia, quam professi erant, negligebant regulam, verum et externis fieret formidabilis quosdam quidem favoribus dulcibus alliciens, quosdam vel indignatione vel ecclesiastica districtione mediante compellens.' *Oratio funebris*, fol. a6^{v}.

founding the university[26]. At any rate it is clear that the very beginnings of the university coincided with a carefully conceived programme of economization; a phenomenon observable at other German universities founded in this same period.

It is hazardous to speculate about the potential consequences of Count Eberhard's unrealized plan to remove and relocate the Tübingen Augustinians and replace them with Dominicans in 1478. He would indeed have achieved the same inexpensive expansion of the theological faculty to which the later observant reform of the Augustinians under the learned leadership of men such as Staupitz and Nathin led.[27] But Tübingen would also have borne, together with Cologne, the fury of the humanist assault on the Dominican obscurantists.

A second, and in the long run more significant, move was Count Eberhard's decision to invite the Brethren[28] to his capital at Urach. On 10 July 1477, only a few weeks after the Windesheim Chapter General had approved the addition of the Sindelfingen chapter, the assembled representatives of the German houses,[29] with Gabriel Biel presiding, endorsed the transformation of the church of St Amandus in Urach into a collegiate endowment and its addition to the German Chapter.[30] A few weeks later, testifying to careful planning and preparation, Biel presided, on 17 August 1477 and in the presence of Count Eberhard, over the festive transfer of ownership of the church to the Brethren.[31] Approximately three years later Biel himself succeeded Benedict of Helmstatt as prior.[32]

Count Eberhard continued to promote the cause of the *devotio moderna*. In 1482 he had the court chapel in Tübingen incorporated into the Urach endowment. Biel's later successor in the nominalist

26 See above, p. 22, n. 31.

27 Not only the Württemberg counts but the Augustinian Order as well, must have been interested in this symbiosis. In 1490 a separate lectorate was established in the convent. 'The close liaison between monastery and university found visible expression therein [in the lectorate].' Brecht, 'Das Augustiner-Eremiten-Kloster zu Tübingen', p. 78.

28 The Brethren were also known as 'Gugelherren' or 'Kugelherren' in reference to the 'Gugel' or pointed hood that they wore.

29 St Mark's in Butzbach, Marienthal near Geisenheim, St Mary's at Königstein and St Martin's at Wesel.

30 Meyer, *Die Brüder des gemeinsamen Lebens in Württemberg*, pp. 16ff. (=1, pp. 109ff.).

31 Cless, *Versuch einer kirchlich-politischen Landes- und Cultur-Geschichte von Würtenberg bis zur Reformation in zween Theilen*, vol. 2, pt. 2, p. 281.

32 Fritz Ernst seems to have assumed that Gabriel Biel was immediately elected the first prior. He has probably confused this Urach endowment with St Peter's in the Schönbuch where Biel was indeed the first prior. *Eberhard im Bart*, p. 93.

chair of theology, Wendelin Steinbach, left Urach to represent its collegiate chapter as pastor to the castle residents and as the count's confessor.[33] After accompanying Count Eberhard, Chancellor Vergenhans and Johannes Reuchlin on a trip to Rome, Biel settled in Tübingen in 1482, entering upon the next major phase in his career in close contact with the leadership of the university.

When Biel became the *Ordinarius* for theology on 22 November 1484, he did so without relinquishing his office as prior in Urach. And thus, at the beginning of a chain of tradition extending by way of Wendelin Steinbach to Peter Braun, Biel linked in his person the worlds of the *devotio moderna* and *via moderna*.[34] The Brethren not only ensured the economic feasibility of the University of Tübingen but they were also responsible in a large measure for that distinctive quality of Tübingen's intellectual life which separated the Swabian school from other young south German universities such as Freiburg and Ingolstadt and from the older institutions in Cologne and Heidelberg.

But what of the content of this modern devotion one hundred years and hundreds of miles removed from its late-fourteenth-century cradle in Deventer? Fortunately we are able to reconstruct major features of the Tübingen *devotio moderna* with the aid of a treatise in which Gabriel Biel described and defended the ideals of the Brethren. Although undated, the work must have been written following Biel's entry into the Windesheim Congregation in 1468–9.[35] And it may well have been composed considerably later since Biel wrote as an established spokesman for the movement and described the life of the community with the authority of years of experience. Perhaps it was a programmatic outline intended to accredit and introduce Biel and his brethren to Württemberg in the years during which both the *devotio moderna* and higher learning arrived in Swabia.[36]

[33] Meyer, *Die Brüder des gemeinsamen Lebens in Württemberg*, p. 27 (=1, p. 123).

[34] J. van Ginneken, in an excellent study, made the claim that the label *devotio moderna* originated in conjunction with Geert Groote's adherence to the *via moderna* during his time in Paris. *Geert Groote's Levensbeeld naar de oudste Gegevens bewerkt*, pp. 95ff. Unfortunately Theodore P. van Zijl has followed van Ginneken in this undocumented and undocumentable assertion. See *Gerard Groote, Ascetic and Reformer (1340–1384)*, p. 41.

[35] William J. Courtenay has demonstrated that Biel had not yet joined the Brethren of the Common Life in 1467. But records list him as involved in the new foundation at Marienthal on 1 November 1463. 'Gabriel Biel as Cathedral Preacher at Mainz and his Supposed Sojourn at Marienthal', pp. 146 and 149.

[36] The *Tractatus Magistri Gabrielis Byell de communi vita clericorum* had been noticed by Johannes Haller (2, p. 56). W. M. Landeen reprinted it without commentary in 'Biel's Tractate on the Common Life'.

At first glance one might conclude that the treatise reveals Biel once more as a 'collector'; in this case drawing not on William of Occam but on the apologetic for the Brethren and Sisters of the Common Life written by Gerard Zerbolt of Zutphen (†1398).[37] But Biel made no mention of Gerard, and the charges against which he defended the Windesheim canons were of such traditional nature, stemming as they did from the prohibition of new monastic orders in 1215 and 1274, that parallels to Zerbolt would surface even in an independently developed apologetic.[38] The traditional nature of Biel's defence is clearly visible in his conclusion that the Windesheim canons[39] formed no new order in the technical sense of the term since they neither obeyed the rule nor wore the habit of an order.[40]

Biel's repeated allusions to the *Venerabilis Magister* Jean Gerson – quoted in this treatise with the same deference and authority accorded the *Venerabilis Inceptor* Occam in Biel's commentary on the Sentences – fit the contours of Biel's thought well. He gratefully employed Gerson's ecclesiastical authority because at Constance the Paris chancellor had obtained the condemnation of the Dominican Matthew Grabow's attempt to brand the institution of the common life outside monastic orders a heresy.[41] Biel hoped to demonstrate from the condemnation of the Dominican's charges that the Brethren

37 Zerbolt of Zutphen, 'Super modo vivendi devotorum hominum simul commorantium'.

38 Cf. the first ruling on this issue by Arnold Dickinghe (2 December 1397), which was published by Leonard Korth, 'Die ältesten Gutachten über die Brüderschaft des gemeinsamen Lebens', pp. 14–17. This judgment deals with the question of the propriety of the *lay* branches of the *devotio moderna*, concluding in favour of the movement.

39 From the very outset, rather than referring to the lay movement for which Groote was likewise responsible, Biel defined his 'Order' as 'ordo noster vel institutio communis vite clericorum . . .'. Landeen, ed., *Tractatus Magistri Byell*, p. 79. Paul Mestwerdt detected the culmination of the relationship between adherents of the *devotio moderna* and the thought of the *via moderna* in the fact that Gabriel Biel 'was able to influence the theological attitude of the Brethren in Württemberg to the point that, within the local university context, nominalism became an actual *Ordenstheologie* as demonstrated by the theological path taken by his pupils and Brethren at the University of Tübingen, especially Wendelin Steinbach and Peter Braun'. Mestwerdt, *Die Anfänge des Erasmus*, p. 109.

40 'illi dumtaxat dicuntur habere "ordinem" vel esse in "ordine", qui sub professione certe alicuius regule et susceptione habitus etiam religiosi solent nominari.' Landeen, ed., *Tractatus Magistri Byell*, p. 80.

41 Gerson had in fact repudiated this thesis of Grabow in an opinion of 3 April 1418. 'Super assertionibus Fratris Mathaei Grabon O.P.', *Gerson, Oeuvres*, ed. Glorieux, 10, pp. 70–2; *J. Gersonii Opera omnia*, ed. Du Pin, 1, cols. 467–70. Grabow's *Conclusiones* and retraction are likewise found in the Du Pin edition, *ibid.*, cols. 470–4.

enjoyed official conciliar approbation.[42] He intended to serve notice to potential adversaries that the canons were no longer defenceless, but rather, since the public endorsement by such prominent conciliar fathers as Gerson and Pierre d'Ailly, lived and worked under the protection of the respected doctrinal authority of these Paris theologians.[43] The respect and authority enjoyed by Gerson found graphic expression in his portrayal in company with the four Latin church fathers in the church of St Amandus at Urach. Philologically and theologically, Biel appealed to Gerson for proof that limiting the term 'religiosi' to monastics and 'religio' to a monastic order was nothing short of semantic scandal: there could be only *one* Christian order and that was the exemplary rule according to which Christ had lived.[44]

Aquinas had asserted that it was much better to live under than outside 'religious' vows. In contrast, Biel states: 'It is sufficient for our complete perfection that we live and persevere in the liberty of Christian law under the one Abbot Jesus Christ.'[45] This concept of liberty by no means anticipated Luther's 'freedom of the Christian man'. For Biel the completion of the law remained essential for salvation ('sine quibus non est salus') and he never questioned in a fundamental way the medieval distinction between the law applicable to all Christians (*praecepta evangelica*) and the supplementary gospel guidelines (*consilia evangelica*) established for members of monastic orders. Biel's aim was to prevent the transformation of what was voluntary and dependent on the capabilities of individual Christians into obligations pegged in place by monastic vows.

Because Biel, unlike Geert Groote one hundred years earlier, excluded the lay Brethren and Sisters of the Common Life from consideration, he has presented us with a one-sided, clericalized portrait of the *devotio moderna* adjusted to the Windesheim model. And yet we are reminded of the early years of the movement by his insistence that Christian liberty consisted above all in following the apostolic admonition that 'everyone remain in the state in which he

[42] At the Council 'predicta institutio communis vite fuit proposita, examinata, probata et declarata . . .' Landeen, ed., *Tractatus Magistri Byell*, p. 80.

[43] 'vivere sub umbra eorum, quorum auctoritas et doctrina abinde nos defendere potest et tueri.' *Ibid.*, p. 82, Cf. Ps. 91.1.

[44] 'sola religio christiana est proprie, vere et anthonomatice dicenda "religio" . . .' *Ibid.*, p. 80; *Gerson, Oeuvres*, ed. Glorieux, 10, p. 70.

[45] 'Nobis interim satis est ad omnem perfectionem stare et vivere in libertate legis christiane sub uno abbate Christo Jhesu . . .' Landeen, ed., *Tractatus Magistri Byell*, p. 81.

was called'.[46] Biel readily admitted that for the most part working laymen and women had decided to enter the common life. But that life was admirably suited to priests as well.[47] He saw no contradiction here[48] and argued that the Brethren had formed a lay movement in the beginning only because the monastic landscape had appeared so bleak at that moment as to make a merger with existing orders seem ill-advised.[49]

Thus the inquisitorial assault from the outside had been repulsed, but at a price: the lay element in the *devotio moderna*, suspect in the face of Beghard and Beguine threats, has been reduced to echoes from the distant past. The mission to schoolboys has been transfigured into a reformation of the clergy. At the same time, theology has advanced to a more central and less anti-intellectual enterprise. Copying is an art, unfortunately seldom mastered, but it is also an office, for thus it is that the sacred writings preach to ever-widening circles.[50] The pastoral office and theological studies have here been drawn into immediate liaison.[51] We can understand how Biel and his successors could fill double offices in their association with Deventer and Tübingen, and how they were able to steer the Modern Devotion into a *via moderna*.

The transplanted Brotherhood withered prematurely due to its own clericalized isolation. Duke Ulrich's greed led to the dissolution of the various houses in 1517. But the tie with this movement largely determined the profile and essence of the theological faculty and the university in its first decades. An affective and anti-speculative

[46] Biel took his key from the word 'observatio' that precedes this text in the Vulgata: 'Circumcisio nihil est, et praeputium nihil est; sed observatio mandatorum Dei. Unusquisque in qua vocatione vocatus est, in ea permaneat.' 1 Cor. 7.19f.

[47] 'Et quamquam hec communis vita indifferenter omnibus suadetur precipue tamen eis qui in sortem Domini electi sunt, hoc est clericis . . .' Landeen, ed., *Tractatus Magistri Byell*, p. 84.

[48] His account of the expansion of the movement in north Germany should be compared with Post's reservations regarding the legal forms approved by the pope. Post, *The Modern Devotion*, pp. 427 and 437.

[49] Landeen, ed., *Tractatus Magistri Byell*, pp. 87f.

[50] 'qui voce tacemus scripto predicamus damusque operam ut sancti libri et sacre littere multiplicentur et venia[n]t in usus plurimorum ex quibus verbum salutis populo deinceps possit ministrari. Quomodo enim predicabunter nisi legantur et quomodo legentur nisi scribantur. Quamquam prochdolor his diebus scriptores multiplicati sunt super numerum. Et ut Hieronimus conqueritur, Scribimus indocti doctique poemata passim.' Landeen, ed., *Tractatus Magistri Byell*, p. 91. J. G. R. Acquoy had described even the beginnings of the movement as a community of copyists. See *Het Klooster te Windesheim en zijn invloed*, vol. 1, pp. 43ff.

[51] Typical of the clericalization we have indicated is the fact that Biel paid no attention here to the problem of vernacular translations of texts, a theme to which Gerard Zerbolt had devoted an entire chapter (VII) in his apologetic. See above, n. 37.

theology, oriented toward scripture and the church fathers, equipped its students for service in a church that was structured around the clerical office. In these academic circles the reconciliation of pope and curia with the church as represented in the council could once more be presupposed, making the preceding century's great problems of structural reform appear to have been resolved long since. No trace is left of the earlier mood of apocalyptic urgency.[52]

In full confidence that the mending of the Schism and the apparent burial of the Hussite hatchet now allowed for both the *causa unionis* and the *causa fidei*, for ecclesiastical union and doctrinal unity, to be checked off the conciliar agenda, attention centred on the third point of the Constance platform, the *causa reformationis*. But what did 'Reformation' entail, what ideal of reform carried the Modern Devotion all the way to Paris and southern Germany?

For the masters of the 'first Tübingen school', 'reformation' meant above all the promotion of personal integrity and scholarship through the union of scholarly inquiry and devotion. Such an assertion neither denies nor obscures the obvious fact that Count Eberhard's new institution served other purposes as well. The university was conceived as an aid to the reunion of a divided Württemberg and as a training school for jurists fit to replace clerics as the officials, counsellors and judges who were needed to conduct the internal and external affairs of state. The faculty of theology was cast in an ancillary role. Its task was to train pastors able to foster personal reform among the faithful, and, within the university, to devote itself especially to problems of theological ethics. A revision of our understanding of the Deventer Movement on the eve of the Reformation and a view of its wide appeal and impressive adaptibility reveal the fertile crest where medieval scholasticism and the northern Renaissance give rise to a 'pious enlightenment'. Short-lived though it was, it mirrors the hope for reform of church and society – at a time when the structures of the church were still believed to be sound and firm.

52 With regard to this apocalyptic mood the *sermones* of Pierre d'Ailly are extremely revealing. See, for example, the *Sermo de sancto Francisco*: 'Huic autem prophetiae (scil. Abbatis Joachimi de Floris) mihi salvo meliori iudicio concordare videtur illa beati Johannis visio, quam sub tuba quinti angeli, id est sub persecutione temporis quinti, in Apocalipsi se vidisse testatur. . . . Ubi correspondenter ad praemissa, tria tanguntur. Nam primo ostenditur, qualiter ecclesia lapsa est culpabiliter, quia ipsa est stella, quae prius lucebat in coelo per virtutis excellentiam et nunc cecidit in terram per iniquitatis ruinam. . . . Secundo tangitur, qualiter ecclesia punienda est crudeliter, . . . Tertio subiungitur, qualiter ecclesia praeservanda est salubriter, quia dicitur: "Et praeceptum est illis, ne laederent" "nisi tantum homines qui non habent signum dei in frontibus suis" (Rev. 9.4).' Petrus de Alliaco, *Tractatus et Sermones*, fol. c7^{v}.

5

Patterns of thought on the eve of upheaval

WHATEVER THE influence of a historiographically harried Tübingen humanism upon the European scene, by any assessment it shaped the university's atmosphere between 1477 and 1516 in a peripheral manner at best. Elsewhere on the continent, humanism had allied itself by 1500 with two and occasionally with all three of the 'biblical languages', and 'eloquence' had long since ceased to mean mere elegance or nimble-tongued Latinity. Against this background the contemporary adulatory hymns addressed to Tübingen's provincial *poeta*, Heinrich Bebel, must be savoured with a grain of salt. They can best be admitted, if not as *testimonium paupertatis*, then as *testimonium abundantiae*: as witnesses to that epoch's passion for praise and praising.

On the other hand, the 'academy of Thomas Anshelm' flourished intermittently alongside the university only to disintegrate in the wake of Anshelm's flight to Hagenau in the summer of 1516. It is true that Christopher Scheurl, for a long time leader of the Nuremberg humanist circle, could report nearly three years later to Melanchthon in Wittenberg about a Frankfurt meeting of Melanchthon's former Tübingen colleagues and disciples.[1] But such passing mention cannot disguise the fact that Melanchthon never managed to found a Tübingen sodality comparable to those in the university towns of Heidelberg, Erfurt or Vienna or to the *sodalitas Augustana* or *Staupitziana* in the bustling commercial centres of Augsburg and Nuremberg.

Tübingen occupies at best a modest niche in the as yet little-studied history[2] of this fascinating preliminary form of the later scientific

[1] Frankfurt 'quo audio convenire tuos Tubingos'. Letter of 10 April 1519; *Melanchthons Briefwechsel*, ed. Clemen, 1, p. 64.

[2] See Hummel, *Die humanistischen Sodalitäten und ihr Einfluss auf die Entwicklung des Bildungswesens der Reformationszeit*. In contrast to the other, local foundations, the *sodalitas litteraria Danubiana* in Vienna, founded by Conrad Celtis in 1497, had a supraregional membership in its second phase. See *Der Briefwechsel des Konrad Celtis*, ed. Rupprich, pp. 300 and 310. Cf. Spitz, *Conrad Celtis, the German Arch-Humanist*, and *idem*, 'The Course of German Humanism', pp. 403f.

academies. At the universities the *humaniora* were not integrated as a regular discipline in the field of *Philosophia naturalis*, where physics stretched into metaphysics, nor in the sphere of theology, where exegesis led to ethics. Instead, they functioned only as a propaedeutic 'elective' discipline which aided in mastering the *trivium* as preparation for the *Baccalaureus artium* examinations. Like her older sisters, the university in Tübingen reacted with coy reservation to the overtures of humanist curricular reforms. This reserve was the stimulus for Melanchthon's complaint in 1518 that he could endure Tübingen no longer, being forced to behave more as schoolmaster than as professor.[3]

Superimposed on his duties as copy-reader for Anshelm, Melanchthon's probable position as head tutor in the nominalist *bursa* must have taxed his intellectual energy and versatility to the limit. His former companion, Johannes Oecolampadius (†1531),[4] in whose company he had once enthusiastically devoured Greek authors,[5] had long since wandered by way of Heidelberg to the new centre of European humanism at Basel.[6] Their exchanges of books and ideas soon gave way to competition; at first within the bounds of the usual humanist 'rivalry' (*aemulatio*)[7] but later sobered by the tensions of the Eucharistic controversy and the swelling divergence between Wittenberg and Zürich. During his Tübingen period, however, the humanist Melanchthon clearly had to play second fiddle to Oecolampadius.

During his last weeks in Tübingen (May 1518) Melanchthon announced plans for an improved edition of Aristotle in the conclusion to his Greek grammar.[8] This announcement invites misinterpretation[9] for it actually testifies more to his desire to fill the vacuum left by Anshelm's departure than to the flowering of humanism in Tübingen. The work was not planned as the showpiece of a

[3] See above, p. 19.

[4] He matriculated at Tübingen on 9 April 1513 as 'magister Johannes Icolumbadius de Winsperg'. Hermelink, *Die Matrikeln*, 1, p. 194, no. 112.

[5] *CR* 4, cols. 720f.

[6] Born in Weinsberg, which at that time belonged to the Palatinate, Oecolampadius turned toward Württemberg in 1512. Not only did he study with Reuchlin in Stuttgart, but with careful deliberation also dedicated his first volume of sermons to the patron – 'Doctissimus es Moecenas' – and chancellor of Württemberg, Dr Gregory Lamparter. Cf. Finke, *Die Tübinger Juristenfakultät*, pp. 146–8; here p. 147.

[7] It was the Tübingen alumnus Oecolampadius who called for priestly veneration of Erasmus in his epilogue to the *Novum Instrumentum*: 'hunc verum theologum vero honore, quo Apostolus presbyteros coli vult certatim adornemus . . .' Basel, February 1516; Staehelin, *Briefe*, 1, p. 28.

[8] *CR* 1, col. 26.

[9] See Maurer, *Der junge Melanchthon*, 1, pp. 76f.

Tübingen sodality, but provided Melanchthon with a deep breath of imported cultural oxygen in the rarified Tübingen atmosphere. For aside from the mathematician and astronomer, Johann Stöffler (†1531), the university could boast no professor with the European-wide significance of the now-departed Biel or Summenhart.[10] The Tübingen editorial contingent consisted of only Melanchthon, George Simler and Franciscus Stadianus; the renowned figures all came from outside Tübingen: Reuchlin, Pirckheimer, Capito and Oecolampadius.

It is even more important to recognize that this proposed edition of Aristotle was not merely part of a *humanist* anti-scholastic offensive.[11] To free Aristotle from the Christianizing straitjacket of the *via antiqua*[12] and to permit him to speak as an unbaptized ancient was an express concern of the *nominalists* which made it possible for Melanchthon to fuse his humanist spirit with his enthusiasm for the Tübingen *via moderna*.

This realization yields a significant insight but not the final word on Melanchthon's development. Our present interest in the plan 'ad instauranda Aristotelica' is an indirect one: the projected new edition of Aristotle serves as a backdrop against which we can measure the importance, impact and 'density' of humanism in Tübingen. There can be no doubt that enthusiasm for ancient history and literature and for the fusion of dialectics and eloquence as expressed in veneration for the heroes of three successive student generations – Conrad Celtis,[13] Johannes Reuchlin and Desiderius Erasmus – found more complete expression in Melanchthon than in Heinrich Bebel. But Tübingen's essential feature and most significant legacy to Wittenberg was not the product of these scholarly passions alone. Paul

[10] See Haller, 1, p. 263–75.

[11] Maurer, *Der junge Melanchthon*, 1, pp. 75f.

[12] A most informative passage in this regard is found in 2 Sent. q. 1 art. 3 of the commentary on the Sentences by Peter of Candia: 'Sed ‹quia› aliqui theologi volunt Aristotelem catholicum facere, dicunt, quod nunquam fuit sua opinio, quod mundus eternaliter fuerit, sed potius sensit oppositum, quod ex suis principiis nituntur probare.' After Peter had described the motives for this 'Catholic' interpretation of Aristotle, he closed this portion of his account with the following words: 'Et ista sunt motiva dicentium, Aristotelem sensisse, mundum temporaliter a Deo productum, aliter sibi contradixisset, quod non est putandum in tanto philosopho. – Sed salva ipsorum reverentia, ista motiva non concludunt suum propositum. Et ideo ad ista respondendo dico duo. Dico primo, quod mundum fuisse eternum fuit de mente Aristotelis. Secundo dico, quod eternitas mundi suis principiis non repugnat.' Ehrle, *Der Sentenzenkommentar Peters von Candia, des Pisaner Papstes Alexanders V*, pp. 66f.

[13] See the letter, 'Ad Conradum Celtem, primum in Germanis poetam laureatum' by Michael Köchlin († ca. 1512), Tübingen, 23 March 1500. *Der Briefwechsel des Konrad Celtis*, ed. Rupprich, pp. 389–91; here p. 391.

Joachimsen's comments on the precipitate of Reuchlin's religious philosophy apply to humanist education in a more general way: 'The university at Tübingen is not involved. As Luther made his debut it had already become primarily a guardian of the old heirlooms . . .'[14]

The 'old legacy' enjoyed a continuing creative influence in a manner totally different from that of literary humanism. The edition of Aristotle was not the sole seed sown in Tübingen to bear fruit first in Wittenberg. The death of his friend, Hieronymus Schürpf (†1554), whom Melanchthon venerated 'like a father'[15] and who had preceded him to Wittenberg in 1502, led Melanchthon to reflect on the continuity between the two universities. Not only had Schürpf emerged publicly as Luther's legal counsel at the Diet of Worms but he also served Melanchthon in the same capacity throughout the formative years of the Reformation. This position placed Schürpf on a collision course with Carlstadt during the Wittenberg crises of 1521–2[16] and invested him with considerable influence as Melanchthon's mentor in the pursuit of a proper relationship between biblical, canon and Roman law.[17]

On 7 August 1554, two months after Schürpf's death, Melanchthon published a remarkable eulogy that opened with the prayerful plea that God 'would kindle His light in the hearts of many in order that He might be properly known and that His Wisdom, as manifested in law, might be perceived'.[18] The assessment of Schürpf's significance that followed emphasized the formative power of the University of Tübingen as a harbinger of the Wittenberg Reformation. Melanchthon described how the young Schürpf, aided by his father's cordial friendship with Vergenhans and Summenhart and the even earlier patronage of his mother's relative, the influential chancellor of Württemberg, Gregory Lamparter, found a ready welcome in Tübingen. He owed his excellent, source-oriented[19] acquaintance with both canon and Roman law[20] to his teachers, Conrad Ebinger (†1535) and the rhetorically gifted Johann Lupffdich (†1518). 'But at the same time he heard the theologian Summenhart, whose lectures

[14] 'Zwei Universitätsgeschichten', p. 413; also in *Gesammelte Aufsätze*, p. 272.

[15] 'tanquam patrem diligo et colo, Deoque gratias ago, quod hunc mihi non solum huius doctrinae monstratorem, sed totius vitae rectorem dedit.' *CR* 11, col 918.

[16] Schaich-Klose, *D. Hieronymus Schürpf*, pp. 25–8.

[17] Kisch, *Melanchthons Rechts- und Soziallehre*, pp. 62–7.

[18] 'Ac Deum precamur, ut in multorum pectoribus accendat lucem, qua ipse recte agnoscetur, et sapientia eius monstrata in legibus consideretur.' *CR* 12, col. 88; text in Kisch, *Melanchthons Rechts- und Soziallehre*, appendix 13, p. 290, lines 73–5.

[19] Finke, *Die Tübinger Juristenfakultät*, pp. 113–18.

[20] Haller, 2, pp. 49–51; Finke, *Die Tübinger Juristenfakultät*, pp. 149–52.

were attended by other law students; for he [Summenhart] attempted to free the teaching of the church from the deceptive trappings of useless disputations and from a superstitious interpretation of human juridical traditions.'[21]

We shall return later to this stream of formative influence that justifies talk of a 'first Tübingen School'. This was an academic tradition characterized by groundbreaking scholarly activity between the fronts of theology and law where Gabriel Biel and especially Conrad Summenhart addressed fiery issues of social ethics that alternately smouldered and flamed during the entire sixteenth century. With deliberate calm they staked out a *via media* in Tübingen disputations; a mediating path that held its own course in the passionately contested controversy between the *mos italicus* and the *mos gallicus*. We are dealing here with that *Wegestreit* which had flared up between a philosophy of law based primarily on the glosses of the great medieval commentators and a school of law which pursued matters to their sources and original intent by the application of historical–critical criteria.[22]

In painstaking detail Guido Kisch has demonstrated from the sources how the history of jurisprudence shaped an entire epoch of intellectual history in the sixteenth century. It is an epoch 'in which the study of law defended or indeed for the first time captured a field position in opposition to theology . . .'[23] The shift from the medieval to the modern era is clearly visible in this process. A similar struggle commenced in Tübingen when theologians began to reclaim, as innately theological, certain practical social and ethical issues then within the jurisdiction of the canon lawyers. Not only the extensive treatment of the obligation of restitution in the fourth book of Biel's *Collectorium* but also Summenhart's *Septipertitum opus de contractibus* and his unjustifiably neglected treatise *De decimis* merit particular consideration in this regard.[24] The Tübingen school's interest in these issues links it to the *mos gallicus*, being connected by a common interest in up-to-date administration of justice and by the rejection of

21 *CR* 12, col. 90; Kisch, *Melanchthons Rechts- und Soziallehre*, appendix 13, p. 292, lines 127–44.

22 See the standard work by Stintzing, *Geschichte der deutschen Rechtswissenschaft*, vol. 1, pp. 106–45, and the concise summary in Wieacker, *Privatrechtsgeschichte der Neuzeit*, pp. 36–8. Cf. above all the subtle analysis by Guido Kisch in the context of the university that served as a prototype for Tübingen: *Humanismus und Jurisprudenz. Der Kampf zwischen mos italicus und mos gallicus an der Universität Basel.*

23 Kisch, *Erasmus und die Jurisprudenz seiner Zeit*, p. 51.

24 See the bibliographical references in Finke, *Die Tübinger Juristenfakultät*, pp. 239–41.

metahistorical legal philosophies that confused a human, historically evolved law with immutable and divine justice.[25]

A comprehensive verdict on the significance of the Tübingen school must await a more detailed account of its effect on the soon-to-be-divided camps, especially on Eck in Ingolstadt and Melanchthon in Wittenberg. For the present it is important to establish that Melanchthon did not distort Tübingen's past when he pointed out in his eulogy of Hieronymus Schürpf that Summenhart had subjected the historically evolved *traditiones humanae* to a severe scrutiny aimed at demythologizing divine law and, contrary to canonist pretentions, unmasking its largely human origins and urgent need of reform.

Melanchthon added still another important observation. Summenhart had been, in this regard, 'Gersonis imitator'; a pupil, indeed a disciple, of Gerson.[26] This fifteenth-century addition to the church fathers who was venerated, quoted, copied and edited by Geiler in Strassburg[27] and Wimpfeling in Heidelberg,[28] became the patron of the Tübingen *via media*. However, the former points of opposition between *via moderna* and *via antiqua* were by no means neglected, eliminated or surmounted. The differences in epistemology and in the relation between reason and revelation remained as conspicuous as ever. But the explosive potential of the *via moderna* was dissipated, deactivated on three sides. In the first place, a common basis with the *via antiqua* was established in dealing theologically with social ethics. John Duns Scotus' fourth book on the Sentences, which had been almost completely overlooked by Occam, displaced Aquinas for the Tübingen *via antiqua* as a mutually acceptable source-book on social and ethical issues. Secondly, both 'ways' gratefully absorbed Jean Gerson's carefully drafted criticism of canon law and lawyers, since this criticism sought answers based on the criteria of Christian charity and reason to questions that had long found apparent resolution, or indeed evaded examination, under the protective umbrella of divine law. And finally Gerson left his mark on the Tübingen theology as the defender of the *devotio moderna* at Constance. Without denying basic

25 This traditional scholastic distinction by no means resulted from a new historical sensitivity but nevertheless provided opportunity to employ the humanist discovery of 'anachronism'. Cf. Gilmore, *Humanists and Jurists*, p. 63.

26 Kisch, *Melanchthons Rechts- und Soziallehre*, p. 292, line 138.

27 See Douglass, *Justification in Late Medieval Preaching. A Study of John Geiler of Keisersberg*, pp. 18ff., 40ff., 213ff.

28 'Wimpfeling, wie schon sein Meister Geiler von Keisersberg, gehört zu Gersons geradlinigen Fortsetzern, zu seinen Verbreitern, Herausgebern, Verteidigern.' Herding, *Wimpfelings Adolescentia*, p. 110.

points of conflict, the Tübingen *via moderna* and the *via antiqua*, with their major representatives, Biel and Summenhart, converged in their common appropriation of Duns Scotus and Gerson.

In the case of the modern way yet another factor entered the picture. The mingling of *devotio moderna* and *via moderna* so characteristic of the Tübingen landscape sought a synthesis of piety and scholarship, thereby rounding the specific contours and sharp profile of the nominalist platform. In part the trend toward equalization and equilibrium can be traced to nominalist confidence in the effort to transcend the strife between the schools. On the other hand, we can observe the results of a pious reconciliation of offensive contradictions in the church's teaching, defusing the explosive potential of 'nominalism'. Liaison with the *via moderna* was not indispensible for the mere promotion of an individualistic piety; the *devotio moderna* was fully capable of meeting that challenge with its own resources. Rather it was the programmatic attempt by the *devotio moderna* to level the wall separating monastic and profane society that required the cooperation of the *via moderna* for its completion. For it was in the *via moderna* that the clear distinction between the realms of the experience of faith and the observation of the world helped legitimize a world-centred devotion which could maintain its rights against its older sister, the traditional church-oriented piety. So outrageous a sibling shocked the elders; those reformers who had been brought up in the *via antiqua* easily but unjustifiably branded it libertinism and Epicureanism.

Summenhart's desire to demythologize the so-called divine law found acceptance in the south German cities and in Melanchthon's Wittenberg in the wake of the elevation of the principle of *sola scriptura* to the standard of truth for both the sphere of faith and the realm of the world. In similar fashion Biel's nominalism found added vitality and validity in Luther's Wittenberg as the Pauline doctrine of justification cleared the way for a new piety which was no longer the regulating and levelling force it had been for the *devotio moderna* but a form of piety staked out in the Augustinian renaissance as both a seed-bed and a fruit of theology.

6

The Augustine renaissance in the later Middle Ages

There is probably no phase of medieval intellectual life that could not be portrayed as having reassessed and redigested the Augustinian legacy. Yet, in the middle of the fourteenth century we encounter a novel appropriation of that heritage which permitted Augustine to speak not merely as one of the four church fathers but also as an eminent gospel exegete. In seeking a proper understanding of this development, researchers have already encountered considerable difficulties. An 'Augustinian school' has been christened amid a mixture of enthusiasm and conviction[1] but the subsequent explorations have been marred by question-marks and outright gaps in the documentary log.[2] The final resolution of key problems must await intensive source study based on new and reliable editions equipped to deal critically with questions of textual transmission.[3]

Whereas the term 'schola moderna Augustiniana' has quite properly entered the historian's vocabulary to stay,[4] the interpretation of the unmistakable references to an 'Augustinian school' rests for the present on working hypotheses.[5] And answers to the questions surrounding this 'Augustinian school' must be pursued in conjunc-

[1] Drawing from Karl Werner's, *Die Scholastik des späteren Mittelalters,* Carl Stange stressed at the beginning of this century the significance of Augustinian theology for Luther's development in an article that has left few traces in later scholarship, most likely due to Otto Scheel's sharp rejection of its thesis. Stange, 'Über Luthers Beziehungen zur Theologie seines Ordens'; and 'Luther über Gregor von Rimini'. Cf. van Rhijn, 'Luther en Gregorius van Rimini'; and Scheel, *Die Entwicklung Luthers bis zum Abschluss der Vorlesung über den Römerbrief,* esp. p. 215, n. 143. The discussion was revived by Alphons Victor Müller, *Luthers theologische Quellen,* p. ix. Cf. the point-by-point critique of Müller by Eduard Stakemeier, *Der Kampf um Augustin. Augustinus und die Augustiner auf dem Tridentinum,* pp. 36ff. Stakemeier expanded the thesis of an 'Augustinian doctrinal tradition'. *Ibid.,* pp. 49ff. and 130ff.

[2] See Hubert Jedin in his review of Stakemeier in *Theologische Revue* 37 (1938), pp. 429f.

[3] 'Fordert nicht allein die literarische Aufarbeitung der Augustinertheologie des 14. und 15. Jahrhunderts mindestens ein Jahrzehnt unausgesetzter Handschriftenforschung?' Jedin, *Girolamo Seripando,* vol. 1, pp. viiif.

[4] See Zumkeller, 'Die Augustinerschule des Mittelalters'.

[5] Set forth cautiously in Zumkeller, 'Die Augustinertheologen Simon Fidati von Cascia und Hugolin von Orvieto und Martin Luthers Kritik an Aristoteles'.

tion with the study of the transmission and reception of the Augustinian corpus both within and without the Augustinian order. In this regard the fourteenth century once more constitutes a historical watershed.

The first pebbles were cast into the pond by the nearly simultaneous beginnings of an academic Augustinianism mirrored in the writings of Thomas Bradwardine (†1349) and Gregory of Rimini (†1358); an Augustinianism linked in a manner as yet unexplained with English proto-humanism[6] and early Italian humanism respectively.[7] For all their differences, both men pursued the renewal of dogmatic theology, in conflict with the *doctores moderni* and supported by Augustine's anti-Pelagian writings.

Bradwardine's concern was apparently not a reform-inspired recovery of a tradition-obscured Augustine. He hoped rather to expose the hopelessly isolated position of Pelagius and the *pelagiani moderni* by surrounding them with a solid wall of Catholic tradition. Yet Bradwardine considered Augustine an eminent *doctor catholicus*[8] and medium for Christian truth. Seeking the 'intent of scripture and of its expositors'[9] and extolling the consensus of the church,[10] Bradwardine could not escape the fact that his key informants (from Anselm, Bernard, Hugh of St Victor and Peter Lombard through to Thomas and Scotus) had all turned to Augustine when arriving at authentic and substantial assertions.

Thus, despite Bradwardine's respect for the other *doctores*, Augustine remained the star witness to be summoned at the outset of every proceeding in the court of doctrine. For with regard to the central issue of theology, salvation through Christ *sola gratia*, Augustine had

[6] See Smalley, *English Friars and Antiquity in the Early Fourteenth Century*, pp. 6ff.; 299ff.; here pp. 73f. The tradition of the 'prisci theologi' – from Hermes Trismegistos to Virgil and Ovid – as convincingly demonstrated by John O'Malley for the Augustinian Order's Giles of Viterbo (†1532) and linked by O'Malley to Ficino and Pico, had already played a significant role for Bradwardine. *Giles of Viterbo on Church and Reform. A Study in Renaissance Thought*, pp. 55ff., 29f. Even though Bradwardine, in quoting Ovid, left the question unanswered as to whether one should read the poet 'ad autoritatem vel ad voluptatem', the answer was clear to him: Ovid belonged to the tradition of the *sapientes* which stretched back as far as Enoch. *Thomae Bradwardini De causa Dei contra Pelagium et de virtute causarum ad suos Mertonensis libri tres*, ed. Savilius, lib. 1 cap. 1 cor. 35; pp. 73D–76D. The alternative *auctoritas/voluptas* helps us to define the category 'proto' as a preliminary form of humanism.

[7] See Arbesmann, *Der Augustiner-Eremitenorden und der Beginn der humanistischen Bewegung*, pp. 15ff. and 73ff.

[8] *De causa Dei*, lib. 3 cap. 52; p. 855A.

[9] 'mens scripturae canonicae et doctorum.' *De causa Dei*, lib. 1 cap. 43; p. 401D.

[10] 'intellectus communis ecclesiae et ecclesiasticorum doctorum.' *De causa Dei*, lib. 1 cap. 45; p. 426E.

walked both biographically and theologically in the footsteps of St Paul. 'As far as the statement, "grace that is dependent on works is no grace",[11] is concerned, all doctors of the Catholic church are most profoundly of one mind. But Augustine emerged from their midst as the herald of grace, as its indefatigable champion; because he had once been, like Paul, an unbeliever, indeed a blasphemer and enemy of the grace of Jesus Christ. But then he was overcome and converted by that very grace which precedes every work, and thus he imitated the Apostle in a unique way.'[12]

Augustine so dominated Bradwardine's appeals to tradition that the Englishman's *De causa Dei* may be considered a large-scale attempt to offer an outline of theology disguised as a commentary on Augustine. Even where contemporary theological issues forced him to forge new answers, Bradwardine's language was more profoundly moulded in Augustinianisms than the mere length of his quotations can indicate. The pivotal point was the conviction that 'man is justified by faith alone without prior merit';[13] a tenet in which the rejection of 'prevenient' works served a dual purpose. On the one hand it repudiated that doctrine of justification which assumed that God's initial gift of grace could be earned *ex puris naturalibus*, i.e. without the aid of grace, although admittedly only by the generosity of God (*de congruo*). Bradwardine countered energetically with the argument that such a merit *de congruo* was a fraud on the part of the modern Pelagians and that the concept of a merit *de condigno* did not even merit discussion:

In general usage as well as in terminology peculiar to academics, we should also realize that the concept of actual or full merit [*de condigno*] can be applied variously to both good and evil. For on the one hand, a sinner rightfully merits eternal punishment because his sin is so evil that for the sake of his wickedness alone the everlasting penalty could be imposed without causing any injustice. But on the other hand, no one rightfully merits eternal life because no human work can be so good or so meritorious before God that its

[11] Cf. Rom. 11.6.

[12] 'In hac etiam sententia ['si gratia sit ex operibus, iam non est gratia'] omnes doctores catholici unanimiter sunt concordes, inter quos Augustinus; *quia* sicut Apostolus primo fuit infidelis et blasphemus et inimicus gratiae Jesu Christi, *postquam praeventus eadem gratia similiter est conversus, quodammodo singulariter imitatus Apostolum,* factus est gratiae laudator, gratiae magnificus ac strenuus propugnator.' Bradwardine, *De causa Dei*, lib. 1 cap. 35; p. 311B–C.

[13] 'Sola fide sine operibus praecedentibus fit homo iustus.' *De causa Dei*, lib. 1 cap. 43; p. 394B.

author deserves eternal life for the sake of his goodness or merit alone, in the complete absence of grace.[14]

Probably alluding to Robert Holcot's use of the distinction between *mereri* and *promereri* to disentangle the merits preceding and succeeding justification,[15] Bradwardine delineated the basic heresy of the modern Pelagians. They had illicitly enriched the quality of human actions prior to the emancipating and enabling act of justification, and elevated human achievements to the same level as works performed in the state of grace. In the process, the deep chasm between the friend and enemy of God, bridgeable only by prevenient grace, had been 'removed' by semantic sleight of hand.[16]

Next comes the second assertion of the phrase 'by faith alone without prevenient works', 'Sola fide' rejects only those works performed prior to justification since a living faith matures into fruits meriting God's reward as *dona Dei*.[17] Close attention must be paid to the sequence of action in Luke 22.61 where 'the Lord turned and looked at Peter. And Peter remembered the word of the Lord . . .' The turning, indeed, the 'conversio' of the Lord preceded Peter's change of heart.[18] In this manner God kindles genuine contrition in a sinner's heart which in due course flashes into flames of reciprocal love. The sinner's loving response contrasts so radically with his previous attitude and makes its presence felt in such a novel manner that he knows with a great degree of probability that he has become a child of God.[19]

[14] 'Pro modo quoque loquendi communi omnium proprioque doctorum ulterius est sciendum, quod mereri de condigno diversimode sumitur in bono et in malo. Dicitur enim quod quis peccans meretur condigne poenam aeternam, quia tam malum est illud peccatum, quod ex sola eius malitia poena aeterna sine omni iuris iniuria infligi poterit sic peccanti. Dicitur autem quod nullus meretur condigne vitam aeternam, quia nullius opus est tam bonum aut tam meritorium apud deum, ut ei ex illius solius bonitate aut merito vita aeterna sine omni gratia debeatur.' *De causa Dei*, lib. 1 cap. 39; p. 360B.

[15] *Super libros Sapientiae*, Lectio 116A–B.

[16] 'Item si quis carens gratia potest mereri gratiam primam de congruo et habens gratiam potest mereri augmentum suae gratiae tantum de congruo, non autem de condigno, carens gratia posset similiter primam gratiam promereri, sicut habens gratiam, gratiam suam augeri.' *De causa Dei*, lib. 1 cap. 39; p. 338D.

[17] *Ibid.*, lib. 1 cap. 43; p. 407D–E.

[18] *Ibid.*, p. 395E. Cf. Augustine, *De gratia et libero arbitrio* (c. 427), cap. v. 10; *PL* 44, col. 887, line 45.

[19] 'est mihi probabile quod homo verisimiliter potest scire, saltem secundum praesentem iustitiam, se esse in gratia et dignum Dei amore, per hoc scilicet quod diligit Deum ex toto corde, . . . velletque voluntatem divinam in omnibus adimplere . . . tantum gratuito propter ipsum, et per alia signa multa.' Bradwardine, *De causa Dei*, lib. 1 cap. 39; p. 338B.

But this experience offers at best mere assurance of grace. In the same doctrine of predestination that asserts prevenient grace to be unmerited, the path to assurance of ultimate salvation is blocked by the uncertainty of the grace of perseverance (*donum perseverantiae*). In the final analysis Bradwardine was also governed by the phrase that was to dominate late medieval theology and piety: 'Man knows not whether he merits love or hate' (Eccl. 9.1). The fire of first grace kindles no assurance of the eternal flame of perseverance.

Although the final version of Gregory of Rimini's *Lectura in primo et secundo Sententiarum* must have been produced enough later to permit reference to Bradwardine's *De causa Dei*,[20] the two authors were as far removed from each other as were the *via antiqua* and *moderna*. Against this background the parallels between these two works with their common programmatic Augustinian orientation become even more striking.

We begin with an inconspicuous item; yet at the same time a discovery that continued to make history up to the Leipzig Disputation (1519).[21] Confronted with Pelagianizing quotations from the letter *Ad Demetriadem*,[22] ascribed by medieval manuscripts to Jerome, Bradwardine referred to aspects of Jerome's style of thought, as well as statements by Augustine and Bede, and concluded: 'That letter cannot have been written by Jerome but must be attributed to Pelagius or one of his godless, heretical adherents.'[23]

Though referring only to Augustine and adducing no internal textual evidence, Gregory arrived at a similar conclusion: 'neither this passage nor the letter from which it is taken is the work of Jerome; it comes rather from Pelagius'.[24] The offending notion for which the

[20] For the chronology of the major works of Thomas Bradwardine and Gregory of Rimini as well as their relationship to each other, see Courtenay, 'John of Mirecourt and Gregory of Rimini on whether God can undo the Past', 2, pp. 150, 157; *idem*, 'Some notes on Robert of Halifax, O.F.M.', p. 139; *idem*, 'Alexander Langeley, O.F.M.', p. 100, n. 16; and *idem*, *Adam Wodeham. An Introduction to his Life and Writings*, pp. 117f. The priority of Bradwardine's treatise, which I assumed from the outset, remains valid; see Oberman, *Archbishop Thomas Bradwardine, a Fourteenth-Century Augustinian*, p. 214.

[21] In addition to Gregory's references to Bradwardine that I judged to be critical in nature (*Archbishop Thomas Bradwardine*, pp. 215ff.), Courtenay detects a development 'in favor of Bradwardine's position' in Gregory's treatment of the central question of the omnipotence of God (regarding the *futura contingentia* which have become history) after 1344. Courtenay, 'John of Mirecourt', 2, p. 160.

[22] *PL* 30, cols. 15–45; 33, cols. 1099–120. See de Plinval, *Pélage, ses écrits, sa vie et sa réforme*, p. 26, n. 2.

[23] 'Illa epistola non est beati Ieronymi, sed Pelagii aut alicuius Pelagiani haeretici et profani.' *De causa Dei*, lib. 1 cap. 35; p. 313B.

[24] 'nec verba illa nec epistola in qua continentur, fuerunt Hieronymi, sed Pelagii.' Gregory, *Sent.* II d. 26–8 q. 1 art. 1, line 3; reprinted edn, fol. 92P.

authority of Jerome had been improperly usurped was an assertion that good works could be performed without grace.[25] Gregory took his counter-argument from the example of Peter cited by Bradwardine wherein Peter's change of heart followed Christ's look of love.[26]

Augustine's *De spiritu et litera* further documents this theme with its portrayal of Christ not merely as the end of the Old Testament sacramental and ceremonial law[27] but as the termination of the tyranny of the law in general, since spirit and grace alone can satisfy the law's demands.[28] But if the principle of election, the *ratio praedestinationis*, lies not within man but in God's inscrutable free will, then the unwelcome but inescapable issue of the fate of children dying without benefit of baptism arises. The 'Augustinian' rigour with which Gregory met the objections of moralistic sensibility, and his steadfast embrace of grace as alone able to equip for eternal life, earned him the label of 'child abuser' (*tortor infantium*). But by the same logic his English counterpart Bradwardine also deserved the dubious distinction.[29]

That Bradwardine left behind few theological traces, compared to Gregory and to the extent of Bradwardine's own mathematical legacy,[30] is explained by Oxford's increasing isolation in the wake of the Hundred Years War, by the yawning generation gap dug by the ravages of one of the worst of the European plagues and by the fact that Bradwardine belonged to no monastic order and hence lacked a regular and ordered following. But it was perhaps more decisive that in attempting metaphysically to strengthen 'prevenient grace' with

[25] Bede (†735) warned against reference to the virtuousness of the philosophers as proof of the unblemished goodness of human nature (*PL* 30, col. 15). The later Augustine underscored the uniqueness of Christ. Looking back over his earlier works he regretted (*Retractationes*, lib. 1 cap. 4 §3, lines 4–7; *CSEL* 36, lines 23f.) not having presented Christ clearly enough as the sole path to God. See Nygren, *Das Prädestinationsproblem in der Theologie Augustins*, p. 189.

[26] Gregory, *Sent.* II, fol. 98G–H.

[27] Bradwardine, *De causa Dei*, lib. 1 cap. 43; pp. 392E–393C.

[28] Gregory, *Sent.* II, fol. 100C–D.

[29] Bradwardine, *De causa* Dei, lib. 1 cap. 39; pp. 335E–356A. Cf. Gregory, *Sent.* II d. 30–4 q. 3; fols. 115J–116K.

[30] We owe an interesting piece of evidence to the fact that Eck was originally obviously inclined toward humanist pursuits. Proud of his archival research, Eck reported, 'Bravardinus dicitur multas rationes contra conclusionem istam [Christus non potuit esse mendax] induxisse; sed undequaque feci scrutinium, non potui tamen eas habere.' *Chrysopassus praedestinationis*, cent. 6 cap. 24. Dr Venicio Marcolino (Tübingen) kindly brought my attention to the fact that Eck knew Gregory not only through Capreolus, as I conjectured in *Scientia Augustiniana*, Festschrift Adolar Zumkeller, p. 355, n. 30, but that he had owned a copy of the 1503 Venice edition of Gregory's commentary on the Sentences since October 1510. See Johannes Eck, *Explanatio psalmi vigesimi* (1538).

the doctrine of divine omnipotence, Bradwardine remained indebted to the *via antiqua*.

Gregory of Rimini on the other hand managed to combine Augustine's teaching with the same contemporary, indeed modern,[31] philosophical and intellectual initiatives upon which his opponents, the contemporary 'Pelagians', had constructed their soteriology. This led Gregory to depart from the example of Aquinas and Bradwardine in extricating the doctrine of predestination from the cramped pigeonhole of systematic theology which it was sharing with divine providence. His nominalist antipathy toward attempted abstract–speculative penetration into divine being and essence[32] and his corresponding predilection for divine self-revelation inclined him towards the reassignment of predestination to christology[33] and thereby to soteriology.[34]

When, on the eve of the Council of Trent, Gregory and Bradwardine reappeared in a single retrospective glance at the close of years of controversy over and in Augustine's name, the Englishman was 'reduced' to the chronicler of a supposedly outlasted Pelagian wave of the fourteenth century[35] while Gregory was promoted as Augustine's greatest champion ('maximus et studiosissimus divi Augustini propugnator').[36] But such words of praise by no means implied that their author, the Franciscan conciliar theologian Andreas de Vega (†1549), was prepared to follow in the theological footsteps of the *propugnator Augustini*. For here we have reached the end of that era which can be called an Augustinian renaissance insofar as one's

[31] See the chapter titled 'Nominalismus: Experientia und die Geburt der Neuzeit' in my opusculum *Contra vanam curiositatem*, pp. 33–8.

[32] Wolfhart Pannenberg has offered a different view by portraying Gregory as an exponent of 'Augustine's deterministic doctrine of predestination' and he detects in Gregory, as in all of nominalism, a reversion to a stage of development prior to Duns Scotus: 'Die von Skotus als falsch erkannte Antithese zwischen Determinismus und Synergismus trat wieder hervor.' *Die Prädestinationslehre des Duns Skotus*, pp. 143f.

[33] 'Sicut humana natura in Christo ex eterna gratuita praedestinatione divina *unita* est verbo et absque peccato comcepta et nata, sic quicumque baptisati sunt – sive antequam credant ut pueri, sive postquam crediderunt ut provecti hoc ex gratuita eorum praedestinatione consecuti sunt.' Gregory, *Sent.* I d. 40–1 q. 1 art. 2; fol. 159A.

[34] Despite all reservations regarding Martin Schüler's evaluation of Bradwardine's theology as 'determinism' and his lack of emphasis on the parallels to Gregory of Rimini, he must be credited with having delineated the contrast between Bradwardine and the 'redemptive history' orientation of Gregory's theology. *Prädestination, Sünde und Freiheit bei Gregor von Rimini*, p. 31.

[35] 'Revixit [Pelagianism] et postea in Scotia teste magistro Thoma Bradabaerdino decano Londoviarum in Summa contra Pelagianos.' Andreas de Vega, *Opusculum de iustificatione, gratia et meritis*, a.VI; fol. 147.

[36] *Ibid.*

closeness to truth in general and to the gospel in particular was measured against one's proximity to Augustine.

The first edition of the *Opera Omnia Augustini*, published in Basel by Johannes Amerbach (†1513) and the product of editorial teamwork stretching over the years between 1490 and 1506, was certainly one of the high points in the late medieval Augustinian revival.[37] It constituted both the end of an era and a new beginning in the transmission of Augustine. Yet echoes of the earlier impressive and comprehensive Gregorian interpretation of Augustine can still be detected in the early Wittenberg theology. Within the Augustinian order the legacy of Gregory of Rimini had been transmitted as far as Erfurt[38] and in 1508 the statutes of the university in Wittenberg provided for a course of study in a *via Gregorii*.[39] Outside the order we find the *princeps Thomistarum*, Johannes Capreolus (†1444), not merely copying Gregory by the page but thoroughly blending material from Gregory and Thomas,[40] concentrating on the characteristically Gregorian issue of the impossibility of good works ('bona opera in genere sine gratia').[41] Gabriel Biel, on the other hand, quoted Gregory less extensively and by no means with approval. Only on scattered questions, in abbreviated but accurate form, did Biel take account of Gregory's theology.

But now that the Amerbach edition was being sold at the book fairs in Leipzig and Frankfurt, the coming generation had no desire to travel the detour through Gregory's writings in order to make Augustine's acquaintance. One result is visible in Johannes Eck's

37 Aside from the preceding sale of individual volumes, a press run of two hundred, i.e. 2,200 individual volumes in the eleven-volume edition, appears to have left the Amerbach printing shop. At least this seems to me the proper interpretation of 'pariter' in Conrad Pellikan's note: 'Fuerunt tunc pariter impressi a Magistro Amorbachio Joanne duo millia exemplariorum et ducenta in undecim tomis.' Although Amerbach was concerned about this huge capital investment, on 14 April 1506 he managed to persuade Koberger in Nuremberg to take 1,600 copies. But this lot not only consisted of the Augustine edition but also contained the *Margarita philosophica* of Gregory Reisch and the Amerbach edition of Hugo Cardinalis. *Das Chronikon des Konrad Pellikan*, ed. Riggenbach, p. 27.

38 See my essay, 'Headwaters of the Reformation: Initia Lutheri – Initia Reformationis', pp. 69–85. For Bartholomaeus of Usingen's high opinion of Gregory see Kleineidam, *Universitas Studii Erffordensis*, 2, pp. 148 and 227.

39 See Karl Bauer, *Die Wittenberger Universitätstheologie und die Anfänge der deutschen Reformation*, pp. 41ff.

40 'Unter seinem Einfluss scheint Capreolus im hl. Thomas weithin vor allem die augustinischen Elemente gesehen zu haben.' Stegmüller, 'Gratia sanans. Zum Schicksal des Augustinismus in der Salmantizenserschule', pp. 402f. Cf. Grabmann, 'Johannes Capreolus O.P., der "Princeps Thomistarum"', pp. 387f. and n. 61.

41 See Oberman, *The Harvest of Medieval Theology*, pp. 141–4.

treatment of the doctrine of predestination – his *Chrysopassus praedestinationis* of 1512 (Augsburg 1514). The achievements of the source-oriented fourteenth-century Augustinian studies are noticeably absent. And thus Eck unquestioningly assumed Jerome's authorship for the Pelagianizing *Epistola ad Demetriadem*.[42] Seven years before Luther arrived at the same conclusion, though propelled by different motives, Eck considered the 'best medieval expert on Augustine'[43] (Gregory of Rimini) a dissonant choirboy in the scholastic chorus.[44]

Both architects of the Wittenberg theology had made Gregory's acquaintance at least briefly in the course of their educations: Luther through the mediation of Gabriel Biel; Carlstadt as a follower of Capreolus. But for partisans and opponents alike, the increased accessibility of Augustine's works quite understandably meant the demise of the fourteenth-century Augustine interpretation.[45] Ten years after the completion of the Amerbach edition, Erasmus transformed the horizon for his loyal circle of humanists by advancing Jerome and not Augustine as the guiding light of the theological renaissance. He announced his intention in a letter to Pope Leo X on 21 May 1515: 'I am doing my best to encourage Jerome's reemergence' ('sedulo adnitor ut Hieronymus renascatur') because 'we consider him to be almost the sole Latin theologian deserving that title'.[46]

Erasmus' Augustine edition of 1528–9 marked another shift in

[42] *Chrysopassus*, cent. 3 cap. 79, referring to the lengthy preceding quotation: 'bonus usus liberi arbitrii fuit in multis philosophis gentilium, ut dicit beatus Hieronymus ad Demetriadem virginem'; *ibid.*, cent. 2 cap. 13. Since Capreolus was an important channel for Gregory's theology outside the Augustinian Order and made copious excerpts from the relevant *distinctio* of Gregory, it is important to point out that Capreolus ignored Gregory's exposure of the *Epistola ad Demetriadem* as Pelagian. A collation reveals the following: Gregory, *Sent.* II: fol. 96 Eff. = Capreolus, *Defensiones* IV: 287ff.; fol. 98G = 298; fol. 99A = 300.

[43] Trapp, 'Augustinian Theology of the Fourteenth Century', pp. 188f.

[44] 'Gregorius Ariminensis valens ille doctor more suo hic sit singularis . . .' *Chrysopassus*, cent. 3 cap. 79. Cf. 'quamvis et in hoc Gregorius ceteris adversetur.' *Ibid.*

[45] In the dedicatory epistle to Staupitz that Carlstadt added to his commentary on Augustine's *De spiritu et litera*, he recounted how he had purchased his first set of the *Opera Augustini* on 13 January 1517 in Leipzig, having been stimulated by one of Luther's interpretations of the African bishop. See Kähler, *Karlstadt und Augustin*, p. 5, lines 4f. He confessed that he had previously owned none of the editions of the fathers. *Ibid.*, p. 5, line 1. Kähler demonstrated that Carlstadt used the Amerbach edition (Basel) of 1492 for the letters of Augustine and cautiously hypothesized that he had used the Paris reprint of 1515 for the *Opuscula* (vol. 8). *Ibid.*, p. 54, n. 1. Luchesius Smits has since shown that the supposed existence of this Paris edition rests on an error in the catalogue of the Bodleian Library; *Saint Augustin dans l'oeuvre de Jean Calvin*, vol. 1, pp. 197–9.

[46] 'Perspiciebam divum Hieronymum sic apud Latinos esse theologorum principem, ut hunc prope solum habeamus theologi dignum cognomine . . .' *Opus Epistolarum*, ed. Allen, 2, pp. 88, line 292 and 86, lines 220ff.

emphasis since it returned Augustine to a more conventional position as one among the many fathers of the church edited by Erasmus: Cyprian (1520), Arnobius (1522), Hilary (1523), Jerome (1524–6), Irenaeus (1526), and Ambrose (1527). When the time arrived for a new edition of Jerome in 1524 (third edition 1533, sixth edition 1565), Erasmus was unwilling to retract a single line of his extensive introduction of 1516 with its programmatic comparison of Jerome and Augustine,[47] destined to help refashion the contemporary image of Augustine.[48] If by 1524 Jerome had become the standard-bearer for all the forces of the Renaissance at the outset of the controversy with Luther,[49] we must recall that as early as 1515 Erasmus had established the precedent for Jerome's new position by proclaiming him 'summus theologus', and the embodiment of the Renaissance ideal.[50] But even where Augustine was by no means displaced – reform Catholicism

[47] 'Franciscus Philelphus, arrepta velut censoria virgula, Augustino tribuit dialecticae palmam, eloquentiae Hieronymo. Non est meum Augustini laudibus quicquam decerpere: verum illud ipsa res clamitat, Hieronymum Augustino non minus antecelluisse dialectica, quam precessit eloquentia; nec minus eruditione superiorem fuisse, quam dicendi laude.' 'Eximii doctoris Hieronymi Stridonensis vita', in *Opus Epistolarum divi Hieronymi Stridonensis* (Basel, 1516, Paris, 1533), vol. 10 I. Cf. the dedicatory 'Epistola nuncupatoria' addressed to William Warham, Archbishop of Canterbury and dated 1 April 1516: 'Aureum flumen habet, locupletissimam bibliothecam habet, quisquis unum habet Hieronymum.' Jerome is to be considered 'inter theologos summus'. *Ibid.*, fol. 4D and 4C. Cf. *Opus Epistolarum*, ed. Allen, 2, p. 220, lines 358f. and 328. Luther probably had reference to these pages when he wrote to Spalatin on 19 October 1516: 'Ego sane in hoc dissentire ab Erasmo non dubito, quod Augustino in scripturis interpretandis tantum posthabeo Hieronymum, quantum ipse Augustinum in omnibus Hieronymo posthabet.' *WABr* 1, p. 70, lines 17–19.

[48] At the same time that he was preparing for the battle against the Wittenberg theology, a struggle taking shape programmatically around 'Paul and Augustine', Johannes Eck was also engaged in a protest against an inadequate appreciation of Augustine. Well aware of Erasmus' influence, he took Erasmus' position in the matter as a provocation: 'ut omnes ferme docti prorsus sint Erasmiani, cucullatis paucis demptis et theologastris'. *Opus Epistolarum*, ed. Allen, 3, p. 209, lines 23–5, February 1518. In addition to three reservations regarding the manner in which Erasmus' textual criticism in his *Novum Instrumentum* seemed to threaten the doctrine of inspiration, Eck also felt that Augustine's authority had been undermined: 'Augustini doctrinam eminentissimam in primis post sacrum canonem ac Ecclesiae sanctae decreta suscipio et veneror . . . Noli ergo, Erasme, tantum Ecclesiae lumen, quo post primas Ecclesiae columnas nullum fuit illustrius, tuo iudicio obtenebrare.' *Ibid.*, p. 211, lines 81–96.

[49] If we compare the dedicatory epistle of 1 June 1524 with the *Vita Hieronymi* of 1516, Erasmus' implicit understanding of his own times becomes visible. Just as Staupitz could affirm the relevance of Augustine's significance by an appeal to 'Augustinus noster', so Erasmus spoke of 'noster Hieronymus'. *Opus Epistolarum*, ed. Allen, 5, p. 466, line 64.

[50] The relationship between Augustine and Jerome forms a major theme in the excellent study by Charles Béné, *Érasme et Saint Augustin ou l'influence de Saint Augustin sur l'humanisme d'Érasme*. Although he correctly points out that Erasmus

itself considered Augustine an excellent basis for mediation between the parties of reform and Reformation – he was reshaped with humanist candour. The most important Catholic participant at the Regensburg Colloquy, Gasparo Contarini (†1542)[51] took the unprecedented liberty, shortly before his death, of transforming Augustine's doctrine of predestination into a universalism introduced with the explicit antithesis: 'Augustine stressed indeed . . ., but I am of the opinion . . .'[52]

Thus in a century of confessional entrenchment, Augustine's authority waned either in the light of a direct return to scripture or in the course of constructing a broader patristic basis. A new and more distant relationship to Augustine prevailed[53] while the Basel editions of Amerbach and Erasmus – according to the current state of knowledge[54] – failed to inspire a comprehensive acquaintance[55] with the total Augustinian corpus comparable to that which had characterized the Augustinian renaissance of the fourteenth century.[56]

We have ventured to trace a broad arc from the turbulent fourteenth century to the no less tempestuous sixteenth in order to construct a framework for investigating to what extent Augustine served as a guiding light or at least as a companion to the Reformation, the Counter-Reformation, and also to the Renaissance (including its Erasmian Jerome-centred reorientation of Augustine's legacy). The impression conveyed is that precisely in that era which is commonly termed the 'dawn of modern Europe', Augustine seemed threatened with destruction in a battle of dogma, his writings used as a quarry for the *ex post facto* fortification of already established

deployed the works of Jerome and Augustine over the years with equal respect but on different fronts (see *ibid.*, pp. 88–95 and 328–33), Béné does not take account of the above-mentioned unequivocal statements which term Jerome a 'theologus summus' and which stem from Erasmus' period of most intensive text-critical work.

51 Franz Dittrich, *Gasparo Contarini 1483–1542*, p. 839.

52 Scholion to Rom. 11.28f., 'Scholia in epistolas divi Pauli', in Gasparo Contarini, *Opera*, p. 444.

53 Cf. Oberman, 'Headwaters of the Reformation', p. 88.

54 Pontien Polman, *L'Élement historique dans la controverse religieuse du XVIe siècle*, remains the point of departure for necessary further research.

55 The florilegium of Joachim Westphal, *Collectanea sententiarum D. Aurelii Augustini* illustrates the understandably eclectic spectrum of points of interest in the wake of the theological debates.

56 Luther knew Augustine, at least 'his' Augustine, well enough to determine – 'gravius offendi omnes' – the *De vera et falsa poenitentia* to be pseudo-Augustinian in October 1516: 'Est enim . . . nihil ab Augustini eruditione et sensu remotius.' *WABr* 1, p. 65, lines 24–6. It had been included as genuine not only in the 1489 Strassburg edition of the *Opuscula Augustini*, which Luther had studied in 1509 (*WA* 9, p. 4, no. 13), but also in volume eight of the Amerbach edition which Luther was using in the autumn of 1516 (*WABr* 1, p. 70, line 12).

confessional positions. Calvin was not the only reformer to claim Augustine for his own theological edifice under the motto: 'plane nobiscum est Augustinus'.[57] Indeed, the phrase could serve as a caption for an entire epoch endeavouring to come to terms with its scholastic past.[58]

Having sketched the historical context, we turn to two Tübingen theologians, Wendelin Steinbach (†1519) and Johann von Staupitz (†1524), each of whom in his own manner permitted Augustine a voice in his theology. At the time, their use of Augustine established the arena in which the tug of war over his authority would soon escalate to the Reformation conflict.

A student of Biel and the conscientious editor of his works, Steinbach had taught theology at Tübingen since 1486 and continued to influence the Tübingen climate until 1517 in his capacity as Biel's successor and 'headmaster' of the modernist 'school'. Johann von Staupitz arrived at Tübingen much later (1497) to assume the duties of prior at the Augustinian monastery which Andreas Proles had won to the reform congregation of that order in 1483. Together with Jacob Lemp, Staupitz received the doctorate in theology in 1500 under the sponsorship of Steinbach, who also entered the event in the faculty's statute book and delivered the festive oration at the graduation celebration.[59] Tübingen was merely a temporary station for Staupitz. We must nonetheless consider the manner in which his new academic environment affected him; above all the influence of the *via moderna*.

In various ways Staupitz's writings represent a specific stage in the already outlined history of the late medieval appropriation of Augustine's works. Unlike the devotees of academic Augustinianism, Staupitz did not draw Augustine into the scholastic battle of *auctoritates*. Instead, without explicit citation, he thoroughly absorbed the content of Augustine's thought in the course of interpreting the Apostle Paul. Educated at the Thomistically inclined University of

[57] For Calvin's appeal to Augustine see the *Institutio*, lib. 3, cap. 4 §33; *Calvini Opera Selecta*, ed. Barth and Niesel, vol. 4, p. 125, line 16. Cited by Smits, *S. Augustin dans l'oeuvre de J. Calvin*, 1, p. 271.

[58] This should not be taken to mean that Augustine was received and applied uncritically. It is possible to find phrases such as 'constet hic hallucinari Augustinum'. Smits, *S. Augustin*, 1, p. 268. And Melanchthon and Luther wrote from Wittenberg to Brenz: 'Tu adhuc haeres in Augustini imaginatione . . .' *WABr* 6, p. 99, line 3; mid-May 1531. Cited by Braunisch, *Die Theologie der Rechtfertigung im 'Enchiridion' (1538) des Johannes Gropper*, p. 382, n. 133.

[59] See Feld, *Martin Luthers und Wendelin Steinbachs Vorlesungen über den Hebräerbrief*, p. 5. n. 9. For Steinbach's life and works see *Steinbach, Opera exegetica*, ed. Feld, 1, pp. xi–xlv.

Cologne, Staupitz had not yet developed his specific style in the scholastically organized and citation-filled sermons on Job (1498). But during the years which followed he succeeded in transforming theology into proclamation, using language so saturated with Augustinianisms that any methodical attempt to extricate the quotations and allusions must be conducted with utmost caution in order to avoid shattering the unity of his style and artful composition. He subordinated exegesis to piety and learnedness to pastoral concern, permitting the Augustinian legacy a voice in preaching election by grace.

One of the ripest fruits of this later creative period and at the same time a high-point in the homiletical precipitation from the late medieval Augustine renaissance was the *Libellus de exsecutione aeternae praedestinationis* (1517).[60] Yet his Nuremberg audience experienced these sermons not only as a climax but also – as reported to Luther by Staupitz's patron and protector, Christopher Scheurl[61] – as a new evangelical beginning.[62] We find one clear reference to 'Augustinus noster' where Staupitz implicitly contrasted the 'summus theologus' of his own order to Erasmus' image of Jerome.[63] But aside from that allusion, Staupitz explicitly mentions Augustine only once and then not in a citation but in order to discredit a *dictum vulgare*. This maxim, 'widely attributed to our Augustine', is indefensible in its usual sense: 'If you are not predestined, then see to it that you become predestined (si non es praedestinatus, fac ut praedestineris).' Staupitz explained his condemnation of the proverb: 'sine poenitentia sunt

[60] This work resulted from sermons preached at Nuremberg during the Advent season in 1516. Christopher Scheurl's German translation left the Nuremberg press of Friedrich Peypus on 19 January 1517, shortly before the Latin version. See *Johann von Staupitz, Sämtliche Schriften*, vol. 2, p. 42. A description of both Nuremberg editions may be found in Grossmann, 'Bibliographie der Werke Christoph Scheurls', here nos. 46 and 42, p. 665. Cf. the references in Kolde, *Die deutsche Augustiner-Congregation und Johann von Staupitz*, p. 274, n. 2. Scheurl's translation was also printed in *Johann von Staupitzens sämmtliche Werke*, ed. Knaake, vol. 1, pp. 136–84.

[61] 'Praedicavit autem amicissimus noster executionem aeternae praedestinationis tanto quidem populi applausu, tanto concursu, quantum vix dicere audeo . . ., ut uno verbo dicam, publice asserunt huius simile antea non audisse . . .; alii Pauli discipulum, immo linguam, alii evangelii praeconem et verum theologum cognominant. . . .' *WABr* 1, p. 84, lines 10–16; 2 January 1517.

[62] Our analysis is based largely on the *Libellus* (=*Tractatus de exsecutione aeternae praedestinationis*), not merely because it presents a systematic outline of Staupitz's theology, but also because we have here a Latin text from Staupitz himself, which permits easier comparison with the theological tradition.

[63] 'Nam et Augustinus noster, in culmine luminis naturae ambulans, nec suspicari poterat, quid sacramenti haberet: "Verbum caro factum est."' *Libellus*, cap. 4 §17. 'Noster' may also indicate a reaction to Jacob Wimpfeling's treatise, *De integritate* (1505) in which he denied any link between the Augustinian Order and Augustine.

dona et vocationes Dei' (Rom. 11.29). Christopher Scheurl, a friend of Staupitz since their days in Wittenberg, a Nuremberg patrician humanist and member of the *sodalitas Staupitziana*, translated as follows: 'this common proverb, ascribed to our Augustine, should by no means be championed in its literal sense: "if you are not predestined, endeavour to be predestined"; on the contrary, God's gifts and his call are beyond human contrition'.[64]

At first glance Scheurl appears to have undertaken a wilful and considerable contraction. Certainly Staupitz had no intention of departing from the medieval exegetical tradition which read 'sine poenitentia' as 'sine immutatione' (*Glossa ordinaria*), 'sine mutabilitate' (Lyra) or as 'unwanckelbar' ('unwavering' – Luther)[65] and thus referred this Pauline text to God's faithfulness and not to human contrition. Only Staupitz's solution to the second problem raised by the text shows that Scheurl, although reproducing Staupitz's statement in abbreviated form, did indeed remain true to Staupitz's intention.

Although the origin and transmission of this 'Augustinian adage' requires further investigation,[66] its use has been variously documented in the years following the appearance of Staupitz's sermons on predestination.[67] And two years previously, Johannes Eck's *Chrysopassus Praedestinationis* had appeared in Augsburg describing this proverb as a 'teaching of Augustine which is better known than the history of Troy'.[68] Although it cannot be proven that

[64] 'diser gemein spruch, so unserm Augustino zugeschriben wirdet, in dem buchsteblich sinn mit nichte mag vertedingt werden: Bistu nit fürsehen, so schaf, domit du fürsehen werdest; wan auserhalbs der busswürkung sein die gaben und fordrung Gots.' *Libellus*, cap. 5 §28. Cf. the translation by Paul Nyhus in Oberman, ed., *Forerunners of the Reformation*, p. 181: 'For the gifts and call of God are not the result of penance.'

[65] See the *apparatus criticus* for *WA* 56, p. 114, lines 10f.

[66] Richard Wetzel kindly referred me to Hugo Cardinalis' gloss on Romans 8.30 (expositio glossae); *Postilla utriusque Testamenti*, vol. 6, s.v.

[67] In Johannes Altenstaig's *Vocabularius Theologie*, a reference work dedicated to Staupitz, the article 'Praedestinatio' was based to a large degree on Eck's *Chryssopassus* and Biel's *Collectorium* (fol. 201ra). The 'dictum' was no longer ascribed to Augustine but was still supported with a quotation from (Pseudo-)Augustine: 'Unde quidam doctor: Si non es praedestinatus, fac ut praedestineris. Unde in potestate tua est damnari vel salvari. Nam Christus dixit: "Si vis ad vitam ingredi, serva mandata" [Matth. 19.17]. "Novit deus mutare sententiam, si tu noveris mutare vitam,"' Pseudo-Augustine, *Sermo* 29, §2; *PL* 39, col. 1802. (Caesarius Arelatensis, *Sermo* 109, §2; *CChr* 103, p. 452.) See the *apparatus criticus* for Biel's *Collectorium* I d. 41 q. 1 art. 3 dub. 5 N 8f.; Werbeck and Hofmann edn, 1, p. 735.

[68] 'Ex data distinctione clare potest haberi verus sensus propositionis divi Augustini, quae est notior alias historia Troiana: "Si non es praedestinatus, fac ut praedestineris"; quod de praedestinatione simpliciter non potest intelligi, secundum quam nullus de novo potest praedestinari . . . Recipit ergo veritatem, quando

Staupitz had reference to this passage by Eck (I consider such an allusion likely), still Staupitz's position may be taken as a reply to the Pelagianizing reinterpretation epitomized by Eck. In complete agreement with Gabriel Biel on justification, Eck would certainly deny that predestination could be earned in the strict sense of the word. But he would add that God has obliged himself in his goodness to accept the good works performed in a state of grace and to reward them with eternal life. Hence, reversing Scheurl's translation would properly capture Eck's position: 'If you are not predestined, endeavour to be predestined; for only within contrition are found the gifts and call of God.'

Staupitz had taken precisely the opposite course in his Nuremberg sermon cycle on Romans 8.28–39. In his gracious predestination God has pledged himself to call (*vocatio*), justify (*iustificatio*) and fully sanctify (*magnificatio; glorificatio*) the elect in Christ.[69] This decision to save precedes all human works and even the very existence of human works, and originates in a covenant of God which can never be revoked; an obligation which in this sense is 'sine poenitentia Dei'.[70] But this means at the same time – and here Staupitz pursued a genuinely Augustinian theme which we have found emphasized in Bradwardine and Gregory – that God's *vocatio* and *conversio* precede the conversion of the elect; indeed, they evoke and cause that conversion.[71] Hence in this regard God's summons is indeed 'sine poenitentia hominis'.

Like Bradwardine and Gregory, Eck stressed the sequence of action

intelligitur de praedestinatione secundum quid et secundum praesentem iusticiam, et est sensus: *Si non es praedestinatus*, scilicet per praesentem gratiam, *fac* poenitendo et displicentiam de peccatis habendo *ut praedestineris* gratiam acquirendo, a qua diceris praedestinatus secundum praesentem iusticiam.' *Chrysopassus*, cent. 1 cap. 66. In Eck's commentary on the Sentences (1542) the *facere quod in se est* clearly constitutes the *ratio praedestinationis. In primum librum Sententiarum annotatiunculae D. Iohanne Eckio praelectore anno ab Christo nato 1542*, ed. Moore, p. 120, lines 27f.

69 'Cum autem iustificatio gratia est, non natura, acceptatio operum in gratia ad meritum gratia, et Christi merita nostra sunt facta gratia, merito universa vita christiani gratiae tribuitur, et in ipso deletur quod naturae rationali concedunt, puta dominium operum a principio usque in finem; siquidem operis christiani principium est praedestinatio, medium iustificatio, finis glorificatio seu magnificatio, quae gratiae sunt effectus, non naturae.' *Libellus*, cap. 8 §52. See in this regard especially Steinmetz, *Misericordia Dei*, pp. 51ff.

70 We find the same relationship between Staupitz's intention (cap. 5, §28) and Scheurl's translation (*busswürkung* = *poenitentia hominis*) in Luther's roughly contemporary commentary on Rom. 11.29 where he refuted the (Pseudo-) Augustine quotation cited by Eck (and Biel). *WA* 56, p. 440, lines 2–8.

71 See Vignaux, *Justification et prédestination au XIV*^e^ *siècle*, pp. 141–75.

in his exposition of Zach. 1.3,[72] thereby placing a proper preparation by means of repentance, prior to the advent of grace. In contrast Staupitz insisted that God's 'conversion' toward the sinner precedes the latter's change of heart. In this manner, human conversion necessarily follows – in the course of predestination's realization in history (*exsecutio*).[73] Accordingly, the scholastic term, 'gratia gratum faciens', referring to the sacramental grace that makes us pleasing to God, required reinterpretation: in this context grace is the divine election itself, a process by which God becomes pleasing, worthy of love, indeed, a friend to the sinner.[74] It is the *necessitas* of God's faithfulness[75] that connects the various stages along the path of the elect to God (Rom. 8.30) and makes it possible to perceive that the love one receives is a sign of one's election:[76] 'From that point on God appears sweet to us' (Scheurl).[77] Hence the *signa praedestinationis* are also *signa caritatis;*[78] the stirrings of affection are tokens of election.

To Staupitz's theological frame of mind these signs of love and of progress in sanctification are mystical experiences granted to supplement[79] justification. Nevertheless, justification and sanctification are linked through divine election in a reliable (*necessarie*) sequence as set forth in the Pauline 'golden chain' (Rom. 8.28ff.).

Staupitz here collided with that scholastic tradition which fundamentally rejected the possibility of inferring one's predestination from one's performance of good works (*syllogismus practicus*). This

[72] 'Totus discursus patet per illud Zachariae primo [Zach. 1.3]: "Convertimini ad me et ego convertar ad vos." Primo dicit "convertimini" et dein "convertar": Notetur ordo littere, sicut iureconsulti solent hoc profunde pensare. Ac si diceret deus per Prophetam: *Convertimini ad me* praeparando et disponendo per contritionem: *et ego convertar ad vos* per gratiam.' *Chrysopassus*, cent. 3 cap. 51.

[73] In this regard see especially Ernst Wolf, *Staupitz und Luther*, pp. 54 and 229ff. Cf. Steinmetz, *Misericordia Dei*, pp. 97–104.

[74] 'Iterum cernis quod gratia gratum faciens non est illa qua deo placemus, sed qua deus nobis placet et gratus est. Quapropter divinae electioni tribue gratum facere te deo, iustificationi gratum facere deum tibi.' *Libellus*, cap. 16 §131.

[75] 'Verum hi, quos praedestinavit libere, sunt necessaria consequentia in tempore ad fidem efficaci voluntate vocati . . .' *Libellus*, cap. 5, §24. Cf. cap. 6 §§22 and 27; cap. 8 §45.

[76] *Libellus*, cap. 13 §92; 'indicium salutis', cap. 14 §106; 'signa rectae fidei', cap. 21 §196; in addition the 'manifestationes spiritus', cap. 15 §§107ff.

[77] 'von dannen ist uns got sues' (Scheurl); 'Inde Deus suavis nobis factus est', *Libellus*, cap. 10 §64.

[78] 'Indicia amoris' (*Libellus*, cap. 14 §§114 and 121); 'signum amoris' (cap. 18 §133); 'singularia signa' for the proficient (cap. 15 §117). Staupitz advised cautiously: 'Neque enim ipsemet sapiens dulcedinem dei novit aliis saporem explanare et satis informare, ut et ipsi sapiant; quippe quod solo experimento discitur, stilum doctrinae non habet.' Cap. 15, §110.

[79] See *Libellus*, cap. 18 §§161 and 145. In addition, the article 'Goldene Kette', in the *Lexikon der Alten Welt*, cols. 1108–9.

tradition argued that good works within and without the state of grace are not experientially 'different' or distinguishable; without exception, its proponents employed Eccl. 9.1 as its central biblical proof text: 'No one knows whether he merits God's love or his hatred.'[80]

Eccl. 9.1 demands our special attention because Staupitz's understanding of this verse both sheds light on his relationship to late medieval theology and piety, and promises aid in examining the even more complicated issues of his Catholicity[81] and his significance for the Reformation.[82]

At first glance Staupitz's interpretation of this verse in the 1516 sermons seems to fit seamlessly into the late medieval web constructed around the basic and pedagogically necessary insistence on the uncertainty of salvation and grace. For he noted that God's working in history is veiled in obscurity so that 'No one knows whether he merits God's love or his hatred.'[83]

This exposition, however, was no isolated passage in Staupitz's sermon. The context dealt with the heart of the Christian faith ('ista credere est de necessitate salutis')[84] which he summarized in referring to the twofold word of God: God's self-revelation as power (*potentia*) and as mercy (*misericordia*).[85] Departing from tradition,[86] including Augustine,[87] Staupitz applied the *potentia Dei* only to God's omnipo-

[80] The exegesis and use of this verse merits a special study. Gabriel Biel considered his treatment to have been representative (ut tradunt doctores): 'charitas et cetere virtutes infuse a nobis experimentaliter cognosci non possunt'. *Canonis misse expositio*, Lect. 86P; Oberman and Courtenay edn., 4, p. 137. See the index to that edition for Biel's frequent use of this text.

[81] Adolar Zumkeller considered this teaching of the 'uncertainty of our salvation' and the rejection of (Luther's) fiducial faith as proof that Staupitz 'is completely Catholic'. See 'Das Ungenügen der menschlichen Werke bei den deutschen Predigern des Spätmittelalters', p. 300; *idem*, 'Die Augustinerschule des Mittelalters', p. 256.

[82] Oswald Bayer has focused on Luther's interpretation of Eccl. 9.1 in 1516 and 1518 as a key to understanding his 'evangelical experience'. *Promissio. Geschichte der reformatorischen Wende in Luthers Theologie*, p. 75, n. 261 and p. 216.

[83] 'Currit in factis humanis tam absconditum iudicium dei, ut nemo sciat, an amore dei odiove dignus sit, et nihilominus peccatorum contra se clamorem semper audiat.' *Libellus*, cap. 17 §142. Cf. *Staupitzens Werke*, ed. Knaake, p. 164, lines 35ff; cf. pp. 69, line 25; 19, line 21; and 70, lines 4ff.

[84] *Libellus*, cap. 17 §145.

[85] Staupitz is here interpreting Ps. 61.12f.: 'Semel locutus est Deus; duo haec audivi: Quia potestas Dei est, et tibi, Domine, misericordia.' (The Vulgate continues: 'Quia tu reddes unicuique juxta opera sua.') *Libellus*, cap. 17 §136.

[86] Staupitz does not explicitly mention the following clause of verse 13 ('quia tu . . .') which in the exegetical tradition led to the pair *iustitia–misericordia* (see *Libellus*, cap. 17 §37). But the verse is implicitly included in the contrast *misericordia–miseria* (*opera sua*, i.e. *peccata*).

[87] 'Hunc humilat, et hunc exaltat: hunc humilat potestate; illum exaltat misericordia

tence in the creation *ex nihilo* and his subsequent maintenance of creation. But apart from the fallen creature's capacity to perceive that God exists and is the origin and end of all things, the omnipotence of God remains hidden and inaccessible to man: at the summit of the human capacity to know, man can only discover his ignorance.[88] By restricting the Thomistic expansion of the natural cognition of God and approaching the nominalist concept of the inscrutability of divine omnipotence (*potentia absoluta Dei*), Staupitz interpreted Eccl. 9.1 as testimony to the hiddenness of God (*absconditum iudicium*).[89] But then, in emphatic contrast, the revelation of God's mercy in the incarnation shatters man's basic inability to assess his works through God's eyes. Man discovers himself a sinner whose good works can only be considered the gift of God.

Expanding our survey to incorporate parallel passages from his complete corpus, we find that Eccl. 9.1 served a threefold purpose for Staupitz. In the first place, it directed itself against all forms of arrogance and presumption ('ut nemo glorietur').[90] At the same time it offered consolation for those burdened by awareness of their sinfulness. The first mark of God's mercy is the sinner's perception of his unrighteousness; assurance of his own righteousness comes only as the result of exceptional and special revelation.[91] And lastly, applied positively, the passage meant that God is incalculable and yet merits and demands man's trust. In this context Staupitz clearly pointed out that the sacraments were specifically instituted in order to awaken, if not certitude, then at least a certain hope (*certa spes*).[92] Eccl. 9.1 had served the preceding tradition as 'exhibit A' for a

. . . Time ergo et treme eius potestatem, sed spera eius misericordiam.' *Enarrationes in Psalmos*, Ps. 61, §20; *CChr* 39, p. 788, lines 14–22.

88 'Ecce hic finis totius studii philosophici: cognoscere ignorantiam nostram.' *Libellus*, cap. 17 §140.

89 Regarding election he noted emphatically, 'haud sine inscrutabili iustitia dei'. *Libellus*, cap. 14 §99, Cf. *Staupitzens Werke*, ed. Knaake 1, p. 69, line 25.

90 1 Cor. 3.21. *Libellus*, cap. 17 §141. Cf., *Staupitz, Tübinger Predigten*, ed. Buchwald and Wolf, p. 23, lines 3–12; Cf. pp. 59, lines 37–42; 205, line 37–206, line 2. Cf. *Staupitzens Werke*, ed. Knaake, p. 69, line 18.

91 'Inde procedit primum divinae misericordiae testimonium, quod quilibet se cognoscit peccatorem – nemo novit absque revelatione se esse iustum; et aliud, quod misericordia dei omnium bonorum moralium est primum principium et ultimus finis.' *Libellus*, cap. 17 §143. Cf. *Staupitzens Werke*, ed. Knaake, pp. 69, line 22; 70, lines 9f.

92 'Ideo habet dilectionem stabilem et spem vivam. Et quamvis non possit homo sua inquisitione certitudinem habere, an dei odio amoreve dignus sit, potest tamen per infallibilia signa ad hoc instituta certam facere spem et eiicere desperationem, quae maxima tribulatio animae est, quae innititur quaestioni de sui electione . . .' *Libellus*,. cap. 23 §238.

conjectural faith[93] and in the process encouraged introspection. Staupitz considered any faith in the outcome of such analysis to be misplaced, because not our works but God's sacraments mirror his mercy until the final moment of death; impossible, because we cannot penetrate the *iustitia abscondita* of God; and superfluous, since Eccl. 9.1 by no means imagines the human conscience to be a *tabula rasa*. Indeed, if misused as a call for introspection, the verse could serve only to sharpen the already present self-indictment.

In the *Büchlein von der Nachfolgung* the devil's temptations climax in his use of Eccl. 9.1 against Christ, who asserted, 'I am the son of God.' Believers who follow Christ's example will find themselves made fearful and unsure by the devil; unsettled 'by unnecessary fear arising from the fact that a man never knows whether he be worthy of God's love or his hatred'.[94] There could have been no more effective method of refuting the traditional exegesis than by placing it in the mouth of the devil.

But how can the systematic search for the *signa caritatis*, for the signs within us, be linked with Staupitz's exegesis of Eccl. 9.1 and above all with the reference to the sacramental *signa instituta* contained in that exegesis? The answer to this problem, one of the most difficult in Staupitz research, seems to me to lie in the above description of the temptations that beset the dying. The seventh temptation which, along with the ninth, treats of the diabolical abuse of the doctrine of predestination, results from a 'presumptuous confidence in God's mercy'. It is presumptuous (*stulta*)[95] because 'no one is saved by his own righteousness as a result of his works, but only by divine mercy and grace . . .'[96] The passage would be difficult

[93] See Nicolaus de Lyra, *Postilla super totam Bibliam*, vol. 3, s. v.

[94] In 'unordenlicher forchte, die dorauss enspringt, das der mensch nymmer weiss, ab er der liebe, ader aber des hass gots wirdig sey', *Staupitzens Werke*, ed. Knaake, p. 66, lines 26ff.

[95] In *Libellus*, cap. 19 §170 Staupitz introduced as a potential objection to preaching predestination the claim that it 'sit occasio stultae confidentiae in deum'. Staupitz's response was firm: 'Praedicatio praedestinationis veram libertatem, qua nos Christus liberos fecit, erigit.'

[96] 'nymand wirdt selig auss seiner gerechtickeit, umb seiner werck willen, sunder allein auss gotlicher barmhertzickeit, auss gnaden, . . .' *Staupitzens Werke*, ed. Knaake, p. 66, lines 6–12. It is this passage especially that may have led Zumkeller to distinguish Staupitz clearly from Luther. But Luther revealed, even in his later years, his profound indebtedness to precisely the pastoral theology formulated in these last three temptations. We should at the same time take note of a very revealing text that indicates the degree to which Luther shared Staupitz's concern to avoid both an excessively lighthearted *fiducia* (*contemptus*) and *desperatio*. This text also discloses that Eccl. 9.1, placed in the devil's mouth, leads to a *contemptus* of human works in the seventh temptation and, as with the Epicureans, to *desperatio* in the ninth temptation outlined by Staupitz. *WA* 43, p. 458, lines 20–5.

to understand and to reconcile with the central theme of Staupitz's theology, characterized by David Steinmetz as 'sola misericordia Dei', if we fail to pay close attention to precisely which point Staupitz attacked as false. At issue was the diabolical attempt to arouse excessive confidence in divine mercy toward us (*pro nobis*) and thereby to bypass Christ who is in us (*in nobis*).[97] The significance of Staupitz's implications and theological conclusions here will concern us at a later point.

For the present, however, we must keep in mind that whoever undertakes a reinterpretation of such a central passage of scripture as Eccl. 9.1, and thereby tampers with a pivotal point in late medieval theology,[98] has set much more in motion than is apparent from a single verse. Nevertheless the question remains whether Staupitz's broadly conceived attempt to fit the individual's life of faith into God's plan of salvation could furnish the consolation he hoped to provide with his evidence of the mercy of God (*testimonium misericordiae*). For at least the second part of the *Libellus* is an example of the pastorally oriented late medieval consolation literature.[99] It reaches its climax in the penultimate chapter with the counsel that assurance of salvation can be had where one indicts oneself but justifies one's neighbour ('magnam certitudinem suae salutis consecutus est, qui bona aliorum, mala sua crebre intuens se damnare, reliquos iustificare solitus est').[100] In this case consolation follows the sinner's steady listening (*semper audiat*) to the indictment against himself, his attention to God's verdict on his sin and, in effect, his ratification of that verdict. In this manner the sinner's self-righteousness yields to God's justification.[101]

[97] 'Also lernet er trost ym leiden Christi tzu suchen, ane das man werde ein glid Christi, das falsch ist.' *Staupitzens Werke*, p. 66, lines 13f.

[98] Eccl. 9.1 employed as encouragement in the struggle with death: 'also findest im grundt keine leichtere vberwindung der anfechtigung, das einem menschen seine eigne tugendte tzu wolgefallen vnnd das vortrawen tzu gote torrechte vormessenheit worde, also die dir vom creutze geben, das ist bedencken, das du nicht weist, ab du ye was got gefellig gethan vnd volbracht habst'. *Von der nachfolgung*, cap. 8; *Staupitzens Werke*, ed. Knaake, p. 70, lines 6–10.

[99] 'Enumeratis certis quae ad salutem sunt necessaria et necessario credenda pro consecutione eiusdem, pro ulteriori nostra consolatione sublevemus intuitum mentis in manifestationem spiritus, antequam felicitatis tempus, quod futuri exspectamus, adsit.' *Libellus*, cap. 15 §107.

[100] *Libellus*, cap. 23 §246. Cf. Luther: 'Secundo paratur per intuitum et contemplationem speciosissimae iusticiae, qua quis in pulchritudine et specie iusticiae meditatus in eam ardescit et rapitur, incipitque cum Salomone fieri amator sapientiae, cuius pulchritudinem viderat. Haec facit vere poenitentem, quia amore iusticiae id facit, et hii sunt digni absolutione . . .' *WA* 1, p. 319, lines 27–31.

[101] In similar fashion Staupitz's interpretation of the exchange between Christ and the malefactor on the cross (Luke 23.39–42) and the latter's vindication of God as an

This was the path taken by Luther after his own *Dictata super Psalterium*, a path which was to extricate him from the pit of pious introspection.[102] And only against the backdrop of these occasionally very extensive parallels[103] does it become completely clear that Staupitz's answer to the same question had a different orientation. Indeed, in some respects he suggested a solution diametrically opposed to Luther's in describing the second evidence of God's mercy. Not by referring to the verdict of God in Christ (*extra nos*) but by stressing the work of God in us (*in nobis*) did he offer support to the sinner – a new footing based on the fact that 'the mercy of God is the beginning and end of all temporal things'.[104] Luther developed the *extra nos* of Christ's righteousness in a positive sense from the mystical tradition of the *excessus mentis* and *raptus*[105] wherein we are drawn out of and placed outside ourselves.[106] Yet Staupitz turned to the same tradition to describe the manner in which the Mosaic law overwhelms: 'It robs man of himself, draws him into a life of illusion and makes off with his liberty',[107] and the even more powerful effect of the law of Christ: 'It seizes the whole man and completely alienates him from himself.'[108] In Luther's treatise on freedom it is precisely *libertas* or freedom from the law that Christ brings as a dowry to the 'marriage' of justification. But Luther based that freedom on the *iustitia aliena* or extrinsic righteousness of Christ (*extra nos*).[109]

For Staupitz, an Augustinian emphasis on the internal quality of grace which, by returning us to ourselves, makes us capable of free and spontaneous action in contrast to the alienating effects of the law, appeared in yet another context: in connection with the capacity to identify good works; a capacity resulting from the coincidence of the

anticipation of God's last judgment. *Von der nachfolgung*, cap. 9; *Staupitzens Werke*, ed. Knaake, pp. 69, lines 31ff. and 71, lines 13, 18 and 23.

102 Scholion for Ps. 50.6; *WA* 3, p. 290, lines 7ff., continued in the commentary on Rom. 9.3 in *WA* 56, p. 393, lines 14–17. Regarding the *Dictata* see especially the careful exposition by Reinhard Schwarz, *Vorgeschichte der reformatorischen Busstheologie*, pp. 228–47.

103 Cf. Staupitz, *Libellus*, De matrimonio Christi et christiani (cap. 9) with Luther's use of this image in his treatise on the 'Freedom of the Christian', especially the common concluding question: 'Quomodo autem nobis adveniat nostreitas meritorum Christi . . .' *Libellus*, cap. 9 §53; *WA* 7, pp. 54, lines 31–56, line 14.

104 'das die barmherzikeit gots aller sitlichen dingk erst anfangk und letstes end ist' (Scheurl). Cf. *Libellus*, cap. 17 §143.

105 See my article, 'Simul gemitus et raptus. Luther and Mysticism', pp. 233ff.

106 See in this regard especially zur Mühlen, *Nos extra nos. Luthers Theologie zwischen Mystik und Scholastik*, pp. 101ff. and 198ff.

107 'spoliat hominem seipso, rapit extra se, tollit libertatem.' *Libellus*, cap. 16 §123.

108 'rapit totum hominem sibimet et totaliter extra seipsum ponit.' *Libellus*, cap. 16 §126.

109 *WA* 7, p. 55, line 19.

operation and effect of grace. Whereas the first of the two signs of *misericordia* leads to the discovery that man stands as a sinner before God, the second reveals that our good works originate in Christ[110] and return to him.[111] In this manner the *syllogismus practicus* results, confirming the existence of a formerly impossible but now vital loving bond to Christ which finds expression in human works.[112]

Staupitz was concerned above all to eliminate any sort of confidence in human works and to exalt the work of Christ as the sole basis for the crown of eternal life. Not our own inevitably limited[113] merits, which are dependent on God's more gracious *acceptatio*,[114] but rather the work of Christ is the foundation and object of our hope.[115] Even in the state of grace our works remain so inadequate[116] that they require the *acceptatio divina*. Staupitz had arrived at a doctrine of a *duplex iustitia*, but of a different sort from that developed in the pre-Tridentine epoch by Gropper (†1559) and Seripando (†1563).[117] In Staupitz's understanding of the *commercium admirabile*, the righteousness of Christ was not, as with Gropper and Seripando, a foreign righteousness or *iustitia aliena extra nos*, but was, like our own righteousness, a *iustitia in nobis*.

The newly created, internal and dual righteousness now expresses

[110] 'et aliud, quod misericordia dei omnium bonorum moralium est primum principium et ultimus finis. [144] Et sicut facta sunt omnia in esse naturali per verbum aeternum, ita sunt in esse morali facta per idem verbum incarnatum.' Staupitz, *Libellus*, cap. 17 §§143–4.

[111] *Ibid.*, cap. 8 §50.

[112] Echoes in the preceding tradition are not found in Aquinas (*STh* I–II q. 112 5 ad 5; Eccl. 9.1 in *sed contra*!) but in the Pseudo-Bonaventure: 'Et debemus considerare quatuor signa, quibus electos suos signat Deus. Est enim virtus pignus vel pretium salvationis. Sicut enim qui habet pretium, rem potest emere; et sicut qui habet arrham vel pignus sufficiens, certus est de solutione: sic qui habet virtutem, vel gratiam gratuitam, securus est de aeterna salvatione. De hoc pignore habetur: *Signati estis spiritu promissionis sancto*, scilicet gratiae, *qui est pignus hereditatis nostrae.*' *Opusculum diaeta salutis*, tit. 5 cap. 1 in *S. Bonaventurae Opera omnia*, ed. Peltier, vol. 8, p. 292.

[113] *Libellus*, cap. 7 §43.

[114] *Ibid.*, cap. 8 §50.

[115] *Ibid.*, cap. 7 §43; 8 §§50 and 52. 'Opera bona in gratia facta' possess no condignity and Staupitz avoided the expression 'de congruo'.

[116] See Zumkeller, 'Das Ungenügen der menschlichen Werke', pp. 300f. Steinmetz has pointed, in contrast to E. Wolf, to non-Thomistic elements in Staupitz's theology. See *Misericordia Dei*, pp. 26f.

[117] See Walter Lipgens, *Kardinal Johannes Gropper (1503–1559) und die Anfänge der Katholischen Reform in Deutschland*, pp. 100–8, 192–203. For clarification see Braunisch, *Theologie der Rechtfertigung*, pp. 419ff. On Seripando's defence of the *duplex iustitia* at the Council of Trent see Walther von Loewenich, *Duplex iustitia. Luthers Stellung zu einer Unionsformel des 16. Jahrunderts*, pp. 78–81 and the literature, p. 78, n. 149.

itself in works of love that testify to their source. Because not merely meritorious (*digna*) works but even good works (*bona opera*) result from the efficacy of the love of Christ, it can be said of the believer's works of love that: 'if love is pure, then the works of love (*signa amoris*) are also pure; but the works of a false love are flawed'.[118] One important point can now be clarified: although Staupitz's remark about the cross of Christ would help to shape history by opening Luther's eyes to a Christ *extra nos*, he himself could have had in mind only a meditative glimpse of the cross that imparts courage and confidence in an *internal* spiritual remoulding through Christ and the radiance of his death on the cross. A sentence written in 1515 thoroughly supports this view: 'He [Christ] is the snake on the tree, the beholding of which destroys the venom of death . . .'[119] The effect was in the beholding, in a *recordari*, in being inwardly affected.

And thus no matter how much Staupitz proclaimed his understanding of an unconditional gift of mercy (*gratuita misericordia*) and of Christian faith as confidence in the work of Christ, he was still unable to shatter the anthropological fetters of pious introspection which he recognized, as we do today, to be the key problem of late medieval piety.[120] Only an awareness of the ambiguity of even the deepest religious experience and the realization that precisely the pursuit of the *signa praedestinationis* can be a diabolical temptation permit one fully to appreciate the mercy of God.

We find the main theme of Staupitz's pastoral theology in abbreviated form in a letter contemporaneous with his treatise on predestination and written to the prior of the Erfurt Augustinians, Johannes Lang: 'Though Fortune deserts you may grace enlighten you and may

[118] 'Si castus est, et signa ipsa casta sunt; si impurus est amor, et ipsa quoque signa impura sunt.' *Libellus*, cap. 15 §115.

[119] *Von der nachfolgung*, cap. 6; *Staupitzens Werke*, ed. Knaake, p. 62, lines 22f.

[120] The 'most widely read book of devotion in the late middle ages' according to Herbert Grundmann in *RGG* 4, p. 466, the *Meditationes vitae Iesu Christi* by Ludolf of Saxony (†1377 in Strassburg), which was reprinted sixty times after 1472, can be considered typical in its use of Eccl. 9.1: '*Nescit homo finem suum; sed sicut piscis capitur hamo, et sicut avis comprehenditur laqueo, sic homo capitur in tempore malo* . . . Quia ergo tempus iudicii et etiam mortis est incertum, ideo debemus semper esse parati ad ipsum expectandum et semper esse in continua solicitudine, ne improvisi inveniamur in morte . . . Habeamus igitur in memoria, quia mundus fallax, vita brevis, finis dubius, exitus horribilis, iudex terribilis, poena interminabilis; et haec semper nos terreant, et ad vigilandum inducant . . . Haec itaque scientes et illam diem semper suspectam habentes faciamus nunc de nobisipsis iudicium praeoccupando faciem Domini in confessione et iustitia, perficiendo dignos fructus poenitentiae, ut Deum nobis propitium inveniamus et benignum.' *Vita Iesu Christi*, II, cap. 45 §§12–14, pp. 544f.

God's righteousness condemn you, yet lead you to salvation.'[121] Although one's own righteousness in God's eyes cannot be determined (Eccl. 9.1),[122] our discovery of our sinfulness is proof of God's mercy, for it is not our good works but solely our sin that Christ expects as a dowry in our marriage with him.[123] The righteousness that Christ provides in that union does not contrast with a *iustitia Dei* of the last judgment, the measure of our good works. Rather the *iustitia Dei* of which Staupitz spoke entered the service of divine mercy long before the foundation of the world was laid. As early as the Salzburg sermons of 1512, Staupitz had maintained that all God's actions flow from the 'fountain of mercy', from God's eternal, gracious election.[124] On the basis of that eternal election God pledged himself to summon and to save his chosen people. In the faithfulness with which he fulfils his promises God demonstrates his righteousness.[125] The Augustinian vicar-general's favourite maxim, 'Tuus sum, salvum me fac' (Ps. 118.94), had ceased to be a petitionary prayer as it had been for his order's spiritual master Augustine,[126]

121 'Interim fortuna te deserat, gratia illustret, justitia te damnet, immo salvet, Adam te morti, Christus vitae aeternae generet.' 14 November 1516. Kolde, *Augustiner-Congregation*, p. 439.

122 The much-discussed statement by Luther, 'peccator secundum rem iustus secundum spem, peccator revera, iustus vero per imputationem Dei miserentis' (*WA* 1, p. 149, lines 9–11) was prefaced with the words: 'Cum iusticia fidelium sit in Deo abscondita, peccatum vero eorum manifestum in seipsis, verum est non nisi iustos damnari atque peccatores et meretrices salvari.' *WA* 1, p. 148, lines 35–7 (September 1516). With reference, *inter alia*, to Eccl. 9.1, the subsequent train of thought asserted that the fact that our merits (i.e. *iusticia*) are unknown to us (i.e. hidden from us) should not lead us to despair. *WA* 1, p. 149, lines 33f. and 36 to p. 150, line 2.

123 *Libellus*, cap. 10 §§66 and 69. The Dominican Jacob von Hoogstraten's criticism of Luther's understanding of the 'commercium admirabile' could likewise be levelled at Staupitz in that Hoogstraten dismissed with disgust the 'cogaturque Christus, velit nolit (nimirum matrimonii iure), purulentam ac scabiosam sponsam thalamo suo castus sponsus admittere'. *Contra Lutheranos*, lib. 3 disp 1; fol. 4^{r}; Pijper, ed., *Primitiae pontificiae theologorum neerlandicorum Disputationes contra Lutherum*, pp. 607f. Cf. Staupitz's stress, indeed, stipulation, that the soul is a 'meretrix'. *Libellus*, cap. 15 §114. But where Hoogstraten can hold against Luther that no 'munditia sponsae' followed, this attack does not apply to Staupitz. *Contra Lutheranos*, p. 610. Hoogstraten thus assists us in identifying the difference between Luther's 'simul iustus et peccator' and Staupitz's 'simul purus et impurus'. *Libellus*, cap. 17 §141 and 19 §173.

124 'prunn der parmhertzykait' (Salzburg, St Peter, Cod. b V 8, fol. 3^{r}).

125 'opus demum iustissimum, in quo redditur promissum, servatur iusiurandum.' *Libellus*, cap. 15 §98. Cf. Christ as 'debitor salutis' in cap. 9 §22; 6 §33. Cf. the preliminary forms of the medieval 'covenant theology' in Augustine: 'Fidelis ille [Deus] factus est debitor.' *Enarrationes in Psalmos*, Ps. 119, §1; *CChr* 40, p. 1601, line 11.

126 Augustine rejected the 'tuus sum' as an excessively audacious (*familiarius*) claim to a special status, for indeed the whole world belongs to God. Hence the 'tuus sum' is

and had become a demand,[127] claiming the faithfulness of God and holding him to his promise of election that he complete the process of salvation begun in justification.

Following in Augustine's footsteps, Bradwardine and Gregory of Rimini had entered the lists against the Pelagians of the fourteenth century, asserting that the *sola gratia* aspect of justification was illustrated in Peter's conversion in response to the *conversio Dei*; to Jesus' act of turning to look at Peter. Staupitz took another giant step along that path by fetching the academic–dogmatic doctrine of predestination from the speculative eternity of 'before the foundation of the world' and bringing it into the kerygmatic 'now' of preaching. If Gregory's teaching on predestination had already been clearly christologically oriented, with Staupitz it became the centrepiece in the proclamation of the *hic et nunc* pursuing and conquering will of God.

A quotation from the Salzburg sermons demonstrates this more exquisitely and appealingly than could any systematic analysis. Staupitz began by mentioning and surprisingly enough, nearly equating, the two traditional scriptural types for the elect and the reprobate: 'With regard to their repentance, Judas and Peter were not very dissimilar.' He continued: 'This was the difference between Peter and Judas: Peter accepted the look of mercy and trusted in the mercy of God, whereas Judas despaired over his sin. Had Judas trusted in God's mercy, he would also have found succour.'[128] Whereas the contemplation of the crucified One was understood in the *Büchlein von der Nachfolgung* as a *recordatio* and inward affectedness, in the Salzburg sermons it represented a 'fiducial faith' or confidence in the forgiveness of God that seemed 'Lutheran' to Catholic theologians. From these apparently unsystematic and rhe-

to be understood not in contrast to other men but in opposition to one's former tyranny over oneself: 'Meus esse volui et perditum me feci.' *Enarrationes in Psalmos*, Ps. 118, Sermo 21, §6; *CChr* 41, pp. 1734, line 8–1735, line 12.

[127] Carlstadt's threefold exposition of Staupitz's motto is significant. Initially remaining within the framework of Augustine's exegesis, he then heightened the 'familiarius' charge by observing that only rarely could one say, 'tuus sum'. In his third analysis he noted in the spirit of the *Theologia Deutsch*, and of Staupitz's discipleship of suffering, 'Tuus sum, *tormenta suscipio*, salvum fac.' Kähler, *Karlstadt und Augustin*, pp. 6, line 25; 8, lines 25f.; 9, lines 8, 23f. Carlstadt's threefold interpretation hence remains within the context of petitionary prayer. See also Spitz, 'Headwaters of the Reformation', pp. 93–101.

[128] 'das was [war] die unterschidung Petri und Judas: Petrus hat angenumen den plick der parmhertzikait, und vertraut in die parmhertzikait gots, aber Judas verzagt yn seinen sünten [Sünden]; hiet [hätte] Judas vertraut yn die parmhertzikait, im [ihm] wär auch geholffen warn [worden].' Salzburg, St Peter, Cod. b V 8, fol. 32^{r-v}.

torically moving statements we observe how far Staupitz had wandered from that which scholars have postulated as an Augustinian determinism. The doctrine of predestination had no specific speculative face value for Staupitz but helped – along with Scotist–nominalist theses on God's covenant – to trace the Christ-event to its very origin in the eternal divine decree, to its source in the fountain of mercy. Considered alone, the equation of Peter with Judas would scarcely lead one to expect a homiletical application of the doctrine of election. A Pelagianizing shift of initiative in salvation from God to man would seem a far more likely interpretation. But for Staupitz it was precisely divine election, which included Christ's coming in spirit and in flesh, that excluded any form of merit reckoning (Eccl. 9.1), and invited the sinner to entrust himself to God's prevenient grace.

Even this skein of ideas indicates that the Augustinian renaissance, as embodied in the works and influence of Johann von Staupitz, should not be confused with a repristination of Augustine. Challenged *and* enriched by the development of theology and piety in the late middle ages, the Augustinian revival could participate in the reform efforts of its era while ostensibly better equipped institutions, such as the universities and the monastic orders, revealed their inadequacy for the task.

Throughout the Middle Ages the phrase, 'nemo scit . . .' (Eccl. 9.1) had been a stimulus for exhortation and exegesis alike. With the aid of an unusual coalition between Augustinianism and Aristotelianism, the same destination had been reached from two different points of departure. Whereas one tradition clung to a 'grace of perseverance' whereby uncertainty persisted to the very end, the other considered the chain of *scire–scientia–evidentia* essential. An Augustinian capacity to persist in uncertainty (*donum perseverantiae*) and an Aristotelian understanding of knowledge and knowing combined to forge and temper the flaming sword (Gen. 3.24) that guarded the entrance to God's hidden council-chamber. Only a single bridge crossed the gaping chasm between God's power (*potentia*) and his willingness to save (*misericordia*): the rope bridge of the *certitudo spei*, a theology of hope for the dying.

Sixteenth-century developments illustrate just how vastly difficult the mastery of the problem of the uncertainty of salvation was and remained. Although the left wing of the Reformation found, along with Luther,[129] an 'answer' to the 'nemo scit' dilemma in rejecting

129 For Luther see the abbreviated formulation, 'contra spem in spem' in his exposition of Ps. 4.3; *WA* 5, pp. 84, line 33–85, line 5 (1519–20); p. 84, line 39.

introspection, the problem proved to have been postponed rather than solved. A different passage – 'The spirit [wind] blows where he wishes' (cf. John 3.8) – assumed the medieval role of Eccl. 9.1, but the entire play was shifted to the ecclesiastical *sacramental* stage.

Our historical survey facilitates the definition of Staupitz's position and significance since the central issue of his epoch was also the central concern of his theology. The heart of the theology of this 'herald of grace and the cross' – as Luther was to style Staupitz in retrospect[130] – was a product of the tense opposition of Eccl. 9.1 and Psalm 118.94. A silent and sealed heaven occupied by an inaccessible and incalculable God (Eccl. 9.1) contrasted with a confident, indeed audacious proximity to that same God (Ps. 118.94). From these dialectical threads the web of Staupitz's theology derived its form. Eccl. 9.1 retained a purposeful validity in demonstrating that God is inaccessible via the intelligent introspection of a *homo sciens*. That meant abandoning the influential medieval interpretation (Lyra) according to which a good *(con-) scientia* permitted at least a 'conjectural' assurance. The Augustinian legacy's battle against the Pelagian insistence on self-determination delivered the dogmatic foundation for a pastoral 'No' to human striving for advance bookings in the celestial theatre *coram Deo*.

In direct contrast, the gracious gospel of election reveals how God makes it possible for the *homo sapiens* to claim the *gratis* box seats already set aside for him. By minimizing the concept of a *donum perseverantiae*,[131] Staupitz was able to take an important step beyond Augustine and the fourteenth-century recovery of Augustine. For in the eternal decree of predestination Christ becomes man's *debitor* whom God the father and his virgin mother *must* abandon to cohabitation with the sinner.[132] Not the traditional image of marriage but the obligation, the *must*, merits emphasis here; for it justifies addressing God audaciously with: 'Tuus sum' and claiming the accompanying *right* to salvation: 'Salvum me fac!'

The far-reaching consequences of this line of thought are impossible to overlook. For with the aid of Augustine, Augustine has been surpassed by overturning the keystone of medieval piety: the plain-

[130] 'Praeco gratiae et crucis.' *WABr* 2, p. 264, line 48; Luther to Staupitz, 9 February 1521.

[131] E. Wolf has already noted Staupitz's suppression of the *donum perseverantiae*; *Staupitz und Luther*, pp. 68 and n. 1; 62, and n. 3. I have used the term 'minimizing' in view of the petition for confirmation in faith (!) found in *Von der nachfolgung*, cap. 13; *Staupitzens Werke*, ed. Knaake, pp. 83, lines 27–33; 84, lines 25–34.

[132] 'O mein mueter, die zeit yst hie, ych mues peyligen.' Salzburg, St Peter, Cod. b V 8, fol. 5^v (1512).

tive plea, 'Lord, grant that I may some day be reckoned among thy elect.'

It would be amiss to assume that Staupitz applied his motto only to the 'final farewell', relating it exclusively to the moment when the departing soul entrusts his spirit with confidence into the hand of God 'from which no one can snatch or steal . . . for I am thine, save me. Amen'.[133] For all of reality is present in its most concentrated form at the deathbed, and conversely, in the midst of life we are surrounded by death.

Despite the controversy surrounding the posthumously published *Von dem heyligen rechten Christlichen glauben* (1525), one passage can indisputably pass for authentic Staupitzian solace and captures the burden of his pastor's heart: 'We have clear knowledge; if we believe in Christ we have Christ and shall not perish but attain eternal life. Such are those who have been drawn to Christ by the father who has obliged Christ to save them, ensuring that not a single one of them should be lost.'[134]

Tübingen also bore the mark of the Augustine revival which we have pursued as far as Wittenberg. It was fully predictable that Augustine should have been a respected and much-quoted authority at a medieval university. And the works of the chief representatives of both *viae* at Tübingen, Conrad Summenhart and Gabriel Biel, abundantly justify such anticipation.

Yet a new scholarly situation had arisen with the critical edition of Augustine by Johannes Amerbach. This, the first nearly complete edition of Augustine's works, in effect hurled the gauntlet at the feet of the adherents of the *via moderna* who had long since earned a reputation as the modern opponents of Augustine (*pelagiani moderni*). That the major challenger had already emerged from their own nominalist ranks in the person of Gregory of Rimini only reinforced the summons to theological combat.

In reaching its summit with Gabriel Biel, the Tübingen modern way had by no means arrived at its final destination. Luther's word construction 'wittenbergescere'[135] as a description for the attraction

133 'dorauss nymandt tzucken ader rauben kan . . . dann dein bin ich, mach mich selig. Amen.' *Von der nachfolgung*, cap. 15; *Staupitzens Werke*, ed. Knaake, p. 88, lines 16–18.

134 'Wir haben klaren beschayd, glauben wir in Christum, so haben wir Christum, werden nicht verloren, vberkummen das ewig leben, das sein die, die der vater zu Christo gezogen hat, vnd Christo sie selig zumachen auffgelegt, Also das nit einer auss jn verlorn werdt.' Cap. 5; *Staupitzens Werke*, ed. Knaake, p. 125, lines 21–5.

135 *WABr* 12, p. 14, lines 6–9; 4 October 1518 to the Wittenberg circle (Carlstadt, Amsdorf, Melanchthon, Beckmann among others).

exerted by the Wittenberg theology could even be modified to apply to Tübingen, producing the term 'gabrielescere'. In addition to his demonstrable influence on Luther's teachers in Erfurt, Biel also continued to shape intellectual currents in his own university, not merely through his writings but through the unbroken succession of his students Wendelin Steinbach (†1519) and Martin Plantsch (†1533), as well as Steinbach's pupil Gallus Müller (†1546), who succeeded Plantsch as parish priest in Tübingen (1526). Even Paris was penetrated by the spirit of the Biel school when Müller had the final twenty-eight *distinctiones* of Biel's *Collectorium* published by Jodocus Badius,[136] the printer chosen by the Sorbonne to publish the Leipzig Disputation.[137]

The major editor of Biel's works was Wendelin Steinbach, who not only supplemented his master's *magnum opus*, the *Collectorium*, but deserves the major credit for the widespread influence of the Biel school.[138] Born in Butzbach (Hesse) in 1454, Steinbach entered the local St Markusstift of the Brethren of the Common Life. His provost, Gabriel Biel, took him along to Württemberg and became his academic master. There Steinbach personally experienced both the festive beginnings (1477) and the bitter end (1517) of the *devotio moderna*'s forty-year history of service to Württemberg and its university. In 1516 Duke Ulrich succeeded in gaining the approval of Pope Leo X for the dissolution of all houses of the Brethren in Württemberg, ostensibly in order to endow a choir for his court in Stuttgart. When, in conjunction with this event, Steinbach was evicted from his quarters in the castle of Hohentübingen[139] upon completing his lectures on Hebrews (1517), an epoch ended abruptly;

[136] In a most unusual dedicatory letter to Martin Plantsch (Tübingen, 30 June 1520), Johannes Brassicanus used a variation of the 'modus loquendi' category in order to distinguish between language suitable to the epochs *ante* and *post Erasmum*, without disguising his joy at being an Erasmian: 'DEO OPTIMO MAXIMO gratias dico quas, in suam imaginem Poeta factus, potest atque debet, quod me GERMANUM fecit, quod me ERASMICO, hoc est omni bonarum literarum genere florentissimo tempore nasci voluit. Alia tempora, alii scribendi modi . . . Ex aedibus nostris Philosophicis. Tubingae.' Dedicatory epistle for Steinbach's *Gabrielis Byel Supplementum in octo et viginti distinctiones ultimas Quarti Magistri Sententiarum*, ed. Gallus Müller (Paris, 1521).

[137] Bos, *Luther in het oordeel van de Sorbonne*, pp. 32f.

[138] See Steiff, *Buchdruck*, pp. 55–71. The undated reissue of the *Epithoma* (1500 or 1501) and the excerpt from the complete *Expositio*, the so-called *Expositio brevis*, should be added to the list. *Ibid.*, pp. 72f.

[139] See Feld, *Hebräerbrief*, pp. 4–18 for a reconstruction of these events. For literature regarding the dissolution of the houses of the Brethren see *ibid.*, p. 16, n. 79.

two decades in which Gabriel Biel had been most prominently present even following his death in 1495.[140]

For all his loyalty to his master, Steinbach's lectures on Galatians (1513) offer us insight into the transformation occasioned by the new exegetical tools and a new scholarly atmosphere. Together with his final series of lectures, devoted to the letter to the Hebrews, his treatment of Galatians presents an unusual opportunity to evaluate the range and significance of the Augustine revival by comparison with Staupitz, who, educated in the Cologne *via antiqua*, confronted Augustine constantly within the context of his own monastic order.

At first, the Augustinian Eremite Staupitz would seem to have exchanged places with the Biel disciple Steinbach. For whereas Staupitz borrowed the terminology of the Scotists and nominalists to defend the importance of God's firm obligation (*debitum*) to the elect, Steinbach emphasized the gift of grace at the expense of stress on the divine covenant and obligation. A decisive reason for this astonishing emphasis on the part of a student of Biel may well lie in the fact that Steinbach had worked through the Augustinian corpus in his personal copy of the Amerbach edition.[141] Steinbach, like many of his contemporaries, could not afford to ignore the new level of scholarship attained with the publication of this edition. He cited the bishop of Hippo by the page and far more than all other fathers and *doctores* of the church. And these long quotations were no longer introduced as mere proof texts without regard for their context and intent, but rather, were cited together with a careful indication of the individual work and the specific flow of the discussion from which they were taken.

Aristotle took a rear seat in Steinbach's lectures on Galatians, a fact which cannot be completely explained by his scriptural subject matter, since the passages of admonition and counsel in the epistle would in fact have lent themselves well to citations of at least the *Nicomachean Ethics*. The content of Steinbach's interpretation of Paul was established when, supported by an appeal to Augustine, he

140 Steinbach reserved the question of guilt to the Last Judgment in a plaintive sigh at the end of his lectures on Hebrews, an exclamation remarkable precisely for its restraint: 'ex causa quam divino relinquam et tradidi iudicio.' Fol. 213v; cited by Feld, *Steinbach, Opera exegetica*, 1, p. xiii, n. 20.

141 Steinbach's personal copy of the Amerbach edition bearing his annotations is held by the University Library in Tübingen. Of course it is impossible definitely to attribute underlining to a specific user. Yet the marking of one passage ('Neminem velim sic amplecti omnia mea, ut me sequatur, nisi in his, in quibis me non errare perspexerit', in *De dono perseverantiae*, II, 21) corresponds well to Steinbach's attitude towards Augustine. Amerbach edition, vol. 10, fol. x3r.

called the position taken by the backsliding Galatians a false hope, 'as if the gospel of grace without the law of works is insufficient for salvation'.[142] The false teachers are pseudo-apostles who confuse the law with the gospel and thereby detract from Christ as the fulfilment of the law.[143]

Steinbach's mentor, Gabriel Biel, had understood the process of justification in such a way that the sinner, by doing his utmost (*facere quod in se est*), could perform a good work, at least so far as can be judged materially or externally (*quoad substantiam actus*). Even without a proper intention, which flows from love for God, and therefore without any *claim* to a reward, man could still earn a first infusion of grace due to God's generosity (*de congruo*). Only with the aid of this first grace was man capable of performing acceptable works of love that were meritorious in the true sense of the word (*de condigno*).[144]

Under the influence of Augustine's exegesis of the Pauline epistles, Steinbach does indeed appear to have departed from Biel. Not in regard to the teaching that the infusion of grace is necessary for good works to be performed out of love – for Biel and all the *doctores* had shared that view – but in his assertion that a human action in the absence of a transformation by grace is next to useless since it is not unleashed and sustained by a faith active in love.[145] God's grace or love, Steinbach concluded from the writings of Augustine, not only facilitates but is an irrevocable prerequisite for performing works of love.[146]

Despite this 'panegyric on grace' it would be totally misleading to

[142] 'gracia sola remittuntur homini peccata sine lege factorum . . .' *Opera exegetica*, 1, p. 6, lines 7f.; cf. p. 7, lines 12f. and 20; p. 24, lines 4f.; p. 149, line 25 *et passim*. 'Docui [Paulus] solam fidem Christi iustificare hominem, et hoc per promissionem factam Abrahe et per Moysen . . . Et Abacuk inquit: "ex fide iustum vivere coram Deo" non ex lege.' *Ibid.*, p. 152, lines 23–153, line 1. Cf. 'lex non salvat, sed fides Christi'. *Ibid.*, p. 153, line 30.

[143] 'Nichil autem prodest circumcisio ei, qui circumciditur post evangelii susceptionem, ut pseudo [apostoli] voluerunt, ponendo in lege spem salutis, quasi evangelium gracie sine lege factorum non sufficiat.' *Opera exegetica*, 1, p. 248, lines 1–3; cf. *ibid.*, p. 7, line 28 to 8, line 2. The 'false apostles' are also characterized by their confusion of law and gospel: 'Vos autem commiscetis unam alteri', i.e. the *lex factorum* with the *lex gracie*. *Ibid.*, p. 248, line 27; cf. p. 205, line 10.

[144] See *The Harvest of Medieval Theology*, pp. 175ff.

[145] 'sua benedicta incarnacione nobis meruit et infundit per Spiritum Sanctum donum caritatis, quo legem implere ad intencionem legislatoris possimus. Fides enim per caritatem operatur. Que si non habetur, fides mortua est et informis. Sine hac nec nove legis littera salvat, eciam si ad substanciam operis servetur, ut manifeste docet Apostolus.' *Opera exegetica*, 1, p. 259, lines 2–7.

[146] 'Sed caritas requiritur ad actus substanciam, quo diligimus Deum, et non solum ad promptificandam potenciam.' *Ibid.*, p. 269, lines 5f.

portray Steinbach as an anti-Pelagian in an Augustinian sense. For Steinbach certainly did not answer in an Augustinian vein the decisive control question which asks whether a human being minus grace can do nothing but continue in a deluded resistance against God. Had Steinbach sided with Augustine here, he would have indeed clearly sidestepped Biel. One cannot charge Steinbach with ignoring the anti-Pelagian Augustine or refusing to take a position. Nor can he be accused of having attempted – as he might have been inclined to do by his own tradition – to reduce the various Augustines to a common middle ground. On the contrary: Augustine's approach proved so powerful to Steinbach that he found himself compelled to recognize the doctrine of man's absolute dependence on the grace of God as the correct interpretation of Augustine's theology. Given that realization, Steinbach also felt obliged to demonstrate the conformity of Augustine's exegesis with the teaching of the Apostle Paul.

Steinbach applied his theological scalpel at a completely different point: he ascribed the continuity and even conformity between Paul and Augustine to their mutual *modus loquendi*,[147] thereby attacking the tradition that identified the form of an expression with its content. Thomas Bradwardine had insisted that the *doctores'* mode of expression regarding man's capacity to merit grace was inseparably bound up with the substance of this assertion. Hence, so far as Bradwardine was concerned, to sacrifice the form of expression meant the surrender of its content.[148] In contrast, skilled in supposition logic, Steinbach applied his nominalist tradition in order to elevate the distinction between subject matter and expression, between formulation and object, to a principle of interpretation. The nominalist reliance on specifically tailored terminology had often attracted the wrath of the *via antiqua* and had been the main cause of the Paris condemnations.[149] This reliance on terminological advances, which prompted the introduction of the label 'terminista', first as an insult and then as a proud self-designation,[150] led to a clarification of scholarly language within the *Artes* and was used to tame the

[147] 'Hoc loquendi modo operacio, que non est formata caritate, non dicitur esse aliquid meritorie, et fides informis fides ficta, ut supra, nominatur, quia non meritoria.' *Opera exegetica*, 1, p. 259, lines 14–16. 'Consequenter, quia secundum vulgatissimum modum loquendi beati Augustini . . . et similiter Apostoli, non est vera virtus sine caritate, et secundum Apostolum, operationes que non sunt secundum Deum, non dicuntur esse aliquid, sed nichil' (2 Cor. 10.17). *Ibid.*, p. 262, lines 24–8.

[148] See Bradwardine, *De Causa Dei*, lib. 1 cap. 39; p. 360B; cf. *ibid.*, pp. 352B and 353B.

[149] See Paqué, *Das Pariser Nominalistenstatut*, pp. 105ff.

[150] See *Werden und Wertung der Reformation*, appendix IV, 2.

otherwise uncontrollable metaphysical speculation in the field of dogmatics.

We are supplied with ample source material in this regard, and it exposes the once popular talk of nominalist logical hairsplitting as a misnomer for a serious academic exercise. With Steinbach we witness those 'terminist' tools applied to the exegesis of scripture and the fathers. Occam had already pointed out, appealing to Peter Lombard, that both scripture and the fathers were in complete agreement so far as content was concerned and yet used differing terminology. In response to the metaphysical depersonalization of God by Pope John XXII, who thereby invested with his papal authority a basic principle of the *via antiqua*, Occam defended the programmatic modernist distinction between *potentia Dei absoluta* and *potentia Dei ordinata*[151] in order to highlight the sovereignty of God and the contingency of the creature.[152] The *moderni* emphasized this distinction without claiming insight into God's essence; rather, they did so in order to salvage God's self-disclosure, transmitted in the church's tradition, from the

[151] 'Ista doctrina [John XXII] patenter asserit, non latenter, quod Deus non potest aliquid facere de potentia absoluta, quod non facit de potentia ordinata, quia omnia sunt ordinata a Deo. Ex quo sequitur evidenter quod nulla creatura potest aliquid facere, quod non facit; et ita omnia de necessitate eveniunt et nihil penitus contingenter, sicut quamplures infideles et antiqui haeretici docuerunt, et adhuc occulti haeretici et laici et vetulae tenent, saepe per argumenta sua etiam litteratos viros et in sacris litteris peritos concertantes. Uterque autem errorum praedictorum scripturis divinis repugnat aperte . . .' *Tractatus contra Benedictum* (1337/8), cap. 3; in *Ockham, Opera politica*, ed. Offler, 3, p. 231, lines 30–8.

[152] 'Ad cuius evidentiam ad praesens breviter est sciendum, quod ad recte intelligendum distinctionem de potentia Dei absoluta et ordinata non intendunt quod in Deo sint diversae potentiae, quarum una est absoluta et alia ordinata, per quarum unam potest Deus aliqua, quae non potest per aliam. Sed intendunt solummodo quod Deus posset aliqua, quae non ordinavit se facturum; quemadmodum posset aliqua facere, quae non praevidit se facturum, quia non est ea facturus: quae tamen, si faceret, et praeordinasset et praescivisset se facturum. Non ergo sunt tales potentiae in Deo diversae; sed quemadmodum, ut dicit Magister Sententiarum libro i, di, xlv: *Sacra [scriptura] de voluntate [Dei] variis modis consuevit loqui; et non est voluntas Dei diversa, sed locutio diversa est de voluntate, quia nomine voluntatis diversa accipit*, sic scripturae divinae et sanctorum diversimode loquuntur de potentia Dei, et tamen potentia Dei est una, et non diversa. Et ideo, licet potentia Dei sit una, tamen propter diversam locutionem dicitur quod Deus aliqua potest de potentia absoluta, quae tamen numquam faciet de potentia ordinata (hoc est, de facto numquam faciet): quemadmodum essentia et potentia, et similiter esse et posse, non sunt diversa in Deo, et tamen Deus potest multa, non obstante quod non sint illa multa, quae potest. Potest enim facere et fecit creaturas, scilicet caelum et terram et alia, et tamen non illa, quae fecit, et illa, quae faciet.

Qualiter autem non propter diversitatem potentiarum in Deo, sed propter diversitatem locutionis (hoc est, propter diversum modum accipiendi vocabula vel vocabulum) sit dicendum quod Deus posset aliqua de potentia absoluta, quae numquam faciet, non posset verbis brevibus explicari. . . .' *Tractatus contra Benedictum*, cap. 3; *Ockham, Opera politica*, ed. Offler, 3, pp. 233, line 37–234, line 23.

grip of alienating ontological speculation, and to allow it a voice in theology. Accordingly, the fundamental nominalist distinction between *potentia absoluta* and *potentia ordinata* took account of the varying language of scripture and ensured that the revealed plan of salvation remained contingent history instead of becoming a necessary self-expression of a divine essence.

Thus an emphasis on the *modus loquendi* was central to the legitimation of a cornerstone in Occam's system of thought, filling a role that can be traced all the way to Gabriel Biel and Wendelin Steinbach. For Occam, God's contingent nature determined the essence of his creature, which could likewise realize its potential contingently according to its own free capacity. And for Steinbach the *modus loquendi*[153] likewise helped to preserve human freedom of action against any form of determinism.

His point of departure was the assertion that scripture does not contradict itself and that all the apostles were of one mind on the question of salvation: Peter had not criticized Paul but extracted the true Catholic significance of his fellow apostle's words when he noted 'that our dear brother Paul wrote to you according to the wisdom given him, . . . there are some things in them [his letters] hard to understand . . .' (2 Peter 3.15f.).[154] Paul, a mighty preacher and warrior for grace, found himself doing battle zealously with those heretics who maintained that human nature, free will and proper instruction sufficed for salvation. In opposition to them and to future Pelagians, he had elevated the *sola fide*.[155] Furthermore, both his

153 For a discussion of what previous interpreters of Gal. 4.24 meant in skirting the Greek term 'allegory' by employing 'circumloquendo', Steinbach referred his reader to his commentary on 2 Corinthians (not yet rediscovered). See *Opera exegetica*, 1, p. 231, lines 19–23. In that work he must have dealt with the problem of the 'modus loquendi' specifically, as he probably did also in his no longer extant commentary on Romans mentioned in the lectures on Hebrews. See *ibid.*, p. xv, n. 27.

154 'Cum tamen Paulus de salute nil aliud senserit a ceteris apostolis, quodque non datur nisi viventibus legi Dei, ut Christus ait Mt 19[.17]: "Si vis ad vitam ingredi, serva mandata" . . . Hic Petrus Paulum non taxat, nec de falso reprehendit, sed Pauli sentenciam sanam et katholicam suis verbis extrusit.' *Opera exegetica*, 1, p. 133, lines 20–7. 'Nec ceteri apostoli eius dicta correxerunt, sed elucidarunt prout oportunum fuit contra emergentes hereses ex non intelligencia verborum eius. Oportet itaque textum per textum exponere, quia nulla est repugnancia canonice scriptura sane intellecte.' *Ibid.*, p. 134, lines 9–12.

155 'Verum Paulus specialis gracie predicator et propugnator inexpugnabilis quandoque magno fidei zelo de gracia et fide loquens loco et tempore oportunis visus est quibusdam hereticis gracie ac caritatis infuse inimicis (dicentibus sufficere hominis naturam, liberum arbitrium et doctrinam ad hominis iustificationem, que omnia sunt gracie, absque dono caritatis infuso per Spiritum Sanctum, hiis et similibus visus est) dicere, quod sola fides sufficiat.' *Opera exegetica*, 1, pp. 132, line 19–133, line 1.

apologetic mission *and* his pastoral office had motivated him to write in that manner to those who otherwise would have been abandoned to despair, bowed beneath the unbearable burden of sin.[156] Only the uneducated fail to see that the apostles and the fathers appeared to use immoderate language for the sake of their special pastoral or apologetic task. And that had also been the case with Augustine when he had turned to face the enemies of grace: in that context he had often exaggerated, but only apparently so.[157]

An important shift in the understanding of Augustine has come to light at this juncture. Rather than attempt to harmonize the embattled and supposedly immoderate anti-Pelagian voice of the later Augustine with that of the younger Augustine found in works such as *De libero arbitrio*, Steinbach chose to back the *doctor gratiae* by appealing to Paul for support. Augustine's teaching was not intemperate but inspired by the Holy Spirit. It is the *modus loquendi* that must be taken into account; an insight that could now be understood and applied due to the terminological progress of the 'modern' theology.[158]

The modernists had developed their own *modus loquendi* with their distinction between 'full' (*de condigno*) and 'partial' (*de congruo*) merit. Thanks to this distinction, the apparent incongruities and severities of the doctrines of justification taught by Paul and Augustine vanished. Where the Apostle taught that we are justified by faith alone without works he was completely correct but had in mind only the beginnings of faith which then enable the sinner to perform genuinely good works meriting a legitimate reward in God's eyes.[159]

Thus works do not 'cause' justification but 'merely' presuppose

[156] 'Alia Paulus vere protulit ob eam causam, ne quis desperet de peccatis commissis, non ut animaret homines ad peccatum.' *Opera exegetica*, 1, p. 133, lines 10f.

[157] 'Et sepe numero, cum sancti errorem aliquem funditus enervare volunt aut veritatem aliquam in lucem ponere, cui plerique contradicunt aut contradicere presumunt, quasi excessivo videntur uti sermone aut nonnumquam subobscuro, ne qualemcumque errandi relinquant occasionem. Ita Paulus, cum de fide, que est inicium omnis boni et sperandarum rerum substancia, loquitur, quasi sola sufficiat loqui videtur indoctis.' *Opera exegetica*, 1, p. 134, lines 12–17. 'Augustinus disputando contra inimicos gracie et caritatis infuse sepe numero excessive locutus esse videtur, salvo nostro loquendi modo nunc solito de merito congrui et condigni.' *Ibid.*, p. 135, lines 2–4; cf. p. 210, lines 5–12.

[158] 'Quod nisi attendatur in dictis Augustini et Apostoli, videntur totum dare Deo, semoto libero arbitrio. Cuius contrarium uterque tenet. Sumus enim adiutores Dei, et unusquisque propriam mercedem accipiet secundum suum laborem, 1 Cor 3.' *Opera exegetica* 1, p. 206, lines 6–9.

[159] 'Insuper dicit [Augustinus] Apostolum velle, quod "ex fide iustificatur homo, non ex operibus", quia ipsa fides prima datur, ex qua impetrantur cetera, que proprie opera nuncupantur, in quibus iuste vivitur; cum tamen utrumque sane possit concedi, salvo nunc currente modo loquendi theologorum.' *Opera exegetica*, 1, p. 135, lines 18–21.

it.[160] Faith is a gift of God for which man must prepare himself. Although Abraham's faith was reckoned to him as righteousness (Rom. 4.3), that by no means implies that no good works preceded the transaction. Abraham had first lived properly according to the natural law and then endeavoured with all his might to believe God. Because God withholds his grace from no one who does his best, it was revealed to Abraham that his faith alone without works could not please God.[161] In contrast to Biel and the traditional teaching, Steinbach did not reject a *sola fide* justification but accepted it as the *modus loquendi* of the Apostle Paul and of Augustine. But he considered it sufficient only for the 'beginning Christian', who is still unaware that faith without works by no means satisfies God.

Steinbach presents us with the unique case in which a Pauline justification *sola fide* provides a basis for a semi-Pelagian *meritum de congruo*. According to the *modus loquendi* of the 'modern' theologians, Abraham had been a good man before he believed and precisely on that basis merited his first faith. But the Holy Spirit chose to avoid that manner of speaking in the wise foreknowledge that later heretical Pelagians would cling to such a formulation in order to ascribe their justification to their own merits: 'But today it is not misleading to say that the sinner merits justification *de congruo* by his good works, . . . even though the Apostle says that grace is given *gratis* and not on the basis of merit.'[162] For 'as today's *doctores* say, we merit

[160] 'Sic sumendo nomen "opus", katholicum est dicere, quod opera inchoant et precedunt meritum proprie dictum. Hinc De gracia novi testamenti c. 30, ait: Ex hoc incipiunt bona opera, *ex quo* iustificamur; non *quia* precesserunt, iustificamur.' *Opera exegetica*, 1, p. 135, lines 25–8 (my italics).

[161] 'negatur consequencia, quod credere Deo non fuerit Abrahe reputatum ad iusticiam. Inicium enim conversionis Abrahe ad Deum fuit per fidem, qua Deum cognovit et eius voluntatem. Cognito Deo et eius voluntate illi se obtemperanter conformare studuit, Deum super omnia diligendo; et quia "facientem quod in se est non deserit Deus in hiis, que sunt ad salutem necessaria", illustratus fuit a Deo, quod sine dono Dei infuso, quod caritas nominatur, eciam per fidem solam Deo placere non posset.' *Opera exegetica*, 1, p. 129, lines 25–31. 'Voluit acta imperato credere Deo, et illud suum credere Deo actu voluntatis imperativo reputatum et estimatum est ei a Deo benignissimo, qui non refugit confugientes ad se, tamquam disposicio de congruo sufficiens ex beneplacito Dei ad iusticiam fidei et gracie infusionem, non precedentibus legis operibus, . . .' *Ibid.*, p. 130, lines 1–5; cf. lines 24–29.

[162] 'ita potest dici de Abraham: Quia vir bonus erat sequendo legem nature, meruit credere, eciam antequam crederet. Verum ille modus loquendi non est a Spiritu Sancto positus, quia prescivit futuros hereticos potentes ex hoc sumere fomentum erroris sui, quasi merita sint sua et non gracie divine. Et tamen hodie non est absonum dicere, quod peccator mereatur bonis operibus de genere vel impetret de congruo a Deo iustificari et graciam sibi infundi, licet Apostolus dicat graciam "gratis" dari et "non ex merito".' *Opera exegetica*, 1, p. 136, lines 1–7; cf. p. 210, lines 8–12.

additional grace *de condigno* but the first outpouring of grace occurs *de congruo*'.[163]

We can observe clearly in these conspicuous departures from tradition how one of Gabriel Biel's students met the challenge of the Augustinian renaissance. Steinbach utilized the interpretative tool of the *modus loquendi* to defuse the threat to tradition posed by Paul and Augustine and at the same time to admit the validity of their concerns. In weighing the alternatives of grace versus works he found it necessary to make considerable apparent concessions to Augustine, but in actual fact he accurately represented and defended the doctrine of his own master Gabriel. For Biel had also stressed that God alone can justify. But he qualified this by noting that man must do his best in order to obtain *de congruo* the first grace of God and then, standing on that foundation, muster renewed strength successfully to pass the test of God's throne of judgment on the strength of genuine (*de condigno*) merits.[164]

Steinbach thought the *modus loquendi* of the 'modern' theologians to be collectively backed by scripture's specific use of language (*mos scripturae*). This *modus loquendi* of scripture can be illustrated by two of its especially characteristic features. Scripture directs its exhortations and admonitions at everyone without distinction even though such counsel may directly affect only a few: although all the Galatians were reprimanded by the Apostle Paul, not all were backsliders, for the genuine elect had remained steadfast. However Steinbach attached a fundamentally different meaning to 'election' from that of Staupitz. For the disciple of Biel, election meant not divine predestination but God's foreknowledge, his preview of who will take advantage of the offer of grace and who will rebel.[165]

163 'Meremur enim gracie augmentum, ut hodie dicunt doctores, merito condigni, et gracie prime infusionem merito congrui, quod aliqui nominant quandam impetracionem et non meritum, quia meritum innititur iusticie premiantis, sed impetracio liberalitati donantis.' *Opera exegetica*, 1, p. 136, lines 14–18. Cf. the conclusion of Lectio 17: 'Ex hiis nunc facile claret intellectus verborum Apostoli, cum inquit: "Credidit Abraham Deo." Non inquit: "in Deum", quia inicium fecit fide informi, qua meruit de congruo iustificari et ita in Deum credere fide per dilectionem operante etc.' *Ibid.*, p. 137, lines 31–4.

164 See *The Harvest of Medieval Theology*, pp. 169ff.

165 'More scripture omnibus loquitur, cum tamen sermo suus dumtaxat ad aliquos pertineat. Hunc enim morem tenet scriptura in corripiendo et arguendo. Non enim qui fuere ad vitam presciti, predestinati et vocati secundum propositum Dei relapsi sunt, sed aliqui tantum, qui dumtaxat generali vocacione (que omnibus patuit signo visibili) vocati fuerunt ad fidem, quos Deus prescivit non permansuros, vocati, non quia ab eterno electi, sed ut eligantur secundum presentem iusticiam tantum. Quibus proprie non debetur hereditas, quia numquam habebunt eam, cum non sunt ab eterno ad gloriam predestinati.' *Opera exegetica*, 1, p. 204, lines 9–16; cf. p. 246, lines 10–15.

Lest we overlook the significance of the free will in cooperating with grace in the second part of the process of justification, Steinbach warned, we must take account of a further scriptural mode of speaking. We can observe from scripture the distinction between a *cognitio Dei activa* and *cognitio Dei passiva*. Prior to the creation of the world God foresaw (*cognitio activa*) which of his creatures he would aid along the path to knowledge of himself (*cognitio passiva*). But this 'predestination' has nothing to do with determining who would be able to persist in faith. Both the active and passive knowledge of God applied to the Galatians, for 'God knew them and they had known God in return.'[166] And yet they had deserted Christ, unable to distinguish between law and gospel or to tell the era of the Old Testament from that of the New.[167]

It must be noted that Steinbach's reasoning runs directly opposite to that of Luther, who explained his evangelical experience in terms of a distinction between *iustitia Dei activa* and *iustitia Dei passiva*.[168] For Luther permitted God to retain both these righteousnesses as his own without exception or diminution. In contrast, Steinbach warned against dismissing such a typically scriptural manner of speaking and thereby ascribing to God what in reality has been left to our free capacity to obey.[169] If we pay insufficient attention to the *modus loquendi* of scripture we run the risk, especially with Paul and no less with Augustine, of misinterpreting God's will to mean that he uses men as mere tools, disengaging their free will. But such is certainly not the case, for then there would remain no role for merits.[170]

[166] 'Ad illa legis figuralis opera post Dei cognicionem activam et passivam anhelabant, seducti per pseudoapostolos iudaisantes, ponendo enim in eis spem salutis. Ideo non poterant salvari tamquam infideles.' *Opera exegetica*, 1, p. 204, lines 28–31.

[167] 'Quid vobis prodest, o Galathe, cognicio Dei activa et passiva et quod reliquistis idolatriam, cum iam post evangelium confugitis ad legis opera, seducti per pseudo [apostolos], nescientes distinguere inter tempus et tempus, quo legalia fuere vel necessaria, vel utilia, vel egena et infirma sine fructu etc. Hoc enim a vobis repellit Christum etc., qui vos vocavit ad inicium conversionis.' *Opera exegetica*, 1, p. 205, lines 8–12.

[168] See *WA* 54, pp. 185, line 19–186, line 7 (1545).

[169] 'Est communis tropus scripture, quo per efficientem id, quod efficitur, significatur, maxime cum de Deo aliquid dicitur, quod ei secundum proprietatem locucionis convenire non potest . . .' *Opera exegetica*, 1, p. 205, lines 14–16. 'Ita in proposito, cum clamare dicitur in cordibus nostris Spiritus Sanctus, qui datus est nobis, intelligitur i.e.: facit nos clamare. Quomodo facit? Meritorie et secundum Deum per gracie infusionem. Hoc enim est facere Dei, cuius perfecta sunt opera. Item clamare in spiritu Dei vel ipsum clamare in nobis est ei per fidem obtemperare. Clamat in illis, qui eum obtemperanter audiunt per fidem formatam.' *Ibid.*, p. 205, lines 19–24.

[170] 'Sumus enim adiutores Dei, et unusquisque propriam mercedem accipiet secundum suum laborem, 1 Cor 3.' *Opera exegetica*, 1, p. 206, lines 7–9. Just as he later (p. 275, lines 21f.) took Jerome to task, Steinbach was here admonishing Augustine, who

active + passive cognition of G-d

We find no basic shifts of emphasis in Steinbach's commentary on Hebrews of 1516–17. But one aspect of this later work merits attention. In the appendix, Steinbach devoted more effort to refuting Gregory of Rimini, who had not even been mentioned in the 1513 lecture on Galatians, than to any of the other medieval *doctores*. This preoccupation with Gregory becomes understandable when we consider that Gregory viewed what Steinbach treated as a mere interpretive and case-specific mode, namely the *modus loquendi* of Augustine and St Paul, as their eternally valid doctrine. No other medieval theologian could have posed a more serious threat to the validity of Steinbach's exegesis.

Steinbach was acquainted with Gregory's theology long before writing his commentary on Hebrews. Biel had cited Gregory in his *Collectorium* – edited by Steinbach (1501) – in regard to an entire range of questions, and distinctly rejected Gregory's understanding of the relationship between grace and free will: he had underestimated man's free will, whereas Thomas Aquinas had dealt in a more judicious manner with the issue.[171] But Steinbach appeared to have turned his attention more directly to Gregory before his lectures on Hebrews ended; for Biel had never quoted him to the extent and with the precision of the appendix to the lectures.

The appearance of Eck's *Chrysopassus* (1514) may indeed have sharpened Steinbach's interest in Gregory. It seems more likely, however, that Gregory attracted the attention of both Steinbach and Eck from atop the crest of the Augustinian renaissance and that Steinbach's discourse with Gregory was influenced by the discussion surrounding the Wittenberg theology in 1517.[172] Contacts between

had failed to take note of this scriptural *tropus* ('per efficientem id, quod efficitur, significatur') when he claimed that Paul had backpedalled on the issue. This *tropus* should be assumed only in company with direct assertions by God; here we are dealing with anthropomorphisms that *secundum proprietatem sermonis* are not suited to God. *Ibid.*, p. 209, lines 19–25.

171 'Nam est opinio Gregorii de Arimino, qui parum attribuens libero arbitrio . . . tenet quod nullus homo in statu presenti stante etiam generali influentia dei potest absque speciali dei auxilio agere actum moraliter bonum.' *Collectorium*, II dist. 28 q.1 A. 'Beatus Thomas prima secundae q. 109 fere per omnes articulos eiusdem questionis videtur temperantius loqui . . .' *Ibid.*, B.

172 My attempt to establish the significance of the *schola Augustiniana moderna*, initiated by Gregory of Rimini, in the development of the Wittenberg theology – set forth in 'Headwaters of the Reformation', esp. p. 82 – has met with cautious and carefully studied criticism from David C. Steinmetz. See 'Luther and the Late Medieval Augustinians: Another Look', pp. 255–9. Steinmetz himself noted (p. 247, n. 8) that at the time of his writing only the text of my article and not the (probably decisive) footnotes were available to him. But I am also of the opinion that determining the extent of the fifteenth- and sixteenth-century influence of what I have termed the *via*

Tübingen and the young university in Wittenberg by way of the Observant Augustinian monastery in Tübingen are known to have continued even after Staupitz left his post as prior for Wittenberg. Two Tübingen *magistri*, Dionysius Bickel and Sigismund Epp, accompanied him to Saxony, where they lectured on Lombard's Sentences, returning to Tübingen later to receive their doctoral berets.[173] Whatever the ties between Tübingen and Wittenberg, it is clear that Gregory was not merely known during this period but was considered a serious theological challenge. The Tübingen reply to that challenge may also have been a response to the very beginnings of a Reformation theology in Wittenberg.[174]

NB

Gregorii – an influence both as an *Ordenstheologie* and as a radically anti-Pelagian interpretation of Augustine – requires further work with the sources and above all the publication of sources. Only then can both scholarly scepticism and understandable confessional resistance be overcome with firmly established results of research. See my introduction to the series, 'Spätmittelalter und Reformation', in the *Bibliographie zur Geschichte und Theologie des Augustiner-Eremitenordens bis zum Beginn der Reformation*, pp. v–xiii. But Steinbach's testimony to the challenge posed by Gregory and his *sequaces* at the outset of the sixteenth century is a further tile in the mosaic portrait which is far from complete.

173 Steinbach himself entered Bickel's date of graduation as 12 February 1504 and Epp's as 27 November 1504 in the statute book of the theological faculty. Cf. *Opera exegetica*, 1, pp. xxxiiif., n. 104. On Epp see Bauer, *Die Wittenberger Universitätstheologie*, pp. 11f. Julius Köstlin lists both Epp and Bickel as successive deans of the Wittenberg faculty of arts in 1503; entering Epp as an Augustinian Eremite and Bickel as *Magister artium* and *Baccalaureus theologiae* 'ex Weyla Suevo'. *Die Baccalaurei und Magistri der Wittenberger Philosophischen Fakultät*, p. 21. By 1504/5 Epp was serving as rector in Tübingen (Hermelink *Matrikeln*, p. 145). It is probably not too far-fetched to link Pellikan's remark that during Staupitz's priorate in Tübingen the Augustinian monks all attended the lectures of the Scotist, Paulus Scriptoris ('acutissimus Scotista') at the university with the fact that Staupitz's fellow monk, Epp, lectured in the *via Scoti* at the newly founded university in Wittenberg. Staupitz's own education in the Thomistically oriented *via antiqua* of the University of Cologne can likewise be reconciled with his later preference for the *acceptatio* doctrine when we consider that the Tübingen *via antiqua* under Scriptoris and Summenhart was Scotist-oriented with strong ties to the *via moderna*. See Pellikan's *Chronikon*, p. 12, line 15.

174 'Non veretur *quidam* dicere tenentes questionis partem affirmativam contraire decretis patrum et conciliorum, doctrine apostolice, ac favere errori Pelagii. Fundat se cum suis sequacibus in dictis Augustini per eum citatis. Ni fallar, non attendit ille doctor, quod beatus Augustinus volens radicitus enervare errores illos vel istos, abundancius nonnumquam loquitur, minus volens, plus dicens . . . citra mendacium et simulacionem, quodque pro suo more familiari sibi alio utitur loquendi modo contra infideles et supectos de heresi, aliter ad fideles iam eruditos in fide, qui non querunt erroris fomentum, sed veritatis cognicionem.' Fol. 215^{r}; cited by Feld, *Hebräerbrief*, pp. 201f. Feld identifies the 'quidam' at the opening of the 'Dubitatio generalis' (Lectio 65–70 in the appendix to *Hebräerbrief*) with Gregory of Rimini, most likely because Steinbach in subsequent passages explicitly identified the opinion ascribed to this unknown *Doctor* with that held by Gregory. But we may well be dealing here with a first reaction to the Wittenberg theology of 1517, an

Steinbach's previous work on the letter to the Galatians had equipped him well to confront Gregory. It merely remained for him to demonstrate that Gregory had not paid sufficient attention to Augustine's specific *modus loquendi*. Above all, Steinbach objected vigorously to Gregory's distinction between an *auxilium generale* and *auxilium speciale*, which made every human initiative toward justification totally dependent on the assistance of divine grace and traced not merely meritorious works but all good works to the power of God.[175]

Steinbach took no exception to Gregory so far as God's general assistance was concerned. Divine providence provides for both creature and creation through the *auxilium generale*. But the special assistance of grace (*auxilium speciale*) which Gregory postulated eliminated human participation to a degree unacceptable to Steinbach.[176] Aside from a few exceptions that are theologically irrelevant, God endeavours to bring sinners to repentance via normal channels: by wooing their hearts. He stimulates but does not compel; he knocks at the door and is ready to help anyone who opens that door.[177] Only the restriction of the *auxilium speciale* to God's first offer of grace in the process of justification, and proper attention to

assumption which also explains why Steinbach offered his treatment of Gregory as a supplement to his lectures on Hebrews and why he dealt with Gregory anonymously at first and then mentioned him by name in subsequent treatment. That Luther's theses for the *Disputatio contra scholasticam theologiam* (1517) could have been accessible to Steinbach finds support in Luther's letters to Johannes Lang on 4 September 1517 (*WABr* 1, p. 103, esp. line 12) and to Christopher Scheurl on 11 September 1517 (*WABr* 1, p. 106, line 36), in which he noted that he had submitted the theses for the disputation to a wide circle of colleagues for their evaluation. Steinbach's 'Dubitatio' lends additional support to Ernst Kähler's thesis that the discussion surrounding 'Gregory's Augustinianism' began 'no later than the spring of 1517' in Wittenberg. Kähler, *Karlstadt und Augustin*, p. 22* and p. 22*, n. 5.

175 Steinbach noted in regard to Gregory's insistence on the necessity of an 'auxilium speciale' for meritorious as well as all good works: 'De quo non habetur certa doctrina vel auctoritas solida.' Fol. 224^{r}. All quotations from Steinbach's commentary on Hebrews refer to the MS. Tübingen University Library Mc 201.

176 'Cur vero illi non solum suadeantur, sed eciam persuadeantur obtemperare vocacioni, divini est iudicii. Dei est dare et pulsare, hominis est sui liberi arbitrii consentire, accipere vel aperire; et id quod accipit, Dei est et a Deo habetur, nec sine Deo. Deus personam hominis non accipit, sed vult omnes homines iuvare et salvare voluntate beneplaciti antecedente, ut habet communis sentencia doctorum.' Fol. 224^{v}. Steinbach repeatedly indicated that he had difficulty understanding Gregory's intent: 'Hanc differentiam non facile capio.' 'Verum Gregorii mentem non plene capio.' Fol. 225^{v}.

177 'Stat ad ostium et pulsat iuvare paratus volentem aut non recalcitrantem.' Fol. 228^{v}. 'Cui id non placet, fingat alium modum loquendi, ut intelligantur dicta patrum et sanctorum de auxilio Dei generali et speciali, licet illis vocabulis raro vel nunquam usi sint priores nostri in suis scriptis, nec Augustinus. Forte curiositas adinvenit.' *Ibid.*

Augustine's specific *modus loquendi* could make Steinbach ready to accept Gregory's position without reservation.[178]

We are now able to define Steinbach's position regarding various matters more precisely:

1. In contrast to the preceding tradition, it is significant that Steinbach, in his own way, defended Augustine. Whereas scholastics learned from Bonaventure that Augustine had occasionally spoken *abundantius* in reaction to Pelagius, and although Scotus even charged him with intemperate language,[179] Steinbach stressed that Augustine was guilty of only an apparent misdemeanour. In actual fact he had utilized an apologetically and pastorally defined *modus loquendi* present in the Pauline epistles; a manner of speech that owed its origin to the inspiration of scripture through the Holy Spirit. Until the triumph over Pelagius – for Steinbach an event recorded in the completed chronicle of the fifth century – this mode of speaking had been both legitimate and necessary. Just as the Christian world reckoned history in periods *ante Christum* and *post Christum*, so Steinbach assigned a proper *modus loquendi* to each of the epochs *ante* and *post Pelagium*.[180]

Proper consideration of this chronological watershed gave Steinbach his proof that Paul and Augustine appeared to have overreacted only when viewed through an improperly ground lens of church history. The later scholastic theology with its modern *modus loquendi* had finally made possible – for the period *post Pelagium* – an exegesis true to scripture. Thus it became possible once more to mesh the

[178] 'plus concurrit et coagit causa prima ad cuiusvis effectus boni productionem, voluntate beneplaciti consequente, quam quevis causa secunda. Hoc modo facile possent teneri proposiciones Gregorii, saltem in ea parte, ubi loquuntur de adiutorio Dei speciali et supposito modo loquendi beati Augustini sibi familiari de actibus bonis et de actu moraliter bono et de vera virtute et similibus.' Fol. 229^v.

[179] See my introduction to the series 'Spätmittelalter und Reformation', in *Bibliographie zur Geschichte und Theologies des Augustiner-Eremitenordens*, pp. xif., and additional literature *ibid.*, p. xi, n. 16. See also Luther: 'S. Augustinus schreibt, dass der freie Wille ohn Gottes Gnad und den heiligen Geist nichts mehr kann und vermag denn sündigen. Welcher Spruch die Schultheologen hart dringet, wiewol sie sagen, Augustinus habe hyperbolice geredt und zu viel gethan.' *WATR* 6, no. 6682; cf. *WA* 1, p. 224, line 7 (1517). In his controversy with Melanchthon in 1536 Luther insisted 'eum [Augustine] nobiscum sentire' and rejected Melanchthon's remark that 'Augustinus ut apparet, extra disputationes commodius sensit quam loquitur in disputationibus.' *WABr* 12, pp. 191, lines 1f. and 193, lines 90f.

[180] On the one hand, the Holy Spirit avoids certain thoroughly Catholic formulations because the Pelagian heresy still lurks about. (See above, note 162) On the other hand, he may choose more pointed expressions precisely in order to neutralize that danger. Hence, for example, 'Deus est qui operatur in nobis velle et operari, Phil 2, sive perficere, ubi apostolus hunc futurum errorem elidere studuit, quem spiritu revelante previdit.' Commentary on Hebrews, fol. 229^r.

soteriological gears of human responsibility and divine initiative and relieve the misalignment introduced by an anachronistic exegesis.

2. Thus Steinbach's relationship to Staupitz also becomes intelligible. It is perhaps symbolic that precisely a *strange* hand should have entered a phrase from the Psalms on the front page of Steinbach's commentary on Galatians: 'Deus, in nomine tuo, salvum me fac' (Ps. 53.3).[181] For Staupitz the parallel version, 'Tuus sum, salvum me fac' served as a concise expression of a firm confidence in God's sovereign completion of his own eternal election by grace. The phrase would have possessed a radically different meaning for Steinbach. In reaction to the Judaizing Galatians who placed their hope in fulfilling the *old* law, Steinbach felt that the core of Pauline theology lay in the genuine Christian hope of merits gained by fulfilling the *new* law.[182] Because God has not predestined the elect but merely foreseen in all eternity how they would set their free will in motion in space and time, the *viator* faces ethical demands until the very end of his path; remaining uncertain as long as he lives on earth whether he has produced the necessary meritorious works. For, as Steinbach stressed, 'incertus est finis hominis'.[183]

3. Steinbach's soteriology can certainly not be termed 'un-Catholic' especially if one is willing to define the term 'Catholic' from the perspective of the Council of Trent.[184] On one page after another, Steinbach demonstrated and stressed the necessity of divine grace – in 1513 as well as in 1516–17. He sought a harmonization of grace and the humanness of man which might avoid degrading the sinner to a mere executive organ of the will of God. The sinner must remain free to decide at the outset whether to grant access to his heart to a God who knocks and whether he will continue to the end as a *cooperator* with and aide (*adiutor*) to that God. For that reason the believer also remains unsure of his salvation until the end, for he has bought his freedom at the expense of his assurance of salvation.

From Augustine, Steinbach took the view that the Apostle Paul emphasized justification by grace and not by works (Eph. 2.8f.) in order to prevent men from ever claiming a full and complete merit for

181 *Opera exegetica*, 1, p. xlvi.

182 'Nos enim non ex lege, sed fide Christi per dilectionem operante spem iusticie, i.e. remuneracionem operum iusticie, que est gracia gratumfaciens vel caritas per Spiritum Sanctum infusa, expectamus . . .' Cf. 2 Tim. 4.8. *Opera exegetica*, 1, pp. 250, line 24–251, line 1.

183 'incertus est finis hominis, Ecclesiastis 9. Quis novit Dei iudicia? Abissus multa.' *Opera exegetica*, 1, p. 300, line 30; cf. p. 294, lines 22–6.

184 See the same conclusion with reference to Gabriel Biel in my epilogue to *The Harvest of Medieval Theology*, pp. 423–8.

themselves. He at times avoided the technical term, *meritum de condigno* in favour of the label that won approval at Trent, *meritum proprie dictum* – merit in the strict sense of the word. There can be no talk of such genuine and full merit during the first halting steps of the sinner's approach to God. Only a Pelagian could want to insist that, 'I have merited this in the full sense of the word (*promerui*)'.[185] But renouncing a *promereri* did not mean, to Steinbach or to the Council of Trent, a denial of the possibility, indeed, of the responsibility to prepare oneself for grace granted *de congruo*.[186]

What we have encountered in Steinbach is not a Tübingen theology in a strict sense, for it approaches to a surprising degree the position of Erasmus in his conflict with Luther. Erasmus revalued the Pelagian position – and history generally supports this effort – in contrast to the unflattering portrait by Augustine that dominated the middle ages.[187] He placed the Scotists close to, indeed, almost to the left of

185 'Promerui et ideo accepi.' *PL* 38, cols. 916f.; *Opera exegetica*, 1, p. 231, line 12.

186 See my article, 'Das tridentinische Rechtfertigungsdekret im Lichte spätmittelalterlicher Theologie', p. 278. In addition to the reservations voiced by Hanns Rückert, the critique by Valens Heynck, 'Die Bedeutung von "mereri" and "promereri" bei dem Konzilstheologen Andreas de Vega OFM', deserves notice. Heynck could establish no technical distinction between 'mereri' and 'promereri' in the case of Vega. But he shares my opinion that the Council of Trent's intent was 'unmistakable': 'to understand the "promereri" in the sense of a *meritum de condigno*'. *Ibid.*, p. 237. In chapter 8 of the decretal on justification we find: 'nihil eorum quae iustificationem praecedunt, sive fides, sive opera, ipsam iustificationis gratiam promeretur.' (Denzinger and Schönmetzer, *Enchiridion Symbolorum*, no. 1532 [801].) But such was no semantic innovation nor had the verb 'promereri' been endowed with a meaning for which there was no precedent. Among the references to the term's firm mooring in tradition we must pay close attention to Peter Lombard: '*Existimo enim*, id est scio, *quod passiones huius temporis*, id est temporales et momentaneae simul omnes, *non sunt condignae*, id est sufficientes, si districte ageretur nobiscum, *ad* promerendam *futuram gloriam*. Tribulatio namque est cum fine, merces sine fine erit, et multo maior erit tibi gloria quam hic labor.' *Collectanea in epistulas d. Pauli*, in epist. Ad Rom. 8.18; *PL* 191, cols. 1441f. Cf. William of Auxerre: 'Ad primum ergo obiectum dicimus, quod non sunt condignae passiones huius temporis ad futuram gloriam, scilicet ad promerendum, sicut dicit Glossa, id est ad proportionaliter [sic!] merendum; sunt enim tamen condignae ad simpliciter [sic!] merendum.' *Summa aurea*, lib. 3 tract. 16 cap. unic q. 2 ad 1, fol. 221^{v}.

187 'Quid senserint Pelagiani nescio, tantum ex verbis ago, quae ex libris Juliani refert Augustinus, quae mea sententia potuissent commoda interpretatione pro veris haberi, magnaque pars huius contentionis ex verbis nasci videtur potius quam ex re ipsa, et huiusmodi λογομαχίαι facile exeunt in rixam, si quid accesserit humanae contentionis.' *Hyperaspistes Diatribae adversus servum arbitrium Martini Lutheri* (Basel, 20 February 1526) in *LB* 10, col. 1524C–D; cited by Charles Trinkaus, 'Erasmus, Augustine and the Nominalists', p. 12, n. 18. Erasmus not only made Augustine's '*excessive*' language appear humanly understandable as had already been the case in the medieval tradition, but also employed it as an aid to a historically valid and just verdict on Pelagius.

Pelagius in view of their even higher estimation of the human free will. And the terminology that Erasmus used to justify classifying the Scotists to the left of Pelagius is worthy of attention: they maintained that good works do not, to be sure, merit first grace *de condigno* but nevertheless that 'de congruo *promereantur* gratiam gratum facientem'.[188]

Erasmus rejected as too harsh the alternative extreme – represented by Gregory of Rimini, Carlstadt and Luther – which taught that all human works are sinful in the absence of grace.[189] If properly used, Erasmus asserted, the creative gifts of God can call forth God's compassion. But Erasmus further believed he had found a *via media* by stressing a second special assistance of grace by which God, out of pure compassion, urges the sinner who can claim no merit (*nihil promeritum*) to repentance.[190] Thus it was not in a denial of a *meritum de congruo*, through which the believer could provoke (*provocet*) or call forth further grace, that Erasmus parted company with the Scotists. Rather, it was in his repudiation, along with Holcot, Biel, Steinbach and the Council of Trent, of a *promereri* within the preparation for first grace. This term should be reserved for full merit which originates in the special activity of God's grace ('iuxta quod promeretur').[191] All men, at some point in their lives, hear the call of God's grace. If followed, that call leads to conversion and makes the sinner a candidate (*candidatum quendam*) for the grace that guides him to perfection.[192] So far as the grace that is offered to every human being is concerned, Erasmus accepted as valid the principle that God does not deny his grace to those who do their utmost ('facientibus quod in se est Deus non denegat gratiam'). Hence no one need despair but

[188] 'Qui Scoti placitis addicti sunt,proniores sunt in favorem liberi arbitrii, cuius tantam vim esse credunt, ut homo nondum accepta gratia, quae peccatum abolet, naturae viribus exercere posset opera moraliter, ut vocant, bona, quibus non de condigno, sed de congruo promereantur *gratiam* gratum facientem; sic enim illi loquuntur.' *De libero arbitrio* ed. von Walter, p. 26, line 15–p. 27, line 2. Cf. *Hyperaspistes*, *LB* 10, col. 1531C.

[189] Erasmus made a further distinction between the *opinio durior* – not difficult to identify with Gregory of Rimini and Carlstadt – and the *opinio durissima* of Luther: 'Itaque cum his duabus postremis potissimum erit conflictatio.' *De libero arbitrio*, *LB* 9, col. 1224C; von Walter edn, p. 31, lines 12f. Cf. McSorley, 'Erasmus versus Luther. Compounding the Reformation Tragedy?', pp. 113f.

[190] 'Altera est gratia peculiaris, qua deus ex sua misericordia peccatorem nihil promeritum stimulat ad resipiscentiam, sic tamen, ut nondum infundat gratiam illam supremam, quae abolet peccatum ac deo gratum facit hominem.' *LB* 9, col. 1223F; von Walter edn, p. 29, lines 16–20.

[191] *LB* 9, col. 1223D; von Walter edn, p. 28, line 15.

[192] *LB* 9, col. 1224A; von Walter edn, p. 30, line 1.

neither is anyone assured of salvation, for all devout Christians live in constant striving between fear and hope.[193]

Erasmus basically shared Steinbach's opinion that the *recentiores doctores* had made the 'excessive' assertions of Augustine – and Pelagius! – tolerable by distinguishing between the *meritum de congruo* and *meritum de condigno*.[194] But Erasmus was far too non-dogmatic an exegete and far too conscious of the relative factor in history to canonize any given *modus loquendi* for all time.[195]

4. It is probable that Steinbach's treatment and refutation of Gregory of Rimini in the *Dubitatio* that he appended to his lecture on Hebrews was written with a certain Augustinian monk of Wittenberg in mind. In terms of content, he had already endeavoured in his lectures on Galatians (1513) to refute the radical interpretation of Paul and Augustine with the same arguments later directed exclusively at Gregory. However, both series of lectures indicate that the Augustine renaissance led Steinbach to an image of Augustine more historically accurate than that of his master Gabriel Biel, while failing to free the Tübingen *via moderna* from its reputation for semi-Pelagianism. Like Biel, Steinbach sought to harmonize a *sola gratia* with human works-righteousness. The historical classification of portions of Luther's *Dictata super Psalterium* (1513–15) is facilitated by Steinbach's roughly contemporary commentary.[196] But we must also read Luther's com-

193 Cf. *LB* 10, col. 1534F. McSorley has charged Erasmus with a 'lack of sensitivity to this Neo-Semipelagianism' (Occam–Biel). I am prepared to accept his label for the Occamistic doctrine of justification, although personally preferring 'Semipelagianism' in order to keep the terminological inflation to a minimum. See McSorley, 'Erasmus versus Luther', p. 115; cf. p. 112.

194 'Augustinus adversus Pelagianos decertans, studio gratiae tam parum tribuit libera arbitrio, ut nomine tribuat aliquid verius quam re. Rursus cum iisdem dimicans, qui dicebant infantes nihil damnationis contrahere ex peccato primorum parentum, ait illos, si sine baptismo decesserint, aeternis ignibus exurendos. Utramque sententiam posteriores Theologi moderati sunt, aliquanto plus tribuentes libero arbitrio quam ille tribuebat, ac distinguentes meritum congruum a merito condigno, fidem acquisitam a fide infusa, voluntatem perfectam ab imperfecta.' *LB* 10, col. 1534D–E. Cf. *ibid.*, col. 1532C–F.

195 We should indeed speak according to the *modus loquendi* of scripture and the fathers – 'certe loquamur more Scripturarum, more Sanctorum Patrum' – but also take account of the pastorally varying *modi* of scripture by dealing differently with an obstinate sinner than with someone who, burdened by the weight of his sins, doubts the forgiveness of God. *LB* 10, col. 1536C–E.

196 With the young Luther we find Biel's 'pactum' concept filled with Augustinian 'promissio', but even there the *meritum de congruo* appears. See Luther's scholion on Ps. 113.9: 'non nobis Domine, non nobis'. *WA* 4, pp. 261, line 25–262, line 17. Regarding the exegesis of this passage see Bayer, *Promissio*, pp. 128–35. Luther rejected the *meritum de congruo* for the first time as early as 1516, and not in 1518–20. See my article, 'Facientibus quod in se est Deus non denegat gratiam', p. 338.

mentary on Romans with different eyes, if we wish to avoid interpreting his use of the term *modus loquendi* in isolation from contemporary exegesis. Luther's attack – in conjunction with Carlstadt – on all the *doctores* who relativized Augustine because of his allegedly intemperate language was a direct result of having employed the *modus loquendi* of Paul and Augustine as a permanently valid key for understanding all of scripture rather than as the tool of a bygone epoch of church history. For Luther, the *modus loquendi* of the Apostle and his faithful interpreters remained valid *post Pelagium* because that fifth-century controversy belonged as much to Luther's present as the church's past. Since Pelagianism arises continually in the natural theology of the sinner's heart, an anti-Pelagian *modus loquendi* is the mode of speaking for all authentic theology.[197]

Augustine was eagerly read in Wittenberg as well as Tübingen, and the Augustinian revival left tangible traces on both sides. In increasingly specific interaction with Gregory of Rimini and with each other, minds parted company over the legitimacy of a radically anti-Pelagian interpretation of Augustine and its employment in the service of an emerging Reformation theology. Those thinkers educated in the 'Tübingen school' also parted company, but returned to fill the vacuum in three successive waves directed and sponsored in varying degrees by Counter-Reformation Constance and Vienna, by the city reformations of Zürich and Strassburg and ultimately by Lutheran Wittenberg and Stuttgart.

[197] Luther's stress on the 'modus loquendi *theologicus*' can only be fully understood in the context of the entire late medieval debate surrounding the 'modus loquendi'. Cf. my article, 'Reformation: Epoche oder Episode'.

Part II

THE GRAPES OF WRATH

7

A theology of turmoil: the ferment of ideas

IN THE YEARS following 1516 the political and social instability of its Württemberg environment began increasingly to affect the university at Tübingen. Neither the deposition of Duke Ulrich in 1519 nor the political expertise of the initial imperial vice-regent, the Netherlander Maximilian of Zevenbergen, brought the hoped-for calm. Charles V could indeed be convinced to ratify the Tübingen Treaty (1520), due partially to the persuasion of Gregory Lamparter, formerly Ulrich's chancellor and now an imperial commissioner doubling as an unofficial lobbyist for the interests of an occupied and debt-ridden Württemberg. But in view of many domestic and foreign policy difficulties, any such attempted annexation by Austria promised little in the way of lasting solutions. *Anschluss* at Habsburg hands was an intolerable threat to France and the Swiss Confederation and before long aroused anxiety in free cities such as Constance and Strassburg. Above all, the prospect threatened Bavaria. In Württemberg itself, Count Eberhard's policy of reunion had taken root too firmly to allow Swabian self-confidence to be shunted lightly aside. Social and religious ferment stirred up by opposition to foreign domination could only be expected to swell the ranks of the supporters of the deposed duke.

Only after Duke Ulrich's return in 1534 was the split of the university into ducal and imperial factions healed. As an eyewitness reported to Ambrosius Blarer, those elements of the population not represented in the territorial diet greeted the change of regime with applause. Blarer, the future reformer of south Württemberg,[1] described the entry of Duke Ulrich and his troops into Tübingen: 'Tübingen and its castle surrendered last Wednesday [20 May] . . . just after they had arrived and fired several shots . . . When the duke

[1] Toward the end of August 1534 the duke decided to commit the Reformation of the lands 'ob der Steig', south of Stuttgart, to Ambrosius Blarer, who made Tübingen his base of operation. Keim, *Ambrosius Blarer, der schwäbische Reformator*, p. 63. His Lutheran colleague, Erhard Schnepf (†1558), was entrusted with the reform of the 'Unterland', operating from Stuttgart.

rode into town (so he [Blarer's informant] told me), there arose a roar of exultation from young and old, man and woman, the like of which had never been heard before.'[2]

Blarer himself found considerable openness to the message of the Reformation within the general population when he made his own entry into the university town on the Neckar. The theological faculty made an equally powerful though precisely opposite impression: Blarer called it an Augean stable.[3]

Assigned the Herculean task of reorganizing the university,[4] Blarer's reform programme encountered the unrelenting resistance of professors intent on defending their venerable medieval traditions against the Reformation's innovations.[5] There could be little question of his duplicating, even figuratively, his mythological precursor's feat in the space of 'one day' – the real question was whether the stable could be mucked out at all without putting its occupants out to pasture.

The university dispatched a delegation headed by its oldest and, in terms of tenure, senior theologian, Peter Braun, to the duke[6] in a vain attempt to ward off the threatened reform measures.[7] Braun represented both the *via moderna* and the *devotio moderna* in the tradition of Biel and Steinbach, and his case rested on a plea that theological

[2] 'Tubingen Stadt und Schloss hat sich ergeben uff vergangen mittwoch . . . glich als man dafür kommen und ettlich schutz gethon . . . War der hertzog eingeritten (so sagte er [Blarer's informant] mir), das sölich gross frödengschray von jungen, alten, weyb und man gewesen, das dergleichen nie gehört sey.' Blarer to Heinrich of Ulm, Constance, 23 May 1534; Schiess, *Briefwechsel*, 1, p. 499.

[3] '. . . plebs hic evangelio Christi satis magno numero accedit. Ex theologis unus solus est D. Ba[l]thassar Wilpergensis [Käuf(f)elin], quocum mihi conveniat; caeteri ad unum omnes iunctis copiis veritatem oppugnant et, quantum possunt, expugnant, et facile coniicis, mi frater, quo in fimoso bubili verser et quod mihi Augiae stabulum repurgandum sit . . .' Blarer to Heinrich Bullinger, Tübingen, 5 October 1534; Schiess, *Briefwechsel*, 1, p. 563.

[4] Along with Simon Grynaeus; see Roth, *Urkunden*, p. 165. The duke's message to the university of 11 November 1534 informing then that Grynaeus and Blarer had been assigned the task of visitation and reform of the university is found in Haller, 2, p. 209, appendix 16; cf. p. 130.

[5] 'Fervent nunc reformandi ac melius instituendi gymnasii conatus; parturiunt huius proceres remorarum nonnihil abmandatis heri ad principem Petro [Peter Braun] seniore theologo et Baltassare [Käuffelin].' Blarer to Martin Bucer, Tübingen, 10 December 1534; Schiess, *Briefwechsel*, 1, p. 610. Blarer and the duke were forced to deal with the resistance of the university's leading lights once more on 6 and 7 January 1535 according to Blarer's report to Bullinger: 'Gymnasii proceres in omnia se torquent, ut veterem studiorum tenorem et ordinem retineant.' *Ibid.*, p. 622.

[6] For a description of this event from the perspective of the university see Roth, *Urkunden*, pp. 161–3.

[7] In addition to Braun, Balthasar Käuffelin (†1559) represented the university's position in the matter.

continuity should not be sacrificed for the sake of an even more 'modern' theology. The threat of a new *Wegestreit* was banished only by the ducal confirmation of the university's privileges on 3 November 1536, nearly two years after the promulgation of the university's new statutes on 30 January 1535, and by the forced retirement of the professorial die-hards.[8]

But the Tübingen professors were not merely the victims of the socio-political turmoil of the period; they were the source of some of the ferment. And at one focal point Tübingen theologians became so directly involved that they helped devise the immediate prerequisites for the development of a genuine *theologia moderna*. Both Gabriel Biel (†1495) and Conrad Summenhart (†1502) were not satisfied with mere awareness of the social evils of their age but sought to confront injustices with the means at their disposal and to employ their influence to bring about improvement. Biel took up a perennial peasant lament when he found the feudal nobility guilty of frustrating the peasantry in the exercise of their natural rights and activities such as hunting and fishing, of forcing them to absorb the damage caused by wild game, and of restricting peasant access to forests and meadows.[9] Let the rulers, he fulminated, who never cease to ruminate on new and ingenious methods with which to burden their subjects, ponder God's judgment on Ahab and Jezebel for the theft of Naboth's vineyard: for such lords are no protectors but mere thieves and tyrants.[10] 'Perhaps then they will restrain their rapacity and relieve the oppression of the poor.'[11]

If Biel had allowed himself the luxury of an unusually sharp tone of rebuke, Summenhart minced no words when he decided to devote more than his previous passing glance to a topic of highly charged

[8] The faculty members dismissed in this manner were granted generous severance settlements; see Roth, *Urkunden*, p. 184. Braun received a pension of eighty fl. – about two-thirds of a full professor's salary (see Kuhn, *Die Studenten der Universität Tübingen*, 1, p. 54) – and retained his seat in the university council. Blarer informed Bullinger on 15 February that the 'Gymnasii reformatio' had been ordered, affecting especially the canonists in addition to the theologians: 'unus solus canonum lector in schola retinebitur.' Schiess, *Briefwechsel*, 1, p. 653f.

[9] *Collectorium*, IV dist. 15 q. 5 art. 2 concl. 5; Werbeck and Hofmann edn, vol. 4, pt. 2, pp. 99f. Angelus de Clavasio, quoted by Biel, expressed more moderate and less fundamental criticism. *Ibid.*, pp. 99, line 10–100, line 44. Cf. Angelus de Clavasio, *Summa angelica de casibus conscientiae*, s. v. 'Restitutio' I §12, fol. 296vb; see also s.v. 'venatio'; *ibid.*, fol. 341ra.

[10] 1 Kings (*III Regum*) 21.15–19.

[11] 'Forsitan temperarent cupiditates suas et gravamina in pauperes.' Biel, *Collectorium*, IV dist. 15 q. 5 art. 2 concl. 5 corr. 3; Werbeck and Hoffman edn, vol. 4, pt. 2, p. 100, lines 43f.

relevance.[12] In questioning the divine legitimacy of mandatory tithes, Summenhart took up a social issue that resurfaced persistently in the canons of peasant grievances. But this subject, the theme of a hitherto unexamined Summenhart treatise,[13] was by no means of vital interest to peasants alone. The tithe affected all strata of society and was among the key factors behind the striving for reform and Reformation which in the following years led to an increasingly volatile situation.

In view of the mixture of claims on the part of church and state, it is nearly impossible to distinguish between the obligations of tithe and taxation in late medieval feudal Europe, especially in the colourfully chequered empire. Thus Summenhart found it necessary to shore up his position with an immediate reference to Romans 13 and a clear denial of any intended questioning of the ruler's right to tax. Yet, although Summenhart was clearly no revolutionary, he had broached an issue which not only found prominent display in peasant petitions and Anabaptist apologetics, but which even furnished a legal basis for an accord between city fathers and peasant horde in 1525.[14] And in the long run the new foundation for the tithe obligation that was developed later during the Reformation also furnished the theoretical justification for the secularization of ecclesiastical property.

The matter was of such sensitivity that Summenhart preferred to have his discussion of it entrusted only to the discretion of prudent father confessors and not to the laity in general. It is our good fortune to be able to examine his text from a double perspective. The university library at Tübingen possesses a copy of Summenhart's treatise on tithes published by Heinrich Gran (Hagenau, 1500) and bound with his *Septipertitum opus de contractibus*.[15] It is a volume decorated with refined and artfully executed marginal illustrations and notations that testify to the extensive erudition of the annotator.

[12] 'propter materiae periculositatem protestor . . .' See following note.

[13] *Tractatulus bipartitus de decimis defensivus opinionis theologorum adversus communiter canonistas de quotta decimarum, si debita sit de iure divino vel humano*, per Conradum Summenhart de Calw, artium atque sacrae theologiae professorem in alma universitate Tuwingensi ordinarie in theologia legentem, editus et ibidem lectus solemniterque anno domini 1497 per eundem disputatus (Hagenau [Heinrich Gran], 1500).

[14] An instructive example of such a compromise between city and peasants is found in the *Urkundenbuch der Stadt Heilbronn*, vol. 4, compiled by M. von Rauch, pp. 132–41. With the approval of the city council the peasants had sacked the Carmelite monastery in Heilbronn while the council confiscated the convent's lands and placed them under the administration of the 'Pflegern des geistlichen Säckels'. *Ibid.*, p. 136.

[15] The numerous marginal comments added to the treatise on tithes in the Tübingen UB copy testify to the relevance of the theme in contrast to the major work of the volume, on interest and usury, which lacks annotation. Both works were presented as separate disputations in Tübingen (the *Tractatulus bipartitus de decimis* in 1497), although they were later published together in 1500.

These illustrations and marginal comments are the work of the first owner of this volume,[16] Ambrosius Blarer (1492–1564), the later Swabian reformer and initial but unsuccessful administrator of the Tübingen university reorganization of 1535.[17] Under a Bebel hexametre[18] on the title page he noted in gratitude: 'I, brother Ambrosius Blarer, purchased this book in Tübingen in the year 1515 with a gift from my dear mother, Catherine Blarer.'[19] At the time of purchase Blarer was a young monk at Alpirsbach[20] who busied himself learning Greek and Hebrew while maintaining enthusiastic contact with Melanchthon in Tübingen.[21] His recently acquired language skills left their mark on the marginal notes in which he captured the most compelling arguments and summarized Summenhart's sentiments in alternating red and black ink applied in an intentional interplay of fine and broad pen strokes.[22]

The reader approaching Summenhart's treatise under the spell of a stubbornly transmitted image of scholastic disputations full of logical sophistry[23] and devoid of all vitality is in for a surprise. Even before the heightened social unrest, expressed in uprisings in Alsace (1498),

16 In his earliest letter (1509?) Blarer requested 'min liebe mutter' to send painting colours. Apparently, like his monastic brother, the painter Hans Halfinger, he was engaged in artistic pursuits. Schiess, *Briefwechsel*, 1, pp. 1f.

17 Haller was correct to point out that Roth 'willkürlich und fälschlich' added the caption, 'Herzog Ulrich's Ordnung' to the programme of reform of 30 January 1535. Haller, 2, p. 130; Roth, *Urkunden*, pp. 176–85. 'Herzog Ulrichs zweite Ordnung' of 3 November 1536 first established 'ain luttere Ordnung' for the university. *Ibid.*, p. 187.

18 See above, pp. 20–1.

19 'Comparatus est is liber Tubingae/per me F. Ambrosium Blarer/impendio Caterinae/ Blarerin pientis/simae meae/matris/anno/1515/1 floreno, X solidis.' I am indebted to my colleague Hansmartin Decker-Hauff for his aid in securing from the Stuttgart police laboratory a legible reproduction of this heavily soiled entry.

20 Blarer registered at Tübingen on 17 January 1505, having not yet reached the age of thirteen. See Hermelink, *Die Matrikeln*, 1, p. 146, no. 38. He was awarded the degree of *Baccalaureus* on 24 December 1511 and *Magister* on 24 June 1513, in both cases as a member of the Alpirsbach convent. See Roth, *Urkunden*, p. 164, n. 1.

21 See the evidence of affectionate attachment in Melanchthon's letter from Tübingen of 1 January 1515: 'Docto et religioso viro . . . Monacho suo.' *CR* 1, col. 7.

22 Blarer added illustrations of, among other items, Summenhart's interpretation of the two tables of the Mosaic law (fol. 1^{v}); St Thomas (fol. 5^{v}); an incense censer (fol. 6^{r}); a goblet (fol. 9^{v}); a church decorated for its consecration with a three-pointed flag (fol. 12^{r}); a tiara and sword to mark the discussion of the issue of papal power (fol. 17^{r}); two drawings of the emperor at the term *Donatio Constantini* (illustrations which were clearly intended to portray Maximilian by imitating his hair style and the shape of his nose), one appearing singly (fol. 3^{r}) and the other together with the pope (fol. 20^{r}); a drawing of a downcast and wounded Panormitanus opposite an argument 'contra Panormitanum' (fol. 19^{v}); and a Swiss halberd (fol. 38^{r}). Ornamental designs also appear frequently, added to emphasize important passages, organize argumentation or integrate marginalia.

23 See above, note 15.

in Bruchsal (1502) and in the Rems valley (1514), began to creep toward Tübingen, Summenhart had perceived the decisive importance of the tithe issue and no longer treated it peripherally under the juridical banner, *De contractibus*. The central question was whether theology, independent of canon lawyers and on the basis of its own sources, was competent to decide whether the tithe obligation belonged to the jurisdiction of divine or human law.[24]

Summenhart had no intention of sheltering the theologians from critique. They had permitted the ticklish issue of tithes to go unattended for too long to warrant further delay.[25] With broadly conceived argumentation he sought to demonstrate that the tithe obligation established in the Old Testament had been fulfilled and abolished in Christ.[26] Christ had put an end to the temporally bound Jewish judicial and ceremonial law while affirming with equal vigour the force of the moral law contained in the ten commandments. There is no trace of any reaffirmation of the tithe obligation in the gospel. If then, despite the above, the authority of divine law is still to be claimed in support of the tithe obligation, the tithe would have to be anchored in the natural law that is inscribed on every human heart and to which all men are at all times subject. But natural law also offers no foundation for a mandatory tithe.

Turning on his opponents, Summenhart flung the words of Christ at them: 'Woe to you, scribes and Pharisees, hypocrites! For you tithe mint and dill and cummin and have neglected the weightier matters of the law . . .' The conclusion of Jesus' castigation was certainly familiar enough to his listeners to justify its omission: 'you . . . have neglected . . . justice, mercy and faith'.[27] Blarer's marginal response to this reproach is enlightening: 'he is going after the canonists here'.[28] But Blarer censured not only the act, but the motive: 'These canonist hypocrites act out of "scorn" for the oppressed.'[29]

24 See the programmatic thoughts in the introductory chapter to the *Tractatus de decimis*: 'Melius quippe noverunt qui divinam professi sunt legem, quid de divina lege sit, quam qui humanam, adeo ut etiam si in humanis legibus scriptum inveniatur aliquid de divina fore lege, id quomodo intelligendum sit, melius divinae legis arbitrabitur professor.' 'Praefatio.'

25 'Et quia magistri nostri (scil. divinae legis) valde breviter super hoc transierunt quasi nihil tangentes, . . . placuit mihi materiam ipsam profundius intrando diffusius examinare . . .' *Ibid*.

26 The entire first part of the treatise was devoted to this issue.

27 Matth. 23.23.

28 'Notat canonistas.' Fol. 2ra. The target was enlarged later to include all lawyers: 'Adverte optimum argumentum contra iuristas, quibus congrue dici possunt verba Christi, Mathei 23: "Ve vobis scribae etc."' Fol. 13^{r}.

29 'ex schmytzis.' Fol. 2ra. The middle high German 'schmitzen' or 'schmytzen' ranges from 'to strike' (schlagen) to 'to slander' (verleumden); see Grimm, *Deutsches*

The remainder of Summenhart's recital contained arguments that must have made sense to and awakened approval on the part of a much wider public. Clearly intended to excite emotions beyond the walls of the lecture hall was the argument that if the tithe was indeed anchored in divine law, such an obligation should find universal recognition. But what should be done with the Italians, who were required to pay no tithes? If this obligation were truly of divine institution, then all of Italy was living in mortal sin; to say nothing of the popes and bishops who permitted such scandal! To counter that this exception rested on common law proved to be of little help, for convention carried no weight *vis-à-vis* the laws of the Lord: 'consuetudo contra precepta dei non valet'.[30]

Following the discussion with obvious sympathy, Blarer singled out this 'Italian argument' for special attention. Its overtones harmonized with the swelling strain of national and anti-Rome sentiment north of the Alps.[31] Where Summenhart repulsed the insistence of canonists such as Innocent IV and Antonius de Butrio that those who denied the divine precept of the tithe were heretics, Blarer noted pointedly: 'Innocent and Antonius thereby condemn the theologians before they have understood them.'[32] When Antonius was charged by Summenhart with having contradicted himself, Blarer added: 'Antonius has fallen into a pit dug with his own hands.'[33] With its humanist propensity for the epigrammatic,[34] this marginal comment also suggests the contours of the humanist front against a jurisprudence perverted by canon law.[35]

But Blarer's openness to the new learning by no means led him to condemn all scholastic theologizing. His marginal notes illustrate his

Wörterbuch, vol. 9, cols. 1100–4. The term 'schmytzen' might also be early 'Yiddish' and stem from a Hebrew root. Reuchlin interpreted the verb 'schadash' as: 'Insinuans, portendens, innuens' and added: 'nota infamia'. *De rudimentis hebraicis*, lib. 2, p. 524.

30 *Werden und Wertung der Reformation*, p. 395.

31 Blarer's marginal comment: 'Tota Italia non observat preceptum de danda quotta decimarum, non tamen ob hoc damnanda est.' Fol. 4^r.

32 'Hii ergo, puta Innocentius et Anthonius de Butrio, theologos damnant, priusquam intelligant.' Fol. 5^r.

33 'Incidit in foveam, quam fecit.' Fol. 5^r.

34 With his collection of *Adagia*, Erasmus provided considerable impetus for the pursuit of epigrammatic wisdom. He explained the significance of proverbs in his dedicatory epistle to Lord Mountjoy in the first edition of the *Adagiorum Collectanea* (Paris, 1500). *Opus Epistolarum*, ed. Allen, 1, pp. 289ff.; cf. the excellent annotated translation with its play on 'verbosity' and 'proverbosity' in *The Correspondence of Erasmus*, ed. Mynors, Thomson, Ferguson, 1, pp. 255–66; here p. 266, lines 305f.

35 For the attack by Italian humanists on the scholastic–canonistic legal tradition see Gilmore, *Humanists and Jurists*, pp. 61–86.

willingness to retrace the scholastic course of thought; they illuminate his theological sensitivity to the critical junctures in Summenhart's chain of reasoning. Thus he singled out the claim that a constitution bearing the approval of *both* pope and council is of greater authority than one endorsed by the pope alone.[36] The implications of Summenhart's assertion were not lost on Blarer: clothing it in a conciliarist thesis, Summenhart has established the logical basis for asserting the theologian's competence critically to review ecclesiastical and even papal decisions. And if the pope imagines he has found support in divine law for insisting on the payment of tithes while theologians, appealing to Paul and the authority of the first apostolic council, teach the liberty of the Christian from the law, then one should heed the doctors of theology and not the pope.[37] A papal doctrinal decision does not merit *ipso facto* acceptance as a ruling from the highest court in the *corpus Christianum*, but must first be interpreted theologically and integrated into the valid tradition of that church.

Summenhart chose not to pursue this explosive assertion since his purpose was to demonstrate the canonists' lack of competence in dealing with theological questions. Likewise, varying ecclesiological positions, such as the disparity between the canonist popes and a conciliar canon lawyer such as Panormitanus, were of secondary importance to the Tübingen professor.[38] Despite certain similarities between Summenhart's ecclesiology and that of Panormitanus, the latter was no doctrinal authority for Summenhart, but continued to occupy a position behind enemy lines, among the canonists. And according to Summenhart's concluding arguments, an error by Panormitanus simply verified the unreliability of all canonists, indeed, of all lawyers. Had not Panormitanus charged theologians with teaching that the New Testament made the tithe a matter of individual volition? To have done so would have constituted a most scandalous violation of their oaths as doctors of theology, for was not

36 Blarer: 'Constitutio a solo papa facta differat a constitutione a papa cum approbatione concilii facta.' Fol. 20^{v}.

37 Citing Panormitanus: 'quod ubi dictum alicuius sancti iuvatur auctoritate iuris divini, potius ei quam constitutioni summi pontificis standum est . . .' (fol. 38va), Summenhart concluded: 'Sequeretur quod predicte opinioni theologorum potius standum esset quam constitutioni summi pontificis saltem crude intellecte, que potius est exponenda et sane intellegenda.' Fol. 38vb.

38 The basic outline of Panormitanus' ecclesiology is especially visible in his commentary to c. Significasti. See the text and commentary in Nörr, *Kirche und Konzil bei Nicolaus de Tudeschis (Panormitanus)*, pp. 104–6. The decisive authority of a scripturally-supported *dictum* (*ibid.*, p. 176), which Summenhart derived from Panormitanus, is the axis of Luther's appeal to pope and Council and explains both its sincerity and its limits.

this the heresy of Wyclif, the teaching that paying tithes was no more than voluntary almsgiving?[39]

Summenhart rejected this indictment as a crude misunderstanding since he considered the payment of tithes to be an obligation of love not dependent on human whim. Although he denied a basis for the tithe in divine law he did recognize its foundation in the positive law of custom. All Christians were expected to contribute to the church that which was really necessary for its functioning, a duty of love which Christ had reaffirmed, not revoked. This was at the same time a historically evolved customary legal responsibility that could not be abandoned or reinstituted arbitrarily. A just and adequate tithe guaranteed the pastor's living and aided the poor. On these grounds the tithe was no matter for debate. But attempts to expand the grain tithe to a ground rent independent of harvest yields[40] perverted the basic principle.

Yet the medieval tax structure rested on precisely this extension of an otherwise valid principle, and such expansion soon led to considerable social unrest in German-speaking regions. Summenhart thought it essential to point out that increases in customary dues could gain legal validity only with the consent of all concerned. If a pastor introduced tithe obligations that exceeded his and the parish's actual requirements, or attempted to expand the tithe to non-agricultural goods, it was no sin to refuse such payments; rather it was the priest who sinned.[41]

Summenhart's treatment of the tithe issue yielded two contradictory consequences for the life of the church. In the confessional there was no need to conceal the tithe's weakened legal foundation, because a conscience plagued by the refusal to pay unjustly demanded dues needed consolation and comfort.[42] But in the pulpit, the fact that the tithe had no basis in divine law was to be dodged discreetly. The duty to inform and instruct could not be ignored. But the dissemination of this particular information could only serve to confirm the weaker brethren and sisters in their already questionable

39 'Et hoc eis imponere est eis imponere abiuratum errorem Johannis Wickleff, inter cuius articulos quadragintaocto ille fuit unus, quo dixit, quod decime essent pure elemosine.' Fol. 39ra–b^. See article 18 of Wyclif's forty-five (!) condemned theses. Denzinger and Schönmetzer, eds., *Enchiridion Symbolorum*, no. 1168 (598).

40 Fol. 22^{v} ff.

41 'non peccant, si postquam sunt exacti solum a suo plebano ad solutionem quotte de omnibus, recusant eam dare, dummodo non indigeat illa decima exacta; imo in casu tali natus esset ipse exigens peccare.' Fol. 24ra.

42 'Nam errantes et scrupulosos dirigere et quietare est opus misericordie . . .' Fol. 37^{va-b}.

anti-clericalism and to escalate the stage-whisper campaign against a materially bloated church to even greater heights of spitefulness.[43]

We have lingered at length over this treatise because, as Summenhart apparently realized, it assembled the building blocks for a revolutionary theology. In the wake of his frontal attack on the canonists, who, like the Pharisees, had burdened the people with unconscionable loads, he appealed to theologians to take their own task seriously and to console and edify the consciences of the laity. Unfazed and intellectually incorruptible, he risked acquiring a reputation as a revolutionary in the eyes of professors and students dependent on ecclesiastical benefices. And by publishing his academic disputations he flouted his own restrictions on the flow of information: anyone, including the educated layman, could now read for himself that the tithe lacked any foundation in divine law.

Some idea of the limited effectiveness of Summenhart's daring thrust is evident from the fact that the treatise disappeared from public view even before the armed resistance of the 'Poor Conrad' uprising (1514). And Nicholas Baselius described the conspiracy of Bruchsal (1502) in his supplement to Vergenhans' *Chronicle* (1516)[44] with such a mixture of disgust and fear that openness to Summenhart's bold theses among those academics belonging to the elite of society could scarcely have been very extensive.[45] In contrast to the repeated reprintings of the massive and moderate portion of the volume, the *Septipertitum opus de contractibus*, the slender treatise on tithes found no second publisher.[46]

It is difficult to determine with certainty the degree to which Summenhart influenced his listeners in Tübingen in his role as professor. But it was not the great uprisings of 1524–5 that first saw priests becoming spokesmen for the underprivileged of society[47] who suffered the most under the steadily rising dues and tithes.[48] And

[43] 'laici, qui oppido sunt infesti, clericis alias graviter ferunt, quod clerici multa temporalia possideant, et eos de cupiditate solent sugillare, inciperent iam institutionem sinistre interpretari, quasi ex cupiditate originaliter processissent, non necessitate.' Fol. 38ra.

[44] On Nicholas Baselius see above, p. 15, n. 2.

[45] Vergenhans, *Chronicle*, fol. 305^{r-v}.

[46] Haller, 1, p. 178.

[47] See Maurer, 'Das Verhalten der reformatorisch gesinnten Geistlichen Süddeutschlands im Bauernkrieg 1525. I: Systematische Darstellung des Themas; II: Biographische Darstellung des Themas'. Widespread purges of clergy suspected of having sympathized with the peasants were resumed following Duke Ulrich's return in 1534. See Schiess, *Briefwechsel*, 1, p. 619.

[48] The church was the first target of peasant outrage. See my article 'The Gospel of Social Unrest: 450 Years After the So-Called "German Peasants' War" of 1525'.

there can be no doubt that Summenhart enjoyed an exceptionally positive reputation among the enthusiastic younger humanist generation that led the urban reformations of south Germany. The later Strassburg reformer and longtime associate of Bucer, Wolfgang Capito, undertook the publication of Summenhart's *Summa Physice* as early as 1502, adding a laudatory introduction. And as late as 1552 Melanchthon remembered Summenhart as one of the superbly learned Tübingen theologians who had attempted, within the limitations of his age, to transmit the true teaching of the church.[49] In 1515 Ambrosius Blarer's friendship with Melanchthon induced him to accept his mentor's invitation and travel from Alpirsbach to Tübingen in order 'to partake of his [Melanchthon's] books and knowledge'.[50] Blarer used the opportunity to acquire his own 'Summenhart' from a Tübingen bookseller.

It is important to keep in mind this connection between Summenhart and the reformers of the following generation in order not to confine his legacy to the social unrest of the peasant uprisings. For the Reformation could succeed inside city walls only if the claims and privileges of cloister and parish were eliminated, stripping them of their basis in divine law; privileges that extended far beyond the tithe to include taxes on market produce and merchant wares. Summenhart had certainly not envisioned the limitation and later elimination of such privileges, enforced citizenship for the clergy[51] or the secularization of ecclesiastical property. Yet these developments demonstrate clearly that the entire structure of medieval society was shaken to its foundation where the following two principles were consistently applied: the tithe is based on human and not divine law; and its legitimate application in a given situation depends on common law and custom as determined by the consensus of those affected.

Summenhart remained true to his pre-Reformation principle that lectern and pulpit must not be confused. Unlike the lecture or disputation, in the sermon the whole truth (Summenhart would have said: *all* the truth) need not and should not be proclaimed to the people. Blarer followed Summenhart's reasoning carefully and at the end of the tithe treatise took specific notice of the caution against

49 *Oratio de Eberardo, Duce Wirtebergensi. CR* 11, cols. 1021–30; here col. 1025. Cf. *Oratio de vita Hieronymi Schurfii* in Kisch, *Melanchthons Rechts- und Soziallehre*, pp. 288–97; here p. 292.

50 'Utere libris nostris et ingenio.' Schiess, *Briefwechsel*, 1, p. 6.

51 See Moeller, 'Kleriker als Bürger', pp. 195–224; *idem*, *Pfarrer als Bürger*.

preaching to the people on this subject.[52] With that in view and proudly applying his newly acquired language skills, he summarized the entire work with two Greek sentences. On the title page Blarer wrote: Υπὲρ εὐσεβείας καὶ λάλει καὶ μάνθανε;[53] and at the end of the treatise: 'Ανέχου καὶ ἀπέχου.[54]

The meaning of this two-part maxim is ambiguous and perhaps typical of the intellectual atmosphere of the second decade of the sixteenth century. If one chooses to emphasize the academic freedom for theologizing created by the scholastic disputation where a problem could be treated internally (*disputative*) without binding oneself or getting into a bind externally (*assertive*), then the last lines of the couplets must be stressed:

> Of the fear of the Lord
> Discourse and discern!
> . . .
> Sustain [the truth]
> And restrain [the truth]!

But if, in view of the powerful religious motivation of pre-Reformation humanism, one chooses to stress 'fear of the Lord' or 'piety' as the basic prerequisite for genuine scholarship and learning, the epigram permits the following translation:

> All your speech and study
> must pursue piety.
> . . .
> Endure
> And abstain!

This interpretation emphasizes especially the interiorization and subjective appropriation of the truths that the scholastic educational process objectified. All these truths are here directed toward the one Truth, toward an authentic relationship with God. 'Fear of God' is not merely the beginning of all wisdom but also the never-failing fountain and point of reference. Genuine education requires a learned life of

52 Summenhart, fol. 38r above: 'Non omnis veritas passim predicanda.' Fol. 38r below: 'Non dicendum laicis ius divinum hodie non obligare ad quottam decimarum.'

53 For Blarer's quotation see *Menandri Sententiae*, ed. Jaekel, no. 781, line 78. Hugh Grotius translated the proverb in his edition (*Excerpta ex Tragoediis et Comoediis Graecis*, no. 521) as :'Ea fator et disce quae pietas probat.' Richard Walther rendered it as a moralistic admonition: 'Sprich immer in Ehrfurcht und heiliger Scheu und suche sie ständig zu lernen aufs neu.' *Menanders Denksprüche dreisprachig. Die griechischen und lateinischen Texte*, ed. Walther, no. 521.

54 See below, n. 56.

withdrawal from the desires and distractions of the world in devotion to study.[55]

The second part of the adage was very likely taken from the 'Attic Nights' of Aulus Gellius († before A.D. 165) where its ancient author stressed self-control and tolerance as the two cardinal virtues of the authentic man.[56] With the aid of Blarer's moving letter of 25 July 1522, we can confirm that it was not merely pride in his philological skills that caused him to inscribe these two Greek verses in the work of a Tübingen scholastic. In that letter Ambrosius Blarer first revealed, to his brother Thomas, that he had left the monastery at Alpirsbach.[57] His explanation took the form of an *itinerarium mentis*, a travel journal of the inner development that had brought him to break with his past and forsake the monastery. He had endeavoured to the end of his monastic career, so he reported to Thomas, to combine *pietas* and *tolerantia*. Piety consists in reverence and respect for holy scripture and in a loving eagerness for its company and proclamation; tolerance enabled him to endure the reproaches and insults arising from suspicion of Lutheran sympathies. Blarer had been willing to bear the abuse,[58] but when he was deprived of the privilege of proclamation and the pastorate – and thereby deprived of Christ himself – he found himself suddenly torn by the tension between two ethical principles, a tension his conscience could not overcome.

Just as these two Greek verses had represented an organic unity within Blarer's cloistered world of 1515–16, it was the tension between them, indeed, their confrontation, that forced his shift toward the Reformation in 1522. Public denunciation in the face of the Luther issue could be tolerated so long as the honour of holy scripture remained untouched.[59]

55 William J. Bouwsma termed this a 'Stoic' tendency that found a counterpart in an 'Augustinian' assent to political responsibility. Both were characteristic of humanism; indeed, both tendencies may often be observed struggling for supremacy within one personage of the humanist world. See 'The Two Faces of Humanism, Stoicism and Augustinianism in Renaissance Thought'.

56 This adage was cited by Aulus Gellius in his 'Attic Nights' as a key proverb of the Stoic Epictetus. Aulus Gellius, *Noctes Atticae*, vol. 2, Lib. XVII, 19, §§5–6; p. 528. Translated into Latin as 'sustine et abstine', the proverb corresponds to the German 'leide und meide'. See Büchmann, *Geflügelte Worte*, s.v. 'leiden'. See also *Aulus Gellius. The Attic Nights*, transl. Rolfe, vol. 2, pp. 266–7. Cf. Erasmus, *Adagia*, *LB* II, col. 617A–B.

57 Schiess, *Briefwechsel*, 1, pp. 47–9.

58 '(ut hic transmittam innumeras iniurias . . . quas vel brevi finem habituras sperare poteram vel certe forti animo negligere) . . .' Schiess, *Briefwechsel*, 1, p. 48.

59 'Abierat iam Luteri nomen in publicam eorum omnium execrationem, id quod utcunque forte tulissem, modo divinis literis suum habuissent honorem.' Schiess, *Briefwechsel*, 1, p. 48.

But when they began to decry everything that I had carefully gleaned from the Gospel and from Paul as drawn from Luther and therefore impious and heretical, and when they no longer permitted me to give account of my faith; then it ceased to be an injustice borne by *me* and became an insult to God. And my Christian spirit neither could nor dared tolerate that. As long as hope remained, dear brother, that I could benefit my brethren, I exercised Christian restraint and tolerance. Fully aware of my own liberty, I was willing to Judaize with the Judaizers in the hope that they might some day realize their own freedom.[60]

But as it became clear that patient self-restraint, *modestia ac patientia*, accomplished nothing, Blarer resolved to follow Christ's counsel and to forsake the house that had rejected his words.[61]

In 1534 Duke Ulrich assigned to Ambrosius Blarer the task of reforming south Württemberg. He returned to the university that, thanks to Summenhart and Melanchthon, had provided him with two lasting and fundamental values. By subordinating both *pietas* and *tolerantia* to the obligation of obedience he had succeeded as a monk in harmonizing one with the other. But his newfound obedience to the greatest Abbot now brought evangelical liberty and at the same time, burdened him with the task of ending 'tyranny'.

What Ambrosius had related as his personal experience to his brother, who was bursting with enthusiasm for Luther, was typical of the period of the Reformation's history characterized by the turmoil in Wittenberg during and following Luther's absence. From the approval of clerical marriages to the liberation from monastic vows, the principle of evangelical liberty in lifestyle played a major role.[62] In Wittenberg all participants – Luther, Melanchthon and Carlstadt – had accepted the thesis that Christian freedom was a matter of divine justice. Their concern was to reconcile the principles of Christian liberty with those of Christian love and with the prohibition against giving offence to the weaker brother. Blarer's task, in contrast, had been the reconciliation of Christian liberty with the lofty ethical obligation to tolerance within the monastic community.

Blarer's 'evangelical turning-point' was the product of the tension between his own obedience and his responsibility toward his neighbour. In numerous other individual lives of that epoch, in varying circumstances and under diverse conditions, a struggle of conscience

[60] *Ibid*. Cf. Blarer's 'Wahrhafte Verantwortung' (1523); *Ambrosius Blaurer's des schwäbischen Reformators Leben und Schriften*, ed. Pressel, pp. 5–17; here pp. 7f.
[61] Schiess, *Briefwechsel*, 1, p. 48. Cf. Matth. 10.14; Luke 9.5.
[62] See Bubenheimer, 'Scandalum et ius divinum. Theologische und rechtstheologische Probleme der ersten reformatorischen Innovationen in Wittenberg 1521/22', pp. 328f.

likewise led to pivotal decisions. Blarer found his solution in the supremacy of Christ's admonition to preserve the gospel, preferring that single counsel of Christ to the *consilia evangelica* according to which he had vowed to live as a monk: obedience, poverty and chastity. Only in retrospect does it become clear that his Tübingen teachers, Summenhart and Melanchthon, had supplied the requisite perspectives for his conflict of conscience and the resulting turning-point.

In 1534 Blarer once more faced his theological faculty, a faculty which had not shared his change of heart and which understood piety and tolerance to be superseded and completed in obedience to the church. But apart from this obvious contradiction, the keenness of the confrontation was exacerbated by irony. On both sides the same ethical standards struggled for a chance to refashion faith and the church. For it was not tradition and renewal, conservatism and 'progressiveness' that proved to be the most irreconcilable antagonists. Instead, churchly reform and the reformation of the church battled implacably for the right to rule.

8

The ethics of capitalism: the clash of interests

THE TÜBINGEN SCHOOL'S foray into the field of theological ethics was not restricted to the problems of a south-west Germany beset by social turmoil; Biel and Summenhart also constructed a foundation for a new economic theory. It was an *oeconomia moderna* specifically adapted to the needs of the international commerce of the south German cities. And if we may trust the account of Urbanus Rhegius, the new economic theory attracted international attention through one of its most prominent and vehement advocates, the Ingolstadt professor Johannes Eck.

On 15 July 1515, in Bologna, Eck had been permitted to hold a disputation on the practice of collecting interest and, according to Urbanus Rhegius, won a resounding victory. But in Germany the question of investment interest was the focal point of an acute controversy, a dispute that moved leading businessmen and humanists alike, and not all were as easily convinced of Eck's success as was his Ingolstadt pupil and self-appointed press agent, Urbanus Rhegius. Many opponents of Eck's views on the interest issue eagerly accepted the humanist Johannes Cochleus' eyewitness account of the disputation in which Eck appeared as anything but the victor.[1]

But after Eck returned from Italy and posted the official confirmation of his triumph on the notice board of the Bavarian university,[2] Urbanus Rhegius saw no reason to temper regional pride, and poetically compared his master's Italian conquest to a triumphal procession. In the process the university at Tübingen was permitted to bask in the fame amassed by her former *alumnus*:

[1] Christopher Scheurl had access to a report from Bologna by the former Nuremberg schoolteacher and later opponent of Luther, Johannes Cochlaeus. Scheurl wrote on 25 September 1515 to Johann Rüdiger, *vicarius* at Eichstätt: 'Doctor Eck conclusiones suas disputavit Bononiae, ferunt tamen parum reportasse gloriae, ne dicam ridiculo habitum. Johannes Cocleus, aliquando apud nos ludi magister, de ea re scripsit libellum.' *Christoph Scheurl's Briefbuch. Ein Beitrag zur Geschichte der Reformation und ihrer Zeit*, ed. von Soden and Knaake, vol. 1, p. 144; cf. p. 148.

[2] See Schlecht, 'Dr. Johann Ecks Anfänge', Beilage IV, pp. 34–6; and von Pölnitz, 'Die Beziehungen des Johannes Eck zum Augsburger Kapital', p. 699.

Tübingen rejoice!
For you nourished this child
With the first milk of learning.[3]

The entire poem rings with somewhat smug satisfaction over the blooming state of studies in Germany which even the venerable University of Bologna, Europe's senior institution in Eck's field of disputation (canon law), could no longer deny. This newly earned respect was therefore of interest to more than just Ingolstadt university circles. Eck's victory represented a triumph not only for one of Ingolstadt's professors but for all the recent German university foundations, including Tübingen where Biel and Summenhart had done the spadework for Eck's success. Heinrich Bebel (†1518), the voluble versifier and, since 1497, first incumbent of the chair for poetry and rhetoric at Tübingen,[4] seized the opportunity to celebrate his university and its pupil in a poem that has little to fear from a modern versifying 'renderer':

Our Eck is back, choice friends rejoice!
Exult ye who his love with me enjoy!
Make merry, modern Occam's sect;
For bliss is back, behold your Eck
Bedeckt with praise, bathed in respect,
Unscathed from Italy retrekk'd![5]

Bebel quite properly referred to Eck's education in the *via moderna*. For Eck remained indebted to the modern way all his life despite attempting – in the Tübingen tradition – to overcome the strife between the schools.[6] But Eck's acquaintance with the new Tübingen economic ethic is of even greater importance for our present concerns. Taken from Biel and with 'modern' openmindedness, from Summenhart, Eck adapted these economic principles to the south German world of finance and eloquently defended them at Bologna.

In addition to a main section devoted to economic issues, the Bolognese disputation theses also included a set of afterthoughts or

[3] 'Gaudeto, primo doctrinae lacte, Tubinga,/Nutristi puerum. Vive valeque diu!' Schlecht, 'Dr. Johann Ecks Anfänge', Beilage III, p. 33. Tübingen had to share this honour with Cologne and Freiburg, both recipients of similar praise from Rhegius.

[4] As Eck noted in his *Epistola de ratione studiorum suorum* (1538), Bebel had been his teacher at Tübingen in 'humanioribus literis'. *CCath* 2, p. 41.

[5] 'Ekius advenit, dulces gaudete sodales,/Dicite, quos mecum semper amavit, io!/Secta recens, gaude, deducens nomen ab Occham./Deliciae redit en Ekius ille tuae,/ Incolumen nobis quoniam Itala terra remisit,/Non sine laude tamen, non sine honore viri./ . . . Ex Tibinga, VI. die Novembris, anno etc. XV./Salve, vale, Ecki, omnium charissime.' *CCath* 6, p. 50, lines 5–10, 19f.

[6] See Walter L. Moore, introduction to his edition, *In Primum Librum Sententiarum Annotatiunculae D. Iohanne Eckio*, pp. 10–12.

Impertinentia in which Eck dealt with the theme of penitence and indulgences. Largely ignored by scholars, they represent a preliminary form of Eck's *Obelisci* or marginalia to Luther's indulgence theses of 1517, and practically predestined their author to become an opponent of Luther.[7] But the glimpse of Eck's future, afforded by hindsights to the modern reader of the *Impertinentia,* was denied to Eck's contemporaries of 1515. It was the disputation's own rearward glance that aroused attention and antagonism in attempting to put an end to the question of interest-taking despite moralistic protest and ecclesiastical indecision.

At issue was the legitimacy of profit-making commerce with capital, a practice long accepted in international banking and financial circles but still encountering organized resistance in Germany, especially among humanists. Thus the practice urgently needed the protective rationale of a new theology of capital. A new interpretation of the church's prohibition of usury was required, an interpretation that would permit smooth financing of investments, especially the rapidly expanding long-distance commerce, without the restrictive overhead of a guilty conscience. Ultimately, as merchants began demanding written opinions from professors of theology, the issue could be ignored no longer and the standard canon law solutions finally came under careful scrutiny.

The discrepancy between the church's prohibition of usury and routine business practice had apparently long since found a satisfactory solution as far as the canon lawyers in the Italian financial centres were concerned. Yet merchants in the south German commercial capitals found themselves faced with a grave question of conscience at the beginning of the sixteenth century. Explaining why they could not have simply adopted the Italian solutions is as difficult as the intellectual history of the period is complex. Nor is it essential to our purpose to decide whether public opinion mobilized by humanist moral indignation[8] forced the crisis of conscience; or whether a financial magnate such as Jacob Fugger (†1525), immersed in late medieval piety, sought theological clarification of the issue out of his own devout desire for peace of mind; or whether a desire to

[7] *CCath* 6, pp. 46–8; here pp. 46, line 12–47, line 28.

[8] The humanist agitation in opposition to interest-taking was not limited to south Germany. See Raymond de Roover's account of the clash between John Major (†1550) and the Paris humanists. *La pensée économique des scolastiques. Doctrines et méthodes,* p. 32. For a general treatment of the relationship between theology and trade in the fifteenth century and a careful critique of the Weber thesis, see *idem,* 'The Scholastic Attitude toward Trade and Entrepreneurship', pp. 336–45.

guarantee the incontrovertibility of letters of credit was responsible for the scruples of south German business circles.[9]

All these factors demanded a new economic theory, an *oeconomia moderna*. A series of universities received requests for theological opinions from the Fugger capital of Augsburg. That Tübingen was included was fully predictable in view of the teaching tradition established by Biel and Summenhart. Precisely this pastoral frontier region between theological ethics and political economics, where an investment contract could be branded with the infamy of usury, had caught the Tübingen theological eye. And precisely this 'pastoral' interest in moral and economic theology permits talk of a 'Tübingen school' even for this early period of the university's history.[10]

Concern for a 'theology of commerce' was scarcely a scholarly innovation; modern scholars have simply given too little attention to this aspect of medieval theology. The *via moderna* had already made a considerable impact in this field during its early phase. In the mid-thirteenth century (1255) Thomas Aquinas denounced the claim that the sacrament of baptism owed its efficacy, its ability to impart grace, to divine ordinance and not to the consecrated water. According to the view that Thomas repudiated the sacraments in general function not as a *causa efficiens* but as a necessary prerequisite (*causa sine qua non*) for divine action. God covenantally pledges that all recipients of the sacraments will simultaneously receive grace, but such grace is not 'caused' by the sacraments. For an illustration, sacramental theologians of this persuasion reached into the monetary realm. They offered as an example someone who is prepared to accept a lead coin as payment upon being assured that the piece of lead represents the king's guarantee of one hundred pounds to the bearer on demand. In such a case it is not the coin but the king who 'causes', makes possible and initiates the one hundred pound payment.[11]

William J. Courtenay has quite properly pointed out that this interpretation, assailed by Aquinas in the thirteenth century, won

[9] Götz Freiherr von Pölnitz has pointed out that the financial arrangements for the benefice-buying of Archbishop Albrecht of Mainz and his involvement in the indulgence of 1515 were among the circumstances that induced Fugger to renew the discussion surrounding the issue of interest. 'Jakob Fugger', pp. 16f.

[10] Under the caption, 'Adoption by the Tübingen School . . .' John T. Noonan, Jr, observed: 'The university at the time must have been almost as much a center of liberal economics as centuries later it was to be a center of liberal theology.' *The Scholastic Analysis of Usury*, p. 206; cf. p. 231.

[11] Thomas Aquinas, IV Sent. dist. 1 q. 1 art. 4, ad primam quaestionem. Cf. William J. Courtenay, 'The King and the Leaden Coin. The Economic Background of "sine qua non" Causality', p. 185, n. 1.

wide acceptance in fourteenth- and fifteenth-century nominalism. We have here stumbled upon a theme that shaped and characterized the nominalist world view in matters extending far beyond sacramental theology.[12] And the young Luther made use of this 'face-value tradition' in his first lectures on the Psalms (1513–15) when he employed the image of royally backed currency to illustrate the *sola gratia* nature of justification.[13]

The choice of an example from the financial world by representatives of the nominalist tradition was scarcely accidental. The shift from agricultural barter to urban commerce required a new theory of money. Whereas Aquinas could cling to the causal theory that coins contain an intrinsic value that makes a distinction between the possession of money and its use unthinkable,[14] the new nominalist contractual theory legitimized the introduction of letters of credit and securities.[15]

In his often reprinted treatise on 'The Power and Utility of Money', Gabriel Biel refers to the previous work of the Paris nominalist, Nicholas d'Oresme (†1382) to explain the problem of monetary inflation.[16] In his commentary on the mass he dealt eloquently with the meaning and purpose of the sacraments which are 'backed' by God in precisely the same way that coins are backed by secular authorities.[17] The acceptation doctrine developed by Duns Scotus and borrowed by the nominalists – wherein justification occurs through God's 'acceptance' of a human righteousness inadequate on its own merits – found a clear parallel in the *valor extrinsecus*, the imputed

[12] *Ibid.*, p. 186, n. 3. Cf. *idem*, 'Covenant and Causality in Pierre d'Ailly'.

[13] *WA* 4, pp. 261, line 34–262, line 17 (Scholion on Ps. 113.9; 1515). For analysis and further literature see Bayer, *Promissio. Geschichte der reformatorischen Wende in Luthers Theologie*, pp. 128–43.

[14] *STh* II–II q. 78 art. 1; Courtenay, 'The King and the Leaden Coin', p. 206, n. 66.

[15] Proof of prior involvement in usurious transactions, even in earlier generations, could mean that a commercial company would be forced to forfeit its entire capital. Appealing to Rom. 11.16, *si radix sancta, et rami*, the company's entire capital was declared 'infected'. Biel countered by insisting that the Pauline text did not apply since – parallel to the 'sine qua non' causality discussed by Courtenay – 'pecunia non habet rationem radicis, sed magis materiae sine qua non'. *Collectorium*, IV, dist. 15 q. 11 art. 2 concl. 5 ad 2 Y; Werbeck and Hofmann edn, 4, pt. 2, p. 246, lines 21f.

[16] Oresme was twice cited explicitly: Biel, *Tractatus de potestate et utilitate monetarum*. Robert B. Burke published an English translation, *Treatise on the Power and the Utility of Moneys, by Master Gabriel Biel of Speyer* . . . The Oresme quotation is found on p. 23, line 32 of that translation. The treatise was a separate printing from Biel's *Collectorium*, IV, dist. 15 q. 9; Werbeck and Hoffmann edn, 4, pt. 2; pp. 175–87, with the Oresme quotations at pp. 176 and 181.

[17] Cf. my book, *The Harvest of Medieval Theology*, pp. 373f. Kenneth Hagen has pointed out the significance of the 'Testamentum' for the young Luther. *A Theology of Testament in the Young Luther. The Lectures on Hebrews*, pp. 61ff., 108ff.

value of money.[18] Such parallels made it clear that narrowly limiting our investigation to the history of theology would obscure non-theological preliminary conclusions that shaped and permeated the nominalist world of thought. We would miss correlations between economics and theology that today are hidden by catchwords such as the economically determined 'substructure' and the religious 'superstructure' of society. Thus nominalism also demonstrated its 'modernity' in furnishing the conceptual apparatus necessary to grasp new developments in the monetary system. But the modernist Biel was no radical innovator in his treatise on money. Indeed, in his desire to see the coin's face value correspond as nearly as possible to the inherent value or precious metal content of the coin, he took a rather conservative view.[19] However, Biel also managed to reconcile a 'modern' doctrine of divine acceptation with a very traditional call for optimal growth in human righteousness and good works.[20] The profile of the Tübingen school's first 'headmaster' comes into focus as we watch Biel draw on canon law in order cautiously to further that development upon which the expansion of early capitalism depended: the shift from currency to credit transactions.

Detaching ownership from the possession or use of money had even more far-reaching consequences, because it snapped the hinge on which the traditional definition of usury swung.[21] Canonists and theologians had concluded long before that a distinction must be made between usury, which the Vulgate expressly forbids (Luke 6.35), and 'profit through participation' in the *commenda* contract. The

[18] Raymond de Roover considers the emphasis on the 'valor extrinsecus' or face value to be a dangerous nominalist development which opened the way for arbitrary intervention in the market economy through price controls and even a sort of sales tax. *La Pensée économique des scolastiques*, p. 62f. What I consider to be de Roover's incorrect assessment of nominalism should not be permitted to obscure the enormous contribution he has made in resisting attempts to portray economic forces as autonomous historical determinants. See *Business, Banking and Economic Thought*, p. 332; cf. p. 17, n. 17.

[19] *Collectorium*, IV, dist. 15 q. 9 dub. 1 L; Werbeck and Hofmann edn, 4, pt. 2, 186, lines 19–27.

[20] In light of Wilhelm Ernst's criticism of my portrayal of Gabriel Biel's soteriology, I would like to note here that fixing the 'face value' of good works, indeed paying any attention to them at all, is for Biel purely an act of God's grace. But one should not conclude that Biel had thereby cleared himself of the charge of Pelagianism (I prefer the term 'Semipelagianism'). For the external 'face value' must be matched by a human performance – of lesser value – that God has pledged to reward. For Ernst's view see *Gott und Mensch am Vorabend der Reformation*, pp. 321, 333f. and 388. For a recent response to Ernst see Janz, 'A Reinterpretation of Gabriel Biel on Nature and Grace'.

[21] See McLaughlin, 'The Teaching of the Canonists on Usury (XII, XIII and XIV Centuries)', esp. 1, pp. 98–111.

latter was a legitimate partnership contract creating a *societas* and involving a risk to the investors. But where money was lent risk-free with the stipulation that the principal be repaid with interest, then, in the traditional view, ownership (*proprietas*) and the use of the capital (*possessio*) had been illicitly separated. As Aquinas so clearly demonstrated on the basis of Roman law, this verdict rested on the assumption that money, like wine or grain but unlike a rentable house, was a consumable commodity exhausted by use.[22] Its inherent value or substance consisted in its utilization. Thus usury was fraud because the same object, the licence to employ the capital, was sold twice; once as principal to be repaid and the second time as the utilization itself, to be compensated with interest payments.

The introduction of money 'backed' by external guarantee and the sale of securities or bonds not only meant a considerable expansion of the monetary economy but also made a redefinition of usury necessary, since money could no longer be considered a consumable commodity.[23] Biel remained extremely cautious in his formulations,[24] careful to buttress his position with support from the canonist tradition, especially by appeals to Angelus de Clavasio († ca. 1495). For Luther, Angelus was to become the embodiment of canonist tyranny and his *Summa* shared the fiery fate of the papal bull of excommunication on 10 December 1520. But Biel was able to comb the various canonist conclusions and prohibitions for a theological framework that cleared the way for a commercially up-to-date verdict on the use and misuse of capital.[25]

Conrad Summenhart had likewise taken up the problem of usury, and during Biel's lifetime attempted to clear the air with a series of

[22] *De malo* q. 13 art. 4c. S. Thomae Aquinatis, *Quaestiones disputatae*, vol. 2, p. 637^{b}. See the lucid account by Herbert Johnston, 'On the Meaning of "Consumed in Use" in the Problem of Usury'.

[23] See Biel, *Collectorium*, IV, dist. 15 q. 9 art. 1 not. 2; Werbeck and Hofmann edn, 4 pt. 2; pp. 176–7.

[24] Noonan is correct to consider Biel the point of departure for a redefinition of the census-contract but his conclusion is too far-reaching: 'The extended theory really removed all matter from the usury prohibition.' *The Scholastic Analysis of Usury*, p. 230.

[25] The path was cleared by means of subtle argumentation: 'If someone desires to avoid all risk to his capital and yet to share in the profit . . ., that is clearly usury . . . But if, in contrast, someone is willing to accept the risk of the possible loss of capital and to guarantee the sum to the investor for an agreed-upon price, it is not usury to pay for such security nor to accept payment for the risk assumed. In similar fashion, if one member of a company personally assumes the risk so that the company is no longer liable for losses; then an investor can share in the profits of the company and in this manner free himself from risk.' *Collectorium*, IV, dist. 15 q. 11 art. 3 dub. 10; Werbeck and Hofmann edn, 4, pt. 2, p. 253.

opinions, even if in a more moderate tone than he had employed for the issue of the tithe. He published the results of his years of teaching activity in 1500, bound with the treatise *De decimis*, under the title, *Septipertitum opus de contractibus*.[26] This two-part volume thus documents the Tübingen school's fusion of the social concerns of both *viae*. Although, as the successor of Heynlin of Stein, Summenhart occupied the chair reserved to the *via antiqua*, his thinking was oriented not toward Aquinas but toward the more nominalistically inclined Scotist branch of the *via antiqua*.[27] Thus Summenhart cast his lot with that same Franciscan who had replaced the *Inceptor Venerabilis* as Biel's mentor in questions of moral theology. An intersection of the *viae* in this region should not surprise us. It is precisely this characteristic of the young Tübingen university that permitted scholastic theology a final creative unfolding at the end of the Middle Ages. Summenhart sought a renewed application of a solution that had previously invariably succumbed to massive opposition. He attempted to narrow the definition of usury by forbidding money-lending at interest (*mutuum*) while legitimizing corporative investments. This approach had previously run aground on the insistence that a genuine partnership must include sharing the risks generated by the venture. A limited-liability partnership was nothing but a holding company set up to conceal usury.[28]

At this juncture Summenhart entered the debate armed with his own arguments. He began by demonstrating that the assumption of risk was no requisite characteristic of a legitimate investment partnership.[29] Normally the person possessing capital must also accept the risks of the financial venture, but he also has ways to insure himself against risk. Risk then cannot be an essential component of a valid contract. The crucial factor is not risk but the intention of the lender or investor. From the outside it is impossible to distinguish a risk-free partnership from usury even when the money-

[26] Hagenau: Heinrich Gran.

[27] It may be seen from his *Commentaria in Summam physice Alberti Magni* that he was concerned to 'nudge' the realist tradition back into line with the aid of Scotus – and he was probably more consistent in this objective than was Carlstadt at approximately the same time in Wittenberg. The later reformer at Strassburg, Wolfgang Capito, edited Summenhart's commentary on the basis of a poor manuscript ('dictamine torto'). Against a background of rising humanism, his judgment on the commentary amounted to high praise: 'Optime lector, habes fundamina vera sophie, qualia non etas pristina contribuit . . .' Fol. s5^{v}. Cf. Kittelson, *Wolfgang Capito. From Humanist to Reformer*, p. 14, n. 17.

[28] *Septipertitum opus*, Tract. VI, q. 97, fol. T6^{rb}.

[29] 'non est contra essentiam societatis, quod ponens pecuniam sit liber a periculo eiusdem, . . .' *Ibid.*

lender's intention is not usurious. Only a knowledgeable reader can determine the lender's intent since that intent determines the wording of the contract. In usury the capital is relinquished to the borrower whereas in a genuine partnership (*fraternitas*), the borrower receives a share in ownership so that both parties to the contract have a stake in the capital.[30]

Since the intention of the lender remains concealed from those not privy to the text of the contract, such a contract should still be considered sinful as long as it arouses offence and induces others to improper imitation. Hidden from the modern reader in this fear of causing public offence is that era's unquestioning assumption of a connection between private ethics and public welfare; a concern not limited to urban communities. Even so, in declaring the corporative capital investment contract to be basically legitimate, Summenhart had leaped the decisive barrier to commercial capitalism erected by traditional financial ethics. In his final statement he argued for removing the proscription of usury from underneath the protective sanction of divine law just as he had undermined the divine law foundation for the tithe obligation. But despite having removed all basic impediments to profitable capital investments, Summenhart urged that such contracts not be concluded – moved by socio-psychological consideration for the weaker brother likely to be scandalized by rapid expansion in this area. In his caution he was true to his programmatic endeavour no longer to view ethical problems from the canonist perspective of permissibility, turning instead to the theological perspective of pastoral care.[31] His concern was to 'do justice to economic reality without falling prey to it'.[32]

One segment of Summenhart's chain of reasoning – the thesis that the investor's pure intent preserves him from the sin of usury in charging interest – met with general approval in the ensuing discussion. A second aspect – his caution against arousing public offence – was also accepted but only to lend impetus to the task of reeducating the public. In a reversal of previous reasoning, the 'scandal' was no longer to be charged to the account of the businessman but to be blamed on the confused conscientiousness of an uninformed society.

Precisely this desire to reeducate moved Johannes Eck to popularize a new definition of usury. As a third member of the 'Tübingen School' he belonged to the modernist way, but, typical of Tübingen, had been trained by both Biel and Summenhart. Eck entered the

30 *Ibid.*, q. 97, fol. T6^{va-b}.
31 See Ott, 'Zur Wirtschaftsethik des Konrad Summenhart', p. 2, n. 4.
32 *Ibid.*, p. 27.

debate for the first time in 1514 with both theoretical and practical arguments in defence of a five per cent investment contract. His theoretical contribution consisted of a new variant of the *contractus trinus*, a three-step procedure designed to escape suspicion of usury. In this approach a partnership is first established by means of a basic agreement. A second contract follows, transforming the original participation into an investment made attractive by a potential but non-guaranteed profit. The third agreement sees the non-guaranteed ten per cent return 'sold' for a smaller but risk-free five per cent profit.[33] Greeted with reserve by Thomists and attacked by Jesuits until 1573,[34] the *contractus trinus* triumphed nonetheless and formed the foundation for ecclesiastical approval of the expanding capitalist financial system.[35]

Eck himself thought that his real contribution fell within the field of practical theology. Summenhart had removed a series of significant theoretical scruples and Eck continued his work by making a sharp distinction between the charging of interest and the sin of usury, reinforcing the money-lender's clear conscience. He mollified fears of scandalizing outsiders by insisting that one must always assume the existence of a healthy desire for a corporative business venture instead of a reprehensible usurious intention on the part of the investor – at least until the opposite could be proved. Furthermore, he insisted that theologians should finally have the courage to put an end to a social hypocrisy that clouded a basically unobjectionable

33 See the detailed treatment by Schneid, 'Dr. Johann Eck und das kirchliche Zinsverbot'.

34 In his *Grosser Sermon vom Wucher* (1520) which was to become part two of *Von Kaufshandlung und Wucher* (1524) (*WA* 15, pp. 293–322; pt. 2, pp. 314–20), Luther asked that the believer should loan money without desiring interest in return: 'dass wir willig und gerne leyhen oder borgen sollen, an allen auffsatz und zins.' *WA* 6, pp. 36–60; here p. 47. Cf. *An den christlichen Adel* (1520), *WA* 6, p. 466. Zwingli enjoined every Christian to meet those interest payments to which they had obligated themselves. Yet he rejected the charging of interest, including a five per cent rate, as usury. *ZW* 3, pp. 387, line 15–392, line 6. For the Thomist position and the decision (Rome, 1573) of the Jesuit congregation to accept the *contractus trinus*, see Nelson, *The Idea of Usury. From Tribal Brotherhood to Universal Otherhood*, p. 101.

35 'The near exemption of the merchant and financier from the stigma of usury and from liability to crippling actions by ecclesiastical and secular courts was a prerequisite to the expansion of Europe along capitalist lines. Modern capitalism could not come of age so long as the agents of church and state were able or especially disposed to require merchants and financiers to disgorge their "usuries" and "ill-gotten gains." Indeed, so long as a traditionalist version of usury and restitution controlled public sympathy and official support, neither secure title to his earnings nor a consistently honorable reputation could accrue to the enterpriser. Without these stimuli, his energies could not truly find release.' Nelson, 'The Usurer and the Merchant Prince. Italian Businessmen and the Ecclesiastical Law of Restitution, 1100–1550', p. 121.

forty-year-old business practice; a social hypocrisy that dumped this artificially created problem on to merchant consciences.[36]

But Eck's contemporaries did not always consider his views to be the product of his pastoral concern. The Nuremberg circle, later to be acclaimed as the *sodalitas Staupitziana*, detected in Eck a tool of the Fugger business empire, and their suspicions were not completely unfounded. Although it cannot be proved that the twenty-four-year-old Eck owed his call to Ingolstadt (1510) to Jacob Fugger, ties to this powerful banking family by way of Conrad Peutinger can be demonstrated, and the expenses of both Eck and his servants on the Bologna trip of 1515 were paid for with Augsburg money.[37] At the same time Eck's background in the 'Tübingen school' indicates that we are dealing with a coincidence of interests that permitted his theories on money to meet with grateful acceptance in business circles. Yet, to his earliest opponents, with their deep mistrust of a scholastically flexible use of the oldest and most authentic sources of antiquity and Christianity, Eck must have appeared as an opportunistic Fugger lackey,[38] an academic entrepreneur to be discredited and checked wherever possible.

Ties to Eck's ecclesiastical and academic superiors gave the anti-Eck coalition some prospect of success. But at the outset Eck controlled the throttle. He began with a disputation on the interest issue held on 11 September 1514 in the Fugger-patronized Augsburg Carmelite monastery. He posted the resulting theses in Ingolstadt, probably toward the middle of October, hoping to stimulate a university disputation.[39] But the humanist-inclined and influenced chancellor of the university and bishop of Eichstätt, Gabriel of Eyb, immediately forbad until further notice any public university disputation on the subject.[40]

The prohibition provided only a brief cease-fire. Both sides devoted all their energies to mobilizing the scholarly world in support of their viewpoints. During the ten months between Eck's first disputation in Augsburg (September 1514)[41] and the 'Italian solution' of the Bologna

36 Johannes Eck, 'Tractatus de contractu quinque de centum' (1515), University Library, Munich, 2° Cod. ms. 125, argumentum 11, fols. 262^v, 263^v.

37 Von Pölnitz referred to the Bolognese disputation as having been 'deviously staged' by Jacob Fugger. 'Jakob Fugger', p. 17. See also his monumental work, *Jakob Fugger*, vol. 1, pp. 316–18.

38 This humanist interpretation reappears in Protestant accounts with no conspicuous adjustments. See, for example, Roth, *Wilibald Pirkheimer, ein Lebensbild aus dem Zeitalter des Humanismus und der Reformation*, p. 31.

39 Von Pölnitz, 'Die Beziehungen des Johannes Eck', p. 691.

40 Schlecht, 'Dr. Johann Ecks Anfänge', p. 22.

41 Described for the first time by Schlecht, 'Dr. Johann Ecks Anfänge', p. 26.

disputation (12 July 1515), coalitions and connections were cemented which previously have been only partially uncovered. And the University of Tübingen's role in the entire affair remained totally unknown to later scholars. Intervention by the bishop of Eichstätt ensured that theological and juridical factors would take their place alongside questions of economic theory, casting a shadow over university professors' academic autonomy and over the significance of the doctoral office.

Even after the debate over both sets of issues began to subside in the wake of the Bologna disputation and then disappeared from view under the crush of other pressing problems, a veritable web of connections, sympathies and antipathies remained. Such liaisons in turn formed the historically productive human context for the first reactions to the collision between Eck and Luther two and a half years later.

Gabriel of Eyb once more set events in motion in 1517 after Eck had presented him with his *Obelisci* or critical marginalia to Luther's theses, accompanied by a renewed request for a disputation. This time the bishop and chancellor gave his consent: the debate took place in Leipzig in 1519. A comparison of this Leipzig Disputation with Eck's attempted Ingolstadt disputation of 1514 yields interesting insights into the manner in which universities evaluated and passed judgment on disputation theses from other higher schools.

One cannot fairly claim that all the humanists closed ranks against Eck and the Augsburg captains of capitalism during these months of 1514–15. The humanists were divided over the issue. Christopher Scheurl's 'sodalitas Augustiniana' soon took up the battle against Peutinger's 'societas Augustana'. Competition between Augsburg and Nuremberg undoubtedly played a role in this controversy, as did personal animosities. A disgruntled Bernhard Adelmann, who had been deprived of the Augsburg bishop's mitre through Fugger machinations, struck back by persuading Willibald Pirckheimer to publish his translation of Plutarch's admonition against borrowing, *De vitando aere alieno*.[42] It is impossible to identify with precision the pressures that moved Bishop Gabriel of Eyb to forbid Eck's Ingolstadt disputation. Though he may simply have voiced his own conviction

[42] *Plutarch's Moralia*, vol. 10, translated by Harold N. Fowler in the Loeb Classical Library, pp. 315–39. Pirckheimer's translation appeared as 'Über den Wucher den man meiden soll' from the Peypus press in Nuremberg (1515). The title page is reproduced in Eckert, *Willibald Pirckheimer*, p. 229. Cf. Thurnhofer, *Bernhard Adelmann von Adelmannsfelden, Humanist und Luthers Freund (1457–1523)*, p. 53.

in the matter, major influence on the part of Adelmann[43] also seems likely. What remains beyond doubt is that the bishop asked Christopher Scheurl, the central figure in the Nuremberg circle,[44] to gather scholars' opinions on the issue in late autumn of 1514.[45]

Although Scheurl had been asked 'to consult with experts concerning the further course of action', he seemed more intent on uniting his portion of the scholarly world against Eck. For the Nuremburg humanist was convinced that the public welfare was at stake and that Eck's impudence must be checked if scandal was to be avoided.[46] Furthermore, Scheurl had no scruples about announcing that Eck had sold himself to the Augsburg capitalists. There could have been little doubt in the minds of his correspondents as to the sort of conclusions expected in the 'objective' written opinions requested by Scheurl.

Gabriel of Eyb had chosen well in entrusting Scheurl with organizing the resistance against Eck and the Augsburg financial interests. Not only was Scheurl a leading figure in Nuremberg political and art circles as well as being active in ecclesiastical reform efforts, but he also maintained close contact with representatives of the scholarly world outside his city of birth: for he held a doctorate from Bologna in both jurisprudences and was the ex-rector of the fledgling university at Wittenberg.[47] But Eck also exploited the months following his abortive disputation in October 1514 to recruit allies in his cause. Though the dossier of documents and letters from those months is far from complete, even the extant portion indicates that Jacob Fugger and his ally Eck gained the upper hand in the diplomatic battle of wits with Scheurl.

How Eck represented his cause in Rome, Paris and Bologna has been recounted in previous studies.[48] In March 1515 he expressed his willingness to have his theses judged by the German universities in Cologne, Heidelberg, Freiburg, Tübingen, Mainz and Ingolstadt.[49] To

[43] Cf. *Ibid.*, Beilage VII h, p. 144. This letter also contains the first mention, so far as I can determine, of Eck's 'modestia' to which Luther referred with frequent sarcasm.

[44] It is not known whether the label *Sodalitas Staupitziana* was used prior to this point. Ties between Staupitz and Scheurl can be dated at least to Staupitz's presence at Scheurl's graduation ceremonies at Bologna on 23 December 1506. See Wilhelm Graf, *Doktor Christoph Scheurl von Nürnberg*, p. 33.

[45] Scheurl sent Eck's theses to Jodocus Trutvetter on 19 October 1514 and mentioned that the disputation had been forbidden. He then continued with other news, choosing not to comment further on the disputation attempt. *Scheurl's Briefbuch*, 1, p. 134.

[46] *Scheurl's Briefbuch*, 1, pp. 135–7.

[47] See Grossmann, *Humanism in Wittenberg 1485–1517*, pp. 62–5.

[48] Schneid, 'Dr. Johann Eck und das kirchliche Zinsverbot', pp. 321ff., 473ff.; Schlecht, 'Dr. Johann Ecks Anfänge', pp. 25ff.

[49] Von Pölnitz, 'Die Beziehungen des Johannes Eck', p. 694.

date, only Mainz has been shown actually to have taken up Eck's theses, doing so under pressure from Archbishop Albrecht of Mainz.[50] But by a fortunate accident a group of documents relating to the interest controversy of 1514–15[51] escaped the great fire of 1534 which destroyed nearly all the records of the Tübingen university.[52] This file permits the more precise reconstruction of the controversy as it affected the Tübingen theological faculty and sheds light on the gradual shifting of the centre of controversy from the economic to the theological sphere. A memorandum from the ducal chancellor, Dr Gregory Lamparter,[53] dated the Tuesday following Easter in 1514, clearly demonstrates that Tübingen and not Mainz was the first university asked to pass judgment on Eck's theses.[54] An additional and no longer extant document which, on the basis of a Tübingen archivist's comment,[55] had formerly been considered an opinion from the University of Ingolstadt, proves to have been a personal statement sent by Eck to the Tübingen theologians prior to Easter 1514.[56]

Eck had dealt with the charging of interest from a Scotist perspective early in 1514 when he discussed *distinctio* 15 of the fourth book of his lecture on the Sentences. A revised and recopied text of the lecture was completed by 25 May 1514.[57] The missing position paper

50 Chilian Leib, *Historiarum sui temporis ab anno MDII ad annum MDXLVIIII annales* III (1513–1521), p. 631. Leib was a good friend of Pirckheimer and an early (1503) admirer of Staupitz, yet recorded with obvious disapproval: 'gloriatus est, sese Lutherum instituisse, id est, tale nutrivisse monstrum'. *Ibid.*, p. 663. Leib was present at the meeting of the Nuremberg *sodalitas* when the news of Luther's entry into Worms arrived in April 1521. When his host, Hieronymus Ebner (to whom Staupitz had dedicated his treatise on predestination in 1517), asked the counsel of all present regarding the future course of action, Pirckheimer responded to Leib's plea for a cautiously paced conservative reform with a call for radical measures: 'Nain, die Unordnung, so unter uns seind, die werden mit keiner Ordnung, sondern mit Unordnung müssen gebessert werden.' *Ibid.*, p. 662. In 1520 Pirckheimer came to be suspected, with good cause, of having written a slashing satire on Eck, 'The Corner Shaved Down' (*Eccius Dedolatus*. Autore Joanne Francisco Cottalambergio, Poeta laureato. Acta decimo Calendas Martii Anno 1520 in Occipitio Germaniae). Eck responded by having Pirckheimer placed on the papal bull threatening excommunication (15 June 1520) together with Bernhard Adelmann and Lazarus Spengler – all of whom opposed Eck in the controversy over interest in 1514–15!

51 *Werden und Wertung der Reformation*, Appendix v.

52 Haller, 1, pp. 331f. Cf. 2, appendix 10, pp. 186–9.

53 Gregory Lamparter was one of the first Tübingen *Baccalaurei* (October 1477) and became a *Magister artium* on 2 January 1479. He was twice chosen rector of the university, in 1487 as a licentiate and 1493 as a doctor of both laws. See Haller, 1, pp. 142f.

54 *Werden und Wertung der Reformation*, Appendix v, 4.

55 'Dominus Cancellarius Lampard petit supscriptionem consilii, quod Ingolstadtenses socero suo Jacob Augustano in materia contractus impertiti sunt.' *Ibid.*

56 'cuius consilium vos vidistis.' *Ibid.*

57 Eck summarized the most important conclusions, for his listeners' convenience, in a

which Eck sent to Tübingen may well have been his first pronouncement on the issue to reach university circles beyond Ingolstadt. It was accompanied by a letter from Lamparter, who attempted, in a mixture of polite reserve and undisguised pressure, to persuade the Tübingen theologians to support Eck's position. Lamparter made no effort to conceal the fact that Jacob Fugger's interest was at stake and that Fugger had approached Eck for a written opinion.

The Lamparter letter also yields a hitherto unknown piece of evidence that sheds light on several obscure aspects of the troubled reign of Duke Ulrich. For Lamparter described Fugger as 'socer meus' – 'my father-in-law'. The best authority on the Fugger archival materials, Baron Götz von Pölnitz, has recounted Jacob Fugger's patronage of Lamparter and mentioned the rumours of familial ties, but he could find support in the documentary record only for the statement that Lamparter was thought by contemporaries to be a relative and confidant of Fugger,[58] or perhaps his 'in-law'.[59]

Jacob Fugger's financial support for Lamparter was indeed of extraordinary dimensions. The Augsburg financier paid Lamparter's imperial pension 'in five installments totalling 8,000 fl.' in June 1518.[60] In 1521 he paid a princely ransom to release Lamparter, who had been taken hostage in the Absberg–Oettingen feud,[61] and as late as 1524 he interceded for him in Nuremberg.[62] So we can imagine Duke Ulrich's acute disappointment, financially and otherwise, when his attempt to capture Lamparter in Tübingen failed (1516). In the Blaubeuren Treaty of 1516, which the emperor had forcibly extorted from the duke, Ulrich's governing powers had been limited to a degree intolerable for his self-esteem. Viewed in this light, a hostage Lamparter would have been an excellent tool in Ulrich's hand to pressure the emperor, by way of Fugger, to stifle the imperial sentiment within Württemberg, defusing the threat of Ulrich's deposition as duke.

In his Tübingen memorandum Lamparter documented his relationship with Fugger and bequeathed a mystery to subsequent generations. The university chancellery reproduced the notation: 'Fugger, Lamparter's father-in-law'. We know that Jacob Fugger's first and only marriage, with Sybille Artzt, was childless. We can find

treatise that is still unpublished and to which his brother Simon Thaddaeus Eck later referred as the *Tractatus de contractibus usurariis*. Von Pölnitz, 'Die Beziehungen des Johannes Eck', p. 689, n. 18.

58 Von Pölnitz, *Jakob Fugger*, 2, pp. 471 and 480.

59 *Ibid.*, p. 399.

60 *Ibid.*, p. 392.

61 *Ibid.*, p. 480.

62 *Ibid.*, p. 506.

no other solution than to assume that Lamparter's mother-in-law, Mechthilt Belz, who later married the duke's private physician and professor of medicine at Tübingen, Johannes Widmann,[63] was once the mistress of Jacob Fugger. And thus one of the children of Johannes Widmann and Mechthilt Belz was actually the illegitimate offspring of Jacob Fugger, namely, Mechthilt who later married the ducal chancellor, Lamparter.[64] The sudden rise in Lamparter family fortunes, their ties to the imperial court, and Gregory Lamparter's role in the deposition of Duke Ulrich all become more understandable if we assume that Jacob Fugger obviously provided well for his daughter and in the process furthered the ascent of the renowned Widmann–Lamparter family.[65]

But Lamparter's authority as chancellor of Württemberg and his personal ties to the Fuggers were not enough to persuade the university to deliver the urgently desired verdict in favour of Eck's Augsburg patron. We cannot be sure whether Eck's position seemed to the Tübingen theologians to depart too far from Summenhart's cautious course in the *Septipertitum opus de contractibus*[66] which, unlike the *Tractatus de decimis*, tried to navigate around any cause for public scandal. They may also have wished to await the completion by their rector, Jacob Lemp, of a treatise on the same subject, a work known to us only through Lamparter's passing reference.[67] At any rate, Eck did not refer to any previous Tübingen opinion in his letter of 7 February 1515, which is also preserved in the university archives.[68] We should probably interpret Eck's plea for an immediate response as an indication of silence on Tübingen's part up to this point; a silence especially inopportune for Eck since he must have felt increasingly pressured by the lessened space in which to mobilize his forces.[69] Scheurl's similar efforts had certainly not escaped Eck's attention.

63 Haller, 1, pp. 134f.

64 Reproductions of two letters of Mechthilt Widmann in Haller, 1, facing p. 137.

65 Hansmartin Decker-Hauff is pursuing the genealogical consequences of this conclusion. Without his enthusiastic interest and especially without his genealogical knowledge, I would have been unable to ascertain the full significance of Lamparter's comment.

66 Eck recalled Summenhart in his *Tractatus de contractibus usurariis* (1514) with gratitude. *CCath* 2, p. 42, n. 6. The *Tractatus de contractibus* is here incorrectly dated in the year 1515.

67 Lamparter wrote that Lemp was working on a treatise on usury. See *Werden und Wertung der Reformation*, Appendix v, 4. On Lemp see Haller, 2, p. 71. After receiving his M.A., Eck attended lectures in the theological faculty in Tübingen, hearing in addition to Steinbach, Scriptoris, Summenhart and Jacob Lemp. See Wiedemann, *Dr. Johann Eck, Professor der Theologie an der Universität Ingolstadt*, p. 8.

68 *Werden und Wertung der Reformation*, Appendix v, 1.

69 The Bavarian chancellor, Leonhard von Eck, and councillors Jörg von Au and

Eck's letter attempted, in his 'modest' way, to exert pressure on the Tübingen faculty. In its address and closing greeting he explicitly reminded his Tübingen colleagues that he had once studied under them,[70] stressing a lasting bond between them and hoping to draw them into a sense of obligation to himself. He offered to send the second, negative portion of his major treatise on interest, *De contractu quinque de centum*, as soon as the corrected copy was finished; a treatise in which he claimed to have demonstrated that charging interest was nowhere prohibited.[71] The corrected copy was indeed in his hands scarcely one month later. But he also suggested that the Tübingen professors could form their opinion without delay on the basis of the 'Schema' that they already possessed; probably once more thanks to Lamparter's mediation. They could also consult the first and affirmative portion of *De contractu* already in their hands, a treatise in which Eck had argued for the propriety of a five per cent interest charge.[72]

Eck voiced his confidence that the response from Tübingen would both serve the glory of God and the salvation of men and magnify the renown of the university. But he urged them to hurry with their reply since he had sent the same materials to his former professors at Cologne. A committee had already been formed to consider the case and the theological faculty there had pledged full support. His further remarks give us some idea of the intensity of efforts by Eck and probably by Fugger, since the Tübingen faculty had first dealt with his interest issue soon after Easter in 1514.

In issuing his disputation prohibition the following autumn, Bishop Gabriel of Eyb had appealed to the authority of an opinion from the theological faculty of the university at Mainz. This evaluation had been requested, if not by Jacob Fugger himself, then, according to Chilian Leib, by Cardinal Albrecht, the archbishop of

Anselm Göttinger were active in Eck's cause. Von Pölnitz, 'Die Beziehungen des Johann Eck', p. 694.

70 *Werden und Wertung der Reformation*, Appendix v, 1.

71 Thus the reference to the 'argumenta in partem negativam'. See *ibid*. The first 'century' is found in the University Library, Munich, 2° Cod. ms. 125, fols. 241–65 and the complete work *ibid.*, fols. 95–239. Schneid, 'Dr. Johann Eck und das kirchliche Zinsverbot', pp. 321ff., 473ff.

72 'Schema (sckemma) nostrum' probably referred to the already posted disputation theses that were normally termed 'scheda'. 'Faetura' likely had reference to the *Tractatus de contractibus usurariis*, the summary of the lectures on Duns Scotus finished on 25 May 1514 with its flattering comments on Summenhart – flattering at least to Tübingen readers. (See n. 66.) The 'pars affirmativa' is the first 'century' of the later *Contractus quinque de centum*.

Mainz, who was heavily in debt to Fugger.[73] But Eck now informed the Tübingen theologians that Bishop Gabriel and his advisor (Adelmann!) had misunderstood the Mainz statement and that Eck found it necessary to take up direct contact with that university. In a craftily weighed response composed with amazing alacrity his correspondents then established that Eck's position in no way ran counter to divine or human law, giving their approval for a disputation. A copy of this response was available to the Tübingen theologians from Eck's uncle, Martin Maier at Rottenburg, upstream from Tübingen.

But Eck was much less pleased at the Mainz recommendation that the type of contract approved of in his treatise be avoided. The Mainz opinion evaded the essential problem: were entrepreneurs to be considered usurers deserving of excommunication if they persisted in concluding investment contracts according to the now standard procedure? The controversy over investment interest had long ceased to be a matter for mere academic debate and now constituted one of the most pressing problems in Augsburg business practice. The theologians in Mainz had finally met their obligation to take a stand on the issue, and Eck expected his Tübingen colleagues to do the same.[74]

The Mainz response of January 1515 to Eck's second request was then transmitted to Tübingen, even if in a poor copy.[75] It consisted of two letters; one a more formal memorandum addressed to the theological faculty at Ingolstadt and the other a detailed letter to Eck that dealt in careful sequence with three of Eck's questions. In the formal statement the Ingolstadt theologians were assured that Mainz had no fundamental reservations against a five per cent interest rate fixed in the manner advocated by Eck and that any attempt to hinder a disputation on the subject would meet with disapproval.[76] The readers were referred to the personal letter to Eck for a discussion of the chief theological aspects of the issue.

In examining that letter,[77] we are immediately impressed by the speed with which the Mainz theologians responded to Eck's treatise on interest. Within a few days, a work that Eck, in his proverbial

[73] We find in the minutes of the Mainz cathedral chapter for 26 March 1515 a reference to the level of indebtedness reached by Albrecht. In order to cover a debt, he found himself forced to raise new funds and requested a loan of 4,000 fl. from the chapter, 'da die Messe und die Zahlung an Fugger bevorstehe'. *Die Protokolle des Mainzer Domkapitels*, ed. Herrmann, vol. 3, p. 29.

[74] Lamparter regarded the actual controversy as more a problem of conscience than of economic theory. *Werden und Wertung der Reformation*, Appendix v, 4.

[75] 'Copiam . . . satis mendosam.' *Ibid.*, v, 1.

[76] *Ibid.*, v, 2.

[77] *Ibid.*, v, 3.

modesty, had called a *faetura* or premature offspring, had been circulated, read and evaluated. But a closer look renders this expeditious treatment somewhat less surprising. Generally treated with polite respect, Eck's arguments never posed a threat to the position defended in Mainz, where theory and practice, in this case 'scholastic theology' and 'official church doctrine', remained basically separate. Like Summenhart, the theologians at Mainz by no means rejected the theoretical legitimacy of investment interest. They merely argued that such a practice unnecessarily confused the consciences of the faithful. So long as Holy Mother Church failed to deliver a dogmatic decision in the matter, they judged it better to abstain from collecting interest.

In false modesty, the Mainz theological faculty sidestepped its duty to assist in the clarification of a vital contemporary issue and declined to venture from behind the moat of dogmatic definitions. Thus, refusal in the face of future challenges would reduce the theological faculties to jousting fields for theoreticians. The Mainz opinion concluded with the comment that 'some of us are indeed able to hold and defend this [Eck's] position *scholastice*';[78] an attempt at appeasement that can only underscore the Mainz position astride the fence of financial ethics. But they were certainly not alone in dodging the issue. No response from Tübingen is known nor did the University of Paris reply.[79] Even Pope Leo X, wooed by both Jacob Fugger and Eck,[80] refused comment on this delicate issue, and the reform council meeting in the Lateran since 1512 ended its laborious discussion of the issue of usury in April 1515 without reaching any clear conclusions.[81]

Fifty more years of controversy and indecision passed before the church finally assented to the practice of charging interest.[82] But the consciences of the faithful – set on edge by the decrees of the Fourth Lateran Council (1215) and the Council of Lyon (1274) – had been left in the lurch so long that the world of *haute finance* had long since developed its own ethics. It was the business sector which, long

78 'Sunt enim et apud nos qui eam scholastice et tenere et defensare possent.' *Ibid.*

79 See von Pölnitz, 'Die Beziehungen des Johannes Eck', p. 700.

80 Schlecht, 'Dr. Johann Ecks Anfänge', p. 29.

81 See the bull, 'Inter multiplices' of the tenth session of 4 May 1515. Denzinger and Schönmetzer, eds., *Enchiridion Symbolorum*, nos. 1442–4 (739). Cf. Bauer, 'Diskussionen um die Zins- und Wucherfrage auf dem Konstanzer Konzil'.

82 See Noonan, *The Scholastic Analysis of Usury*, pp. 220f. In the Reformed, 'urban' camp, the reorientation should probably be located chronologically somewhere between Zwingli and Bullinger. See the convincing judgment by J. Wayne Baker, 'Zwingli grudgingly allowed *Zins*; Bullinger sanctified the practice of taking the honorable *Zins* or *Wucher*.' 'Heinrich Bullinger and the Idea of Usury', p. 66.

before the peasants and the proletariat, was the first social stratum to be left to its own devices in ethical questions.[83] However we assess Eck's own motives, he had good reason to be disappointed by what the Mainz theologians, in unconscious irony, termed a 'clear statement'.

We should not overlook a further aspect of significance for the *Causa Lutheri*. From its academic origins in the 'first Tübingen school', the debate expanded as a result of Eck's investment controversy to become an issue of intense public interest and in its final phase underwent an important change in emphasis. Eck's disputation was originally a question of economic theory that directed attention to problems of pastoral theology, but its prohibition by the bishop of Eichstätt had great future import. At stake was the episcopal right to interfere with a university disputation: Can the *Ordinarius loci* forbid a disputation by a properly installed and sworn *doctor* at an official, papally approved university?[84]

Eck linked the above question with the issue of the universities' relationship to each other: should one university proclaim itself judge over another and, indeed, over its proposed disputations? The professors at Mainz eventually denied that they had ever intended to hinder an Ingolstadt disputation in any way. And they proceeded to defend the right of any *doctor* to voice his opinion at any time in a university disputation, especially where theological ethics were under discussion and so long as he remained within the bounds of the Catholic faith.

In connection with Eck's debate with the Mainz theologians and their concluding opinion we encounter another statement that gives the now rediscovered letter containing it a significance extending far beyond the issues current at its composition. Bishop Gabriel and Christopher Scheurl had argued that academic disputations become intolerable for church and society when they threaten to confuse the faithful – in this case, the businessmen.[85] Eck was now assured that disputations cause no public offence (*scandalum*); rather they help to eliminate error and put an end to the silly chatter of uneducated preachers. It is the duty and obligation of a *doctor* of holy scripture to accompany critically the proclamation and preaching of the church. Three years later *Doctor* Martin Luther directed this same argument

[83] F. X. Funk found it impossible 'to credit the Reformation with any sort of decisive significance in the interest issue. . . .' *Zins und Wucher. Eine Moraltheologische Abhandlung*, p. 104.

[84] *Werden und Wertung der Reformation*, Appendix v, 3.

[85] Cf. *Scheurl's Briefbuch*, 1, pp. 135f.

against Archbishop Albrecht and Eck himself in defence of his call for a disputation on the indulgence issue.

The theological faculty at Mainz had also distinguished between pragmatic evaluation of the situation and a statement of principle in response to Eck's potentially inflammatory question regarding the extent of episcopal authority. As far as the prohibition of the Ingolstadt disputation was concerned, they thought it essential to determine whether Gabriel of Eyb had acted as bishop or as university chancellor. As chancellor he could legitimately forbid an academic disputation but as bishop he could not since the biretta of a *doctor* at a university founded with papal authority outranked a bishop's mitre.

The Tübingen documents make it clear that the significance of the doctoral office and the privileges and powers associated with it had become a matter for serious debate three years before Luther posted his Wittenberg theses. Eck insisted that in matters of theological ethics, the doctor of theology – and not only the specialists in canon law, Summenhart would have added immediately – has a right to announce, present and defend his opinion publicly and unimpeded. But in situations where the church has already distinguished Catholic truth from heresy, this privilege is suspended. It is in this light that the anti-Hussite oath in the statutes of the new German universities must be viewed.[86]

Nearly three years to the day after Eck posted his interest theses in Ingolstadt,[87] Luther's indulgence theses were made public in Wittenberg in the same traditional manner. The Wittenberg disputation, like the Ingolstadt, never took place. When Luther forwarded his theses to his ecclesiastical superiors in Germany, Archbishop Albrecht and his bishop, Hieronymus Schulz (Brandenburg) he was not seeking their approval but – to apply the theory of his future opponent Eck – merely informing them of his plans. The announcement and realization of a disputation on indulgences could not be affected by the reaction of the bishop, or in Luther's case, of the archbishop.[88] With

[86] For Tübingen see Roth, *Urkunden*, p. 258. In Paris an additional oath was made mandatory on 3 March 1497. The Sorbonne decided to accept no masters who were unwilling to swear an oath affirming the immaculate conception. Defections to the (Dominican) opponents of this doctrine were to be punished with immediate dismissal. Du Plessis d'Argentré, *Collectio judiciorum*, vol. 1, pt. 2, pp. 333f. See also Feret, *La Faculté de Théologie de Paris et ses docteurs les plus célèbres, Moyen-âge*, vol. 4, pp. 136ff.

[87] 'Reverendissimus Eystetensis interposito mandato disputari vetuit.' Chilian Leib in *Beyträge zur Geschichte und Literatur 7*, p. 631. Cf. *Scheurls Briefbuch*, 1, p. 134.

[88] The Tübingen documents make it possible to evaluate the arguments brought forth in the discussion between Hans Volz and Erwin Iserloh about the posting of the 95 Theses of 1517. Iserloh argues that Volz has separated too widely two key aspects; (a)

the academic clarification through disputation and (b) Luther's effort via ecclesiastical channels 'inviting' Archbishop Albrecht to withdraw immediately his *Instructio summaria*. Iserloh, *Luther zwischen Reform und Reformation. Der Thesenanschlag fand nicht statt*, p. 47; translated by Jared Wicks, *The Theses Were Not Posted: Luther Between Reform and Reformation*, p. 54. Volz, 'Erzbischof Albrecht von Mainz und Martin Luthers 95 Thesen', p. 214. But the following points are to be considered:

(1) Luther appended his 'disputationes' as a postscript intended to inform the archbishop about the state of the scholarly discussion: *WABr* 1, p. 112, lines 66–8. In the main section of the letter (*ibid.*, p. 112, lines 55ff.), Luther's concern was to convince the archbishop to intervene in his function as an officer of the church to regulate the abuses. Thus we are indeed dealing with 'two paths . . ., that Luther pursued independently of each other'. Volz, 'Erzbischof Albrecht', p. 214.

(2) In his letter to Elector Frederick on 21 November 1518 Luther insisted expressly – the unusually formal phrase, 'manu propria', as well as the 'ista ego feci', lends a notarial character to the letter (*WABr* 1, p. 246, line 419; p. 245, line 366) – that he had not prepared the attack on indulgences on behalf of someone else and then published it (*ederem*) at a later point. *Ibid.*, p. 245, lines 361–6.

(3) Luther stressed what he considered a decisive point: that not even his closest friends were aware of the matter. 'cum huius disputationis nullus etiam amicorum fuerit conscius'. *WABr* 1, p. 245, lines 358f. Only Archbishop Albrecht and his own *ordinarius loci* were informed by private letter prior to the publication ('antequam disputationem ederem'; *WABr* 1, p. 245, line 362). As early as the beginning of November Luther hesitated to permit his theses (*positiones nostras*) to be sent to Spalatin at that time – i.e. on 31 October – for these same reasons. *WABr* 1, p. 118, lines 9ff. Luther must have been concerned above all that this eminently theological matter should not appear as a political move on the part of Frederick against Archbishop Albrecht. See *WABr* 1, p. 146, lines 80–3 (to Spalatin, 15 February 1518).

(4) In response to critics of Iserloh we must keep in mind that Luther was not speaking over Frederick's head to a wider audience nor manoeuvring tactically in his letter to the elector. Paying attention to the precise sequence of events will help to avoid a misinterpretation, i.e. will prevent discounting the explosive political dimension of this 'causa stantis et cadentis ecclesiae'.

(5) But in response to Iserloh, we must point out two weak links in his argumentation. Firstly, at one point he translates 'disputatio' as 'Disputationsabsicht'. But on 31 October 1517 Luther did not claim that his closest friends knew nothing of his 'intended disputation'; rather he insisted that none of them had prior knowledge (were not *conscius*) of the theses – variously termed *positiones, propositiones, disputationes* or *disputatio*. Luther wrote the theses independently, without conferring with, for example, Spalatin, his friend and link with the elector. This does not at all preclude the posting of the theses on the doors of the Wittenberg castle church, which indeed was the normal internal academic procedure. It establishes merely the purity of his own theological motivation. Secondly, it appears to me that Iserloh has not taken account of Luther's concern to make clear to the archbishop that the *Instructio* erroneously assumed the validity of points of doctrine that *had been* called into question in the academic world, including Wittenberg. Luther's argumentation would have lost its penetrating force and urgency if he had left the impression that his theses were merely intended for private circulation. He could only expect to be effective if he could send the archbishop 'disputationes' that evidenced not merely a private opinion but reported the state of the academic debate. Hence his signature: 'Doctor S. Theologie vocatus'. As a doctor of theology conscious of his vocation, Luther surprisingly proves to be in basic agreement with Eck's opinion of two years previously with regard to the privileges and obligations of the doctoral office!

(6) It was Iserloh's declared intention to demonstrate the credibility of Luther, contradicated by Melanchthon's later report about the posting of the 95 Theses. We are now able to regard Iserloh's intention as accomplished and still take Melanch-

good justification Luther could defend his right to discuss freely relevant theological questions within a papally approved university, and to do so *scholastice*, which in those months still meant a dogmatically non-binding discussion as far as Luther was concerned.[89] At the request of Bishop Gabriel of Eyb, Eck compiled a set of notes on Luther's theses, the *Obelisci*, which followed the channels established in the dispute over investment interest to reach Archbishop Albrecht and then, via Adelmann, gained Luther's attention. In this initial response to Luther, Eck labelled the Wittenberg professor 'a disseminator of the Bohemian virus',[90] laying his finger on the crucial passage of the academic oath. In tainting Luther with the charge of heresy, Eck hoped to deprive him of the immunity of his office and the forensic freedom offered by the academic disputation.

And thus a curious reversal of roles ensued when Eck took up the cry of his former opponents and voiced his fear that Luther's critique of the indulgence dealers would scandalize the public. For his part, Luther adopted Eck's defence that no offence could result from exercising his right as a doctor of theology, especially since his theses were not intended for publication in German but restricted by their language to educated circles. If they managed to scandalize the pseudo-academic, obscurantist inhabitants of the province of the lettered, then they had accomplished their purpose; for Eck himself had argued that such disputations help to avoid scandal and elimin-

thon's account as credible. Any other interpretation would contradict the academic conventions of the day and significantly dilute the force of Luther's urgent warning to the archbishop.

(7) Not only Luther himself but the university asserts – in an official document – that the disputation was carried through in Wittenberg. *D. Martini Lutheri Opera Latina, var. arg.*, II, p. 426.

In view of these seven considerations we must conclude that the 95 Theses were both posted and debated.

[89] *WA* 1, p. 528, lines 27–31; the dedicatory epistle for the *Resolutiones disputationum* addressed to Pope Leo X, May 1518. So far as is known to me, no one has taken account of the fact that Luther had good reason to expect sympathy in Paris not only for his ecclesiology but also for his theses on indulgences. Only one year prior to the Leipzig Disputation, on 6 May 1518, the Sorbonne criticized and corrected, from the perspective of the *via moderna*, the theory that a direct link existed between the coin 'that rings in the coffer' and the liberation of the soul from purgatory. Du Plessis d'Argentré, *Collectio Judiciorum*, vol. 1, pt. 2, pp. 355f. This decision may permit us to assume a phase in the controversy during which the Sorbonne treated the Luther affair as an attack by an Augustinian on the Dominicans. Such was the view of Erasmus at about the same time and he was likewise sympathetic to the opponents of the Dominicans. See *Opus Epistolarum*, ed. Allen, 3, pp. 408–10 (no. 892); 17 October 1518.

[90] 'quod nihil aliud est quam Bohemicum virus effundere.' Eck, *Obeliscus* 18; *WA* 1, p. 302, lines 15f.

ate error.[91] When Eck succeeded in eliciting Luther's approval of certain Hussite tenets at the Leipzig Disputation of 1519, he could be assured that his move would gain the immediate attention of academics. And indeed, two theological faculties soon declared themselves willing to condemn Luther, with Eck's *Alma Mater*, Cologne, leading the charge just as it had been the first to promise Eck full support in the controversy over interest.[92]

In the summer of 1515, under the patronage of Augsburg capitalist interests,[93] Eck finally achieved in Bologna what had been denied him in Ingolstadt. His choice of Bologna was not arbitrary since the Italians could only be expected to scratch their heads over German passions aroused by an issue that had long since ceased to trouble Italian consciences.

But the Bologna disputation ended the German academic debate over interest on capital investments, and Eck had mended his Eichstätt episcopal fences before Luther came into public view.[94] The flattering inclusion of Bishop Gabriel on a list of the fifty most important German *eruditi* which Eck published in 1515 had certainly not missed its mark: the episcopal eye.[95] The leaders of the Nuremberg opposition likewise reconciled their differences with Eck and Fugger, and Scheurl even received Eck into the circle of his correspondents and friends.[96] But the Nuremberg–Wittenberg, anti-Fugger/Eck axis of 1514–15 remobilized rapidly – in Luther's opinion, too

91 Eck's twenty-sixth *Obeliscus* directed against Luther's sixty-seventh thesis. *WA* 1, p. 311, lines 1–25.

92 *Werden und Wertung der Reformation*, Appendix v, 1.

93 Von Pölnitz, 'Die Beziehungen des Johannes Eck', p. 697.

94 In his report to Gabriel of Eyb on his Vienna disputation (18–19 August 1516) Eck stressed that the disputation was designed 'exercitii gratia paradoxa hec disputasse', hence was only an 'exercitium scholasticum'. He added, 'Veneror enim in te eum locum, quem tenes in ecclesia Dei magnum utique et praepollentem . . .' Johannes Eck, *Disputatio Viennae Pannoniae habita* (1517), *CCath* 6, p. 16, lines 23–4, p. 21, lines 32–4.

95 In a volume of collected writings that has escaped previous notice, *Orationes tres non inelegantes*, Eck published an address delivered in Ingolstadt in mid-October 1515, a speech that is also interesting because it offers Eck's selection of the leading men of letters of his age, including Gabriel of Eyb, 'omnino in hoc albo connumerandus'. *Ibid.*, fol. B4^{r}. Cf. Eck's words one year later, 24 October 1516, in *CCath* 6, pp. 11f. The list apparently also represents Eck's attempt to plug gaps in an earlier speech. On that occasion he had omitted Gabriel of Eyb and honoured higher authorities, specifically Cardinal Matthaeus Lang ('meus olim Tibingae . . . condiscipulus') and the archbishop of Mainz, Albrecht of Brandenburg, whom Eck honoured with the epithet: 'Magno omnium assensu et favore creatus est.' *Orationes*, fols. B 1^{r}; B 3^{r}.

96 Scheurl reported to Trutvetter on 13 March 1516 that he had patched up his relationship with Eck. He set about attempting to kindle a similar friendship between Eck and Trutvetter, just as he was to do a short time later with Luther. *Scheurl's Briefbuch*, 1, p. 153.

rapidly[97] – when the theses on indulgences appeared in Nuremberg in 1517.

Yet the conflict with Luther may have opened with Eck enjoying a head start traceable to the 1514–15 controversy. Not only did he face Luther as an experienced disputant, but he also had at his disposal a mass of connections and academic contacts in Germany as well as abroad.[98] A Swabian by choice and a Tübingen alumnus, Eck had outgrown the provincial limitations of his former *Alma Mater* and acquired such a national and international reputation that Luther could scarcely have found a more powerful opponent north of the Alps. Eck's original advantage did not dwindle[99] until the Zürich Reformation transformed the disputation system, by transferring the office of debate judge from academic or ecclesiastical authorities to city magistrates under the guidance of holy scripture.[100] His subsequent role in the Counter-Reformation rested on the authority of the Hapsburgs and the ecclesiastical hierarchy instead of the authority of the office of *doctor* of sacred theology he had once defended so fervently.

We must abandon our look into Eck's future and return to his Swabian *Alma Mater*, especially to the theological faculty that had accomplished so much in arbitrating the strife of the *viae* and linking scholarly inquiry with piety. Theologians at Tübingen chose a spectator's role. Having delivered the theoretical basis for the renewed attempt to legitimize certain forms of moneylending, the Tübingen theological faculty then lapsed into a state of indecision which neither the controversy surrounding Reuchlin nor the tempest aroused by Luther was able to dispel. Nicholas Baselius hoped to convince the readers of his supplement to Vergenhans' *Chronicle* that the university at Tübingen had forged a golden chain linking Gabriel Biel to Wendelin Steinbach and Conrad Summenhart, and then to Johannes Eck,[101] and had in fact built a bridge from the middle ages to the modern era. Although Baselius' image enjoyed understandable popularity with previous historians of the university, we can only conclude that Tübingen first emerged from indecision after the Reformation arrived. Only then could the great tradition of the 'first

97 *WABr* 1, p. 152, lines 6–20; Luther to Scheurl, 5 March 1518.

98 *CCath* 6, p. 3, lines 4–10.

99 Eck never ceased to be a significant threat to the Reformation. On the contrary, even outside Wittenberg circles he earned a reputation among the Swiss reformers as a champion of the 'old faith' alongside Fabri – a reputation confirmed at the Baden Disputation.

100 See below, pp. 187ff.

101 *Werden und Wertung der Reformation*, Appendix II.

Tübingen school' be resumed gradually under the banner of the 'new faith'.

In applying the label *moderna* to the various aspects of Tübingen's intellectual life, we employed the term to mean nothing more than 'new' in the context of that era. Baselius was not completely mistaken to single out ideas and individuals in Tübingen's intellectual history that were of more than local importance and transcended the bounds of their own epoch. But this legacy was not transmitted by members of the Tübingen intellectual community itself; indeed, the *moderni* were so caught up in the struggle against the invading spirit of the new era that they failed to perceive the lines of continuity. The history of ideas furnishes ample proof that nothing ages so rapidly nor is so inclined toward tenacious conservatism than a self-proclaimed 'modern' movement fascinated by its own 'break-throughs' and hence easily overtaken and displaced by younger and more energetic suitors for the minds of men. In Tübingen's case it was the newly arrived spirits of humanism and the Reformation that burst upon the recalcitrant *moderni.*

In contemplating Tübingen's shrinking influence upon the outside world, which at first suggests the waning of creative energy, we must consider that, like the twentieth-century ivory tower, the sixteenth-century university enjoyed no scholarly immunity against the turmoil that occupied its environs. Ever since the death of Eberhard im Bart (1496), Württemberg had experienced peasant unrest that culminated in 1524–5 when the government forsook Stuttgart for Tübingen. It is true that the extensive uprising of 'Poor Conrad' (1514), which was centred in the Rems valley east of Stuttgart, lacked the programmatic clarity and keenness of the peasant revolts associated with the *Bundschuh* in the diocese of Speyer (1502).[102] The Rems valley rebellion was characterized above all by a less stridently revolutionary call to elevate divine justice to the rule and standard of a reordered society.[103] But both the 'Poor Conrad' movement and the Speyer *Bundschuh* resulted from the great social shortcomings and political tensions which had overtaken Württemberg since before the turn of the century, and which were intensified by political and economic mismanagement, especially during the first reign of Duke Ulrich (1503–19).

The political significance of the Tübingen Treaty (8 July 1514) has

102 For the *Bundschuh*'s plans and the programme of Thirteen Articles see Vergenhans, *Chronicle*, fols. 305^{r}f.

103 See the exemplary study by Heinrich Öhler, 'Der Aufstand des Armen Konrad im Jahr 1514', pp. 482ff.

been inflated by the intervening centuries of history and historiography. To a coolly calculating Duke Ulrich, the agreement merely represented a temporary alliance with the territorial estates in order to gain the upper hand in the peasant uprisings. Dr Gregory Lamparter, an advocate for the Württemberg estates at the deposition of Eberhard II in 1498 and probably already one of the most influential men in Württemberg thanks to the emperor, was still one of Duke Ulrich's most trusted advisors. But his influence declined rapidly as Dr Ambrosius Volland began his ascent. Volland was entrusted with the administration of the duke's new policy aimed at a *Gleichschaltung* of the territorial estates.[104]

The emperor pronounced the imperial ban on Duke Ulrich on 11 October 1516. Amid growing tension in Württemberg, Ulrich succeeded in negotiating at heavy cost and with the backing of the Württemberg cities, what turned out to be a three-year imperial reprieve in the Treaty of Blaubeuren on 22 October. But Ulrich employed the time he had purchased not as an opportunity to reduce internal tensions but to reduce the landed nobility to political impotence wherever possible. He must have regarded his Chancellor Lamparter as the personification of that opposition which had conspired with the emperor and the urban elite to bring about his humiliation at Blaubeuren. Lamparter would surely have shared with Conrad Vaut and Sebastian Breuning the dubious honour of being one of the first 'martyrs in the struggle of the [Württemberg] territorial estates against despotism'[105] had he not eluded capture in Tübingen by fleeing to the imperial court.

A political situation so precarious, especially for a university, helps to explain Thomas Anshelm's sudden and hitherto mysterious move from Tübingen to Hagenau. Even before coming to Tübingen, while still in Pforzheim, he had published the *Ordnung* drawn up by the territorial diet on the basis of the Esslingen Accord [1492].[106] Anshelm adorned his edition of this historic decree with splendid ornamentation, presenting it as a Magna Carta in which the active participation in government asserted by the estates in deposing Duke Ulrich's uncle, Eberhard II (1496–8), could find a fitting repository. Even though the Esslingen Accord was never fully transformed into political reality and soon lost all validity, Thomas Anshelm had

[104] Thus Walter Grube, *Der Stuttgarter Landtag 1457–1957. Von den Landständen zum demokratischen Parlament*, p. 100.

[105] *Ibid.*, p. 103.

[106] *Ibid.*, pp. 62f.; Alberts, 'Reuchlins Drucker, Thomas Anshelm, mit besonderer Berücksichtigung seiner Pforzheimer Presse', p. 236.

marked himself as the estates' publisher, associating himself with a movement for autonomy that corresponded well to the aims of imperial policy. Thus Anshelm was the central figure for a humanist circle in Tübingen that remained loyal to the emperor and whose leading light, Johannes Reuchlin, was implicated as an important member of the 'conspiracy' against Ulrich in the confession extracted by torture from Conrad Vaut.

Although Anshelm avoided any form of personal opposition to the duke, Tübingen could offer him no protection after Ulrich voided the Blaubeuren treaty, and after Anshelm had violated an imperial mandate by publishing the second edition of Reuchlin's *Defensio* against Pfefferkorn (9 July 1513). So he moved to the imperial free city of Hagenau from which Maximilian had appealed to the Württemberg estates to release the captives illegally imprisoned by Ulrich. For how could a publisher whose copyright enjoyed at best a ten-year imperial guarantee have continued his trade under a prince whose future rule seemed totally unpredictable and who had been threatened with and temporarily placed under the imperial ban? Moreover, Hagenau promised Anshelm the opportunity to expand his portfolio of humanist writings with the publication of the works of Melanchthon, Erasmus, Mosellanus and Brassicanus in addition to Reuchlin.[107]

Anshelm's speedy retreat from Tübingen is a far better symbol of the end of an epoch in the history of the university than is the long overdue removal of Duke Ulrich in 1519. New impulses would hereafter reach the university only from the outside. The coming academic generation at Tübingen, up to this point poised in hesitant anticipation, scattered before its members could establish themselves at the university. The defensive stance of the former *moderni* in the face of new scholarly currents temporarily obscured Tübingen's most important contribution in the field of social ethics. First nurtured under the protective eye of Eberhard im Bart, the university recovered its former bloom only when Duke Christopher relieved the tense relationship between university and territorial prince after Ulrich's death (1550).

Philipp Melanchthon had been well advised in the summer of 1518 when his great-uncle Reuchlin[108] counselled him to accept the call to

[107] The word 'trotz' should probably read 'dank' in the description by Alberts: 'Betrachtet man die letzten Jahre der Anshelmschen Tätigkeit, so sieht man, dass er trotz der Übersiedlung nach Hagenau weiterhin feste Verbindungen zu dem alten Kreis der Humanisten unterhielt.' 'Reuchlins Drucker', p. 224.

[108] See Hannemann, 'Reuchlin und die Berufung Melanchthons nach Wittenberg', p. 127.

the new university at Wittenberg; well advised despite his later desire to return to Tübingen. The monk at Hirsau, and Tübingen alumnus, Nicholas Baselius, could still extol his *Alma Mater* as the mother of the German renaissance in 1516,[109] but she soon demonstrated her inability to keep pace with an energetic and pervasive new spirit. Melanchthon was not wrong to label the University of Wittenberg a 'colonia Tubingensis' in his memorial oration for Eberhard im Bart,[110] but the daughter had long since shown herself to be more intellectually alert and alluring than her mother.

Yet the 'first Tübingen school' left a lasting mark on future socio-economic theory in two ways. In the tradition leading from Biel through Summenhart to Eck, theological theory took notice of early capitalist practice. An emphasis on the theology professor's right to dispute scholastically, free of episcopal interference, emerged as a by-product of special importance for the Reformation.

As a second aspect of its legacy, this Tübingen tradition served notice to the academic world that canon law was divine only where it accorded with scripture. By far the greatest portion of canon law was thereby unmasked as mere statutory legislation which, having been enacted in the past, can and must be altered or abolished in the future. Herein lay the fundamental significance of Summenhart's treatise *De decimis*. The general proscription of interest-taking finds as little support in scripture as does the tithe obligation in divine law. The standard for all decisions in the realm of economics is the obligation of love imposed on every believer. With his unambiguous voice, Summenhart distanced himself, to his great credit, from the silence of his theologian successors who obviously owed a response to Lamparter, Fugger and Eck. His stance was likewise far removed from the attempt to equate divine and statutory law as found in the opinion formulated by the theological faculty at Mainz on 17 December 1517 in response to Luther's indulgence theses and at the request of Archbishop Albrecht. For these Mainz professors agreed that a papal statute should be treated as if it had issued from the mouth of Peter or from God himself.[111]

Summenhart's treatment of the tithe issue was a far more courageous venture than Eck's defence of the professor's privileges in

[109] See *Werden und Wertung der Reformation*, Appendix II.

[110] *CR* 11, col. 1023.

[111] Herrmann, 'Miscellen zur Reformationsgeschichte. Aus Mainzer Akten', p. 267. The Mainz theologians rested their case on canon law: 'Nemini est de sedis apostolicae iudicio iudicare, aut illius sentenciam retractare permissum, uidelicet propter Romanae ecclesiae primatum, Christi munere in beato Petro apostolo divinitus collocatum.' *CIC*, 1, Decr. Grat. c. 30 C. XVII q. 4; p. 823.

teaching and research. In the final analysis Eck could ignore his bishop, confidently building on the powerful connections of Jacob Fugger and assured that his theology contained no daring proposals that might eventually endanger the ecclesiastical property structure. Indeed, Eck merely pursued the *ex post facto* approbation of a business practice long customary in Augsburg and the other European financial centres.

Thus, both with regard to the 'captains of capitalism', through its alumnus Eck, and with regard to the peasant prophets and city reformers through the voice of Summenhart, the 'Tübingen school', with its specific blend of devotion and scholarly inquiry, helped to shape the history of the Reformation, even if historically more indirectly than and within a different theological framework from that of the reformers of Wittenberg.

9

The power of witchcraft: devil and devotion

CENTURIES OF pseudo-historical propaganda have acquainted us with the image of a medieval *Mater Ecclesia* and her handmaiden *Theologia* straying benighted into a dead-end street on the dark and frozen eve of the Reformation; a plight from which true religion was miraculously guided into the dawn of the modern era by the morning star of the wise men of Wittenberg. The chief exhibit in the Reformation hall of heroics has consisted, on the one hand, of a Protestant tableau portraying the breathtaking descent of Truth into a hostile late medieval terrain devoid of historical points of contact. But the exhibition displays other scenes also. Indeed, the opposite wall of the Reformation gallery has been *re*fitted only in recent decades with the so-called ecumenical image of Luther.

Although drawn from another perspective, the new ecumenical portrait carries the same message and only confirms its Protestant counterpart. Its Catholic predecessor in the exhibit – cracked, faded and above all, out of style – had been masterfully painted by Heinrich Denifle. Denifle had portrayed Luther's Reformation as a smokescreen for his libido,[1] as if Luther had tried to legitimize his insurmountable and incessant concupiscence with the doctrine of the sinner's justification *sola fide*, freeing him from his *Anfechtungen* to marry Catherine von Bora. In contrast, the new Catholic portrait honours Luther – and modern Catholics show themselves particularly indebted to Joseph Lortz – by depicting him as an 'earnest and devout man of prayer'. But the background of the Lortz Luther-portrait[2] has been overlooked in the flush of ecumenical euphoria: Denifle's libido has become Lortz's nominalism. Born and brought up under the sinister constellation of nominalism, Luther was in Lortz's

[1] 'Luther dachte, sprach, schrieb allmählich unter dem Druck und Trieb der bösen Lust . . .' *Luther und Luthertum in der ersten Entwicklung*, vol. 1, pt. 1, pp. 95f. Translated in Raymund Volz, *Luther and Lutherdom*, vol. 1 (pt. 1 only), p. 105.

[2] Walther von Loewenich argues that 'die Urteile von Lortz über Luther im Laufe der Jahre zunehmend mehr das Positive an Luther betonen'. 'Zum Gedächtnis an Joseph Lortz', p. 47.

view predestined by this radically 'un-Catholic' theology[3] to heresy and the destruction of the unity of the church. Thus both confessional armies have engaged in a war of words in the no-man's-land between the Middle Ages and the modern era. The shelling has disfigured the terrain beyond recognition.[4]

Obviously the established results of research require considerable time to penetrate the confessional consciousness. To aid this permeation process we might sketch a more complete picture of the *via moderna*, a panorama that is not limited to the late medieval university lecture hall. It is easy to turn one's back on those bygone phases of scholarly strife which in themselves are difficult to relive mentally, but which in our age demand a seemingly indefensible expenditure of time and mental effort to reconstruct. But whether we can dissociate ourselves from the tangle of witchcraft, superstition and hysteria that snakes its way through the intervening centuries, challenging us to come to terms with our common past, is another matter. Nominalism invaded precisely this area of life and thus demonstrated a non-academic vitality that has previously escaped our attention.

In an attempt to dispel the hysteria surrounding the first execution for witchcraft in Tübingen, the Biel student and parish priest Martin Plantsch preached a series of sermons in the Tübingen Collegiate Church in 1505 and published them two years later in treatise form. Because we have no definite information regarding this Tübingen witchcraft trial, in order to illustrate the urgency which surrounded Plantsch's preaching we must rely on a roughly contemporary case in which a woman's simple piety confronted the persecution and prosecution mentality of neighbours and authorities alike. We shall consider the fate of Anna Spülerin of Ringingen,[5] who became ensnared in a trial for witchcraft with consequences extending over a ten-year period (ca. 1505–18) and as far as the imperial supreme court. The account of this case is of singular importance since we have here, from a woman's perspective, a description of procedures known to us only in countless other documents from the pens of men whose emotions had been laced into a judicial corset.

[3] *The Reformation in Germany*, transl. Ronald Walls, 1, p. 488 (*Die Reformation in Deutschland*, p. 437). See Denifle's earlier and more detailed treatment, 1, pt. 2, pp. 591–612. In his most recent Luther study, Erwin Iserloh indeed admits: 'Luther überwindet den Ockhamismus in Rückbesinnung auf Augustinus.' But Iserloh finds sufficient shortcomings to warrant the thesis that 'Luther bleibt aber zugleich dem Ockhamismus verhaftet.' *Luther und die Reformation. Beiträge zu einem ökumenischen Lutherverständnis*, pp. 39, 42.

[4] Cf. *The Harvest of Medieval Theology*, pp. 423f.

[5] Between Ulm and Ehingen, six km north of the Danube.

Anna Spülerin's mother had been arrested the previous year on suspicion of witchcraft, and the daughter's outraged reaction had made her conspicuous. She was arrested and transported to Blaubeuren where she was incarcerated pending investigation, fully confident that she could clear herself upon interrogation.[6]

But who else should appear that evening than the torturer and executioner of the honourable city council here at Ulm. He dealt harshly, cruelly, inhumanly and unwomanly with her, desiring only to hear her confess that she was a [witch]. But since she knew herself to be free and innocent of this charge, she refused to incriminate herself with any falsehood or to admit anything, but rather placed her hope in the Almighty God.

Thereafter she was taken into another cell and not once, twice, three or four times but indeed inhumanly and gruesomely tormented: all her limbs being mutilated and being robbed of her mental faculties and her five senses to the extent that she never fully recovered her sight and hearing. And thus her agony was increased to such an inhuman level that she was overcome with terror, expecting never to leave that place alive, even though, deprived of her sight, she was unable to survey the full extent of her mutilation.

But such torture was unsatisfactory since it had yielded no results and the prefect arrived from Tübingen with yet another executioner. The prefect did his best to convince her to incriminate herself and thereby put an end to her torment. He addressed her amicably and inquired why she resisted so – she should really confess her guilt. For when she had once departed this life, the inhabitants of Ringingen, every single one of them, should and would endow a mass for her. To which she answered that the prefect would in that case please to thank them, but as far as she was concerned, she was completely confident of her innocence. Since the prefect had failed to extract anything from her, he started over again and insisted that her mother had admitted Anna's guilt by confessing that Anna too was a witch. Anna denied this and countered that she knew well that her mother could say nothing bad about her and had not done so. She was convinced of her complete innocence of every charge brought against her and stood unrelentingly steadfast upon the truth, refusing to depart from it.

When they had perceived this, they continued to assail her vigorously with tales attributed to her mother and threatened to break every bone in her body. And although she more than once kindly asked them why they still accused her and whether they indeed desired to drive her to falsehood, they neither accepted nor comprehended her words. Instead they incessantly maintained that she was a witch and would have nothing but her confession, despite having never produced one genuine scrap of evidence against her. One of her accusers who was present had indeed spoken up and asked her where the shirt of Our Lady that had been in the church of Ringingen had

[6] The account is included in Soldan and Heppe, *Geschichte der Hexenprozesse*, 1, pp. 483–5. The outcome of the action for damages is unknown.

been taken, for she, he maintained, knew very well who had ripped it to shreds. She then asked whether someone had accused her of this act. When the prefect responded that he simply knew what had happened and that a little bird had told him, she insisted once more that she was a victim of injustice and totally innocent of this affair. By their leave, if anyone maintained that she had done anything of the sort, then she would be willing to die for it. But no one could possibly desire to accuse her further of such a thing. Thereupon they departed, threatening to return the next morning and interrogate her with even greater cruelty and torture. In addition, she was afterward transferred to an even harsher and more intolerable prison.

When they had all departed it occurred to her to take refuge in Him who possessed the power to aid her, namely Almighty God and his Mother, Mary, Queen of Heaven. With fervour and from the depths of her heart she called on both to deliver her, in view of her innocence and for the sake of justice and truth, from that severe and harsh imprisonment and to preserve her from speaking falsehood. This her prayer and also her vows to undertake pilgrimages to St Leonard and to other places were heard by Almighty God: between the tenth and eleventh hours of that same night she was released from prison.

And after all this – after she had been carried off to prison upon denunciation by the inhabitants of Ringingen, tortured with all severity, gruesomeness and barbarity, maimed and stripped of her mental powers and senses, and in addition robbed of her reputation and health, she fell into a great and insurmountable sorrow – for she could neither feed herself nor her children as she had done previously, nor could her husband resume marital intercourse with her as before. Therefore she made the urgent request that the inhabitants of Ringingen be obliged to compensate her according to her needs and her dignity for her pain, agony, humiliation and injury she had endured. Should such not be amicably attainable, then she hopes that justice might be done to her reasonable demand in the course of judicial proceedings.

The Anna Spülerin case was no anomaly, except perhaps in the fact that she lived to tell her tale, indeed, to tell it to the highest court in the empire. Her trial for witchcraft announces a wave of persecution that flooded Europe in complete indifference to confessional boundaries.

With its mixture of fear, superstition, ideology and religious conviction, the witchcraft hysteria demanded a response from the academic world; a reply which all too often employed current popular opinion, or 'common sense', rather than making use of the ivory tower to develop a critical perspective on the issue.

Against this historical backdrop we turn our attention to the preacher of the Tübingen Collegiate Church, Martin Plantsch (†1533). Perhaps no other alumnus of Tübingen remained so closely associated with the history of the university from its beginnings until the eve of the Reformation. Indeed, as 'plebanus'[7] of the city church, whose collegiate chapter provided benefices for university faculty members, he was qualified to represent the university alongside its chancellor.

Plantsch matriculated with the very first student generation at the founding of the university[8] (*Magister Artium* in February 1483) and was admitted, along with Wendelin Steinbach, to the degree of *cursor biblicus*, or lecturer on the Old and New Testaments, on 27 April 1486.[9] He graduated to doctor of theology in 1494 after he had already served as dean of the arts faculty in 1488 and as rector of the university through the winter of 1489–90. When, after pastorates in Gültlingen and Dusslingen, he became pastor at the Tübingen Collegiate Church, he soon gained a reputation as a superb preacher who conscientiously combined theological scholarship with the parish ministry. Heinrich Bebel even reported that Plantsch 'was considered above all a great preacher, indeed, the best of his time'.[10] Since neither that epoch nor Heinrich Bebel were known for their miserliness in bestowing praise on orators and poets, we are lucky to be able to measure Plantsch's significance by means of his series of sermons on the witchcraft hysteria,[11] published in 1507. Appearing under the title, *Opusculum de sagis maleficis Martini Plantsch concionatoris Tubingensis*, it seems at first glance to be part of the long-established *genre* of writings directed against magic and the occult arts. But the work reveals a conscious extension and application of the basic tenets of the *via moderna* to the many-faceted field of popular piety, testifying to the intellectual power and pastoral vitality of the modern way. And the term 'popular piety' calls our attention to that particular spiritual grey area between orthodox theology and superstition that has largely eluded the grasp of scholarship to this day. From those

[7] The financial importance of this office is clear from the fact that Plantsch received an income of 200 fl. coupled with a benefice of 40 fl. The provost, who was also the chancellor of the university, received 300 fl. while the dean derived only 110 fl. from his office. The salary of a typical professor during these early years of the university ranged between 60 and 120 fl. per annum. See Rauscher, ed., *Württembergische Visitationsakten*, vol. 1, p. 190. Plantsch died on 18 July 1533.

[8] Hermelink, *Die Matrikeln*, 1, p. 14, no. 223.

[9] 'Dominus Wendalinus Steinbach de Butzbach . . . die 27ª Aprilis anni Christi 1486, principiavit in bibliam, una cum magistro Martino Plantsch de Dornstetten . . .' University Archives, Tübingen, XII, 21f. 10ª.

[10] In the dedicatory epistle to Peter Jakobi, provost at Backnang: 'quo mihi inter concionatores nostrae tempestatis principem locum moereri [sic] visus est'. Martin Plantsch, *Opusculum de sagis maleficis*, fol. a2ᵛ.

[11] Among Plantsch's listeners was Johannes Altenstaig who explicitly referred to Plantsch as a charismatic preacher. *Vocabularius Theologie*, s.v. 'Maleficium'.

muddied waters Plantsch set out to distill the clear water of truth and discard the sediment of superstition.

But first a warning to the reader. If reading historical sources – even those of our own contemporary era – demands a general willingness to enter the world of the author and don the garb of his assumptions, then the case at hand will tax the reader to the limits of his sensitivity.[12] We shall be tested especially since we ourselves have not yet succeeded in draining the swamplands between superstition and faith, parapsychology and scientifically apprehended reality. Hence it is easy for our inner defences to blind us to a pursuit of enlightenment in a distant past that we fancy ourselves to have outgrown long ago.

Our treatise on the 'malevolent masters of the occult' has not been entirely overlooked by past scholars. W. G. Soldan revealed a greater analytical acuity in his impressive *Geschichte der Hexenprozesse* in the last century than did the later beneficiaries of his work to whom Plantsch remained no more than a name. For Soldan recognized Plantsch's concern 'to enlighten and instruct'.[13] In contrast, Johannes Haller considered Plantsch's work 'an unadulterated portrait of the crassest superstition which had at that point ensnared even the most learned minds'. But Haller also noted that the Tübingen pastor's 'special intention is to show that magic can only be effective where the divine will permits and that one should commit himself to the will of God rather than employ counter-magic'.[14]

This estimation recognizes the treatise's pastoral framework but fails to give credit to Plantsch's essential motive: to shatter scientifically the spell of witchcraft. Haller was perhaps misled by Bebel's

[12] For an overview of the state of research in this area, see Russell, *Witchcraft in the Middle Ages*. Henry Chadwick has eloquently portrayed and documented the prehistory of the medieval ecclesiastical decisions and prohibitions in his *Priscillian of Avila. The Occult and the Charismatic in the Early Church*.

Keith Thomas deals with England between 1500 and 1700 but with observations and conclusions valid for the continent, transcending confessional limits. See *Religion and the Decline of Magic. Studies in Popular Beliefs in Sixteenth and Seventeenth Century England*. Thomas demonstrates that the Reformation in England indeed began in the name of a struggle against superstition, exorcism and magic in the church (p. 74), but that Protestants and Catholics in the mid-sixteenth century had become 'equally vehement in their hostility to popular magic, and both denounced it in terms that would have been approved by their medieval predecessors'. *Ibid.*, p. 258; cf. pp. 499f. In a significant review of Raoul Manselli, *La Religion populaire au moyen age. Problèmes de méthode et d'histoire*, L. Genicot describes the state of research and quite legitimately warns against separating 'religion populaire' ('efficacité'-oriented) too widely from 'religion savante' ('verité'-oriented).

[13] Soldan and Heppe, *Geschichte der Hexenprozesse*, 2, p. 209.

[14] Haller, 1, p. 195.

dedicatory lines which chiefly extolled Plantsch – using Luther's later label for Gerson[15] – as a *doctor* of consolation.[16] But Bebel also praised him for having 'denounced, confuted and shattered the pestiferous superstition and execrable perfidy of sorceresses and witches'.[17]

Were this the extent of Plantsch's efforts, the treatise could quickly be reshelved amid the seemingly endless rows of anti-sorcery publications, scarcely disturbing the dust of centuries. But in that case, Plantsch's purpose would have been thoroughly misunderstood.

The work of H. C. Erik Midelfort on witch-hunting in south-west Germany represents a considerable advance. Midelfort realizes that an adequate evaluation of Plantsch depends in part on explicit recognition of his firm adherence to the Biel school. He is also the first scholar to ask whether a deeper penetration into the differences between *via moderna* and *via antiqua* might not bring to light diverging views of witchcraft.[18] However, in writing social history, Midelfort can justify limiting himself to the most essential conclusion: that Plantsch emphasized witchcraft's subjection to divine providence so much that he virtually ignored the various means of punishing it.[19] Midelfort also broaches the thesis that, in the wake of a 'Tübingen sermon tradition', the opinions developed by Plantsch in Catholic Tübingen were adopted in the Lutheran Tübingen of Johannes Brenz thirty years later.[20]

In Plantsch's own epoch, Johannes Hiltebrandt (†1514) grasped the priest's purpose more accurately than had Bebel. Hiltebrandt, a humanistically educated reader for the Anshelm press and colleague of Melanchthon, felt obliged to apologize in his epilogue[21] for the sober theologian's Latin employed by Plantsch. In Hiltebrandt's view, 'rather than write for an elite and refined circle', this learned theologian 'preferred to demonstrate to a wide audience, and espe-

[15] *WATR* 2, no. 1351.

[16] 'egregius consolandi atque persuadendi artifex Martinus noster . . . ad sanctam patientiam cohortetur . . .' Fol. a3^r.

[17] 'prudenter sagarum et maleficarum pestiferam superstitionem et execrandam perfidiam detestetur, confutet et confringat . . .' Fol. a3^r. But in the epigram written to accompany the treatise, Bebel revealed his awareness that Plantsch's theme was actually the *credulitas* of the witches and their surroundings.

[18] *Witch Hunting in Southwestern Germany 1562–1684. The Social and Intellectual Foundations*, p. 236, n. 7.

[19] *Ibid.*, p. 35.

[20] 'The views that Plantsch expressed at Catholic Tübingen became the traditional and accepted ones at Lutheran Tübingen thirty years later.' *Ibid.*, p. 36.

[21] The epilogue is followed by a list of corrections, by no means a mere catalogue of typographical errata but rather a collection of improvements on formulations – especially in Bebel's introduction – from the perspective of advanced humanist erudition. Regarding Hiltebrandt see Steiff, *Buchdruck*, pp. 21f.

cially to pastors, an easy way to lead a people that is stupid and prone to error away from its superstitious obsession with witchcraft'.[22]

To be sure, Plantsch did not share this humanist condescension toward the less educated – priests included! Furthermore, the lower social classes held no monopoly on 'stupidity', as the authorities in the Anna Spülerin case convincingly demonstrated. Nonetheless Hiltebrandt had penetrated to the essence of the issue. He and Plantsch were not concerned with the *crudelitas* of the witches but with the *credulitas* of those who believed in the witches' powers over men and matter.[23] What means did Plantsch employ in this struggle against superstition, a campaign inspired by the pyre of the first victim of the witchcraft craze in Tübingen?

Plantsch was a pupil of the *via moderna*, of Occam,[24] Gerson and his own 'distinguished teacher' Biel.[25] He therefore united the contributions of theology and the natural sciences and appealed to church, scripture and the fathers[26] in pursuing his purpose. An anti-dualistic view of nature was his point of departure. Augustine aided him in his formulation of the absolute sovereignty of God, while Occam furnished thoughts on the extent of human responsibility subsisting under that sovereignty (fol. a 7r). That the devil was obliged first to fetch divine consent for his torment of Job (fol. a 8r) demonstrated to Plantsch and, as he hoped, to his audience, that everything happening to men is traceable to God. Whether welcomed by men or

22 Fol. g5r.

23 This *vana credulitas*, literally 'groundless credulity', is a sin peculiar to the uneducated masses, and formed a counterpart to the *vana curiositas* which Gerson and the nominalists laid at the feet of largely academic circles. But since the original meaning of *curiositas* implied a desire to penetrate beyond God's self-revelation into the divine *secreta*, the word – commonly applied by the Latin fathers to the heathen philosophers – came to refer to the 'superstition' of the common man as well. Hence Plantsch described those who preferred to trust the tales of 'old wives' instead of the church and its *doctores* with the words, 'Vanis curiositatibus intendunt'. Fol. c7r.

24 'magnus ille et venerabilis inceptor Guilhelmus Occam . . . Quem imitatur venerabilis et precellens Gabriel Biel prepositus olim sancti petri in silva, . . .' Fol. a7r.

25 'Quomodo autem diabolus faciat huiusmodi apparentias et illusiones, pulchre declarat eximius magister et preceptor meus Gabriel in suo secundo di. VIII q. II reducens huiusmodi illusiones ad tres modos.' Fol. c4v. For differences between Plantsch and Biel see below, n. 62.

26 The structure of Plantsch's sermons and his style of argumentation are far less scholastic than that of his master Gabriel Biel. The three-part outline encompasses (1) three *veritates* with their practical consequences or *documenta* (fols. a4r–c6r); (2) ten reasons why God permits diabolical threats and injuries to humans (fols. c6r–e5r); (3) eight possible *remedia* based on two fundamental considerations (fols. e5r–g2r). One final question is appended to the conclusion (fols. g2r–g4r), an inquiry that would appear as a *dubium* in a scholastic outline. The entire structure lacks formal scholastic and external divisions; the transitions are smooth and inconspicuous – probably a mark of the original sermon form.

apparently injurious, even if the work of demons or evil men, without the consent and authorization of God nothing can occur.

Such considerations led to two practical conclusions. In the first place, a Christian need fear no one beside God; no man, no witch nor sorcerer (fol. b 3r). Secondly, one should attribute everything that one is 'called upon' to endure to the righteous will of God and not to the stars, demons, witches or sorcerers of fate (fol. b 3v). Man should endure the hand of God and not rebel against his holy will even when God makes use of the devil and his demons.[27]

The most significant passages for the history of ideas now follow, pages that turn this treatise into a stimulating document.[28] Plantsch deployed the entire nominalist arsenal, with its characteristic theory of causality, to liberate and demythologize. We can better understand the struggle involved if we recall that the *via antiqua* attributed an 'inherent momentum' to the second causes (*causae secundae*) originally set in motion by God, the 'Prime Mover'. This inherent momentum then determines by intrinsic necessity the further course of motion. In the supernatural realm such a view corresponded to the conception that the means to salvation – e.g. good works caused by grace or the consecrated water, bread and wine – are endowed with an inherent efficacy.

The *via moderna*, on the other hand, maintained that good works must first be accepted by God before they can achieve their effect, i.e. to obtain additional grace, and ultimately, to attain celestial beatitude. Likewise the sacramental efficacy of the water of baptism and the elements of the Eucharist is founded on God's covenant with the church, on the *pactum cum ecclesia* wherein God pledged himself to grant his grace with each imparting of the sacraments. Indeed the sacramental elements possess no causal efficacy and are not *causae efficientes* but *causae sine qua non* for divine grace. We recall in this context the example from what we have termed the *oeconomia moderna*,[29] likewise dependent on a covenant principle,[30] whereby money is no longer measured by its inherent value but is accepted as payment on the basis of its 'backing' by a sovereign.

Aware of all these elements, recently rediscovered, and laboriously stripped of layers of grimy caricature and confessional distortion, we are prepared to evaluate an as yet unnoticed area of activity for

[27] 'qui hec duo pensat documenta, sufficiens habet incitamentum pacientiae in quacumque adversitate.' Fol. b4v.

[28] Fols. c1r–c6r.

[29] See above, pp. 128ff.

[30] Thus Courtenay, 'The King and the Leaden Coin', p. 209.

nominalism: the debunking of the powers attributed to witches and demons.

Plantsch's new initiative in the first part of his *Opusculum* becomes the major focus of our interest. The second and third parts of the sermon series deal with the reasons why God permits demonic activity in this world and discuss the remedies effective against such activity. These remedies are indeed significant for the history of piety but do not represent specifically nominalist traits. They find clear parallels in the nearly contemporaneous work of Johannes Trithemius (†1516), the *Antipalus maleficiorum*, which, unlike Plantsch's sermons, preserved the conceptual presuppositions of the *Malleus maleficarum* (ca. 1487).[31] Where parallels do persist between Plantsch and Trithemius, as in the antidotes for witchcraft, they constitute no proof of direct dependence but rather point to a common and broader tradition.[32]

Trithemius certainly attempted in his own way to enlighten, when he suggested 'that occasionally the demon-possessed *also* suffer from corporal maladies' and therefore an exorcist should 'possess medical knowledge'.[33] For his larger purpose was to clear the way for legitimate investigation by distinguishing between black and white magic. Plantsch, in contrast, pinpointed the central synapse of the medieval witchcraft hysteria in the first and fundamental portion of his treatise. Current research into the phenomenon of the witchcraft scares repeatedly points to the importance of the seldom absent attempts to explain the witch's powers as an illegitimate *charisma* stemming from a *pactum illicitum*, an ecclesiastically proscribed pact with the devil.

The significance of this explanation of occult powers is illustrated by the prominence given to it in the already mentioned *Malleus maleficarum* ('the witches' hammer'), one of the most widely distributed writings of the period. Composed by the Dominican inquisitors Heinrich Krämer (Institoris) and Jacob Sprenger, who conducted in Plantsch's own diocese of Constance a witch-hunt so intensive that forty-eight 'witches' had been executed by the end of the 1480s,[34] the work proclaimed the pact with the devil to be an essential component of all witchcraft.[35]

[31] Hansen, *Quellen und Untersuchungen zur Geschichte des Hexenwahns und der Hexenverfolgung im Mittelalter*, pp. 291ff.

[32] Arnold, *Johannes Trithemius (1462–1516)*, pp. 196–9.

[33] *Ibid.*, p. 198.

[34] Karl O. Müller, 'Heinrich Institoris, der Verfasser des Hexenhammers, und seine Tätigkeit als Hexeninquisitor in Ravensburg im Herbst 1484', p. 397, n. 2.

[35] See Shumaker, *The Occult Sciences in the Renaissance. A Study in Intellectual Patterns*,

Without expressly mentioning the Dominican inquisitors and their 'hammer' but with marked abstention from the intellectual tools of their trade, Plantsch set about to hammer the witchcraft delusion into the ground of the *via moderna*, defying the theological and philosophical presuppositions of the *via antiqua* so doggedly defended by the Dominicans.

Plantsch employed the same concept that dominated the nominalist 'acceptatio' soteriology as his point of departure for a demonic 'counter-soteriology': just as 'divine acceptance' made it possible to bestow merit on meritless human works,[36] so the evil powers of this world possess only delegated, received or 'accepted' power.[37] They are no more 'efficient causes' in their evil activity than are good works with respect to gaining celestial bliss. Their weapons are mere means dependent on God's 'temporary' concession of efficacy.[38]

Witches attempt basically four things, according to Plantsch: to influence the weather through storms, hail and thunder; to practice telekinesis and *locomotio* – for example, when they ride their broomsticks to the witches' sabbath at the haunted meadow;[39] to inflict physical injury; and, finally, to turn their victim's inner life into chaos. Witches themselves claim to accomplish these effects through a repertoire of four means (*media*): through the use of magically charmed images, symbols, magical incantations and through the deviant use of natural materials such as spices, powder, stones, roots and in many cases, poisons.[40] Plantsch wove in as a warning a

pp. 72f. Cf. the introductory collection of readings edited by Kors and Peters, *Witchcraft in Europe 1100–1700*, p. 130. Midelfort warned that the influence and authority of the *Malleus* 'have been greatly exaggerated by most scholars', but also noted that 'the late Middle Ages did indeed make two fundamental contributions to the witch hunt, notably the idea that all magic involved a pact with the devil', and the concept of a 'massive, organized witch cult' which threatened Christendom. *Witch Hunting*, pp. 22, 20.

36 See above, p. 85.

37 'nullam haberet in eum [Christum] potestatem, nisi eam a deo accepisset . . .' Fol. b1ʳ; cf. fol. a8ʳ.

38 'Quis enim impacienter ferret illa onera, quae iustus deus et cuius omnia iudicia recta sunt, qui sanctus est in omnibus operibus suis, sibi imponit, licet per homines, diabolos vel alias creaturas tamquam per media portanda. . . .' Fol. b4ᵛ.

39 'ad montem foeni, vulgo "Heuberg" dictum, ubi choreisando laeta celebrent convivia. . . .' Fol. b5ʳ. The reference here is to one of the highest peaks of the Black Forest, although Tübingen also possesses, even today, a 'Heuberg'. Indeed, nearly every locality once could have pointed to its 'Heuberg', 'Bockberg' or 'Blocksberg'.

40 See the collection, 'Zaubersegen und zauberische Mittel', in Ulrich Jahn, *Hexenwesen und Zauberei in Pommern*, pp. 40–196. Cf. the entry 'Segen' in Bächtold-Stäubli, ed., *Handwörterbuch des deutschen Aberglaubens*, vol. 7, cols. 1582–620.

plaintive account from his home town of Dornstetten (Black Forest) where a witch's love potion had proved to be a lethal poison.[41]

We have thus far reproduced ideas from Plantsch that illustrate his firm footing in the faith of his age, which appears to the modern reader as merely so much superstition. But we now approach the point where our preacher tackled the issue from the nominalist tradition as transmitted above all through his *Magister* Gabriel.

At first his arguments appear to follow an ordinary trajectory: the witches abuse the church's rituals of exorcism and benediction as well as the sacraments of the Eucharist and baptism, the church's relics, Easter candles and so forth, in order to lend power to their potions.[42] But unlike the Dominican witch-hunters, Plantsch did not insist that such misuse of the church's rites placed the 'effects' of the sacraments at the perverse disposal of the devil. On the contrary, such 'magic' is groundless fantasy because the sacraments and *sacramentalia* of the church simply defy such simple 'disposition': in short, they are 'non-negotiable'. The words of consecration have no power or efficacy of themselves but are signs of God's promise according to which he pledges to impart his grace to each person who properly receives the sacraments.[43]

The witches' chants and charms are no such signs of God's promise because they use sacramental phrases inappropriately instead of *rite* or according to divine institution. In the first place, signs cannot be divorced from the things signified, and in this case the object signified is God's efficacy, which will not permit itself to be applied outside of its sphere of validity (the divine covenant with the church), to say nothing of permitting manipulation at the hands of witches.[44]

[41] Fol. b6^{v}.

[42] 'Nam aliquando ad carmina recipiunt benedictiones seu exorcismos, aliquando sacramenta ecclesiae. Saepe etiam ad illa media applicant missas, aliquando, quod horrendum est, venerabile eucharistiae sacramentum, aliquando sacramenta ecclesiae ut aquam baptismatis, cereum pascalem, sanctorum reliquias et sic de consimilibus.' Fol. b6^{v}.

[43] 'ita deus sacramenta sua instituit, quod quicumque illa rite susceperit, ipse deus velit animae suae infundere gratiam, vel gratiam prius habitam augere.' Fol. b6^{v}. Very compactly but at the same time vividly portrayed by Biel in his *Canonis misse expositio*, Lectio 47T; Oberman and Courtenay edn, 2, p. 226.

[44] 'Neque pars eius, neque aliae quelibet consecrationes aut benedictiones effectum suum habent ex se, sed ex operatione et ordinatione instituentis dei, qui suis assistit signis efficiendo quod signant. Sed nullibi legitur, quod dominus deus missam vel partem eius aut aliquod sacramentum, vel orationem aliquam vel ieiunium seu aliquod bonum opus istituerit ad dandum robur et efficaciam talibus mediis incantatorum, quae media tam vetus quam novum testamentum reprobat. Igitur vanam et derisione dignum est dicere, quod haec media vim agendi consequantur ex officio missae vel consimilibus.' Fols. b8^{v}–c1^{r}.

The sacraments are not storage batteries whose terminals can be harnessed by means of a satanic transformer to perverse ends. They are personalized channels for God's gift of grace.

Regarding the so-called 'spells' with their purported healing powers, there can be no thought of these possessing supernatural powers since such powers are reserved to the church's sacraments. One can only conclude, then, that whatever effectiveness magical incantations and spells may have results from purely natural processes. Hence such phrases should yield precisely the same effects coming from the mouth of an 'ordinary citizen' as when spoken by witches around a seething cauldron. Witches may mysteriously adorn their spells with whatever intricate and impressive intonation they please; it all makes no difference, for a phrase is a phrase and a saying is just that: something said. Whether whispered by full moon or candlelight, by witch or good Christian, when considered from the perspective of natural science, a given sentence has precisely the same effect in each case, since it always crosses in the same manner the space between a mouth and one or more pairs of ears.[45] This means that where a supposed magic spell has healed a sick person, anyone using the same formula has at his or her disposal precisely the same power to heal.[46] This same nominalist demythologizing cleaver trims the superstitious fat from all magical *media* whether they be secret spells or wax figures: none of these means possesses any mysterious immanent powers.

Plantsch's double debunking based on the 'non-transferability' of divine power in both supernatural and natural spheres reached its limits in his conviction that demonic witchcraft did indeed exist. The devil has instituted his own sacraments 'backed' with his own powers in the course of his persistent attempts to imitate his divine Rival. The decisive difference lies in the fact that although Satan can promise to give his 'sacraments' effective power, he possesses no means of guaranteeing his promise in the manner in which God guarantees the sacraments of the church.[47] Satan has only as much power as God is willing *ad hoc* to grant him.

45 See below, n. 65.

46 'Recte ergo sicut partes eiusdem aeris sunt eiusdem speciei specialissimae substantialis. Ita verba in oedem aere prolata in se sunt eiusdem speciei specialissimae; quapropter si tua verba prolata naturaliter sanant hanc infirmitatem, et mea sanabunt eandem, non obstante quod in auribus audientium aliter sonent verba mea et tua.' Fol. b7r.

47 'ita verba maleficarum non operantur effectus sequentes, sed diabolus sic assistens suis sacramentis. Est tamen magna differentia inter sacramenta dei et daemonis. Quia sacramentis dei semper assistit deus operando effectum, quem signant, cum

Recast in terms of our example from the realm of coinage: the devil's money is highly inflated and his fiscal policy bankrupt. He cannot correct the problem. Why should men and women credulously continue to accept the counterfeit currency of the witchcraft delusion? Witches themselves have no power at all: they can only cause mischief when it is expressly permitted them. The 'pact with the devil', which until this point had formed a standard element in the inquisitorial interrogations and all outbreaks of witchcraft hysteria, has simply ceased to exist for Plantsch.[48]

In conclusion, Plantsch pointed out that much of what circulates under the label of magic is the result of natural phenomena which the devil has marketed as mysterious and magical. Perhaps Plantsch had in mind the first Tübingen execution for witchcraft when he warned that 'even today' Satan can assume the form of an innocent human being, unjustly destroying an unblemished reputation and resulting in imprisonment and torture.[49]

Plantsch's goal of rational enlightenment became even more conspicuous where he denied that offspring could issue from a supposed sexual union between a woman and the devil. He insisted that witchcraft could not be inherited according to the sense in which inheritance is normally understood. For a witch could not really have sexual intercourse with a demon or with the devil himself since neither spirit has a genuine body capable of producing sperm. No, the 'best' the devil could do would be to malevolently collect and preserve semen from a man and artificially inseminate a 'witch'.[50] But

legitime conferuntur et suscipiuntur. Diabolus autem non potest semper suis assistere sacramentis operando semper effectus suos, sed solum quando deus sibi dat potestatem operando et admittit productionem talium effectuum . . .' Fol. c1^r–c1^v.

48 Plantsch mentioned the 'pactum diaboli' only once and then solely to expose the fictitiousness of this allegedly satanic arrangement: 'si aliquando vera dicit aut . . . simulat, omnia ficte et decipiendi animo agit, . . .' Fol. e6^v.

49 'Sic adhuc hodie ad diffamandum hominem innocentem potest in eius specie assumpta apparere et ea operari ratione, cuius malam famam incidat, unde capiatur, torqueatur etc.' Fol. c3^r.

50 'Quomodo autem daemon possit exercere actum carnis vel eundem pati in corpore assumpto, facile coniici potest ex hiis, quae de generatione supra immediate dicta sunt. Sicut enim potest ab alio viro colligere semen et conservare, quantum deus permittit in sua naturali dispositione, et postea vasi mulieris infundere, unde sequi potest generatio prolis, ita apparendo in copore muliebri, potest formare vasculum sexui foemineo debitum ac calefacere ipsum etc., prout sibi a deo permittitur, in ipsum quoque recipere semen decisum a viro, quamvis in tali corpore daemonis non fiat generatio prolis ex semine in ipsum assumpto ex causa dicta, quia tale corpus non est vivum.' Fol. c3^v.

the offspring of this 'union' would still be a completely human child like every other baby.[51]

Admittedly, Plantsch's call for soberness and reason had little effect. In the subsequent explosive excesses known to us as the witch-hunts, extending from south Germany to New England,[52] it was precisely the belief in inherited demonic possession which made possible the arrest of entire families and their subsequent 'painful interrogation'. Just how timely was Plantsch's warning, is well illustrated by the Spülerin case. Anna Spülerin was arrested not merely because her outrage made her suspect, but because her mother had already been arrested for witchcraft. The judicial 'interrogator' was finally forced to admit his inability to extort an admission of guilt and she left the prison marked for life, physically unable to nurse her child or resume marital relations with her husband.[53] In a charge of demonic parentage the burden of proof lay on the shoulders of the accused! Plantsch hoped to shift that burden of proof to the prosecutor.

Encouraged by Trithemius,[54] Cornelius Agrippa of Nettesheim (†1535) devoted more attention than did Martin Plantsch both to the demonically oriented black magic and to the scientifically courted white magic.[55] But on the central point concerning the offspring of a satanic sexual union he fully agreed with the Tübingen pastor. More significantly, Agrippa furnished us with an important clue to the identity of the enemy both men had in mind:[56] according to Agrippa

[51] 'Nec vere generant, quia semen ab illo corpore diffusum non est genitum ex digestione cibi facta in tali corpore, sed aliunde assumptum seu collectum a viro vivente et postea proiectum in matricem mulieris, cui conmiscetur, unde proles sequens non est daemonis, sed illius, a quo semen colligit.' Fol. c2^{v}.

[52] The year 1692 witnessed the peak of the 'infamous witchcraft hysteria', especially in Salem, Massachusetts. Ahlstrom, *A Religious History of the American People*, p. 161. Increase Mather (1639–1723), president of Harvard College since 1685 and, together with his son Cotton (1663–1728), a pillar of strength for the 'rule of the saints', knew and used the *Malleus maleficarum*. See Chadwick Hansen, *Witchcraft at Salem*, p. 6.

[53] See above, p. 161.

[54] Walker, *Spiritual and Demonic Magic from Ficino to Campanella*, p. 85, n. 1. Cf. the still useful work by Silbernagel, *Johannes Trithemius*, pp. 135–58.

[55] Thorndike, *History of Magic and Experimental Science*, vol. 5, pp. 128ff. In the excellent monograph cited above, Walker demonstrated that Trithemius and Agrippa stood in a Neoplatonic tradition of astrological magic moulded by Ficino and Pico, a tradition which accepted as factual precisely the magical effect of spoken spells (*vis verborum*) that was repudiated by Plantsch's nominalist *pactum*-theory.

[56] That Agrippa's *De occulta philosophia libris tres* ([Cologne], 1533) was already completed in 1510 is evident from the date of the enthusiastic preface by Trithemius (April 1510). After aligning himself more closely with the Reformation, Agrippa modified his thinking and published a retraction of this earlier work in his *De incertitudine et vanitate scientiarum declamatio invectiva* (n.p., 1531), on which the following discussion is based. For the key concepts of *De occulta philosophia* see

one should not primarily pursue the education of the simple captives of folk superstition, but rather persist in the struggle against the assortment of ideas and errors intentionally propagated by the Dominican inquisitors. In 1519 the Dominican Nicholas Savini, at that time active as an inquisitor in Germany, took Agrippa to task for defending a peasant woman suspected of witchcraft. Agrippa pointed out that no evidence had been introduced against the woman. 'The evidence against her is fully adequate', replied Savini, 'for her mother was burned as a witch.' This reasoning having failed to impress Agrippa, Savini appealed to 'the *Maleus maleficarum* and the peripatetic theology'. Insisting on the validity of his 'evidence', Savini maintained that sorceresses not only consecrate their children to the demons immediately following birth but 'become pregnant through intercourse with the *incubus* and pass on their witchcraft in this way'.[57]

Agrippa responded by noting the heresy of his opponent's assertions: the Dominican had implicitly denied the power of the sacrament of baptism to transform all its recipients from companions of Satan to children of God. Despite all the unanswered questions surrounding Agrippa's relationship to the Reformation, this statement of one of its central concerns should be clear enough. In addition, his explicit mention of the 'peripatetic theology' as indicative of Savini's unreliability fits the state of the controversy in 1519 quite well; a situation portrayed unretouched by Agrippa in his *De incertitudine* (1531).

The Wittenberg theology had been freed from Aristotelian guardianship by the joint effort of Luther, Carlstadt and Lang, who had combined the cause of the Reformation with an attack on the authority of Aristotle. And Melanchthon, who before leaving Tübingen had been enthusiastic about his plan for a 'purified' edition of Aristotle,[58] later defended the utility of the Leipzig Disputation (1519) in a letter to Oecolampadius with a reference to the need to combat the peripatetic theology.[59] Furthermore, since the Jetzer

Nauert, *Agrippa and the Crisis of Renaissance Thought*, pp. 201ff., esp. pp. 261–3; Walker, *Spiritual and Demonic Magic*, pp. 90–6; Shumaker, *The Occult Sciences in the Renaissance*, pp. 134–57.

[57] *De incertitudine et vanitate scientiarum*, cap. 96; German translation in Soldan and Heppe, eds., *Geschichte der Hexenprozesse*, 1, pp. 486f.

[58] See *CR* 1, col. 26; cf. *CR* 11, col. 20.

[59] 'Haec vero disceptandi provincia primum non ob aliud suscepta est, nisi ut palam fieret, inter veterem et Christi theologiam ac noviciam et Aristotelicam quantum intersit.' Wittenberg, 21 July 1519; Staehelin, *Briefe*, 1, p. 98, lines 29–31.

affair,[60] the Reuchlin controversy, and the formation of the common front between Sylvester Prierias, Cardinal Cajetan and the inquisitor Jacob van Hoogstraten, the Dominicans had become a symbol for the repressive and irreformable papal church within broad segments of society.

A comparison of Plantsch and Agrippa proves instructive because the parallels between them illuminate likewise their divergent dispositions. Both attacked the Dominican-produced *Malleus maleficarum*, both endeavoured to introduce a breath of liberal rationality into the theory and practice of the Inquisition. But with his reference to baptism, Agrippa advocated the theological alternative to the Catholic ecclesiastical system. In contrast, Plantsch shunned all explicit confrontation and never directly criticized the Inquisition or its 'Manual of Operations' for witch-baiting, preferring instead to concentrate on the effects of Dominican anti-witch warfare on popular superstition. Whereas Agrippa sought to expose the heresy of the heresy-hunters, Plantsch – still operating within the framework of the *Wegestreit* – endeavoured to mobilize and harness the intellectual forces of the *via moderna* for an invasion of the territory of demonology and magic which had long been occupied solely by the Dominican army of the *via antiqua*.

The common ground between Agrippa and Plantsch by no means implies an orientation shared by both nominalism and the Reformation. Nominalist schooling indeed bore Reformation fruit in a unique way, in the person of Martin Luther. The genealogy is apparent in the questions he asked of scripture and the answers he found in scripture. But the fifteenth-century nominalist theological tradition which transmitted Occam's legacy via the Tübingen school of Biel and Steinbach rested on a firm confidence in existing ecclesiastical structures, a confidence that Luther very early subordinated to his overriding commitment to the scriptural marks of the true church.[61]

Martin Plantsch was the last explicit mouthpiece for the Tübingen *via moderna*[62] prior to the Reformation. His sermons of 1505 clearly

[60] See von Greyerz, 'Der Jetzerprozess und die Humanisten'.

[61] See Hendrix, *Ecclesia in via. Ecclesiological Developments in the Medieval Psalms Exegesis and the Dictata super Psalterium (1513–1515) of Martin Luther*, pp. 243ff.

[62] A detailed comparison with Gabriel Biel not only confirms the fact that Plantsch was a pupil of Biel but also reveals accents specific to Plantsch. Compared to Biel's treatment, Plantsch gave less consideration to the idea of a *pactum diaboli*. See *Collectorium*, II, dist. 8 q. 2 art. 4 dub. 2 L; Gabriel Biel, *Epitome et collectorium ex Occamo circa quatuor sententiarum Libros*, fols. ff3^{rb}–ff3^{va}. See also Biel's assumption of an *assistentia occulta*, which however we must distinguish from the *influentia generalis*. Cf. *Canonis misse expositio*, Lectio 4 F; Oberman and Courtenay edn, 1, p. 36. On the

and irrefutably demonstrate his unquestioning respect for the authority of the church. His loyalty is distinctly visible in the fact that he took both the commandments of God and the precepts of the church as a unitary foundation for a Christian ethic, which in turn established the framework and limits of his rational critique of the witchcraft hysteria. In one of the most beautiful passages of the second part of his work,[63] Plantsch swung the discussion – probably once more in conscious contrast – from the *Malleus maleficarum* to the *malleus Dei*, from whipping witches to scourging sin: what we are called upon to endure comes to us from the 'hammer' of God, not the mischief of witches. We should trust God as we would a physician whose distasteful medicine we faithfully swallow in hope of recovering our eternal health and salvation.[64]

Plantsch extended this same confidence in God to his *Mater Ecclesia* and expected the same of all faithful Christians. In the concluding portion, dealing with the antidotes to the *media* of magic, Plantsch drew his line of demarcation between the believing and the superstitious use of such antidotes in the authority granted to the church to 'institute' remedies, just as Christ had once instituted the sacraments. The dividing line between faith and superstition followed the principle that God alone frees the believer from the power of witchcraft. To believe certain forms, intonations or locations to be decisive for the success of a 'remedy' made one a slave of superstition. That one should face north and not east, remain in one's house and not go to the wine cellar, whisper rather than speak the words aloud, remain seated instead of standing, wear the talisman around the neck but

other hand both Plantsch and Biel agreed fully in their opinion of astrology. See *Collectorium*, II, dist. 14 q. 1 art. 3 dub. 3 P; Biel, *Epitome*, fol. hh 5vb–hh6^{rb}.

63 This threefold division is a subjective one because Plantsch and his publisher inserted no external indication of the transitions between sections. But the introductory sentence of what I have termed the 'concluding part' seems to me to justify the divisions. Fol. $e5^{r}$.

64 'Dic mihi, quid amari habes tibi datum a medico deo, quod prius in calice non biberit suo; si tibi offertur contumelia, prior cum daemones eiiceret, audivit: "In Beelcebub eiecit daemonia"; si dolores abominaris, prius ipse flagellatus, coronatus, crucifixus est; si mortem times, mortuus est; si genus mortis horrescis, ignominiosissimam mortem subiit. Et ut uno dicam verbo: quicquid tribulationis, quicquid adversitatis tibi iste de coelo medicus pro medicina offert, ipse prius idem assumpsit. Unde si contra medicum talem murmuras, si medicum hunc blasphemas, si medicinam eius inepte repellis, quae spes salutis, quae spes vitae tibi esse potest?' Fols. $d8^{v}$–$e1^{r}$. Cf. the same imagery by Luther from the same period but centred on the word of promise rather than the example: 'Est enim simile sicut cum aegroto. Qui promittenti medico certissimam sanitatem credit et precepto eius obediens interim in spe promissae sanitatis abstinet ab iis, que prohibita sunt ei ne promissam sanitatem impediat et morbus augeat, donec impleat medicus, quod promisit' (referring to Rom. 4.7). *WA* 56, p. 272, lines 3–7.

never over one's heart – to follow such instructions was 'superstitious', inappropriate, and glorified neither God nor the saints.[65]

The assurance that certain devotional exercises achieve certain effects is superstitious delusion, except when it can be shown that such practices have been authorized. Certain prayers are more effectual than others because they have been instituted by Christ (the Lord's Prayer) or the angels (Ave Maria), the apostles (Credo), the fathers, the saints or the church (the canonical hours and liturgical prayers linked to indulgences).[66] Thus the antidotes are primarily cries for help that give all glory to God. No counter-magic can accomplish what God alone can do: send the devil packing. Appeals to the saints likewise suited Plantsch's framework, since in venerating the saints one reveres and praises God.[67] Because it became a hotly contested issue in the early years of the Reformation, we shall return later to this traditional understanding of the reverence due the saints.

Even though, by present-day standards, Plantsch retained a con-

[65] 'Sic si quis putat remedia aliqua talia plus efficatia, si in ortu solis vel ante quam post, aut si verso vultu ad septentrionem quam ad austrum vel meridiem, aut in cellario plus quam domo, aut plus sub arbore quam divo, vel magis efficatia in bivio quam campo, aut si susurrata quam expresse et intelligibiliter dicta, aut plus sedendo quam stando prolata, aut si portetur in collo aut lumbasio plus quam in sinu, superstitiosus est: illae enim observantiae et consimiles nec ad rem nec ad dei aut sanctorum laudem pertinent, ideoque sicut stulte ita et vane illis admiscentur, per quae a deo solo liberationis effectus expectatur.' Fol. e8^{r}.

[66] 'Verumtamen si in huiusmodi remediis sint orationes exorcismi aut alia non prohibita nec speciem mali habentia, illae assumantur observantiae, quae sanctorum atque dei laudem respiciunt, non reprobandae sunt. Ut cum orando credis hanc tuam orationem plus exaudiendam pro impetrando aliquo suffragio quam aliam consimilem sensum habentem; et hoc ideo credis, quia haec oratio quam assumis, est a Christo instituta ut Pater noster, vel ab angelo pronunciata ut salutatio angelica, aut apostolis composita ut Simbolum, vel a patribus sicut orationes prophetarum, aut a sanctis et ab ecclesia catholica sicut horae canonice, vigiliae mortuorum et caetera publice in ecclesia ordinata, vel quia est specialibus privilegiis indulgentiarum dotata. Non prohibeo talem orationem prae aliis assumendam, aut credere plus aliis esse impetraturam, quia qui huiusmodi orationes Christi, sanctorum vel ecclesiae prae ceteris ideo assumit, quia ab ispsis institutae, in hoc specialem deo et sanctis honorem, ideo non mirum, si plus tales orationes quam alias orando exaudiantur a deo.' Fols. e8^{r}–e8^{v}. Cf. the basic passage from Gabriel Biel, *Canonis misse expositio*, Lectio 57 B; Oberman and Courtenay edn, 2, p. 394 with a reference to Gerson, *De oratione* (ed. Du Pin, 3, p. 248B–C) = *Epistola 37* to his brother Jean the Celestine, 28 September 1416; *Gerson, Oeuvres*, ed. Glorieux, 2, pp. 170f. See also Steinbach's disputation on *sacramentalia* and *sacramenta* (causa sine qua non!) with its concluding theses concerning their superstitious misuse (1500). *Steinbach, Opera exegetica*, ed. Feld, 1, pp. xxvif. Cf. *ibid.*, pp. 217, line 22–218, line 8.

[67] 'In his enim omnibus et consimilibus spes non in verbis, rebus, observantiis, sed in deo et sanctis ecclesiaeque orationibus figitur, ad quorum reverentiam vel humilem obedientiam haec aguntur, imo in sole deo, quia reverentia sanctis exhibita in deum redundat, nec aliud in sanctis quam deum reveremur atque laudamus.' Fol. e8^{v}.

siderable measure of credulity about witchcraft, it becomes clear that, owing to his nominalist training, he was well suited to scorn the tools of witchcraft as mere apparent causes. At the same time his modernist background aided him in removing the remedies against witchcraft from underneath their awe-filled awning of superstition.[68] Words of prayer, consecrated water and flickering candles by themselves heal nothing and cause nothing. They can have only the 'effect' of the royal insignia that protect the traveller from the dangers of the road: such signs have no force or power apart from signifying the royal government that guarantees protection.[69]

Following Plantsch's train of thought, we find ourselves in the company of a different set of ideas from those of Trithemius' *Antipalus*, which was completed one year after Plantsch published his *Opusculum*. Trithemius ascribed an independent significance and supernatural causality to both the tools of witchcraft and their corresponding antidotes, clearly separating himself from Plantsch's radically theocentric understanding of an 'imputed' covenantal causation. Trithemius' widely read and influential work portrayed the defensive weapons against demon attack not as the protective insignia of Almighty God but as potent amulets. When a new edition of the *Antipalus* appeared a century later in Mainz (1605), after the deletion, by its Jesuit editor (Busaeus), of those passages which appeared too magical,[70] a 'witch's dagger' remained which exerted a more pointed influence on its century than the 'hammer' of the previous one, but which stood in the same tradition and did as much to further the witchcraft craze as its Dominican predecessor had done.[71]

The influence of the *Malleus maleficarum* awaits detailed investigation, but in German-speaking areas it certainly helped to direct the growth and consolidation of what were at that time far from estab-

68 'Notanter autem pensandum est, quod dixi, ut scilicet a solo deo liberationis effectus expectetur. Non enim credendum est, quod verba prolata vel aqua benedicta, cereus ardens et similia inducant sanitatem fugatis daemonibus, sed solus deus per orationem, verba et alia invocatus fugat daemonia.' Fol. f1^{r}.

69 'Recte enim sicut ambulans habens signum regis, liber est ab hostibus, non quia signum, quod defert, securitatem praestet aut hostes fuget, sed potentia regis hanc securitatem reddit, ita huiusmodi licita media non sua virtute fugant daemones et ab eisdem liberant, sed dei omnipotens virtus, quae per talia media veneratur atque colitur, fugat et liberat a maleficiis . . .' Fol. f1^{r}.

70 Walker cites good reasons for viewing at least the third part of the *Steganographia*, which appeared one year later (1606), as a 'treatise on demonic magic'. *Spiritual and Demonic Magic*, p. 89.

71 'In seinem *Antipalus* steht Trithemius ganz auf dem Standpunkte des Hexenhammers . . .' Silbernagel, *Johannes Trithemius*, p. 156.

lished views on demonology. However important social or economic factors may be for understanding the total phenomenon, no component was by itself as significant for the sudden expansion of the witchcraft persecutions as was the bull *Summis* issued by Innocent VIII in 1484 or the dissemination of the Dominican 'witch-hunter's handbook' that appeared three years later. Innocent's bull bestowed the church's official blessing on witch-burning much as the crusades had earned the ecclesiastical seal of approval several centuries earlier; a kind of 'causa Dei' medal or *bulla*. The *Malleus* forged the collective force of canonical and canonist authorities into a powerful tool.[72] Its two Dominican authors, Jacob Sprenger and Heinrich Krämer, were authorized to compile their own manual since the bull *Summis* had already named them judges in witchcraft trials within the ecclesiastical provinces of Mainz, Cologne, Trier, Salzburg and Bremen. In addition, they had been placed under imperial protection in their function as inquisitors [1486] and received the express endorsement of the theological faculty at Cologne on 19 May 1487.[73]

Although already in the fifteenth century Sebastian Brant's *Narrenschiff*,[74] and shortly thereafter Thomas Murner's *Schelmenzunft* and *Narrenbeschwörung*,[75] had directed satiric shafts at the witchcraft craze, satire proved too mild a weapon to combat the growing fury of persecution. Instead, the theories of the Inquisition won a broad popular foundation.

72 Any monocausal theory proves inadequate to explain the complex phenomenon of the witchcraft trials of the sixteenth century. In connection with their origins in the fifteenth century we must especially emphasize the role of the ecclesiastical authorities. But that still does not justify talk of manipulation 'from above'. Wanda von Baeyer-Katte, who estimates that about one million trials for witchcraft took place between 1450 and 1730, has argued that 'an enlightened attitude toward the witchcraft trials rose from the bottom to the top [of society]'. She explains the phrase 'from the bottom' by asserting that 'the lower the level of literary education, the less one believes in witchcraft'. 'Die historischen Hexenprozesse. Der verbürokratisierte Massenwahn', pp. 223, 224. We can find little support for this thesis.

73 Cf. the literature listed in Löhr, *Die Kölner Dominikanerschule vom 14. bis 16. Jahrhundert*, pp. 104f.

74 'And then, when comes the bright New Year,/The one who gifts does not receive/Will fear a year when he must grieve/And other superstitious fancy,/ Palm-reading, e'en ornithomancy,/Or symbols, signs, and books of dreams,/Or search for things by Luna's beams,/Or black arts done with pomp and show./There's not a thing men wouldn't know . . . Yet naught it is but blasphemy/To treat such matters frivolously,/To force th' Almighty we'd aspire/And bend His will to our desire./God's love and favor now have fled,/We seek the devil's art instead.' *The Ship of Fools by Sebastian Brant*, transl. Zeydel, pp. 218–19; cf. *Sebastian Brants Narrenschiff*, ed. Zarncke, pp. 64, lines 42–50, 65, lines 87–92.

75 See Thomas Murner, *Die Narrenbeschwörung* (1512): [46] 'Ein hagel sieden'; [83] 'Thürung der heiligen'. *Thomas Murners Deutsche Schriften*, ed. Spanier, vol. 2, pp. 288ff., 404ff.

Martin Plantsch's sermons, which may also represent a Tübingen response to the Cologne approval of the *Malleus maleficarum*,[76] were potentially more efficacious than satire in probing the intellectual presuppositions of the Dominican 'hammer'. Yet Plantsch's efforts enjoyed no more success than had Brant's or Murner's barbs. The clouds of the battle of 'obscure men' had not settled solely over the heads of the supposedly obscurantist Dominicans at Cologne but had overshadowed and obscured the authority of every academic master who claimed to have cornered the market on truth or undertook where possible the renewal of scholasticism. Plantsch found it impossible to succeed against the combined forces of pope and popular superstition, emperor and Inquisition.

Yet on another front his observations did prove their relevance. His Catholic loyalty to and respect for the church bore fruit in the thesis that all methods instituted by the church, and therefore inspired by the Holy Spirit, may reasonably and effectively be employed in the struggle against demonic forces. Relics, holy water, consecrated salt, candles, palm branches, lamps blessed on the eve of Easter: all these, as we noted, have no effectiveness of themselves. Rather, they all draw their power from their institution by the intercession of the church, the Bride of Christ whom God never abandons and whose prayers he never rejects because he governs her through the Holy Spirit.[77] To employ *these* weapons is not merely authorized, but meritorious.[78]

Unlike the seven sacraments, these *sacramentalia* do not work *ex opere operato* on the basis of their having been officially imparted and

[76] The surprising appeal by Plantsch to Aquinas' *Summa* three times in the course of his treatment of the issue of the *remedia* against witchcraft can perhaps be explained as an attempt to play off the Dominican order's 'house theologian' against the two authors of the *Malleus*. See fols. e8^{v}; f1^{v}; g3^{r}.

[77] 'Haec omnia iam dicta remedia non habent efficatiam ex se, sed precipue ex institutione et petitione ecclesiae, sponsae Christi, cui semper assistit deus, qui eam in suis precibus non repellit, quia Spiritu Sancto eam regit.' Fol. g1^{r}. The *sacramentalia* do not work *ex opere operato* as do the sacraments but primarily by virtue of their institution through the church and secondarily on the condition that the victim of demonic assault has attained true *contritio*, a condition explicitly not required in the sacrament of penance: 'Quicumque enim debita intentione ea suscipit a legitime conferente, intentione scilicet hac per huiusmodi susceptionem velle consequi ea, propter quae instituta sunt, et non ponit obicem contrarium illi effectui – id est, non habet actuale propositum vel complacentiam peccati mortalis aut dissensum recipiendi sacramentum – , ille semper consequitur gratiam, et sic sanitatem animae, etiam si non habeat interius motum bonum interiorem, sicut declarari potest de infante baptisato. Et haec remedia sic efficacia a deo solo instituta sunt.' Fol. g2^{v}.

[78] 'Iccirco talibus uti secundum ecclesiae ordinationem ne dum licitum est, sed etiam meritorium.' Fol. g1^{r}.

partaken,[79] but are dependent on the qualification and preparation of their recipients, i.e. they work *ex opere operantis*. But he who employs these ecclesiastically sanctioned defences against demons should not rely excessively on his competence or his own faith but rather appeal to the faith of the entire church and its merits. Plantsch made the distinction completely clear in regard to the use of holy water:[80] the merits and faith of the whole church exceed those of an individual just as the efficacy of the church's ritual of exorcism exceeds that of the individual believer's pious behaviour. Hence general criticism of these *devotionalia* is out of place – they become superstition only in the absence of an intention to honour God and the saints.[81] Although Plantsch by no means questioned the significance of the *sacramentalia*, he pointed out once more at the conclusion of his treatise that only the sacraments are always effective, because no *pactum Dei* exists for the *sacramentalia* and God has not obliged himself to ensure their efficacy.[82] Hence these supplements to the sacraments contrast with the witches' claims for the infallibility of their magical efforts. Returning to his point of departure, Plantsch noted that, collectively considered, the defensive weapons of the church are all forms of prayer in which the believer threatened by evil powers places his

79 Fol. g2v.

80 'Primo quod aqua benedicta et caetera ab ecclesia instituta, non sunt ab ecclesia contemnenda, licet non sint sacramenta nec habeant efficaciam ex opere operato; quia effectum habent non solum ex merito et fide utentis sed ecclesiae totius. Unde sicut non est parvipendenda fides, meritum et oratio totius ecclesiae, sic nec ab ea instituta. Et quanto plus valet meritum et fides totius ecclesiae quam unius personae, tanto cerimoniae universalis ecclesiae praecellunt devotionem singulorum.' Fol. f3r. Plantsch referred here to Petrus de Palude (†1342), IV Sent. d. 2 q. 1 art. 2, who was also held in high esteem by Biel. That he deserves to be classified as a 'Thomist' has been disputed; see Roensch, *Early Thomistic School*, pp. 124–31. See also the two theses of Wendelin Steinbach from a disputation on the *sacramentalia* (1500) which Helmut Feld has transcribed from manuscript Mc 185 of the University Library, Tübingen: 'Sicut non est parvipendenda ecclesia [*crossed out*: meritum] fides aut preces ad Dominum fuse, ita nec sacramentalia pleraque ab ea aut eius ministris rite instituta, generales quoque et laudate ceremonie divinitus inspirate, tametsi effectum habeant non ex opere operato, sed [*crossed out*: per modum fidei et meriti] ex opere operantis (fol. 222v). Aqua benedicta et similibus sane utitur ecclesia contra demonia et venialia peccata (fol. 224v).' *Steinbach, Opera exegetica* 1, p. xxvii.

81 'Ad includendum debitam intentionem, ita scilicet honorandi deum, ecclesiam et sanctos dei . . .' Fol. g1r.

82 'Alia sunt remedia minora, quae dicuntur sacramentalia, quae non sunt ita efficacia, nec ita certa, quod semper sequatur effectus, propter quem instituta sunt, cum ab hominibus in usum sumuntur, sed requiritur certa dispositio in ministrante vel assumente, secundum meritum devotionem aut motum bonum interiorem, vel sequitur effectus aliquando ex mera liberalitate donantis dei absque pacto de assistendo et operando semper huiusmodi effectum ad assumptionem illorum.' Fol. g2v.

hope on the author, Almighty God himself, and not merely on the means of defence.[83]

Aside from the brief but programmatically pertinent discussion by Midelfort, Plantsch's sermons have played no role in previous studies of late medieval intellectual history. Nevertheless they merit our attention. They offer a 'modern' weapon against the witchcraft delusion in which the philosophical reinterpretation of second causes – their consistent subordination to God's contingent activity – was united with the theological stress on God's covenantal pledge to form a programme of demystification. The sermons undermine not merely the delusion of the common people in their erroneous credulity towards the demonic powers of anti- and extra-ecclesiastical forces. The lofty churchly superstitions which endowed the church's exorcising *media* with a magical, autonomous efficacy, also came under fire.

By the end of the sixteenth century Plantsch could hardly have marketed his 'rational' ideas under the seal of wholesome Catholic theology. Belief in witches and witchcraft had become too closely identified with orthodoxy, indeed, with the orthodox theologies and hierarchies of *all* the confessions! But even during his lifetime, pointed criticism appeared from a totally different source. The sacramental doctrine in which the functioning of God's covenant was dependent on the cooperation of the sinner, became the target of the Wittenberg theology, coming under attack even where 'cooperation' was defined 'merely' as an absence of resistance to grace. From Luther's perspective, such a teaching was a *pactum illicitum*, a conspiracy with the devil to annul the cross of Christ. This confrontation then sparked an explosion over the *pactum cum ecclesia*: the controversy over what constituted the true church.

In south Germany the target of the first critical clamour was not the Catholic doctrine of justification, but what was perceived as an excessively 'magical' view of the church's sacraments and *sacramentalia*. The devotional aids and *sacramentalia* gave rise to a far more powerful critique in that area, which included Plantsch's own diocese of Constance with a protest epicentre in Zürich, than can be detected in Wittenberg. For Tübingen's Plantsch we must stress that his doctrine regarding the *sacramentalia* assumed as its basic principle that

83 'Et ex his primo patet differentia inter exorcismos et cerimonias ecclesiae, et exorcismos et observantias incantatorum, quia in primis solum invocatur nomen divinum, nec spes aliqua nisi in solum deum ponitur, a quo effectus expectatur, ne admiscetur illis aliquid falsum vel vanum ad dei vel sanctorum honorem non pertinens. In cerimoniis autem et exorcismis maleficorum inseruntur vel quae ad invocationem daemonum pertinent, vel falsa aut non intelligibilia atque vana, spes quoque in alio quam in deo ponitur, et effectus a diabolo expectatur.' Fol. g4r.

the practices of the church, whether exorcism or touching relics, burning candles or sprinkling holy water, were effective because they glorify God, his saints and his church. These forms of devotion are prayerful entreaties (not magic), directed to God, instituted and sanctioned by his church, the Bride of Christ who intercedes in the company of her saints before the throne of God on behalf of the individual believer.

Thus, before the veneration of the saints and icons came to symbolize the superstitious adulteration of the gospel[84] and became the subject of countless Protestant leaflets and theological tracts, Plantsch had offered, on the very eve of the Reformation, a critical and 'fully Catholic'[85] defence of the veneration of the saints. Armed in this fashion, Plantsch was a fine choice to travel to Zürich in 1523 as a member of the bishop of Constance's delegation assigned the task of arresting the errant course of Zwingli's reformation.

At the end of this chapter we recall Erik Midelfort's observations regarding a sermon style specific to Tübingen[86] which managed to escape the revolutionary changes of the Reformation. It is true that in the Württemberg reformer Johannes Brenz we find attempts at rational enlightenment that resemble those of Plantsch: the omnipotent God delegates power only temporarily, and superstition ascribes more powers to witches than they actually possess.[87] But aside from these common themes it is difficult to test the thesis of a continuity in sermon style, since Plantsch reworked his spoken sermons into a written treatise.

We can, however, compare the content of both these theologians' thought by considering their understanding of Job, the Old Testament character who represented for both Plantsch and Brenz the believer assailed by demonic powers. Plantsch took Job as evidence that even when handed over to temporary torment at the hands of

84 'Aber – Gott klag ich es – mein Herz ist von Jugend auf in Ehrerbietung und Hochachtung vor den Bildern erzogen worden und auch so aufgewachsen . . . Gott möge mir seine Gnade geben, dass ich die Teufelsköpfe [images] – die gewöhnlich in der Kirche Heilige genannt werden – nicht mehr fürchte als Stein und Holz; und Gott gebe, dass ich Stein und Holz nicht dem Schein und Namen nach als Heilige verehre. Amen.' Andreas Carlstadt, *Von Abtuhung der Bilder und das keyn Bedtler unther den Christen seyn sollen, 1522*, ed. H. Lietzmann, p. 19, lines 19–37.

85 I use this term in the same sense as Joseph Lortz who, however, could only see nominalism as a typical form of late medieval 'lack of clarity' that was 'no longer fully catholic' or was even 'radically uncatholic'. *The Reformation in Germany*, 1, pp. 196, 199 (=1, pp. 173, 176 in *Die Reformation in Deutschland*, 4th edn). Cf. Hubert Jedin's theological critique of Lortz, 'Zur Aufgabe des Kirchengeschichtsschreibers', p. 28.

86 See above, p. 164.

87 Midelfort stresses the parallels in sermon construction. See *Witch Hunting*, pp. 34ff.

Satan, the believer can never be wrested from the supreme sovereignty exercised by God. In contrast, for Brenz, Job typified the Christian believer who experiences the hand of God in the midst of daily threats from the devil and finds his faith in God's mercy strengthened by the suffering he endures: 'In their essence the cross and God are inseparable.'[88] Whereas for Plantsch, faith and the religious application of the *sacramentalia* constituted the divinely and ecclesiastically ordained defence against the power of Satan and conspiracies of witches, Brenz considered faith itself to the guarantee that the devil and his entire staff of demons would leave no stone unturned in their campaign against the believer.

Brenz can be described as having disenfranchised the demonic world through the application of the *theologia crucis*. Plantsch and Brenz moved in different worlds where the one described faith as a shield against the devil's darts and the other portrayed that same shield as a target inviting those satanic shafts. But neither denied the reality of the demonic world; rather, both sought to fix the limits of the devil's power and the boundaries of his parade-ground.

One central theme merits a special concluding glance. It is a mark of the 'first Tübingen school' in which, despite all structural changes and reforms within and without the university, we espy a thread of continuity in the perception of the theological task, a constant line leading from the university's founding years into the epoch following the Württemberg reformation. Both before and after, theology and theologians at Tübingen refused to withdraw into the ivory tower of scholarship but sought to shape the piety and devotion that form the indispensable foundation for faith. The tension between a *devotio perennis* and an academic theology can be traced under varying labels through the history of the Tübingen theological faculty even to the present. Aside from occasional invasions on the part of scholasticism, scholastic Protestant orthodoxy, and a self-proclaimed presuppositionless theological scholarship, this union has been not a burden but a fertile basis for a 'Tübingen school' which served both church and scholarship in their pursuit of the *praxis pietatis*.

[88] Brecht, *Die frühe Theologie des Johannes Brenz*, p. 160; cf. pp. 154, 158.

Part III

NEW JERUSALEM WITHIN THE OLD WALLS

10

Magistri and magistracy: the old and new masters

POPULAR PIETY forms the vital substratum of all theology. It fashions the domestic climate in which future theologians are nurtured and it also determines the response and range of influence enjoyed by a new theological 'school'. The history of Mariology provides a convincing example of the enormous creative power of a piety that managed to triumph over periodic resistance from 'high' theology. By winning the coming generation of theologians as its most enthusiastic publicists and advocates before the bar of academic theology, the new veneration for the Virgin overcame what had previously passed for immutable dogma.[1]

The stream of theology which finds its channels in teaching and preaching according to scripture and tradition forms different currents. But any theology whose course skirts popular piety can at best leave its mark on centuries of academia or impress posterity in a delayed reaction; in its own epoch it is powerless to move and mould history.

In the course of confessional conflict the sixteenth century witnessed the mobilization of the area of popular devotion we have come to call lay piety. The rapid expansion of the educational system, from elementary schools to universities, produced the same effect on the general population as had the growth of scholarship in the urban upper classes and at the courts of the nobility. The aspiring, educated segments of society now found themselves able to articulate their religious needs, a capability once largely limited to the clergy. Among both groups, a peculiar fluctuation can be observed between a condescending criticism of the religious life of the 'plebs' and a sense of solidarity with a populace either deceived, intentionally imprisoned in ignorance or oppressed by religious and secular authorities.

The multifaceted Reformation movement offered three therapies for these three maladies afflicting the masses. In combating, with Luther, the *deception* of the faithful, the preaching of the gospel

[1] See Rusch, 'Mariologische Wertungen', pp. 129–50.

received absolute priority. Hence Luther could suggest the otherwise incomprehensible compromise that he abandon his criticism of the indulgence system and the doctrine of the church's treasury of merits in return for complete and guaranteed freedom to proclaim the gospel of free grace *sola fide*.

Those reformers who considered the educational aspirations of the Renaissance as both a signal and a basis for a renewal of the church concentrated their attack on the *enforced ignorance* of the common folk and transformed the preaching of the gospel into a pedagogical mission. Attempting to enlighten the laity and reorient their devotional practices to conform with scripture turned the veneration of the saints and the use of icons into cardinal illustrations of the confusion that had entered the relationship between Creator and creature.

The struggle against the *oppression* of the people led to an emphasis on the validity and priority of divine justice at the expense of ecclesiastical statutes and placed the issue of tithes on the centre of the stage. In a tradition whose proponents ranged from Reublin, Grebel and Schappeler to Thomas Müntzer this controversy proved to be of special significance for the peasant revolts.

Yet amid such varied accents one goal remained fundamental and common to all: the liberation of consciences which, deceived and seduced into self-righteousness, had been enslaved for the purpose of exploitation. No matter how scholarly and desk-bound the coordinates of Luther's evangelical experience may appear to modern Luther scholars, the object of his theology was the renewal of lay piety. The surprising reception enjoyed by his ideas, at least until 1522, indicates his success in presenting the doctrine of justification as the springboard for true piety. That he did not immediately demand an end to the veneration of saints and images, or even, at first, to the excesses of the indulgence trade, in no way contradicts Luther's pursuit of true piety. For he was convinced that such practices would lose their credibility and popularity, becoming superfluous once true faith was understood to be the fulfilment of the law. The breeding ground for anguished efforts to court divine favour would be drained in every soul that knew God's favour to be guaranteed in faith. As long as the church's preaching remained obedient to the Gospel, the reformation of popular piety had no need of legalistic props: once its vital trunk had been resuscitated, the dead branches would drop of their own accord.

Despite similarities in basic outline, the Reformation, when introduced to south Germany and Switzerland, followed a different course from that at Wittenberg. Concern to maintain and further the common weal conferred a public relevance on the practice of piety which invested the questions of the veneration of saints and images with a special urgency from the outset. Top priority went not to unmasking deception and exploitation but to promoting obedience to the will of God as proclaimed in scripture. Invariably the first conflicts arose over forms of expressing faith such as the 'Ave Maria' and the veneration of saints and not over one of the ninety-five theses; to say nothing of the issue of justification *sola fide*.

The young German universities did not escape the surge of criticism of a deceived people ignorant through no fault of its own. Divided by the strife between the *via antiqua* and *via moderna* imported from Oxford and Paris, the German schools' reputation and scholarly influence had reached rock bottom. Thus humanist complaints about scholastic 'narrow-mindedness' and 'hairsplitting' as captured in the slogan, 'a notion for every noggin', easily turned the academic establishment into an object of public ridicule. In Tübingen such taunts, though perhaps not eliminated, had at least been quieted by the two ways' agreement to disagree. Such peaceful coexistence permitted an intensified development of each *via*'s specific assets and complemented a mutual concern for the promotion of piety and the reform of church practice.

But before long a new challenge arrived from the south. Humanism knocked at university portals advertising a solution to the educational crisis of the age: a curriculum based on the classical languages. The crop of para-university academies and *sodalitates* that sprang up all over Europe documents the imminence of the challenge faced by the universities. It is perhaps dangerous to speculate regarding the perils that would have awaited the established schools had the humanist pedagogical programme succeeded in establishing an elitist detour around the university. The universities may, in that case, have found themselves facing the prospect of reduction to mere professional schools training pastors, lawyers and physicians.

A long overdue change of course became possible in Tübingen after the flight of Duke Ulrich and change of governments in 1519. A new incumbent occupied Bebel's chair of rhetoric that same year, and in 1521 not only were new chairs for Greek and Hebrew established but the Swabian *Magister magistrorum*, Johannes Reuchlin, was persuaded to pass his remaining days in Tübingen. Furthermore, despite only partial realization, the reform statutes of 1525 offer us a realistic notion of attempts at renewal in the faculty of arts.

The image of the academic masters had scarcely begun to improve following their accommodation to the new scholarly ideals, although the tradition-oriented theologians conceded very little, when a new movement appeared at the edge of the diocese of Constance. Bishop Hugh of Landenberg (1496–1528) faced the challenge of the 'new masters' in Zürich who threatened to usurp decision-making powers previously reserved to bishops and academic *magistri* at papally approved universities.

It was the recurring question of the veneration of saints, a devotional practice so eloquently championed by Martin Plantsch in his 1505 sermons, that stimulated the Zürich innovations. For the intervening years had witnessed a growing uneasiness in this regard that had unsettled the celestial hierarchy of the church's superstructure; a construction well buttressed by scholastic theology and understood to constitute the link between God and the terrestrial community of the faithful. Although merely a peripheral aspect in present-day study of the Christian communities of belief, in the 1520s the veneration of the saints irritated the nerve-point where piety and ecclesiology intersect. Conflict first arose when concern was voiced that Christian love was being lavished on long-deceased saints while believers on this earth languished in need.[2]

This controversy attracted the public eye through the so-called 'first Zürich disputation' of 29 January 1523. The object of special attention in recent research, this disputation has afforded scholars an opportunity both to study the appearance of the fledgling left wing of the Swiss Reformation[3] and to demonstrate the Zürich debate's prototypical significance. Bernd Moeller terms this public disputation, based on scripture and held during a session of the city council,[4] the 'founding assembly of the evangelical church of Zürich'.[5] It was likewise the precursor of a series of disputations in which Moeller

[2] See the statement submitted to the Zürich city council on 13 September 1522 by Pastor Rudolf Ammann in which he defended himself against attacks attributed to him by the bishop of Constance. Egli, *Acten*, no. 271.

[3] Cf. Walton, *Zwingli's Theocracy*, pp. 133–8. In addition see Goeters, 'Die Vorgeschichte des Täufertums in Zürich'. Goeters considers the 'Simon Stumpf case', Stumpf's outcry ('man sei keinen Zehnten schuldig') and his imprisonment to have given rise to the disputation. *Ibid.*, pp. 246, 252. For further literature see Stayer et al., 'From Monogenesis to Polygenesis: The Historical Discussion of Anabaptist Origins', pp. 93–100; and Fast, 'Reformation durch Provokation. Predigtstörungen in den ersten Jahren der Reformation in der Schweiz'.

[4] 'vor gesessnem radt' in the words of Magister Erhard Hegenwald's account, which was 'written down in my home after the session'. *ZW* 1, p. 479, lines 1–6 and p. 480, line 9.

[5] Moeller, 'Zwinglis Disputationen. Studien zu den Anfängen der Kirchenbildung und des Synodalwesens im Protestantismus', 1, p. 319.

detects the 'origins of the Reformed church'.[6] But compared with the examination of far-ranging questions regarding the historical significance of the event, study of the actual course of the disputation has seemed less attractive. And it has been a prominent and predictable tendency of earlier Zwingli research to cast the man and his personality in the title role of a smoothly executed dramatic piece. According to this scenario, Zwingli's performance at the disputation swept the representatives of the bishop of Constance into the wings, relegating them to film extras[7] engaged in a useless battle 'to bring the debacle to an end'.[8]

But to perceive the disputation as 'Zwingli's invention' and to tailor the account around the triumph of the Swiss reformer blurs the profile of the powers and parties shaping the debate. One detail of the otherwise thoroughly studied background of the 'first Zürich disputation' has likely been overlooked precisely because it does not fit the image of 'Zwingli's Zürich'.

On 20 January 1523 Glarean complained in a letter to Zwingli that the Zürich reformer had given him the wrong date for his anticipated debate with Fabri: 'I talked with Oecolampadius and he expects to

[6] Bernd Moeller, 'Die Ursprünge der reformierten Kirche', p. 651.

[7] Thus it is understandable that Steven E. Ozment could refer to 'rigged disputations, veritable charades tacitly agreed to in advance, as happened in Nürnberg, Zurich and Constance'. *The Reformation in the Cities. The Appeal of Protestantism to Sixteenth-Century Germany and Switzerland*, p. 125. The tension and trembling with which the conclusion of the Zürich disputation was awaited – according to the accounts of the day's events – as well as the joyful sense of relief after the announcement of the 'ordinance on preaching' on the afternoon of 29 January 1523 indicate that Zwingli and his followers at least were less than sure of the outcome. From Zwingli's perspective the disputation was more likely to be 'rugged' than 'rigged'. See also Rudolf Pfister, 'Kirche und Glaube auf der Ersten Zürcher Disputation vom 29. Januar 1523', p. 557. Not only the outcome, but even the precise date and format of the proceedings were unclear to Zwingli. Leonhard von Muralt has pointed to 'the tension, the quivering, the quaking', of the days preceding and following the announcement of the Bern disputation (17 November 1527). 'Stadtgemeinde und Reformation in der Schweiz', pp. 372–4.

[8] Baur, *Zwinglis Theologie. Ihr Werden und ihr System*, vol. 1, pp. 174–98; esp. p. 193. Cf. his earlier work *Die erste Züricher Disputation*. An English translation of the Hegenwald account of the disputation is found in *Ulrich Zwingli (1484–1531). Selected Works*, ed. Jackson, pp. 40–117. For the disputation's promulgation decree, see *ibid.*, pp. 43–4; for the council's conclusions, pp. 92–3; for Zwingli's sixty-seven theses, pp. 111–17.

One source – though mentioned by Finsler in *ZW* 1, p. 478 – has never received proper recognition: the Latin version of the disputation by Rudolph Gwalther, the husband of Zwingli's daughter Regula and the state-church oriented successor of Bullinger. In the second volume of his *Opera Huldrychi Zwingli* (=*Opp. Zw.*), Gwalther was, to be sure, dependent on Bullinger's history of the Reformation but apparently also had access to his own sources. But above all the Latin translation makes it possible to clarify ambiguous expressions. *Ibid.*, fols. 607^r–623^r.

come, although he is not yet sure. But your letter announcing the disputation for the 20th of January has led us completely astray. I had eagerly passed it around to friends and those who read it and have now travelled to Zürich in vain will be likely to be angry with me . . .'[9]

Zwingli may have been misinformed regarding the form of the disputation as well, expecting to assume a university professor's function as moderator and judge of a debate over his own theses. Oecolampadius criticized him sharply for such presumption and in so doing was probably dependent on information from Zwingli himself.[10] We shall consider later how much importance should be ascribed to the futile journey of Glarean's friends from Basel to Zürich. For the present we note merely that the proclamation and planning of the disputation were so completely a project of the city council, especially of the lesser council and Mayor Marx Röist, that Zwingli was caught by surprise when the date was set or postponed. Oecolampadius' reaction permits the further conjecture that Zwingli had been falsely informed on the form of the debate: while he prepared for a disputation complete with a series of academic theses, Röist and the lesser council had in mind a public hearing for two conflicting parties. We would thus be well advised not to assume concerted action on the part of Zwingli and the appropriate magistrates, but to endeavour to view the events from the perspectives of the parties participating.

In order to evaluate the full significance of the actual disputation, we must first consider the political context within which it occurred. We are concerned above all with the circumstances facing the town council in its attempt to serve the public welfare while steering between the emerging ecclesiastical parties.

Even the specific character of the event that took place in the Zürich

[9] 'Cum Oecolaempadio locutus sum. Habet in animo, ut veniat, quamquam certus non est. Mirum in modum fefellit nos charta tua, in qua scripseras XIII. Kalendas Februarias venturam disputationem. Eam cum ubique sedulus apud amicos circumferrem, quidam viderunt ac Tigurum iverunt, fortassis mihi infensi, cum celeritas tua et te et me fefellerit.' *ZW* 8, pp. 8, line 28–9, line 4.

[10] 'Rumor autem narrabat fore apud vos disputationem te praeside.' *ZW* 8, p. 5, lines 14f.; Basel, 17 January 1523. Visions of a para-academic disputation might also have been the source of the irritation in Basel, 'ubi tota universitas esset', that was reported by Glarean. *Ibid.*, p. 7, lines 8f. Erasmus also responded to Zwingli's first notice, sent before the disputation was changed to 29 January. Zwingli had apparently requested the presence of academics from outside Zürich but Erasmus declined the invitation, noting that the matter was of concern to Zürich alone: 'rem unius oppidi esse'. *Ibid.*, p. 9, line 17.

town hall defies simple definition.[11] The difficulty does not result from a lack of historical source material, even though no officially verified minutes of the session exist.[12] The availability of such records would scarcely simplify the historian's task. For the formal definition of what was happening in Zürich on 29 January 1523 was itself one of the points for debate and later proved to have been the decisive theme of the disputation.

From the vantage point of the 'Two Hundred',[13] the combined greater and lesser councils, the motive for the debate lay in the threats to public peace posed by the 'discord and division among those who proclaim the word of God from the pulpit to the common people'. These were the words used in promulgating the disputation on 3 January and in the summation concluded on the afternoon of 29 January. The latter document clearly indicates that the council considered the encounter to be a judicial investigation or hearing. 'They [we] desire to bring to confrontation and interrogate those who accuse each other of false teaching, in order to see which, if any of them, prove to be good and loyal citizens.' Because no one appeared who was willing to accuse Zwingli of preaching heresy, the council decided that he should be permitted to continue to proclaim the Gospel as before 'so long as and to the extent that he pleased, until he – and [not the council] – be acquainted with a superior doctrine'.[14]

[11] The agenda for a session of the Constance cathedral chapter on 15 January 1523 suggests 'diaeta' as the proper label for the external structure: 'Ex parte diete per Thuricenses . . . statuta . . . pro disputatione d. Ulrici Zwingli in negocio Luterano statuta.' Krebs, *Protokolle*, no. 7510.

[12] Egli made use of the following sources in producing his edition of the accounts of the Zürich Disputation of 29 January 1523: Erhard Hegenwald, *Handlung der Versammlung* (3 March 1523), served as the basis; Johann Fabri's report to the government in Innsbruck on 6 February 1523 was consulted for the footnotes in addition to Fabri's *Ain warlich underrichtung, wie es zů Zürch auff den neündzweintzigsten tag des monats Januarii nechstverschynen ergangen sey* (10 March 1523) which was directed against Hegenwald's account. *ZW* 1, p. 483, n. 1. To Egli's sources must be added the account by Gwalther as discussed above, n. 8, and a second edition of the Fabri report, *Ain warlich underrichtung, wie es zu Zürch by dem Zwinglin uff den nün undzwentzigsten tag des monats Januarii nest verschinen ergangen sey* (Zentralbibliothek Zürich Zw 205). Compared to this text, the edition used by Egli is incomplete, lacking two folia and ending abruptly on fol. GIII.

[13] In order to understand the decisive year 1523 it must be noted that even the most recent research has tended to identify too closely Zwingli's intentions with the city council's policy as represented by Mayor Marx Röist; viewing both as constituting a common front against the episcopal delegation. Only the emergence of a fourth party from the ranks of the radical Zwinglians led by Conrad Grebel, Felix Manz and others, pushed Zwingli and the council, as personified by Marx Röist's son and successor, Diethelm, into a closer embrace.

[14] *ZW* 1, p. 471, lines 2f. Text of the announcement *ibid.*, pp. 466–8; the summation, pp. 469–71. Cf. G. Finsler's modern German translation in *Ulrich Zwingli. Eine Auswahl*

The decree concluded by repeating[15] the council's mandate of 1520[16] which made holy scripture the sole basis for preaching and instituted heavy penalties for priests who disparaged others as 'heretics'.[17]

In announcing the disputation on 3 January, the mayor and the Two Hundred set forth their claims to authority. They linked their *ius pacificandi* or responsibility to maintain public peace and order – which no right-thinking citizen would deny – to the *ius iudicandi*. Exercising the latter right of judgment in disputes was now claimed as the task of the political panels of the city; scholarly institutions and their educated members must be satisfied with no more than a supportive and advisory function in the council's deliberations. The bishop of Constance might also [!] send representatives: 'We shall listen attentively there in such company of learned men as we see fit. And depending on what holy scripture and the truth reveal, we shall permit each to return home, commanding one party to desist from their preaching in order that each individual might not begin to proclaim from the pulpit all manner of ideas appearing proper to himself but lacking foundation in the true holy scripture. We shall also inform our gracious Lord, the bishop of Constance, of the same, so that his Grace or his representatives might be present, should they so desire.'[18]

It was not the introduction of the principle of *sola scriptura*[19] which was up for debate. That principle had been valid since the late autumn of 1520, although it was reinforced here: 'Should, however, anyone continue to resist and fail to corroborate his doctrine from holy scripture, we shall proceed against him according to our good judgment, more severely than we would in our compassion prefer.'[20] In contrast to this repetition of a long familiar reality, a hint of an attitude of reform bearing the mark of Zwingli's immediate influence appears in the final sentence of the proclamation. Here the council expressed confidence that scripture would expound itself, making it

aus seinen Schriften, pp. 140–2 and the English translation by McLouth in *Ulrich Zwingli. Selected Works*, p. 93.

15 See below, n. 67.

16 See Bullinger's report concerning the events of 1520: *Heinrich Bullingers Reformationsgeschichte*, ed. Hottinger and Vögeli, vol. 1, p. 32, no. 11.

17 For the discussion surrounding the trustworthiness of Bullinger's account see Farner, *Huldrych Zwingli*, vol. 3, pp. 206–17. Cf. the even earlier discussion by Egli in *ZW* 7, p. 366, n. 4.

18 *ZW* 1, p. 467, lines 11–19. Cf. *Zwingli. Selected Works*, p. 44 and *Zwingli. Eine Auswahl aus seinen Schriften*, p. 141.

19 Egli, 'Zur Einführung des Schriftprinzips in der Schweiz', p. 333.

20 *ZW* 1, pp. 467, line 19–468, line 2.

possible for the council to pass judgment in the light of scripture and permitting the councillors to move and work as 'sons of the Light'.[21]

One might expect to discover this 'innovation of Reformed theology' once more in the summation composed at the end of the special council session. But such was not the case, for that decree redistributed the accents of the proclamation of 3 January. From the council's perspective, the just-completed assembly had witnessed no disputation in an academic sense, but had been limited to a *judicial proceeding*. Furthermore, it had taken the familiar form of an interrogation by confrontation in order to determine which of the two conflicting parties might prove to be the 'good citizen', i.e. obedient to the council.[22] Those who persisted in disturbing public peace and order with scripturally unfounded charges of heresy must reckon with harsh consequences.[23] We no longer find any mention of self-expounding scripture or of the council as its mouthpiece.

Emil Egli pointed out that the mandate to preach on the foundation of scripture alone, which he called the 'Zürich disputation decision' or the 'reformation mandate', became an example for all of Switzerland and south Germany.[24] Thus Egli and Moeller have offered related theses on the influence of the Zürich reformation. One stressed the prototypical significance of the council's *decision* to encourage evangelical preaching, while the other underscored the historical importance of the council session itself, the *assembly* that gave birth to the decision. Both, however, agreed on the historical significance of the events in Zürich. Fritz Blanke expressed that consensus in an as yet unchallenged and concise sentence: 'Zürich became evangelical by city council decree in January 1523.'[25] The question of what is meant by an 'evangelicalism' that owed its existence to a council decree must await later clarification.

As far as the council's perception of its political responsibility was concerned, the disputation resulted in no 'mandate for reformation'

21 'Wir sind ouch gůtter hoffnung zů gott dem almechtigen, er werde die, so das liecht der warheit also ernstlich sůchent, mit demselben gnedencklich erlüchten, unnd das wir dan nachin in dem liecht als sün des liechts wandlen.' *ZW* 1, p. 468, lines 2–6.

22 'welliche als die gehorsamen erschinen.' *ZW* 1, p. 470, line 14.

23 *ZW* 1, p. 471, lines 8f.; cf. p. 467, lines 19ff.

24 Egli, 'Zur Einführung des Schriftprinzips', p. 338. The 'mandate on preaching' is comparable in its paradigmatic effect to the Zürich matrimonial decree of 10 May 1525 (replacing the episcopal matrimonial court), the influence of which spread via French-speaking Switzerland to Geneva. Köhler, *Zürcher Ehegericht und Genfer Konsistorium*, vol. 1, pp. 25f. With its detailed account of this itinerary, this work remains, despite earlier criticism, an exemplary monument of historical research.

25 *Brüder in Christo. Die Geschichte der ältesten Täufergemeinde (Zollikon 1525)*, p. 5. Translated by Nordenhaug, *Brothers in Christ*, p. 7.

or 'introduction of the scripture-based sermon' in the sense of the Reformation, but rather in a pacification decree. Seen historically, the council's conclusions represented the first 'Interim' of the Reformation era. For the sake of ending the tumultuous interruption of sermons and provocation from the pulpit, the excesses of theological controversy were placed under civic legal jurisdiction[26] and classified as 'slander'. The theological dispute's day in court permitted the judges assembled in council session to promise protection to Zwingli and his preaching. This assurance was intended to last until someone should 'inform him of a superior doctrine'.[27] Since 'him' referred to Zwingli and not to the council itself, the council's judicial impartiality was at the same time preserved and emphasized.

Thus the council's concluding decree of 29 January should not be interpreted as the civic authorities' partisan blessing for Zwingli's theological programme, but as a refuge for *all* office-holders, so long as they could demonstrate a scriptural foundation for their preaching.[28] This was not the Reformation concept of the self-evident exposition of scripture. Insistence on formal agreement with scripture was sufficient for the council. The efforts of the bishop's representatives to demonstrate the biblical foundation of ecclesiastical tradition indicate that even this compromise position created serious difficulties for the Catholic delegation.

Thus we are dealing with an adaptation of the decree on preaching passed in the autumn of 1520 and not the 'introduction of Reformation preaching' as interpreted by Zwingli and many later historians of the Reformation. The same mayor who issued the council's verdict on the disputation in his own name, Marx Röist, later proved unyielding when the Zwinglian party attempted to give substance to the call for *formal* agreement with scripture by endeavouring to redecorate the interior of Zürich's churches in basic white. Not until the day of his death, 15 June 1524, was the decree, 'What should be done with the church's images'[29] issued[30] and his son Diethelm, mayor

[26] See the statements by the Tübingen alumnus (1481) Ulrich Zasius (†1535) in his revised edition of the Freiburg city code. *Neue Stadtrechte und Statuten der Stadt Freiburg im Breisgau*, Traktat v, fol. 93^{rv}.

[27] *ZW* 1, p. 471, line 2.

[28] 'anders nüt fürnemmen noch predigen, dann was sy mit dem heiligen euangelion unnd sust rechter göttlicher geschrifft beweren mögen.' *ZW* 1, p. 471, lines 5–7. See also Augustijn, 'Allein das heilig Evangelium, Het mandaat van het Reichsregiment 6 maart 1523'.

[29] 'Wie man mit den kilchengötzen handeln soll.' Egli, *Acten*, no. 546.

[30] 'Es ist recht wahrscheinlich, dass allein Markus Röists Tod den Bruch mit Zwingli und seinen kirchlichen Plänen verhinderte.' Jacob, *Politische Führungsschicht und Reformation. Untersuchungen zur Reformation in Zürich 1519–1528*, p. 235. Jacob cites

from 1525 to 1544, first brought partisan support for Zwingli to that office.[31]

When the Basel city council passed a statute on preaching at the end of May 1523, it followed Zürich's lead[32] and laid down an unambiguous principle of formal agreement with scripture. This Basel action likewise constituted an 'Interim' to remain in effect 'until further instruction'.[33] The council also desired to draw the line between freedom of proclamation and subversive pulpit-provocation threatening the public welfare. The 'holy Gospel and doctrine of God alone'[34] was to be proclaimed not merely in the city parishes but in the monasteries as well. The council specified that this excluded all forms of agitation, all 'teaching, disputing and useless rubbish' contrary to the Gospel, 'whether written by Luther or other doctors whoever they might be . . .'[35] Thus a desire to avoid wild 'disputations' and to impart order to the winnowing of true and false faith and doctrine stood behind the concept that every pastor should, in principle, be prepared to defend his preaching to his colleagues on the basis of scripture.

But Basel faced greater difficulties due to the presence within its walls of a papally privileged and flourishing university with its traditional right of disputation. These problems were illustrated by the alliance between university[36] and cathedral chapter[37] in opposition to a disputation announced by Oecolampadius for 30 August

the chronicle of Bernhard Wyss: 'Das ufrumen der götzen was herrn Marx Röisten gar widrig und ein gros crüz . . .' *Die Chronik des Bernhard Wyss 1519–1530*, ed. Finsler, pp. 40f. Jacob, *Politische Führungsschicht*, p. 236.

31 Against Norman Birnbaum's 'united front of artisans and merchants behind Zwingli' ('The Zwinglian Reformation in Zürich', p. 24), Jacob concludes: 'Die Stellungnahme für oder gegen die Reformation ging aber gesamthaft über alle zünftischen, berufsmässigen und sozialen Schranken und Bindungen ebenso hinweg wie über die familiären.' *Politische Führungsschicht*, p. 116.

32 See 'Das erste predigtmandat des basler rats' in *AGBR* 1, pp. 65–9; here p. 65, note a.

33 *AGBR* 1, p. 67, line 2.

34 *Ibid.*, line 7.

35 'leeren, disputation und stempanien . . . sy syen von dem Luther oder anderen doctoribus, wer die syen, geschriben . . .' *Ibid.*, lines 12–14. For a comparison between the 'mandates on preaching' issued in Zürich, Basel, Strassburg and Constance, see Rublack, *Die Einführung der Reformation in Konstanz von den Anfängen bis zum Abschluss 1531*, p. 244. Rublack notes that it cannot be established that any of the other three 'mandates' were known in Constance.

36 The university protested against a disputation, whether conducted in Latin or German, and affirmed its compliance with the 'ordinances and decrees of the holy Roman and apostolic church'. *AGBR* 1, p. 76, lines 7f.

37 When the cathedral chapter learned of rumours that Oecolampadius, after initial hesitation (see *ZW* 7, p. 116, n. 8), planned to post his theses with the approval of the council and mayor, the chapter lodged an unsuccessful protest with the council. *AGBR* 1, p. 75, lines 7f.

1523. But the university overplayed its hand. The disputation was held, its theses – which also gained Erasmus' approval[38] – were zealously copied, and four recalcitrant theology professors were dismissed.[39] Oecolampadius' only recently reaffirmed aversion to 'academic' disputations[40] demonstrates that the Zürich example had not found imitation as a disputation in the usual sense, i.e. as a mere competition of minds; rather that it had been perceived and copied as a chance to take public account of the state of faith.

The Zürich council's strategy of attempting to master an explosive situation by establishing formal criteria was neither a decision to remain neutral in the larger Swiss context nor a policy aimed only at maintaining the *status quo*. All historians who have pointed to the Swiss city council decrees of this period as the legal basis for the introduction of 'evangelical' preaching have been correct. But it is extremely important that the term 'evangelical' should not be interpreted from the perspective of later developments or on the basis of the theological programme of the major urban reformer involved. At least for Zürich in the year 1523,[41] the council decree must be understood as an assertion of political authority, a warning against jeopardizing the unity and public welfare of the city for the sake of 'free' and uninhibited preaching.

Thus the decision to permit Oecolampadius' Basel disputation was fully consistent with the intent of the decree on preaching, since the first duty it demanded of the citizen was a willingness to confront

[38] 'Oecolampadius heri disputavit, equidem feliciter . . .' Erasmus to Zwingli, Basel, 31 August 1523; *ZW* 8, p. 117, lines 25f. Staehelin and Allen read *et quidem* instead of *equidem*. Staehelin, *Briefe*, 1, pp. 251f.; *Opus Epistolarum*, ed. Allen, 5, p. 330.

[39] Vischer, *Geschichte der Universität Basel*, pp. 230, 261.

[40] Previously Melanchthon had felt compelled to defend the utility of the Leipzig Disputation in a letter to Oecolampadius on 21 July 1519. Staehelin, *Briefe*, 1, p. 98. And the Basel reformer had only recently informed Caspar Hedio of his deep scepticism regarding such confrontations in a letter of 21 January 1523: 'Nam quid parit disputatio quam disceptationem? Quid disceptatio? Lites. Quid lites? Odium. Ubi odium, quomodo veritati salvus est locus?' *Ibid.*, p. 203. See above, n. 10.

[41] Such a precise time index is crucial for our understanding of the process of fermentation and clarification. The duration of the various phases in different cities was not at all identical. In Zürich the interim period came to a close in October 1523, but Basel had not yet reached that stage. Regarding the 'turning-point' between two eras in Basel early in 1529, see Roth, *Durchbruch und Festsetzung der Reformation in Basel*, pp. 26–56, 25.

When Geneva reached a comparable stage of development ten years later in March 1533, the agreement insuring 'biblical preaching' appeared as anything but 'freedom of preaching' when viewed from another, more 'advanced' perspective (Bern!). See Locher's concise commentary, '"La charte de la préréforme" – oder ihrer Abwürgung.' 'Von Bern nach Genf. Die Ursachen der Spannung zwischen zwinglischer und calvinistischer Reformation', p. 82.

one's opponents in the presence of the city council, defending one's views from scripture. On the other hand, it was an equally consistent application of the decree to demand that the respected printer Adam Petri recant under oath when one of the 'Lutheran' products of his press disparaged the people of Lucerne and that city's preachers as 'impious'.[42]

After the edict of Worms had finally been posted in Strassburg on 30 September 1521 in the wake of extensive debate, that city's council received a complaint against the 'evangelical' preaching of the friar Tilman of Lyn, submitted by his superior in the Carmelite order. The title of Tilman's treatise of defence in early 1522 was at the same time a manifesto: 'Tilman of Lyn's Appeal to the Council and Inhabitants of this City to Devote Themselves to the Cause of Evangelical Truth and Protect it from its Enemies'. His defence documents an effort independent of Zürich and inspired by Luther – as his editors have shown – to persuade the city magistrates to permit and protect the free proclamation of the gospel.[43]

When Wolfgang Capito and Matthaeus Zell (†1548) petitioned the Strassburg magistrates on 17 September 1523, the text of their request may well reflect the reasoning that moved a majority on the councils in Zürich and Basel to mandate 'Gospel' preaching. For Capito and Zell explicitly requested the council to 'sponsor a hearing and discussion' by means of a disputation based on holy scripture.[44]

Furthermore, within Switzerland this new application of the disputation was not introduced by the Zürich reform faction. As early as 1522 the Catholic traditionalists had considered it a suitable device to contain the expanding Reformation. Owing no doubt to preoccupation with events in Zürich, researchers have overlooked the October 1522 decision by the Catholic party in Solothurn to summon the schoolmaster Melchior Macrinus to a disputation on the sacrifice of the Eucharist and the priestly office. Macrinus immediately reported to Zwingli that the Solothurn city council was prepared to intercede on his behalf and, should it prove impossible to reach an accord between the parties, to appeal to Zwingli and his associates as

[42] 8 June 1523; *AGBR* 1, pp. 69–72; here p. 70, line 13.

[43] See Lienhard and Rott, 'Die Anfänge der evangelischen Predigt in Strassburg und ihr erstes Manifest: Der Aufruf des Karmeliterlesemeisters Tilman von Lyn (Anfang 1522)', pp. 68ff.

[44] See Baum, *Capito und Butzer, Strassburgs Reformatoren*, p. 231. In his psychologically penetrating biography, Kittelson doubts whether Capito seriously sought a disputation. *Wolfgang Capito*, p. 102. Cf. Chrisman, *Strasbourg and the Reform. A Study in the Process of Change*, pp. 108–11.

competent arbitrators.[45] As we have seen from Glarean's reaction to Zwingli's original and misleading invitation, Zwingli probably originally imagined that his role in the Zürich disputation would resemble this Solothurn proposal.

Other Swiss and south German cities issued similar council mandates, formally establishing the 'Gospel' sermon, and in the process staking out sufficient political manoeuvring space to prevent uproar and division.[46] In steady succession we encounter similar interim phases during which biblical preaching was permitted or even prescribed. But none of these ordinances documents a political intent to make a city 'evangelical' in any sense consistent with the medieval and Catholic understanding of the term. Nor should the reference to a succession be understood to establish Zürich's chronological priority in introducing such an interim. That 'Zwingli's innovation' involved a city-council-organized disputation was not necessarily peculiar to Zürich. Although the Capito–Zell petition may be understood as inspired by the first Zürich disputation, Tilman of Lyn had demanded such a disputation two years before. The impulse leading to the Zürich disputation may well have originated in Strassburg, especially since we know that increasing tensions in the autumn of 1523 also led to attacks on images in the churches of Strassburg; attacks that were perceived in Zürich as an instigation to similar action.[47]

Comparing parallel measures in various cities has made us aware of a need to distinguish between the political and theological perspectives of events. The decisions and verdicts of the year 1523 permit us to define even more precisely the degree of autonomy asserted by the

[45] Macrinus sought contact with Zwingli for the first time on 30 September 1522, turning to him as the 'Swiss Erasmus', the champion of the 'christiana atque evangelica philosophia'. Cf. *ZW* 7, pp. 589–90, 595.

[46] The Nuremberg council pursued this same political line during this period. Although, unlike Basel, it had no resistance from a university *inter muros* to contend with, Nuremberg found itself in an even more exposed position internally and externally due to its status as an imperial city and seat of the imperial regime. The 'Grosser Nürnberger Ratschlag' (1524) was addressed to the council itself. *Andreas Osiander d.Ä., Gesamtausgabe*, ed. Müller and Seebass, vol. 1, p. 319, line 3.

[47] This is my understanding of the statements by witnesses in the council minutes of September 1523 according to which Thoma Kleinbrötli, an opponent of the removal of the images, had allegedly expressed a desire in response to Leo Jud's iconoclastic preaching, to 'shove the images in the laps [of the iconoclasts] and ship them off to Strassburg . . .' Egli, *Acten*, no. 416. I am indebted to my colleague Thomas A. Brady, Jr, for the reference to the Strassburg events that are most likely implied in this statement in Reuss, ed., 'Les Collectanées de Daniel Specklin', no. 2239. It is probably to these events that Bucer referred in *Grund und Ursach* (1524). *Bucers Deutsche Schriften*, 1, p. 273, lines 26–36.

Zürich city council in response to Zwingli's reform programme. We turn our attention first to an item that heretofore seemed to confirm the basic identification of Zwingli's reformation with the Zürich council's reform measures. The third day of January 1523 witnessed not only the proclamation of the 'first Zürich disputation' but also the selection of a four-man commission intended to monitor the products of Zürich's printing presses.[48] In addition to two *Obristmeister* from city council circles,[49] this board of censorship included two canons from the collegiate chapter. The result was a committee composed of Zwingli and three of his supporters drawn from the Zürich elite: Zwingli's patron, the canon Heinrich Utinger (†1536);[50] the later mayor (1524–41), Heinrich Walder;[51] and Rudolf Binder, a member of the lesser council (1491–1538).[52]

As a gesture of support for the simultaneously proclaimed 'freedom to preach the Gospel' and obligation to desist from calumny, the appointment of the commission represented a further limitation of the spiritual jurisdiction of the bishop of Constance. It served the interests of the various reform parties; those of Zwingli as well as the council. But Zürich was not alone in seeking autonomy from its spiritual overlord. As an imperial city, Strassburg found itself in the more complicated situation of having to deal with the demands of both its bishop and the Edict of Worms and gained a head start on Zürich in developing countermeasures to attain and assure autonomy.[53]

Although the composition of the censorship committee points to Zwingli's close ties with the council and to the strength of his following in this period, the very decision to hold the disputation and the language of the council's summation decree rule out any sugges-

[48] Fabian, *Geheime Räte in Zürich, Bern, Basel und Schaffhausen*, p. 33.

[49] Heinrich Walder and Meister Binder had already been entrusted by the council on 29 October with the task of tracing the source of two 'scandalous' publications, which proved to be products of the Froschauer press. Egli, *Acten*, no. 284.

[50] See ZW 7, p. 110, n. 1. Cf. Myconius' report to Zwingli, Lucerne, 8 January 1521; ZW 7, p. 424, lines 27f.

[51] Jacob, *Politische Führungsschicht*, p. 289. Cf. Morf, *Zunftverfassung, Obrigkeit und Kirche von Waldmann bis Zwingli*, pp. 83, 86.

[52] Jacob, *Politische Führungsschicht*, pp. 133–5.

[53] Although the Edict of Worms (30 May 1521) with its prohibition of Lutheran publications was only published in Strassburg after a four-month delay, the modifications made to it provide the clearest indication of the influence acquired by the evangelical party. The city council had demanded in December 1522 the return of the 'evangelical' publications confiscated by the episcopal officials and then confiscated the entire edition of Murner's satire, *Vom Grossen Lutherischen Narren* which had just appeared from the Grüninger press. See Rapp, *Réformes et Réformation à Strasbourg. Église et société dans le Diocèse de Strasbourg (1450–1525)*, p. 474.

tions of a change of course on the council's part. In fact, a council mandate of 26 February 1523 dealing with the issue of Lenten fasting renewed[54] the ordinance 'that no one eat meat except out of necessity, during the previously established days and times of abstinence'. The council appealed to no ecclesiastical legislation in support of the measure but pointed to their obligation to prevent 'a lot of scandal, strife and bad will' in Zürich and to avoid diplomatic repercussions within the Swiss Confederation.[55] The issue's explosive potential was illustrated by the March uproar in Ötenbach where Leo Jud, *Leutpriester* (people's priest) at St Peter's for scarcely a month,[56] was reviled as a 'rogues' preacher' and 'meat eater'.[57] The council endeavoured resolutely to wriggle past the threats from all sides[58] while remaining within the narrow confines of its policy of neutrality.

When September brought the iconoclastic invasion of St Peter's, the council lost little time in punishing the offenders. Although an invitation was issued on 15 October to a disputation 'over mass and idols', the image-breakers had to 'remain in their prison'.[59] On 27 October the council released, as a result of this so-called 'second disputation' (26–28 October), a strict decree against changes in the mass and the removal of images of the saints 'pending further instruction which, God willing, his Word will reveal . . .'[60]

The greater council's decision of 11 January 1524 to appropriate the lesser council's competence to judge whether preaching conformed to scripture[61] certainly contained a measure of criticism of the moderate course previously followed by the lesser council.[62] Thus we are compelled to differentiate further when speaking of the 'council's policy'. For already on 22 October 1523 Adam Sprüngli had been forced to answer for his criticism of the lesser council. The target of Sprüngli's attack was the council's foot-dragging response to Ludwig Hätzer's denunciation of a priest loyal to the old faith. Sprüngli was accused of having complained that there were not even fourteen (out of forty-eight) members of the council willing to work for the evangelical cause. Sprüngli noted that it had now been a year since the free proclamation of the Gospel had been mandated, and insisted

54 See the mandate of 9 April 1522; Egli, *Acten*, no. 237. Cf. *ibid.*, nos. 232 to 236.
55 *Ibid.*, no. 339.
56 See Wyss, *Leo Jud. Seine Entwicklung zum Reformator 1519 bis 1523*, p. 132.
57 Egli, *Acten*, no. 345 (p. 120).
58 *Ibid.*, no. 416. Cf. above, n. 47.
59 *Ibid.*, no. 430.
60 *Ibid.*, no. 436; renewed on 13 and 23 December. *Ibid.*, nos. 458, 464.
61 *Ibid.*, no. 480.
62 Jacob, *Politische Führungschicht*, pp. 73, 79.

that offenders against that ordinance be summoned before the *greater* council and punished.[63] Sprüngli got his wish the following January.[64] But the events of 11 January 1524 point to more than a loss of influence for the Catholic party in the council. The greater council's decision to take the reins also focuses attention on the lesser council's attempt at an independent policy as late as 1523.[65]

We must expand our account in order to avoid portraying the so-called 'introduction of the Reformation' in Zürich as a simple choice between Zwingli and the bishop of Constance. Three additional points claim our attention. In the first place, the accusation levelled at Adam Sprüngli implies more than the tensions arising from the administration by the Two Hundred of the decree on Gospel preaching. For he referred to an action by the council 'one year ago'. If we may take the testimony of the witness literally, Sprüngli could not have had either the promulgation or the summation of the 'first Zürich disputation' in mind. But it had been nearly one year since Bishop Hugh had requested the council to intervene in order to calm tensions and prevent schism in the Dominican nunnery at Ötenbach.[66] The council took up the question and concluded, undoubtedly contrary to the bishop's hopes, that the nuns should be free to choose confessors from among either the monastic or parish clergy. The council merely stipulated that neither parish priest nor mendicant confessor 'preach anything other than that which can be supported by the holy word of God and the gospel'.[67]

Thus the announcement and concluding decree of the 'first Zürich

63 Egli, *Acten*, no. 434.

64 *Ibid.*, no. 480.

65 W. Jacob finds Sprüngli's estimate 'not entirely credible – or [Sprüngli] is counting only those who were unconditionally evangelical . . .' *Politische Führungsschicht*, p. 79, n. 36. But Jacob also assumes the presence of a relatively powerful minority in favour of the Reformation: 'It must have been roughly identical with the political elite . . .' *Ibid.*, pp. 81f. In my opinion the struggle was concerned at the same time with the question of what 'Reformation' implied for Zürich and at what pace it could be accomplished without giving rise to 'discord'. And even if Sprüngli's standard for determining the 'evangelical' members of the council was extremely high, it remains significant that he favoured, on the basis of his standard, precisely that which was turned into policy on 11 January 1524.

66 It was here that Zwingli had preached his sermon on the 'Clarity and Certainty of God's Word' in the summer of 1522, an event which triggered so much unrest that the bishop and council were forced to intervene to still the uproar. See the detailed comments by Finsler in *Die Chronik des Bernhard Wyss*, pp. 38f. Cf. Egli in *ZW* 1, pp. 328f.

67 Egli, *Acten*, no. 301 (1 December 1522); cf. no. 291 (13 November 1522). This decision represents not merely the repetition of the preceding decree regarding preaching (November? 1520) but also the anticipation of the promulgations of 3 and 29 January 1523. *ZW* 1, p. 470, line 4. Cf. Pestalozzi, *Leo Judä*, p. 17.

disputation' a few months later neither broke with the past nor broached the homiletical pattern of the future, however significantly those statements may have influenced history. To the council's eyes these decrees and decisions constituted no more than a patient and plain repetition of an established principle, the same approach adopted towards the issues of Lenten fasting and saints' images. Concessions to the evangelical party depended on proof of its partisans' contribution to the political–religious unity embodied in the *bonum commune*, the common weal.

The second point is not far distant from the first. Although the campaign to make Gospel preaching normative has dominated previous analyses, we should not overlook the prominent place accorded the issue of foreign alliances and the mercenary trade in council deliberations during the years in which the Reformation gained the upper hand in Zürich. Domestic and foreign policy became more closely identified in the wake of the defeat at Marignano (1515). The traditional class-oriented distribution of political roles in the city was so shattered by the domestic repercussions of this foreign policy debacle, that granting greater political responsibility to the representatives of the artisan guilds became inevitable.[68]

The realization that the public welfare depended on avoiding all military entanglements grew; foreign policy adventures ceased to be politic. One year after concluding an alliance with the pope on 9 December 1514, the Zürich council chose the setting of the Confederation's assembly at Lucerne to announce that it would enter no future foreign alliances. Zwingli's call to Zürich in 1518 enjoyed the support of the papal party, which, strengthened by the events of Marignano, rejected all further foreign obligations.[69]

The events of 1515 were repeated in 1521 when Zürich resolved to spurn the alliance offered by Francis I. The issue grew heated when the French king expanded his campaign to gain the services of Swiss mercenaries as a result of his defeat in the German imperial election and his inability to intervene as Hapsburg control tightened around Württemberg. Some indication of the intensity of French efforts is apparent from day-to-day conversation and the political agenda in Zürich, where the council dealt nearly every week with rumours and corroborated reports testifying to the strength of the French faction within the city walls. Again and again reports of unrest among the 'common folk' surfaced; turmoil which was unleashed partially

[68] Morf, *Zunftverfassung und Obrigkeit*, pp. 12f. Cf. the final chapter, 'Obrigkeit und Pensionenfrage', *ibid.*, pp. 64–76.

[69] Farner, *Huldrych Zwingli*, 3, pp. 222–36; here p. 222.

through the desire to enlist in foreign pay and was to some degree the result of popular mistrust of certain political leaders suspected of secretly pocketing French *pensions*.[70] On the political level, the anti-French policy of Cardinal Schinner gave rise to party labels such as 'cardinalist' and 'papal' in opposition to the friends of the French in Zürich. But such political terms paralleled and even converged with labels from the religious scene where the Zwinglians, attacked as 'heretics', responded by hurling the epithet 'idolater' at the devotees of the saints and their images. One incident illustrates both the political ferment in the Zürich city state and the occasionally veiled conjunction of the political and religious fronts. In March 1523 the council received a report of a pro-French demonstration in which a *fleur-de-lis* had been drawn on a wall and then kissed. And none other than the radical Zwinglian Adam Sprüngli, who might be expected to be *anti*-French, complained to the council that an opposing mob had 'smeared said lily with filth' and thereby disgraced it.[71]

To understand the relationship between the Zürich council and the bishop of Constance, and the background for the appearance of the Constance delegation in Zürich on 29 January 1523, it is essential to know that the pope owed money for the services of Zürich mercenaries. And the bishop of Constance understood how to play this trump card in dealing with the city. On the other hand, the Zürich drive for emancipation from the spiritual jurisdiction of Constance by no means induced the council to abandon its political neutrality and seek a confrontation with Rome. Ever more impatiently the council reminded Constance of the papal arrears. The episcopal chancellery responded, often through the papal nuncio Ennius, with assurances of the pope's gratitude to the Zürich authorities;[72] later with the promise that the money would soon arrive, and finally by insisting that a Fugger draft was already under way.[73] By 27 April 1523, with no money in sight, the council expressed for the first time the suspicion that the papal poverty might result from anti-Zürich church politics, hinting that the circumstances almost led one to believe that the pope either planned to renege on his debts or took pleasure in watching opposition to the council grow inside Zürich's walls.[74] And thus the question of paid foreign agents had become fully intertwined with the religious controversy!

[70] Egli, *Acten*, no. 350.
[71] *Ibid.*, no. 352 (March 1523).
[72] *Ibid.*, no. 279.
[73] *Ibid.*, no. 281 (19 October 1522).
[74] *Ibid.*, no. 357. Cf. no. 295.

Fridolin Ryff's entry for 1521 in his Basel chronicle also applies to a three-year period in Zürich's history: 'Thus, when the citizens of Basel returned home [from the Italian campaign], great dissension arose as one opposed the other, the one being of the papal party, the other French . . . People began to band together, splitting the citizenry into parties and forcing the councillors to respond. They issued a mandate forbidding anyone to provoke, revile or insult another, decreeing instead that all behave as befits good citizens and live in wholesome peace and harmony. But it did little good and one party continued against another . . . In the above year, soon after the dissension broke out among the citizens, and with conflict occurring daily, all sorts of rumours of bribery began to circulate among the people.'[75]

The council's efforts to prohibit foreign enlistment, and the common man's suspicion that certain citizens in privileged positions were for sale to foreign powers, created a climate of mistrust, unrest and conspiracy in Zürich as well; an atmosphere that cannot be easily distinguished from the religious ferment. It demonstrates above all the narrow limits constricting the policy of the lesser council during these years and the political necessity to maintain order in the midst of all the pressure for religious reform.

A third and no less decisive item is the social instability accompanying the drive for religious reform. Amid all the problems facing the citizens of Zürich, the agitation against paying tithes demanded a response from the council. By early 1523 the challenge to the council's authority could no longer be ignored. It would not be too daring to view the petitions for emancipation from tithes as chronicling the emergence of the fourth party, later to be decried as 'Anabaptists' or 'Catabaptists'. On 19 March 1523 a group in Witikon petitioned for freedom from paying tithes in order to be able to support[76] their own parish priest, Wilhelm Reublin, who had been active there as pastor since Christmas 1522.[77] More than two years before the traditional 'hour of birth' of Anabaptism (21 January 1525),[78] the first contours of

[75] 'Die Chronik des Fridolin Ryff 1514–1541, mit der Fortsetzung des Peter Ryff 1543–1585', p. 29.

[76] Egli, *Acten*, no. 351.

[77] See Goeters, 'Die Vorgeschichte des Täufertums in Zürich', p. 247; Stayer, 'Reublin and Brötli: The Revolutionary Beginnings of Swiss Anabaptism', p. 84. A second centre of unrest was Höngg, where the parish priest Simon Stumpf was alleged to have said in neighbouring Affoltern that 'man sei keinen Zehnten schuldig'. Egli, *Acten*, no. 267.

[78] Blanke, *Brüder in Christo*, p. 22, Nordenhaug translation, p. 20.

confessing congregations became visible. These groups[79] desired, like Zwingli, to see the preaching of the Gospel 'taken seriously' and thus advocated the elimination of 'idols' and superfluous masses. They also sought to realize that political–religious community over which the city of Zürich claimed sole control as the divinely appointed and legitimate human authority. But in opposition to the council the emerging radicals pursued that political–religious community on the village and prefecture level. This conflict set off more than mere theological explosions: it threatened Zürich's claims of sovereignty over its cantonal *Hinterland* and undermined the unity of city and countryside.[80]

On the political level, the council countered the challenges to paying tithes by declaring itself, as the secular authority, the future recipient of what was formerly due to the spiritual authority.[81] Zwingli disappointed his radical followers when he advised the council shortly before the second disputation that abolishing the tithe would 'clearly damage and lead to the decline of the city and entire community'. But Zwingli added theological force to his economic analysis with his assurance that 'divine wisdom' would reveal a solution that would 'benefit everyone and injure no one'.[82]

In one of the most significant of his early letters (summer 1523), Conrad Grebel vented his outrage over the city council's hesitation in the central questions of faith as well as the issue of the tithe.[83] But Grebel's criticism was only formally addressed to the city politicians; *de facto* the council basked in the confidence that their position enjoyed the backing of Zwingli's theological authority. One month later Grebel risked his first substantial criticism of Zwingli. The exposition of Zwingli's disputation theses, his *Usslegen*, had just appeared, and earned Grebel's praise as 'a genuinely Christian book'.

79 See the account and documentation in Williams, *The Radical Reformation*, pp. 120–7.

80 Cf. *ZW* 4, p. 479, lines 6–9. Norman Birnbaum assumes a population of 5,000 for the city of Zürich itself in the year 1519. He refers to Schnyder, *Die Bevölkerung der Stadt und Landschaft Zürich vom 14. bis 17. Jahrhundert*. His conclusion that the 'discrepancy' between city and countryside with regard to participation in government 'acted as a political irritant' is confirmed here. Birnbaum, 'The Zwinglian Reformation in Zürich', p. 17. But 'political' must be understood broadly enough to include church policy in this regard.

81 Egli, *Acten*, no. 426.

82 *Ibid.*, no. 425 (September 1523). For Zwingli's position on interest and the *Früchtekauf*, a form of capital investment in which interest was paid in the form of a percentage of the harvest yield, see Ramp, *Das Zinsproblem. Eine historische Untersuchung*, pp. 59–81. Cf. the broader, excellent study by Nelson, *The Idea of Usury*, pp. 65ff.

83 To Vadian, Zürich, 17 June. Von Muralt and Schmid, eds., *Quellen zur Geschichte der Täufer in der Schweiz*, vol. 1, p. 1, lines 11f.

But Grebel balked abruptly at Zwingli's treatment of the tithe issue: 'I can give him no more honest, true and Gospel-based answer than that the Zürich senators are tyrants who in no way differ from the unbaptized heathen.'[84] Here, on the level of Christian practice, the protest against tyranny and the arguments against the divine law legitimacy of tithes presented by Summenhart to his academic audience and underlined by Ambrosius Blarer,[85] reappear. But Summenhart's stipulation that such teaching not be openly preached to the laity has fallen by the wayside.

Wilhelm Reublin, who was baptized with Grebel in 1525, had already been conspicuous in the Zürich countryside, hovering close to the fires of agitation wherever they might smoulder within the Zürich prefectures. When Reublin registered in Tübingen on 21 August 1509, Summenhart had long since died; but his teaching continued as a vital tradition and his writings could still be purchased. Whatever Reublin absorbed from such sources during his studies in Tübingen first bore fruit when Summenhart's attack on the tyranny of the canonists was developed into Reublin's attack on a church ruled according to the standard of canon law.

That evolution took place after Reublin became the *Leutpriester* at St Alban's in Basel in 1521. The chronicler Fridolin Ryff characterized his activity there under the rubric: 'How the gospel began here . . .'. Reublin now recognized as Christian only a church obedient to scripture. He offered to defend himself against charges of heresy in a disputation where he could 'give account on the basis of the scripture'.[86] Threatened with the loss of his pastorate he took up contact with the city-state of Zürich and began new pastoral duties at Witikon in December 1522. The council decree exiling him as an Anabaptist on 21 January 1525 brought that two-year phase in Reublin's life to an end.[87] But that same decree of exile for the Zürich

[84] 'Gentes mundi dixi tyrannos patriae nostrae, quos patres conscriptos vocant, rectius patres decimantes vocaturi.' To Vadian, Zürich, 15 July. *Quellen zur Geschichte der Täufer in der Schweiz*, vol. 1, p. 2, lines 17–19. Grebel cited with understandable enthusiasm the treatise by Jacob Strauss, 'Wider den unchristlichen Wucher' (1523), which could only serve to confirm his own opinions. See also Oyer, 'The Influence of Jacob Strauss on the Anabaptists', p. 79.

In the Basel 'Orthodoxenvermahnung' of 1529 the members of the synod were required both to pledge to abjure 'rebaptism' and to admonish the faithful to fulfil their tithe obligations. *AGBR* 3, pp. 30–3.

[85] See above, pp. 115ff.

[86] 'Die Chronik des Fridolin Ryff', p. 33, line 11; p. 24.

[87] Wyss mentioned Reublin's arrival in a spirit of goodwill, contrasting with the cutting account by Wyss' modern editor, Finsler, in *Die Chronik des Bernhard Wyss*, p. 20, n. 2. The earlier literature is cited there; in addition, see Goeters, 'Die Vorgeschichte des Täufertums in Zürich', p. 247.

Anabaptists also made clear the council's unwillingness to sponsor further discussion and disputation,[88] thus marking the end of the first chapter in the history of the Reformation in Zürich.[89]

[88] Egli, *Acten*, no. 624.
[89] The utility of holding a disputation was debated in Zürich for the last time in 1597; in this case supported with far more enthusiasm by the bishop of Constance, Cardinal Andreas, than by the city council. But with the bishop's death on 12 November 1600, the extensive and revealing manoeuvring for acceptable conditions came to an end. See the account and further literature in Pfister, *Kirchengeschichte der Schweiz*, vol. 2, pp. 407–9.

11

The great visitation: bishop and city

IF THE EVENTS of 29 January 1523 appeared to the Zürich Two Hundred as a special council session to which the representatives of the bishop and members of the academic community had been courteously invited, Zwingli approached that session with different expectations. He had come to participate in an ecclesiastical synod at which the clergy and the representatives of city and countryside had assembled to determine, on their own authority and with the aid of Zwingli's sixty-seven hurriedly composed theses, the specific content of the existing mandate to preach nothing that conflicted with scripture. The objections of the Constance delegation made it impossible to establish specific points of doctrine. Yet the 'synod' led to the emergence, perhaps even the discovery, of a new ecclesiology and left the local municipal congregation with a new sense of identity as the legitimate representative of the universal church.

In contrast to the now commonly accepted thesis of Emil Egli, our analysis has shown that the council did not decree complete freedom of preaching but merely sought to standardize the teaching issuing from Zürich pulpits. For the interim, 'Gospel' or 'evangelical' meant no more than 'that which is defensible from holy scripture'. Zwingli thus had grounds for disappointment at the outcome on 29 January. The council declined to elevate his theology to the standard for Zürich's Gospel. In the absence of objections from the assembly, the council did clear Zwingli of any taint of heresy. But we must repeat that, far from being Reformation-oriented in Zwingli's sense, the action of the council simply aimed to determine the bounds for preaching that would serve and be tolerated by the common weal.

Bernd Moeller's success in redirecting attention from the mandate on Gospel preaching to the organizational structure of the disputation and its legal implications is a significant advance in interpretation. If the preliminary form tested in Strassburg is disregarded, Moeller's carefully formulated conclusion is valid: 'A sort of "discovery" was made in Zürich in January 1523.'[1] In Moeller's view the discovery consisted in the novel combination of two traditional elements: the early church's provincial synods and medieval university disputations. In the process, 'the traditional form was adopted where it proved useful and dropped where it hindered'.[2]

Despite its firm place in Reformation historiography, the term 'disputation' scarcely fits the 'discovery' of January 1523, especially when applied to the 'second disputation' in October where, after opening the session, Mayor Marx Röist relinquished his presiding role to academically proven *doctores*. As a caption for one item on the agenda for 29 January, the term 'disputation'[3] is perfectly valid. But the actual course of events forces us to distinguish between the agenda and the session furnishing the setting for that agenda. What we are provisionally terming a 'synod of clerics',[4] and what the civic authorities considered to be a 'special session' of the city council, was called in order to make a disputation possible. That purpose was clear even to Zwingli. His hastily written theses actually pointed to a debate, in his words, a *certamen*.[5] Zwingli must have so emphasized this aspect of the coming assembly to Oecolampadius that the latter felt obliged to warn him of the uselessness of such learned competition.[6] To Zwingli's great disappointment no opponent could be found who was willing to debate his theses, and although a controversy of great import followed, indeed the 'hearing' intended by the council took place, still Zwingli's disputation never occurred.

In Constance the announcement was likewise interpreted as an invitation to a disputation, a battle of minds that the bishop and his advisers fully intended to sidestep.[7] But no disputation resulted and

1 Moeller, 'Zwinglis Disputationen', 1, p. 304.

2 *Ibid.*, p. 305.

3 In the loose rather than lucid language of Reformation scholarship, a distinction is made between a period of 'disputations' and a subsequent phase of 'religious colloquies'. Yet the latter were disputations as well, the difference being that the 'disputation' as the initiation of local political action sought victory by defeat whereas the 'colloquy' as an instrument of national or even imperial policy sought unity by compromise.

4 On 9 April 1522 the council expressed its willingness, in response to episcopal admonition, to enforce the Lenten regulations. But the council also requested that the bishop convene a interregional synod of the clergy as soon as possible in order to deliberate on the issue of the fast. See Egli, *Acten*, no. 236. We must conclude: 'Episcopo deliberante senatus convenit' – when the bishop declined to follow up, the council considered itself justified in seeking a solution on the local level.

5 *ZW* 8, p. 4, line 12.

6 See Oecolampadius' letter to Zwingli on 17 January 1523; *ZW* 8, pp. 5f.

7 Luther also reported to Spalatin in late January that Zwingli had announced a disputation. *WABr* 3, p. 24, line 12. On 16 February 1523, with the aid of hindsight, Hans von der Planitz informed Elector Frederick that a council had taken place.

even had one taken place, it would not justify talk of Zwingli's 'discovery'. Just how devoid of novelty such a development would have been is indicated by the Constance chapter's far from groundless apprehension that what had been announced as a hearing would indeed turn into a disputation. It was well known in Constance that the planned city council special session had been preceded by controversies between clerics and non-clerics in Zürich. We have information concerning a series of such events that escalated from agitation to confrontation and ultimately to disputations. Three of them reveal links with Zwingli and two incidents involved the recently elected *Leutpriester* at St Peter's, Leo Jud.

Jud had been Zwingli's companion as a student in Basel and his successor at Einsiedeln before becoming his 'left-hand man', a friend to the radical Zwinglian party. It was Leo Jud who broke the Lenten fast in 1522 in the printer Froschauer's house[8] while Zwingli looked on. Jud had earned a reputation for interrupting sermons and a name as a 'Gospel' agitator. Indeed, Georg Finsler and Oskar Farner regard his dispute with the prior of the Zürich Augustinians as the immediate stimulus for the 'first Zürich disputation'.[9]

Yet the visitation carried out in Zürich by an episcopal delegation from Constance (7–9 April 1522)[10] in the wake of the Froschauer evening 'break-fast' was more significant for subsequent events than was Jud's contentiousness. When the episcopal legate summoned the entire Zürich clergy to the collegiate chapter hall on 8 April, obviously to reprimand them, Zwingli sought opportunity for discussion. His attempt failed when the bishop's representative abruptly left the room. Zwingli managed, with the help of his supporters, to gain admission and a hearing at the city council session with the Constance delegation the following day. Zwingli avoided any form of dispute[11] but very adroitly insisted that the bishop's delegates discharge their obligation as episcopal examiners, thereby ensuring that his right and duty to answer for his preaching would be respected.[12] And although in this case the ecclesiastical visitation and political consultations were scheduled for two different days, clearly separat-

Wülcker and Virck, eds., *Des Kursächsischen Rathes Hans von der Planitz Berichte aus dem Reichsregiment in Nürnberg 1521–1523*, p. 375.

8 Egli, *Acten*, no. 233.

9 *Die Chronik des Bernhard Wyss*, ed. Finsler, p. 12, n. 3. Likewise Farner, *Zwingli*, 3, p. 330. In greater detail in Pestalozzi, *Leo Judä*, p. 17.

10 *ZW* 1, pp. 137–54.

11 *ZW* 1, p. 146, lines 36–40.

12 *ZW* 1, pp. 147, 16–20.

ing the spheres of competence, still it was becoming apparent that the city council would have to take the initiative in the future reformation of the civic organism.

Three months later, on 16 July 1522, Zwingli debated against the Observant Franciscan, François Lambert (†1530),[13] in the same collegiate chapter hall. On 15 July, in the *Fraumünster*, Zwingli had interrupted Lambert's sermon[14] on the intercession of the Virgin and the saints by shouting at the top of his lungs: 'That's where you're wrong, brother.'[15] The next day's disputation, coming at Lambert's initiative, can still be classified as a private debate. But five days later, on 21 July, it was the city council that called for what has come to be known as the 'disputation with the Zürich mendicants'.[16] It is precisely the council's role and its significance which have been overlooked in previous accounts.

The oldest contemporary chronicle reversed the accent: the so-called 'first Zürich disputation' found only brief mention in conjunction with the veneration of the saints while the debate of the preceding July was recorded in detail.[17]

Zwingli and the lectors of the three mendicant houses were summoned by the council to appear before a committee of the lesser council, probably the privy council.[18] The collegiate chapter of the *Grossmünster*, the two remaining *Leutpriester* and a master of philosophy and bachelor of theology, Conrad Schmid (M.A. Tübingen, 1504), were also invited, with Schmid probably functioning as a consultant (*peritus*). Thus, several months before the general summons of the clergy of city and countryside on 29 January 1523, the council had attempted to master the situation by confronting the monastic academic elite with Zwingli. It is not unreasonable to conclude that *the first Zürich disputation took place on 21 July 1522*. And it is in comparison to that event that the so-called 'first Zürich disputation' of 29 January 1523 merits more precise examination. Both

[13] Following his disputation with Zwingli, Lambert travelled to see Erasmus in Basel and then visited Luther in Wittenberg. He died as professor of theology at the first university founded as a Protestant institution, Marburg (founded 1527). See Gerhard Müller, *Franz Lambert von Avignon und die Reformation in Hessen*.

[14] François Lambert arrived in Zürich on 12 July and preached four times in the *Fraumünster*. See in addition Moser, 'Franz Lamberts Reise durch die Schweiz im Jahre 1522'. Lambert's debate with Zwingli was his last disputation in the Franciscan cowl.

[15] 'Bruder, da irrest du.' *Die Chronik des Bernhard Wyss*, ed. Finsler, p. 16.

[16] Zwingli himself was the source of the designation 'contest'. *ZW* 7, p. 549, n. 4.

[17] *Die Chronik des Bernhard Wyss*, ed. Finsler, pp. 12, 17–20.

[18] Fabian refers to two decisions from the year 1522 that dealt with the role of the privy council in matters of faith. *Geheime Räte*, pp. 26ff.

sessions not merely enjoyed the city council's approval but were actually initiated by the council. In both cases the council functioned as judge in determining the outcome of the disputation or 'face-to-face hearing'.[19] As was later the case, in January 1523, the council concluded the July disputation of 1522 with the advice: 'Yes, gentlemen of religion, it is the opinion of the council that you should from this time on preach the holy Gospel, Saint Paul and the prophets that constitute holy scripture and leave Scotus and Thomas and the like alone.'[20]

These three events, first the 'visitation debacle' of 9 April, next the confrontation with the mendicants on 21 July 1522, and last the 'synod of clerics' on 29 January 1523, mark three stages in the shift from spiritual jurisdiction by the bishop of Constance to the Zürich city council's appropriation of the arbitrator's office. On the occasion of the first episcopal visitation in April 1522, Zwingli had his hands full gaining even a hearing before the council. By 16 July he found himself receiving the council's invitation.[21] Mayor Marx Röist had initially hoped to avoid increased tensions by calmly asking Zwingli and the mendicants 'to get along amiably with one another'. Responsible for preserving public concord, he wished to leave the verdict on this theological altercation to the collegiate chapter. Only Zwingli's protest[22] and pressure by the 'evangelical' councillors ultimately led to the ordinance on gospel preaching.

[19] The council summoned the lectors of the three mendicant orders on the evening of 21 July 1522. After lengthy debate, the disputants and spectators were asked to leave the chamber; they were 'usgestelt' in order to permit the council to reach its verdict. 'Und als man wider hinin kam, do redt burgermeister Roust, si soltend miteinandren früntlich faren, und wenn eim teil etwas angelegen were, soltend si für probst und capitel Zürich komen.' *Die Chronik des Bernhard Wyss*, ed. Finsler, pp. 17, 18f.

[20] *Ibid.*, p. 19. Zwingli informed Beatus Rhenanus: 'Mandatum erat, ut relictis Thomabus, Scotis reliquisque id farinae doctoribus unis sacris literis nitantur que scilicet intra biblia contineantur.' Zürich, 30 July 1522; *ZW* 7, p. 549, lines 3–5. The Dominican lector lost little time in moving from Zürich to Lucerne. *Ibid.*, p. 555, line 34. That this *first* disputation did not take place in the council chambers does not detract from its official character. The first sessions of the *Ehegericht* were also held outside city hall in the rectory of the *Fraumünster*. See Köhler, *Zürcher Ehegericht*, 1, p. 32.

[21] The previous obscurity surrounding this affair can be traced to the ambiguity of the term 'senatus' in Zwingli's account. Where he wrote 'persuasum quoque senatui, ne ego vocarer' (*ZW* 1, p. 143, line 23), this means that the *lesser* council found it unnecessary to summon Zwingli. The 'cives', in this case also called 'plebs', (*ibid.*, lines 25f.), i.e. the Two Hundred, then overturned that decision. *ZW* 1, p. 144, lines 9–11; cf. lines 5f. The town clerk thought it sufficient simply to record that Zwingli, as a representative of the parish clergy, had 'also been heard'. Egli, *Acten*, no. 236.

[22] Zwingli's protest against the implicit equating of his office with that of the mendicant *Lectores* documents his high esteem for the 'episcopal' office of the *Leutpriester*: 'Ich

Thus it was not the elevation of *scripture* to the sole standard for preaching that distinguished the 'synod of clerics' on 29 January 1523 from those which had come earlier. Neither the holding of a *council-sponsored* disputation nor the language of its concluding verdict was novel. Because historians have read that verdict through Zwingli's eyes and judged him the victor, one sentence from this document has received special attention – the concession that Zwingli might continue to preach and teach 'as before'. Although his theology was thereby exonerated of the taint of heresy, this stamp of approval was no seal of exclusive validity and in no way implied Zwingli's appointment as the sole spokesman for Zürich theology. Zwingli may indeed have detected his call to that office in the council's verdict; but he was forced to await the gradual shift in the composition of the greater and lesser councils in the following years before actually assuming the post.

In 1523, in complete accord with the policy of the lesser council and especially of Mayor Marx Röist, *both* parties were dismissed with the injunction to desist, under threat of the most severe penalties, from charging others with heresy and from slander.[23] The majority in the lesser council continued to limit their intervention to peace-keeping even after the 'second Zürich disputation'. But on 11 January 1524 the Two Hundred put an end to the foot-dragging by assuming in the future full responsibility not merely for the basic legislation but also for the practical administration of the ordinance on preaching. Four years of legislative procedure reached their conclusion.

When juxtaposed with the series of political developments that preceded it, the January 1523 'synod of clerics' seems similar to its predecessors. We will not discern its specific characteristics on the structural level. When viewed from the council's perspective, the innovation is quantitative, but should not be lightly dismissed: a new political reality has emerged, no longer founded on deliberations by Zürich's elite or privy council sessions, but the aftermath of a mobilization of the entire clergy of the city and countryside. This political development holds implications for both domestic and foreign policy. Indeed, in shaking off the claims of Constance to spiritual jurisdiction, the rest of the diocese to which Zürich belonged became foreign territory.

bin in diser statt Zürich bischof und pfarrer und mir ist die seelsorg bevolen; ich han darum geschworen und die münch nit . . .' *Die Chronik des Bernhard Wyss*, ed. Finsler, p. 19.

[23] 'einanderen hinfür dheins wegs [keineswegs] schmützen, ketzeren, noch andere schmachwort zůreden.' *ZW* 1, p. 471, lines 7f.

Already in 1522 Mayor Röist had been forced to abandon his attempt to dump the theological controversy in the lap of the collegiate chapter at the *Grossmünster*, the local ecclesiastical authorities. On 3 January 1523 he watched his second attempt to master the situation crumble: the failure of a 'policy of containment' that would have limited the issue to the sessions of the lesser council. When the setting shifted to the council of the Two Hundred on 29 January, the move had ramifications both for the course of the Reformation in Zürich and for future events in Europe. It owed that significance not to any basic structural innovations but to Zwingli's theological interpretation of the day's events. We shall adopt the term, Zwingli's 'discovery', but we apply it not to the political reality engineered by the lesser council: it relates properly to the 'redemptive history' interpretation of that reality, an interpretation that was laboriously but unwittingly extracted from Zwingli by the Constance delegation.

But before we turn to this decisive aspect of the day's events, we must consider the composition and instructions of the episcopal delegation from Constance. Having received the Zürich invitation on 15 January, at Bishop Hugh's behest the cathedral chapter deliberated the issue of participation in the coming *diaeta*. The chapter had fundamental reservations. Should it participate, either personally or represented by other 'experienced, learned persons', in a session where a city council would interfere in matters of the holy faith that were no business of the laity?

Probably unwilling to be accomplices in such impropriety, the chapter recommended to the bishop that, in the event that he did not personally make the trip, he should send good and experienced theologians well versed in scripture. Their mission should be restricted to hearing grievances in conjunction with the councillors. Should the Zürich council go so far as to usurp the office of judge and declare one party the victor, then the bishop's delegates should 'in no case interfere or make concessions on their own authority but insist that they lacked further instructions from his Grace'.[24]

The composition of the delegation also presented problems. Although the bishop had originally envisioned a two-man mission, in the end four men left Constance for Zürich. Their names and biographies shed light on the earnestness with which Constance viewed the developments in Zürich. Although Fabri was unquestionably the actual leader of the delegation, Sir Fritz Jacob von Anwyl

[24] Krebs, *Protokolle*, no. 7510.

(† ca. 1535) formally headed the embassy[25] and delivered an elegant and conciliatory inaugural speech concisely outlining the mandate entrusted to the delegation by the Constance cathedral chapter.

An experienced diplomat and since 1501 a regular 'ambassador' for the bishop at the assemblies of the Swiss Confederation, Sir Fritz Jacob had been named personal adviser to Duke Ulrich of Württemberg in the critical year 1519 while the duke was endeavouring to hold his own with the aid of Swiss mercenaries against the superior strength of the Swabian League.[26] Increasingly concerned with religious issues,[27] Sir Fritz Jacob embraced Zwingli's cause soon after the January 'disputation'[28] and promoted the introduction of the Reformation in his prefecture of Bischofszell.[29] His second son and namesake was named chief prefect in Tübingen in 1536 following Duke Ulrich's return to Württemberg.[30]

Sir Fritz Jacob was cast in the role of a diplomatically skilled but non-academically educated *orator*. The three remaining members of the commission, all educated in Tübingen, formed its panel of theological experts and solid core. The doctor of canon and civil law, Georg Vergenhans,[31] was added to the group at the express desire of the bishop of Constance.[32] Vergenhans appears in none of the reports

25 See Emil Egli, 'Ritter Fritz Jakob von Anwyl, ein thurgauischer Edelmann und Verehrer Zwinglis'.

26 The council must have remembered well Sir Fritz Jacob's visit to Zürich less than four years earlier, in March 1519, when Duke Ulrich entrusted him, accompanied by *Burgvogt* Stelzer of Tübingen and others, with the delicate task of apologizing for the duke's illicit recruiting of mercenaries without the council's knowledge. See Feyler, 'Die Beziehungen des Hauses Württemberg zur schweizerischen Eidgenossenschaft in der ersten Hälfte des xvi. Jahrhunderts', p. 108.

27 Joachim von Grüt sketched a character portrait for Zwingli in April 1522. *ZW* 7, p. 505, lines 1–9.

28 Although toward the end of the session he somewhat ambiguously contradicted Fabri, triggering a burst of laughter, Sir Fritz Jacob must have still enjoyed the confidence of the bishop at this point. At sometime between 24 July and 2 October 1523 he resigned as episcopal *Hofmeister*. See Krebs, *Protokolle*, no 7819, where he is listed for the first time as 'althoffmaister'.

29 For his interpretation of his 'conversion', see *Die Vadianische Briefsammlung der Stadtbibliothek St. Gallen*, ed. Arbenz, vol. 4, p. 40.

30 In this capacity, with ducal support, he broke up the logjam into which the university had drifted when its chancellor, Ambrosius Widmann, fled from Tübingen, yet refused to surrender his right to grant degrees. See Volz, 'Luthers und Melanchthons Beteiligung an der Tübinger Universitätsreform im Jahre 1538'.

31 Registered along with Philip Vergenhans in Tübingen between 31 May and 5 June 1480 in the same matriculation book in which their uncle, Johannes Vergenhans (Nauclerus), had entered the names of the first students. Out of respect for their uncle, they were exempted from paying the registration fees: 'Nil dederunt ob honorem domini D. Vergenhans.' Hermelink, *Die Matrikeln*, 1, p. 30, no. 12. Cf. Haller, 1, p. 256 and 2, p. 98.

32 Krebs, *Protokolle*, no. 7518.

on the actual course of the disputation, certainly not due to a lack of issues pertinent to the expertise of a canon lawyer. More probably, his silence resulted from his strict adherence to the mandate of the bishop and chapter that permitted participation in a hearing but not in a disputation. Such a regard for his instructions contrasted with a more flexible interpretation by the remaining two delegates and was no accident. Vergenhans continued to demonstrate his deep loyalty to tradition during subsequent months when the evangelical movement made rapid gains in the diocese and became an ever more serious threat to existing order. Thus on 26 August 1523 he favoured the dismissal without hearing of the Constance preacher Wanner, who had been accused of distributing 'Lutersche materi' and questioning 'important articles dealing with the veneration of the saints and the Mother of God'.[33]

As we shall see, Vergenhans' determined rejection of the Reformation may well have been decisive in establishing episcopal policy. A more unaccommodating attitude finally prevailed when Vergenhans was elected dean on 10 November 1523 by the chapter and without delay confirmed by Bishop Hugh the next day.[34] The chapter and bishop thereby resolutely put behind them the mediation attempts of April 1522 and January 1523 and moved towards confrontation with the Reformation. Even though the bishop and his cathedral chapter were eventually forced to undertake a two-phase flight from Constance in the years 1526–7, within the Württemberg portion of the diocese a *temporary* Counter-Reformation could be introduced thanks to the protection of the Austrian regime.

In the middle of the crisis complicated in 1523 by growing strain between town and bishop as well as within the chapter, a third participant in the mission to Zürich also figured prominently in events in Constance. He was Martin Plantsch,[35] priest at the Tübingen Collegiate Church[36] and author of the treatise against the

[33] For the Wanner affair, which occupied the attention of the chapter for a period of months, see Willburger, *Die Konstanzer Bischöfe Hugo von Landenberg, Balthasar Merklin, Johann von Lupfen (1496–1537) und die Glaubensspaltung*, pp. 78–85. See also the comprehensive biographical information on Wanner in Rublack, *Die Einführung der Reformation in Konstanz*, pp. 213f.

[34] Krebs, *Protokolle*, nos. 7784, 7786.

[35] The satire, *Die lutherisch strebkatz*, lists the professor of theology, Jacob Lemp, instead of Plantsch. Schade, ed., *Satiren und Pasquille aus der Reformationszeit*, 3, pp. 112–35; here pp. 124f. He may have been confused with Sir Fritz *Jacob*, but it is more likely that the author's source referred to an unidentified Tübingen member of the delegation for which he substituted Lemp's name.

[36] Whether merely repeating a rumour or not, Luther informed Spalatin that the bishop of Constance had originally invited Gregor Reisch (†1525) but then rejected him as an

witchcraft hysteria. For many years a representative of his bishop as arbitrator in ecclesiastical litigation in the Tübingen area, in 1521 he had been asked by the cathedral chapter to accept a vacant post as preacher in Constance, 'in view of his skill, aptness and priestly manner'.[37] Canon Vergenhans, whose uncle 'Nauclerus' had headed the university when Plantsch registered as a 'charter' student in the winter term of 1477,[38] may have influenced the chapter's choice. His hand may also have been involved in Plantsch's appointment to the 1523 Zürich embassy.

Plantsch had quite understandably chosen to decline the position offered to him in 1521 and to remain in Tübingen. To replace him the chapter appointed Johannes Wanner[39] who was soon to become the focus of evangelical agitation in Constance. In 1523 Plantsch did accept the post in the Zürich delegation. But his role there was a modest one and his name appears only twice in the records of the session. When he interrupted his return trip to stop in Constance and consented to the bishop's request to preach in the cathedral on Candlemas (2 February), he found his path to the pulpit blocked by his 'successor' on the list of candidates to occupy that pastoral office, Johannes Wanner.[40] According to the minutes of the later chapter session, Plantsch had acceded to Wanner's request to see his sermon notes in advance and the young preacher had discovered to his dismay that his Tübingen counterpart planned to employ the three points of his sermon to demonstrate the validity of calling on the saints and the Virgin and to argue that Christ was sacrificed in the mass. Furthermore, Plantsch intended to assert that decrees passed by church councils enjoyed full authority,[41] or, to follow Wanner's more pointed description, that 'patristic decrees are no less authoritative than the gospel and holy scripture'.[42] Wanner defended his interference, appealing to his desire to enlighten his congregation gradually and to avoid dissension. Plantsch represented a threat to

'enemy of the Gospel' and turned to the Tübingen 'plebanus', or *Leutpriester*, Plantsch. *WABr* 3, p. 24, lines 12–15.

[37] 15 November 1521; Krebs, *Protokolle*, no. 6911.

[38] Hermelink, *Die Matrikeln*, 1, p. 14, no. 223.

[39] The bishop's lengthy hesitation in filling this position was probably not the result of cautious circumspection (Willburger, *Die Konstanzer Bischöfe*, p. 79) but due to his interest in the income from this benefice. Krebs, *Protokolle*, no. 6974.

[40] A summary of literature and carefully weighed account of the situation can be found in Rublack, *Die Einführung der Reformation in Konstanz*, pp. 221ff.

[41] Krebs, *Protokolle*, no. 7545.

[42] '3^{m} quod patrum decretis non esset minor auctoritas quam evangelio et sacris literis.' Letter of 12 March 1523 from Constance to Thomas Blarer; Schiess, *Briefwechsel*, 1, p. 78.

Wanner's timetable for the reeducation of his congregation: he had not yet completed the catechism required by the third point and not yet begun to deal with the other two.[43]

This altercation stretched the already tense relationship between bishop and city council almost to the breaking point and had far-reaching theological consequences. The subsequent interrogation of Wanner before the chapter and bishop centred on Plantsch's second and third assertions; theses well suited to delineate the boundaries – then still fluid – between reform and Reformation. The issues broached by Plantsch seemed custom-designed to distinguish the Erasmian attempt at reform through education and enlightenment from a fundamental criticism of the church's dogmatic tradition. And the question of the authority of church councils had formed a major theme of the just concluded Zürich 'synod of clerics'.

Already acquainted with Plantsch in his capacity as episcopal ambassador, we turn to the fourth member of the delegation, Johannes Fabri, who merits the greatest credit for such clarification as did result from the session. Johannes Heigerlin, the son of a smith, had registered at Tübingen on 22 October 1505 as 'Johannes Fabri ex Leutkirch'. Twenty-seven years old, he arrived in Tübingen ten months later than his future Protestant opponent, Ambrosius Blarer.[44] Like his teacher, Jacob Lemp, Fabri combined theological and legal studies and, upon becoming a doctor of both canon and civil law at Freiburg around 1510,[45] was fully equipped for an ecclesiastical career. His experience as an episcopal official in Basel beginning in 1513 provided practical preparation for his subsequent post as vicar general in the diocese of Constance from 1518 to 1523.[46] After ten years as bishop of Vienna, the politically talented and theologically productive Fabri died in 1541.[47]

43 'under denen artickeln er der predicant die zwen noch nie angetascht unnd den dritten noch nit zuend gebracht hab.' Krebs, *Protokolle*, no. 7545.

44 Hermelink, *Die Matrikeln*, 1, p. 150, no. 4; Blarer matriculated on 17 January. *Ibid.*, p. 146, no. 38. Helbling, *Dr. Johann Fabri*, pp. 3f. There is abundant material with autobiographical information in Staub, *Dr. Johann Fabri, Generalvikar von Konstanz (1518–1523), bis zum offenen Kampf gegen M. Luther (August 1522)*, pp. 23–36.

45 The precise date is uncertain and could have been as late as early 1511. Staub, *Dr. Johann Fabri*, p. 17, n. 28.

46 Unlike Helbling, Staub did not attempt to ignore Fabri's multiple benefices and his resulting absentee administration. Staub, *Dr. Johann Fabri*, pp. 17f., 21f., 139f., 167–70. His pursuit of these benefices is frequently reflected in the minutes of the cathedral chapter, as are the vain attempts by the chapter to control the accumulation. Only after he entered the service of Archduke Ferdinand did the chapter become more conciliatory. Krebs, *Protokolle*, no. 8029.

47 See Helbling's eulogy: 'In den letzten Lebensjahren konnte der Humanismus für Fabri unmöglich Ziel und Zweck, nur noch Mittel zum Zweck sein: seine Seele und

Due to his education and the office he held, Fabri had become influential in ecclesiastical politics. His connections with Rome – Prierias, Catharinus and Cajetan – and with the house of Habsburg rivalled those of Eck. He surpassed even his own bishop in political pull since he was less directly involved in local political strife in Constance. Dr Fabri was unquestionably the actual leader of the delegation to Zürich.[48]

Fabri had journeyed to Rome at the same time as his early rival Eck in the late autumn of 1521. While there, he published a generously documented treatise against Luther, dedicating it to the recently elected Pope Adrian VI.[49] Judging from the opening lines of the admonition to Luther appended to that volume (1522), one can imagine Fabri's reaction as he read the January 1523 invitation to the Zürich 'hearing' shortly after his return from Rome: 'My dear Martin, most beloved in Jesus, you will have comprehended well enough in the past years how useless the modern public disputations are for establishing truth. For truth never dawns with ease upon the billowing passions of agitated minds. The spirit of truth extends itself more readily to calm and tranquil spirits untainted by ambition . . .'[50] Fabri could count on the complete approval of Erasmian circles for these reservations regarding the utility of disputations, since academic calm and scholarly exchange formed the humanist topsoil so essential for the cultivation of the *bonae literae*. And Oecolampadius turned to

das Beste seiner Persönlichkeit galt der Reform und Wiederherstellung der Kirche.' *Dr. Johann Fabri*, p. 11.

48 His influence is visible in the composition of the delegation. Plantsch's selection is understandable in light of a letter by Fabri to Johannes Brassicanus in Tübingen. The Constance vicar general requested on 9 April 1519 that greetings be passed on to Plantsch and Lemp, who 'replaced' Plantsch in the *Strebkatz*. See Staub, *Dr. Johann Fabri*, pp. 94, 110, n. 157; Helbling, *Dr. Johann Fabri*, p. 151, no. 11; and above, n. 35.

49 *Opus adversus nova quaedam et a christiana religione prorsus aliena dogmata Martini Lutheri* (Rome, 1522). A second printing appeared in Leipzig in 1523, after Cardinal Matthaeus Schinner sent a copy of the rapidly out-of-print Rome edition to Duke George of Saxony on 29 August 1522. Staub, *Dr. Johann Fabri*, pp. 166, 174, n. 53. A third edition dedicated to Archbishop Hermann von Wied appeared in Cologne in 1524 with the new title, *Malleus in haeresim Lutheranam*, and has been edited in a critical edition by A. Naegele, *Dr. Johann Fabri, Generalvikar von Konstanz, Malleus in haeresim Lutheranam (1524)*. The Cologne Dominican, Johannes von Romberch, was responsible for the retitling with its allusion not only to Fabri's father's occupation as a smith (*CCath* 23/24, p. 5, n. 4), but also to the Dominican *Malleus Maleficarum*.

50 'Quam inutiles sint disputationes illae nostrorum temporum publicae ad inveniendam veritatem, opinor, satis annis superioribus es expertus, Martine in Iesu carissime. Nam veritas inter tumultuantes illos animorum aestus haud facile illucescit. Sedatis autem et tranquillis animis, nulla ambitionis labe infectis, spiritus ille veritatis se prodit libentius . . .' *CCath* 23/24, p. 23, lines 7–12.

these same arguments in attempting to dissuade Zwingli from his disputation plans.[51]

Conrad Summenhart's plea, 'O wretch that I am, who will deliver me from contentious theology (*rixosa theologia*)', was a comment intended to criticize a scholastic theology that contributed nothing to the edification of the soul or the church.[52] Fabri employed the same expression twenty-five years later to characterize Luther's boldness in forcing theological issues into the public spotlight, thereby scandalizing the weaker members of the body of Christ.[53] Such a contrast in assessing the public dimension of theology reflects a characteristic of Zwingli's 'discovery' that should not be underestimated: like the violation of the Lenten fast in Froschauer's house which preceded it and the sermon interruptions which followed, the 'disputation' of 29 January 1523 was a publicly effective demonstration, a deliberate form of agitation. In his attack on Luther, Fabri stressed that a theologian should not depend solely on his own opinion.[54] Nor should he interpret the approval of large groups of laity as confirmation of his theological orthodoxy. The illumination of the Holy Spirit is essential to the understanding of the scripture it inspired.[55]

Thus laymen need the spirit of wisdom and knowledge. But how can laymen distinguish truth from the error scattered throughout heretical writings? And even where this spirit of truth may be present in laymen, there remain certain dogmas and 'mysteries' that laymen and even priests should not approach too closely.[56] This viewpoint accorded well with a stipulation in the mandate given to the episcopal delegation: 'it is not fitting that the lay citizens of Zürich should deal with and decide matters of doctrine'.[57] Thus Fabri appears to have been more than merely the bishop's executive agent, consultant or

Fabri

[51] See above, n. 6.

[52] Johann von Staupitz recalled this lament by Summenhart: 'quis me miserum tandem liberabit ab ista rixosa theologia?' (the allusion is to Rom. 7.24) as reported in Melchior Adam, *Vitae Germanorum theologorum* (1620), p. 12f.; cited by Haller, 2, p. 65.

[53] 'At non rixosa illa theologia, quae non sine gravissimo pusillorum scandalo noviter inter nostros Germanos, et ita ut, velim nolim, dicere cogor, Dei sermonem inter eosdem scommatibus athleticis esse conspersum.' *CCath* 23/24, p. 24, lines 11–14.

[54] 'non perinde tutum esse putarim a receptis iam pridem illorum sententiis privata auctoritate dissentire . . .' *Ibid.*, p. 23, lines 24f.

[55] 'In explanatione sacrae scripturae semper sancti Spiritus inspiratione egemus, ut, cuius instinctu scripta sunt, illius revelatione pandantur, . . .' *Ibid.*, p. 53, lines 26–8.

[56] 'Sed demus sapientiae spiritum in laicis esse, tamen et id verum est, quod "in ecclesia dogmata secretiora sunt, quae adire nex ipsis sacerdotibus liceat," . . . Per quae datur intelligi secretiora scripturarum a laicis ut plurimum indigne tractari . . .' *Ibid.*, p. 54, lines 13–15, 28f.

[57] Krebs, *Protokolle*, no. 7510. Cf. in contrast Fabri's account, *ZW* 1, p. 496, n. 7.

right-hand man: he may have determined even the language in which important theological–ecclesiastical decisions were expressed.

When Sir Fritz Jacob von Anwyl, the political adviser, Vergenhans, the canon lawyer, and Plantsch, the 'experienced' pastor, entered Zürich on the evening of 28 January together with Dr Fabri, they came to conduct a visitation and attend a hearing sponsored by the city council, but not to expound or decide questions of doctrine.[58] Yet the delegation could not have been more carefully chosen and better equipped to survive a tough debate.

The polite communication to the episcopal chancellery inviting participation in the Zürich 'synod' restated the central issue that had been clarified in Mayor Röist's verdict of 21 July: holy scripture would quite naturally form the sole basis for the proceedings. Only a single trace remained of the council's former hesitation to pass judgment on theological questions or of a preference to leave such a responsibility to specialists.[59] The council now voiced its hope that 'God would fill those who earnestly seek the light of truth with that light'.

Could this be the innovation we are seeking? Has the council, illuminated by the Spirit, claimed the function of the hierarchy of the church? Not at all! That assumption would place us on the same erroneous path taken by past scholars, bypassing an understanding of the further course of the debate.[60]

Let us first summarize the course of events. In opening the session Mayor Röist made it unmistakably clear that the council had arranged for a disputation at Zwingli's suggestion. It was to be 'a disputation in the German language and before the greater council at Zürich',[61] an occasion at which anyone could accuse Zwingli without fear and at which Zwingli could be challenged to justify his teaching or be branded a heretic.

Although Zwingli thereupon three times invited his opponents to

58 Thus Fabri in his report to the Austrian government in Innsbruck regarding the first Zürich disputation. Mayer, 'Die Disputation zu Zürich am 29. Januar 1523', p. 185; cf. p. 56.

59 When Magister Jacob Edlibach, a canon at the *Grossmünster*, interjected his controversy with Zwingli into the proceedings of 29 January, even though it had already been dealt with at an earlier session of the chapter, Zwingli insisted that it be discussed 'here, before my lords of the council'. *ZW* 1, p. 543, line 31. And 'some of the councillors' supported him although the opposition proved strong enough for the matter to be tabled for possible discussion in a future chapter session. *ZW* 1, p. 544, lines 7 and 10f.

60 *ZW* 1, p. 468, lines 2–6; cf. p. 482, lines 18–21.

61 *ZW* 1, p. 484, lines 13f.; Gwalther: 'liberam et publicam coram Diacosiorum consessu disputationem instituit . . .' *Opp. Zw.* 2, fol. 608^{v}.

voice their complaints,[62] no disputation materialized. Zwingli, who had expressed pleasure that Johannes Fabri would be coming to Zürich and would by his presence lend a special radiance and lustre to the occasion,[63] was disappointed. Fabri dodged the anticipated confrontation by first referring to the general council of the empire planned for that same year with 'half of the judges coming from the secular and half from the spiritual estate'.[64] The vicar general then immediately proposed to substitute for the planned council-sponsored disputation an academic debate to be judged by the same three universities that had already ruled on the outcome of the Luther–Eck debate at Leipzig.[65] Seconded by Plantsch,[66] Fabri finally suggested that the city council, Zwingli and he himself each name one judge to a panel that would reach a final verdict.[67]

Although noting his rejection of Zwingli's theses, Fabri was unwilling to depart from the episcopal instructions – which in all likelihood he had helped to compose – and consistently refused to accept uneducated laymen as judges. Thus the council had no alternative but to conclude, contrary to all embellishment by later historians, that the disputation had not taken place because 'no one raised any objections against him [Zwingli]'.[68] For lack of objection the council declared Zwingli's message permissible and placed *all* participants who could support their preaching from scripture under the council's protection against calumny.[69]

The 'first Zürich disputation' could be quietly dismissed as the 'most important disputation never to take place' had not a *dispute* developed that our sources quite properly term a 'discussion'.[70] Only during this discourse did Zwingli make his 'discovery' and this exchange alone justifies the prominence accorded the Zürich 'synod of clerics' as a historical event.

62 *ZW* 1, p. 501, line 7.
63 *ZW* 8, p. 4, lines 14f.
64 *ZW* 1, p. 492, line 3. Fabri could point to a preliminary draft of the decree of the Diet of Nuremberg that mentioned Strassburg, Mainz, Cologne or Metz as possible venues. In an opinion written for the privy council, Constance was mentioned as a further potential site. *Ibid.*, n. 1.
65 Fabri listed Paris, Cologne and Louvain. *ZW* 1, p. 493, lines 1f.
66 See *ZW* 1, p. 559, lines 15–18. Zwingli responded stonily to Plantsch, insisting that he could understand scripture in no other way than 'wie sy sich selbst durch den geist gottes usslegt; bdarff keins menschlichen urteils'. *Ibid.*, lines 20f.
67 *ZW* 1, p. 563, n. 10. The later unofficial 'recording secretary' Hegenwald failed to mention that the city of Zürich was also to take part in the decision and provide one judge. *Ibid.*, p. 558, lines 7f.
68 *ZW* 1, p. 470, line 17.
69 *ZW* 1, p. 471, line 7.
70 Note Gwalther's concluding sentence: 'Et haec quidem totius disputationis aut colloquii istius summa est.' *Opp. Zw.* 2, fol. 623^{r}.

For as it became clear that the 'disputation' would not materialize, Zwingli either consciously or unconsciously reached for inflammatory phrases from the abusive language of the inn and the direct provocation of the streets. Fabri's attempt to reserve the problem of law and order to the jurisdiction of the entire church and its appropriate channels instead of this local assembly[71] provoked Zwingli's wrath. For that was precisely the kind of evasion one heard daily. The 'bigwigs', the bishops and prelates, were withholding the Gospel from the 'common man'.[72] The 'despotic prelates and bishops'[73] or – Zwingli hammered home his point – the 'bigwigs'[74] were not at all interested in a council but merely wanted to string the 'poor folk' along.[75]

Although even this pointed assault failed to goad any of Zwingli's opponents into a counter-attack, a heckler's exclamation indicates how much social dynamite had been ignited in Zwingli's massive anti-clerical outburst. Someone shouted, 'What's happened to the bigwigs who parade so bravely through the streets? Show your colours! Here's the man! You make fine speeches from behind your wine glasses but here no one opens his mouth.'[76]

[71] Well aware of the political issues agitating Zürich, Fabri pointed out that decisions made there could not be binding on other segments of the universal church. Only a general council could really banish 'Zwytracht'. *ZW* 1, p. 491, lines 13–17. But as far as Zwingli and his followers were concerned, that universal church had fallen into the hands of pope, cardinals and prelates when they had usurped the doctrinal office. If the Gospel could only once more enjoy its unhindered proclamation, then the church could once more 'be illuminated by the word of God and be of one mind and accord'. *ZW* 1, p. 497, lines 3f.

[72] *ZW* 1, p. 496, line 10; Gwalther translated: 'mitrati illi et saeculari potentia armati episcopi et ecclesiarum proceres'. *Ibid.*, n. 4. But his erudite Latin was, of course, incapable of handling the task of translation. *Opp. Zw.* 2, fol. 610^{v}. At another point Gwalther rendered 'grosse hansen' as 'magnates'. *ZW* 1, p. 497, line 11; *Opp. Zw.* 2, fol. 611^{r}.

[73] *ZW* 1, p. 495, lines 20f.

[74] *ZW* 1, p. 497, line 11.

[75] *ZW* 1, p. 497, line 6.

[76] 'Wo sind nun die grossen hansen, die uff der gassen so dapffer bochen! Tretten nun harfür! Hie ist der man! Ir künt all wol hinder dem win reden, aber hie will sich keiner regen.' *ZW* 1, p. 500, lines 19–21.

In a Nuremberg pamphlet of April (?) 1525, *An die Versammlung gemeiner Bauernschaft*, which reveals Zwingli's influence in its principles of reform, the secular princes are called the 'grosse herren' in contrast with the socially oppressed, the 'armen'. Laube, Seiffert *et al.*, eds., *Flugschriften der Bauernkriegszeit*, p. 122, lines 8 and 18.

For Thomas Müntzer the 'armen' and 'das arme Volk' are, as with Zwingli, primarily the common folk who have been led astray by the 'scribes' and only secondarily the economically exploited segments of society. Both the spiritual and temporal lords are the 'grosse Hansen' for Müntzer. His *Ausgedrückte Entblössung* (late July 1524) carried the term 'grosse hansen' in its title. *Thomas Müntzer, Schriften und Briefe*, ed. Franz, p. 267, line 10.

We must focus closely upon the circumstances that prompted such taunts. A reference to 'bigwigs' and thoughts of the innumerable financial obligations all clerics owed to or collected for their bishop must have stirred the minds of more than just the radicals in the Zwinglian party. Resistance to the episcopal jurisdiction personified in Fabri and Canon Vergenhans was considerable. The opposition directed itself with equal vigour against the fines for living in concubinage, which were assessed annually as if they were taxes;[77] against the countless mandatory payments for non-recurring official services at confirmations and church consecrations, which had only recently been denounced and boycotted as simony; and above all against the greater and lesser tithes that were encountering increasing resistance as a form of tyranny.

The heckler's shout, which was greeted by a burst of laughter, was merely the prelude to an increasingly critical confrontation. Jacob Wagner,[78] a pastor in Nefftenbach in the canton of Zürich, rose and reminded his listeners that his colleague, Urban Wyss had been imprisoned on the authority of an episcopal mandate affirming the validity of 'human ordinances'.[79] Wyss's crime was to have condemned appeals to the Virgin and the saints as human precepts contrary to the Gospel. Wagner argued that, since no one had contradicted Zwingli's theses, from that point on one dared proclaim only the pure Gospel free of human ordinances. He saw clearly that the spiritual jurisdiction of Constance would thereby be shaken to its foundation and that the tremors would be felt outside the diocese as well. Wagner explained, 'I raise this point because the good pastor of Fislysbach [Wyss] is our brother and I would very much like to have explained to me how I am supposed to react to the episcopal mandate according to which this pastor has been condemned.'[80] Wagner's complaint marks a turning-point in the day's events that was to give

[77] See Vasella, *Reform and Reformation in der Schweiz*, pp. 24–48.

[78] He was apparently the priest mentioned in Zwingli's *Apologeticus Archeteles* who had accused Melchior Fattlin, a rather conservative colleague of Vergenhans in the Constance cathedral chapter, of simony for having demanded, 'according to long-standing custom', payment for the consecration of a new church near Nefftenbach. *ZW* 1, p. 310, n. 1; Egli, *Acten*, no. 459.

[79] Wagner used the expression 'constitutiones humanae' (*ZW* 1, p. 501, line 20) which points to the episcopal encyclical of 10 August in which the 'menschlichen satzungen, ordnungen und guoten gewohhaiten' of the church were defended and confirmed as fully valid. Strickler, *Actensammlung*, no. 464. It is possible that he also had reference to the letter of 24 May 1522 from the Constance chapter to the Zürich council. Egli, *Acten*, no. 251.

[80] *ZW* 1, p. 502, lines 5–7.

the assembly of clerics a significance for ecclesiastical law that reached far beyond Zürich.

Here, where Zürich's local tensions threatened rebellion against the diocesan hierarchy, Fabri could no longer persist in his (self-) assigned role as observer. By his own admission personally affected by the charge that 'a bishop of Constance had forbidden the preaching of the gospel', he confessed to Sir Fritz Jacob von Anwyl that he could not permit the remark to stand unchallenged.[81] He saw no alternative but to point out publicly that not only the bishop, in whose name he had come to listen and observe, but also he himself, as vicar general responsible for the spiritual jurisdiction of the diocese of Constance, had been the target of the attack.[82] He hoped that his response would not be construed as participation in the announced disputation, but in any event, the cause of truth demanded that he defend himself.[83] In other words, Fabri claimed the same right of self-defence (*satisfactio*) that Oecolampadius had recommended to Zwingli *in place of* a disputation. Hence Fabri sought to evade Zwingli's theses by recalling his own 'fatherly' visit to Pastor Wyss during which he had attempted to demonstrate the scriptural basis for the 'intercession by and appellation to the dear saints and Mother of God'. Zwingli seized the opportunity for debate and asked Fabri to recount those scriptural reasons that had allegedly led Pastor Wyss to recant; noting that he himself had dealt with this theme in his theses proclaiming Christ the sole mediator.[84]

Had Fabri been amenable to a debate, he would have been well advised to yield the floor to Dr Martin Plantsch, who already in 1505 had developed a Catholic doctrine of the veneration of the saints, teaching that the saints themselves point the believer to Christ.[85] But Fabri had no intention of debating individual questions of doctrine. His strategy was to question the fundamental legitimacy of the assembly in which he was participating. He confessed to a tactical

[81] *ZW* 1, p. 505; cf. pp. 502–4. Whether the choice of delegates was tactically wise seems questionable to me. In estimating the reaction to this 'Tübingen delegation', account should have been taken of the sentiments of the Swiss. Zwingli exploited the divided state of the diocese of Constance since the Swabian War (1499) to underscore Swiss sensitivity to Swabian domination of the diocesan hierarchy: 'lieben bischoff imm Schwytzer- unnd Schwabenland'. *ZW* 2, p. 282, lines 16f. But in his generosity Zwingli was willing – alongside the usual 'uppigen und selenlosen bůben' – to entertain the possibility of 'frommen' among the *Schwaben*! *Ibid.*, p. 283, lines 1f.

[82] See Helbling, *Dr Johann Fabri*, pp. 8f.

[83] *ZW* 1, p. 502, lines 11–13.

[84] See *ZW* 1, p. 460, lines 12–17.

[85] See above, p. 182.

error in his previous remarks[86] and retreated to his basic argument that this 'small and extraordinary assembly' possessed no competence to decide matters pertaining to the entire church. Such issues should be brought before a general council just as the proper interpretation of scripture was a matter to be undertaken by universities such as Paris, Cologne and Louvain.[87]

Plantsch followed suit. When the time came to deal with 'his' theme of appeals to the saints, he appealed – in contrast to his authority in the Tübingen struggle with the *via antiqua* – to the miracles by which the saints daily demonstrate their ability to aid.[88]

The front had shifted for Plantsch. Because he now faced heresy and not superstition, his argument required modification. He emphasized the church's experience and authority, for the church is as infallibly founded on the Holy Spirit as were the authors of holy scripture. Christ's assurance that 'he who hears you, hears me' (Luke 10.16) applied to the words of bishop and pope who, as successors of the twelve apostles, 'govern the Christian church just as the Roman church has for many hundreds of years been a mother of all the other churches'.[89] And with that the bishop's representatives had made their point and thereupon rested their case, refusing to budge from that position for the rest of the session.

The 'disputation' was now a clear failure. Zwingli's theses had not become the object of debate, not even the three that dealt with the veneration of the saints. Yet precisely in the defeat lay the germ of Zwingli's realization of the real significance of the day's events. For in their insistence on a general council, the Tübingen episcopal delegation forced the clarification of the January synod's claim to Gospel authority.

Fabri insisted that grievances and questions of ritual and ceremony be decided for the entire church by a general council and the conclusions examined for their scriptural basis by the universities. Faced with this challenge, Zwingli proclaimed the 'Christian assembly' in Zürich competent in *both* instances. For him the Zürich synod was a general council capable of concluding with full authority that which Fabri reserved to the universities and papal councils. The renewal of theology and the church could begin in Zürich on the basis of holy scripture and possess validity for the entire church 'because the Holy Spirit does not say one thing today and something else

[86] ZW 1, p. 508, lines 1–8.
[87] ZW 1, pp. 510, lines 27ff. and 511, lines 20–2.
[88] ZW 1, p. 536, lines 2–6.
[89] ZW 1, p. 534, lines 17–22.

tomorrow'.[90] The Spirit could not deliver a different diagnosis and remedy to a future council. Hence, Zwingli concluded, the universities are unnecessary as supreme judges in determining truth for we have here and now our infallible and impartial judge, holy scripture, 'which cannot lie nor deceive'.[91] It is true that the *doctores* present must apply their philological knowledge to ensure that the scripture is employed correctly.[92] But confidence in the validity of the synod's results rests on the knowledge that 'so many Christian hearts' were present[93] and open to the illumination of the Spirit. For in the final analysis, 'in this hall we undoubtedly have a Christian assembly'.[94]

Just as Fabri had accused Luther of assailing the entire church from the narrow foundation of his own authority, so he now informed Zwingli that the Zürich session involved only a limited local convocation not competent to make decisions for the entire church. Zwingli reversed Fabri's argumentation and wriggled free of the potential *Anfechtung* – the same self-doubt that plagued Luther all his life – by appealing to the citizens of Zürich to glimpse the grace of God's election, to recognize God's gift and mandate as embodied in this synod: 'You people of Zürich should consider as the grace and vocation of God the fact that such a thing has been undertaken in your city to the praise and honour of God and the truth.'[95] Compared with Zwingli's intention, Fabri's disparaging label, 'local synod', seems misleading and inaccurate. From Zwingli's standpoint, 'general synod' was a far more suitable term since the assembly's agenda included the discussion, conclusion and celebration by proxy of the inauguration of reformation for the universal church.

All relevant issues lie within the competence of such a synod and find their clarification there through the illumination of holy scripture. But Zwingli's synodal principle was first applied practically at the second Zürich disputation, which was convoked in order to discuss the controversy over the mass and the images of the saints. The first 'Christian assembly' succeeded only in formulating the

90 *ZW* 1, p. 514, line 9.
91 *ZW* 1, p. 498, lines 3f.
92 The scholars present were to follow in the original languages the passages cited. Zwingli's expression, 'hören und lassen vorlesen' was rendered by Gwalther as 'audire et legere, ut videant'. *ZW* 1, p. 499, lines 5f.; *Opp. Zw.* 2, fol. 611^{r}.
93 *ZW* 1, p. 499, line 8.
94 *ZW* 1, p. 495, lines 10f.
95 *ZW* 1, p. 499, lines 14–17. 'ir von Zürich solt das für eine grosse gnad und berůffung gottes achten, das sölichs in üwer statt, got und der warheit zu lob und eeren, ist fürgenummen.' Gwalther translated: 'singulare divinae gratiae et vocationis indicium'. *Opp. Zw.* 2, fol. 611^{r}.

synod's claim of competence to establish truth for the whole church and in transferring to the assembly of the faithful the university's authority as an independent court of appeal. In reviewing our observations up to this point we must conclude that our working hypothesis under the label 'synod of clerics' understates the phenomenon which far more deserves to be called the *first 'evangelical' general synod*.

But not until his ecclesiological exchange with Fabri and the episcopal delegation did the novel aspect of this convocation dawn on Zwingli. Only then did he develop an interpretation that set the day's events into the framework of God's providential government of the world. That Mayor Röist, as a representative of the political powers, did not and could not share this conviction, is apparent. But the Constance delegation's involuntary role as midwife at the emergence of Zwingli's 'discovery' permits us a glimpse of the origins of the Swiss Reformation. For here, just as in the entire Reformed tradition, ecclesiology appropriated top priority from soteriology.

The relationship between city council and synod first found explicit definition at the second 'synod' session in October. But that task of definition hovered briefly on the January horizon when Zwingli reached for the same text from Matthew that Summenhart had employed twenty-five years earlier against the canonists and their teaching on tithes: 'Our Lord Christ knew very well that some day these "bigwigs" who load the poor with intolerable burdens would sit on the throne of Moses.'[96] But Zwingli used this text to support a fundamental rejection of all church laws: 'We want to be free of them in order not to burden our consciences with them.'[97] With that rejection the passage of new legislation would be inevitable, and the first ruling was written when the council, in its concluding statement, proclaimed Zwingli's preaching free of heresy.

Just as Johannes Fabri had provoked Zwingli to identify the Zürich convocation with a general council in January, provocation by Zwingli's radical following helped him to clarify the proper relationship between Zürich's city council and church in October. His conclusions prompt us once more to submit our facile assumption of a 'council-sponsored disputation' to the discipline of historical reality. When Zwingli announced that the council would determine how the issue of the mass could best be resolved, Simon Stumpf, pastor in Höngg since 1520 and, like Reublin, an opponent of the tithe,

[96] *ZW* 1, p. 538, lines 17–20; cf. Matth. 23.2–4.

[97] 'wir wollen fry in dem sin, unser conscientzen damit nüt zu beschwären.' *ZW* 1, p. 536, lines 23f.

protested: 'That decision belongs to the Holy Spirit and not the council. Should the city council rule in opposition to God, I will live and teach in defiance of the council.' Zwingli's reply is significant: 'That is correct. I would also preach and act in opposition in that case. But I have not attributed any privilege of judgment to the council. Neither the council nor anyone else in this world shall pass judgment on the word of God. And this assembly has not been convened by the council in order to pass judgment on scripture but rather to permit the council to inform itself and learn from scripture whether or not the mass is a sacrifice. Only then will the council consider the measures necessary to avoid tumult and uproar.'[98] Zwingli distinguished between the synod, which has subjected itself to the verdict of scripture, and the city council, which would take the executive action required by the synod's scripturally based doctrinal conclusions. Zwingli could not rule out the possibility of conflict between the two bodies, but he was confident that the council's political will could be harnessed to the causes of the Reformation.[99]

The situation in a series of other south German imperial cities assumed a different outlook when, in the wake of the Peasant's War (1524–5) and the Augsburg Interim (1548), a sense of responsibility for the political welfare of a city or region led city councils to adopt measures opposed to the convictions of scripture-citing preachers.[100] A look at such later developments confirms our resolve to avoid viewing even the early stages of the Reformation from the vantage point of the evangelical party alone. Zwingli recognized the political interests of the city council as responsibilities distinct from his own and made legitimate by the requirements of the common weal. The city council should participate in the synods to provide an organizational framework: convening and adjourning the sessions and presiding over deliberations either in the person of the mayor or by delegating the chair to competent specialists. Since the city council convenes, participates in and observes at the synod in order to remove the 'yoke of the Pharisees' and to take politically responsible action in Zürich, that same general synod which claims the competence to formulate truth for the entire church also functions as a local synod for Zürich and its territories.

98 *ZW* 2, p. 784, lines 19–26.

99 In the following years the issue of the independence of the local church *vis-à-vis* the city council became as important as it had once been in regard to the bishop of Constance.

100 For Strassburg see especially the thoroughly documented study by Thomas A. Brady, Jr, *Ruling Class, Regime, and Reformation at Strasbourg, 1520–1555*.

This synod, with its two faces, toward the church of Zürich and toward the universal church, has only one judge: holy scripture. The judge is joined by the *doctores* as consultants, the general clergy as its constitutive membership and the city council as its executive arm. But together all of these are 'brethren in Christ'. Neither bishop, general church council, pope nor city council could preside as judge over the assembly's deliberations. The innovation introduced by the 1523 assembly consisted in the elevation of scripture from a canon of reference to an immediate and sufficient assurance of doctrinal rectitude which would lead the 'brethren in Christ' to truth: 'We have here an infallible and impartial judge, namely holy scripture.'[101] With such claims Zwingli and his brethren assailed not only the ecclesiastical 'bigwigs' but also the pretensions of university professors and theological faculties. Whereas Dr Fabri addressed Zwingli, with what were certainly intentionally chosen words, as 'Master Ulrich',[102] the Zürich reformer could remain confident of the support of a majority of the Two Hundred, which directed a declaration of independence at the old masters: 'We have no need of Cologne, Paris or Louvain for we trust in the words of the Apostle James who assured us that "if any of you lacks wisdom, let him ask God and it will be given to him"' (James 1.5f.).[103]

Sir Fritz Jacob von Anwyl may not have enjoyed a formal higher education but he grasped the significance of the battle between the old and the new masters and discovered a biblical parallel for the condescending attitude of the academic *magistri*. Approximately three years after he had left the bishop's service and made public his evangelical sympathies he reacted, in a letter dated 14 August 1526, to the latest news from the Diet at Speyer[104] with a description of the cities' opposition to the imperial mandate ratified by the 'antichristian bishops'. In a letter to Vadian he cloaked his concluding assessment of the situation in a prayer:

> Father, I thank you that you have hidden these things from the wise of this world and revealed them to the simple (Matt. 11.25, Luke 10.21). And although the godless take this word of our Lord as just one more proverb and jestingly say, 'the guildmasters, there are the simple!' yet this proverb has now been realized and found application in the cities' reply. . . .[105]

101 *ZW* 1, p. 498, lines 2f.
102 *ZW* 1, p. 489, lines 1f.
103 *ZW* 1, p. 499, line 20.
104 See Fabian, *Die Entstehung des Schmalkaldischen Bundes und seiner Verfassung 1524/29–1531/33*, lines 44ff.
105 *Vadianische Briefsammlung*, ed. Arbenz, 4, p. 39.

The revolt of the cities, most rapidly consolidated, though not initiated, in Zürich, demonstrated the limits of the old and traditional authorities. The universities were too closely identified with those authorities to permit the Tübingen members of the episcopal delegation to stem the tide. For the moment, they were left with no choice but to accept an unwelcome role as a catalyst in the synthesis of a new ecclesiology. Scarcely more than ten years later, after plans for founding new 'city-universities' had foundered everywhere, when attacks against 'bigwigs' had long ceased to be aimed at the *magistri* alone, and when a new relationship to tradition had been carved out, the university at Tübingen was once more courted by the representatives of the cities. Bucer, Capito, Blarer and Zwingli's successor Bullinger all searched for ways to enlist the academic institutions and tradition to serve the progress of the Reformation. They endeavoured to reorganize the university, to defeat both scholastic and profane investigation, and thereby to subordinate science to wisdom and wisdom to faith.

If the phrase 'brethren in Christ' had not already gained a firm place in history as the term chosen by the Zollikon Anabaptists to describe themselves,[106] it would serve well as a description for Zwingli's 'discovery'. More than two years before the emergence of this first Anabaptist congregation (ca. 1525), Zwingli programmatically and intentionally, it seems to me, addressed the 'Christian assembly' with the words: 'Devout brethren in Christ'.[107] Mayor Röist opened his remarks with the conventional titles required by protocol: 'Most learned, worthy, noble, exalted, honourable, wise and spiritual lords and friends'.[108] Sir Fritz Jacob von Anwyl also observed diplomatic convention by including the city council in his salutation, adding the adjective 'prudent' (*fürsichtig*).[109]

Zwingli's salutation implied that the event in which all participated was not merely a special council session, but a 'Christian assembly' of equally privileged colleagues subject to the authority of scripture.[110] His greeting encompassed all present, including the episcopal delegation; despite the fact that the 'Devout brethren' might seem to mesh poorly with his description of the pope, bishops and prelates as

[106] Blanke, *Brüder in Christo*, p. 83; Nordenhaug translation, p. 71.
[107] *ZW* 1, p. 486, line 11. In the summer of 1523 Zwingli discussed the term 'Brüder in Christo' in his exegesis of the 27th article, making allusion to Hebrews 2.11. See *ZW* 2, p. 253, line 21.
[108] *ZW* 1, p. 483, lines 9f.
[109] *ZW* 1, p. 485, line 5.
[110] See his address to the nuns in Ötenbach in 1522 and 1524; *ZW* 1, pp. 338, line 10 and 339, line 24.

'bigwigs'.[111] With its sharp contrast, Fabri's greeting impresses on us the degree of novelty Zwingli had just introduced: 'Most learned, worthy, noble, exalted, gracious, wise, etc.! My good brother and lord, Master Ulrich charges and complains . . .'[112] For Fabri consistently addressed the city council, even when he referred to Zwingli as his brother. His language accorded fully with his proposition that the city council, Zwingli, and Fabri's own delegation represented three separate audiences meeting in the Zürich town hall. But Zwingli's phrase, 'brethren in Christ', prevailed and had become a common, indeed almost liturgical, formula by the time of the so-called 'second disputation' in October.

Admittedly neither Mayor Röist, who opened the October session, nor Joachim Vadian (†1551) who, together with Sebastian Hofmeister (†1533) and Christopher Schappeler (†1551)[113] had been named by Röist to preside over the deliberations, could bring themselves to use such language.[114] Indeed, the foreign guests generally hesitated on this point.[115] But the proclamation for the session on 26 October announced the goal of the meeting as an attempt to find ways to live together as 'brethren in Christ Jesus'.[116]

A further stage of development is Zwingli's extension of his confidence in Zürich's election as the birthplace of reformation – a belief only hinted at in January – to the October assembly of the 'brethren': 'Faithful, elect, beloved brethren in Christ Jesus our Lord'.[117] The new salutation articulated that crucial question that was to help shape the course of the Reformation in the coming decades. In that same October assembly Leo Jud stressed the potential tension between a truth-seeking (and under the guidance of the Holy Spirit, 'truth-finding') 'general synod' of the brethren in Christ and the local political powers in their function as a Christian magistrate. At first Jud directed his remarks past the city council to the assembled clergy,

111 *ZW* 1, p. 497, lines 22 and 11; p. 506, line 4.

112 *ZW* 1, p. 489, lines 1–3.

113 Hofmeister became a Franciscan at Schaffhausen. He had studied in Paris and served as lector for the Franciscans in Zürich 1520–2. He died in 1533 as the reformer of Zofingen. See *RE* 8, pp. 241f. Schappeler is known to us as the later co-author of the *Twelve Articles* of the Swabian peasants. See Brecht, 'Der theologische Hintergrund der Zwölf Artikel der Bauernschaft in Schwaben von 1525. Christoph Schappelers und Sebastian Lotzers Beitrag zum Bauernkrieg'.

114 *ZW* 2, pp. 676, lines 17f. and 677, line 17. Cf. Röist's introduction on 27 and 28 October; *ZW* 2, pp. 731, lines 30f. and 785, lines 4 and 15.

115 Sebastian Hofmeister was the only exception but he was not a complete outsider, having spent three years in Zürich. *ZW* 2, pp. 691, line 33 and 715, line 34.

116 *ZW* 2, p. 679, line 29.

117 *ZW* 2, 680, lines 11f. Cf. pp. 732, lines 6f. and 799, line 4.

addressing them as 'My beloved brethren in Christ' and admonishing them to preach the gospel faithfully and valiantly (*styff*).[118] Then he turned to the council: 'My Lords of the council at Zürich', you should, as is fitting for Christians, remain true to the true doctrine and protect it, ensuring that your mandate is followed in Zürich and the region for which you are responsible. Should that happen, God will certainly be with you for all eternity 'just as he stands by his elect'.[119] Jud noted that the city council could demonstrate that it stood on the side of the elect simply by reversing its previous verdict and releasing the iconoclasts imprisoned following the invasion of St Peter's during the preceding month.[120]

But the council chose to deny itself membership among Jud's brethren in Christ. On 4 November 1523 the imprisoned ringleaders of the attack on the images were banned for two years.[121] Ludwig Hätzer, who introduced his notes recording this judicial session of the council with the plea: 'O God, deliver the captives!' soon collided head-on with the civic authorities. Together with his like-minded comrades, Simon Stumpf, Wilhelm Reublin, Felix Manz and Conrad Grebel, Hätzer would probably not have hesitated to determine who were numbered among the true brethren in Christ. The council, at any rate, was not. Its members subsequently refused to warm to the concept of constructing a state church of the elect. Only then did Hätzer and his friends decide in favour of a 'community of the few'.[122]

In October as in January 1523, Zwingli found himself confronted with an independent city council policy. For his part, Mayor Röist was in no hurry to testify to his membership among the 'brethren', and he responded coolly to Jud's challenge to demonstrate his election. Content to rely on the intercession of others seeking the aid of Almighty God, he readily and pragmatically admitted his inability to speak authoritatively on the matter, arguing that he would resemble a blind man describing colours. He was indeed convinced that the word of God should be proclaimed in a reasonable and sober manner. But he chose to conclude with a simple request that 'all concerned might pray to God for the success of the matter'.[123] And early in the following year (1524), the greater council itself assumed

[118] *ZW* 2, p. 799, lines 24ff.
[119] *ZW* 2, p. 800, lines 5–10.
[120] See above, p. 202.
[121] Egli, *Acten*, no. 442.
[122] Blanke, *Brüder in Christo*, pp. 12f.; Nordenhaug translation, p. 13.
[123] *ZW* 2, p. 802, lines 4–8.

the supervision of the mandate on Gospel preaching. In the long run, the Zürich Reformation could tolerate no colour-blindness in high places.

We can now summarize the results of our investigation:

1. The *first Zürich disputation* took place not on 29 January 1523 but on 21 July 1522 when a committee of the lesser council passed the ordinance stipulating scripturally based preaching by both parties in the emerging Reformation.

2. In the city council's eyes and hence in a formal juridical sense, the so-called 'first Zürich disputation' of 29 January 1523 was a special session of the council and consequently was quite properly referred to in Constance as a *diaeta*.

3. The disputation which had formed the sole item on the special session's agenda never materialized. Because no one was prepared to charge Zwingli with heresy, the council ruled that Zwingli could continue 'as long and to the extent he pleased until someone could instruct him in a better doctrine'. The session was neither the first nor the second Zürich disputation – it was no disputation at all.

4. The Zürich magistracy, which was still largely dominated by the lesser council in 1523, should not be considered as the political arm of Ulrich Zwingli's reformation. Zwingli was caught very much by surprise when the council shifted the assembly to 29 January, nine days later than he had expected. Oecolampadius' sharp critique of Zwingli's plans for an academic disputation permits us to reconstruct Zwingli's original expectations: Zwingli himself planned to preside in order to defend his theses in the manner of a university professor. In contrast, the actual proclamation announced a council-sponsored disputation with Mayor Röist presiding. Zwingli endeavoured in vain to focus the deliberations on his theses. He had in mind a Swiss version of the Leipzig Disputation between Luther and Eck (1519). Neither Zwingli's plans for a disputation nor the council's decision to adjudicate matters of faith pertaining to public peace are radically innovative or a breach with medieval tradition: they do not mark the 'reformation break-through' which scholarship has hitherto related to 29 January 1523.

Admittedly newsworthy was the fact that Zwingli plotted an academic disputation in a city without a university just as the city council claimed judicial rights which in the empire the emperor exercised at the imperial Diet: even in the hard politicking during the Augsburg Diet of 1530 none of the parties ever challenged the claim of the emperor to be 'von Rechtswegen Richter' – as Charles V wrote to the pope on 14 July.

5. Distracted from his original goal by the episcopal delegation's stance and provoked by continual references to the sole competence of a supraregional general church council, Zwingli first conferred upon the event its special significance for Reformation history during the course of the debate. It was neither as professor nor as politician, but as prophet that Zwingli placed the convocation into the framework of church history; viewing it as the first evangelical general synod and an authoritative representation of the Church Universal. *This* was Zwingli's 'discovery'.

6. 'Disputations' as such were by no means a uniquely evangelical weapon: Solothurn before 1522 and Baden afterwards (1526) are two out of a series of Catholic disputations against heretics as had been held against Jewish rabbis for centuries.

7. Zwingli's prophetic interpretation of the events suddenly confronting him should not be dismissed as irrelevant *Schwärmerei*, at best of interest to professional church historians. A firm grasp of Zwingli's theological perspective on the Reformation in Zürich is as indispensable to our understanding of the local developments as is the general study of theological factors for the comprehension of the Reformation period as a whole. Any one-sided analysis thereof – theological, social, legal, political or military – distorts our sense of a century marked, perhaps uniquely so, by the immediate impact of ideas and ideals. The result of the Marburg Colloquy (1529) – or the lack of results! – should *pars pro toto* warn the modern historian to take seriously the factor of Reformation theology, a theology that followed its own 'laws' despite the obvious need for political unity.

8. The city council considered the assembly to be anything but a synod of the 'brethren in Christ'. And they were right! This became fully apparent when the peasant revolts of the 1520s and again the Interim of the 1540s revealed the fundamental divergence of interest between the 'faithful' and the body politic as to the religious and political goals. The context for the history of both city and Reformation was formed by a symbiosis between their specific interests, but that symbiosis was an interim, a *temporary* coalition. There exists indeed continuity between the late medieval *Corpus Christianum* and the new evangelical urban church. Yet discontinuity is also apparent. Each defined the basis of the common weal in a different manner: in the 'obedience of faith' on the one hand and a 'sense of civic virtue' on the other.

A shared vision on the part of church and civic authorities, and the political mandate of the 'brethren in Christ', would eventually emanate from Zürich[124] to influence English Puritanism[125] and, for a time, to help mould the commonwealth of Puritan New England.[126] But the mainstream of the Reformed tradition was formed and shaped by other experiences, by the events of the 1540s when the conflict between the confessing church community and the Christian civic authority grew clear,[127] coinciding with the beginnings of a decline in the cities' economic and political importance. Strassburg and Geneva managed to develop their own historically potent existence as independent 'communities under the cross' of exile and the exiled.[128] Calvin's historical significance lies above all in the fact that he showed to the innumerable refugee congregations forced into exile

124 We must take account not only of the subsequent but also of the preceding history of the Reformed tradition. As James S. Preus put it: 'Carlstadt had tried to begin in Germany what was later done in the Swiss Confederation . . . at Zurich, Basel, and Geneva: institute a reformation in cooperation with the city magistracy. Due to decisive political differences . . ., Carlstadt's project did not take root,' *Carlstadt's Ordinaciones and Luther's Liberty. A Study of the Wittenberg Movement 1521–1522*, p. 83.

125 See Hill, *Puritanism and Revolution*; Paul, *The Lord Protector, Religion and Politics in the Life of Oliver Cromwell*; Locher, 'Zwinglis Einfluss in England und Schottland. Daten und Probleme'; Walton, 'The Institutionalization of the Reformation at Zurich', pp. 506–11.

126 See Miller, *The New England Mind: The Seventeenth Century*.

127 I know of no document that permits such profound insight into the painful process of separation of *two* urban movements of reform, temporarily linked so closely as to be scarcely distinguishable, as the letter of Martin Bucer to Jacob Sturm in Strassburg, written from England on 13 May 1549; discovered and carefully edited by Jean Rott. Asserting 'Domini est terra, ideo et patria', as a basis for the political mandate of believers, Bucer accused Sturm of having bowed during the Interim to political pressure instead of the will of God. A minority qualified by true faith fully deserves decision-making influence out of proportion to its numerical strength: 'debebat eorum hic sententia maxime valere, in quibis Christus maxime vivat; etiam si numero pars horum minima esset . . .' The common weal once more became the subject of discussion; the faithful know best what is good for the whole city: 'Scimus quid iudex vivorum et mortuorum a nobis postulet, quid promittat sibi obtemperantibus, quid minetur iussa sua contemnentibus.' Rott, 'Un recueil de correspondences strasbourgeoises', pp. 809–18; here p. 810. No single sentence could so clearly illuminate Bucer's distance from Luther's political ethic.

It would be mistaken to assume that a radical break occurred in Bucer's development from a 'theocrat' to the founder of a 'free church'. For the germ of this letter may be found in the petition, 'Vom mangel der Religion, an deren alles hanget' (August 1532), edited by B. Bellardi in *Martin Bucers Deutsche Schriften*, vol. 4, pp. 452–62. And at the end of his career Bucer wrote a theocratic *utopia*, a comprehensive plan for the reformation of England, *De regno Christi* (1550). The break in continuity consisted in adjustment to political developments but the goals remained unchanged. It is symbolic of the continuity in Bucer's thought that – having been won for the Reformation at Luther's Heidelberg Disputation – at the end of his life (†February 1551) he extended invitations to a public disputation at Cambridge on 6 August 1550. He had also been prepared to go to Tübingen for a disputation, at that time (1524) still termed a 'hearing'. See *Handel mit Cunrat Treger*, ed. J. Müller in *Martin Bucers Deutsche Schriften*, vol. 2, p. 125, line 34.

128 See Locher, 'Von Bern nach Genf', here pp. 84–6.

a path[129] that avoided both the theocratic state-church of Zürich under Zwingli's successors, Bullinger and Gwalther, and the apolitical flight from the world that characterized major portions of the Anabaptist movement. But this achievement was purchased at heavy cost. The political dimension of the doctrine of election yielded to the personalized doctrine of predestination, proclaimed in the following century by the Reformed synod of Dordrecht (1618–19).[130] Indeed, at this first Reformed general synod to follow that of Zürich, the most important advance in the development of political theology on the long path from Augustine to Calvin was reversed in one stroke.[131]

129 See the relevant comments on a 'theology of exile' by Walzer, *The Revolution of the Saints. A Study in the Origins of Radical Politics*, p. 117.

130 Among the parallels between Zürich and Dordrecht, special attention should be given to the criticism of academic theology. The partisan but highly interesting history of the background of the Synod of Dordrecht, published as *Praefatio ad Reformatas Christi Ecclesias*, reveals that that assembly opposed the influence of the young university at Leiden as being destructive in the same manner as once had seemed the case in Paris or Tübingen. *Acta synodi nationalis in nomine Domini nostri Iesu Christi, authoritate illustr. et praepotentum DD. Ordinum Generalium Foederati Belgii provinciarum Dordrechti habitae anno 1618 et 1619*, fol. IV^{v}.

131 See Calvin's political testament in his last sermon series, begun two years prior to his death (1564). *Predigten über das 2. Buch Samuelis*, ed. Rückert, pp. 104f. Cf. the translation and analysis in my article, 'Die "Extra"-Dimension in der Theologie Calvins', pp. 328f.

12

The onset of the Counter-Reformation

THE REVOLT of the 'new masters' produced more than mere consternation on the part of the old. Johannes Fabri[1] was sufficiently impressed by the potential of a Christian assembly such as he had experienced in Zürich to fall back on a variation long legitimate in church law, the diocesan synod,[2] as a weapon against the threatened erosion of the authority of the church of Rome. The deliberations of an assembly of the bishops of the south German dioceses seemed most likely to prove effective against the mounting heresy. We do know that the bishops of Constance, Augsburg and Strassburg assembled in Tübingen in May 1523, although the report of this session gives no further details.[3]

The plan to convene the clergy of various areas may have been discussed there. Fabri reported to the Constance cathedral chapter on 30 July 1523 concerning this proposal. He related that he had summoned the parish clergy of all Württemberg to Tübingen and Esslingen and impressed the provisions of the Edict of Worms and the decree of the Diet of Nuremberg on those assembled.[4] Repre-

[1] Fabri research remains in an incipient stage. The evaluation of the period from 1523 to his death in 1541 requires access to his still unpublished political correspondence for those years. But we are on firmer ground regarding his significance for the Roman curia, both as a reporter supplementing the papal legates and as a warrior against Protestantism. See Gerhard Müller, *Die römische Kurie und die Reformation 1523–1534*, p. 53.

[2] Odette Pontal points out that the Fourth Lateran Council prescribed periodic diocesan synods that would be responsible not only for church discipline but also for religious education; educational responsibilities that devolved upon the theological seminaries in the seventeenth century. Pontal defines these synods as 'Une réunion périodique officielle et obligatoire des membres du clergé diocésain ayant charge d'âmes, autour de leur évêque ou de son représentant, cette réunion ayant pour but d'informer et de contrôler ce clergé.' *Les statuts synodaux*, p. 27. Provincial synods, in contrast, were held irregularly and infrequently. *Ibid.*, p. 29.

[3] Karl Th. Keim reported, without indicating his sources: 'Man wandte sich an die Städte, Luthern Manches zugestehend, man wandte sich an den Klerus, um ihn zu ermahnen, man verschärfte den Priestereid, man erliess Citationen.' *Schwäbische Reformationsgeschichte bis zum Augsburger Reichstag*, p. 26.

[4] This 'clerics' *Convent*' may have been held in conjunction with the territorial diet at Stuttgart on 4 March. In that case it was the expansion of the circle of fifteen prelates

sented by a committee,[5] the Württemberg clergy accepted the mandates against the Lutheran heresy 'submissively and with good will', reporting that only a few within their ranks were 'followers of the Lutheran sect'. At the same time they considered assistance by the authorities in suppressing the 'sectarians' to be most desirable.

The Dutch pope, Adrian VI (1522–3), may be reproached with some justification for his failure to press for the convening of diocesan or provincial synods during those decisive years;[6] despite the respect merited by the 'confession' which his nuncio Chieregati read in Nuremberg on 3 January 1523: 'all of us, prelates as well as clergy, have strayed from the path of justice. . . .' Fabri's initiatives stand out against a context of indecision; his attempt to bring the Württemberg clergy to a new corporative pledge of loyalty indicates that he had accurately assessed the challenge posed by the Reformation. Unlike the other theological combatants, Fabri not only utilized polemical writings but also resisted the Reformation by anchoring the theological defence within the organizational life of the church. The Achilles heel of the new movement was its lack of an ecclesiastical superstructure to connect its local strongholds. But Fabri's goal in these measures was certainly not identical with the renewal through democratization that led the Zürich 'brethren in Christ' to charge that the highest echelons of the ecclesiastical hierarchy were composed of 'bigwigs'. Fabri aimed instead to fortify the church's defences by reinforcing its hierarchical structure and improving the education of the clergy.

Fabri knew of radical aspirations within the evangelical party even prior to his trip to Rome in 1521. But he dismissed them in passing as being 'more Lutheran than Zwingli' ('Zwinglio Lutheranior').[7] In January 1523, he saw with his own eyes that he was dealing with a successful and potentially far-reaching mutiny. With the aid of 'Zwingli and his friends', an entire section of the diocese of Constance threatened to forsake the episcopal embrace permanently. Far more clearly and, above all, more rapidly, than most of his comrades-in-arms, Fabri perceived that he was facing more than a mere temporary wave of enthusiasm or a revised edition of one of the

represented in the Stuttgart *Landtag*. The extirpation of the 'lutherischer sect' first appeared on the *Landtag*'s agenda on 15 June 1524, receiving the assembly's approbation. Grube, *Stuttgarter Landtag*, pp. 131 and 135.

5 'durch ir botschafften erschynen.' Krebs, *Protokolle*, no. 7721.

6 Thus Müller, *Die römische Kurie*, p. 14.

7 Letter to Wilhelm Falconi, 10 October 1521; printed in Horawitz, *Johann Heigerlin (genannt Faber), Bischof von Wien, bis zum Regensburger Convent*, pp. 83–220; here p. 175.

medieval heresies that church and state had long since brought under control. He realized that the mobilizing troops of the Reformation could be combated only through a network of political alliances coordinated with a careful internal reinforcement of the Catholic church. Thus Fabri's efforts in Württemberg marked the first stage on the road to the Regensburg Union concluded between Archduke Ferdinand of Austria, the Bavarian dukes and the south German bishops in June 1524 for the purpose of enforcing the Edict of Worms.

In view of these efforts, we can understand how Fabri could symbolize for the south German reformers precisely what Johannes Eck represented to Luther and his Wittenberg colleagues: the central strategist and 'chief whip' of the Counter-Reformation.[8] Fabri himself had no intention of sharing top billing in the Catholic resistance but hoped to leave Eck behind him in a competition that neither explicitly acknowledged. Potential compensation at Zürich for Eck's head start gained at the Leipzig Disputation evaporated into the disputation-free January Swiss air, proscribed by the Constance cathedral chapter's instructions that Fabri helped to construct. Until Ferdinand's election as king of the Romans in 1530, the same year that Fabri was consecrated bishop of Vienna, the former vicar general in Constance indeed operated some of the most important levers of power in the empire as an advisor to the archduke. But at the same time the continually shifting contours of the anti-Habsburg coalition prevented him from asserting widespread influence in Germany. As Eck's south German counterpart, he consistently advocated the early convening of a council that could have had only one purpose: the condemnation of the reformers in order to halt the diabolical erosion of church discipline. But under no circumstances, Fabri added in reference to the Zürich events of 1523, should this council permit the participation of the 'new masters'.[9]

[8] Johannes Botzheim, the leader of the pro-Wanner reform faction of the Constance cathedral chapter, considered Fabri to be the behind-the-scenes strategist and chief of operations for the anti-Luther alliance of bishops and princes: 'D. Margarita furit in negotio Lutherano, id quod apud nos facit Faber et per hunc aliquot episcopi et principes.' Constance, 24 August 1523. *Opus Epistolarum*, ed. Allen, 5, pp. 323, line 37–324, line 28.

[9] In his advice to Pope Paul III regarding the preparations for the council called for Mantua, the *Praeparatoria futuri universalis nuper indicti concilii* (1536), Fabri recommended that the pope should have fifty to one hundred copies of the *Acta* of the councils of Constance and Basel brought to Mantua, in order to prove to his opponents that no 'cobblers, tailors, brick-layers and such folk' had ever had a voice or vote in previous councils. This was especially important to Fabri because he was convinced that the Zürich model of a 'town council' had been adopted by most Protestants: 'Illis enim habitis licebit videre, in prioribus conciliis non sedisse neque vocem dedisse sutores, sartores, caementarios et huis generi homines, id quod

Even as early as 1523, in Fabri's final year as vicar general in Constance, a new and sharply formulated oath was introduced for all prospective priests in the diocese of Constance. The text of this new 'parsons' pledge' – to use the words of the Constance town clerk, Jörg Vögeli[10] – merits full-length reproduction here because it documents in a unique way the transformation of the medieval Catholic church into the Roman Catholic church. Already in this early phase, the Reformation understanding of the church as a community of believers gathered around word and sacrament was uncompromisingly repudiated. From the busy loom of medieval concepts of the true church, one single strand was now to be followed as the unique delineation of orthodoxy.

I confess the true, catholic and apostolic faith and swear by Almighty God and by this His holy gospel that I have hitherto remained with heart and mouth in the unity of the holy catholic church and the fellowship of the supreme bishop of Rome and that I shall in the future remain steadfastly therein. I shall also uniformly observe the regulations of the holy canons and salutary deliberations [decisions] and conclusions of the councils of the godfearing mother church[11] and do not nor shall not assent to the doctrines condemned by that same Christian Roman church, nor to any new heresies or perverse teachings, especially the Lutheran arch-heresy and its adherents.

To all of them and to each one in particular I wish malice and intend to resist them out of free will and a non-dissembling, pure spirit. And in no way shall I shield those who hold to, dispute, protect, preach or take up either secretly or publicly – by any sort of request, ruling, appearance or deception – their teachings, which are erroneous and devoid of love.

But Fabri realized that compliance with an oath was no substitute for the acquisition of a solid theological foundation. He would have been pleased to draw both of the universities to which he felt attached

maxime fieri et observari volunt adversarii fere omnes.' *Concilium Tridentinum*, 4, pp. 10–23; here, p. 17, lines 3–6.

10 In his history of the Constance Reformation, Jörg Vögeli – who was exiled from Constance in 1548 and died in Zürich in 1562 – reported that the 'nüwen pfaffenaid' had been introduced because 'die vorige huldung, die die pfaffen von alter gethon hattent, nit styf gnueg bunde'. But according to Vögeli, the initiative came not from the vicar general but from the suffragan, Dr Melchoir Fattlin (†1548). Vögeli, *Was zue Constantz dess Evangelii halben gehandelt ist von anno 1519–1536 [1538]*, in Jörg Vögeli, *Schriften zur Reformation in Konstanz*, ed. A. Vögeli, vol. 1, p. 84; vol. 2, pt. 2, pp. 867f., n. 29.

11 Willburger's translation, which has the priests swearing obedience to Mother Church 'and councils', suppresses Vögeli's stress on the fact that the reference was not to any and all councils – e.g. the French council at Pisa (1511/12) or even Zwingli's Zürich 'council' (1523) – but to the councils of Holy Mother Church: 'beschlüssen der gotsachtigen muetterkirchen concilien . . .' Vögeli, *Schriften*, 1, p. 84. For the text of the oath see Willburger, *Die Konstanzer Bischöfe*, pp. 108f.

as an alumnus, Tübingen and Freiburg, into his work of reform. And after he had accepted the call to become councillor and confessor to Archduke Ferdinand of Austria on 1 August 1523, he found himself in a position to integrate the two universities, which now stood under Austrian control, into his anti-Reformation campaign.[12] One of the best opportunities for the universities to prove their readiness to take up the cause of the Roman church emerged from plans for a disputation in the Swiss town of Baden in 1526. The university at Freiburg joined Zürich's council in ignoring Fabri's urging and declined to attend. Tübingen, however, experienced in the ways of the recalcitrant Swiss, did not disappoint Fabri and sent a four-professor delegation to participate in a confrontation that Fabri and Eck managed to turn into the Swiss 'Diet of Worms'.[13]

For all the political caution exercised by the University of Tübingen during the weeks preceding Duke Ulrich's deposition (April 1519),[14] the theological faculty did not hesitate to reveal its sympathies in the incipient confessional conflict. Jacob Lemp, invited to Baden as Fabri's honoured teacher, had already earned a reputation as an opponent of the Lutheran heresies. But his reputation also earned him the abuse of the Reformation-inspired pamphleteers. Lemp appeared in the satire, *Ain schöner dialogus*, as the target of the taunts of the 'Lutheran peasants' Fritz and Cunz.[15] In the *Luterisch Strebkatz* (winter 1524–5), the pope showered an eager and willing Lemp with praise but the ostensibly neutral and obviously evangelical 'Genius' or guardian spirit clearly condemned him:

Pope to Lemp:
O Lemp, you dear old sophist you,
  Think up a crafty trick or two
To catch that monk and him confound,
  For I'm convinced he's devil-bound.
He scatters all my best allies,
  As fools, I fear, we'll be despised.

[12] I suspect that Fabri's strategy inspired Ferdinand's plan to include the universities in the preparations for a national council set to convene in Speyer in late 1524. Electors, princes and the estates with universities were specifically requested to have their 'gelerte, erbare, erfarne und verstandige rethe [Räte]' comb the writings of the 'innovators' and prepare to discuss their doctrines at the synod. *Deutsche Reichstagsakten*, 4, p. 605, lines 1–5.

[13] The phrase was coined by Walther Köhler, *Zwingli und Luther. Ihr Streit über das Abendmahl nach seinen politischen und religiösen Beziehungen*, 1, p. 327.

[14] Haller, 1, pp. 295f. Regarding Ferdinand's desire to gain control of the administration of Württemberg in 1522 in return for assuming the expenses of the Swabian League's military effort, see the section 'Die Württembergische Frage' in Hauswirth, *Landgraf Philipp von Hessen und Zwingli*, pp. 22–6.

[15] See *Ain schöner Dialogus* in Schade, *Satiren und Pasquille*, 2, pp. 119–27.

And yet, I hope your bellowing
  Reduces him to cowering.
And if at that you should succeed,
  A red hat shall reward your deed;
An extra special card'nal's seat
  With gleaming ducat gold replete.

Lemp:

O Father, you most holy man,
  I've always done the best I can.
In Tübingen they know full well
  How in the lib'ral arts I'm swell;
And doctor of the Holy Writ.
  And for your Holy Benefit
I'll gladly give both life and limb
  And shout them down with all my *vim*
As heretics and impious strays.
  Now, I've been mixed up in the fray
Since Luther and his connivees
  Conspired to steal the holy keys
That fit the lock to heaven's gate
  And Peter's heir's chair decorate:
As is well known, I did inveigh
  Against that crime without delay.

Genius:

My dearest Lemp, your tale is true,
  You proved your skill in Zür'ch anew.
Your roaring mug so failed you there
  That neither growl nor bark it blared.
We've never heard from you as much
  As one word which true scripture touched.
Proverbial you are for sure,
  Contented dog in your manure.
But when the barnyard you forsake,
  You tremble, jitter, shake and quake
And bite your tongue to hide your fear.
  Hence my advice to you, my dear:
Pipe down, my friend, it's now high time,
  Lest whimp'ring turn to pantomime.
You only serve to demonstrate,
  Isaiah's still quite up-to-date
Where he refers to silent hounds
  Whose slumber lets the shepherd down.
But read the verse and rest assured
  That you belong in that same herd.
But as for now, I've had my say:
  Your sickly aid's worth less each day.[16]

[16] Schade, *Satiren und Pasquille,* 3, pp. 124f. Cf. Is. 56.11.

Tübingen's Lemp has been chosen here to personify the unrepentant and, above all, unteachable old scholastics who, thanks to the 'Magistri nostri' of the *Letters of Obscure Men*, had long since acquired a public image as having been immunized against genuine education. It was of utmost importance to the young Counter-Reformation forces that they shake off this unwelcome caricature. As part of the Austrian government's total plan to expand the universities located in its territories and to orient them to contemporary questions such as the Reformation and the Turkish menace, the year 1524 witnessed attempts to modernize the universities of Vienna[17] and Freiburg and to render them serviceable to state interests.

In 1525 Tübingen also experienced an attempt at reorganization[18] that envisioned the suppression of the two *viae* anchored in the charter of the faculty of arts.[19] But accomplishing by decree a university reform that attacks the most basic scholarly forms and principles is always unrealistic, unless the things jettisoned are forms from the past that scholars themselves have long since abandoned as meaningless. Tübingen's supra-regional academic importance had rested for too many years on the creative coalition between the two ways to permit that coalition's simple undoing without adequate replacement.

Moves against the two *viae* are understandable in light of the humanist scorn and evangelical satire which played off the two scholastic 'sects' against each other in order to make the humanist and proto-protestant programmes more attractive as means to 'reunion'. Such polemics stemming from the passions of past controversy dominate the images current even today, since modern historiography developed under the tutelage of the victorious parties in the struggles. But in Tübingen the two ways were a scholarly matter of course due to the *esprit de corps* shown by Biel and Summenhart or Lemp and Steinbach. And as far as the *via moderna* is concerned, its

[17] The expansion was to have been achieved in close conjunction with stricter controls on orthodoxy, according to a proposal by Eck (1523): 'Constituantur inquisitores super universitate Viennensi.' *Acta Reformationis Catholicae*, ed. Pfeilschifter, vol. 1, p. 149, line 35.

[18] 'Ordinatio Regis Ferdinandi 1525.' Roth, *Urkunden*, pp. 141–52.

[19] Roth, *Urkunden*, p. 147. See Schreiber, *Geschichte der Albert-Ludwigs-Universität zu Freiburg im Breisgau*, vol. 1, p. 37.

In Ingolstadt the *Wegestreit*, which had been creating unrest during the summer of 1514, was laid to rest shortly thereafter: 'in den Protokollen [of the faculty of arts, 1515–17] fehlen jetzt schon die Parteinamen'. Seifert, *Die Universität Ingolstadt im 15. und 16. Jahrhundert*, p. 78. But it remains open to question whether the controversy had not merely been transferred from the arts faculty to the *bursae*; see the following note.

most important contributions – overcoming the gap between scientific activity and observation while levelling the university's ivory tower – have yet to be surpassed by any other form of modernity. That the programmatic nominalist initiative stagnated in academic theory and came under attack from the humanist 'third way', has denied the *via moderna*, with its scholarly orientation so essential to every vital university, a just evaluation.

Tübingen's nominalism experienced no sudden interruption nor did it suddenly vanish from the university scene. The vitality of the modern way's scholarly tradition even in the face of the new educational movements is underscored by Martin Plantsch's decision to endow stipends for the benefit of needy students who had chosen to follow the *via moderna*.[20] Nor could the measures of the year 1525 dislodge the two *viae*. The minutes of the visitation conducted in the *bursae* of both ways on 15 August 1531 describe the situation. In addition to the usual 'abuses' such as cutting classes, excessive festivities and the misuse of a certain vessel not intended to function as a urinal, the complaints dealt with the methods of instruction. We discover in the report[21] that the two *viae* had preserved their individual identities,[22] with each using a different textbook for the introductory lectures on dialectics. In the *via antiqua* the *Summulae*

[20] The endowment, called the *Martinstift*, was confirmed by the university on 3 September 1511 with stipends for nine students. After discussions in Stuttgart, Plantsch later requested that they be made equally available to students from both *bursae*. Fritz Ernst, *Die wirtschaftliche Ausstattung der Universität Tübingen in ihren ersten Jahrzehnten (1477–1537)*, pp. 103f. A. Vögeli reported twelve to eighteen recipients, citing Anton Weis, *ADB* 26, p. 241. See Vögeli, *Schriften*, vol. 2, pt. 2, p. 912, n. 93. In 1516 Jacob Strylin of Urach, a canon at the Tübingen *Stiftskirche*, bequeathed a sum to endow scholarships for four students, one of whom was to be in orders and two of the remaining three to be chosen from the 'modern way'. Ernst, *Die wirtschaftliche Ausstattung*, p. 104. Ernst's information is contradictory at some points and he explained Plantsch's desire to expand the endowment by his supposed adherence to the *via antiqua*. *Ibid.*, p. 103, n. 362. For all aspects of the Plantsch endowment see 'Die Martinianische Stiftung', in *Die Württembergischen Familien-Stiftungen*, Heft 4 (Stuttgart, 1853), pp. 3f.; On Strylin's endowment, *ibid.*, Heft 10 (Stuttgart, 1854), pp. 1–99.

In Ingolstadt Johann Permeter von Adorf (†1505) left a sum that was used after 1515 to aid the *via antiqua*: 'das der allt wege sein rector, dechant und doctor haben mogen'. Seifert, *Die Universität Ingolstadt*, p. 46, n. 29.

[21] Haller, 2, p. 182.

[22] In a very interesting autobiography, the lawyer Johann Kingsattler recounted how, during his rectorate, he was forced to leave Tübingen along with his wife and children from October 1530 to May 1531 because of the plague. But his absence and the epidemic did not mean that teaching activities were completely disrupted. The two *bursae* were transferred to two locations far from Tübingen, to Blaubeuren and Neuenbürg: 'Et bursa Antiquorum sive Realium in Plabeuren, bursa Modernorum seu Nominalium in Novo Castro vulgo Neuenpürg sedem locavit. Sed doctores et alii qui non tenentur esse apud bursas, disgregati sunt.' Haller, 2, p. 223.

logicales of Petrus Hispanus (†1277)[23] were employed as they had been since the beginnings of the university. Here the visitation committee could find nothing objectionable. But in the *via moderna* the textbook on dialectics then in use was written by Rudolph Agricola (†1485),[24] a friend of Reuchlin with ties to *devotio moderna* circles. The choice demonstrated the adaptability and openness characteristic of Tübingen nominalism until well into the sixteenth century. For precisely that reason the commission took this discovery very seriously and a university decree of 6 September 1531 prohibited the further use of the modernist Agricola by an instructor in either *bursa* under penalty of the loss of his position.[25]

Although Ferdinand's nearly simultaneous efforts on behalf of renewal at the universities in Vienna, Freiburg and Tübingen reveal a consistent policy designed to mobilize all pedagogical forces to confront the immense problems of the age, different accents are perceptible at each university. Ferdinand hoped to transform the Vienna university into a cultural centre on the European periphery. At the same time he wished to impress on European consciences that the Turkish armies were no mere potential and shadowy danger but actually stood *ante portas*, demanding an immediate intellectual and financial counter-offensive. The situation at Freiburg was dominated by the fact that the citizens and the university – in the person of Ulrich Zasius – had registered complaints with the Austrian officials clearly showing how inadequately the university had immunized itself against the 'Lutheran venom'. Fabri's request of 27 January 1524 did indeed receive a speedy response from the theological faculty in the form of a written judgment on Zwingli's theology issued on 7

[23] Peter of Spain, later Pope John XXI, wrote the *Summulae Logicales* around 1250. See Prantl, *Geschichte der Logik im Abendlande*, 3, pp. 32–74; critical ed. by de Rijk, *Peter of Spain (Petrus Hispanus Portugalensis), Tractatus, called afterward Summule logicales*.

[24] Agricola, born in Baflo near Groningen, an acquaintance both of Wessel Gansfort and of the rector at Deventer, Alexander Hegius, completed his introduction to dialectics, *De inventione dialectica*, in 1479. See IJsewijn, 'The Coming of Humanism to the Low Countries', pp. 261f., 284f. For Agricola's significance see Ong, *Ramus, Method, and the Decay of Dialogue. From the Art of Discourse to the Art of Reason*; and Breen, *Christianity and Humanism*, pp. 98f.

[25] Haller, 2, p. 182. As progressive as Agricola's *De inventione dialectica* may have been, not all the leading humanist pedagogues approved of it; and for various reasons. Erasmus, who took the expression 'philosophia Christi' from Agricola and proudly recalled for the rest of his life that he had heard Agricola in Deventer one year before the latter's death (1484), complained that the *Dialectica* had been 'published in mutilated form'. See Stupperich, *Erasmus von Rotterdam und seine Welt*, p. 26. A concise account of the basic differences is found in Tracy, *Erasmus. The Growth of a Mind*, pp. 70–2. Wimpfeling even considered Agricola's text less suited to beginners than that of Peter of Spain. Letter of 1521, cited by Herding, *Wimpfelings Adolescentia*, p. 68.

April. But only following a personal visit by the archduke and his privy councillor Fabri on 13 May 1524 could the university senate be convinced to accede to a request to 'prepare and refute a list of the innovators' ecclesiological teachings' for the coming 'diet'. Even so, the fruits of this reluctant undertaking, the *Dogmata quaedam nova*, were too late to meet the deadline established for their completion. The compilers then appended at their own initiative a list of twenty-two points that urged, with the same clarity employed in refuting the 'innovators', the pressing necessity of ecclesiastical reform measures.[26]

Despite the circle of Erasmians who supported this Freiburg drive for reform, the *bonae literae* never properly flourished in the Freiburg of the 1530s. Erasmus complained about the climate and wine, but also lamented that the study of theology was pursued ineffectively and the languages were cultivated with mediocrity there. Given such conditions, Erasmus concluded that he 'would rather live among the Turks'. Spoiled by his background in the Low Countries and the Rhenish metropolis Basel, he brooded like a modern social historian over the disastrous consequences of Freiburg's remoteness from the Rhine, the source of life's wealth and wisdom.[27] A guess at his assessment of the Tübingen of the 1530s, given our already acquired acquaintance with conditions there, requires little more than a mediocre imagination!

The Tübingen statutes of 1525 never gained the support of all sectors of the university. The humanist Nestor, Johannes Reuchlin, who died in 1522, never enjoyed the influence he had anticipated when he accepted his chair one year before. As the new tone faded, one potential aid to the success of the programme of 1525 with its stress on languages and history, disintegrated. And when the statutes were reinforced in 1531, the changes were undertaken with so little understanding for the challenges of the new era that precisely the most modern aspect of instruction, Agricola's textbook on dialectics, was struck from the curriculum.

The new statutes of 1525 were not intended to topple from its position a discipline so essential to scholasticism in the fundamental training of all students. The encouragement of logical thinking and conceptual clarity remained a goal of university instruction, corres-

[26] Schreiber, *Geschichte der Albert-Ludwigs-Universität*, vol. 2, pp. 3–40; here p. 12. The 'national council' planned for St Martin's Day 1524 is probably the 'Reichstag' referred to here.

[27] 'inter Turcas habitare mallem.' Letter to Glarean, 6 September 1535; *Opus Epistolarum*, ed. Allen, 11, p. 228, line 1.

ponding roughly to the *philosophicum* that continued to place a common foundation and vocabulary at the disposal of students at many European universities even following the Second World War. But the *moderni* had insisted that the 'classical' authors such as Aristotle and Avicenna not be employed merely as targets for developing the reader's logical acumen but that they be read for their own sake and interpreted from the texts themselves. Hence the modernists also recommended reading Lefèvre d'Étaples' commentary on Aristotle.[28]

No real contradiction exists between the critique directed at Aristotle by the Erfurt 'Gabrielists' and this Tübingen use of Aristotle. Jodocus Trutvetter of Eisenach and Bartholomaeus of Usingen had shaped the *via moderna* in Erfurt ever since their victory in a quodlibetal disputation in 1497, doing so independently of Biel but being, like him, oriented toward Occam.[29] For neither Erfurt professor did the rejection of the *via antiqua* mean disdain for its authorities, including Thomas and Scotus. They pursued instead a new clarity of thought and definition within the field of philosophy; a clarification to be achieved with the aid of the Aristotelian corpus. At the same time they insisted that the boundaries between philosophy and theology be respected, since outside the realm of reason Aristotle proved to be an untrustworthy guide. Therein lay another parallel between the *via moderna* at Erfurt and at Tübingen. Respecting this frontier presented a point of contact to the following generation with its criticism of scholasticism and its concern to combat useless dispute over metaphysical questions irrelevant to devout experience.[30]

The Tübingen statutes of 1525 explained the restrictions on dialectics by condemning as vain *curiositas* any intellectual acuity that bypassed the text for the sake of demonstrating the professor's own cleverness.[31] This rationale must have been immediately intelligible to the Biel student and member of the advisory commission, Martin Plantsch, for he stood in the Tübingen tradition where perception of precisely these dangers in the medieval scholarly process had been

[28] Roth, *Urkunden*, pp. 147f. On Lefèvre's Aristotle interpretation, see Rice, *The Prefatory Epistles*, pp. xi–xxv; here xviiif.

[29] See Erich Kleineidam, *Universitas Studii Erffordensis*, 2, pp. 147f.

[30] Erasmus summarized this accusation in a letter of 5 September 1520 from Louvain to Pirckheimer, speaking for a generation that soon found itself unable to distinguish between different kinds of scholasticism': 'Hactenus ad scholasticam ac disputatricem theologiam frigebant ac nauseabant piae mentes, et mox ad Evangelicae veritatis gustum ceperant hilarescere . . .' *Opus Epistolarum*, ed. Allen, 4, p. 336, lines 71–3.

[31] Roth, *Urkunden*, p. 147. See my account in *Contra vanam curiositatem*, pp. 33–8.

sharpened both by the *devotio moderna* and by the authority of the highly respected Jean Gerson. Had this concern been integrated with Agricola's attempted renewal of dialectics – a reform combining formal logic with the basic principles of rhetoric – a synthesis between scholastic and humanist educational ideals might indeed have emerged to give epochal significance to the statutes of 1525. The publication of Agricola's 'Oration on the Birth of Christ' by the Tübingen instructor 'in poesi and oratoria', Caspar Volland[32] indicates that such an integration was not completely illusory early in 1527.[33]

But the times were not propitious for a programmatic renewal. Reform came to a standstill before a series of obstacles. The blossoming of the *bonae literae* required at least a modicum of academic tranquility which – as Erasmus correctly feared – was precluded by religious and political agitation. The plague that twice hounded Tübingen's last pre-Reformation rector from the city (1520 and 1530), can perhaps be counted among the 'normal' interruptions of instruction.[34] But there is certainly no room under that same rubric of 'normality' for the peasant revolts, which reached a climax in 1525 and disrupted routines all over Württemberg. And although the Swabian League regained control of the situation by military force, its victory failed to restore the desired political stability. Rumours that Duke Ulrich was on the march and had allied himself with the malcontent elements of the land in order to wrest Württemberg from Habsburg hands circulated constantly until the very eve of his actual return.[35] For its part, the Habsburg regime in Stuttgart did its best to

[32] Born in Groningen, as was Agricola, Volland accepted the duties of *Stadtschreiber* in Tübingen prior to his return to the university to teach law. He appears in the records as *Stadtschreiber* in 1533, 1536 and 1537. See Seigel, *Gericht und Rat in Tübingen. Von den Anfängen bis zur Einführung der Gemeindeverfassung 1818–1822*, p. 165.

[33] *Longe elegantissima oratio de nativitate Christi a Rodolpho Agricola phrysio Heydelbergae dicta* (Tübingen, 1527). In his dedicatory epistle to Georg von Haus, the imperial legate, Volland explicitly referred to Agricola's *De inventione dialectica*. This sermon must have seemed undisguisedly biblical to all theologians from the *via moderna* since Agricola stressed that the Gospel of Christmas contradicts all human speculation in its theme: 'qui cum sermo sit dei patris, iacet factus pro nobis infans expersque sermonis.' *Longe elegantissima oratio de nativitate Christi*, fol. A3^r.

When compared with Geert Groote's 'Sermo de nativitate Domini' of one hundred years previously – also known as *De quattuor generibus meditabilium* – with its carefully considered epistemological theme: 'Talis est Scriptura qualis est scribens: mitis est et humilis corde et rursus alta et sublimis', Agricola's Advent sermon seems even less academic, although Groote expressly wrote for the simple *devoti. Gerardo Groote, Il trattato 'De quattuor generibus meditabilium'*, ed. Tolomio, p. 50, lines 91–3.

[34] See above, n. 22.

[35] The rumours were based on knowledge of Duke Ulrich's efforts to ally himself with various peasant bands during the peasant revolts. See Zimmermann, *Der grosse*

ensure that the uprisings were not forgotten. Systematic purges aimed at all sympathizers in the peasant cause, especially those among the clergy,[36] commenced.

They had scarcely ended when the next threat to stability appeared. After the Habsburg vice-regent in Stuttgart requested as early as 1 October 1528 that the theological faculty in Tübingen conduct a disputation on the Anabaptist issue,[37] 'four *doctores* and preachers' from Tübingen were summoned in January 1530 to deal with Anabaptists incarcerated in Stuttgart. In addition to two unnamed theologians – probably Lemp and Braun – Gallus Müller and Balthasar Käuffelin were cited to Stuttgart and expressly freed from their teaching duties by the university senate[38] in order to 'reeducate' the Anabaptists and advise the government! Tübingen's first public burning of Anabaptists took place in the marketplace that same year.[39] The fear of religious conspiracies circulating through the government and among the elite of city and countryside – often accompanied by suspicions of Jewish involvement – had obviously converged with a horror at the prospect of renewed social conflagrations. Amid the populace, sympathy for the Reformation grew to the degree that at the beginning of 1530, Stuttgart found it necessary to inform Vienna that the majority of the people of Württemberg had taken up the Reformation cause.[40]

In April 1525 the rebellious peasants rejected Duke Ulrich's offer of alliance, an offer intended to make his return to Württemberg possible. The alliance was turned down on the grounds that it was

deutsche Bauernkrieg, pp. 240f. Regarding the actual conclusion of an agreement achieved on 9 May 1525 in Herrenberg, see Franz, *Der deutsche Bauernkrieg*, p. 221.

36 See the careful summary by Maurer, 'Das Verhalten der reformatorisch gesinnten Geistlichen Süddeutschlands', 1, pp. 299–325.

37 Printed in Bossert, 'Augustin Bader von Augsburg, der Prophet und König, und seine Genossen nach den Prozessakten von 1530', Appendices; the text is found on p. 19. The government laboured under the mistaken conviction that a widespread conspiratorial network lay behind the Anabaptist agitation; a conspiracy behind which they thought they detected Duke Ulrich's machinations, effected via Jewish channels! See the account, *ibid.*, pp. 317ff. and the appendix, p. 52.

38 *Ibid.*, pp. 23, 36f. Cf. Hermelink, *Die Theologische Fakultät*, p. 203.

39 Martin Brecht discusses the historical background of the authorities' preoccupation with the Anabaptists in his introduction to Johannes Brenz, 'Ob eyn weltliche Oberkeyt . . . möge die Widerteuffer . . . zum Tod richten lassen' (1528). *Johannes Brenz, Frühschriften*, ed. Brecht, Schäfer and Wolf, vol. 2, pp. 472–5. Brecht concludes that Bossert failed to substantiate 'clearly' his thesis that Brenz's opinion influenced the Austrian regime. *Ibid.*, p. 474.

40 See the report by Hans von der Planitz, the representative of electoral Saxony to the imperial government in Esslingen; cited in Rauscher, *Württembergische Reformationsgeschichte*, p. 54.

'self-serving' and hence 'not suitable to the cause of God'.[41] But early in the following decade a large portion of the populace was ready to forget the bad experiences with the duke. After the dissolution of the Swabian League on 2 February 1534 and the resulting attenuation of Austrian power, the rumours that the duke was under way and an 'uprising of the common rabble' near at hand quickened. A group of the ruling elite of society that still adhered to the old faith thought it prudent to flee. Broader and more Protestant-inclined segments of the population greeted the impending changes with enthusiasm[42] in what proved to be an illusory hope of gaining a more active role in civic life.

Duke Ulrich's return in May 1534 inaugurated a new era in the history of the university. Taking the fullest advantage of the converging interests of the pope, Francis I and England – all intent on containing Habsburg expansion – Ulrich was able to return with the military support of Philip of Hesse and the financial backing of both the French and the city of Strassburg.[43] He returned to a land that formed the keystone in the strategic but fragile cruciform vaulting supported on various Protestant pillars: the south German cities, the Swiss areas inclined toward Zwingli, and the Lutheran regions. This multiplicity of religious and political interests helped to reinstate Ulrich in his territories but also complicated and obstructed the uniform introduction of the Reformation into both the territory and the university.

Ulrich chose an administratively practical solution for the land of Württemberg. He assigned ecclesiastical reorganization in its northern portion to the Lutheran theologian Erhard Schnepf and sought for the southern territories a reformer capable of taking the interests of Württemberg's Swiss and south German neighbours to heart. That reformer was the Tübingen alumnus, Ambrosius Blarer, who was known to be linked to Strassburg by way of Jacob Sturm, Martin Bucer and Wolfgang Capito while maintaining close ties with his home town of Constance and with Zürich. Even after Zwingli's death

41 Letter of Rutger Rescius, cited in a letter from Joh. de Fevyn to Francisco Cranevelt, Bruges, 9 April 1525. de Vocht, ed., *Literae virorum eruditorum ad Franciscum Craneveldium 1522–1528*, pp. 415ff.

42 Grube, *Der Stuttgarter Landtag*, pp. 174, 193.

43 I am indebted to Thomas A. Brady, Jr (University of Oregon) for calling this to my attention. Regarding the exaggerated significance of the Kaaden Accord between Ferdinand and Ulrich (29 June 1534) for interpreting the duke's position *vis-à-vis* Blarer and the Swiss Reformation, an interpretation employed by Rückert and more recent scholars to explain Ulrich's religious policy, see Bofinger, 'Kirche und werdender Territorialstaat. Eine Untersuchung zur Kirchenreform Herzog Ulrichs von Württemberg', pp. 116ff.

at Kappel (1531), communication between Blarer and Zwingli's successor, Heinrich Bullinger, continued as they actively exchanged experiences and reflections. Until Luther and Bucer managed to construct a bridge between the south German cities and Wittenberg in the Wittenberg Concord of May 1536 – an agreement on the Eucharistic question that left the Zwinglian party completely isolated – Blarer enjoyed the confidence of leaders in both Zürich and Strassburg. Hence he seemed ideally suited to carry out Duke Ulrich's policy.

Along with Blarer, Master Simon Grynaeus (†1541) of Basel was entrusted with the reform of the university on 11 November 1534. But even when first acquainted with the task through the mediation of Bucer and Capito in July 1534, Grynaeus evinced little enthusiasm. He could scarcely have been disappointed that the Basel city council granted him only a temporary leave of absence and recalled him, despite intensive efforts by the Strassburg reformers and Blarer's urgent pleas, only seven months later, toward the end of June 1535. Trusted by the Strassburg reformers and with his not uncritical but nevertheless friendly ties with the Swiss leadership, Grynaeus offered many of the same political advantages as Blarer. But despite his Swabian background, he felt too great an obligation to quiet scholarly work in Basel – until recently he had been assisting in the production of Erasmian editions – to allow himself to be devoured by the administrative activity of university reform. What this colleague and comrade-in-arms with extensive university experience meant to Blarer is evident from Blarer's repeated but unsuccessful efforts to retain his services. Yet the former monk of Alpirsbach never approached the prophetic severity employed one year later by Guillaume Farel to overcome Calvin's thirst for scholarship: 'Your studies are merely a pretence! If you refuse to join us in devoting yourself to this work, the Lord will curse you for seeking yourself rather than Christ.'[44]

For four years (1534–7) Blarer struggled to fill his dual office[45] and to reconcile the theological contradictions that threatened to limit the Reformation's range of influence and political power. Ironically enough, Blarer's first opponents at the university were those who had already resisted Fabri's reform plans. In 1525 Fabri had attempted to reunite the intellectual forces of the university for the struggle against the Reformation but at the expense of the *via moderna*. When

[44] *CR* 49, col. 125; cf. 59, col. 26.
[45] Brecht, 'Ambrosius Blarer's Wirksamkeit in Schwaben', pp. 154–63.

Blarer undertook to sell the same plan under the Reformation label in late 1534, the university once more resisted with all the power at its disposal. Blarer wrote to Bullinger on 7 January 1535 in language that was certainly readily understood in Zürich: 'The bigwig professors twist and squirm in every way possible in order to preserve the old university.'[46]

Blarer managed to win Duke Ulrich's support for his suggestion that the recalcitrant members of the theological faculty be relieved of their teaching duties. The late medieval university could not be harnessed to the cause of the Reformation without nudging from the state. At the same time there were definite limits to the ability of external authorities to influence the internal affairs of the university. For although the German universities were all founded by external governmental authorities,[47] they had also obtained the same privilege held by their predecessors elsewhere in Europe: the right to organize and govern themselves as autonomous academic corporations.[48] Thus any sort of reform depended on intramural cooperation for which careful negotiations were essential. The process could be influenced from the outside only by invoking the right of visitation pertaining either to church or state.[49]

Not even Duke Ulrich could summarily eject from the university those professors whom he had suspended from teaching.[50] How much less could Fabri have hoped to accomplish from Vienna in 1523–4 as he endeavoured, in the service of a ruler foreign to Württemberg, to equip the university with a new curriculum for the defence of the old faith? Furthermore, the virulence of the rapidly escalating religious conflict led him to attempt to marshal all scholarly forces without delay. He had personally discovered in Zürich and explained in his *Malleus* that it was essential to construct a completely new hierarchy of authorities from scripture and the fathers to replace the former mixture of canon law, quotations from Aristotle and the church's doctrinal rulings.

[46] 'Gymnasii proceres in omnia se torquent, ut veterem studiorum tenorem et ordinem retineant.' Schiess, *Briefwechsel*, 1, p. 622, line 9.

[47] See Rückbrod, *Universität und Kollegium, Baugeschichte und Bautyp*, p. 32.

[48] 'die Universitates [sind] autonome Körperschaften demokratischer Struktur.' *Ibid.*, p. 11.

[49] Ulrich's announcement of 11 November 1534 appointed 'Superintendents' *in addition to* Blarer and Grynaeus. Haller, 2, p. 209. In a report of the first discussions both men were termed ducal visitators, 'visitatores et legati principis', and were probably called 'reformatores' as well. Roth, *Urkunden*, p. 162. The reformation was expected to correct existing defects without difficulty, according to the text, 'modo universitas reciperet pietatem et evangelium'. *Ibid.*, p. 161.

[50] For the specific measures undertaken, see Haller, 1, pp. 335f.

But unfortunately for Fabri's designs, the requisite foundation for such a scholarly upheaval was missing, and not merely in Tübingen, as Erasmus testified. In its absence, Fabri was obliged to cooperate with those forces content to employ the traditional and time-tested methods of pursuing truth even in the face of modern challenges. Yet his plans for liberalizing the *Artes* and equipping theology for battle could be realized only in the context of a university where the rejuvenation of theology was organically bound to philological and historical research. Tübingen failed Fabri. At the death in 1541 of this first-generation counter-reformer feared above all others in the south German territories, his Tübingen *Alma Mater* had long since become a training ground for Protestant pastors.

Although Tübingen failed as a fountain-head of Catholic renewal, it did become an armoury for the Counter-Reformation.[51] In addition to the personal participation of Tübingen professors in direct confrontation with the evangelical standard-bearers, especially at Zürich and Baden, Tübingen became a bastion of Counter-Reformation publishing activity. The publications from the press of Tübingen's first long-term publisher, Ulrich Morhart, during the years 1523–34 clearly testify to the town's new role. Admittedly, during Morhart's first year in Tübingen we do find six editions, some actually printed in Strassburg, that indicate a more progressive scholarly atmosphere: Valla's *Elegantiarum libri*, two commentaries on the Bible by Melanchthon, the *Expurgatio* of the polyhistor Johannes Stöffler and the second edition of Erasmus' *Novum Testamentum*.

But in examining the publications after 1524, it becomes obvious that Tübingen had developed into an anti-evangelical centre of publication from which the south German intelligentsia could be readily influenced. One treatise after another left Morhart's press, with the works of Cochlaeus, Schatzgeier, Eck, Emser, and, of course, Fabri himself, well represented. In both German and Latin, polemical arrows such as Fabri's *Sandtprieve* (1526) and Schatzgeier's *Traductio sathanae* (1530) shot from the university town on the Neckar. Prior to the appearance of Emser's translation of the New Testament on 31 August 1532, a total of thirty-three anti-Reformation polemical writings[52] appeared. Ironically, the dire necessity of the crisis of 1525 that induced the Habsburg government to leave Stuttgart for refuge

[51] Krebs, *Protokolle*, no. 7722.

[52] We have not included here the Cochlaeus edition no. 161, *Sieben Kopffe Martini Luthers* (n.p., n.d.), which was a reprint of the Leipzig edition of 1529 (or Dresden, 1531) and may have appeared in Tübingen between 1532 and 1534. Steiff, *Buchdruck*, p. 197.

in Tübingen also produced the 'miracle' of a Tübingen Luther publication: the reformer's denunciation of the peasants, the *Ermanunge zum frid auff die zwölff Artikel der Bauerschafft in Schwaben*.[53] From the government's perspective, regardless of whether Luther's 'admonition' 'resulted in its author's intended sedative effect on the peasants or shattered Luther's authority in their eyes, it would have proved useful to the authorities'.[54]

But the victory achieved in Tübingen under the Habsburg banner was a temporary triumph. Less than ten years later a second epoch in Tübingen's intellectual life ended under the influence of Duke Ulrich. Reminiscent of the sudden withering of the tender blossom of Tübingen humanism when the Anshelm circle scattered in 1516, and of the banning of the *devotio moderna* in 1517, Ulrich's return now meant the end of the collective effort against the Reformation. But in contrast to 1516–17, Ulrich's latest intervention produced no polarization of the sort that forced a new epoch in Tübingen's intellectual history into direct confrontation with the old. Rather than experiencing a sudden and enthusiastic awakening, the university entered a tenacious struggle overshadowed by the duke's immense pretensions to the exercise of authority prior to the Augsburg Interim. He removed the university town from Habsburg control with a flourish, reissuing on 10 July 1534 the same ordinance against bearing arms that Archduke Ferdinand had published eight years previously. Printed by Morhart, it now appeared under the authority of 'Ulrich, by the grace of God, Duke of Württemberg . . .'[55]

Neither Jacob Lemp nor Martin Plantsch lived to see this reversal. In quick succession both had died in 1532–3, leaving reputations as men of the Counter-Reformation's first hour who had entered the lists in Zürich and Baden on behalf of something which had been considered modern in their student days, during the early years of the University of Tübingen, but which now appeared conservative, if not reactionary. As the shadows appeared on Tübingen's intellectual horizon, Reuchlin was fetched in his old age from Ingolstadt to Tübingen in order to lend his great reputation to the sinking image of the university and to stimulate ebbing enrolment figures. The prayer that he entrusted to paper shortly before his death expressed both censure of the present and confidence in the future: 'Truth will

53 The *Admonition* was quickly reprinted in Augsburg and the Tübingen printing was copied from that edition. It also appeared in Nuremberg, Strassburg, Erfurt, Zwickau, Leipzig, Speyer and Mainz. See *WA* 18, pp. 282ff.

54 Steiff, *Buchdruck*, p. 150.

55 Steiff, *Buchdruck*, pp. 137–93; here p. 192.

emanate from this land, the light will shine and drive away the darkness that the sophist plague has spread abroad for four hundred years. And I, old man that I am, would remain alert; Hasten, O Lord to my aid.'[56]

It now became the task of Ambrosius Blarer, commissioned by the duke of Württemberg, to accomplish what had frustrated the Swabian harbinger of Hebrew wisdom and champion of new learning between Agricola and Erasmus: the elimination of 'four hundred years of darkness'. Blarer was no dark-horse candidate for the task but an alumnus of Tübingen and first-generation recruit in the Reformation ranks. An enthusiastic admirer of classical literature under Melanchthon's tutelage in Tübingen, he lost no time in distancing himself from Fabri's Habsburg-oriented course after his flight from the monastery at Alpirsbach and relocation in Constance.

Like Eck in Wittenberg, the Constance vicar general Fabri had acquired fame among the south German and Swiss reformers as one of the strategists of the Counter-Reformation. One of his letters, accidentally intercepted and forwarded to Zwingli by Blarer,[57] documents Fabri's innermost intentions. Written, it seems, to a close friend in Mainz, the letter asserted the urgency of the battle against the Lutheran heresy, especially since it had now spread to his own diocese and because a much 'worse Luther' had arisen in Zürich in the person of Ulrich Zwingli.[58]

Like Fabri, Blarer began astonishingly early to consider the conflict irreconcilable and the fronts unbridgeable. His marginal notes to the intercepted missive, drawn in the same artistic hand with which he had once annotated Summenhart's tithe treatise, are much more revealing than the cover letter he enclosed for Zwingli. A sketch of a fly-like insect on the margin succinctly illustrates Blarer's verdict on Fabri's rejection of the Wittenberg theology. Guilty, in Blarer's eyes, of despising the Gospel, Fabri was assigned, in allusion to Eccl. 10, the symbol of the fly or fool, a reference to those 'bigwigs' who would be deposed and removed from power in God's good time: 'Folly is set in many high places, and the rich sit in a low place. I have seen slaves on horses, and princes walking on foot like slaves . . .'

For Blarer, the ejection of the Habsburgs from Württemberg in 1534 meant the dawn of the day of the Lord. It was now time to summon

[56] Haller, 1, p. 312.

[57] Blarer described Fabri's letter, dated 3 June 1523, as an 'epistola Fabri ad quendam Moguntinensem plane digna Fabro'. *ZW* 8, p. 97, n. 2.

[58] 'apud Tigurinos novus Lutherus exoritur, qui tanto gravior est, quanto austeriorem populum habet.' *Ibid.*, p. 98, lines 39f.

all energy in order to eradicate the remnants of popery with its incense, crucifixes and images, for even 'dead flies make the perfumer's ointment stink'.[59]

[59] The editor, Walther Köhler, quite correctly points to Eccl. 10.1 (*ZW* 8, p. 99, line 28) because the passage continues (v. 3): 'Even when the fool walks on the road, he lacks sense, and he says to every one that he is a fool.' But his note should have been attached to Fabri's preceding sentence: 'In brevi stupidas illius allegorias [Lutheri] adgrediar.' *ZW* 8, p. 98, line 28.

13

The Reformation: a German tragedy?

THE SIXTEENTH CENTURY had a special affection for aphoristic wisdom.[1] Blarer's epigrammatic marginal comments, made either in enthusiastic approval of Summenhart's theological social theory or in mischievous denunciation of Fabri's rejection of the Reformation, typify the style of that period. Not only Erasmus, but also his theological, psychological and cultural counterpart in Wittenberg prized proverbs.[2] Yet, significantly enough, Luther preferred the vernacular wisdom of the peasant's hearth and artisan's workshop to Erasmian adages. For Luther, such proverbs expressed an unbroken empirical tradition of folk and worldly wisdom which the learned lords of the university had scholastically emptied of all signs of life and then proudly refilled with their own absurdities whisked from a classical bag of mythological tricks. That sort of educational veneer, an *eruditio vana et curiosa*, contrasted unfavourably with the tart vernacular folk wisdom.

It was precisely Luther's medieval and scholastic education that freed him to appreciate the worldly wisdom of the populace alongside holy scripture. The Erasmian humanists took up the opposite position, recognizing as wise only that which had established its worth under the watchful eye of classical antiquity. With the dross of medieval barbarity burned away in the fires of erudition, this refined classical wisdom could now be introduced to its proper purpose and destination: contemporary religious devotion. The disputed legitima-

[1] The use of proverbs from scripture and the ancients is especially characteristic of the pedagogically motivated curricular reforms in the Latin schools. See Herding, *Wimpfelings Adolescentia*, pp. 76f. Melanchthon offered lectures on the wisdom literature, especially the book of Proverbs, over a period of thirty years beginning in 1524, and enjoyed great success with attendances ranging between 400 and 500 students.

[2] Luther was not alone in this interest. Natalie Zemon Davis has remarked on the collections of medieval 'Proverbes ruraux et vulgaux' of the sixteenth century: 'Learned interest in proverbs intensified in a way that would not be seen again in Europe until the romantic national movements of the late eighteenth and nineteenth centuries . . .' *Society and Culture in Early Modern France. Eight Essays*, pp. 227–67; here p. 233.

cy of secular wisdom was established not in conjunction with the controversy over free will, but in the course of determining the relationship between Christian faith and the profane world. The simultaneous recognition of a distinct *divine* wisdom accessible only in Gospel faith neither threatened nor impaired the legitimacy of a *secular* wisdom.

Here we have touched on the fundamental issue which demanded response from all parties in the Reformation and over which they parted company: determining the precise interdependence between the kingdom of Christ and the structures of profane society. The intertwining of these two realms is not a problem that has been coaxed into prominence by modern historiographical or theological heuristics, obscuring the real concerns of the Reformation. It actually held the minds of the Reformation era in suspense from the very beginning.[3] Efforts were under way everywhere, whether in approval or rejection of the Wittenberg, Zürich or later Genevan models, to unravel the spiritual–secular community of the medieval *Respublica Christiana* and to reweave its constituent strands around scripture.

We would eliminate an entire dimension of the forces that agitated Europe in that century if we were to reduce the Reformation to a question of political emancipation and possibilities of upward social mobility.[4] Within the urban setting we would be left with an outline of Reformation history sketching the one-dimensional sequence of upward pressures exerted by once underprivileged groups, especially the petty and unincorporated artisans; a striving which, frustrated and unnerved by princely territorial politics, ultimately shared the

[3] The systematic theological category of the 'doctrine of two kingdoms' cannot do justice to political realities, even in the Lutheran territories. It obscures the historical diversity of the sixteenth century. Anabaptist research has achieved a methodological head start by refusing to define 'Anabaptism' and the 'Anabaptist view of social and political authority' (*Obrigkeitslehre*) without considering geographical variants. At the same time scholars have refused to be satisfied with a mere 'bunt zusammengewürfeltes Spektrum von Auffassungen'. See Hillerbrand, *Die politische Ethik des oberdeutschen Täufertuns*, pp. 3–5, 81. See also Stayer, *Anabaptists and the Sword*, pp. 13–23, 335–7; cf. *idem*, 'Reflections and Retractions on *Anabaptists and the Sword*'.

The alternatives within Protestantism between 'Wittenberg' and 'Zürich' found their clearest expression in Zwingli's letter of 4 May 1528 to Blarer. The Zürich reformer described the tasks and sphere of competence of the Christian magistrate within a Christian society by rejecting Luther's thesis, 'regnum Christi non esse externum'. *ZW* 9, pp. 451–67; here p. 452, line 23.

[4] See Febvre's conclusion which bypasses the distinction between 'motivation' and 'results': 'Une religion mieux adaptée à leurs besoins nouveaux, mieux accordée aux conditions modifiées de leur existence sociale–voilà ce que la Réforme accomplit finalement.' *Au Coeur religieux du XVIe siècle*, p. 26.

fate of the peasant rebellions. Recognizing the correlation[5] between both spheres by no means renders 'external conditions' insignificant, because only the recognition of such a correlation illuminates the spectrum of possibilities for restructuring society, including the geopolitically dependent components.

From the Habsburg perspective, the 'German question' appeared to have been brought under control by the end of the 1520s. The emperor had made his peace with the pope, settled his differences with the king of France and engineered his brother Ferdinand's election as king of the Romans. The urban reformations of south Germany had by this point passed their respective apogees and their proudest successes were now history.[6] But Habsburg hegemony in Germany was seriously threatened when, contrary to all expectations,[7] Duke Ulrich succeeded in wresting Württemberg from Habsburg control in 1534, thereby opening an entire *territorium* to the Reformation. The urban reformers of south Germany once more gained an opportunity to influence the construction and consolidation of a reformed ecclesiastical structure according to their own convictions. By investigating the struggle for control of the University of Tübingen in the years 1534–6, we can examine in greater detail these events of such great significance for the entire German Reformation. The evolution of a philistine *bourgeoisie* into an urban ruling caste and ultimately into loyal subjects in a territorial church and state, when studied through the microscope of the university,

[5] Paul Tillich has made the concept of correlation the cornerstone of his systematic theology in order to relate philosophy and theology: 'The method of correlation explains the contents of the Christian faith through existential questions and theological answers in mutual interdependence.' *Systematic Theology*, vol. 1, p. 60. Due to the fixed ontological structure of his anthropology in which the finite and the infinite of necessity define and intertwine themselves, Tillich has overlooked the fact that 'correlation' must not of necessity be fitted with the theoretical principles of the *via antiqua*. On the contrary, the concept is well suited to the task of opening one's eyes to the diversity and contingency of the consequences of historical facts and factors. Himself a representative of the German *via antiqua*, he continued the *Wegestreit* into our own time. See Tillich's sharp repudiation of nominalism as a type of positivism. *Systematic Theology*, vol. 1, pp. 77f.; vol. 2, pp. 9f., 19.

[6] See Hans Baron, 'Religion and Politics in the German Imperial Cities during the Reformation', pp. 413f.

[7] Bucer's fears on the eve of the battle at Lauffen leave little to the imagination: 'Atrox praelium ut committatur, verendum. O domine Iesu, adsis nobis; profliga istos furores bellicos, da pace tue frui! Quod ni faciat, quid putas impendere Germaniae? Vereor, vereor, rursus committi Caesarem et Francum idque in nostris visceribus.' Schiess, *Briefwechsel*, 1, p. 494 (no. 417); to Blarer, from Strassburg, 30 April 1534. Cf. the letter of 9 May: 'Quanto in periculo es, o Germania!' *Ibid.*, p. 494 (no. 418).

cannot be reconciled with a widespread value-judgment that makes the Reformation a 'German tragedy'.[8]

An academic perspective on these developments initially seems unpromising, since the Reformation's first wave of victory in the German territories bypassed the universities. The 'natural' system of communication utilized the network of Observant monasteries of the Augustinian Eremites,[9] its first enthusiastic impulses from Wittenberg being transmitted to the Erfurt and Nuremberg houses. The movement soon won the attention of humanist circles in those cities. Interested observers or even sympathizers were before long using the excellent humanist communications network to transmit information about reformation innovations.[10]

But the academic establishment reacted coolly. To be sure, cooperation between the theological faculty of the University of Wittenberg and the local Augustinian monastery helped to launch Luther's dive into the turbulent waters of church politics, but that same coalition failed as a springboard to other universities. At the Heidelberg convocation of the Augustinian congregation in the spring of 1518 only Luther's younger colleagues applauded his presentation of

[8] Under the caption 'Germany misses its chance', Karl August Meissinger charged that Luther had no programme of national scope to offer in 1521: 'He evaded this task.' *Luther. Die deutsche Tragödie 1521*, p. 185. According to Meissinger, this tragic retreat into the interior is typical of what is customarily termed German idealism. 'But the withdrawal originated in the position assumed by Luther which led to his failure in 1521.' (*Ibid.*, p. 186.) But if this reproach is valid at all for 1521, then it is equally applicable to the Luther of 1517 and to the early phase following the Leitzkau sermon of 1512 (*WA* 1, pp. 10–17), because from the very beginning Luther counted on the force of the unhindered proclamation of the Gospel to shape events. The 'great tragedy' is rather that Luther's legacy could so thoroughly be shrouded by the modern continuation of the *via antiqua* in German idealism.

[9] As the *regens studii* Luther had ample and early opportunity to instruct the young monks of his own convent in Wittenberg. (See *WABr* 1, p. 72, line 7; Luther was named not only district vicar but also *regens studii* in Wittenberg at the Gotha chapter held on 29 April 1515. Cf. *Epistolae Langianae*, ed. Knaake and Hering, pp. 8f. cf. *WABr* 12, p. 2, n. 5.) In the spring of 1516 he gained an additional 'promoter' in the person of Johannes Lang, the prior of the Erfurt house. Johann von Staupitz cleared a path for Luther's contacts with the Nuremberg *sodalitas*. In addition, five recently discovered letters from 'Frater Karolus Rose Augustinianus' (†1526) indicate the manner in which the Nuremberg Augustinian monastery functioned as a disseminator of Lutheran ideas after 1523. See Rott, 'La Réforme à Nuremberg et à Strasbourg', pp. 116–21. In 1525 Wenceslas Linck published a tract in Altenburg that closed an Augustinian triangle: Linck edited Lang's account of the first martyrdom of a 'Protestant' Augustinian, Saint [!] Hendrik of Zutphen (1524): *Histoira* [!], *wie S. Heinrich von Zutphan newlich yn Dittmars umbs Euangelions willen gemartert und gestorben ist*. See the bibliography compiled by Lorz, *Bibliographia Linckiana, Bibliographie der gedruckten Schriften Dr Wenzeslaus Lincks (1483–1547)*, p. 65 (no. 24). On Hendrik of Zutphen see Carl Bertheau in *RE* 21, pp. 737–42.

[10] See Moeller, 'Die deutschen Humanisten und die Anfänge der Reformation'.

theses setting forth a biblical theology based on Paul and Augustine. As an expression of his consternation but with greater impertinence than he could have realized at the time, one of Luther's Heidelberg colleagues (probably the young doctor of theology Georg Nider) commented on the link between the Christian life and Christ's suffering as set forth in Luther's *theologia crucis* by exclaiming, 'If the peasants catch wind of this . . .' they would stone Luther on the spot.[11]

On the whole, the academics present in Heidelberg found Luther's theology alien (*peregrina*) and were probably alienated by it as well.[12] The university at Ingolstadt, and soon afterwards the University of Leipzig, came under the influence of Johannes Eck. Even in Erfurt the Wittenberg model of cooperation between monastery and theological faculty collapsed after Johannes Lang, Luther's first genuine disciple and the prior of the Erfurt Augustinians, failed in his efforts to convert Luther's former academic masters.[13] His following in Erfurt was restricted for the most part to students who viewed the new theology largely as a weapon against the authority of the *magistri*, ultimately heading not toward the reform but toward the ruin of the university.[14] Condemnations coming from Cologne and Louvain in the wake of the Leipzig Disputation could not have been surprising in view of the dominance of Luther's Dominican arch-adversaries there.[15] Nor was the respected *Alma Mater* of all the German universities, Paris, prepared to take a positive or even neutral position regarding Luther, despite the rumours to that effect which circulated until the last moment in Zürich and Wittenberg.[16] The Sorbonne

[11] *WABr* 1, p. 173, lines 28f.; to Spalatin from Wittenberg, 18 May 1518.

[12] See *ibid.*, lines 2f. In a programmatic settling of accounts with the Paris 'terminists', Faber Stapulensis (Lefèvre d'Étaples) criticized their instruction as 'peregrina' – meaning not 'alienating' but 'irrelevant'. *Organon*, 'Praefatio' (Paris, 1503), fol. 1^v (written 1501); cited by Renaudet, *Préréforme et humanisme à Paris*, p. 415, n. 3.

[13] Luther's theology was totally unacceptable to the Erfurt academics: 'Errfordiensibus mea Theologia Est Bis Mortem Crambe.' *WABr* 1, p. 173, lines 29f.

[14] See Kleineidam, *Universitas Studii Erffordiensis*, 2, pp. 259–69. Robert W. Scribner describes the occasionally considerable tensions within the Erfurt city council arising from political and economic factors. Seen from the perspective of municipal policy, the student protests were no mere intra-university affair but fit into the context of the unrest and disorder that had put the city on edge for decades. In addition to the conservative wing of protest represented by Lang, there was also a Lutheran opposition that 'lost its association with peace and order, . . . [and was] willing, if necessary, to challenge the government and provoke disturbance. Scribner, 'Civic Unity and the Reformation in Erfurt', pp. 52f. Cf. *idem*, 'The Erasmians and the Beginning of the Reformation in Erfurt', pp. 14–20.

[15] See the excellent account by Karel Blockx, *De veroordeling van Maarten Luther door de theologische faculteit te Leuven in 1519*.

[16] See above, p. 150, n. 89.

requested the minutes of the Leipzig Disputation in order to condemn Luther explicitly in a special publication.[17]

Luther's drive for reformation began with a failure on the academic front when he found himself unable to strike up a dialogue with his own academic colleagues. He had addressed his indulgence theses to three groups. He first posted them hoping to win a hearing in Wittenberg itself. In addition, he sent them not only to his *ordinarius loci*, the bishop of Brandenburg, but also to the archbishop of Mainz, as an expression of his earnest concern and in an attempt to persuade the archbishop to withdraw his instructions to the indulgence preachers. And in the third place, Luther sent his theses to a series of his colleagues outside Wittenberg in order to convince members of other universities on the issue. He failed in the last two purposes, and the assumption that he posted the theses on the portals of the castle church has come under attack, at least in certain circles of Catholic Luther-scholarship.[18]

But the Reformation made rapid progress in the cities, above all in south Germany. It was a coalition between city preaching endowments and municipal Latin schools,[19] not the universities, which opened doors and unlocked consciences for the new movement in Nuremberg and Strassburg, Zürich and Constance. The universities in the surrounding territories regarded the new doctrine with reserve or even hostility. At Freiburg the university did demand church reform and acceded only reluctantly to the Habsburg educational and

[17] See Bos, *Luther in het oordeel van de Sorbonne*, pp. 32f., 39. See also Glarean's letter to Zwingli of 1 November 1520 and to Myconius of 7 April 1521 in *ZW* 7, p. 362 and *ibid.*, n. 9.

[18] See above, pp. 148–9.

[19] Johann Eberlin von Günzburg forcefully stressed the role of the teachers in the Latin schools in the portrait of the family tree of the Reformation contained in his *15 Bundsgenossen* (n.p., n.d.; first printed in Basel by Pamphilus Gengenbach, 1521). Reuchlin and Erasmus 'laid the cornerstone of all salvation' with support from Wimpfeling and Geiler in the Alsace, Ulrich Krafft in Ulm and Oecolampadius in Swabia. They were followed by the 'pious schoolmasters in many localities': Crato (Kraft) and Sapidus in Schlettstadt, Michael Hilspach in Hagenau, Spinnler and Gerbel in Pforzheim, Brassicanus, Sr, and Heinrich Mann in Tübingen, Giles Krautwasser in Stuttgart and Horb, Johann Schmidlin (Faber) in Memmingen, Johannes Cochlaeus in Nuremberg and Nesenus in Frankfurt. They prepared the way for the arrival of Luther and Hutten, 'both of them native German, highly learned and Christian men'. *Johann Eberlin von Günzburg, Ausgewählte Schriften*, ed. Enders, vol. 1, pp. 3f. Modern accounts of the history of the Reformation have credited the influence of the urban preaching endowments with nearly epochal significance. But, significant as this phenomenon may be for illustrating the emancipation of the late medieval city, it was only after the new trends in education transmitted by the Latin schools found a forum in the municipal preaching endowments that an important prerequisite for the 'reeducation' of urban society was met.

ecclesiastical policy inspired by Fabri. But Tübingen's university had been a dependable cornerstone of that policy from the beginning because, unlike the humanist desertion of the university in favour of elitist research academies, the Fabri plan promised the university a significant role in the education of future generations.

Tübingen became a bulwark of the Counter-Reformation. Its castle served as a prison for priests denounced as evangelical innovators and suspected of having broken their oath of loyalty sworn – since 1523 – to the 'Roman' church. The most important anti-Reformation treatises, long since suppressed in surrounding cities, enjoyed unabated publication from the Morhart press, which was Tübingen's only printing establishment and the only one for miles around loyal to Rome. Tübingen professors appeared at Zürich and Baden to stem the tide of Reformation and the university furnished inquisitors from its own ranks for the first Anabaptist trials in Württemberg.[20] Tübingen was bound to its medieval past; the future threatened to skirt the university altogether in order to establish new intellectual ganglia in the politically independent cities with the culturally and intellectually alert circles. And it was in those urban intellectual circles that the universities received a public image still popular today. They were caricatured as arrogant, irrelevant, anti-social and reactionary. In short, humanist circles researched, developed and handily marketed the ivory tower image. Thus, when the master craftsmen gained control of city hall, they too took measure of the academic masters' gowns and, not surprisingly, discovered them to be mere cosmetic coverings for minds distended by arrogance. They immediately undertook to tailor them to a size and style more suitable to the common weal.

The treasures of the scholastic tradition could be packed away in the warehouse. There was no market for them among the already established *bourgeoisie*, to say nothing of the rising artisans who had gained a measure of independence in the greater and lesser councils after decades of laborious bargaining with the power brokers of church and society. From their new vantage-point on top of the city hall the new masters could exult in a growing awareness that they were the initiators of a new era; able as a cooperative and collective

[20] See G. Bossert and G. Bossert, Jr, eds., *Quellen zur Geschichte der Wiedertäufer*, vol. 1, pp. 919f. Following Ulrich's restoration, 'Christian preachers' were entrusted with the task of instructing the Anabaptists in order to convince them of the 'error' of their way. See Schraepler, *Die rechtliche Behandlung der Täufer in der deutschen Schweiz, Südwestdeutschland und Hessen 1525–1618*, p. 31.

citizenry at least to regulate, if not actually to realize, their own destiny.

On the national scene, the high tide of urban autonomy came at the imperial diets of 1524 and 1526 when the cities' impressive opposition finally extracted from the emperor a mild interpretation of the Edict of Worms, pledging them to enforce it merely in a manner 'for which each [estate] could confidently hope to answer before God and the Imperial Majesty'.[21] But the cities soon found themselves militarily intimidated, and their not uncommon involvement in the peasant uprisings further compromised their position. The ironic final verdict came from that court of justice that we euphemistically term the Interim, exposing the ideology of urban autonomy as a romantic remnant of the Middle Ages. The peasant revolts of the 1520s not only impeded the territorial expansion of the Reformation but were also fought at the expense of the theocratic pretensions of the cities.

Unlike the successful formation of the Swiss Confederation that had occurred earlier, or the victorious war for independence later fought by the seven United Provinces in the Netherlands,[22] the growing national sentiment in south Germany faced no foreign domination, and that sentiment never coalesced sufficiently to unite city and countryside. The myth of a Holy Roman Empire of the German Nation that chained the leadership of Germany to the medieval past while other European nation-states were emerging, crippled the Schmalkaldic League's will to resist in the 1540s. Furthermore, already in the second decade of the century the cities' drive for unification slowed under the heavy mortgage of the imperial insignia and the fealty they signified. Although fully occupied on three fronts – warring against the Turks, diplomatically engaged by the French, and ultimately forced to move militarily against the pope

[21] Friedensburg, *Der Reichstag zu Speier 1526*, appendix xii, pp. 536, 391. For the background of this formula, which was first introduced by the electors but then supported in a determined and decisive manner by the cities, see *ibid.*, pp. 379–87.

[22] Prior to Charles V's abdication it was possible even in the as yet dis-United Provinces of the Habsburg Netherlands for the emperor to play off the estates and various factions in city and countryside against each other. See for a general account the excellent outline by Smit, 'The Netherlands Revolution', esp. p. 32. This 'provincialism' in the true sense of the word permitted only scattered resistance. Only after the central government actually became, or proved capable of being portrayed as, foreign domination, an image aided by the symbolic religious axis between 'Rome' and 'Madrid', did transregional uprisings occur. But the development from provincialism to nationalism which occurred in the Netherlands under Philip II could very easily have reversed itself had it not been for the Duke of Alba's rule of terror. Smit, *ibid.*, p. 49. Cf. Smit's earlier summary of relevant literature, 'The Present Position of Studies Regarding the Revolt of the Netherlands'.

– Charles V nevertheless had the energy to forbid the German 'national council' planned for November 1524 and favoured by his brother Ferdinand as well as by the cities.[23] The empire and its claims sufficed to turn the participation in diets called by the cities into conflicts of conscience (Ulm 1526) and to prevent the Christian *Burgrecht* alliance from expanding into a major league of cities crossing imperial frontiers.[24]

The modern German tragedy does not begin with the birth of Bismarck's empire and Hitler's apocalyptic imperial vision.[25] Already during the first third of the sixteenth century the myth of emperor and empire impeded the most progressive efforts to overcome the limitations of local political constellations as the Reformation gained entry to Strassburg and Constance in 1523 and to Nuremberg, Ulm and Augsburg in 1524.[26] Despite the mortgage held by the empire, urban potential was impressively evident at the imperial diets, supported by electoral Saxony, Hesse and Brandenburg-Ansbach.[27] Yet only a few years later, on the eve of the coronations of Charles as emperor and Ferdinand as King of the Romans in 1530, the councils

[23] See the petition of the cities to the estates assembled at the third Nuremberg Diet on 6 April 1524. *Deutsche Reichstagsakten*, 4, p. 508, lines 19–26.

[24] For the collapse of Zwingli's 'campaign strategy' (1525–6; *ZW* 3, pp. 539–83) which foresaw the conclusion of 'civic leagues' (*Burgrechte*) with Zürich, Strassburg, Constance, Lindau, St Gallen and Schaffhausen, see Bender, *Zwinglis Reformationsbündnisse*, pp. 161–75.

[25] Erich Kahler's account of the character and history of the German people avoids such a restricted perspective only by adding another *fable convenue*: 'Luther had brought the individual and his God closer together by denying the Church its mediating role between them, but at the same time he drew society and God further apart. In the Lutheran view, God was no longer present in the community as a living force. God had created the social order but then stepped back from it, leaving its administration entirely in the hands of the secular authorities. As a result, German society could never become a true community. It could only evolve into an increasingly elaborate hierarchy in which an unbroken chain of command extended from princes, kings, and emperors down to the lowliest subject. At one stroke, Luther created the ideology that gave rise to the unlimited authority of the modern German ruler and the unlimited obedience of the modern German citizen.' *The Germans*, p. 214. Regarding the tyrannical power of the *fable convenue* see Liebing, 'Perspectivische Verzeichnungen. Über die Haltbarkeit der *fable convenue* in der Kirchengeschichte', pp. 298 and 305.

[26] Heinrich Schmidt's fine phrase is valid only for the political elite in the 'better' areas of the towns: 'In den Gassen von Nürnberg, Augsburg und Ulm *ist* das Reich, in dessen Ordnung das Heil der Welt begründet ist . . .' *Die deutschen Städtechroniken als Spiegel des bürgerlichen Selbstverständnisses im Spätmittelalter*, p. 71.

[27] The cities' strategy in April 1524 as well as August 1526, which was echoed in the prayer of thanks by Sir Fritz Jacob von Anwyl, should serve as a warning against any attempt to establish the significance of the cities for the success of the Reformation solely from the later and more sober perspectives of 1529–31 and 1547–51.

of the leading cities could be described with the phrase: 'Senatu deliberante Germania periit.'[28]

Another Germany had long been emerging to compete with the cities in the political power struggle. The reconquest of Württemberg by Duke Ulrich in 1534 was a turning point of grave consequence for the 'German question'. Although Ulrich's return met with approval in Zürich and Nuremberg and was heavily underwritten by Strassburg,[29] it represented the beginning of a new epoch in which the cities were to be reduced to subject territorial administrative centres unable to pursue their own political inclinations.

Tübingen also acquired considerable strategic importance as a territorial university in 1534, an importance it had never managed to attain as a citadel of the Counter-Reformation. In Wittenberg, Luther and Melanchthon refused to join Carlstadt on the popular bandwagon of scorn for the universities. They considered success in reforming the university at Tübingen crucial to the fate of all south Germany.[30] Yet, although the Wittenberg theology would ultimately leave its stamp on Tübingen, for the moment, men from urban and south German backgrounds ran the machinery of reform in Tübingen.

Although its importance for Ulrich's internal religious policy has probably been overestimated, the Kaaden Accord of 29 June 1534 did grant imperial approval to the reconquest of Württemberg after mediation on the part of electoral Saxony, Hesse and Archduke Ferdinand.[31] As its price, this retroactive legitimation extracted from Ulrich the reluctant concession that future dukes of Württemberg would assume the status of vassals of the Austrian archdukes. An earlier draft of the treaty also included a clause forbidding the toleration of 'sacramentarians, Anabaptists or other unchristian

[28] It is apparent from the accounts of the alliances between cities that already sufficiently complicated negotiations were threatened to breaking-point by controversy over the order in which the various parties were to affix their signatures. Should they sign in the chronological order of their entry into the alliance or should the customary ranking within the empire be followed? Regarding the significance of the question of rank and order of seating at conferences of the cities see Hauswirth, *Landgraf Philipp von Hessen und Zwingli*, pp. 133f. and Exkurs IV, p. 268.

[29] Thomas A. Brady, Jr (University of Oregon) informed me that Strassburg shouldered about twenty-five per cent of the foreign funding in support of the reconquest of Württemberg.

[30] *WABr* 7, pp. 10–12; Wittenberg, 17 December 1534.

[31] See especially the fruitful dissertation by Wilhelm Bofinger, 'Oberdeutschtum und württembergische Reformation. Die Sozialgestalt der Kirche als Problem der Theologie- und Kirchengeschichte der Reformationszeit' and the literature cited there. At present only the second part has been published, as 'Kirche und werdender Territorialstaat'.

sects'; a proscription that left undefined whether a joint campaign against internal threats to the empire – such as the peasant uprisings and the Münsterite Kingdom – was intended, or whether political alliances with the Swiss were likewise excluded. The paragraph has remained controversial ever since.[32] In any case, it was clear to Ulrich that the treaty granted him an unrestricted *ius reformandi*, for he emphasized that his 'conscience remained untroubled and free of scruples' in ensuring the pure and undefiled preaching of the Gospel and the introduction of a new Christian order 'meeting the requirements of the age'.[33]

Ulrich reasoned in a similar vein in his mandate for the reform of the University of Tübingen, a task he committed to the care of reformers who would have passed for 'sacramentarians' even outside Wittenberg. Even during his exile, Ulrich had been a major force behind the conciliatory alliance policies of Landgrave Philip of Hesse, and had provided the impetus for Philip's convening of the Marburg Colloquy.[34] Hence the Stuttgart Eucharistic Concord between Blarer and Schnepf[35] can be fully explained without resort to theories of outside influence.

Favourably disposed toward the political theology of the Swiss and south German Reformation as a consequence of his anti-Habsburg strategy, Ulrich conceded to Blarer and Grynaeus a policy of university appointments to their own liking. And for their part, the urban reformers, led by Bucer and Capito, scurried to the fore: Bucer provided Blarer with detailed suggestions in 1534[36] and by 1535 was

[32] For the various stages of the negotiations surrounding the paragraph dealing with religious affairs, discussions extending from the sessions at Annaberg (ducal Saxony, 6 June 1534) to the conclusion of the Kaaden Accord, see Bofinger, 'Kirche und werdender Territorialstaat', pp. 101–21.

[33] *Ibid.*, p. 120.

[34] See Köhler, *Zwingli und Luther. Ihr Streit über das Abendmahl nach seinen politischen und religiösen Beziehungen*, vol. 2, p. 24.

[35] Blarer and Schnepf having reached agreement on the wording, Duke Ulrich immediately had it recorded in writing, signed by both reformers and sent via Jacob Sturm to the Strassburg reformers: 'Wir bekennend, dass uss vermögen diser wort: "Diss ist min lib, diss ist min blut", der lib und das blut Christi warhaftliklich, "hoc est: essentialiter et substantive, non autem qualitative vel quantitative vel localiter", im nachtmal gegenwirtig siend und geben werdind.' Köhler, *Zwingli und Luther*, 2, pp. 330–55; here p. 337.

[36] Bucer kept his comments concerning the university succinct: 'Thibingae quid sit, tu nosti melius.' Schiess, *Briefwechsel*, 1, p. 512 (no. 430). He was especially concerned that Blarer should remain on good terms with Schnepf regarding territorial policies, for if he did not, Johannes Brenz might be called to replace him! He should be aware of the deviousness of the papists in favouring the Lutheran Eucharistic rite. But the Eucharistic liturgy used by the Lutherans in Reutlingen is acceptable; 'I abhor only the elevation and the celebrant's robes.' *Ibid.*, p. 511.

pressing for his own appointment to a Tübingen professorship.[37] There is much to indicate that a south German academic alternative to Wittenberg and Marburg was in the planning stages.

The attempt failed, with consequences both fortunate and unfortunate, all meriting our attention. The adverse consequences can be recited briefly given the widespread consensus of today's scholars. Duke Ulrich and the urban wing of the alliance that restored him to power in Württemberg drifted steadily apart between 1534 and 1536, and the ideal of municipal ecclesiastical autonomy gave way to that of the supreme episcopacy of the territorial prince. The failure of the urban congregational principle was no personal failure on the part of Ambrosius Blarer,[38] because, as the representative of south German and especially Strassburg plans, he backed a programme that was sure to collide with the consolidation of ducal interests. The Kaaden Accord in no way forbad Ulrich to permit the influence of Blarer, Bucer and Bullinger in his territories, and had it done so it would have caused him little concern. Likewise, in mounting his campaign against those urban reform ideals, Ulrich felt no need of the authority of treaty stipulations. He could simply follow the example of Count Eberhard's ecclesiastical policy which aimed to achieve territorial unity and stability by insisting on a reformed but loyal church.

Later tensions could in part be perceived at the outset in 1534. Bucer's candidate became Ulrich's choice to reform south Württemberg and, in temporary tandem with Grynaeus, the University of Tübingen. But Bucer had suggested that a Württemberg synod be charged with making that choice;[39] a proposal less than pleasing to a

[37] Concerned that Brenz might be called to Tübingen (a concern fully justified by the events of the following year: see below, n. 41), Blarer wrote to Bucer from Tübingen on 23 October 1535: 'Ich hab alle tag ein flissig nachdencken, mit was ursachen ich den fursten bewegen mochte, das er dich beruffete.' Moeller, 'Neue Nachträge', p. 71, lines 17–19; cf. Schiess, *Briefwechsel*, 1, p. 733 (no. 627). Blarer's additional comment that he could be sure of convincing the duke were Grynaeus present (Moeller, 'Neue Nachträge', p. 71, line 20), probably referred to Bucer's complaint of 5 September 1535 that Grynaeus had opposed an appointment for the Strassburg reformer. But Bucer had already come to terms with that outcome: 'Sed dominus noluit me; alium vult, et stultus non agnoscit.' Schiess, *Briefwechsel*, 1, p. 736 (no. 630).

[38] With a wide-ranging perspective Bofinger considers both 'foreign' policy factors (the role of electoral Saxony and the Swabian League) and the domestic situation (the court party!). He concludes: 'So war Blarer, allem Anscheine nach in Gegensatz zu Schnepf, in die Rolle versetzt worden, letztes Hindernis einer konsequenten Verstaatlichung des Kirchenwesens zu sein.' 'Kirche und werdender Territorialstaat', pp. 124f.

[39] *Ibid.*, p. 125. The restructuring of the church in Württemberg was also influenced from Zürich. On 31 October Blarer thanked Bullinger for having sent a copy of the

duke intent on fulfilling his self-appointed office as *defensor ecclesiae Württembergicae*.[40] And Ulrich was also busy systematically expanding the visitatorial office formerly claimed by Count Eberhard in his monastery reforms, extending that office to apply to the entire church structure. In the course of two years the church in Württemberg was drawn securely into the territorial administrative apparatus. Against this absorption the Lutheran reformer of northern Württemberg, Erhard Schnepf, had no reservations[41] so long as the free proclamation of the gospel was assured.[42]

The acute disadvantages of this Württemberg *Fürstenreformation*, undertaken by the territorial prince and accomplished with the aid of an expanded civil service and increasing interference in both ecclesiastical appointments and the formulation of doctrine, may be taken as representative for all the German territories. The shadow side of the princely Reformation included above all reduced urban autonomy and an increasing willingness, resulting from a false understanding of Luther's doctrine of the two kingdoms, to concede to the territorial prince an entire range of powers as accoutrements to his *ius reformandi*, independent of any control by church or theology. The prince as a provisional bishop (*Notbischof*) eventually assumed the supreme episcopacy and was transformed from a *Landesvater* into a fully fledged sovereign.

The Reformation has been termed an 'urban event'.[43] This observa-

Zürich synodal ordinance. Schiess, *Briefwechsel*, 1, p. 593 (no. 487); cited in Brecht, *Kirchenordnung und Kirchenzucht in Württemberg vom 16. bis zum 18. Jahrhundert*, p. 11.

40 The privilege of protection and defence (*Schutz- und Schirmrecht*) included both the obligations of the territorial lord to his subjects and the exercise of his duties as prefect or temporal steward (*Vogt*) for the monasteries and ecclesiastical properties of his territory. See Dietmar Willoweit's references to Hieronymus Schürpf and Ulrich Zasius in *Rechtsgrundlagen der Territorialgewalt. Landesobrigkeit, Herrschaftsrechte und Territorium in der Rechtswissenschaft der Neuzeit*, pp. 63–78.

41 This basic attitude was reinforced rather than weakened by the arrival of Johannes Brenz, Blarer's replacement, in November 1536. Martin Brecht does not hesitate to criticize sharply Brenz's willingness to accept government control of the church. 'Anfänge reformatorischer Kirchenordnung und Sittenzucht bei Johannes Brenz', pp. 346f.; cf. Brecht, *Kirchenordnung und Kirchenzucht*, pp. 40–9. See also Harrison, 'Melanchthon's Role in the Reform of the University of Tübingen'.

42 By 22 January 1538 the Constance city council had been informed that Blarer wanted to leave the service of the duke. But the council expressed uncertainty as to whether 'the prince might not be displeased in the matter'. Moeller, 'Nachträge zum Blarer-Briefwechsel', no. 30 (794a), p. 42.

43 'the German Reformation was an urban event at once literary, technological and oratorical.' Dickens, *The German Nation and Martin Luther*, p. 182. This quotation would be misleading if we did not add that Dickens posits a second Reformation in the years between 1525 and 1535 (–40), a Reformation of the princes: 'Thus a second Reformation, stabilizing yet sterilizing, followed upon the popular and enthusiastic

tion overlooks the fact that not the cities but rather the princely imperial estates made possible the Protestant victory at the Diet of Augsburg in 1555. And the reconquest of Württemberg was the first tangible success of the Schmalkaldic League that outlasted the Interim (1547–8) to frustrate the imperial strategy for returning Germany to the Catholic fold.

For the first and muted phase of Luther's influence prior to the Diet of Worms (1521) we should not underestimate the importance of the monasteries, especially those of the Augustinian Observants, as centres for theological exchange. During the second period of its expansion, at least until the Peace of Nuremberg in 1532, the Reformation admittedly merits the 'urban' label. Yet in the legally decisive question of achieving imperial legitimacy, the cities inclined toward the new movement won no more than a secret promise from the emperor to suspend cases pending against evangelical imperial estates in the Imperial Supreme Court until a council could be held. And that success came only with the determined support of electoral Saxony.[44] Only where the imperial and free cities were able to ally themselves with the surrounding territory, as was the case with Augsburg in 1537,[45] were they able to maintain independence in the face of the Edict of Worms.

Against this backdrop Hanns Rückert's observation is still valid: 'If one inquires to whom the German Reformation owed the hard-fought triumph in the battle for self-preservation won in the Peace of Augsburg, one must reply: to the Reformation's conjunction with the prior opposition of the imperial estates to the centralized authority of the Habsburg emperors.'[46] Today, to be sure, we would no longer speak unreservedly of a 'triumph', since the reformation of the church succeeded only partially with respect to geography and was compelled to compromise at various stages on its path to power.

But the imperial estates alone did not win legitimacy[47] for the Reformation, and by himself Luther could have accomplished even less. The miracle of the movement's survival becomes clear only

Reformation of the cities.' *Ibid.*, p. 196. Basil Hall ('The Reformation City') reaches similar conclusions, basing the most convincing portion of his essay on his thorough preliminary studies on Calvin.

44 For the context of imperial politics see Rabe, *Reichsbund und Interim. Die Verfassungs- und Religionspolitik Karls V. und der Reichstag von Augsburg 1547/1548*, esp. pp. 90f.

45 See Friedrich Roth, *Augsburgs Reformationsgeschichte*, vol. 2, pp. 318f.

46 Rückert, 'Die Bedeutung der württembergischen Reformation', pp. 272f.; reprinted in *idem*, *Vorträge und Aufsätze*, p. 244.

47 See Selge, 'Das Autoritätengefüge der westlichen Christenheit im Lutherkonflikt 1517 bis 1521', p. 519.

when we take many factors into account which together formed a safety net preventing the catastrophic outcome anticipated by all. These include the enormous surface reduction of Europe due to the Turkish threat, making imperial unity and willingness to compromise imperative; the rivalry between Francis I and Charles V, which was interrupted but not eliminated by the Peace of Cambrai (3 August 1529); England's totally unexpected exit from the stage of Catholic Europe;[48] and last but not least the bitter conflicts between emperor and pope (Clement VII) which found unhappy dramatization in the sack of Rome (May 1527). Smoothed over, to be sure, by the coronation of Charles V in Bologna (24 February 1530), nevertheless these battles were fuelled by such fundamentally different concepts of reform that they left their mark on the last session of the Council of Trent.[49]

In addition to this web of foreign factors, we must consider the internal imperial situation. The prospect from the princely courts is reflected in the report by Erasmus – who was well situated to compile an ecclesiastical weather map of Europe at the close of 1518 – after the first exchange of blows between Luther and Rome (Prierias) and after the announcement of the disputation to be held at Leipzig. Erasmus concluded: Papal absolutism in its current form is the plague of Christendom. Yet it would be useless to attack this ulcer publicly (*aperte*) for 'Such was and remains a matter for the princes! But I fear that the princes would rather join forces with the pope in order to secure themselves a share of the spoils.'[50] This was indeed a realistic

[48] On 3 November 1529 Parliament was opened in London with an address by the newly appointed Lord Chancellor, Thomas More. His speech initiated a series of reform measures that led to the drafting of the reform statutes of 1532. After outlining four types of anticlericalism, the fourth being the 'anticlericalism of heresy', J. J. Scarisbrick concludes that the autumn of 1529 was the decisive period in which 'Henry VIII threw in his lot with this anticlericalism which could never have made full progress without him'. *Henry VIII*, p. 245. With convincing documentation, G. R. Elton describes events of the transition years 1529–31 as a process in which Cromwell replaced Wolsey by skilfully combining his base in Parliament with the royal support gained when he entered royal service following the conclusion of Parliament in December 1529 (but prior to April 1530). *The Tudor Revolution in Government. Administrative Changes in the Reign of Henry VIII*, p. 83.

[49] See the second of the two letters that Emperor Ferdinand I sent to Pope Pius IV on 3 March 1563. Ferdinand traced the crisis faced by the council to the fact that there were actually two councils in session, 'one in Trent and one in Rome: the cardinals who surround the pope'. Jedin, *Geschichte des Konzils von Trient*, vol. 4, pt. 1, p. 262. The emperor considered the cause of the crisis to lie 'in the pope's fear of a conciliar reform of the entire curial system . . . To the pope, such intervention by the council in his personal sphere appeared as an attempt to establish the validity of the concilar doctrine of the supremacy of the council over the pope.' *Ibid.*, p. 263.

[50] 'Video τὴν τοῦ Ρομάνου 'Αρχιερέως (ut nunc est ea sedes) μοναρχίαν pestem esse

assessment of the situation, based on recent history. For had not the curia succeeded in disbanding the Council of Basel (1431–49) and neutralizing the partial successes of the conciliar movement through an entire series of national concordats?[51]

The further course of the Reformation, although far from invalidating Erasmus' political analysis, demonstrated that the princes were no longer able to arrange matters quietly and bilaterally with the pope. A new factor, missed by Erasmus but suggested by the tiny word *aperte*, 'openly', was now involved: Luther took to the stage of church politics at the Leipzig Disputation and then appeared before the Diet of Worms. In the wake of these most important events in the early years of the Reformation, he mobilized public opinion and demonstrated the political explosiveness of the pursuit of truth in contrast to its restriction by Erasmus to the polite and learned exchange of correspondence and *convivium*.

A different public had emerged when the educational forces encouraged by Erasmus himself began to produce a new and self-confident elite of theologians and jurists, of politically active preachers and learned councillors, upon whom the princes depended for the expansion of their *ius territoriale*. None of this in any way denies the role played by political egoism in the decisive alliance between the Reformation and the emerging territorial states. Although clearly present, the effect of such self-interest was the reverse of that suggested by Erasmus in 1518. Criticism of Rome, with all its late medieval precedents, now led to an ideologically reinforced community of interests between those pressing for church reform and the proponents of political pragmatism. This was an ideological coalition that made negotiating reform measures and sharing the territorial spoils with the pope superfluous.[52]

Christianismi . . . Sed tamen haud scio an expediat hoc ulcus aperte tangere. Principum hoc erat negocium; sed vereor ne hi cum Pontifice colludant, in praedae partem venturi.' *Opus Epistolarum*, ed. Allen, 3, p. 409, line 16–410, line 21 (no. 872); letter to Johannes Lang, Louvain, 17 October 1518.

51 Since students of Summenhart have overlooked his 'Ode to the Council of Constance' dated Tübingen, 9 September 1499, it merits special mention. It documents both the intellectual context within which Erasmus' thesis that 'structural reform of the church is a matter for princes' must be understood and the sense of shock that must have emanated from Leipzig when Luther undermined the lofty authority of the council with his assertion of conciliar fallibility. The treatise could perhaps best be titled: 'Alios synodorum conventus facile adumbret.' Datum Tubingen nonis Septembris Anno MCCCCXCIX. *Concilium Constantiense. Acta et decreta* (Hagenau: Heinrich Gran for Johann Rynman, 1500), fol. a1^{v}.

52 Any across-the-board judgment on those princes inclined toward or clearly favourable to the evangelical cause that brands them 'political realists' or 'opportunists',

The south German cities chose another path, based on the new, emerging public, when they attempted to realize a union of politics and religion within their own walls. They proposed their own municipal congregations as representative of the universal church, and developed a political theology centred around the *bonum commune*. This was a political theology in manifest extension of the late medieval urban ideology, seeking the seamless fusion of the horizontal dimension of divine justice with the righteousness of faith – all within the framework of the public welfare. It was impossible to foresee in the early years of the Reformation that, due to their municipal church structure, the cities would collide with the emerging territorial churches. Such lack of prescience permitted the recovery of Württemberg by Duke Ulrich to be financed and furthered by leading cities of south Germany.[53]

The years 1534–6 were decisive because then for the first time it became clear that two forms of reformed church structure had crystallized and that a test of strength must ensue. But the political theology represented by Blarer and directed above all by Strassburg was better suited to the struggle for liberation than the political–religious consolidation of a reconquered duchy. When Blarer departed uncompensated for the wilderness, that is, when he left Tübingen to prosecute the urban Reformation elsewhere, his strategy of reformation through the construction and reconstruction of local municipal congregations had already been displaced by reformation 'from above' with its official visitations and confiscation of ecclesiastical property. In the secular sphere, a parallel hope for the revival of the power and influence of the Württemberg estates ran aground on Ulrich's resolute pursuit of territorial centralization.

But should these developments be dismissed as a 'German tragedy' – as our modern and enlightened appreciation of democracy and civil rights might demand? Such a judgment can be supported only through careful examination of the reverse side of the urban political theology. In a recent monograph, Steven E. Ozment has proposed in lively language the thesis that the third and fourth decades of the

fails to deal adequately with a series of figures of the first phases of the Reformation – because the 'real' situation following the Edict of Worms was not clear even to contemporary political observers.

53 Regarding the alliance between Ulm, Augsburg and Nuremberg of 21 May 1533 for the purpose of 'preserving religion and enforcing the public peace', as well as Ulm's support in June 1533 for the Hessian strategy aimed at breaking up the Swabian League, see Wille, *Philipp der Grossmüthige von Hessen und die Restitution Ulrichs von Wirtemberg 1526–1535*, pp. 120f.

sixteenth century brought a transformation in which the 'freedom fighters' of the 1520s reverted to 'new papists' and the liberation from troubled consciences originally proclaimed in Wittenberg and Zürich was exchanged for the new burdens of clericalistic orthodoxy and orthopraxis.[54] A. G. Dickens has also postulated two reformations: an urban movement of the 1520s and the 'stabilizing yet sterilizing' princely Reformation of the third decade.[55] When these two portraits are superimposed, the image of a Constantinian fall arises, evoking the spectre of the bloodless institutionalization of the *spirit* as the price demanded for the expansion of the inclusive church. For behind the unassuming word 'sterile' lurks a barely disguised disappointment at the actual outcome of the Reformation. This disappointment is not uncommonly sublimated by constructing a lineage beginning with Luther and leading up to Bismarck or Hitler.

But applying the image of a Constantinian fall of the church distorts the Reformation and revolution in the church of the sixteenth century just as it falsifies the evolution of an imperial church in the fourth century. Even positing a contrast between the liberating rediscovery of holy scripture and a later infiltration by biblicism is untenable. For the aspects of the south German Reformation that we attempt to denote the slippery but irreplaceable concept of 'biblicism' represent not a relapse but an important, indeed, decisive continuation of concepts[56] encountered in the first Tübingen school, especially in Conrad Summenhart.[57] His frontal attack on the biblical basis for the tithe obligations and the ten per cent church tax not only had social consequences, as the peasant revolts of the 1520s clearly demonstrated, but also possessed enormous theological and political explosive potential, as illustrated by the flood of pamphlets and broadsheets sweeping away the obstacles to the Reformation.

Summenhart used the general lament about the heavy burden of ecclesiastical obligations to indict a tyranny over consciences. He put that lament in the words of Christ: 'Woe to you lawyers as well! For you burden men with unbearable loads while you yourselves refuse to lay a finger to those loads' (Luke 11.46; cf. Matth. 23.23). In the struggle against the unbearable burden of church law, Summenhart aimed not to liberate the Christian conscience from the law but rather

[54] *The Reformation in the Cities*, pp. 164ff.
[55] See above, n. 43.
[56] The ambivalence of such points of continuity is captured aptly, indeed, aphoristically, by Ozment: 'Late medieval developments were a threshold as well as a foothold.' *The Reformation in the Cities*, p. 118.
[57] See Chapter 7.

to trim to a theologically valid compass a body of legislation bloated by canonists and their canons. The urban reformers restricted that scope of validity even more narrowly, identifying it with the canon of scripture. But like Summenhart they had no intention of abolishing the law entirely; rather they endeavoured to proclaim, to preach for the first time an authentic law – making it all the more binding on the individual and, in view of the threat of divine penalty, upon the community. At the same time they introduced a major difference, teaching that, although obedience to God might indeed often turn away divine wrath, God's loving attention no longer came in response to human merit.

The process is thus better described as a 'reorientation of church law toward the word of God and a whetting of Christian consciences', than with the image of liberation at the hands of Ozment's 'freedom fighters'. The believer's conscience, that formerly left the confessional burdened by the innumerable stipulations of the church's canon law, now merely exchanged that load in the south German urban Reformation for a new and absolute obligation to observe God's law recorded in the canon of scripture.

But we must carefully avoid yet another image. It is not at all true that the original ideal of the priesthood of all believers fell prey to a new clericalism as the first wave of enthusiasm ebbed. The 'brethren' christened by Zwingli in 1523 in Zürich – two years before a different brotherhood accepted adult baptism in Zollikon[58] – were indeed all equal as elect of God. Yet they were summoned and superintended by a single 'shepherd' soon to be titled 'episcopus'.

This consciousness of clerical office had a different foundation from that in the Middle Ages when a priest's special status stemmed from the responsibility entrusted him in speaking the transforming words 'hoc est corpus meum', an office bestowed on no layman, indeed, withheld from even the holy mother Mary. Just as the Eucharistic mystery required protection from pollution at lay hands, so not all Christian truth could be revealed to the laity in the sermon. Thus Summenhart expressly warned against transmitting his attack on the tithe to the laity, since laymen were incapable of properly handling this Christian truth and might prostitute it as an excuse for tumult.[59]

To the degree that they had experienced a humanistic phase and had been influenced by Erasmian ideals of scholarship, the urban reformers came to their task with another sort of elitist consciousness

[58] See Blanke, *Brüder in Christo*, p. 82; Nordenhaug translation, p. 71.
[59] See above, pp. 123f.

stemming from their status as citizens of an erudite republic of letters liberated from the barbarities of the *vulgus profanum*.[60] They preferred the dignified pursuit of knowledge in academies to the 'puerile' task of instructing ignorant students. Where they did accept university posts, they favoured the exalted label 'academia' to the terms *universitas* or *studium generale* that were clouded with 'medieval' connotations.[61]

These humanists and urban reformers extolled, in conscious opposition to the university, the ideals of private exchange instead of public disputation. They preferred to communicate in personal letters to learned equals; letters revealing a devotion to *modestia* in expressing *opiniones* that contrast sharply with the *assertiones immodestae* of their professorial targets of abuse.[62] When the rupture between Luther and Erasmus found expression in these same terms, *assertio* and *opinio*,[63] the humanist-inclined leaders within the urban Reformation had already consciously leaped the wall that had once separated them from their public. At the same time they retained a special status as scriptural experts from the republic of letters. This status expressed itself in their sense of a call, as scholarly servants of the Gospel, to be apostolic guardians and shepherds. Just as the priest once brought about the presence of Christ with his proclamation of the Eucharistic words of consecration, so the new preachers summoned the presence of Christ in proclaiming the Gospel.[64] Thus the rediscovery of the Gospel fused organically with an appropriation of

60 Luther's colleague, Otto Beckmann, wrote a confidential letter on 24 February 1519 to Spalatin in order to influence Luther to abstain from criticizing the pope *coram vulgo*. Kolde, ed., *Analecta Lutherana*, pp. 6f. Apparently Beckmann was responding to a concerned inquiry from Spalatin. Neither wished to involve the *vulgus profanum*, which could only make genuine understanding (*pax*!) and princely diplomacy more difficult.

61 Cf. Petry, 'Die Reformation als Epoche der deutschen Universitätsgeschichte', p. 344.

62 Erasmus' verdict on Eobanus is typical: 'Rara avis, eximia doctrina sine supercilio.' Letter to Helius Eobanus Hessus, 19 October 1518; *Opus Epistolarum*, ed. Allen, 3, p. 412, lines 12f. (no. 874).

63 Dietrich Kerlen's difficulty in doing justice to his subject probably results from his decision to limit himself to material from the period 1524–5. *Assertio. Die Entwicklung von Luthers theologischem Anspruch und der Streit mit Erasmus von Rotterdam*. Erasmus' viewpoint appears as early as his letter to Johannes Lang of 12 October 1518. Unfortunately, the preceding letter from Lang to Erasmus is no longer extant, a missive in which Luther's early pupil (cf. the letter from Petreius to Lang, 8 May 1512: 'Sancte Lange et sancte Martine orato pro me . . .' Kolde, *Analecta Lutherana*, p. 4) unsuccessfully sought to recruit Erasmus for the Wittenberg Augustinian circle – Staupitz, Luther, Lang.

64 See Locher, 'Praedicatio verbi Dei est verbum Dei. Heinrich Bullinger zwischen Luther und Zwingli. Ein Beitrag zu seiner Theologie'.

the authority belonging to New Testament offices of ecclesiastical leadership. One of the first to deplore this tendency, even before it became a commonplace of Anabaptist criticism, was Duke Ulrich's choice for reformer of Montbéliard, Pierre Toussain (†1573).[65] On 17 December 1524 he informed Guillaume Farel in a letter written from Basel that 'the [new pastors] permit themselves to be honoured as apostles, evangelists and bishops and use who knows what other titles, [all of] which shed more light on their arrogance than their learning'.[66]

This novel type of reformed clericalism founded on the pastoral responsibility entrusted to the clergy was of a different nature from the medieval clericalism of whispered words of consecration. But it proved to be no less intolerant than its medieval precedents when political theology began to ignore the limits of the pastoral office and declared the Gospel to be no more and no less than a function of the *bonum commune*.[67] As long as the urban reformers managed to mobilize public opinion against the old clericalism, only the most clairvoyant observers, such as Pierre Toussain, perceived the prospect of a sudden reversion. But certainly one aspect of the shadow side of the 'urban event' we call the Reformation was the fact that the concept of the priesthood of all believers risked extinction from the very beginning, despite the many worthy democratic impulses nurtured inside city walls.[68]

[65] On Toussain see *Opus Epistolarum*, ed. Allen, 6, pp. 52f., n. for line 8. Regarding his activity as the first 'superintendent' in Montbéliard (1541–71), see Debard, 'Les visites ecclésiastiques dans l'Église Luthérienne de la principauté de Montbéliard du XVIe au XVIIIe siècle', pp. 42ff., 67.

[66] 'Item faciunt se vocari Apostolos, Evangelistas et episcopos, et je ne scé quelz aultres titres plus plain[s] d'arrogance que de science.' Herminjard, *Correspondence des Réformateurs*, 1, p. 313 (no. 131).

[67] Bucer's insistence on the right of decision reserved to a minority specially qualified by its faith (*pars sanior*) as set forth in his letter to Jacob Sturm of 13 May 1549 may have been influenced by the monastic tradition. Cf. Elsener, 'Zur Geschichte des Majoritätsprinzips (Pars maior und Pars sanior), insbesondere nach schweizerischen Quellen'. For the canonistic interpretation of the pair 'pars maior et sanior' in the event of disputed elections, see *ibid.*, pp. 109f. Cf. *idem*, 'Das Majoritätsprinzip in konfessionellen Angelegenheiten und die Religionsverträge der schweizerischen Eidgenossenschaft vom 16. bis 18. Jahrhundert'.

[68] Nor did Calvin represent a turning-point. Modern Calvin scholars generally admit that he was no democrat but often add an important qualifying comment to the effect that he was no theoretician of *modern* democracy nor advocate of *popular* sovereignty. See the historiographical essay by Hermann Vahle, 'Calvinismus und Demokratie im Spiegel der Forschung'. Even Vahle adds such a qualifying sentence: Calvin was, to be sure, no democrat but he 'furthered the religious-individual and political liberty of the people . . .' *Ibid.*, p. 197. The entire *opus* of Robert Kingdon has been overlooked here: Kingdon has demonstrated that Calvin repressed existing democratic institutions in Geneva. Viewed from this perspective, one can understand why 'Genevans

The appalling experience of the Third Reich inclines historians to assume that what went wrong with the Reformation was Luther's sell-out to the princes: this salves forever the German religious conscience. A contrast between a supposedly legalistic, clericalistic and sterile 'princes' Reformation' and the earlier 'creative' and so-called democratic phase is the natural and therefore not sufficiently examined consequence of this historical outlook. But there is another plane upon which the supposed creativity and sterility of the 'two Reformations' can be examined. The names of the two reformers nominated in Strassburg and appointed by Duke Ulrich to reorganize the University of Tübingen in 1534, Blarer and Grynaeus, were connected with two other attempts to harness universities to the cause of the urban Reformation. From these plans for Strassburg and Basel, which also enjoyed the support of Bucer, we can surmise what the success of the urban Reformation's pedagogical programme might have meant for theology and scholarship in general.

Through Bucer's mediation, the merchant Peter Buffler established on 14 April 1534 an endowment to be located in Strassburg and intended to train theologians from the south German area.[69] Bucer subsequently tried to expand the existing endowment into a university complete with 'all faculties', an institution intended as a Strassburg counterpart to Wittenberg and Marburg. But he was soon informed by the former *Ammeister* and current *Scholarch* or superintendent of municipal educational affairs, Klaus Kniebis, of the restrictions placed on scholarship by the needs of the *bonum commune*. Kniebis pointed out that the founding of a university complete with all disciplines was no task for the city since the public interest in higher education extended only to that which was 'necessary to maintain the common welfare'.[70] The natural sciences were especially superfluous, Kniebis explained, since scripture teaches that they distract from faith in God who rules over all nature and who instructs in holy scripture concerning all nature.[71]

who did not want to trade catholic clerical tyranny for a new protestant yoke' drove Calvin out of the city in 1538. 'Was the Protestant Reformation a Revolution? The Case of Geneva', p. 214. For continuing tendencies exhibited by a 'democratic wing' of Calvinism *after* Calvin, see Vahle, 'Calvinismus und Demokratie', p. 206.

69 Ficker, 'Die Anfänge der akademischen Studien in Strassburg', pp. 25–74; including detailed information from the Thomasarchives; *ibid.*, pp. 55–61. *Idem*, *Erste Lehr- und Lernbücher des höheren Unterrichts in Strassburg (1534–1542)*; supplemented by Walther Köhler in *Zwingliana* 3 (1918, pt 1), pp. 348f.

70 Kohls, *Die Schule bei Martin Bucer in ihrem Verhältnis zu Kirche und Obrigkeit*, p. 80.

71 'Dann die *heylig schrifft* die naturlich philosophiam ansiehet, *als ob sy von dem glauben jn gott (der vber die natur ist vnd leret) abziehet.*' Strasbourg, Thomasarchives, no. 324,

A perilous mingling of terrestrial and celestial wisdom in this manner, a combination occasionally visible in our own century in certain forms of religious opposition to Darwinism, cannot be debited to Bucer's account. Yet Bucer was also a champion of the urban ideology centred on the *bonum commune*. He too intended to establish a Christian university in Strassburg which, although independent of the city, would nevertheless be so integrated with the church that little room remained for secular research. The profane world with all the sciences relating to it was to have been firmly subordinated to theology. Given this point of view, the age of natural science and technology could gain a foothold and establish itself only in the course of a struggle against the church and theology.[72]

The hazards involved in crossing the frontier between university and church became obvious five years later when Bucer travelled to Basel to support his friend and colleague Grynaeus in opposing the new statutes with which the city council had demanded the incorporation of Basel's clergy into the university[73] as a further step in the late medieval policy of 'communalization'.[74] Grynaeus advocated instead that the church and its ministers, in their collective capacity as guardian of the university, be granted the right to choose professors. Although at the outset Bucer supported Grynaeus' efforts, he ultimately gave his reluctant approval to the council's design. But his

fol. 1^r; quoted according to Kohls, *Die Schule bei Martin Bucer*, p. 82. Limits were also placed on dialectics: 'als vil die zu der theology vnd vuffmerkens zu haben dienet, das man nit durch die dialecticam verfuret vnd jn perversam sententiam propositionem fidei geführt werde . . .' Thomasarchives, no. 324, fol 1^r; Kohls, p. 227, no. 70.

72 Ignoring the intentions and assertions of the representatives of the *via moderna* – indeed, reversing their campaign to free the experience and observation of the world from the metaphysical grip of the *via antiqua* – Hans Blumenberg concludes that a religion that 'in the medieval wake of its concern for the infinite power and absolute freedom of its God, destroyed by itself the conditions it had established for man's relationship to the world around him; such a religion inevitably fails to give man his due by departing from its presuppositions in this contradictory manner'. *Säkularisierung und Selbstbehauptung*, p. 134. Although labelled an 'expanded and revised edition of *Die Legitimität der Neuzeit*, parts one and two', the basic conclusions remain unchanged from the earlier work. But note the concessions made to Occamism in the new edition of part three, *Der Prozess der theoretischen Neugierde*, pp. 150f.

73 Although in Wittenberg Carlstadt had been one of the first to shed the academic gown, in Basel he proved willing to support the claims of the university and 'mit eigenem Beispiel trotz des Widerstandes der Geistlichkeit dem Ratsbeschluss zum Durchbruch zu verhelfen . . .' Bubenheimer, *Consonantia Theologiae et Iurisprudentiae. Andreas Bodenstein von Karlstadt als Theologe und Jurist zwischen Scholastik und Reformation*, p. 258.

74 I am indebted to my colleague, Gottfried Seebass, for this fitting parallel concept to 'territorialization'. It is especially well suited to characterize the element of continuity in the urban politics of the late Middle Ages and Reformation.

endorsement was contingent upon a guarantee of the priority of theology over all other disciplines and the assurance that the theological faculty, chaired by the city's head pastor or 'bishop' (*Antistes*!), would supervise the other faculties 'so that . . . indeed in all faculties the religion of Christ might be faithfully furthered'.[75]

The ordinance restructuring the University of Basel unequivocally rejected this proposed domination by the ecclesiastical and theological *domini*.[76] Bucer learned from the rector and the appropriate delegates from the city council that his suggestion violated 'the custom, usage and liberty of all universities' and signified a reversion to the Middle Ages because 'a great tyranny, like that of the papacy, would proceed' from placing such power over the university in the hands of the clergy.[77]

These efforts by the Strassburg reformers to influence the restructuring of universities overtaken by the Reformation aids us in the proper evaluation of the efforts of Blarer and Grynaeus at Tübingen. The resistance that both encountered in Tübingen can only partially be attributed to scholastic stubbornness and a propensity for things of the past – to some degree the professors justifiably feared for the loss of their academic freedom. Duke Ulrich's explicit confirmation of their academic rights and privileges on 16 January 1536 may be viewed as a direct answer to such qualms.[78] But beyond that, we must realize above all that the displacement of the 'urban Reformation' by the 'princes' Reformation' not only brought stability but also produced anything but sterility for the sciences. In the princely Reformation, space was reserved for the investigation of profane and natural phenomena despite attempts to couple them to the *bonum commune*, preserving the breathing room they urgently needed in view of theology's self-confident pretensions to leadership. If the common

[75] Cited by Kohls, *Die Schule bei Martin Bucer*, p. 110. These Strassburg initiatives should be viewed within the larger French context that saw municipal academies and schools established at approximately this period: Angoulême, 1516; Lyon, 1527; Dijon, 1531; Bordeaux, 1533. Jacques Le Goff considers the conflict between universities and these 'collèges des villes' from a social history perspective as a 'forme de conflicts entre les universités nobiliaires et les villes embourgeoisées'. 'La conception française de l'université a l'époque de la Renaissance', p. 99. But because Le Goff considers the bourgeoisie to be the 'moteur du progrès culturel', he portrays the University of Paris in the most sombre shades.

[76] In Grynaeus' opposition, supported by Myconius, Andreas Staehelin correctly detects an attempt to achieve an untrammelled theocracy. *Geschichte der Universität Basel 1632–1818*, vol. 2, p. 394.

[77] See the 'Responsio data Argentinensibus 1539', University Library, Basel, AA I, 42b; quoted and analysed in detail in Kohls, *Die Schule bei Martin Bucer*, pp. 111f.

[78] Roth, *Urkunden*, pp. 185–98.

weal required the amputation of the natural sciences in the context of sixteenth-century Reformation society, application of the same criterion of relevance today would likely result in the expulsion of the humanities and theology. There was no conceivable room for the natural sciences within the narrow-minded perspective of a *bonum commune* appropriated by the church. Even if Ulrich can in no way be credited with stimulating a golden period for the university,[79] at least Tübingen's 'higher school' survived into the age of scholarship's reawakening with 'all faculties' intact.[80]

The preservation of the university, and the recognition of the equality of all its disciplines, was a point of contention outside the struggle between city reformers and the territorial prince for the right of reformation. The conflict over the proper structure of the kingdom of Christ extended beyond the socio-political aspects that have enjoyed the one-sided attention of previous research. That conflict opened channels that lead by way of the Copernican respect for technology and progress to the modern understanding of the universe. And the old conflict between the *via antiqua* and *via moderna* played an astonishing role in that process, even though the sixteenth-century participants and modern historians alike were and continue to be convinced that the *Wegestreit* had been laid to rest as antiquated. For in that *Wegestreit* decisions were made concerning the future of

[79] Even after departing from Tübingen, Grynaeus kept himself informed concerning the reorganization of the university. We possess a dismal report from Joachim Camerarius describing the prevailing crisis of scholarship and political pressure in October 1538. *Simonis Grynaei Epistolae*, ed. Streuber, p. 30 (no. XXII). In Leipzig, the reform of the university was accomplished only after the accession of Maurice of Saxony (18 August 1541) and after Camerarius arrived from Tübingen where he had held the chair for both Latin and Greek as well as rhetoric (1535–41) but 'had not become firmly rooted in the teaching faculty'. Helbig, *Die Reformation der Universität Leipzig im 16. Jahrhundert*, p. 65.

[80] Accounts of the impact of the Reformation on the universities are as diverse as the evaluations of the Reformation itself. Whereas Johannes Janssen compiled materials to demonstrate the decline of scholarship and education in the wake of the Reformation, Hanns Rückert pointed to the educational breakthrough accompanying Luther's arrival on the scene, going so far as to assert that 'Luther war, wie überall, so auch auf diesem Gebiet der einzig wirklich schöpferische Geist unter den Führern der Reformation', 'Die Stellung der Reformation zur mittelalterlichen Universität', p. 91.

It is correct to connect the reform of the University of Wittenberg with the beginnings of Luther's activity and to view his programme for 'disentangling' philosophy and theology as a liberation for *both* spheres. Rückert, 'Die Stellung der Reformation', p. 90. But when we eliminate the negative verdicts on late medieval scholasticism and begin to perceive the subtle shading that has long gone unnoticed beneath the sharp black and white contrast stemming from the humanist sense of a rebirth, then Luther's effort to disentangle philosophy and theology finds its historical niche in the medieval *Wegestreit*.

research and teaching which we have without reason customarily attributed to the rational spirit of the Enlightenment alone.

Whereas the *via antiqua*, in which nearly all the leading urban reformers were educated, called for the subordination of all sciences to theology, the *via moderna* favoured relative autonomy for both natural science and theology, for *scientia* and *sapientia*. To be sure, no effort was made in the Middle Ages to release sciences from a general profession of Christian belief. But an analogous campaign did take place, a campaign for release from the bear-hug of metaphysical speculation which, according to the nominalists, choked *both* physics and theology.

Within the realm of theology the *via moderna* opposed attempted speculative incursion beyond the frontiers of human reason into the revelation of God: a campaign *contra vanam curiositatem*. Regarding the natural sciences (*philosophia naturalis*), the modernists stressed the reliability and assertive force of *experientia* as *experimentum*. What we term the empirical observation of the natural world was shielded from dogmatic theology with the aid of a new view of causation. The path leading from the Paris nominalists, Jean Buridan († after 1358)[81] and Nicholas Oresme (†1382)[82] to Copernicus (†1543) and Galileo (†1642), proved to be a long trail indeed, filled with detours due to inadequate technological tools and filled also with supplementary experience of the world.[83]

81 'Was Buridan an die Stelle der Finalität im Naturgeschehen setzt, ist also nichts anderes als das Naturgesetz im modernen Sinn. Das ist ein Schritt von fundamentaler Bedeutung.' Maier, *Studien zur Naturphilosophie der Spätscholastik*, vol. 4, p. 334 and n. 27.

82 Marshall Clagett offers a careful discussion of Oresme's importance as a natural scientist in the comprehensive introduction to his edition, *Nicole Oresme and the Medieval Geometry of Qualities and Motions*, pp. 3–121. His general effort to avoid inflating Oresme as a 'forerunner of modern science' allows him nevertheless to capture his genuine originality: 'Although Oresme had no interest in experimental measurement, still he did try, for the most part, to present a naturalistic mechanism for the explanation of phenomena and certainly the wave of the future rolled in that direction.' *Ibid.*, p. 121. For biographical details see Edward Grant's introduction to *Nicole Oresme, De proportionibus proportionum and Ad pauca respicientes*, pp. 3–10.

83 Eric Cochrane has impressively countered the widespread thesis that the Renaissance impeded or at least failed to encourage the development of the natural sciences: '. . . it may now be possible to say that humanism facilitated the birth of Galilean science – at least in providing the particular forms assumed by the scientific revolution in Italy'. 'Science and Humanism in the Italian Renaissance', pp. 1049f. I am inclined to believe, however, that the educational programme of the Renaissance had drawn such wide circles that, during Galileo's seventeenth century (†1642), 'humanism' formed a non-specific part of the standard equipment of every educated 'gentleman'. For this development in the reception of Italian humanism in England, see Hay, 'England and the Humanities in the Fifteenth Century', pp. 362ff. So far as Copernicus is concerned, previous attempts to interpret his scientific attitude – and

John Murdoch has rightly labelled the attempt to construct a direct and unbroken chain of tradition in this matter as 'precursoritis' and thereby expanded our list of known historiographical fixations.[84] But his warning need not conceal the fact that the cornerstone for the demythologizing of God and nature was laid in the late Middle Ages; an observation that helps to explain why Christian Europe became the centre of technological progress. Three principles of nominalism bore fruit in this demythologizing process: (1) the priority of the individual phenomenon constituting reality; (2) the inductive method that transformed the preconceived opinions into scientific liabilities *par excellence*; and above all, (3) the distinction between the unknown God discernible only in his self-revelation and the equally unknown natural world, which however is discoverable with the aid of reason and experience.

The intense struggle surrounding faith and the church limited the progress of the natural sciences during the age of the Reformation. Indeed, some enlightened accomplishments of the eve of the Reformation were mislaid by the scholarly community in the mêlée that followed. Thus the Jesuit Friedrich von Spee noted in 1631: 'It is nearly impossible to believe the sort of superstition, envy, calumny, slander, gossip and the like that is found among the Germans. The authorities make no effort to punish such things nor are they censured in sermons. Thus the suspicion of witchcraft invades the world. All the divine punishments that God has threatened in holy scripture are thought to stem from the witches. God and nature do nothing any more, for the witches are responsible for it all.'[85] It was precisely this type of witchcraft mythology against which the Biel disciple Martin Plantsch had thundered in the Tübingen Collegiate Church as early as 1505; seeking to expose its absurdity with the aid of nominalist arguments.[86] Likewise, refusing to permit the biblical view of the world to derail his pursuit of scientific progress, the Wittenberg professor of astronomy, Rheticus, travelled to see Copernicus in order to convince him to publish his book, *De revolutionibus*.[87]

thereby that of the century preceding Galileo – as having been 'humanist' in nature are unconvincing. See Knoll, 'The World of the Young Copernicus. Society, Science and the University', pp. 25–7.

84 See Murdoch, 'Philosophy and the Enterprise of Science in the Later Middle Ages'.

85 Hammes, *Hexenwahn und Hexenprozesse*, p. 9.

86 See above, Chapter 9.

87 See Burmeister, *Georg Joachim Rhetikus 1514–1574. Eine Bio-Bibliographie*, vol. 1, pp. 44f. Rheticus' trip from Wittenberg to see Copernicus in Frauenburg (Prussia) was made possible by Caspar Cruciger (†1548), Luther's trusted colleague and co-editor of the first volume of the Wittenberg *Opera Omnia* (1545ff.). Cf. the chronological table in Burmeister, *Georg Joachin Rheticus*, vol. 2, p. 93.

Should we still be tempted to doubt that this initiative testifies to the influence of the Wittenberg *via moderna*, it is certainly no accident that one of Luther's disciples, the Nuremberg pastor Andreas Osiander, was the first to publish this work, supplemented by Osiander's own foreword.[88] Osiander has often been reproached for having termed Copernicus' revolutionary heliocentricism a hypothesis, but he remained true to the empirical tradition of nominalism when he dealt with the Copernican 'projection' – which was only subsequently verified by Galileo, Kepler and Newton – as not yet scientifically secure.[89]

The upsurge of piety and the powerful emphasis on holy scripture that accompanied the Reformation meant that the nominalist division of scholarly labour would yield only a thin crop within the field of natural science. For the time being, the potential of that division of labour was concentrated within the field of theology.

From Luther's viewpoint, the Zwinglian-led urban undermining of a proper Eucharistic theology was the result of a stubborn insistence on *via antiqua* principles that found a temporary respite only with the Wittenberg Concord of 1536. But that same stubborn insistence on principles of the old way helped to end Ambrosius Blarer's stay in Tübingen in that same year.

In a basic assessment of the lasting significance of the *via moderna*, or 'terminism', to use his own label, Luther pointed out that the resolution of the question of universals in favour of the *individuum* was the decisive characteristic. But in his day the modern way meant a faithful scriptural exegesis expounding scripture *in terminis propriis* without reading into it one's own clever thoughts. Precisely that kind of subjective adulteration had ensued when the medieval church reinterpreted the Eucharist as a sacrifice and transformed the sacrament, instituted by Christ with the symbols of the bread and wine, into a mass that denied the cup to the laity.

Although Luther originally applied the legacy of the *via moderna* against those loyal to Rome, soon after 1525 he turned precisely the same arguments against Carlstadt, Zwingli and all those he denounced as 'enthusiasts'. For in his view, just as the *via antiqua* position on universals refused a historically established, unique

[88] *Nicolai Copernici Thorunensis De revolutionibus orbium caelestium libri sex*, ed. F. Zeller and K. Zeller, vol. 2, pp. 403, line 3–404, line 7. Although the preface was published anonymously, Osiander's name was entered on the first copies so that it was clear to Kepler that Osiander was the author of the preface. See Hirsch, *Theologie Osianders*, appendix I, p. 290 and Seebass, *Bibliographie Osiandrica*, pp. 130f.

[89] See my essay, 'Reformation and Revolution', pp. 413f. For Osiander the alternatives of the *via antiqua* and *via moderna* have receded behind the *via Lutheri*.

existence to the individual man – defining him instead as the manifestation of a trans-temporal idea of man to which one should ascend intellectually – so the sacraments established in scripture were now being spiritualistically and spiritedly distorted in exegesis. Unfortunately the alterations were occurring according to the standard of human wisdom and not in humble subjection to the sure signs (*in certis signis*) to which God has pledged himself.[90]

Luther has often been accused – especially by Luther scholars who themselves draw upon the legacy of the *via antiqua* and are thus understandably in a poor position to do him justice – of having retreated into the Middle Ages with his post-1525 Eucharistic theology.[91] But as far as Luther himself was concerned, he had merely mobilized the 'modern' scientific achievements of Occam's school against 'Rome' and then, without revision, reversion or conversion, against 'Zürich'. His followers adopted his doctrine on the Eucharist without realizing that they were picking up in the process the legacy of a *via moderna* they had long since denounced as scholastic barbarity. The Nuremberg town clerk, Lazarus Spengler (†1534), who faithfully manned one of the most important urban outposts for Wittenberg in the conflict with the Swiss theology, illustrates this unwitting application of the modernist legacy. Fearing that Strassburg too would drift into the Swiss camp, Spengler campaigned, like Luther, on two fronts: against the red biretta of the cardinals[92] and then against Carlstadt, Zwingli and Oecolampadius.[93] Referring to the 'clear language of scripture' in a recently discovered letter dating from the summer of 1526, he complained that these three theologians allowed their human reason to 'promenade through scripture' and thus 'dared to garble God's plain truth . . .'[94]

[90] In 1520, in statements that practically summarize Reformation theology, Luther could still combine ideas (signum *et* memoriale) that became characteristic of the Zürich and south German Reformation after 1525, arousing suspicion of speculative presumption in the expanding Eucharistic controversy: 'his verbis [1 Cor. 11.24] promitto tibi, ante omne meritum et votum tuum, remissionem omnium peccatorum tuorum et vitam aeternam, et ut certissimus de hac mea promissione irrevocabili sis, corpus meum tradam et sanguinem fundam, morte ipsa hanc promissionem confirmaturus et utrunque tibi in signum et memoriale eiusdem promissionis relicturus.' *De captivitate Babylonica*; *WA* 6, p. 515, lines 20–4.

[91] See von Harnack, *History of Dogma*, vol. 7, pp. 248, 260–1. Cf. *Lehrbuch der Dogmengeschichte*, vol. 3, pp. 880, 891.

[92] Letter to Peter Butz, Nuremberg, 24 October 1525; Rott, 'La Réforme à Nuremberg et à Strasbourg', pp. 125f. On Butz (†1531), see *ibid.*, pp. 108f., n. 13.

[93] Letter to Peter Butz, Nuremberg, 14 December 1525; *ibid.*, p. 128.

[94] 'Zwinglein, Oecolampadius und ire anhenger, die mit irer vernunfft also in der schrifft und dem wort Gottes spacyren geen, und die einfeltikait göttlicher warhait zu kruppeln understeen . . .' Letter to Peter Butz, Nuremberg, 10 June 1526; *ibid.*, p. 132.

Luther's impassioned and occasionally coarse campaign against invading the 'plain' text of scripture with lofty ecclesiastical authority and profound academic learnedness had an anti-elitist or even populist spearhead pointed at the scarlet pretensions of the papal church *and* at the ivory parapets of the republic of letters. Both were equally guilty of having swindled the *christifideles*, the simple believers, out of 'their' Bible, the authentic *biblia pauperum*. We must not lose sight of this factor if we wish to avoid falling prey to a romantic, 'democratic'[95] transfiguration of the urban Reformation and an 'anti-authoritarian' disparagement of the 'princes' Reformation'.

It should surprise no one that the *Wegestreit* has been overlooked by scholars as a historically productive factor during the Reformation epoch. For despite their growing controversy and diversification, all parties occupied a common front against their own late medieval roots. In playing off the scholastic and especially the Dominican 'patres' against the 'fathers', they denied the lasting significance of the alternatives disclosed by the conflict between the *viae*, alternatives which even against their will shaped the preconceptions of all concerned.

A persistent pursuit of the university perspective, though not an obvious approach even during the sixteenth century, reveals these repressed and repudiated intellectual foundations. For the harvest of the tradition cultivated by academics who were ridiculed as *viri obscuri* furnished the basic intellectual equipment of the generation that shaped the Reformation epoch. Still, the controversy between the two ways offers no master key for understanding all the differences between the competing Wittenberg and south German Reformation models, much as various socio-political units are incapable of explaining developments comprehensively by themselves.

The attempt at a comprehensive theological interpretation, which has previously centred on the Eucharistic controversy (1525–36), might indeed appear tempting in view of a somewhat speculative connection between 'real presence' and 'Realpolitik'. Yet ultimately it also fails. For delineating the contrasts between the two theologies of the Lord's supper – an endeavour which began in the sixteenth century and remains inescapable today – simply proves inadequate to expose all the social, political and religious interests incorporated in the intra-evangelical dispute. We can only progress when we have learned to distinguish between the specific capacity and contribution

[95] Epigrammatically expressed by Schmidt: 'Das Reich der Reichstädte ist älter, primitiver, mittelalterlicher als der Staat der Fürsten.' *Die deutschen Städtechroniken*, p. 78.

offered by the differing methodologies of intellectual history and social history and after we have also developed interpretative categories that can be translated into both historical vocabularies and subjected to verification by historians of ideas as well as students of social history. Given these criteria of translatability and verifiability, students of Reformation history must abandon interpretative categories that often prove difficult for even historians of ideas to define or grasp, e.g. rationalism, spiritualism, fideism or individualism as well as anachronisms such as 'puritanism' or 'confessionalism'.

Compared with the impressive advances made in analysing the social strata[96] of various cities caught up in the Reformation, the theological assessment of the issues involved has been retarded. We are still dependent on a vocabulary that can be applied only with an uneasy conscience, producing more cosmetic than real progress. Even the term 'south German theology' indiscriminately spans the wide differences between Basel and Strassburg, Schwäbisch-Hall and Heilbronn, Ulm and Zürich, to say nothing of the elusive but supposedly elucidative label 'Melanchthon-Bucerian'.[97]

Profitable incorporation of the theological dimension into a comprehensive interpretation demands a new typology. Mindful of the current state of research, it might usefully employ the already exposed contours of Luther's theology as a foil for the profile of the south German and specifically the urban Reformation. Such a typology could prove to be especially helpful if, in the first place, it skirts systematic theological categories where possible in favour of descriptive interpretative categories, and if, secondly, it is not constructed solely or even primarily from the perspective of the uncompromising post-1525 fronts. Only when we view the Eucharistic controversies as

[96] One must proceed cautiously with talk of the 'corporative structures of the late medieval imperial city' when attempting to demonstrate the presence of 'democratic beginnings'. Thomas A. Brady, Jr has shown that the guilds in Strassburg were anything but 'a democratizing factor in the regime' and that the social tensions were 'only partly veiled by the harmonizing ideology of the leading reformers . . .' *Ruling Class, Regime and Reformation at Strasbourg*, p. 292.

[97] Bernd Moeller defines 'oberdeutsch' geographically as the area 'bounded by the line Esslingen–Ulm–Augsburg in the north and Augsburg–Kaufbeuren–Kempten to the east. To this is added Alsace in the west and German-speaking Switzerland in the south.' 'Die Kirche in den evangelischen freien Städten Oberdeutschlands im Zeitalter der Reformation', p. 148. Not only is 'oberdeutsch' here identified with 'Swiss', but also the critique of Zwingli current among Luther scholars shapes the list of the theological characteristics of the Reformation in 'Oberdeutschland': (1) Sanctification takes on greater significance and the south German reformers were 'somewhat quicker to come to terms with' justification; (2) the south German Reformation reveals a more optimistic anthropology; (3) the south Germans have 'certain spiritualistic and perhaps even [4] rationalistic tendencies'. *Ibid.*, p. 149.

a prism refracting an entire spectrum of components already at work before 1525 does the study of those controversies become a useful tool in pursuing the differences between the 'south German' and Lutheran Reformations.

Seven aspects deserve special attention in this regard:

1. Already in the *initia reformationis* we encounter variations in the image of Luther that point to an autonomous appropriation of the Reformation cause in south Germany. Luther appeared as a prophet and not an apostle, as a witness to and not the measure of the Gospel. Declining the label 'Lutheran' implied no rejection of Luther and was no fearful pretence induced by the imperial edict issued at Worms. Certainly it was not a faint heart that led Erasmus to insist as late as 1519 that he only desired to confront Luther in the same manner 'as we are accustomed to read Cyprian and Jerome, indeed even Peter Lombard'.[98] The preachers of the south German cities did take up the *causa Lutheri* with far greater enthusiasm than Erasmus ever mustered. But in their eyes Luther was no solitary hero, rather one warrior amid a changing assortment of comrades-in-arms.[99]

2. Furthermore, it was the writings of the *young* Luther that seemed to confirm and epitomize the south German reformers' own ambitions. And those writings continued to do so long after Luther himself had moved on to occupy new ground.[100] During the decisive stage of the evolution of a native 'south German' theology, the Luther of the Froben (Basel 1518), Schürer (Strassburg 1519), and Cratander and Petri (Basel 1520) editions appeared on the scene, hawked and read all along the intellectual and commercial highway of the Rhine.[101] For years to come that Luther continued to inspire south Germany: the Luther who, as a young monk, had stood alone against the papal church. The later Luther never held similar sway. But in these same south German eyes he was never credited with developing an independent theological offensive: instead he shared public

[98] Letter to Cardinal Albrecht of Mainz, Louvain, 19 October 1519; appended as a preface to, among other editions, the Petri edition of Luther's work. *Opus Epistolarum*, ed. Allen, 4, p. 100, lines 42–5.

[99] On Johann Eberlin von Günzburg's *15 Bundsgenossen*, see above, n. 19. Even Osiander was able as late as 1530 'to name in one breath Reuchlin, Erasmus and Luther as champions of the Reformation'. Seebass, *Das reformatorische Werk*, p. 72.

[100] Walther Köhler has pointed out that Zwingli's references to the young Luther also worked in reverse. At times Zwingli ascribed 'papal remnants' in the early writings, such as the veneration of saints and belief in purgatory, to the 'mature' Luther (1527). See *Luther und Zwingli*, 1, p. 551, n. 2.

[101] See Benzing, *Lutherbibliographie*, p. 3; Volz, 'Die ersten Sammelausgaben von Lutherschriften und ihre Drucker (1518–1520)'.

attention at the outset with Erasmus and eventually with an entire company of *eruditi* such as Zwingli, Bucer and Melanchthon.

3. The optimism singled out by traditional Luther scholarship as a mark of the south German anthropological views must also take its place amid an assortment of allied factors. Where support for the Reformation was coupled with an expectation of the end of the world, as was variously the case with Luther[102] and his earliest adherents, notably among the Augustinian Eremites,[103] many were inclined to view Luther as an isolated figure and eschatological symbol of great importance. In contrast, Luther appeared in the south German cities not as a sign of the end of time, but as a herald of the 'new times'. Such confidence in the future is not simply the result of an optimistic anthropology[104] but should also be ascribed to the recreative power of the Holy Spirit. Trust in the penetrating power of the new educational ideals as a whole and confidence in the promise of the Spirit, anticipation of both personal emancipation and of social progress, are so closely intertwined that opting for the priority of one impedes our access to both.

4. The *Wegestreit* helps us to understand that strange and complex phenomenon, iconoclasm, which usually accompanied the introduction of the urban reformations. For Erasmus and the Erasmians of our own day and age it is merely proof of the destructive power of the illiterate masses, drawn into the streets by rabble-rousing preachers. For the social historian it manifests the revolt of the poor against the symbols of prosperity and the privileged rich: the wave of iconoclasm which shocked Europe during the French Revolution encourages the transference of motifs from the eighteenth to the sixteenth century. But why, then, does Luther oppose image-breaking whereas the city reformers in Strassburg, Zürich and Geneva insist on the removal of those 'idols'? At this point we should remind ourselves that Luther was a nominalist, reared in the *via moderna*.[105] Whereas the *via antiqua* posited a direct and ontological relationship between the portrait and the portrayed, the *via moderna* understood that link as a mental

[102] See von Campenhausen, 'Reformatorisches Selbstbewusstsein und reformatorisches Geschichtsbewusstsein bei Luther 1517–1522', pp. 138, n. 8 and 141f.; *Tradition und Leben*, pp. 328, 329, n. 58 and 332f.

[103] See above, n. 9.

[104] Gottfried W. Locher has provided a unique service in correcting the use of this label for Zwingli. See the bibliography in the *Zwingliana* issue dedicated to Locher, 13 (1971, no. 2), pp. 370–432; here pp. 425–7.

[105] 'Denn ichs mit den bildestürmen nicht halte.' *WA* 26, p. 509, line 12. Cf. Iserloh, 'Bildfeindlichkeit des Nominalismus und Bildersturm im 16. Jahrhundert', pp. 134–5.

relation lacking any basis in the reality outside the observer. Exactly the same applies to the divergent understanding of the nature and essence of the church.

5. Whereas Luther's ecclesiology was 'anti-papal' and in its earliest phases merely 'anti-papalistic',[106] the south German urban Reformation, due to a long history of power struggles between city and bishop, tended toward an 'anti-episcopal' ecclesiology. Luther sought to overcome curial Catholicism with his Reformation. In contrast, members of the patriciate and upper *bourgeoisie*[107] of the south German cities, in the wake of long-standing efforts at communalization, tended to reject the medieval privileged church that confronted them on every hand. The well-to-do artisan circles of 'new masters'[108] even expressed anti-Catholic sentiments.

6. Another phenomenon is most intimately linked to the above considerations. Whereas Luther directed his stream of criticism above all at the theological failure of the curia and prelates who obstructed the proclamation of the Gospel, the south German Reformation's anti-clericalistic orientation did not preclude the rise of its own new and specific form of clericalism. It is significant that Luther was able to distinguish between the papal mass as a sacrifice instituted by an errant church and the legitimate sacrament of the genuine sacrifice of Christ. Obscured and confused with the mass by the medieval church, the true sacrament was nonetheless never completely lost and hence required nothing more than clarification and restoration.[109] But 'south German' theologians more often simply identified the Eucharist with the service of the mass, leading to the radical rejection of the mass[110] and to uncompromising resistance to the priesthood founded on that mass. In the process, the consecrated status of the priesthood was transferred to the congregation assembled for the purpose of partaking in the biblical Lord's Supper.

106 See my essay, 'Et tibi dabo claves', 2, pp. 103f.

107 See the convincing attempt to define the patriciate as the urban leadership elite in the essay by Ingrid Bátori, 'Das Patriziat der deutschen Stadt. Zu den Forschungsergebnissen über das Patriziat besonders der süddeutschen Städte'.

108 See above, Chapter 10.

109 See 'Ein Brief D. Martin Luthers von seinem Buch der Winkelmessen' (1534). *WA* 38, p. 267, lines 23–37. Cf. already in 1528 the treatise *Vom Abendmahl Christi Bekenntnis. WA* 26, p. 508, lines 30–9.

110 A treatise on the Eucharist (ca. 1523–4) by the Swabian pastor Andreas Keller has gone unnoticed due to having been bound with other writings, including works by Luther. It documents the radical rejection of the mass and summarizes in one sentence the sentiment of the Swiss and southern German city Reformation: 'In der Papisten Messe aber sehen wir und hören nichts dann eytel menschen fünd unnd erdichtungen.' *Ein anzeygung, was für gottzlesterung in der Papisten Messz ist . . . Durch Andreas Keller* (n.p., n.d.), fol. B1^{v}.

7. Luther had streamlined his programme as early as 1517 to emphasize the restoration of an authentic proclamation of the Gospel by means of the almost demagogic, rhythmically repeated phrase, *docendi sunt christiani*, in his indulgence theses.[111] The south German Reformation expanded that limited purpose to include a reordering of the community; seeking to realize the horizontal implications of the gospel within the framework of the *bonum commune*. Based on a view of scripture that considered the divine desire to save and God's provision for justice in time and eternity to have been codified for both individual and community in the canon of scripture, this south German, urban renewal of the church overflowed directly into a reconstruction and restructuring of society.

The seven characteristics described above, without which a typology of the urban Reformation would be unable to maintain its validity and comprehensiveness throughout future research, must be enriched with additional nuances from the perspective of social history and only then subjected to a theological evaluation. But this sequence reverses the presently favoured procedure: the solo flight through the pages of the past, whether undertaken by theologian or intellectual, social or constitutional historian, no longer merits licensing by historical science.

The characteristics of the south German urban Reformation fit to a large degree under the rubric of continuity with the late Middle Ages, a situation receiving due attention in current research. During the beginning stages of the Reformation in the cities we observe an intensification and acceleration of pressures for emancipation from spiritual jurisdiction and episcopal competence in general. Once more the *Wegestreit* aids us in our interpretation. The leading south German urban reformers came almost without exception from the *via antiqua* and were thus prepared to integrate the drive for emancipation of the urban community with the cause of the Gospel. Just as in the academic realm the *via antiqua* would have all disciplines culminate in theology, so the *bonum commune* finds its meaning, purpose and realization in the cause of God.

But asserting a continuity between the late Middle Ages and the Reformation remains a half-truth if not conjoined with an equally perceptive awareness of elements of discontinuity. For the urban *bonum commune* was not merely identified generally with the *causa Dei* but on occasion more specifically with the *properly interpreted* Gospel

[111] Ernst Kähler correctly emphasized the rhetorical force of the ninefold repetition of 'Docendi sunt christiani' in theses 42–51. 'Die 95 Thesen. Inhalt und Bedeutung', p. 123.

and ultimately with the consensus of the community of *true* believers. These broader claims on behalf of the *bonum commune* illuminate the limits to continuity that first became generally visible in the urban crisis of the Interim but which can be traced with the aid of hindsight to the Reformation's very beginnings.[112]

The typology sketched here in conclusion underscores the error of assuming that the conflict between the two *viae* ebbed away as the Middle Ages came to an end. The disparagement and renunciation of the view from the ivory tower leads to a distortion of perspective for which no intellectual history, no matter how subtle, and no social history, however prosopographically and quantitatively comprehensive, can compensate. But the account of the seventy years from the late Middle Ages to the Reformation offered in this study should at the same time point out the danger of attempting to interpret the development from the *Wegestreit* to the Reformation as a necessary, closed process or as a predetermined sequence, as if the confessional struggle emerged from the strife between the schools as a tree from its seed. The amalgam of religious, social and political elements that shaped the century of the Reformation in continually varying compounds cannot and should not be standardized, abstracted and traced to an 'ultimate source' with the aid of the academic perspective. For to do so would be to construct a *universale in re* and to revert once more to the *via antiqua*. In the writing of Reformation history, the struggle between *via antiqua* and *via moderna* continues to shape ideology and history to the very present.

[112] See above, p. 238, n. 127.

Student population at German universities 1385–1540

1. Numbers registered at universities 1385–1540* (five year periods)

	Heidelberg	Cologne	Erfurt	Leipzig	Rostock	Greifswald	Freiburg	Ingolstadt	Tübingen	Wittenberg	Frankfurt	Marburg	Total
1385/90	1252	842	—	—	—	—	—	—	—	—	—	—	2094
1391/95	450	352	668	—	—	—	—	—	—	—	—	—	1470
1396/1400	555	362	983	—	—	—	—	—	—	—	—	—	1890
1401/05	784	360	1130	—	—	—	—	—	—	—	—	—	2274
1406/10	457	464	1346	—	—	—	—	—	—	—	—	—	2267
1411/15	426	509	865	1524	—	—	—	—	—	—	—	—	3324
1416/20	775	652	960	1082	—	—	—	—	—	—	—	—	3855
1421/25	625	1132	1127	1404	794	—	—	—	—	—	—	—	5082
1426/30	578	900	990	940	696	—	—	—	—	—	—	—	4110
1431/35	839	911	896	873	791	—	—	—	—	—	—	—	4 310
1436/40	737	1048	1107	883	437	—	—	—	—	—	—	—	4212
1441/45	619	1138	1544	1442	767	—	—	—	—	—	—	—	5510
1446/50	631	840	1077	1023	689	—	—	—	—	—	—	—	4260
1451/55	666	1005	2066	1767	750	—	—	—	—	—	—	—	6254
1456/60	648	1189	2096	1812	745	528	(214)	—	—	—	—	—	7232
1461/65	469	1348	2022	2002	643	205	453	—	—	—	—	—	7142
1466/70	546	1378	1974	1643	820	199	234	—	—	—	—	—	6794
1471/75	534	1332	1350	1359	967	207	246	717	—	—	—	—	6712
1476/80	569	1735	1409	1470	922	204	200	924	585	—	—	—	8018
1481/85	589	1860	1713	1845	818	215	234	1257	544	—	—	—	9075
1486/90	634	2168	1925	2174	374	366	345	1231	464	—	—	—	9681
1491/95	716	2014	1522	1975	730	217	200	885	527	—	—	—	8786
1496/1500	755	2274	1550	1707	909	295	384	829	428	—	—	—	9131
1501/05	576	1674	1314	2118	922	229	588	491	444	(1204)	—	—	9560
1506/10	762	1591	1348	2250	950	178	596	832	625	878	—	—	10536
1511/15	853	1658	1434	2340	1023	220	578	1061	604	1038	736	—	11545
1516/20	707	1340	1537	1770	810	206	469	1207	458	1714	781	—	10999
1521/25	445	918	271	940	398	127	391	523	351	1069	263	—	5696
1526/30	238	436	125	500	(62)	—	221	423	272	716	141	(109)	3243
1531/35	398	347	303	733	126	—	375	441	301	1061	214	401	4700
1536/40	486	495	357	859	287	—	505	633	444	1674	314	516	6590

2. Numbers of students at German universities 1385–1540 (five year averages)

	Heidelberg	Cologne	Erfurt	Leipzig	Rostock	Greifswald	Freiburg	Ingolstadt	Tübingen	Wittenberg	Frankfurt	Marburg	Total
1385/90	438	—	—	—	—	—	—	—	—	—	—	—	438
1391/95	158	123	292	—	—	—	—	—	—	—	—	—	515
1396/1400	194	126	345	—	—	—	—	—	—	—	—	—	662
1401/05	275	126	395	—	—	—	—	—	—	—	—	—	796
1406/10	159	162	471	—	—	—	—	—	—	—	—	—	793
1411/15	144	179	303	380	—	—	—	—	—	—	—	—	1164
1416/20	271	253	336	378	386	—	—	—	—	—	—	—	1249
1421/25	219	396	394	488	278	—	—	—	—	—	—	—	1778
1426/30	207	315	347	329	243	—	—	—	—	—	—	—	1439
1431/35	294	319	314	305	276	—	—	—	—	—	—	—	1509
1436/40	257	368	387	308	152	—	—	—	—	—	—	—	1474
1441/45	217	398	541	500	233	—	—	—	—	—	—	—	1929
1446/50	221	294	376	355	242	—	—	—	—	—	—	—	1491
1451/55	233	352	723	618	438	—	—	—	—	—	—	—	2189
1456/60	228	467	733	634	436	185	(214)	—	—	—	—	—	2531
1461/65	165	498	709	702	226	89	159	—	—	—	—	—	2499
1466/70	191	483	691	576	287	70	82	—	—	—	—	—	2378
1471/75	187	465	473	476	338	74	86	250	—	—	—	—	2349
1476/80	200	607	494	518	322	72	70	324	256	—	—	—	2807
1481/85	207	651	600	644	287	76	82	439	141	—	—	—	3176
1486/90	222	760	674	760	165	128	121	431	163	—	—	—	3388
1491/95	250	705	532	641	255	76	70	310	184	—	—	—	3075
1496/1500	264	796	543	599	318	103	135	291	151	—	—	—	3196
1501/05	201	586	461	740	322	81	207	172	155	527	—	—	3346
1506/10	266	556	473	789	333	63	208	291	219	308	—	—	3687
1511/15	299	581	502	819	359	77	203	371	212	364	257	—	4041
1516/20	247	469	541	705	284	72	170	422	161	600	273	—	3850
1521/25	156	322	95	331	140	44	147	184	123	379	93	—	1994
1526/30	84	152	44	175	37	—	77	149	95	250	49	47	1135
1531/35	140	121	108	256	44	—	131	154	105	371	75	140	1645
1536/40	170	173	124	301	100	—	177	229	156	586	112	182	2307

* Tables taken from statistics compiled in 1904 by F. Eulenburg. His references to the universities at Trier and Mainz, for which confirmed data are not available, have been omitted. See *Die Frequenz der deutschen Universitäten von ihrer Gründung bis zur Gegenwart* (Leipzig, 1904), pp. 54f. Numbers in parentheses are approximations.

Chronological outline

1340 ff.	The campaign against the 'Pelagiani moderni': Thomas Bradwardine (†1349), Archbishop of Canterbury (after 1348), publishes his treatise *De causa Dei*; Gregory of Rimini (†1358 in Vienna), the General of the Order of Augustinian Eremites (after 1357) releases his commentary on the Sentences in Paris in 1344.
1347	William of Occam (†1349 in Munich) writes his treatise *De imperatorum et pontificum potestate*.
1348	Founding at Prague of the first German university.
1365	Founding of the university at Vienna.
1384	Death of Geert Groote, founder of the *devotio moderna*, in Deventer.
1386	Founding of the reformed monastery of Windesheim near Zwolle, the parent house of the Windesheim Congregation that constituted the monastic branch of the *devotio moderna*.
	Elector Reprecht I of the Palatinate founds the university at Heidelberg, appointing Marsilius of Inghen in the Netherlands to organize the new institution; the Heidelberg *via moderna* becomes known as the *via Marsilii* in a manner analogous to the use of the term *via Gregorii* to refer to the *via moderna* in the statutes of the university at Wittenberg in 1508.
1388	Founding of the university at Cologne.
1392	Founding of the university at Erfurt.
1395	Pope Boniface IX confirms the Windesheim Congregation of the Augustinian canons.
1409	Founding of the university at Leipzig.
1414–18	Council of Constance. Among the most influential theologians at the council are the 'modernist' Cardinal Pierre d'Ailly (†1420) and the chancellor of the University of Paris, Jean Gerson (†1429).
1425	Founding of the university at Louvain.
	The university at Cologne resists the decree of the Elector and Archbishop that philosophical and theological instruction follow the *via modernorum*.
1457	Founding of the university at Freiburg im Breisgau.
1460	Founding of the university at Basel; originally instruction in the *via moderna* alone is permitted; after 1465, the *via antiqua* enjoys equal status.

1472 Founding of the university at Ingolstadt.

1474 On 1 March (according to the French calendar of the time, 1473) the King of France issues the decree against the nominalists, triggering an exodus of the most important teachers that especially benefited the German universities.

1476 Pope Sixtus IV approves on 13 November the establishment of a university at Tübingen.

1477 Count Eberhard I of Württemberg (†1496) announces on 3 July the establishment of his territorial university at Tübingen. The universities at Mainz and Uppsala are also founded in this year. Heynlin von Stein (†1496) is called to positions at Tübingen, beginning his duties as professor in the *via antiqua* and preacher at the Collegiate Church in the spring of 1478.

1478 Upheaval in the European banking world: the Pazzi conspiracy in Rome and Florence threatens the Medici banks; Lorenzo the 'Magnificent' decides to close his affiliated banks in Milan and Bruges.

1481 The King of France retracts the decree against the nominalists. Count Eberhard I issues the first university ordinances for Tübingen.

1482 Johannes Reuchlin (†1522), after a brief period as a teacher at Tübingen, undertakes diplomatic efforts for Count Eberhard I. On 14 December, at Münsingen in the Swabian Jura, Württemberg is reunited after a forty year division; Count Eberhard I governs from Stuttgart.

1483 Johannes Nathin (†1529) who later becomes Luther's teacher at the Augustinian Eremite monastery at Erfurt, comes to Tübingen to reform the monastery there and assume its lectorate.

1484 Gabriel Biel, already at least 65 years of age, is appointed to the university at Tübingen. He becomes the founder and leader of the Tübingen *via moderna*.

1487 The first edition of the *Malleus Maleficarum* (Strassburg).

1489 On 13 October, Conrad Summenhart (†1502) in the *via antiqua* and a Biel student, Wendelin Steinbach (†1519), in the *via moderna*, receive the degree of doctor of theology.

1491 Martin Plantsch (†1533), a Biel student, is appointed preacher at the Collegiate Church in Tübingen.

1492 Gabriel Biel retires as a *doctor emeritus* and takes up the office of provost at the St Peter house of the Brethren of the Common Life at the Hermitage near Tübingen. His successor at the university is his student Wendelin Steinbach.

1496 Gregory Lamparter becomes chancellor to the Duke of Württemberg.

1497 Conrad Summenhart, professor of theology at Tübingen, attacks in a disputation the traditional justification for the obligation to pay tithes.

Johann von Staupitz (†1524) is named prior of the Tübingen Augustinian Eremite monastery; he is awarded the doctorate in theology on 7 July 1500.

1499 Johannes Eck (†1543) studies at the Tübingen university until 1501, the year in which he receives the M.A.

1500 Erasmus' *Adagiorum Collectanea* are published in Paris.

Conrad Summenhart's *Septipertitum opus de contractibus* and *Tractatus de decimis* are printed by Ulrich Gran in Hagenau.

1501 Wendelin Steinbach edits Biel's *Collectorium*; the section *De potestate et utilitate monetarum* (*Collect.* IV d. 15, 1. 9) is published separately in 1516.

At Innsbruck Emperor Maximilian (†1519) honours Heinrich Bebel (†1518), the first professor of rhetoric in Tübingen, as *poeta laureatus*.

1502 Founding of the university at Wittenberg.

1503 Elector Frederick the Wise appoints Johann von Staupitz as professor and first dean of the theological faculty at Wittenberg; Staupitz also succeeds Andreas Proles as vicar general of the German Augustinian Observantine congregation.

1505 Ambrosius Blarer (†1564) and Johann Fabri (†1541) of Leutkirch begin studies at Tübingen. Fabri receives the degree of *doctor utriusque iuris* at Freiburg i. Br. in 1510; Blarer earns the M.A. at Tübingen in June 1513.

Martin Plantsch counters the superstitious witchcraft hysteria from the pulpit of the Collegiate Church on the occasion of Tübingen's first witch-burning; the sermons are published in Latin in 1507.

1506 Johannes Amerbach, Basel printer and publisher, issues *Opera omnia Augustini*.

1507 Johannes Caesar and Wolfgang Capito, the later Strassburg reformer, publish Conrad Summenhart's *Commentaria in Summam physice Alberti Magni*.

1510 Johannes Eck is appointed professor of theology at the university at Ingolstadt.

1512 Philip Melanchthon (†1560) arrives at Tübingen.

1513 In Tübingen, Wendelin Steinbach expounds the Epistle to the Galatians.

Johannes Oecolampadius (†1531), the later Basel reformer, studies at Tübingen until 1515 and learns Hebrew and Greek from Johannes Reuchlin in Stuttgart.

1514 Duke Ulrich's taxation policies trigger in early May the 'Poor Conrad' uprising centred in the Rems Valley.

On 8 July Ulrich reaches an accord with the Württemberg estates at Tübingen.

Jacob Fugger commissions the writing of theological opinions to secure the legitimacy of a five per cent rate of interest.

Johannes Eck completes on 15 May the *Tractatus de contractibus*; his *Chrysopassus Praedestinationis* appears in Augsburg the same year.
In October Eck posts his theses on interest-taking in Ingolstadt.
Tübingen is the first German university to be drawn into the controversy over Eck's theses.

1515 In the spring Eck writes the *Tractatus de contractu quinque de centem*; on 12 June at Bologna he holds a disputation on interest-taking.
Meeting since 1512, the reform council Lateran V considers the issue of usury without reaching any clear conclusions.
German humanist circles are responsible for the publication of the satirical and aggressive *Letters of Obscure Men*, aimed especially at the Cologne Dominicans.
On 13–14 November the Battle of Marignano; the Swiss are defeated and withdraw from the Duchy of Milan.

1516 Nicholas Baselius, a monk at Hirsau, publishes the world chronicle of Johannes Vergenhans (Nauclerus), adding a supplement covering recent events.
After five years in Tübingen, Thomas Anshelm transfers his publishing operations to Hagenau.
In Basel the publisher Johannes Froben prints Erasmus' Greek New Testament.
Erasmus commences his new patristic series with a new edition of the works of Jerome, beginning with the letters.
The *devotio moderna* ceases to exist in Württemberg as an institution.
In the Blaubeuren Treaty of 22 October Emperor Maximilian reaches agreement with the recently outlawed (11 October) Duke Ulrich.

1517 Johann von Staupitz's *Libellus de exsecutione aeternae praedestinationis* is printed in Nuremberg.
Wendelin Steinbach concludes his Tübingen lectures on the Epistle to the Hebrews.
31 October: Luther posts his theses at Wittenberg's Castle Church.

1518 In April Luther's Heidelberg Disputation takes place before the council of the chapter general of the Augustinian Order's Saxon province.
Johannes Fabri assumes the office of vicar general for the diocese of Constance, an office he holds until August 1523.
Philip Melanchthon leaves Tübingen for Wittenberg where he presents his inaugural lecture on 29 August.
Late in the year Ulrich Zwingli (†1531) is chosen *Leutpriester* or salaried priest at Zürich's Grossmünster Church.

1519 Troops of the Swabian League drive Duke Ulrich from Württemberg as the territory falls under Habsburg control.
The Leipzig Disputation; Luther's condemnation by the universities at Cologne (30 August), Louvain (7 November), and Paris (15 April 1521).

1520 Luther writes his *Grosser Sermon vom Wucher* which appears in 1524 as part II of his treatise *Von Kaufhandlung und Wucher*.
Accused of heresy, Johann von Staupitz resigns his office as vicar general of the Augustinian Congregation. He retires to Salzburg to become court preacher to Cardinal-Archbishop Lang and abbot of the Benedictine Archabbey St Peter.
In late autumn the Zürich city council issues a mandate declaring holy scripture to be the foundation for preaching and forbidding priests to decry one another as heretics.

1521 On 8 May Emperor Charles V issues the Edict of Worms which is published only with considerable delay in the imperial cities.
Chairs of Hebrew and Greek are established at the university at Tübingen.
Johannes Reuchlin accepts an appointment at Tübingen.

1522 On 9 January Adrian VI of Utrecht (†1523) becomes the first Dutch pope.
An appeal by the Carmelite lector Tilman von Lyn, published early in the year in Strassburg, is the first manifesto for the inception of evangelical preaching in that city.
From 7–9 April an episcopal delegation from Constance undertakes a visitation in Zürich to deal with the recent violation of the Lenten fast.
Zwingli publishes his first Reformation treatise: *Von Erkiesen und Freiheit der Speisen*.
In Rome Fabri publishes his *Opus adversus nova quaedam et a christiana religione prorsus aliena dogmata Martini Lutheri* which he dedicates to Pope Adrian VI; the second edition appears in Leipzig in 1523; the third (Cologne) is titled *Malleus in haeresim Lutheranam*.
On 5 July Ambrosius Blarer leaves the Benedictine monastery at Alpirsbach.
On 15 July the observant Franciscan François Lambert of Avignon (†1530 as professor of theology in Marburg) preaches in the Fraumünster in Zürich; on 16 July he disputes with Zwingli regarding the veneration of the saints.
On 21 July the Zürich city council arranges a disputation with the Zürich mendicants in which Zwingli also participates: this is actually the 'first Zürich disputation'; the mandate for scriptural preaching is renewed; the council unsuccessfully asks the bishop of Constance to call a provincial council to deal with, among other matters, the issue of fasting.

Andreas Carlstadt publishes the treatise *Von Abtuhung der Bilder und das keyn Bedtler unter den Christen seyn sollen.*

At the end of the year Thomas Murner's satire, *Vom grossen Lutherischen Narren,* appears in Strassburg (Grüninger); the city council confiscates the entire edition in December.

1523 On 3 January the papal nuncio F. Chieregati reads 'Adrian's Confession' at the second Nuremberg Imperial Diet.

On 29 January the so-called 'first Zürich disputation' takes place; a delegation from the bishop of Constance participates in this synod.

During the spring agitation against the veneration of saints and images arises in Strassburg.

In May a conference of bishops from Constance, Augsburg and Strassburg is convened in Tübingen for the purpose of countering the momentum of the Reformation.

In late May the Basel city council issues its decree on preaching modelled on the Zürich precedent.

The Württemberg clergy are corporatively bound by an oath of loyalty to the 'Roman church'.

A call is issued on 15 October to a 'second Zürich disputation' over the issues of 'mass and idols' (26–8 October).

Johannes Fabri enters the service of Archduke Ferdinand of Austria as a privy counsellor.

1524 On 15 June the mandate 'dealing with images in the churches' is issued in Zürich.

The Stuttgart territorial diet approves on 15 June the 'extermination of the Lutheran sect'; Tübingen becomes the publishing centre for anti-Reformation writings.

In June Archduke Ferdinand of Austria, the two Bavarian dukes and the south German bishops conclude the Regensburg Union for the execution of the provisions of the Edict of Worms.

On 15 July in Burgos Charles V forbids the German 'national council' that had been called by the third Nuremberg Imperial Diet early that year and scheduled to convene in November at Speyer.

1525 The Reformation Eucharistic controversy: in October and November 1524 Andreas Carlstadt had published his *Dialogus oder ein gesprechsbüchlein von dem grewlichen und abgöttischen Missbrauch des hochwirdigsten sacraments Jesu Christi* in Basel. Luther answers in December 1524–January 1525 with his treatise *Wider die himmlischen Propheten.*

The beginnings of the Anabaptist movement: on 21 January the first baptisms take place in Zürich and Wilhelm Reublin and others are expelled from the city of Zürich. Reublin had been *Leutpriester* at St Alban's in Basel since 1521 and at Witikon near Zürich since the summer of 1522.

May: the peasant uprisings in Württemberg force the transfer of the seat of government from Stuttgart to Tübingen.

An attempt is made to reorganize the university at Tübingen: the two 'ways' guaranteed in the arts faculty statutes are to be eliminated; the attempt fails.

1526 May: Disputation at Baden (Switzerland); the university at Tübingen sends its four theology professors.

June–August: the Imperial Diet at Speyer; a ruling constraining each imperial estate to act 'in a manner such that each may hope and expect to be able to answer before God and emperor for its conduct'.

1527 Founding of the university at Marburg.

1528 In a letter of 4 May to Ambrosius Blarer, Zwingli criticizes Luther's thesis, *Regnum Christi non esse externum*.

On 1 October the Habsburg governor in Stuttgart calls upon the Tübingen theological faculty to take up the question of the Anabaptist movement; in 1530 the first Anabaptists die at the stake in Tübingen.

1529 The Peace of Cambrai temporarily ends the rivalry between Emperor Charles V and King Francis I.

1530 Pope Clement VII crowns Emperor Charles V in Bologna.

1531 Archduke Ferdinand of Austria is elected King of the Romans.

February: the founding of the Schmalkaldic League.

1532 The Peace of Nuremburg: Protestant imperial estates are promised an end to the cases pending against them before the Imperial Supreme Court.

1533 The endowment of a residence named after Martin Plantsch and intended by him to benefit needy students of the Tübingen *via moderna*.

1534 February: the dissolution of the Swabian League.

March–April: Martin Bucer attempts to establish a university in Strassburg; his efforts fail to overcome the resistance of the city council.

May: with the military support of Landgrave Philip of Hesse, Duke Ulrich returns to Württemberg.

29 June: in the Kaaden Accord Duke Ulrich's restoration is granted imperial approval.

Duke Ulrich appoints administrators for the Reformation in Württemberg: for the southern regions, Ambrosius Blarer and for the north, Erhard Schnepf; the Stuttgart Eucharistic Concord is signed by Schnepf and Blarer on 2 August.

11 November: Duke Ulrich's decree for the reorganization of the university at Tübingen under the leadership of Ambrosius Blarer and the Basel Greek professor Simon Grynaeus (called back to Basel late in 1535).

The final separation of the English church from Rome: in the Act of Supremacy Parliament recognizes the king as head of the Church of England.

1535 30 January: new statutes for the university at Tübingen, originally drafted by Blarer and Grynaeus, are issued.
An intentional 'urban' policy of appointments is introduced in Tübingen.
At the request of Duke Ulrich, Pierre Toussain (†1573) reforms the County of Montbéliard, a Württemberg enclave in modern-day France.

1536 In May Luther and Bucer succeed in bridging the gap between the south German city Reformation and the Wittenberg Reformation by means of their agreement on the Eucharist.

1537 On 11 April Duke Ulrich names, on Melanchthon's advice, Joachim Camerarius (†1574) and Johannes Brenz (†1570) to succeed Blarer in the reorganization of the Tübingen university.

1538 Calvin is forced to leave Geneva.
Ambrosius Blarer is dismissed by Duke Ulrich.

1539 July: Bucer tries in vain to bring the university at Basel under ecclesiastical control.

1543 Andreas Osiander (†1552), a disciple of Luther in Nuremberg, publishes the *magnum opus* of Copernicus (†1543), *De revolutionibus orbium*, together with Osiander's own preface.

1547 The 'armoured' Imperial Diet at Augsburg lasts until 30 June 1548. During the Interim that extends to the Religious Peace of Augsburg in 1555 intensive efforts are made to recatholicize Germany.

1545–7 The first period of the Council of Trent (completed in 1563).

*Bibliography**

Primary sources

Acta capituli Windeshemensis. Acta van de Kapittelvergaderingen der Congregatie van Windesheim. Edited by S. van der Woude. Kerkhistorische Studien, 4. 's-Gravenhage, 1953.

Acta Reformationis Catholicae ecclesiam Germaniae concernentia saeculi XVI. Die Reformverhandlungen des deutschen Episkopats von 1520 bis 1570, vol. 1: *1520–1532*. Edited by G. Pfeilschifter. Regensburg, 1959.

Acta Sanctorum, vol. 7 (Martii, I). Compiled by J. Bollandus, edited by G. Henschenius, D. Papebroch. Antwerp, 1684.

Acta synodi nationalis in nomine Domini nostri Iesu Christi, authoritate illustr. et praepotentum DD. Ordinum Generalium Foederati Belgii provinciarum Dordrechti habitae anno 1618 et 1619. Dordrecht, 1620.

Agricola, Rudolph, *Longe elegantissima oratio de nativitate Christi Heydelbergae dicta, anno a Christo nato MCCCCLXXXVI*. Tübingen, 1527.

Alberts, W. J., Hulshoff, A. L., eds. *Het Frensweger handschrift betreffende de geschiedenis van de moderne devotie*. Groningen, 1958.

Albertus Magnus. *Opera omnia*, vol. 38. Edited by A. Borgnet. Paris: Vivès, 1899.

Alexandri de Hales Summa Theologica, vol. 4. Edited by Pacifico M. Perantoni. Quaracchi, 1948.

Altenstaig, Johannes. *Vocabularius Theologie* . . . Hagenau: Heinrich Gran, 1517.

Alva y Astorga, Pedro de. *Radii solis zeli seraphici coeli veritatis pro immaculatae conceptionis mysterio Virginis Mariae*. Louvain, 1666.

Annalen und Akten der Brüder des gemeinsamen Lebens im Lüchtenhofe zu Hildesheim. Edited by Richard Doebner. Quellen und Darstellungen zur Geschichte Niedersachsens, 9. Hannover, Leipzig, 1903.

Angelus Carleti de Clavasio. *Summa angelica de casibus conscientiae*. Lyon: Jacobus Huguetan, 1516.

Antoninus of Florence. *Summa Theologica*, vol. 2. Verona, 1740: reprinted Graz, 1959.

Antonius de Butrio. *In quinque libros Decretalium commentaria*. Lyon, 1532.

Aristotelis opera cum Averrois commentariis. 9 vols. and 3 suppl. vols. Venice, 1562–74; reprinted Frankfurt a.M., 1962.

* Works included in the list of abbreviations are not cited here.

Aristotelis opera. 5 vols. Edited by Immanuel Bekker. Berlin, 1831–70.

Auctarium chartularii Universitatis Parisiensis, vol. 6: *Liber receptorum nationis Anglicanae (Alemanniae) in Universitate Parisiensi*, tomus unicus: *Liber receptorum nationis Alemanniae ab anno 1425 ad annum 1494*. Edited by A. L. Gabriel, G. C. Boyce. Paris, 1964.

Augustine. *Librorum divi Aurelii Augustini*, partes I–IX. Basel: Amerbach, [1494]–1506. *See also* Westphal, Joachim, *below*.

Baudry, Léon, ed. *La querelle des futurs contingents (Louvain 1465–1475). Textes inédits*. Études de philosophie médiévale, 38. Paris, 1950.

Bebel, Heinrich. *Facetien. Drei Bücher*. Edited by Gustav Bebermeyer. Bibliothek des Literarischen Vereins in Stuttgart, 276. Leipzig, 1931; reprinted Hildesheim, 1967.

Die Bekenntnisschriften der evangelisch-lutherischen Kirche. Herausgegeben im Gedenkjahr der Augsburgischen Konfession 1930. 5th edn, Göttingen, 1963.

Biblia sacra cum glossis, Interlineari et Ordinaria, Nicolai Lyrani Postilla, vols. 2 and 5. Venice, 1588. *See also* Nicholaus de Lyra, *below*.

Biel, Gabriel. *Epithoma expositionis Canonis misse*. Tübingen: Johannes Otmar, [1499].

Canonis misse expositio, vols. 1–4. Edited by H. A. Oberman, W. J. Courtenay. VIEG, 31–4. Wiesbaden, 1963–7.

Epitome et collectorium ex Occamo circa quatuor sententiarum Libros. Tübingen, 1501; Basel, 1508; Basel edn reprinted Frankfurt a.M., 1965.

Collectorium circa quattuor libros Sententiarum. Edited by W. Werbeck, U. Hofmann. Tübingen, 1973ff.

Tractatus de potestate et utilitate monetarum. Edited by J. Adler. Oppenheim, [ca. 1516].

Treatise on the Power and the Utility of Moneys, by Master Gabriel Biel of Speyer. Edited and translated by Robert B. Burke. Philadelphia, Oxford, 1930. *See also* Steinbach *and* Landeen, *below*.

Ambrosius Blaurer's des schwäbischen Reformators Leben und Schriften. Edited by Theodor Pressel. Stuttgart, 1861.

S. Bonaventurae Opera omnia, vols. 8 and 13. Edited by A. C. Peltier. Paris, 1866, 1868.

Bossert, Gustav and Bossert, Gustav, Jr, eds. *Quellen zur Geschichte der Wiedertäufer*, vol. 1: *Herzogtum Württemberg*. QFRG 13. Leipzig, 1930.

Brackert, Helmut, compiler, 'Daten und Materialien zur Hexenverfolgung.' In *Aus der Zeit der Verzweiflung. Zur Genese und Aktualität des Hexenbildes*, pp. 313–440. Edited by Gabriele Becker, Silvia Bovenschen, Helmut Brackert *et al*. Frankfurt a.M., 1977.

Bradwardine, Thomas. *De causa Dei contra Pelagium et de virtute causarum ad suos Mertonenses libri tres*. Edited by H. Savilius. London, 1618; reprinted Frankfurt a.M., 1964.

Sebastian Brants Narrenschiff. Edited by Friedrich Zarncke. Leipzig, 1854.

The Ship of Fools by Sebastian Brant. Translated by E. H. Zeydel. New York, 1944, 1962.

Johannes Brenz, Frühschriften, vol. 2. Edited by Martin Brecht, Gerhard Schäfer, Frieda Wolf. Johannes Brenz, Werke. Eine Studienausgabe. Tübingen, 1974.

Anecdota Brentiana. Ungerdruckte Briefe und Bedenken von Johannes Brenz. Edited by Theodor Pressel. Tübingen, 1868.

Kommentar zum Briefe des Apostels Paulus an die Epheser. Nach der Handschrift der Vaticana, Cod. Pal. lat. 1836. Edited by W. Köhler. Abhandlungen der Heidelberger Akademie der Wissenschaften, phil.-hist. Klasse, 10. Heidelberg, 1935.

Martin Bucers Deutsche Schriften, vol. 2: *Schriften der Jahre 1524–1528;* vol. 4: *Zur auswärtigen Wirksamkeit 1528–1533.* Edited by R. Stupperich. Martini Buceri Opera omnia, I, vols. 2 and 4. Gütersloh, Paris, 1962, 1975.

Martini Buceri Opera Latina, vol. 15: *De regno Christi libri duo.* Edited by F. Wendel. Martini Buceri Opera omnia, II, vol. 15. Gütersloh, Paris, 1955. *See also* Pollet, *below.*

Heinrich Bullingers Reformationsgeschichte nach dem Autographon, vol. 1. Edited by J. H. Hottinger, H. H. Vögeli. Frauenfeld, 1838.

Busche, Hermann von dem. *Dictata pro nominariis collecta ex Proverbiis et Ecclesiastico.* n.p., 1518.

Joannis Calvini Opera Selecta, vol. 4. Edited by Peter Barth, Wilhelm Niesel. 2nd edn, Munich, 1959.

Predigten über das 2. Buch Samuelis. Edited by H. Rückert. Supplementa Calviniana, vol. 1. Neukirchen, 1936–61.

Joachimi Camerarii De vita Philippi Melanchthonis narratio. Edited by Georg Theodor Strobel. Halle a.d. Saale, 1777.

Capreolus, Johannes. *Defensiones theologiae divi Thomae Aquinatis,* vol. 4. Edited by C. Paban, Th. Pègues. Tours, 1903; reprinted Frankfurt a.M., 1967.

Carlstadt, Andreas Bodenstein von. *Von Abtuhung der Bilder und das keyn Bedtler unther den Christen seyn sollen, 1522, und die Wittenberger Beutelordnung.* Edited by H. Lietzmann. Kleine Texte für theologische und philologische Vorlesungen und Übungen, 74. Bonn, 1911.

Karlstadts Schriften aus den Jahren 1523–25, vols. 1 and 2. Edited by Erich Hertzsch. Neudrucke deutscher Literaturwerke des 16. und 17. Jahrhunderts, 325. Halle a.d. Saale, 1956–7.

Celtis, Conrad. *Der Briefwechsel des Konrad Celtis.* Edited by Hans Rupprich. Veröffentlichungen der Kommission zur Erforschung der Geschichte der Reformation und Gegenreformation, Humanistenbriefe, 3. Munich, 1934.

Concilium Constantiense. Acta et decreta. Hagenau: Heinrich Gran for Johann Ryman, 1500.

Concilium Tridentinum. Diariorum, actorum, epistularum, tractatuum nova collectio, vol. 4: *Actorum pars prima: Monumenta concilium praecedentia, trium priorum sessionum acta.* Edited by S. Ehses. Freiburg i.Br., 1904.

Constitutiones Fratrum Heremitarum sancti Augustini ad apostolicorum priuilegiorum forman pro Reformatione Alemanie. [Nürnberg, 1504.]

Contarini, Gasparo. *Opera*. Paris, 1571; reprinted Farnborough, 1968.

Nicolai Copernici Thorunensis De revolutionibus orbium caelestium libri sex. Edited by F. Zeller and Karl Zeller. Nikolaus Kopernikus, Gesamtausgabe, vol. 2. Munich, 1949.

Cranevelt, Francisco, *see* Vocht, Henry de, *below*.

Crusius, Martin. *Annales Suevici sive Chronica rerum gestarum antiquissimae et inclytae Suevicae gentis*. 3 vols. Frankfurt a.M. 1595–6. *See also* Moser, *below*.

Denzinger, Heinrich, Schönmetzer, Adolf, eds. *Enchiridion Symbolorum, Definitionum et Declarationum de Rebus Fidei et Morum*. 34th edn, Freiburg i.Br., 1967. The numbers in parentheses refer to earlier editions.

Deutsche Reichstagsakten unter Kaiser Karl V, vols. 3 and 4. Compiled by A. Wrede. Deutsche Reichstagsakten, Jüngere Reihe, 3 and 4. Gotha, 1901, 1905.

Domenica de' Domenichi, *see* Smolinsky, *below*.

Dumbar, G. *Analecta, seu vetera aliquot scripta inedita ab ipso publici juris facta*, vol. 1. Deventer, 1719.

Joannis Duns Scoti Opera omnia, vol. 7, pt. 2, vols. 9 and 10. Edited by Lucas Wadding. Lyon, 1639; reprinted Hildesheim, 1968.

Diehl, Wilhelm, ed. *Die Schulordnungen des Grossherzogtums Hessen*, vol. 1. Monumenta Germaniae Paedagogica, 27. Berlin, 1903.

Du Plessis d'Argentré, Charles. *Collectio judiciorum de novis erroribus, qui ab initio XII saeculi . . . usque ad annum 1632 in Ecclesia proscripti sunt et notati*, vol. 1, pt 2. Paris, 1728.

Johann Eberlin von Günzburg, Ausgewählte Schriften, vol. 1. Edited by Ludwig Enders. Flugschriften aus der Reformationszeit, 11 = Neudrucke deutscher Literaturwerke des 16. und 17. Jahrhunderts, 139–41. Halle a.d. Saale, 1896.

Eck, Johannes. *Chrysopassus praedestinationis*. Augsburg, 1514.

Orationes tres non inelegantes. Augsburg: Johann Miller, 31 October 1515.

Disputatio Viennae Pannoniae habita (1517). Edited by Th. Virnich. CCath 6. Münster i.W., 1923.

Defensio contra amarulentas D. Andreae Bodenstein Carolstatini invectiones (1518). Edited by J. Greving. CCath 1. Münster i.W., 1919.

Explanatio psalmi vigesimi (1538). Edited by B. Walde. CCath 13. Münster i.W., 1928.

In primum librum Sententiarum annotatiunculae D. Iohanne Eckio praelectore anno ab Christo nato 1542, per dies caniculares, quos alioqui a studiis gravioribus feriari solebat. Edited by Walter L. Moore, Jr. SMRT 13. Leiden, 1976.

Eckermann, Willigis. *Der Physikkommentar Hugolins von Orvieto OESA*. Spätmittelalter und Reformation. Texte und Untersuchungen, 5. Berlin, New York, 1972.

Meister Eckhart, Die Deutschen Werke, vol. 5. Edited by Josef Quint. Stuttgart, 1963.

Erasmus, Desiderius. *Opus Epistolarum Des. Erasmi Roterodami*. 12 vols. Edited by P. S. Allen. Oxford, 1906–58.

The Correspondence of Erasmus, vol. 1: *Letters 1–141 (1484–1500)*. Translated by R. A. B. Mynors, D. F. S. Thompson, annotated by W. K. Ferguson. Collected Works of Erasmus, 1. Toronto, 1974.

Erasmus von Rotterdam, Dialogus cui titulus Ciceronianus sive *De optimo dicendi genere. Der Ciceronianer* oder *Der beste Stil. Ein Dialog – Adagiorum chiliades (Adagia selecta). Mehrere tausend Sprichwörter und sprichwörtliche Redensarten (Auswahl).* Translated and edited by Theresia Payr. Erasmus von Rotterdam, Ausgewählte Schriften (Latin and German), vol. 7. Darmstadt, 1972.

De libero arbitrio διατριβὴ sive collatio. Edited by J. von Walter. Quellenschriften zur Geschichte des Protestantismus, 8. Leipzig, 1910.

Fabri, Johann. *Ain warlich underrichtung, wie es zů Zürch auff den neünundtzweintzigsten tag des monats Januarii nechstverschynen ergangen sey*. n.p., 1523. (Incomplete copy in the Zürich Zentralbibliothek, Zw 202.)

Ein warlich underrichtung, wie es zu Zürch by dem Zwinglin uff den nün undzwentzigsten tag des monats Januarii nest verschinen ergangen sey. n.p., 1523. (Copy in the Zürich Zentralbibliothek, Zw 205.)

Malleus in haeresim Lutheranam (1524). Edited by A. Naegele. Pt 1 = CCath 23/4. Pt 2 (Suppl. by F. Heyer) = CCath 25/6. Münster i.W., 1941, 1952.

Fast, Heinold, ed. *Quellen zur Geschichte der Täufer in der Schweiz*, vol. 2: *Ostschweiz*. Zürich, 1973.

Frensweger handschrift, see Alberts, *above*.

Friedensburg, Walter, ed., *Urkundenbuch der Universität Wittenberg*, pt 1. Geschichtsquellen der Provinz Sachsen und des Freistaates Anhalt, Neue Reihe, 3. Magdeburg, 1926.

Gagliardi, Ernst. 'Zwinglis Predigt wider die Pensionen. 5. März 1525.' *Zwingliana* 3 (1918, 1): 337–47.

M. Wesseli Gansfortii Groningensis rarae et reconditae doctrine viri, qui olim Lux Mundi vulgo dictus fuit, opera . . . omnia. Groningen, 1614; reprinted, Monumenta Humanistica Belgica, 1. Nieuwkoop, 1966.

Gellius, Aulus. *A. Gellii Noctes Atticae*, vol. 2: (Libri XI–XX). Edited by P. K. Marshall. Scriptorum classicorum bibliotheca Oxoniensis. Oxford, 1968.

The Attic Nights, vol. 2. Translated by John C. Rolfe. Loeb Classical Library. Cambridge, Mass., 1960–1.

Gerson, Jean. *Opera omnia*, vol. 4. Cologne: Johannes Koelhoeff, 1484.

Joannis Gersonii Opera omnia . . ., vols. 1 and 3. Edited by L. Ellies Du Pin. Antwerp, 1706.

Jean Gerson, Oeuvres complètes, vols. 3, 5 and 10. Edited by Palémon Glorieux. Paris, 1962, 1963, 1973.

Ioannes Carlerii de Gerson de Mystica Theologia. Edited by André Combes. Thesaurus Mundi. Lucca, 1958.

Jean Gerson, Selections from A Deo exivit, Contra curiositatem studentium and De mystica theologia speculativa (Latin and English). Edited and translated by Steven E. Ozment. Textus minores, 38. Leiden, 1969.

Gess, Felician, ed. *Akten und Briefe zur Kirchenpolitik Herzog Georgs von Sachsen,* vol. 2: *1525–1527*. Schriften der Königlichen Sächsischen Kommission für Geschichte, 22. Leipzig, Berlin, 1917.

Groote, Geert. *Gerardi Magni epistolae*. Edited by W. Mulder. Antwerp, 1933.

Gerardo Groote, Il trattato 'De quattuor generibus meditabilium.' Edited by Ilario Tolomio. Università di Padova, Pubblicazioni dell' istituto di storia della filosofia e del centro per ricerche di filosofia medioevale, N.S., 18, Padua, 1975.

Grotius, Hugh, *Excerpta ex Tragoediis et Comoediis Graecis, tum quae exstant, tum quae perierunt*. Paris, 1626.

Grynaeus, Simon. *Simonis Grynaei, clarissimi quondam Academiae Basiliensis theologi ac philologi Epistolae. Accedit index auctorum eiusdem Grynaei opera et studio editorum*. Edited by Wilhelm Th. Streuber. Basel, 1847.

Hansen, Joseph. *Quellen und Untersuchungen zur Geschichte des Hexenwahns und der Hexenverfolgung im Mittelalter*. Bonn, 1901; reprinted Hildesheim, 1963.

Henricus de Zomeren (Someren). *Epithoma prime partis dyalogi G. ockam que intitulatur de hereticis . . . Recollectum per magistrum Henricum de Zoemeren in Wienna Austrie*. Louvain, 1481.

Herding, Otto, ed. *Jakob Wimpfelings Adolescentia, Jacobi Wimpfelingi Opera selecta*, vol. 1. Munich, 1965.

Hermelink, Heinrich, ed. *Die Matrikeln der Universität Tübingen*, vol. 1: *Die Matrikeln von 1477–1600*. Stuttgart, 1906.

Herminjard, A.-L., ed. *Correspondance des Réformateurs dans les pays de langue française*, vol. 1: *1512–1526*; vol. 9: *1543–1544*. Geneva, Paris, 1866, 1897; reprinted Nieuwkoop, 1965, 1966.

Herrmann, F[ritz]. 'Miscellen zur Reformationsgeschichte. Aus Mainzer Akten.' *ZKG* 23 (1902): 263–8.

Heynlin of Stein, Johann. *Resolutorium dubiorum circa celebrationem missarum occurrentium per venerabilem patrem dominum Johannem de Lapide, doctorem, theologum Parisiensem ordinis Cartusiensis, ex sacrorum canonum probatorumque doctorum sententiis diligenter collectum*. Basel: J. Froben, 1492.

Stephan Hoest, Reden und Briefe (Latin and German), *Quellen zur Geschichte der Scholastik und des Humanismus im 15. Jahrhundert*. Edited by Frank Baron. Humanistische Bibliothek, 2 and 3. Munich, 1971.

Holcot, Robert, *Super libros Sapientiae*. Hagenau, 1494.

Hoogstraten, Jacob von, *see* Jacob of Hoogstraten, *below*.

Hugo de S. Caro Cardinalis. *Postilla utriusque Testamenti*, vol. 6. Basel, 1504.

Hugolin of Orvieto, *see* Eckermann, Willigis, *above*.

Innocent IV. *Apparatus super quinque libros Decretalium*. Venice, 1491.

Jacob of Hoogstraten. *Contra Lutheranos*. In *Primitiae pontificiae theologorum neerlandicorum Disputationes contra Lutherum*, pp. 537–620. Edited by F. Pijper. (Also appeared as Bibliotheca Reformatoria Neerlandica, 3.) The Hague, 's-Gravenhage, 1905.

John of Naples. *F. Ioannis de Neapoli O.P. Quaestiones variae, Parisiis disputatae*. Edited by Dominicus Gravina. Naples, 1618; reprinted Ridgewood, N.J., 1966.

'Quaestio magistri Johannis de Neapoli O.Pr.: *Utrum licite* possit doceri Parisius doctrina fratris Thome quantum ad omnes conclusiones eius.' Edited by Carl Jellouschek. *Xenia Thomistica* 3 (Rome, 1925): 73–104.

Judas Nazarei, *see* Kück, Eduard, *below*.

Kapp, Johann Erhard, ed. *Kleine Nachlese einiger, grössten Theils noch ungedruckter, und sonderlich zur Erläuterung der Reformations-Geschichte nützlicher Urkunden*. Dritter Theil. Leipzig, 1730.

Karlstadt, Andreas, *see* Carlstadt, Andreas Bodenstein von, *above*.

Keller, Andreas. *Ein anzeygung, was für gottzlesterung in der Papisten Messz ist*. n.p., [ca. 1523–4].

Köhler, Walther. *Das Buch der Reformation Huldrych Zwinglis von ihm selbst und gleichzeitigen Quellen erzählt*. Munich, 1926.

Köstlin, Julius, ed. *Die Baccalaurei und Magistri der Wittenberger Philosophischen Fakultät 1503–1517. Aus der Fakultätsmatrikel veröffentlicht*. Osterprogramm der Universität Halle-Wittenberg, 1887. Halle a.d. Saale, 1887.

Kolde, Theodor, ed. *Analecta Lutherana. Briefe und Actenstücke zur Geschichte Luthers. Zugleich ein Supplement zu den bisherigen Sammlungen seines Briefwechsels*. Gotha, 1883.

Kors, Alan C., Peters, Edward, eds. *Witchcraft in Europe 1100–1700. A Documentary History*. Philadelphia, 1972.

Korth, Leonard, ed. 'Die ältesten Gutachten über die Brüderschaft des gemeinsamen Lebens.' *Mittheilungen aus dem Stadtarchiv von Köln* 5 (1888): 1–27.

Kück, Eduard, ed. *Judas Nazarei, Vom alten und neuen Gott, Glauben und Lehre (1521)*. Neudrucke deutscher Literaturwerke des 16. und 17. Jahrhunderts, 142–143 = Flugschriften aus der Reformationszeit, 12. Halle a.d. Saale, 1896.

Landeen, W. M. 'Biel's Tractate on the Common Life' ('Tractatus Magistri Gabrielis Byell de communi vita clericorum'). *Research Studies of Washington State University* 28 (1960): 79–95.

Lang, Johannes. *Epistolae Langianae*. Edited by Joachim K. F. Knaake, Hermann Hering. In Programm Halle a.d. Saale, 1886, pp. 1–12.

Laube, Adolf, Seiffert, Hans Werner, *et al.*, eds. *Flugschriften der Bauernkriegszeit*. Berlin, 1975.

Leib, Chilian. *Historiarum sui temporis ab anno MDII ad annum MDXLVIIII annales*, vol. 3: *(1513–1521)*. In *Beyträge zur Geschichte und Literatur, vorzüglich aus den Schätzen der pfalzbaierischen Centralbibliothek zu München*, vol. 7. Edited by J. Ch. von Aretin. Munich, 1806.

Lenz, Max, ed. *Briefwechsel Landgraf Philipp's des Grossmüthigen von Hessen mit Bucer*, vol. 1. Publicationen aus den k. preussischen Staatsarchiven, 5. Leipzig, 1880.

Lefèvre d'Étaples, Jacques. *The Prefatory Epistles of Jacques Lefèvre d'Étaples and Related Texts*. Edited by Eugene F. Rice, Jr. New York, London, 1972.

Löscher, Valentin Ernst. *Vollständige Reformations-Acta und Documenta*, vol. 2: *Auf das Jahr 1518*. Leipzig, 1723.

Ludolf of Saxony. *Vita Iesu Christi*. Antwerp, 1618.

D. Martini Lutheri Opera Latina, Varii Argumenti, vol. 2, Frankfurt, Erlangen, 1865.

Magnum Bullarium Romanum a Beato Leone Magno usque ad Benedictum XIV, vol. 1. Luxemburg, 1742.

Mandel, Hermann, ed. *Theologia Deutsch*. Quellenschriften zur Geschichte des Protestantismus, 7. Leipzig, 1908.

Mansi, Joannes Dominicus, ed. *Sacrorum conciliorum nova et amplissima collectio*, vol. 22: *1116–1225*. Venice, 1778.

Melanchthons Werke in Auswahl, vol. 3: *Humanistische Schriften*. Edited by R. Münberger. Gütersloh, 1961. Vol. 7, pt. 1: *Ausgewählte Briefe 1517–1526*. Edited by H. Volz. Gütersloh, 1971.

Melanchthons Briefwechsel, vol. 1: *1510–1528*. Edited by Otto Clemen. Supplementa Melanchthoniana, Abt. 6, vol. 1. Leipzig, 1926; reprinted Frankfurt a.M., 1968.

Menandri Sententiae – Comparatio Menandri et Philistionis. Edited by Siegfried Jaekel. Bibliotheca scriptorum Graecorum et Romanorum Teubneriana, Leipzig, 1964.

Menanders Denksprüche dreisprachig. Die griechischen und lateinischen Texte neu herausgegeben und in deutsche Zweizeiler übertragen. Edited by Richard Walther. Munich, 1967.

Molina, Luis de. *Liberi arbitrii cum gratiae donis, divina praescientia, providentia, praedestinatione et reprobatione concordia*. Edited by J. Rabeneck. Oña, Madrid, 1953.

Moser, Johann Jacob. *Martin Crusii Schwäbische Chronick,* aus dem Lateinischen erstmals übersetzt und mit einer Continuation vom Jahr 1596 bis 1733 versehen, vol. 2. Frankfurt a.M., 1733.

Thomas Müntzer, Schriften und Briefe, Kritische Gesamtausgabe. Edited by Günther Franz. QFRG 33. Gütersloh, 1968.

Muralt, Leonhard von, Schmid, Walter, eds. *Quellen zur Geschichte der Täufer in der Schweiz*, vol. 1: *Zürich*. Zürich, 1952.

Murner, Thomas. *Thomas Murners Deutsche Schriften*, vol. 2: *Die Narrenbeschwörung*. Edited by Meier Spanier. Kritische Gesamtausgaben elsässischer Schriftsteller des Mittelalters und der Reformationszeit. Berlin, Leipzig, 1926.

Nicolaus de Lyra. *Postilla super totam Bibliam*, vol. 3. Strassburg, 1492; reprinted Frankfurt a.M., 1971. *See also* Biblia, *above*.

Nicolaus de Tudeschis (Panormitanus). *Lectura domini Nicolai Abbatis Siculi super tertio libro Decretalium*. Basel, 1488.

Occam, William of. *Opera plurima*, vol. 2. Lyon, 1496; reprinted London, 1962.

Guielmi Ockham, Tractatus de imperatorum et pontificum potestate. Edited by W. Mulder. In *Archivum Franciscanum Historicum* 16 (1923): 469–92; 17 (1924): 72–97.

Guillelmi de Ockham Opera politica, vols. 2 and 3. Edited by H. S. Offler. Manchester, 1963 and 1956.

Opus Decretalium cum summariis additis singulis decretalibus. Venice, 1491.

Opus Epistolarum divi Hieronymi Stridonensis cum scholiis Erasmi. Paris, 1533.

Nicole Oresme, De proportionibus proportionum and Ad pauca respicientes (Latin and English). Edited by Edward Grant. Madison, London, 1966.

Nicole Oresme and the Medieval Geometry of Qualities and Motions. A Treatise on the Uniformity and Difformity of Intensities Known as 'Tractatus de configurationibus qualitatum et motuum' (Latin and English). Edited by Marshall Clagett. Madison, London, 1968.

Andreas Osiander d. Ä., Gesamtausgabe, vol. 1: *Schriften und Briefe 1522 bis März 1525.* Edited by Gerhard Müller, Gottfried Seebass. Gütersloh, 1975.

Paltz, Johann von. *Supplementum Coelifodinae.* Erfurt, 1504.

Panormitanus, *see* Nicolaus de Tudeschis, *above.*

Pellikan, Conrad. *Das Chronikon des Konrad Pellikan.* Zur vierten Säkularfeier der Universität Tübingen. Edited by B. Riggenbach. Basel, 1877.

Perez of Valencia, Jacobus. *Centum ac quinquaginta psalmi Davidici cum diligentissima etiam titulorum expositione.* Lyon: Stephan Gueynard, 1518.

Peter of Spain (Petrus Hispanus Portugalensis), Tractatus, called afterwards Summule logicales. Edited by L. M. de Rijk. Philosophical Texts and Studies, 22. Assen, 1972.

Petrus de Palude. *Scriptum in quartum Sententiarum.* Venice, 1493.

Pfeiffer, Gerhard, ed. *Quellen zur Nürnberger Reformationsgeschichte. Von der Duldung liturgischer Änderungen bis zur Ausübung des Kirchenregiments durch den Rat (Juni 1524–Juni 1525).* Einzelarbeiten aus der Kirchengeschichte Bayerns, 45. Nürnberg, 1968.

Pierre d'Ailly (Petrus de Alliaco). *Tractatus et Sermones.* Strassburg, 1490; reprinted Frankfurt a.M., 1971.

Planitz, Hans von der, *see* Wülcker, *below.*

Plantsch, Martin. *Opusculum de sagis maleficis.* Pforzheim: Thomas Anshelm, 1507.

Plutarch. 'On Borrowing.' In *Plutarch's Moralia,* vol. 10, pp. 315–39. Translated by Harold N. Fowler. Loeb Classical Library. Cambridge, Mass., 1960.

Pollet, J. V. *Martin Bucer. Études sur la correspondance. Avec de nombreux textes inédits,* vol. 2. Paris, 1962.

Die Protokolle des Mainzer Domkapitels, vol. 3: *Die Protokolle aus der Zeit des Erzbischofs Albrecht von Brandenburg 1514–1545.* Edited by F. Herrmann. Arbeiten der Historischen Kommission für den Volksstaat Hessen, [3]. Paderborn, 1932.

Rauch, Moriz von, ed. *Urkundenbuch der Stadt Heilbronn,* vol. 4: *Von 1525 bis zum Nürnberger Religionsfrieden im Jahr 1532.* Württembergische Geschichtsquellen, 20. Stuttgart, 1922.

Rauscher, Julius, ed. *Württembergische Visitationsakten,* vol. 1: (*1534*) *1536–1540. Enthaltend die Ämter Stuttgart, Nürtingen, Tübingen, Herrenberg, Wildberg, Urach, Blaubeuren. Göppingen, Schorndorf, Kirchheim, Heidenheim.* Württembergische Geschichtsquellen, 22. Stuttgart, 1932.

Reuchlin, Johannes. *Johann Reuchlins Briefwechsel.* Edited by Ludwig Geiger.

Bibliothek des Literarischen Vereins, 126. Stuttgart, 1875; reprinted Hildesheim, 1962.

De rudimentis hebraicis libri III. Pforzheim: Thomas Anshelm, 1506; reprinted Hildesheim, New York, 1974.

Reuss, Rod., ed. 'Les Collectanées de Daniel Specklin' (continuation and conclusion). *Mittheilungen der Gesellschaft für Erhaltung der geschichtlichen Denkmäler im Elsass*, 2nd series, 14 (1889): 1–178; 201–404.

Rhenanus, Beatus. *Briefwechsel des Beatus Rhenanus*. Edited by Adalbert Horawitz, Karl Hartfelder. Leipzig, 1886; reprinted Hildesheim, 1966.

Richardus de Mediavilla. *Super quatuor libros Sententiarum Petri Lombardi quaestiones subtilissimae*, vol. 4. Brixen, 1591; reprinted Frankfurt a.M., 1963.

Ryff, Fridolin. 'Die Chronik des Fridolin Ryff 1514–1541, mit der Fortsetzung des Peter Ryff 1543–1585.' Edited by W. Vischer, A. Stern. In *Basler Chroniken*, vol. 1, pp. 1–229. Leipzig, 1872.

Schade, Oskar, ed. *Satiren und Pasquille aus der Reformationszeit*, vols. 1–3. 2nd edn, Hannover, 1863; reprinted Hildesheim, 1966.

Scheel, Otto, ed. *Dokumente zu Luthers Entwicklung (bis 1519)*. Sammlung ausgewählter kirchen- und dogmengeschichtlicher Quellenschriften, N.S., 2. 2nd, rev. edn, Tübingen, 1929.

Christoph Scheurl's Briefbuch. Ein Beitrag zur Geschichte der Reformation und ihrer Zeit, vol. 1: *Briefe von 1505–1516*. Edited by F. von Soden, J. K. F. Knaake. Potsdam, 1867; reprinted Aalen, 1962.

Scholz, Richard, ed. *Unbekannte kirchenpolitische Streitschriften aus der Zeit Ludwigs des Bayern (1327–1354)*, vol. 2: *Texte*. Bibliothek des Königlichen Preussischen Historischen Instituts in Rom, 10. Rome, 1914.

Smolinsky, Heribert, ed. *Domenico de' Domenichi und seine Schrift 'De potestate pape et termino eius.'* Vorreformationsgeschichtliche Forschungen, 17. Münster i.W., 1976.

Specklin, Daniel, *see* Reuss, *above*.

Johann von Staupitzens sämmtliche Werke, vol. 1: *Deutsche Schriften*. Edited by J. K. F. Knaake. Potsdam, 1867.

Staupitz, Tübinger Predigten. Edited by Georg Buchwald, Ernst Wolf. QFRG 8. Leipzig, 1927; reprinted New York, 1971.

Decisio questionis de audiencia misse in parrochiali ecclesia dominicis et festivis diebus. Tübingen: J. Otmar, 1500.

Libellus de exsecutione aeternae praedestinationis. Nürnberg: Friedrich Peypus, 1517. In *Johann von Staupitz, Sämtliche Schriften, Abhandlungen, Predigten, Zeugnisse*, vol. 2: *Lateinische Schriften* II. Edited by L. Graf zu Dohna, A. Endriss, R. Wetzel. Spätmittelalter und Reformation, Texte und Untersuchungen, 14. Berlin, New York, 1979.

Steinbach, Wendelin. *Gabrielis Byel Supplementum in octo et viginti distinctiones ultimas Quarti Magistri Sententiarum*. Edited by Gallus Müller. Paris, 1521.

Wendelini Steinbach Opera exegetica quae supersunt omnia, vol. 1: *Commentarius in epistolam S. Pauli ad Galatas*. Edited by Helmut Feld. VIEG 81. Wiesbaden, 1976.

Strickler, Joh., ed. *Actensammlung zur Schweizerischen Reformationsgeschichte in den Jahren 1521–1532 im Anschluss an die gleichzeitigen eidgenössischen Abschiede*, vol. 1: *1521–1528*. Zürich, 1878.

compiler, *Amtliche Sammlung der älteren eidgenössischen Abschiede*, vol. 4, Abt. 1 a. Brugg, 1873.

Summenhart, Conrad. *Oratio funebris*. Tübingen: J. Otmar, 1498.

Septipertitum opus de contractibus pro foro conscientie atque theologico per centum questiones digestum ac . . . quoad pregnantium questionem atque diffcultatem habentium uberiores articulos . . . disputatum. Hagenau: Heinrich Gran, 13 October 1500.

Tractatulus bipartitus de decimis defensivus opinionis theologorum adversus communiter canonistas de quotta decimarum, si debita sit de iure divino vel humano. Hagenau: Heinrich Gran, [1500].

Commentaria in Summan physice Alberti Magni. Hagenau, 1507.

Tauler, Johannes. *Die Predigten Taulers aus der Engelberger und der Freiburger Handschrift sowie aus Schmidts Abschnitten der ehemaligen Strassburger Handschriften*. Edited by Ferdinand Vetter. Deutsche Texte des Mittelalters, 11. Berlin, 1910; reprinted Dublin, Zürich, 1968.

Theologia Deutsch, see Mandel, *above*.

Thomas Aquinas. *Opera omnia*, vol. 31. Edited by S. E. Fretté. Paris: Vivès, 1876.

Quaestiones disputatae, vol. 2. 9th edn, Turin, Rome: Marietti, 1953.

Quaestiones quodlibetales. Edited by R. Spiazzi. 9th edn, Turin, Rome: Marietti, 1956.

Liber de Veritate Catholicae Fidei contra errores Infidelium seu Summa contra Gentiles, vol. 3. Turin, Rome: Marietti, 1961.

Thomas a Kempis. *Thomae Hemerken a Kempis Opera omnia*, vol. 7. Edited by M. Pohl. Freiburg i.Br., 1922.

Trithemius, Johannes. *Annales Hirsaugienses*, vol. 2. St Gallen, 1690.

Vadian (Joachim von Watt). *Die Vadianische Briefsammlung der Stadtbibliothek St. Gallen*, vol. 3: *1523–1525*; vol. 4: *1526–1530*. Edited by Emil Arbenz. *Mitteilungen zur vaterländischen Geschichte*, 27 [3rd series, 7] (1900); 28 [3rd series, 8] (1902).

Vega, Andreas de. *Opusculum de iustificatione, gratia et meritis*. Venice, 1546.

Vocht, Henry de, ed. *Literae virorum eruditorum ad Franciscum Craneveldium 1522–1528*. Humanistica Lovaniensia, 1. Louvain, 1928.

Vögeli, Jörg. *Schriften zur Reformation in Konstanz 1519–1538*, vol. 1; *Texte und Glossar;* vol. 2, pt 1: *Beilagen;* pt 2: *Kommentar und Register*. Edited by A. Vögeli. SKRG 39–41. Tübingen, Basel, 1972, 1973.

Walther, Hans, ed. *Proverbia sententiaeque latinitatis medii aevi. Lateinische Sprichwörter und Sentenzen des Mittelalters in alphabetischer Anordnung*, vol. 5: *Sim–Z*. Carmina medii aevi posterioris Latina, 2, vol. 5. Göttingen, 1967.

Watt, Joachim von, *see* Vadian, *above*.

Westphal, Joachim. *Collectanea sententiarum D. Aurelii Augustini de coena Domini*. Regensburg, 1555.

William of Auxerre. *Summa aurea*. Paris, n.d.
William of Paris. *Opera omnia*, vol. 1. Paris, 1674; reprinted Frankfurt a.M., 1963.
Wimpfeling, Jacob, *see* Herding, *above*.
Wülcker, Ernst, Virck, Hans, eds. *Des kursächsischen Rathes Hans von der Planitz Berichte aus dem Reichsregiment in Nürnberg 1521–1523*. Schriften der Königlich Sächsischen Kommission für Geschichte. Leipzig, 1899.
Wyss, Bernhard. *Die Chronik des Bernhard Wyss 1519–1530*. Edited by Georg Finsler. Quellen zur schweizerischen Reformationsgeschichte, 1. Basel, 1901.
Zasius (Zäsy), Ulrich. *Neue Stadtrechte und Statuten der Stadt Freiburg im Breisgau*. Basel: Adam Petri, 1520; reprinted Aalen, 1968.
Zerbolt of Zutphen, Gerard. 'Super modo vivendi devotorum hominum simul commorantium.' Edited by A. Hyma. *Archief voor de geschiedenis van het Aartsbisdom Utrecht* 52 (1926): 1–100.
Zwingli, Ulrich. *Huldrici Zuinglii Opera. Completa editio prima*, vol. 7; *Epistolarum a Zuinglio ad Zuingliumque scriptarum pars prima*. Edited by Melchior Schuler, Johann Schulthess. Zürich, 1830.
Ulrich Zwingli. Eine Auswahl aus seinen Schriften auf das 400 jährige Jubiläum der Zürcher Reformation. Edited and translated by Georg Finsler, Walther Köhler, Arnold Rüegg. Zürich, 1918.
Ulrich Zwingli (1484–1531). Selected Works. Edited by Samuel M. Jackson, translated by L. McLouth. Philadelphia, 1901, 1972.

Secondary sources

Acquoy, J. G. R. *Het Klooster te Windesheim en zijn invloed*, vol. 1. Utrecht, 1875.
Ahlstrom, Sydney E. *A Religious History of the American People*. New Haven, 1972.
Alberts, Hildegard. 'Reuchlins Drucker, Thomas Anshelm, mit besonderer Berücksichtigung seiner Pforzheimer Presse.' In *Festgabe Reuchlin*, pp. 205–65.
Arbesmann, Rudolph. *Der Augustiner-Eremitenorden und der Beginn der humanistischen Bewegung*. Cassiciacum, 19. Würzburg, 1965.
Arnold, Klaus. *Johannes Trithemius (1462–1516)*. Quellen und Forschungen zur Geschichte des Bistums und Hochstifts Würzburg, 23. Würzburg, 1971.
Assel, Hans-Günther. 'Das kanonische Zinsverbot und der "Geist" des Frühkapitalismus in der Wirtschaftsethik bei Eck und Luther.' Dissertation, Erlangen, 1948.
Augustijn, Cornelis. 'Allein das heilig Evangelium, Het mandaat van het Reichsregiment 6 maart 1523.' *Nederlands Archief voor Kerkgeschiedenis* 48 (1968): 150–65.
Bächtold-Stäubli, Hanns, ed. *Handwörterbuch des deutschen Aberglaubens*, vols. 3 and 7. Handwörterbücher zur deutschen Volkskunde, Abteilung 1: Aberglaube. Berlin and Leipzig, 1930–1 and 1935–6.

Baeyer-Katte, Wanda von. 'Die historischen Hexenprozesse. Der verbürokratisierte Massenwahn.' In *Massenwahn in Geschichte und Gegenwart. Ein Tagungsbericht*, pp. 220–31. Edited by W. Bitter. Stuttgart, 1965.

Baker, Wayne. 'Heinrich Bullinger and the Idea of Usury.' *The Sixteenth Century Journal* 5 (1974): 49–70.

Barge, Hermann. *Andreas Bodenstein von Karlstadt*. Vol. 2: *Karlstadt als Vorkämpfer des laienchristliche Puritanismus*. Leipzig, 1905; reprinted Nieuwkoop, 1968.

Baron, Hans. 'Religion and Politics in the German Imperial Cities during the Reformation.' *The English Historical Review* 52 (1937): 405–27; 614–33.

Bátori, Ingrid. 'Das Patriziat der deutschen Stadt. Zu den Forschungsergebnissen über das Patriziat besonders der süddeutschen Städte.' *Zeitschrift für Stadtgeschichte, Stadtsoziologie und Denkmalpflege* 2 (1975): 1–30.

Bauer, Clemens. 'Conrad Peutingers Gutachten zur Monopolfrage. Eine Untersuchung zur Wandlung der Wirtschaftsanschauungen im Zeitalter der Reformation.' *ARG* 45 (1954): 1–43.

'Diskussionen um die Zins- und Wucherfrage auf dem Konstanzer Konzil.' In *Das Konzil von Konstanz. Beiträge zu seiner Geschichte und Theologie*, pp. 174–86. Edited by A. Franzen, W. Müller. Freiburg i. Br., 1964.

Bauer, Karl. *Die Wittenberger Universitätstheologie und die Anfänge der deutschen Reformation*. Tübingen, 1928.

Bauer, Martin. *Die Erkenntnislehre und der Conceptus entis nach vier Spätschriften des Johannes Gerson*. Monographien zur philosophischen Forschung, 117. Meisenheim am Glan, 1973.

Baum, J. W. *Capito und Butzer, Strassburgs Reformatoren*. Leben und ausgewählte Schriften der Väter und Begründer der reformirten Kirche, 3. Elberfeld, 1860; reprinted Nieuwkoop, 1967.

Baur, August. *Die Erste Züricher Disputation am 29. Januar 1523*. Der evangelische Glaube nach dem Zeugnis der Geschichte. Halle a.d. Saale, 1883.

Zwinglis Theologie. Ihr Werden und ihr System, vol. 1. Halle a.d. Saale, 1885.

Bayer, Oswald. *Promissio. Geschichte der reformatorischen Wende in Luthers Theologie*. Forschungen zur Kirchen- und Dogmengeschichte, 24. Göttingen, 1971.

Becker, Gabriele; Brackert, Helmut; Brauner, Sigrid; Tümmler, Angelika. 'Zum kulturellen Bild und zur realen Situation der Frau im Mittelalter und in der frühen Neuzeit.' In *Aus der Zeit der Verzweiflung. Zur Genese und Aktualität des Hexenbildes*, pp. 11–128. Edited by G. Becker *et al*. Frankfurt a. M., 1977.

Beintker, Horst. *Die Überwindung der Anfechtung bei Luther. Eine Studie zu seiner Theologie nach den Operationes in Psalmos 1519–21*. Theologische Arbeiten, 1. Berlin, 1954.

Bender, Wilhelm. *Zwinglis Reformationsbündnisse. Untersuchungen zur Rechts- und Sozialgeschichte der Burgrechtsverträge eidgenössischer und oberdeutscher Städte zur Ausbreitung und Sicherung der Reformation Huldrych Zwinglis*. Zürich, 1970.

Béné, Charles. *Érasme et Saint Augustin ou l'influence de Saint Augustin sur l'humanisme d'Érasme.* Travaux d'Humanisme et de Renaissance, 103. Geneva, 1969.

Benrath, Gustav Adolf. 'Die Universität der Reformationszeit.' *ARG* 57 (1966): 32–51.

Benzing, Josef. *Lutherbibliographie. Verzeichnis der gedruckten Schriften Martin Luthers bis zu dessen Tod.* Bibliotheca Bibliographica Aureliana, 10, 16, 19. Baden-Baden, 1966.

Bergsten, Torsten. *Balthasar Hubmaier. Seine Stellung zu Reformation und Täufertum 1521–1528.* Acta Universitatis Upsaliensis, Studia Historico-Ecclesiastica Upsaliensia, 3. Kassel, 1961.

Bibliographie zur Geschichte und Theologie des Augustiner-Eremitenordens bis zum Beginn der Reformation. Edited by E. Gindele, H. Geiter, A. Schuler. Spätmittelalter und Reformation, Texte und Untersuchungen, 1. Berlin, New York, 1977.

Biéler, André. *La Pensée économique et sociale de Calvin.* Geneva, 1961.

Birnbaum, Norman. 'The Zwinglian Reformation in Zurich.' *Archives de Sociologie des Religions* 8 (1959): 15–30; also in *Past and Present* 15 (1959): 27–47.

Blanke, Fritz. *Brüder in Christo. Die Geschichte der ältesten Täufergemeinde (Zollikon, 1525).* Zwingli-Bücherei, 71. Zürich, 1955. Translated by Joseph Nordenhaug, *Brothers in Christ.* Scottdale, Pa., 1961.

'Zwingli mit Ambrosius Blarer im Gespräch.' In *Blarer-Gedenkschrift,* pp. 81–6.

Blockx, Karel. *De veroordeling van Maarten Luther door de theologische faculteit te Leuven in 1519* (with summary in German). Verhandelingen van de Koninklijke Vlaamse Academie voor Wetenschappen, Letteren en Schone Kunsten van België, Klasse der Letteren, Verhandeling 31. Brussels, 1958.

Blumenberg, Hans. *Säkularisierung und Selbstbehauptung.* Rev. and exp. edn of *Die Legitimität der Neuzeit,* vols. 1 and 2. Frankfurt a. M., 1974.

Der Prozess der theoretischen Neugierde. Rev. and exp. edn of *Die Legitimität der Neuzeit,* vol. 3. Frankfurt a. M., 1973.

Böhmer, Heinrich. *Luthers Romfahrt.* Leipzig, 1914.

Bofinger, Wilhelm. 'Oberdeutschtum und württembergische Reformation. Die Sozialgestalt der Kirche als Problem der Theologie- und Kirchengeschichte der Reformationszeit.' 2 vols. Dissertation, Tübingen, 1957.

'Kirche und werdender Territorialstaat. Eine Untersuchung zur Kirchenreform Herzog Ulrichs von Württemberg.' *BWKG* 65 (1965): 75–149.

Bopp, Marie-Joseph. *Die evangelischen Geistlichen und Theologen in Elsass und Lothringen von der Reformation bis zur Gegenwart.* Bibliothek familiengeschichtlicher Quellen, 14 = Genealogie und Landesgeschichte, 1. Neustadt a.d. Aisch., 1959–60.

Bornkamm, Heinrich. 'Thesen und Thesenanschlag Luthers.' In *Geist und Geschichte der Reformation.* Festgabe Hanns Rückert, pp. 179–218. Edited by H. Liebing, K. Scholder. Berlin, 1966.

Bos, F. T. *Luther in het oordeel van de Sorbonne. Een onderzoek naar ontstaan, inhoud en werking van de 'Determinatio' (1521) en naar haar verhouding tot de vroegere veroordelingen van Luther.* Amsterdam, 1974.

Bossert, Gustav. 'Augustin Bader von Augsburg, der Prophet und König, und seine Genossen nach den Prozessakten von 1530.' *ARG* 10 (1912/13): 117–65; 209–41; 297–349; appendixes in *ARG* 11 (1914): 19–64; 103–33; 176–99.

'Ökolampad als Seelsorger des Herzogs Ulrich von Württemberg nach seinen Predigten über Psalm 137 im Herbst 1526.' *BWKG* 36 (1932): 208–29.

Bouwsma, William J. *Venice and the Defense of Republican Liberty: Renaissance Values in the Age of the Counter Reformation.* Berkeley, 1968.

'The Two Faces of Humanism. Stoicism and Augustinianism in Renaissance Thought.' In *Itinerarium Italicum*, pp. 3–60.

Brackert, Helmut. '"Unglückliche, was hast du gehofft?" Zu den Hexenbüchern des 15. bis 17. Jahrhunderts.' In *Aus der Zeit der Verzweiflung. Zur Genese und Aktualität des Hexenbildes*, pp. 131–87. Edited by G. Becker *et al.* Frankfurt a. M., 1977.

Brady, Thomas A., Jr. *Ruling Class, Regime and Reformation at Strasbourg, 1520–1555.* SMRT 22. Leiden, 1978.

Braunisch, Reinhard. *Die Theologie der Rechtfertigung im 'Enchiridion' (1538) des Johannes Gropper. Sein kritischer Dialog mit Philipp Melanchthon.* RGST 109. Münster i.W., 1974.

Brecht, Martin. 'Das Augustiner-Eremiten-Kloster zu Tübingen.' In *Mittelalterliches Erbe – Evangelische Verantwortung. Vorträge und Ansprachen zum Gedenken der Gründung des Tübinger Augustinerklosters 1262*, pp. 45–89. Issued by the Evangelisches Stift Tübingen. Tübingen, 1962.

'Ambrosius Blarers Wirksamkeit in Schwaben.' In *Blarer-Gedenkschrift*, pp. 140–71.

'Die Reformation in der Tübinger Vorlesung von Johannes Brenz.' In *Festschrift Reinhold Rau zum 70. Geburtstag am 12. Dezember 1966*, pp. 13–16. Compiled in the Tübingen Stadtarchiv. Kleine Tübinger Schriften, Beiheft 1. Tübingen, 1966.

Die frühe Theologie des Johannes Brenz. Beiträge zur historischen Theologie, 36. Tübingen, 1966.

Kirchenordnung und Kirchenzucht in Württemberg vom 16. bis zum 18. Jahrhundert. Quellen und Forschungen zur württembergischen Kirchengeschichte, 1. Stuttgart, 1967.

'Anfänge reformatorischer Kirchenordnung und Sittenzucht bei Johannes Brenz.' *ZSRG.K* 55 (1969): 322–47.

'Der theologische Hintergrund der Zwölf Artikel der Bauernschaft in Schwaben von 1525. Christoph Schappelers und Sebastian Lotzers Beitrag zum Bauernkrieg.' *ZKG* 85 (1974): 174–208.

Breen, Quirinus. *Christianity and Humanism. Studies in the History of Ideas*, collected and published in his honour. Edited by N. P. Ross. Grand Rapids, 1968.

Bubenheimer, Ulrich. 'Scandalum et ius divinum. Theologische und rechtstheologische Probleme der ersten reformatorischen Innovationen in Wittenberg 1521/22.' *ZSRG.K* 59 (1973): 263–342.

Consonantia Theologiae et Iurisprudentiae. Andreas Bodenstein von Karlstadt als Theologe und Jurist zwischen Scholastik und Reformation. Jus ecclesiasticum, 24. Tübingen, 1977.

Buck, Hermann. *Die Anfänge der Konstanzer Reformationsprozesse, Österreich, Eidgenossenschaft und Schmalkaldischer Bund 1510/22-1531.* SKRG 29/31. Tübingen, 1964.

Büchmann, Georg. *Geflügelte Worte. Der Zitatenschatz des deutschen Volkes.* Edited by W. Rust and G. Haupt. 30th edn. Berlin, 1961.

Burkard, Franz Joseph. *Philosophische Lehrgehalte in Gabriel Biels Sentenzenkommentar unter besonderer Berücksichtigung seiner Erkenntnislehre.* Monographien zur Philosophischen Forschung, 122. Meisenheim am Glan, 1974.

Burmeister, Karl Heinz. *Georg Joachim Rheticus 1514–1574. Eine Bio-Bibliographie,* vol. 1: *Humanist und Wegbereiter der modernen Naturwissenschaften;* vol. 2: *Quellen und Bibliographie.* Wiesbaden, 1967/68.

Campenhausen, Hans Freiherr von. 'Reformatorisches Selbstbewusstsein und reformatorisches Geschichtsbewusstsien bei Luther 1517–1522.' *ARG* 37 (1940): 128–50; reprinted in *idem, Tradition und Leben. Kräfte der Kirchengeschichte. Aufsätze und Vorträge,* pp. 318–42. Tübingen, 1960.

Chadwick, Henry. *Priscillian of Avila. The Occult and the Charismatic in the Early Church.* Oxford, 1976.

Chrisman, Miriam Usher. *Strasbourg and the Reform. A Study in the Process of Change.* Yale Historical Publications, Miscellany, 87. New Haven, 1967.

Clark, Francis. 'A New Appraisal of Late Medieval Theology.' *Gregorianum* 46 (1965): 733–65.

Clemen, Otto. 'Die Luterisch Strebkatz.' *ARG* 2 (1904/5): 78–93.

Cless, David F. *Versuch einer kirchlich-politischen Landes- und Cultur-Geschichte von Württemberg bis zur Reformation,* vol. 2, pt. 2. Schwäbisch Gmünd, 1808.

Clough, Cecil H., ed. *Cultural Aspects of the Italian Renaissance. Essays in Honour of Paul Oskar Kristeller.* Manchester, New York, 1976.

Cochrane, Eric. 'Science and Humanism in the Italian Renaissance.' *The American Historical Review* 81 (1976): 1039–57.

Combes, André. *Essai sur la critique de Ruysbroeck par Gerson,* vol. 3: *L'évolution spontanée de la critique gersonienne (première partie).* Paris, 1959.

Conrad, Ernst. 'Die Lehrstühle der Universität Tübingen und ihre Inhaber (1477–1927).' State-board examination thesis, Tübingen, 1960.

Courtenay, William J. 'Gabriel Biel as Cathedral Preacher at Mainz and His Supposed Sojourn at Marienthal.' *Research Studies of Washington State University* 33 (1965): 145–50.

'Covenant and Causality in Pierre d'Ailly.' *Speculum* 46 (1971): 94–119.

'The King and the Leaden Coin. The Economic Background of "sine qua non" Causality.' *Traditio* 28 (1972): 185–209.

'Nominalism and Late Medieval Thought: A Bibliographical Essay.' *Theological Studies* 33 (1972): 716–34.

'John of Mirecourt and Gregory of Rimini on Whether God Can Undo the Past.' *Recherches de Théologie ancienne et médiévale* 39 (1972): 224–56 (=1); 40 (1973): 147–74 (=2).

'Some Notes on Robert of Halifax, O.F.M.' *Franciscan Studies* 33 (1973): 135–42.

'Alexander Langeley, O.F.M.' *Manuscripta* 18 (1974): 96–104.

'Nominalism and Late Medieval Religion.' In *The Pursuit of Holiness in Late Medieval and Renaissance Religion*, pp. 26–59. Edited by Charles Trinkaus, H. A. Oberman. SMRT 10. Leiden, 1974.

Adam Wodeham. An Introduction to his Life and Writings. SMRT 21. Leiden, 1978.

Dankbaar, Willem F. *Calvin. Sein Weg und Werk*. 2nd edn, Neukirchen, 1966.

Davis, Natalie Zemon. *Society and Culture in Early Modern France. Eight Essays*. London, 1975.

Debard, Jean-Marc. 'Les visites ecclésiastiques dans l'Église Luthérienne de la principauté de Montbéliard du XVIe au XVIIIe siècle.' In *Sensibilité religieuse et discipline ecclésiastique. Les visites pastorales en territoires protestants (Pays rhénans, comté de Montbéliard, pays de Vaud) XVIe–*XVIIIe *siècles*, pp. 41–67. Actes des Journées d'études de Strasbourg, Palais universitaire, avril 1973. Publications de la Société Savante d'Alsace et des Régions de l'Est, Collection 'Recherches et Documents', 21. Strasbourg, 1975.

Decker-Hauff, Hansmartin. 'Die Entstehung der altwürttembergischen Ehrbarkeit 1250–1534.' Dissertation, Vienna, 1946.

'Bausteine zur Reuchlin-Biographie.' In *Festgabe Reuchlin*, pp. 83–107.

Dempsey Douglass, E. Jane, *see* Douglass, E. Jane Dempsey, *below*.

Denifle, Heinrich. *Luther und Luthertum in der ersten Entwicklung*, vol. 1, pts. 1 and 2. 2nd edn, Mainz, 1904, 1906. Translated by Raymund Volz, *Luther and Lutherdom*, vol. 1, pt. 1 only. Somerset, Ohio, 1907.

Dickens, A. G. *The German Nation and Martin Luther*. London, 1974.

Dieckhoff, August Wilhelm. 'Die Theologie des Johann von Staupitz.' *Zeitschrift für kirchliche Wissenschaft und kirchliches Leben* 8 (1887): 169–80; 232–44.

Dittrich, Franz. *Gasparo Contarini 1483–1542*. Braunsberg, 1885; reprinted Nieuwkoop, 1972.

Dolfen, Christian. *Die Stellung des Erasmus von Rotterdam zur scholastischen Methode*. Osnabrück, 1936.

Douglass, E. Jane Dempsey. *Justification in Late Medieval Preaching. A Study of John Geiler of Keisersberg*. SMRT 1. Leiden, 1966.

Eckert, Willehad Paul and Imhoff, Christoph von. *Willibald Pirckheimer, Dürers Freund, im Spiegel seines Lebens, seiner Werke und seiner Umwelt*. Zeugnisse der Buchkunst, 5. Cologne, 1971.

Egli, Emil. 'Regula Zwingli, die Tochter des Reformators, Gemahlin Rudolf Gwalthers.' *Zwingliana* 1 (1903, 1): 323–9.

'Zur Einführung des Schriftprinzips in der Schweiz.' *Zwingliana* 1 (1903, 1): 332–9.

'Ritter Fritz Jakob von Anwyl, ein thurgauischer Edelmann und Verehrer Zwinglis.' *Zwingliana* 2 (1905, 2): 44–51.

Schweizerische Reformationsgeschichte, vol. 1: (*1519–1525*). Edited by Georg Finsler. Zürich, 1910.

Ehmer, Hermann. *Valentin Vannius und die Reformation in Württemberg*. Veröffentlichungen der Kommission für geschichtliche Landeskunde in Baden-Württemberg, B 81. Stuttgart, 1976.

Ehrle, Franz. *Der Sentenzenkommentar Peters von Candia, des Pisaner Papstes Alexanders V. Ein Beitrag zur Scheidung der Schulen in der Scholastik des vierzehnten Jahrhunderts und zur Geschichte des Wegestreites*. Franziskanische Studien, Beiheft 9. Münster i.W., 1925.

Elm, Kaspar. 'Mendikanten und Humanisten im Florenz des Tre- und Quattrocento. Zum Problem der Legitimierung humanistischer Studien in den Bettelorden.' In *Die Humanisten in ihrer politischen und sozialen Umwelt*, pp. 51–85. Edited by O. Herding, R. Stupperich. Deutsche Forschungsgemeinschaft, Kommission für Humanismusforschung, Mitteilung 3. Boppard, 1976.

Elsener, Ferdinand. 'Zur Geschichte des Majoritätsprinzips (Pars maior und Pars sanior), insbesondere nach schweizerischen Quellen.' *ZSRG.K* 42 (1956): 73–116; 560–70.

'Das Majoritätsprinzip in konfessionellen Angelegenheiten und die Religionsverträge der schweizerischen Eidgenossenschaft vom 16. bis 18. Jahrhundert.' *ZSRG.K* 55 (1969): 238–81.

Elton, G. R. *The Tudor Revolution in Government. Administrative Changes in the Reign of Henry VIII*. 6th edn. Cambridge, 1969.

Reformation Europe 1517–1559. The Fontana History of Europe. London, Glasgow, 1963.

Elze, Martin. 'Tübingen, I: Universität.' *RGG* 6: 1064–9.

Epiney-Burgard, Georgette. *Gerard Grote (1340–1384) et les débuts de la devotion moderne*. VIEG 54. Wiesbaden, 1970.

Ernst, Fritz. *Die wirtschaftliche Ausstattung der Universität Tübingen in ihren ersten Jahrzehnten (1477–1537)*. Darstellungen aus der Württembergischen Geschichte, 20. Stuttgart, 1929.

Eberhard im Bart. Die Politik eines deutschen Landesherrn am Ende des Mittelalters. Stuttgart, 1933.

Ernst, Wilhelm. *Gott und Mensch am Vorabend der Reformation. Eine Untersuchung zur Moralphilosophie und -theologie bei Gabriel Biel*. Erfurter Theologische Studien, 28. Leipzig, 1972.

Eulenburg, Franz. *Die Frequenz der deutschen Universitäten von ihrer Gründung bis zur Gegenwart*. Abhandlungen der Königlichen Sächsischen Gesellschaft der Wissenschaften, philolog.-hist. Klasse. Vol. 24, Abhandlung 2. Leipzig, 1904.

Fabian, Ekkehart. *Die Entstehung des Schmalkaldischen Bundes und seiner Verfassung 1524/29–1531/35. Brück, Philipp von Hessen und Jakob Sturm. Darstel-*

lung und Quellen, mit einer Brück-Bibliographie. SKRG 1. 2nd enl. and rev. edn, Tübingen, 1962.

Geheime Räte in Zürich, Bern, Basel und Schaffhausen. Quellen und Untersuchungen zur Staatskirchenrechts- und Verfassungsgeschichte der vier reformierten Orte der Alten Eidgenossenschaft (einschliesslich der Zürcher Notstandsverfassung). Mit Namenlisten 1339/1432–1798 (1800). SKRG 33. Cologne, Vienna, 1974.

Farner, Oskar. *Huldrych Zwingli*, vol. 3: *Seine Verkündigung und ihre ersten Früchte 1520–1525*. Zürich, 1954.

Fast, Heinold. 'Reformation durch Provokation. Predigtstörungen in den ersten Jahren der Reformation in der Schweiz.' In *Umstrittenes Täufertum 1525–1975. Neue Forschungen*, pp. 79–110. Edited by H.-J. Goertz. Göttingen, 1975.

Febvre, Lucien. *Au Coeur religieux du XVIe siècle*. Bibliothèque générale de l'École pratique des hautes études, Section 6. Paris, 1957.

Feckes, Karl. 'Gabriel Biel, der erste grosse Dogmatiker der Universität Tübingen, in seiner wissenschaftlichen Bedeutung.' *Theologische Quartalschrift* 108 (1927): 50–76.

Feld, Helmut. *Martin Luthers und Wendelin Steinbachs Vorlesungen über den Hebräerbrief. Eine Studie zur Geschichte der neutestamentlichen Exegese und Theologie*. VIEG 62. Wiesbaden, 1971.

Feret, P. *La Faculté de Théologie de Paris et ses docteurs les plus célèbres, Moyen-âge*, vol. 4. Paris, 1897.

Feyler, Anna. 'Die Beziehungen des Hauses Württemberg zur schweizerischen Eidgenossenschaft in der ersten Hälfte des XVI. Jahrhunderts.' Zürich, 1905.

Ficker, Johannes. 'Die Anfänge der akademischen Studien in Strassburg.' In *Das Stiftungsfest der Kaiser Wilhelms-Universität Strassburg am 1. Mai 1912*, pp. 23–74. Strassburg. 1912.

Erste Lehr- und Lernbücher des höheren Unterrichts in Strassburg (1534–1542). Strassburg, 1912.

Finke, Karl Konrad. *Die Tübinger Juristenfakultät 1477–1534. Rechtslehrer und Rechtsunterricht von der Gründung der Universität bis zur Einführung der Reformation*. Contubernium, 2. Tübingen, 1972.

Franz, Adolph. *Die Messe im deutschen Mittelalter. Beiträge zur Geschichte der Liturgie und des religiösen Volksleben*. Freiburg i.Br., 1902; reprinted Darmstadt, 1963.

Franz, Günther. *Der deutsche Bauernkrieg*. 10th impr. and exp. edn, Darmstadt, 1975.

Freund, Walter. *Modernus und andere Zeitbegriffe des Mittelalters*. Neue Münstersche Beiträge zur Geschichtsforschung, 4. Cologne, Graz, 1957.

Friedensburg, Walter. *Der Reichstag zu Speier 1526 in Zusammenhang der politischen und kirchlichen Entwicklung Deutschlands im Reformationszeitalter*. Historische Untersuchungen, 5. Berlin, 1887; reprinted edn Nieuwkoop, 1970.

'Dr. Johann Ecks Denkschriften zur deutschen Kirchenreformation 1523.' *Beiträge zur bayerischen Kirchengeschichte* 2 (1896): 159–96; 222–53.

Geschichte der Universität Wittenberg. Halle a.d. Saale, 1917.

Funk, Franz Xaver. *Zins und Wucher. Eine moraltheologische Abhandlung*. Tübingen, 1868.

Gabriel, Astrik L. '"Via antiqua" and "via moderna" and the Migration of Paris Students and Masters to the German Universities in the Fifteenth Century.' In *Antiqui und Moderni. Traditionsbewusstsein und Fortschrittsbewusstsein im späten Mittelalter*, pp. 439–83. Edited by A. Zimmermann. Miscellanea Mediaevalia, 9. Berlin, New York, 1974.

Gäbler, Ulrich. *Huldrych Zwingli im 20. Jahrhundert. Forschungsbericht und annotierte Bibliographie 1897–1972*. Zürich, 1975.

Genicot, L. Review of: Raoul Manselli, *La Religion populaire au moyen âge. Problèmes de méthode et d'histoire* (Montreal, Paris, 1975). *Revue d'Histoire Ecclésiastique* 71 (1976): 470–4.

Gerschmann, Karl-Heinz. '"Antiqui–Novi–Moderni" in den "Epistolae Obscurorum Virorum".' *Archiv für Begriffsgeschichte* 11 (1967): 23–36.

Ghellinck, Joseph de. 'La première édition imprimée des "Opera omnia S. Augustini".' In *Miscellanea J. Gessler*, 1: 530–47. [Antwerp] 1948.

Gierke, Otto von. *Das deutsche Genossenschaftsrecht*. 4 vols. Berlin, 1868–1913.

Gilmore, Myron P. *Humanists and Jurists. Six Studies in the Renaissance*. Cambridge, Mass., 1963.

'Italian Reactions to Erasmian Humanism.' In *Itinerarium Italicum*, pp. 61–115.

Ginneken, J. van. *Geert Groote's Levensbeeld naar de oudste Gegevens bewerkt*. Verhandelingen der Nederlandse Akademia van Wetenschappen, Afdeling Letterkunde, N.S. 57, no. 2. Amsterdam, 1942.

Goeters, J. F. Gerhard. *Ludwig Hätzer (ca. 1500 bis 1529), Spiritualist und Antitrinitarier. Eine Randfigur der frühen Täuferbewegung*. QFRG 25. Gütersloh, 1957.

'Die Vorgeschichte des Täufertums in Zürich.' In *Studien zur Geschichte und Theologie der Reformation*. Festschrift für Ernst Bizer, pp. 239–81. Edited by L. Abramowski, J. F. G. Goeters. Neukirchen, 1969.

Grabmann, Martin. 'Johannes Capreolus, O.P., der "Princeps Thomistarum" (†1444), und seine Stellung in der Geschichte der Thomistenschule.' In *Mittelalterliches Geistesleben. Abhandlungen zur Geschichte der Scholastik und Mystik*, vol. 3, pp. 370–410. Edited by L. Ott. Munich, 1956.

Graf, Wilhelm. *Doktor Christoph Scheurl von Nürnberg*. Beiträge zur Kulturgeschichte des Mittelalters und der Renaissance, 43. Leipzig, 1930; reprinted Hildesheim, 1972.

Grane, Leif. *Contra Gabrielem. Luthers Auseinandersetzung mit Gabriel Biel in der Disputatio Contra Scholasticam Theologiam 1517*. Acta Theologica Danica, 4. Gyldendal, 1962.

'Gregor von Rimini und Luthers Leipziger Disputation.' *Studia Theologica* 22 (1968): 29–49.

'Augustins "Expositio quarundam propositionum ex epistola ad Romanos" in Luthers Römerbriefvorlesung.' *ZThK* 69 (1972): 304–30.

'Divus Paulus et S. Augustinus, interpres eius fidelissimus. Über Luthers

Verhältnis zu Augustin.' In *Festschrift für Ernst Fuchs*, pp. 133–46. Edited by G. Ebeling, E. Jüngel, G. Schunack. Tübingen, 1973.

Modus loquendi theologicus. Luthers Kampf um die Erneuerung der Theologie (1515–1518). Acta theologica Danica, 12. Leiden, 1975.

Greschat, Martin. *Melanchthon neben Luther. Studien zur Gestalt der Rechtfertigungslehre zwischen 1528 und 1537*. Untersuchungen zur Kirchengeschichte, 1. Witten, 1965.

Greyerz, Hans von. 'Der Jetzerprozess und die Humanisten.' *Archiv des Historischen Vereins des Kantons Bern* 31 (1932): 243–99.

Grimm, Jacob and Grimm, Wilhelm. *Deutsches Wörterbuch*, vol. 9. Leipzig, 1899.

Grossmann, Maria. 'Bibliographie der Werke Christoph Scheurls.' *Archiv für Geschichte des Buchwesens* 70 (1969): 658–70.

Humanism in Wittenberg 1485–1517. Bibliotheca humanistica et reformatorica, 11. Nieuwkoop, 1975.

Grube, Walter. *Der Stuttgarter Landtag 1457–1957. Von den Landständen zum demokratischen Parlament*. Stuttgart, 1957.

Haar, Johann. 'Das Wort der Wahrheit. Ein Sermon D. Martin Luthers.' *Luther. Zeitschrift der Luthergesellschaft* 47 (1976): 5–22.

Haas, Martin. *Huldrych Zwingli und seine Zeit. Leben und Werk des Zürcher Reformators*. Zürich, 1969.

Haering, Hermann. 'Johannes Vergenhans, genannt Nauclerus. Erster Rektor der Universität Tübingen und ihr langjähriger Kanzler, Verfasser einer Weltchronik. 1425–1510.' In *Schwäbische Lebensbilder*, vol. 5. Edited by H. Haering. Stuttgart, 1950.

Hagen, Kenneth. *A Theology of Testament in the Young Luther. The Lectures on Hebrews*. SMRT, 12. Leiden, 1974.

Hall, Basil. 'The Reformation City.' *Bulletin of the John Rylands Library* 54 (1971/2): 103–48.

Haller, Johannes. *Die Epochen der deutschen Geschichte*. Stuttgart, 1950 [1923]. Translated by E. W. Dickes, *Epochs of German History*. London, 1930.

Hamm, Berndt. *Promissio, pactum, ordinatio. Freiheit und Selbstbindung Gottes in der scholastischen Gnadenlehre*. Beiträge zur historischen Theologie, 54. Tübingen, 1977.

Hammes, Manfred. *Hexenwahn und Hexenprozesse*. Frankfurt a.M., 1977.

Die Handschriften der Universitätsbibliothek München, vol. 3: *Die Lateinischen mittelalterlichen Handschriften*. [1]: *Die Handschriften aus der Folioreihe*. 1. Hälfte. Edited by N. Daniel *et al*. Wiesbaden, 1974.

Hannemann, Kurt. 'Reuchlin und die Berufung Melanchthons nach Wittenberg.' In *Festgabe Reuchlin*, pp. 108–38.

Hansen, Chadwick. *Witchcraft at Salem*. New York, 1969.

Harnack, Adolf von. *Lehrbuch der Dogmengeschichte*, vol. 3: *Die Entwicklung des kirchlichen Dogmas* 2 and 3. 5th edn, Tübingen, 1932 [1890]. Translated by Neil Buchanan, *History of Dogma*, vol. 7. London, 1903; reprinted New York, 1961.

Harrison, Richard L. 'Melanchthon's Role in the Reformation of the University of Tübingen.' *Church History* 47 (1978): 270–8.

Hauswirth, René. *Landgraf Philipp von Hessen und Zwingli. Voraussetzungen und Geschichte der politischen Beziehungen zwischen Hessen, Strassburg, Konstanz, Ulrich von Württemberg und reformierten Eidgenossen 1526–1531*. SKRG 35. Tübingen, Basel, 1968.

Hay, Denys. 'England and the Humanities in the Fifteenth Century.' In *Itinerarium Italicum*, pp. 305–67.

Heckel, Johannes. *Cura religionis. Ius in sacra – ius circa sacra*. Libelli, 49. 2nd edn, Darmstadt, 1962.

Helbig, Herbert. *Die Reformation der Universität Leipzig im 16. Jahrhundert*. Schriften des Vereins für Reformationsgeschichte, 171, Gütersloh, 1953.

Helbling, Leo. *Dr. Johann Fabri, Generalvikar von Konstanz und Bischof von Wien 1478–1541. Beiträge zu seiner Lebensgeschichte*, RGST 67/8. Münster i.W., 1941.

Held, Friedrich. 'Die Tätigkeit des Ambrosius Blarer im Herzogtum Württemberg in den Jahren 1534–1538. Dargestellt nach seinem Briefwechsel.' *BWKG* 65 (1965): 150–206.

Hendrix, Scott H. *Ecclesia in via. Ecclesiological Developments in the Medieval Psalms Exegesis and the Dictata super Psalterium (1513–1515) of Martin Luther*. SMRT 8. Leiden, 1974.

Herding, Otto. 'Probleme des frühen Humanismus in Deutschland.' *Archiv für Kulturgeschichte* 38 (1956): 344–89.

'Über einige Richtungen in der Erforschung des deutschen Humanismus seit etwa 1950.' In *Humanismusforschung seit 1945. Ein Bericht aus interdisziplinärer Sicht*, pp. 59–110. Edited by A. Buck, Deutsche Forschungsgemeinschaft, Kommission für Humanismusforschung, Mitteilung 2. Boppard, 1975.

Hermelink, Heinrich. 'Die Anfänge des Humanismus in Tübingen.' *Württembergische Vierteljahrshefte für Landesgeschichte* N.S. 15 (1906): 319–36.

Die theologische Fakultät in Tübingen vor der Reformation 1477–1534. Tübingen, 1906.

Geschichte der evangelischen Kirche in Württemberg von der Reformation bis zur Gegenwart. Das Reich Gottes in Wirttemberg. Stuttgart, Tübingen, 1949.

Heynck, Valens. 'Die Bedeutung von "mereri" und "promereri" bei dem Konzilstheologen Andreas de Vega OFM.' *Franziskanische Studien* 50 (1968): 224–38.

Hilgenfeld, Hartmut. *Mittelalterlich-traditionelle Elemente in Luthers Abendmahlsschriften*. Studien zur Dogmengeschichte und Systematischen Theologie, 29. Zürich, 1971.

Hill, [John E.] Christopher. *Puritanism and Revolution. Studies in Interpretation of the English Revolution of the 17th Century*. London, 1958.

Hillerbrand, Hans Joachim. *Die politische Ethik des oberdeutschen Täufertums. Eine Untersuchung zur Relgions- und Geistesgeschichte des Reformationszeitalters*. Beihefte der Zeitschrift für Religions- und Geistesgeschichte, 7. Leiden, Cologne, 1962.

Landgrave Philipp of Hesse (1504–1567). Religion and Politics in the Reformation. Reformation Essays and Studies, 1. St Louis, 1967.

Himmelein, Volker. *Eberhard, der mit dem Barte. Bilder und Stationen aus seinem Leben. Eine biographische Studie zum 500 jährigen Bestehen der Eberhard-Karls-Universität Tübingen.* Tübingen, 1977.

Hirsch, Emanuel. *Die Theologie des Andreas Osiander und ihre geschichtlichen Voraussetzungen.* Göttingen, 1919.

Höffner, Joseph. *Wirtschaftsethik und Monopole im fünfzehnten und sechzehnten Jahrhundert.* Freiburger Staatswissenschaftliche Schriften, 2. Jena, 1941.

Horawitz, Adalbert. *Johann Heigerlin (genannt Faber), Bischof von Wien, bis zum Regensburger Convent.* Sitzungsberichte der kaiserlichen Akademie der Wissenschaften in Wien, phil.-hist. Klasse, 107. Vienna, 1884.

Hossfeld, Max. 'Johannes Heynlin aus Stein. Ein Kapitel aus der Frühzeit des deutschen Humanismus.' *Basler Zeitschrift für Geschichte und Altertumskunde* 5 (1906): 309–56 [=1]; 7 (1908): 79–219 [=2]; 235–398 [=3].

Huizinga, Johan. *Erasmus and the Age of Reformation, with a selection from the letters of Erasmus.* 2nd edn, New York, 1957.

Verzamelde Werken, vol. 6: *Biografie.* Haarlem, 1950.

Hummel, Gerhard. *Die humanistischen Sodalitäten und ihr Einfluss auf die Entwicklung des Bildungswesens der Reformationszeit.* Leipzig, 1940.

Hyma, Albert. *The Brethren of the Common Life.* Grand Rapids, 1950.

The 'Devotio Moderna' or Christian Renaissance (1380–1520). 2nd exp. edn, Hamden, Conn., 1965; reprinted Grand Rapids, [1975].

IJsewijn, Jozef. 'The Coming of Humanism to the Low Countries.' In *Itinerarium Italicum*, pp. 193–301.

Irtenkauf, Wolfgang. 'Bausteine zu einer Biographie des Nikolaus Basellius.' *Zeitschrift für Württembergische Landesgeschichte* 21 (1962): 387–91.

Iserloh, Erwin. *Luther zwischen Reform und Reformation. Der Thesenanschlag fand nicht statt.* 3rd edn, Münster i.W., 1968. Translated by Jared Wicks, *The Theses Were Not Posted: Luther Between Reform and Reformation.* Boston, 1968.

'Bildfeindlichkeit des Nominalismus und Bildersturm im 16. Jahrhundert.' In *Bild – Wort – Symbol in der Theologie*, pp. 119–38. Edited by W. Heinen. Würzburg, 1969.

Luther und die Reformation. Beiträge zu einem ökumenischen Lutherverständnis. Der Christ in der Welt. Eine Enzyklopädie, XI, 4. Aschaffenburg, 1974.

Jacob, Walter. *Politische Führungsschicht und Reformation. Untersuchungen zur Reformation in Zürich 1519–1528.* Zürcher Beiträge zur Reformationsgeschichte, 1. Zürich, 1970.

Jahn, Ulrich. *Hexenwesen und Zauberei in Pommern.* Breslau, 1886.

Jahns, Sigrid. *Frankfurt, Reformation und Schmalkaldischer Bund. Die Reformations-, Reichs- und Bündnispolitik der Reichsstadt Frankfurt am Main 1525–1536.* Studien zur Frankfurter Geschichte, 9. Frankfurt a.M., 1976.

Janssen, Johannes. *Geschichte des deutschen Volkes seit dem Ausgang des Mittelalters*, vol. 1: *Deutschlands allgemeine Zustände beim Ausgang des Mittelalters.* Freiburg i.Br., 1876; vol. 7: *Schulen und Universitäten. Wissen-*

schaft und Bildung bis zum Beginn des dreissigjährigen Krieges. Edited by L. Pastor. Freiburg i.Br., 1893; vol. 8: *Volkswirthschaftliche, gesellschaftliche und religiös-sittliche Zustände. Hexenwesen und Hexenverfolgung bis zum Beginn des dreissigjährigen Krieges*. Freiburg i.Br., 1894. Translated by M. A. Mitchell, A. M. Christie, *History of the German People at the Close of the Middle Ages*. 16 vols. London, 1896–1910 and St Louis, 1907–28.

Janz, Denis. 'A Reinterpretation of Gabriel Biel on Nature and Grace.' *The Sixteenth Century Journal* 8 (1977): 104–8.

Jedin, Hubert. 'Entstehung und Tragweite des Trienter Dekrets über die Bilderverehrung.' *Theologische Quartalschrift* 116 (1935): 143–88; 404–29.

Girolamo Seripando. Sein Leben und Denken im Geisteskampf des 16. Jahrhunderts, vol. 1: *Werdezeit und erster Schaffenstag*. Cassiciacum, 2. Würzburg, 1937.

Review of: Eduard Stakemeier, *Der Kampf um Augustin*. *Theologische Revue* 37 (1938): 425–30.

'Zur Aufgabe des Kirchengeschichtsschreibers.' In *idem*, *Kirche des Glaubens – Kirche der Geschichte. Ausgewählte Aufsätze und Vorträge*, vol. 1, pp. 23–35. Freiburg i.Br., 1966.

Geschichte des Konzils von Trient, vol. 4: *Dritte Tagungsperiode und Abschluss*, pt 1: *Frankreich und der neue Anfang in Trient bis zum Tode der Legaten Gonzaga und Seripando*. Freiburg, Basel, Vienna, 1975.

Joachimsen, Paul. *Geschichtsauffassung und Geschichtsschreibung in Deutschland unter dem Einfluss des Humanismus*, vol. 1. Beiträge zur Kulturgeschichte des Mittelalters und der Renaissance, 6. Leipzig, Berlin, 1910; reprinted Aalen, 1968.

'Zwei Universitätsgeschichten.' *ZKG* 48 (1929): 390–415; reprinted in *idem*, *Gesammelte Aufsätze. Beiträge zu Renaissance, Humanismus und Reformation*, pp. 249–74. Aalen, 1970.

'Der Humanismus und die Entwicklung des deutschen Geistes.' *Deutsche Vierteljahrsschrift für Literaturwissenschaft und Geistesgeschichte* 8 (1930): 419–80; reprinted in *idem*, *Gesammelte Aufsätze*, pp. 325–86.

Johns, Christa Tecklenburg. *Luthers Konzilsidee in ihrer historischen Bedingtheit und ihrem reformatorischen Neuansatz*. Theologische Bibliothek Töpelmann, 10. Berlin, 1966.

Johnston, Herbert. 'On the Meaning of "Consumed in Use" in the Problem of Usury.' *The Modern Schoolman* 30 (1953): 93–108.

Jürgens, Heiko. 'Erudio.' *Archiv für Begriffsgeschichte* 15 (1971): 11–50; printed separately in *Luther: Sol, Ratio, Erudio, Aristoteles*. Probeartikel zum Sachregister der Weimarer Lutherausgabe (Abteilung Schriften). Bonn, 1971.

Kähler, Ernst. *Karlstadt und Augustin. Der Kommentar des Andreas Bodenstein von Karistadt zu Augustins Schrift De spiritu et litera*. Hallische Monographien, 19. Halle a.d. Salle, 1952.

'Die 95 Thesen. Inhalt und Bedeutung.' *Luther, Zeitschrift der Luther-Gesellschaft* 38 (1967): 114–24.

Kahler, Erich. *The Germans*. Edited by R. Kimber and R. Kimber. Princeton, 1974.

Kaufmann, Georg. *Zwei katholische und zwei protestantische Universitäten vom 16.–18. Jahrhundert*. Sitzungsberichte der Bayerischen Akademie der Wissenschaften, philosoph.-philolog. und hist. Klasse, Jahrgang, 1920, Abhandlung 5. Munich, 1920.

Keim, Karl Theodor. *Schwäbische Reformationsgeschichte bis zum Augsburger Reichstag. Mit vorzüglicher Rücksicht auf die entscheidenden Schlussjahre 1528–1531. Mit einem Anhang ungedruckter Reformationsbriefe*. Tübingen, 1855.

Ambrosius Blarer, der schwäbische Reformator. Stuttgart, 1860.

Keller, Alfred. *Die Wiedereinsetzung des Herzogs Ulrich von Württemberg durch den Landgrafen Philipp von Hessen 1533/34*. Marburg, 1912.

Kerlen, Dietrich. *Assertio. Die Entwicklung von Luthers theologischem Anspruch und der Streit mit Erasmus von Rotterdam*. VIEG 78. Wiesbaden, 1976.

Keussen, Hermann. 'Der Dominikaner Matthäus Grabow und die Brüder vom gemeinsamen Leben.' *Mittheilungen aus dem Stadtarchiv von Köln* 5 (1888): 29–47.

'Kleine Mittheilungen.' *Mittheilungen aus dem Stadtarchiv von Köln* 7 (1892): 102–3.

Kingdon, Robert M. 'Was the Protestant Reformation a Revolution? The Case of Geneva.' In *Church, Society and Politics*, pp. 203–22. Edited by D. Baker. Studies in Church History, 12. Oxford, 1975. With slight changes in *Transition and Revolution. Problems and Issues of European Renaissance and Reformation History*, pp. 53–76; with primary source excerpts appended, *ibid.*, pp. 77–107. Edited by R. M. Kingdon. Minneapolis, 1974.

Kisch, Guido. *Humanismus und Jurisprudenz. Der Kampf zwischen mos italicus und mos gallicus an der Universität Basel*. Basler Studien zur Rechtswissenschaft, 42. Basel, 1955.

Erasmus und die Jurisprudenz seiner Zeit. Studien zum humanistischen Rechtsdenken. Basler Studien zur Rechtswissenschaft, 56. Basel, 1960.

Melanchthons Rechts- und Soziallehre. Berlin, 1967.

Kittelson, James M. *Wolfgang Capito. From Humanist to Reformer*. SMRT 17. Leiden, 1975.

Kleineidam, Erich. *Universitas Studii Erffordensis. Überblick über die Geschichte der Universität Erfurt im Mittelalter 1392–1521*, pt. 1: *1392–1460*, pt. 2: *1460–1521*. Erfurter Theologische Studien, 14, 22. Leipzig, 1964, 1969.

'Geschichte der Wissenschaft im mittelalterlichen Erfurt.' In *Geschichte Thüringens*, vol. 2, pt. 2: *Hohes und spätes Mittelalter*, ch. 3, pp. 150–346. Edited by H. Patze, W. Schlesinger. Cologne, Vienna, 1973.

Knod, Gustav C. *Deutsche Studenten in Bologna (1289–1562). Biographischer Index zu den Acta nationis Germanicae universitatis Bononiensis*. Berlin, 1899.

Knoll, Paul W. 'The World of the Young Copernicus. Society, Science, and the University.' In *Science and Society. Past, Present and Future*, pp. 19–44. Edited by N. H. Steneck. Ann Arbor, 1975.

Koch, Joseph. *Durandus de S. Porciano O.P. Forschungen zum Streit um Thomas von Aquin zu Beginn des 14. Jahrhunderts*, vol. 1. Beiträge zur Geschichte der Philosophie des Mittelalters, 26. Münster i.W., 1927.

Köhler, Walther. 'Kleine Beiträge zur Reformationsgeschichte 2: Schweizer und Schweizerbücher in Strassburg.' *Zwingliana* 3 (1918, 1): 348–9.

Zwingli und Luther. Ihr Streit über das Abendmahl nach seinen politischen und religiösen Beziehungen, vol. 1: *Die religiöse und politische Entwicklungen bis zum Marburger Religionsgespräch 1529*; vol. 2: *Vom Beginn der Marburger Verhandlungen 1529 bis zum Abschluss der Wittenberger Konkordie von 1536* (edited by E. Kohlmeyer, H. Bornkamm). QFRG 6 and 7. Leipzig, 1924 and Gütersloh, 1953.

Zürcher Ehegericht und Genfer Konsistorium, vol. 1: *Das Zürcher Ehegericht und seine Auswirkung in der deutschen Schweiz zur Zeit Zwinglis*; vol. 2: *Das Ehe- und Sittengericht in den süddeutschen Reichsstädten, dem Herzogtum Württemberg und in Genf*. Quellen und Abhandlungen zur Schweizerischen Reformationsgeschichte, 7/10. Leipzig, 1932–42.

Kölmel, Wilhelm. *Wilhelm Ockham und seine kirchenpolitischen Schriften*. Essen, 1962.

Kohls, Ernst-Wilhelm. *Die Schule bei Martin Bucer in ihrem Verhältnis zu Kirche und Obrigkeit*. Pädagogische Forschungen. Veröffentlichungen des Comenius-Instituts, 22. Heidelberg, 1963.

Die Theologie des Erasmus, vol. 1: *Textband*. Theologische Zeitschrift, Sonderband I, 1. Basel, 1966.

Luther oder Erasmus. Luthers Theologie in der Auseinandersetzung mit Erasmus, vol. 1. Theologische Zeitschrift, Sonderband 3. Basel, 1972.

Kolde, Theodor. *Die deutsche Augustiner-Congregation und Johann von Staupitz. Ein Beitrag zur Ordens- und Reformationsgeschichte*. Gotha, 1879.

'Camerarius, Joachim, gest. 1574.' In *RE* 3: 687–9.

Krafft, Fritz. 'Renaissance der Naturwissenschaften – Naturwissenschaften der Renaissance. Ein Überblick über die Nachkriegsliteratur.' In *Humanismusforschung seit 1945. Ein Bericht aus interdisziplinärer Sicht*, pp. 111–83. Edited by A. Buck. Deutsche Forschungsgemeinschaft. Kommission für Humanismusforschung, Mitteilung 2. Boppard, 1975.

Kristeller, Paul Oskar. 'The European Diffusion of Italian Humanism.' *Italica* 39 (1962): 1–20; reprinted in *idem*, *Renaissance Thought* II: *Papers on Humanism and the Arts*, pp. 69–88. New York, 1965.

Iter Italicum. A Finding List of Uncatalogued or Incompletely Catalogued Humanistic Manuscripts of the Renaissance in Italian and Other Libraries, vol. 1: *Italy, Agrigento to Novara*; vol. 2: *Italy, Orvieto to Volterra; Vatican City*. London, Leiden, 1965–7.

Kroon, Marijn de. 'Pseudo-Augustin im Mittelalter.' *Augustiniana* 22 (1972): 511–30.

Kuhn, Werner. *Die Studenten der Universität Tübingen zwischen 1477 und 1534. Ihr Studium und ihre spätere Lebensstellung* (Pt. 2). Göppinger Akademische Beiträge, 37/8. Göppingen, 1971.

Kurten, Edmund. *Franz Lambert von Avignon und Nikolaus Herborn*. RGST 72. Münster i.W., 1950.

Le Goff, Jacques. 'La conception française de l'université à l'époque de la Renaissance.' In *Les Universités européennes du XIVe au XVIIIe siècle. Aspects et problemes*, pp. 94–100. Actes du colloque international à l'occasion du VIe centenaire de l'Université Jagellonne de Cracovie, 6–8 Mai 1964, Études et documents, 4 = Commission Internationale pour l'Histoire des Universités, Études et Travaux, 1. Geneva, 1967.

Leff, Gordon. *William of Ockham. The Metamorphosis of Scholastic Discourse.* Manchester, 1975.

Lehmann, Paul. *Merkwürdigkeiten des Abtes Johannes Trithemius.* Sitzungsberichte der Bayerischen Akademie der Wissenschaften, phil.-hist. Klasse, Jahrgang 1961, Heft 2. Munich, 1961.

Lexikon der Alten Welt. Zürich, Stuttgart, 1965.

Liebing, Heinz. 'Perspektivische Verzeichnungen. Über die Haltbarkeit der *fable convenue* in der Kirchengeschichte.' *ZKG* 79 (1968): 289–307.

Lienhard, Marc and Rott, Jean. 'Die Anfänge der evangelischen Predigt in Strassburg und ihr erstes Manifest: Der Aufruf des Karmeliterlesemeisters Tilman von Lyn (Anfang 1522).' In *Bucer und Seine Zeit. Forschungsbeiträge und Bibliographie*, pp. 54–73. Edited by M. de Kroon, F. Krüger. VIEG 80, Wiesbaden, 1976.

Linsenmann, Franz Xaver. *Konrad Summenhart. Ein Culturbild aus den Anfängen der Universität Tübingen. Zur vierten Säcularfeier der Universität Tübingen im Sommer 1877.* Festprogramm der katholisch-theologischen Facultät. Tübingen, 1877.

Lipgens, Walter. *Kardinal Johannes Gropper (1503–1559) und die Anfänge der Katholischen Reform in Deutschland.* RGST 75. Münster i.W., 1951.

Locher, Gottfried W. 'Praedicatio verbi Dei est verbum Dei. Heinrich Bullinger zwischen Luther und Zwingli. Ein Beitrag zu seiner Theologie.' *Zwingliana* 10 (1954, 1): 47–57; reprinted in *idem, Huldrych Zwingli in neuer Sicht. Zehn Beiträge zur Theologie der Zürcher Reformation*, pp. 275–87. Zürich, Stuttgart, 1969.

'Zwinglis Einfluss in England und Schottland. Daten und Probleme.' *Zwingliana* 14 (1975): 165–209.

'Von Bern nach Genf. Die Ursachen der Spannung zwischen zwinglischer und calvinistischer Reformation.' In *Wegen en Gestalten in het Gereformeerd Protestantisme.* Festschrift S. van der Linde, pp. 75–87. Edited by W. Balke, C. Graafland, H. Harkema. Amsterdam, 1976.

Löhr, Gabriel M. *Die Kölner Dominikanerschule vom 14. bis zum 16. Jahrhundert. Mit einer Übersicht über die Gesamtentwicklung.* Cologne, 1948.

Loewenich, Walther von. *Duplex iustitia. Luther's Stellung zu einer Unionsformel des 16. Jahrhunderts.* VIEG 68. Wiesbaden, 1972.

'Zum Gedächtnis an Joseph Lortz.' *Luther. Zeitschrift der Luther-Gesellschaft* 46 (1975): 47–8.

Lortz, Joseph. *Die Reformation in Deutschland*, vol. 1: *Voraussetzungen, Aufbruch, erste Entscheidung.* 1st edn, 1939, 4th edn, Freiburg i. Br., Basel, Vienna, 1962. Translated by Ronald Walls. *The Reformation in Germany.* 2 vols. London, New York, 1968.

Lorz, Jürgen, *Bibliographia Linckiana. Bibliographie der gedruckten Schriften Dr. Wenzeslaus Lincks (1483–1547)*. Bibliotheca Humanistica et Reformatorica, 18. Nieuwkoop, 1977.

Lutz, Samuel. 'Aus dem Schrifttum von Gottfried W. Locher.' *Zwingliana* 13 (1971, 2): 425–9.

McGrade, Arthur S. *The Political Thought of William of Ockham. Personal and Institutional Principles*. London, New York, 1974.

McLaughlin, T. P. 'The Teaching of the Canonists on Usury (XII, XIII and XIV Centuries).' *Mediaeval Studies* 1 (1939): 81–147; 2 (1940): 1–22.

McSorley, Harry J. 'Was Gabriel Biel a Semipelagian?' In *Wahrheit und Verkündigung*, Michael Schmaus zum 70. Geburtstag, pp. 1109–20. Edited by L. Scheffczyk, W. Dettloff, R. Heinzmann. Munich, 1967.

Luthers Lehre vom unfreien Willen. Nach seiner Hauptschrift De Servo Arbitrio im Lichte der biblischen und kirchlichen Tradition. Beiträge zur ökumenischen Theologie, 1. Munich, 1967. Translated as *Luther. Right or Wrong? An Ecumenical–Theological Study of Luther's Major Work, The Bondage of the Will, by a Roman Catholic Scholar*. Minneapolis, 1969.

'Erasmus versus Luther – Compounding the Reformation Tragedy?' In *Catholic Scholars Dialogue with Luther*, pp. 107–17. Edited by J. Wicks. Chicago, 1970.

Maier, Anneliese. *Studien zur Naturphilosophie der Spätscholastik*, vol. 1: *Die Vorläufer Galileis im 14. Jahrhundert*; vol. 4: *Metaphysische Hintergründe der spätscholastischen Naturphilosophie*. Storia e letteratura, 22 and 52. Rome, 1949 and 1955.

March, J. M. 'Cuestiones cuolibetales de la Biblioteca capitular de Tortosa.' *Estudios ecclesiásticos* 5 (1926): 120–63.

Massaut, Jean-Pierre. *Josse Clichtove, l'Humanisme et la réforme du clergé*, vol. 1. Bibliothèque de la Faculté de Philosophie et Lettres de l'Université de Liège, 183. Paris, 1968.

Maurer, Justus. 'Das Verhalten der reformatorisch gesinnten Geistlichen Süddeutschlands im Bauernkrieg 1525,' vol. 1: 'Systematische Darstellung des Themas'; vol. 2: 'Biographische Darstellung des Themas.' Dissertation, Tübingen, 1975.

Maurer, Wilhelm. *Der junge Melanchthon zwischen Humanismus und Reformation*, vol. 1: *Der Humanist*. Göttingen, 1967.

Mayer, Johann G. 'Die Disputation zu Zürich am 29. Januar 1523.' *Katholische Schweizer Blätter* 11 (1895): 51–65; 183–95.

Meissinger, Karl August. *Luther. Die deutsche Tragödie 1521*. Sammlung Dalp, 35. Munich, 1953.

Mestwerdt, Paul. *Die Anfänge des Erasmus. Humanismus und 'devotio moderna'*. Edited by H. von Schubert. Studien zur Kultur und Geschichte der Reformation, 2. Leipzig, 1917.

Meyer, Otto. *Die Brüder des gemeinsamen Lebens in Württemberg 1477–1517*. Stuttgart, [1914]; also appeared in *BWKG* 17 (1913): 97–138 [=1] and 18 (1914): 142–60 [=2].

Midelfort, H. C. Erik. *Witch Hunting in Southwestern Germany 1562–1684. The Social and Intellectual Foundations*. Stanford, 1972.

Miethke, Jürgen. *Ockhams Weg zur Sozialphilosophie*. Berlin, 1969.

Miller, Perry. *The New England Mind. The Seventeenth Century*. 2nd edn, Cambridge, Mass., London, 1954.

Moeller, Bernd. 'Die deutschen Humanisten und die Anfänge der Reformation.' *ZKG* 70 (1959): 46–61; translated by Erik Midelfort and Mark Edwards, Jr, in Moeller, *Imperial Cities and the Reformation. Three Essays*, pp. 19–40. Philadelphia, 1972.

'Die Kirche in den evangelischen freien Städten Oberdeutschlands im Zeitalter der Reformation.' *Zeitschrift für die Geschichte des Oberrheins* 112 [N.S. 73] (1964): 147–62.

'Nachträge zum Blarer-Briefwechsel 1523–1548. Zum 400. Todestag von Ambrosius Blarer am 6. Dezember 1964.' *BWKG* 64 (1964): 3–52.

'Ambrosius Blarer 1492–1564.' In *Blarer-Gedenkschrift*, pp. 11–38.

'Neue Nachträge zum Blarer-Briefwechsel. Zur Reformation der Universität Tübingen 1534–1535.' *BWKG* 68/9 '1968/9): 60–80.

'Zwinglis Disputationen. Studien zu den Anfängen der Kirchenbildung und des Synodalwesens im Protestantismus.' *ZSRG.K* 56 (1970): 275–324; 60 (1974): 213–364.

'Kleriker als Bürger.' *Festschrift für Hermann Heimpel*, vol. 2, pp. 195–224. Göttingen, 1972.

Pfarrer als Bürger. Göttinger Universitätsreden, 56. Göttingen, 1972.

'Die Ursprünge der reformierten Kirche.' *Theologische Literaturzeitung* 100 (1975): 642–53.

Monfrin, Jacques. 'Les lectures de Guillaume Fichet et de Jean Heynlin.' *Bibliothèque d'Humanisme et Renaissance* 17 (1955): 7–23.

Moore, Walter L., Jr. 'Between Mani and Pelagius. Predestination and Justification in the Early Writings of John Eck.' Ph.D. Dissertation, Harvard University, 1967.

Morf, Hans. *Zunftverfassung, Obrigkeit und Kirche in Zürch von Waldmann bis Zwingli*. Mitteilungen der Antiquarischen Gesellschaft in Zürich, vol. 45, Heft 1. Zürich, 1969.

Moser, Andreas. 'Franz Lamberts Reise durch die Schweiz im Jahre 1522.' *Zwingliana* 10 (1957): 467–71.

Moser, Johannes Jakob. *Vitae professorum Tubingensium ordinis theologici, decas prima*. Tübingen, 1718.

Mühlen, Karl-Heinz zur. *Nos extra nos. Luthers Theologie zwischen Mystik und Scholastik*. Beiträge zur Historischen Theologie, 46. Tübingen, 1972.

Mülhaupt, Erwin. '200 Sprichwörter und Sprüche aus Luthers Evangelien- und Psalmenauslegung.' *Luther. Zeitschrift der Luther Gesellschaft* 47 (1976): 23–37.

Müller, Alphons Victor. *Luthers theologische Quellen. Seine Verteidigung gegen Denifle und Grisar*. Giessen, 1912.

Müller, Gerhard. *Franz Lambert von Avignon und die Reformation in Hessen*. Veröffentlichungen der Historischen Kommission für Hesen und Waldeck, 24. Quellen und Darstellungen zur Geschichte des Landgrafen Philipp des Grossmütigen, 4. Marburg, 1958.

Die römische Kurie und die Reformation 1523–1534. Kirche und Politik während des Pontifikates Clemens' VII. QFRG 38. Gütersloh, 1969.

'Die Synode als Fundament der evangelischen Kirche in Hessen. Homberg 1526–1976.' *Jahrbuch der hessischen kirchengeschichtlichen Vereinigung* 27 (1976): 129–46.

Müller, Karl O. 'Heinrich Institoris, der Verfasser des Hexenhammers, und seine Tätigkeit als Hexeninquisitor in Ravensburg im Herbst 1484.' *Württembergische Vierteljahrshefte für Landesgeschichte* N.S. 19 (1910): 397–417.

Müller-Armack, Alfred. 'Holzwege der Universitätsreform. Aus Stätten wissenschaftlicher Bildung werden höhere Schulen.' *Frankfurter Allgemeine Zeitung*, 6 May 1977, pp. 9–10.

Muralt, Leonhard von. 'Stadtgemeinde und Reformation in der Schweiz.' *Zeitschrift für Schweizerische Geschichte* 10 (1930): 349–84.

Murdoch, John. 'Philosophy and the Enterprise of Science in the Later Middle Ages.' In *The Interaction between Science and Philosophy*, pp. 51–74. Edited by Y. Elkana. The Van Leer Jerusalem Foundation Series. Atlantic Highlands, N.J., 1974

Naber, Johanna W. A. *Vrouwenleven in Prae-Reformatietijd bezegeld door den marteldood van Wendelmoet Claesdochter*. 's-Gravenhage, 1927.

Nauert, Charles G., Jr. *Agrippa and the Crisis of Renaissance Thought*. Illinois Studies in the Social Sciences, 55. Urbana, 1965.

Nelson, Benjamin N. 'The Usurer and the Merchant Prince: Italian Businessmen and the Ecclesiastical Law of Restitution, 1100–1550.' *The Journal of Economic History*, Suppl. 7 (1947): 104–22.

The Idea of Usury. From Tribal Brotherhood to Universal Otherhood. Princeton, 1949.

Nörr, Knut Wolfgang. *Kirche und Konzil bei Nicolaus de Tudeschis (Panormitanus)*. Forschungen zur kirchlichen Rechtsgeschichte und zum Kirchenrecht, 4. Cologne, Graz, 1964.

Noonan, John T., Jr. *The Scholastic Analysis of Usury*. Cambridge, Mass., 1957.

Nygren, Gotthard. *Das Prädestinationsproblem in der Theologie Augustins. Eine systematisch-theologische Studie*. Studia theologica Lundensia, 12 = Forschungen zur Kirchen und Dogmengeschichte, 5. Lund, Göttingen, 1956.

Nyhus, Paul L. *The Franciscans in South Germany, 1400–1530: Reform and Revolution*. Transactions of the American Philosophical Society, N.S. 65, pt. 8. Philadelphia, 1975.

Oberman, Heiko Augustinus. *Archbishop Thomas Bradwardine, a Fourteenth Century Augustinian. A Study of His Theology in Its Historical Context*. 2nd edn, Utrecht, 1958.

'Facientibus quod in se est Deus non denegat gratiam. Robert Holcot, O.P. and the Beginnings of Luther's Theology.' *The Harvard Theological Review* 55 (1962): 317–42; reprinted in *The Reformation in Medieval Perspective*, pp. 119–41. Edited by Steven E. Ozment. Chicago, 1971.

The Harvest of Medieval Theology. Gabriel Biel and Late Medieval Nominalism. Cambridge, Mass., 1963; 2nd rev. edn, Grand Rapids, 1967.

'Das tridentinische Rechtfertigungsdekret im Lichte spätmittelalterlicher Theologie.' *ZThK* 61 (1964): 251–82.

Forerunners of the Reformation. The Shape of Late Medieval Thought, illustrated by key documents. Translations by Paul L. Nyhus. New York, 1966.

'Die "Extra"-Dimension in der Theologie Calvins.' In *Geist und Geschichte der Reformation.* Festgabe Hanns Rückert, pp. 323–56. Edited by H. Liebing, K. Scholder. Berlin, 1966.

'Simul gemitus et raptus. Luther and Mysticism.' In *The Reformation in Medieval Perspective,* pp. 219–51. Edited by Steven E. Ozment. Chicago, 1971.

Contra vanam curiositatem. Ein Kapitel der Theologie zwischen Seelenwinkel und Weltall. Theologische Studien, 113. Zürich, 1974.

'Headwaters of the Reformation: Initia Lutheri – Initia Reformationis.' In *Luther and the Dawn of the Modern Era. Papers for the Fourth International Congress for Luther Research,* pp. 40–88. Edited by H. A. Oberman. SHCT 8. Leiden, 1974.

'Tumultus rusticorum. Vom "Klosterkrieg" zum Fürstensieg. Beobachtungen zum Bauernkrieg unter besonderer Berücksichtigung zeitgenössischer Beurteilungen.' *ZKG* 85 (1974): 301–16; extended English version, 'The Gospel of Social Unrest: 450 Years after the So-Called "German Peasants' War" of 1525.' *Harvard Theological Review* 69 (1976): 103–29.

'"Et tibi dabo claves regni caelorum." Kirche und Konzil von Augustin bis Luther. Tendenzen und Ergebnisse, II.' *Nederlands Theologisch Tijdschrift* 29 (1975): 97–118.

'Reformation and Revolution: Copernicus' Discovery in an Era of Change.' In *The Cultural Context of Medieval Learning,* pp. 397–429. Edited by J. E. Murdoch, E. D. Sylla. Boston Studies in the Philosophy of Science, 26 = Synthese Library, 76. Dordrecht, Boston, 1975. Abridged in *The Nature of Scientific Discovery,* pp. 134–69. Edited by O. Gingerich. Washington, 1975.

'Quoscunque tulit foecunda vetustas. Ad Lectorem.' In *Itinerarium Italicum,* pp. ix–xxviii.

'Reformation: Epoche oder Episode.' *ARG* 68 (1977): 56–111.

Öhler, Heinrich. 'Der Aufstand des Armen Konrad im Jahr 1514.' *Württembergische Vierteljahrshefte für Landesgeschichte* 38 (1932): 401–86.

Ogilvie, Margaret H. 'Wessel Gansfort's Theology of Church Government.' *Nederlands Archief voor Kerkgeschiedenis* N.S. 55 (1974/5): 125–50.

Olivier, Daniel. 'Les deux sermons sur la double et triple justice.' *Oecumenica* 3 (1968): 39–69.

O'Malley, John W. *Giles of Viterbo on Church and Reform. A Study in Renaissance Thought.* SMRT 5. Leiden, 1968.

Ong, Walter J. *Ramus. Method and the Decay of Dialogue. From the Art of Discourse to the Art of Reason.* Cambridge, Mass., 1958.

Ott, Hugo. 'Zur Wirtschaftsethik des Konrad Summenhart.' *Vierteljahrschrift für Sozial- und Wirtschaftsgeschichte* 53 (1966): 1–27.

Oyer, John S. 'The Influence of Jacob Strauss on the Anabaptists.' In *The Origins and Characteristics of Anabaptism*. Proceedings of the Colloquium organized by the Faculty of Protestant Theology of Strasburg (20–2 February 1975), pp. 62–82. Edited by Marc Lienhard. International Archives of the History of Ideas, 87. The Hague, 1977.

Ozment, Steven E. *Homo Spiritualis. A Comparative Study of the Anthropology of Johannes Tauler, Jean Gerson and Martin Luther (1509–16), in the Context of their Theological Thought*. SMRT 6. Leiden, 1969.

Mysticism and Dissent. Religious Ideology and Social Protest in the Sixteenth Century. New Haven, London, 1973.

The Reformation in the Cities. The Appeal of Protestantism to Sixteenth-Century Germany and Switzerland. New Haven, London, 1975.

Pannenberg, Wolfhart. *Die Prädestinationslehre des Duns Skotus im Zusammenhang der scholastischen Lehrentwicklung*. Göttingen, 1954.

Paqué, Ruprecht. *Das Pariser Nominalistenstatut. Zur Entstehung des Realitätsbegriff der neuzeitlichen Naturwissenschaft (Occam, Buridan und Petrus Hispanus, Nikolaus von Autrecourt und Gregor von Rimini)*. Quellen und Studien zur Geschichte der Philosophie, 14. Berlin, 1970.

Pastor, Ludwig von. *Geschichte der Päpste seit dem Ausgang des Mittelalters*, vol. 3: *Geschichte der Päpste im Zeitalter der Renaissance von der Wahl Innocenz' VIII. bis zum Tode Julius' II*. 7th edn, Freiburg i.Br., 1924.

Paul, Robert. *The Lord Protector. Religion and Politics in the Life of Oliver Cromwell*. London, 1955.

Paulus, Nicolaus. 'Johann von Staupitz. Seine vorgeblich protestantische Gesinnung.' *Historisches Jahrbuch der Görresgesellschaft* 12 (1891): 309–46.

'Württemberger Hexenpredigten aus dem 16. Jahrhundert.' *Diöcesanarchiv von Schwaben* 15 (1897): 81–5; 107–8.

Payne, John B. *Erasmus. His Theology of the Sacraments*. Richmond, 1970.

Peachey, Paul. *Die soziale Herkunft der Schweizer Täufer in der Reformationszeit. Eine religionssoziologische Untersuchung*. Schriftenreihe des Mennonitischen Geschichtsvereins, 4. Karlsruhe, 1954.

Pestalozzi, Carl. *Heinrich Bullinger. Leben und ausgewählte Schriften*. Leben und ausgewählte Schriften der Väter und Begründer der reformirten Kirche, 5. Elberfeld, 1858. *Register*. Compiled by S. Fischer. Zürich, 1975.

Leo Judä. Leben und Ausgewählte Schriften der Väter und Begründer der reformirten Kirche, 9[2]. Elberfeld, 1860.

Pestalozzi, Theodor. *Die Gegner Zwinglis am Grossmünsterstift in Zürich. Der erste Teil einer Arbeit über: Die katholische Opposition gegen Zwingli in Stadt und Landschaft Zürich 1519–1531, mit einer Einleitung zur Gesamtarbeit*. Schweizer Studien zur Geschichtswissenschaft, 11, Heft 1. Zürich, 1918.

Petry, Ludwig. 'Die Reformation als Epoche der deutschen Universitätsgeschichte. Eine Zwischenbilanz.' In *Festgabe Joseph Lortz*, vol. 2: *Glaube und Geschichte*, pp. 317–53. Edited by E. Iserloh, P. Manns. Baden-Baden, 1958.

Pfister, Rudolf. 'Kirche und Glaube auf der Ersten Zürcher Disputation vom 29. Januar 1523.' *Zwingliana* 13 (1973, 1): 533–69.

Kirchengeschichte der Schweiz, vol. 2: *Von der Reformation bis zum zweiten Villmerger Krieg*. Zürich, 1974.

Plinval, Georges de. *Pélage, ses écrits, sa vie et sa réforme. Étude d'histoire litteraire et religieuse*. Lausanne, 1943.

Pölnitz, Götz Freiherr von. 'Die Bezlehungen des Johannes Eck zum Augsburger Kapital.' *Historisches Jahrbuch der Görresgesellschaft* 60 (1940): 685–706.

Jakob Fugger, vol. 1: *Kaiser, Kirche und Kapital in der oberdeutschen Renaissance*; vol. 2: *Quellen und Erläuterungen*. Tübingen, 1949.

'Jakob Fugger.' In *Jakob Fugger, Kaiser Maximilian und Augsburg 1459–1959*, pp. 5–40. Issued by the City of Augsburg, 1959.

Polman, Pontien. *L'Élement historique dans la controverse religieuse du XVIe siècle*. Gembloux, 1932.

Pontal, Odette. *Les statuts synodaux*. Typologie des sources du moyen âge occidental, 11. Turnhout, 1975.

Poschmann, Bernhard. *Die katholische Frömmigkeit*. Würzburg, 1949.

Post, R. R. *The Modern Devotion. Confrontation with Reformation and Humanism*. SMRT 3. Leiden, 1968.

Posthumus Meyjes, Guillaume Henri Marie. *Jean Gerson. Zijn kerkpolitiek en ecclesiologie*. 's-Gravenhage, 1963.

Potter, G. R. *Zwingli*. Cambridge, 1976.

Prantl, C. *Geschichte der Logik im Abendlande*, vols. 3 and 4. Leipzig, 1867/70; reprinted Graz, 1955.

Preisendanz, Karl. 'Die Bibliothek Johannes Reuchlins.' In *Festgabe Reuchlin*, pp. 35–82.

Preus, James S. *Carlstadt's Ordinaciones and Luther's Liberty. A Study of the Wittenberg Movement 1521–22*. Harvard Theological Studies, 26. Cambridge, Mass., London, 1974.

Rabe, Horst. *Reichsbund und Interim. Die Verfassungs- und Religionspolitik Karls V. und der Reichstag von Augsburg 1547/1548*. Cologne, Vienna, 1971.

Ramp, Ernst. *Das Zinsproblem. Eine historische Untersuchung*. Zürich, 1949.

Rapp, Francis. *Réformes et Réformation à Strasbourg. Église et société dans le Diocèse de Strasbourg (1450–1525)*. Collection de l'Institut des Hautes Études Alsaciennes, 23. Paris, [1974].

Rashdall, Hastings. *The Universities of Europe in the Middle Ages*, revised edition edited by F. M. Powicke, A. B. Emden, vol. 2: *Italy, Spain, France, Germany, Scotland, etc.* 6th edn, Oxford 1964 [1895].

Rau, Reinhold. 'Der Beitrag der Basler Hochschule zu den Anfängen der Universität Tübingen.' *Basler Zeitschrift für Geschichte und Altertumskunde* 52 (1953): 14–36.

'Philipp Melanchthons Tübinger Jahre.' *Tübinger Blätter* 47 (1960): 16–25.

'Über eine Sammlung von Inschriften des 16. Jahrhunderts.' *Zeitschrift für Württembergische Landesgeschichte* 23 (1964): 418–38.

Rauscher, Julius. *Württembergische Reformationsgeschichte*. Württembergische Kirchengeschichte, published by Calwer Verlagsverein, 3. Stuttgart, 1934.

Renaudet, Augustin. *Préréforme et humanisme à Paris pendant les premières guerres d'Italie (1494–1517).* Bibliothèque Elzévirienne, N.S., Études et documents. 2nd edn, Paris, 1953.

Humanisme et Renaissance. Dante, Pétrarque, Standonck, Érasme Lefèvre d'Étaples, Marguerite de Navarre, Rabelais, Guichardin, Giordano Bruno. Travaux d'Humanisme et Renaissance, 30. Geneva, 1958.

Rhijn, Maarten van. *Wessel Gansfort.* 's-Gravenhage, 1917.

'Luther en Gregorius van Rimini.' *Theologisch Tijdschrift* 53 (1919): 238–42.

'Wessel Gansfort te Heidelberg en de strijd tussen de "via antiqua" en de "via moderna".' In *Studiën over Wessel Gansfort en zijn tijd*, pp. 23–37. Utrecht, 1933.

Richardson, Herbert W. *Nun, Witch, Playmate. The Americanization of Sex.* New York, 1971.

Riecke, Karl Viktor von, Hartmann, Julius, compilers, *Statistik der Universität Tübingen.* Stuttgart, 1877.

Ritter, Gerhard. *Studien zur Spätscholastik*, vol. 1: *Marsilius von Inghen und die okkamistische Schule in Deutschland.* Sitzungsberichte der Heidelberger Akademie der Wissenschaften, phil.-hist. Klasse, Jahrgang 1921, Heft 4. Heidelberg, 1921.

Studien zur Spätscholastik, vol. 2: *Via antiqua und via moderna auf den deutschen Universitäten des XV. Jahrhunderts.* Heidelberg, 1922; reprinted Darmstadt, 1975.

Die Heidelberger Universität. Ein Stück deutscher Geschichte, vol. 1: *Das Mittelalter (1386–1508).* Heidelberg, 1936.

Roensch, F. J. *Early Thomistic School.* Dubuque, 1964.

Roover, Raymond de. *The Medici Bank. Its Organization, Management, Operations, and Decline.* Business History Series. New York, London, 1948.

'The Concept of the Just Price. Theory and Economic Policy.' *The Journal of Economic History* 18 (1958): 418–34; reprinted in *Readings in the History of Economic Theory*, pp. 9–21. Edited by I. H. Rima. New York, 1970.

The Rise and Decline of the Medici Bank, 1397–1494. Harvard Studies in Business History, 21. Cambridge, Mass., 1963.

La Pensée économique des scolastiques. Doctrines et méthodes. Montréal, Paris, 1971.

'The Scholastic Attitude toward Trade and Entrepreneurship.' Reprinted from *Explorations in Entrepreneurial History*, 2nd series 1 (1963): 76–87. In *Business, Banking, and Economic Thought in Late Medieval and Early Modern Europe*, pp. 336–54. Edited by J. Kirshner. Chicago, London, 1974.

Roth, Friedrich. *Willibald Pirkheimer, ein Lebensbild aus dem Zeitalter des Humanismus und der Reformation.* Schriften des Vereins für Reformationsgeschichte, 21. Halle, 1887.

Augsburgs Reformationsgeschichte, vol. 2: *1531–1537 bzw. 1540.* Munich, 1904.

Roth, Paul. *Durchbruch und Festsetzung der Reformation in Basel. Eine Darstellung der Politik der Stadt Basel im Jahre 1529*. Basler Beiträge zur Geschichtswissenschaft, 8. Basel, 1942.

Rott, Jean. 'L'humanisme et la réforme pédagogique en Alsace.' In *L'Humanisme en Alsace*. Association Guillaume Budé, congrès de Strasbourg, 20–2 Avril 1938, pp. 64–82. Paris, 1939.

'Un recueil de correspondances strasbourgeoises du XVIe siècle à la bibliothèque de Copenhague (ms. Thott 497, 2°).' *Bulletin philologique et historique (jusqu'à 1610)*, année 1968, vol. 2 (Paris, 1971): 749–818.

'La Réforme à Nuremberg et à Strasbourg: contacts et contrastes (avec des correspondances inédites).' in *Hommage à Dürer. Strasbourg et Nuremberg dans la première moitié du XVIe siècle*. Actes du colloque de Strasbourg (19–20 novembre 1971), pp. 91–142. Publications de la Société Savante d'Alsace et des régions de l'Est. Collection 'Recherches et Documents', 12. Strasbourg, 1972.

Rublack, Hans-Christoph. 'Zwei neugefundene Stücke zum Blarer-Briefwechsel.' *BWKG* 66/7 (1966/7): 27–34.

Die Einführung der Reformation in Konstanz von den Anfängen bis zum Abschluss 1531. QFRG 40 = Veröffentlichungen des Vereins für Kirchengeschichte in der evangelischen Landeskirche in Baden, 27. Heidelberg, Karlsruhe, 1971.

and Scheible, Heinz. 'Matthäus Alber als Reformator Reutlingens. Die neugefundene Beschreibung seines Lebens.' *Reutlinger Geschichtsblätter* N.S. 14 (1976): 44–69.

Rückbrod, Konrad. *Universität und Kollegium, Baugeschichte und Bautyp*. Darmstadt, 1977.

Rückert, Hanns. 'Die Stellung der Reformation zur mittelalterlichen Universität.' In *Die Universität. Ihre Geschichte, Aufgabe und Bedeutung in der Gegenwart*, pp. 63–96. Öffentliche Vorträge der Universität Tübingen, Wintersemester 1932/3. Stuttgart, 1933; reprinted in *idem*, *Vorträge und Aufsätze zur historischen Theologie*, pp. 71–95. Tübingen, 1972.

'Die Bedeutung der württembergischen Reformation für den Gang der deutschen Reformationsgeschichte.' *BWKG* 38 (1934): 267–80; reprinted in *idem*, *Vorträge und Aufsätze*, pp. 239–51. Tübingen, 1972.

'Promereri. Eine Studie zum tridentinischen Rechtfertigungsdekret als Antwort an H. A. Oberman.' *ZThK* 68 (1971): 162–94; reprinted in *idem*, *Vorträge und Aufsätze*, pp. 264–94. Tübingen, 1972.

Rusch, Paulus. 'Mariologische Wertungen.' *Zeitschrift für katholische Theologie* 85 (1963): 129–61.

Russell, Jeffrey Burton. *Witchcraft in the Middle Ages*. Ithaca, 1972.

Scarisbrick, J. J. *Henry VIII*. London, 1968.

Schaich-Klose, Wiebke. *D. Hieronymus Schürpf. Leben und Werk des Wittenberger Reformationsjuristen 1481–1554*. Trogen (Switz.), 1967.

Scheel, Otto. *Die Entwicklung Luthers bis zum Abschluss der Vorlesung über den Römerbrief*. In Schriften des Vereins für Reformationsgeschichte, 100, pp. 63–230. Leipzig, 1910.

Scheib, Otto. 'Die theologischen Diskussionen Huldrych Zwinglis. Zur

Entstehung und Struktur der Relgionsgespräche des 16. Jahrhunderts.' In *Von Konstanz nach Trient. Beiträge zur Geschichte der Kirche von den Reformkonzilien bis zum Tridentinum.* Festgabe August Franzen, pp. 395–417. Edited by R. Bäumer. Munich, Paderborn, Vienna, 1972.

Schepers, Heinrich. Review of: K. A. Sprengard, *Systematisch-historische Untersuchungen zur Philosophie des XIV. Jahrhunderts. Ein Beitrag zur Kritik an der herrschenden spätscholastischen Mediaevistik.* Mainzer Philosophische Forschungen, 3, a/b. Bonn, 1967/8. In *Philosophisches Jahrbuch* 76 (1969): 395–400.

Schlecht, Joseph. 'Dr. Johann Ecks Anfänge.' *Historisches Jahrbuch der Görresgesellschaft* 36 (1915): 1–36.

Schmidt, Heinrich. *Die deutschen Städtechroniken als Spiegel des bürgerlichen Selbstverständnisses im Spätmittelalter.* Schriftenreihe der Historischen Kommission bei der Bayerischen Akademie der Wissenschaften, 3. Göttingen, 1958.

Schmitt, Charles B. *Cicero Scepticus: A Study of the Influence of the Academica in the Renaissance.* International Archives of the History of Ideas, 52. The Hague, 1972.

Schneid, J. 'Dr. Johann Eck und das kirchliche Zinsverbot.' *Historischpolitische Blätter für das katholische Deutschland* 108 (1891, 2): 241–59; 321–35; 473–96; 570–89; 659–81; 789–810.

Schnyder, Werner. *Die Bevölkerung der Stadt und Landschaft Zürich vom 14. bis 17. Jahrhundert. Eine methodologische Studie.* Schweizer Studien zur Geschichtswissenschaft, 14, Heft 1. Zürich, 1925.

Schraepler, Horst W. *Die rechtliche Behandlung der Täufer in der deutschen Schweiz, Südwestdeutschland und Hessen 1525–1618.* Edited by E. Fabian. SKRG 4. Tübingen, 1957.

Schreiber, Heinrich. *Heinrich Loriti Glareanus; seine Freunde und seine Zeit. Biographischer Versuch.* Freiburg i.Br., 1837.

Geschichte der Albert-Ludwigs-Universität zu Freiburg im Breisgau, vol. 1: *Von der Stiftung der Universität bis zur Reformation*; vol. 2: *Von der Kirchenreformation bis zur Aufhebung der Jesuiten.* Freiburg i.Br., 1868.

Schreiner, Klaus. *Sozial- und standesgeschichtliche Untersuchungen zu den Benediktinerkonventen im östlichen Schwarzwald.* Veröffentlichungen der Kommission für geschichtliche Landeskunde in Baden-Württemberg, B 31. Stuttgart, 1964.

'Abt Johannes Trithemius (1462–1516) als Geschichtsschreiber des Klosters Hirsau. Überlieferungsgeschichtliche und quellenkritische Bemerkungen zu den "Annales Hirsaugienses".' *Rheinische Vierteljahrsblätter* 31 (1966/7): 72–138.

Schubert, Hans von. *Lazarus Spengler und die Reformation in Nürnberg.* Edited by Hajo Holborn. QFRG 17. Leipzig, 1934.

Schüler, Martin. *Prädestination, Sünde und Freiheit bei Gregor von Rimini.* Forschungen zur Kirchen- und Geistesgeschichte, 3. Stuttgart, 1934.

Schwarz, Reinhard. *Vorgeschichte der reformatorischen Busstheologie.* Arbeiten zur Kirchengeschichte, 41. Berlin, 1968.

Scribner, Robert W. 'Civic Unity and the Reformation in Erfurt.' *Past and Present* 66 (1975): 29–60.

'The Erasmians and the Beginning of the Reformation in Erfurt.' *The Journal of Religious History* 9 (1976): 3–31.

Seebass, Gottfried. *Das reformatorische Werk des Andreas Osiander. Anhang: Portraits von Andreas Osiander*. Einzelarbeiten aus der Kirchengeschichte Bayerns, 44. Nürnberg, 1967.

'An sint persequendi haeretici? Die Stellung des Johannes Brenz zur Verfolgung und Bestrafung der Täufer.' *BWKG* 70 (1970): 40–99.

Bibliographia Osiandrica. Bibliographie der gedruckten Schriften Andreas Osianders d. Ä. (1496–1552). Nieuwkoop, 1971.

Seifert, Arno. *Die Universität Ingolstadt im 15. und 16. Jahrhundert. Texte und Regesten*. Ludovico Maximilianea, Quellen 1. Berlin, 1973.

Seigel, Rudolf. *Gericht und Rat in Tübingen. Von den Anfängen bis zur Einführung der Gemeindeverfassung 1818–1822*. Veröffentlichungen der Kommission für geschichtliche Landeskunde in Baden-Württemberg, B 13. Stuttgart, 1960.

Selge, Kurt-Victor. 'Das Autoritätengefüge der westlichen Christenheit im Lutherkonflikt 1517 bis 1521.' *Historische Zeitschrift* 223 (1976): 591–617.

Shumaker, Wayne. *The Occult Sciences in the Renaissance. A Study in Intellectual Patterns*. Berkeley, Los Angeles, 1972.

Sider, Ronald J. *Andreas Bodenstein von Karlstadt. The Development of His Thought 1517–1525*. SMRT 11. Leiden, 1974.

Silbernagel, I. *Johannes Trithemius*. Landshut, 1868.

Smalley, Beryl. *English Friars and Antiquity in the Early Fourteenth Century*. Oxford, 1960.

Smit, J. W. 'The Present Position of Studies Regarding the Revolt of the Netherlands.' In *Britain and the Netherlands. Papers Delivered to the Oxford-Netherlands Historical Conference 1959*, pp. 11–28. Edited by J. S. Bromley, E. H. Kossmann. London, 1960.

'The Netherlands Revolution.' In *Preconditions of Revolution in Early Modern Europe*, pp. 19–54. Edited by R. Forster, J. P. Greene. The Johns Hopkins Symposia in History. Baltimore, London, 1970.

Smits, Luchesius. *Saint Augustin dans l'oeuvre de Jean Calvin*, vol. 1: *Étude de critique littéraire*. Assen, 1957.

Soldan, W. G., Heppe, Heinrich. *Geschichte der Hexenprozesse*. 2 vols. Revised and edited by M. Bauer. Bonn, 1911; reprinted Hanau, 1968.

Spitz, Lewis W. *Conrad Celtis, the German Arch-Humanist*. Cambridge, Mass., 1957.

'Headwaters of the Reformation: Studia humanitatis, Luther Senior, et initia reformationis.' In *Luther and the Dawn of the Modern Era. Papers for the Fourth International Congress for Luther Research*, pp. 89–116. Edited by H. A. Oberman. SHCT 8. Leiden, 1974.

'The Course of German Humanism.' In *Itinerarium Italicum*, pp. 371–436.

Sproll, Johann Baptist. 'Die Verfassung des Sankt Georgen-Stifts zu Tübingen und sein Verhältnis zur Universität in dem Zeitraum von 1476–1534.'

Freiburger Diözesan-Archiv 30 [N.S.3] (1902): 105–92; 31 [N.S.4] (1903): 141–97.

Srbik, Robert Ritter von. *Maximilian I. und Gregor Reisch*. Edited by Alphons Lhotsky. Schriften des D. Dr. Franz Josef Mayer-Gunthof-Fonds, 1 (= Archiv für österreichische Geschichte, 122). Heft 2, pp. 1–112 (= 235–340). Vienna, 1961.

Staehelin, Andreas. *Geschichte der Universität Basel 1632–1818*, pt. 2, *Anhang*. Studien zur Geschichte der Wissenschaften in Basel, herausgegeben zum 500 jährigen Jubiläum der Universität Basel 1460–1960, 4/5. Basel, 1957.

Stakemeier, Eduard. *Der Kampf um Augustin. Augustinus und die Augustiner auf dem Tridentinum*. Paderborn, 1937.

Stange, Carl. 'Über Luthers Beziehungen zur Theologie seines Ordens.' *Neue kirchliche Zeitschrift* 11 (1900): 574–85.

'Luther über Gregor von Rimini.' *Neue kirchliche Zeitschrift* 13 (1902): 721–7.

Staub, Ignaz. *Dr. Johann Fabri, Generalvikar von Konstanz (1518–1523), bis zum offenen Kampf gegen M. Luther (August 1522)*. Beilage zum Jahresbericht der Stiftsschule Einsiedeln im Studienjahre 1910/11. Einsiedeln, 1911.

Stayer, James M. *Anabaptists and the Sword*. Lawrence, Kans., 1972; rev. edn, Lawrence, Kans., 1976.

'Die Anfänge des schweizerischen Täufertums im reformierten Kongregationalismus.' In *Umstrittenes Täufertum 1525–1975. Neue Forschungen*, pp. 19–49. Edited by H.-J. Goertz. Göttingen, 1975.

Klaus Deppermann, Werner Packull. 'From Monogenesis to Polygenesis: The Historical Discussion of Anabaptist Origins.' *The Mennonite Quarterly Review* 49 (1975): 83–121.

'Reublin und Brötli: The Revolutionary Beginnings of Swiss Anabaptism.' In *The Origins and Characteristics of Anabaptism*, pp. 83–102. The Hague, 1977. *See* Oyer, *above*.

'Reflections and Retractions on *Anabaptists and the Sword*.' *The Mennonite Quarterly Review* 51 (1977): 196–212. (Reprinted from preface to rev. edn of *Anabaptists and the Sword*, 1976.)

Stegmüller, Friedrich. 'Gratia sanans. Zum Schicksal des Augustinismus in der Salmantizenserschule.' In *Aurelius Augustinus. Die Festschrift der Görres-Gesellschaft zum 1500. Todestag des heiligen Augustinus*, pp. 395–409. Edited by M. Grabmann, J. Mausbach. Cologne, 1930.

Repertorium biblicum medii aevi, vol. 5: *Commentaria. Auctores R–Z*. Madrid, 1955.

Steiff, Karl. *Der erste Buchdruck in Tübingen (1498–1534). Ein Beitrag zur Geschichte der Universität*. Tübingen, 1881; reprinted Nieuwkoop, 1963.

Steinmetz, David Curtis. *Misericordia Dei. The Theology of Johannes von Staupitz in Its Late Medieval Setting*. SMRT 4. Leiden, 1968.

'Luther and the Late Medieval Augustinians: Another Look.' *Concordia Theological Monthly* 44 (1973): 245–60.

Steinmetz, Max. 'Die Konzeption der deutschen Universitäten im Zeitalter von Humanismus und Reformation.' In *Les Universités européennes du XIVe au XVIIIe siècle . . .* (*see* Le Goff, *above*), pp. 114–27. Geneva, 1967.

Stella, Prospero. 'Zwei unedierte Artikel des Johannes von Neapel über das Individuationsprinzip.' *Divus Thomas*, 3rd Series, 29 (1951): 129–66.

Stintzing, Roderich. *Geschichte der deutschen Rechtswissenschaft*, vol. 1. Munich, 1880.

Stolz, E. 'Die Patrone der Universität Tübingen und ihre Fakultäten.' *Theologische Quartalschrift* 108 (1927): 1–49.

Stupperich, Robert. 'Melanchthons Proverbien-Kommentare.' In *Der Kommentar in der Renaissance*, pp. 21–34. Edited by A. Buck, O. Herding. Deutsche Forschungsgemeinschaft, Kommission für Humanismusforschung, Mitteilung 1. Boppard, 1975.

Erasmus von Rotterdam und seine Welt. Berlin, New York, 1977.

Tecklenburg Johns, Christa, *see* Johns, Christa Tecklenburg.

Teufel, Waldemar. *Universitas Studii Tuwingensis. Die Tübinger Universitätsverfassung in vorreformatorischer Zeit (1497–1534)*. Tübingen, 1977.

Thomas, Keith. *Religion and the Decline of Magic. Studies in Popular Beliefs in Sixteenth and Seventeenth Century England*. London, 1971.

Thorndike, S. Lynn. *History of Magic and Experimental Science*, vol. 5. History of Science Society Publications, N.S. 4. New York, 1941.

Thurnhofer, Franz Xaver, *Bernhard Adelmann von Adelmannsfelden, Humanist und Luthers Freund (1457–1523). Ein Lebensbild aus der Zeit der beginnenden Kirchenspaltung in Deutschland*. Erläuterung und Ergänzungen zu Janssens Geschichte des deutschen Volkes, vol. 2, pt. 1. Edited by L. Pastor. Freiburg i.Br., 1900.

Tierney, Brian. *Foundations of the Conciliar Theory. The Contribution of the Medieval Canonists from Gratian to the Great Schism*. Cambridge, 1955, reprinted 1968.

'Ockham, the Conciliar Theory, and the Canonists.' *Journal of the History of Ideas* 15 (1954): 40–70. Reprinted separately as Facet Books, Historical Series, 19. Philadelphia, 1971.

Tillich, Paul. *Systematic Theology*, 2 vols. Chicago, 1951, 1957.

Tracy, James D. *Erasmus. The Growth of a Mind*. Travaux d'Humanisme et Renaissance, 126. Geneva, 1972.

Trapp, Damasus. 'Augustinian Theology of the Fourteenth Century. Notes on Editions, Marginalia, Opinions and Book-Lore.' *Augustiniana* 6 (1956): 146–274.

'Gregory of Rimini: Manuscripts, Editions and Additions.' *Augustiniana* 8 (1958): 425–43.

Trinkaus, Charles. *In Our Image and Likeness. Humanity and Divinity in Italian Humanist Thought*, vol. 1. London, 1970.

'Erasmus, Augustine, and the Nominalists.' *ARG* 67 (1976): 5–32.

Vahle, Hermann. 'Calvinismus und Demokratie im Spiegel der Forschung.' *ARG* 66 (1975): 182–212.

Van der Wansem, C. *Het ontstaan en de geschiedenis der Broederschap van het Gemene Leven tot 1400*. Universiteit te Leuven. Publicaties op het gebied der Geschiedenis en der Philologie, 4, 12. Louvain, 1958.

Vasella, Oskar. *Reform und Reformation in der Schweiz. Zur Würdigung der*

Anfänge der Glaubenskrise. Katholisches Leben und Kämpfen im Zeitalter der Glaubensspaltung, 16. Münster i.W., 1958.

Vignaux, Paul. *Justification et prédestination au XIVe siècle. Duns Scot, Pierre d'Auriole, Guillaume d'Occam, Grégoire de Rimini*. Bibliothèque de l'École des Hautes Études, 48. Paris, 1934.

Vischer, Wilhelm. *Geschichte der Universität Basel von der Gründung 1460 bis zur Reformation 1529*. Im Auftrag der akademischen Regenz zur Feier des vierhundertjährigen Jubiläums. Basel, 1860.

Vocht, Henry de. *History of the Foundation and the Rise of the Collegium Trilingue Lovaniense 1517–1550,* vol. 1: *The Foundation*. Université de Louvain. Recueil de travaux d'histoire et de philologie, 3, fasc. 42 = Humanistica Lovaniensia, 10. Louvain, 1951.

Volz, Hans. 'Die ersten Sammelausgaben von Lutherschriften und ihre Drucker (1518–1520).' *Gutenberg-Jahrbuch* 35 (1960): 185–204.

'Erzbischof Albrecht von Mainz und Martin Luthers 95 Thesen.' *Jahrbuch der Hessischen Kirchengeschichtlichen Vereinigung* 13 (1962): 187–228.

'Martin Luthers Schriften und ihre Druckgeschichte.' *Blätter für pfälzische Kirchengeschichte und religiöse Volkskunde* 39 (1972): 112–33.

'Luthers und Melanchthons Beteiligung an der Tübinger Universitätsreform im Jahre 1538.' In *Theologen und Theologie an der Universität Tübingen. Beiträge zur Geschichte der Evangelisch-Theologischen Fakultät,* pp. 65–95. Edited by Martin Brecht. Contubernium, 15. Tübingen, 1977.

Walker, D. P. *Spiritual and Demonic Magic from Ficino to Campanella*. Studies of the Warburg Institute, 22. London, 1958.

Walton, Robert C. 'The Institutionalization of the Reformation at Zürich.' *Zwingliana* 13 (1972, 2): 497–515.

Zwingli's Theocracy. Toronto, 1967.

Walzer, Michael. *The Revolution of the Saints. A Study in the Origins of Radical Politics*. Cambridge, Mass., 1965.

Weiler, Anton G. 'Antiqui/moderni (via antiqua/via moderna).' In *Historisches Wörterbuch der Philosophie,* vol. 1:407–10. Edited by J. Ritter. Basel, 1971.

Weizsäcker, Carl von. *Lehrer und Unterricht an der evangelisch-theologischen Facultät der Universität Tübingen von der Reformation bis zur Gegenwart*. Zur vierten Säcularfeier der Universität Tübingen im Sommer 1877. Festprogramm der evangelisch-theologischen Facultät. Tübingen, 1877.

Werbeck, Wilfrid. *Jacobus Perez von Valencia. Untersuchungen zu seinem Psalmenkommentar*. Beiträge zur Historischen Theologie, 28. Tübingen, 1959.

'Voraussetzungen und Wesen der scrupulositas im Spätmittelalter.' *ZThK* 68 (1971): 327–50.

Werner, Karl. *Die Scholastik des späteren Mittelalters*, vol. 3: *Der Augustinismus in der Scholastik des späteren Mittelalters*. Vienna, 1883; reprinted New York, 1960.

Weyrauch, Erdmann. 'Strasbourg et la Réforme en Allemagne du Sud.' In *Strasbourg au coeur religieux du XVIe siècle*. Hommage à Lucien Febvre.

Actes du Colloque international de Strasbourg (25–9 mai 1975), pp. 347–68. Edited by G. Livet, F. Rapp. Société Savante d'Alsace et des Régions de l'Est. Collection 'Grandes publications', 12. Strasbourg, 1977.

Widmann, Hans. *Tübingen als Verlagsstadt*. Contubernium, 1. Tübingen, 1971.

Wieacker, Franz. *Privatrechtsgeschichte der Neuzeit*. Göttingen, 1952.

Wiedemann, Theodor. *Dr. Johann Eck, Professor der Theologie an der Universität Ingolstadt*. Regensburg, 1865.

Willburger, August. *Die Konstanzer Bischöfe Hugo von Landenberg, Balthasar Merklin, Johann von Lupfen (1496–1537) und die Glaubensspaltung*. RGST 34/5. Münster i.W., 1917.

Wille, Jakob. *Philipp der Grossmüthige von Hessen und die Restitution Ulrichs von Wirtemberg 1526–1535*. Tübingen, 1882.

Williams, George H. *The Radical Reformation*. Philadelphia, 1962.

Willoweit, Dietmar. *Rechtsgrundlagen der Territorialgewalt. Landesobrigkeit, Herrschaftsrechte und Territorium in der Rechtswissenschaft der Neuzeit*. Forschungen zur deutschen Rechtsgeschichte, 11. Cologne, Vienna, 1975.

Windhorst, Christof. *Täuferisches Taufverständnis. Balthasar Hubmaiers Lehre zwischen traditioneller und reformatorischer Theologie*. SMRT 16. Leiden, 1976.

Wolf, Ernst. *Staupitz und Luther. Ein Beitrag zur Theologie des Johannes von Staupitz und deren Bedeutung für Luthers theologischen Werdegang*. QFRG 9. Leipzig, 1927.

Wolfs, S. P. *Das Groninger 'Religionsgespräch' (1523) und seine Hintergründe*. Utrecht, Nijmegen, 1959.

Die Württembergischen Familien-Stiftungen nebst genealogischen Nachrichten über die zu denselben berechtigten Familien. Heft 4 and 10. Edited by F. F. Faber. Stuttgart, 1853 and 1854.

Wuttke, Dieter. *Deutsche Germanistik und Renaissance-Forschung. Ein Vortrag zur Forschungslage*. Respublica literaria, 3. Bad Homburg v.d.H., 1968.

Wyss, Karl-Heinz. *Leo Jud. Seine Entwicklung zum Reformator 1519–1523*. Europäische Hochschulschriften, Reihe 3: Geschichte und ihre Hilfswissenschaften, 61. Bern, Frankfurt a.M., 1976.

Yoder, John Howard. 'The Turning Point in the Zwinglian Reformation.' *The Mennonite Quarterly Review* 32 (1958): 128–40.

Zenz, Emil. *Die Trierer Universität 1473 bis 1798. Ein Beitrag zur abendländischen Universitätsgeschichte*. Trierer geistesgeschichtliche Studien, 1. Trier, 1949.

Zijl, Theodore P. van. *Gerard Groote, Ascetic and Reformer (1340–1384)*. The Catholic University of America. Studies in Mediaeval History, N.S. 18. Washington, D.C., 1963.

Zimmermann, Wilhelm. *Der grosse deutsche Bauernkrieg*. Volksausgabe. Stuttgart, 1891; reprinted Berlin, 1975.

Zürcher, Christoph. *Konrad Pellikans Wirken in Zürich 1526–1556*. Zürcher Beiträge zur Reformationsgeschichte, 4. Zürich, 1975.

Zumkeller, Adolar. 'Das Ungenügen der menschlichen Werke bei den

deutschen Predigern des Spätmittelalters.' *Zeitschrift für katholische Theologie* 81 (1959): 265–305.
'Die Augustinertheologen Simon Fidati von Cascia und Hugolin von Orvieto und Martin Luthers Kritik an Aristoteles.' *ARG* 54 (1963): 15–37.
'Die Augustinerschule des Mittelalters: Vertreter und philosophisch-theologische Lehre (Übersicht nach dem heutigen Stand der Forschung).' *Analecta Augustiniana* 27 (1964); 167–262.

Index of names and places

Adelmann von Adelmannsfelden, Bernhard († 1523), 139f., 141[50], 145, 150
Adorf, Johann Permeter von († 1505), 247[20]
Adrian VI, Pope (1522–3), 221, 241
Affoltern, Switz., 206[77]
Agricola, Rudolph († 1485), *248–9*, 251, 258
Agrippa of Nettesheim, Cornelius († 1535), *172–4*
Alba, Fernando, Duke of († 1582), 267[22]
Alber, Matthaeus († 1570), 19
Albertus Magnus († 1280), 39[76], 135[27]
Albrecht of Brandenburg, *see* Mainz
Alexander V, Pope, *see* Peter of Candia
Almelo, sisterhouse at, 48
Alpirsbach, monastery of, 20, 117, 125, 254, 258
Alps, 46, 119, 152
Alsace, 117, 265[19], 290[97]
Altenburg, publishing in, 263[9]
Altenstaig, Johannes († after 1525), 77[67], 162[11]
Altmann, Paul (Geraeander), 19
Ambrose of Milan († 397), 40f., 73
Amerbach, Johannes († 1513), *71f.*, 74, 91, 93
Ammann, Rudolf († 1552), 190[2]
Amsdorf, Nicholas of († 1565), 91[135]
Andreas de Vega († 1549), 70, 107[186]
Angelus de Clavasio († ca. 1495), 115[9], 134
Angoulême, 283[75]
Annaberg, ducal or Albertine Saxony, 270[32]
Anselm of Canterbury († 1109), 65
Anshelm, Thomas († 1523), 15[1], 17–20, *57f.*, *154f.*, 164, 257
Antonius de Butrio († 1408), 119
Anwyl, Sir Fritz Jacob von, Senior († ca. 1535), *216f.*, 218[35], 223, 227, 232f., 268[27]
Anwyl, Sir Fritz Jacob von, Junior († 1540), 217
Aquinas, *see* Thomas Aquinas
Aristotle, 29f., 35, 37, 41, *58–60*, 89, 93, 173, 250, 255
Arnobius († 1st third of the 4th c.), 73
Artzt, Sybille, *see* Fugger
Au, Jörg von, 143f.
Augsburg, 57, 131, 138–40, 145, 151, 156, 268, 273, 276[53], 290[97]
—Carmelite monastery at, 138
—episcopal see of, 139, 240
—publishing in, 72, 77, 257[53]
Augustine († 430), 24[6], *64–80*, 84, *87–91*, *93–5*, *98–110*, 159[3], 165, 239, 264
Aulus Gellius († before A.D. 165), 125
Austria (Habsburgs), 10f., 113, 152, 204, 218, 221, 223[58], 242, 244, 246, 248, 251–3, 256–8, 262, 265f., 269f., 273
—Ferdinand, Archduke of (later King of the Romans; Emperor; † 1564), 220[46], 242, 244, 248f., 253[43], 257, 262, 268f., 274[49]
Avicenna († 1037), 250
Avignon, papal residence, 23f., 26

Baden, Switz., 237, 244, 256f., 266
———*see also* Subject index: disputation
Badius, Jodocus († ca. 1534/5), 92
Baflo near Groningen, Netherlands, 248[24]
Basel, 71, 192, 197[35], 198, 200[46], 206, 208, 212, 213[13], 220, 238[124], 249, 280–3, 290
—cathedral chapter, 197
—city council, *197–9*, 254, 282f.
—publishing in, 21, 71f., 74, 199, 212, 265[19], 291
—university of, *31f.*, 34, 40f., 58, 192[10], 197f., 200[46], 254, *282f.*; arts faculty, 32
Baselius (Basellius), Nicholas, *15f.*, 122, 152f., 156
Bavaria, duchy of, 113, 242
Bebel, Heinrich († 1518), *17–19*, 46, 57, 59, 117, 129, 162–4, 189
Beckmann, Otto, 91[135], 279[60]
Bede, the Venerable († 735), 68, 69[25]

Index of modern authors

Subject index